a n   i n t r o d u c t i o n   t o

OPTIONS & FUTURES

second edition

DON M. CHANCE
Virginia Polytechnic Institute and State University

The Dryden Press
Harcourt Brace Jovanovich College Publishers
Fort Worth   Philadelphia   San Diego   New York   Orlando   Austin   San Antonio
Toronto   Montreal   London   Sydney   Tokyo

Acquisitions Editor: Ann Heath
Developmental Editor: Millicent Treloar
Project Editor: Susan Jansen
Design Supervisor: Annette Spadoni
Production Manager: Bob Lange
Permissions Editor: Cindy Lombardo
Director of Editing, Design, and Production: Jane Perkins

Copy Editor: Nancy Maybloom

Library of Congress Cataloging-in-Publication Data

Chance, Don M.
      An introduction to options and futures / Don M. Chance — 2nd
      ed.
        p. cm.
      Includes bibliographical references and index.
      ISBN 0-03-055013-0 (hardcover)
      1. Options (Finance) 2. Futures. 3. Futures market. I. Title.
HG6024.A3C48   1991
332.64'5—dc20

               91-6529
                 CIP

Printed in the United States of America
   4567-016-9876543
Copyright © 1992, 1989 by The Dryden Press.

ISBN 0-03-055013-0

Address orders:
The Dryden Press
Orlando, FL 32887

Address editorial correspondence:
The Dryden Press
301 Commerce Street, Suite 3700
Fort Worth, TX 76102

The Dryden Press
Harcourt Brace Jovanovich

Cover Source Line: © 1986 Tony Armour Photography.

To my family

The Dryden Press Series in Finance

PREFACE

In the first edition of this book, I noted that a separate course in options and futures is a relatively recent phenomenon in business schools. Since that time, the enormous growth in courses of this type has clearly established this subject as an integral part of a solid finance curriculum. Although the course is an elective at most schools, it remains popular among students who want to graduate on the cutting edge of their field. I have found that it brings out the best in many "average" students, and thus is inspiring to teach.

This book is intended to provide a solid foundation in the study of options and futures and many derivative instruments. It presents a balance of the institutional details, theoretical foundations, and practical applications of the field. It does not attempt to teach the reader how to trade; trading cannot be taught from a book. Rather, it provides the information students need to embark on a career that focuses on these instruments.

The primary audience is the advanced undergraduate, although the book has been extensively used at the MBA level, usually supplemented with readings. Undergraduate students are assumed to have had a beginning course in investments; MBA students should be able to use the book after a comprehensive introductory course in corporate finance.

The book assumes only a basic knowledge of time value of money, college algebra, and economic principles. Differential calculus is used in some sections; these are marked with an asterisk (*). This does not necessarily mean that those sections should be skipped. The use of calculus is kept at a very basic level; in most cases, it is used to derive a formula such as the option hedge ratio in Chapter 4. Thus, the formula can be presented without the mathematical details. Material that requires more detailed mathematics appears in an appendix.

The book is designed to be used in a one-semester course. Some instructors, however, may find it difficult to finish the book in one semester. Instructors on the quarter system should be able to cover all the material on either options or futures and a portion of the material on the other. Ideally, a quarter system would provide an opportunity to spend one quarter on options and one quarter on futures.

The subject matter is inherently challenging. Understanding options and futures often requires a different way of thinking than that to which one is accustomed. The book is designed to make the subject as easy as possible without sacrificing important concepts. Although mathematics is used extensively, the level is accessible to most students. In addition, all mathematical principles are illustrated with numerical examples.

Organization

Chapter 1 provides a general introduction to the subject and a brief review of some basic concepts of risk and return and efficient markets.

Part I covers options. It begins with Chapter 2, which presents institutional information about the options markets. Chapter 3 discusses and illustrates the theoretical foundations of option pricing; it establishes the rational principles that must be grasped to understand how options are priced. Chapter 4 deals with option pricing models, specifically the binomial and Black-Scholes models. Chapter 5 covers the basic strategies of buying and selling stock, calls, and puts. Chapter 6 presents advanced trading strategies, which combine other option strategies.

Part II covers futures, and the structure parallels that of Part I. Chapter 7 provides the institutional background on futures markets. Chapter 8 deals with the basic principles of pricing spot instruments. Chapter 9 discusses and illustrates the theoretical principles of futures pricing. Chapter 10 demonstrates how futures can be used in hedging situations. Chapter 11 presents advanced futures strategies, including spread and arbitrage trading.

Part III includes material on both options and futures and deals with a number of advanced and exciting contemporary topics. Chapter 12 covers options on futures, a popular instrument that combines many of the features of options and futures. Chapter 13 explores foreign currency options and futures. Chapter 14 introduces a number of new and exotic instruments that incorporate many characteristics of options and futures. It concludes with a discussion of several key issues of contemporary interest.

Some instructors may wonder why options are covered before futures. Many consider options more difficult, but I believe that notion stems from the advanced mathematics used to develop most continuous-time option pricing models. This book does not employ that level of mathematics. Moreover, I regard options as much more fundamental securities than futures. One can buy a call and sell a put and create a payoff identical to that of the underlying stock or bond, but one cannot create an option from the stock or bond. If the call and put are on a futures, the payoff is like that of the futures. Of course, option payoffs can be created through various dynamic trading strategies, which are covered in Chapter 14, but more restrictive assumptions are required. Thus, I believe options come first in the hierarchy of instruments. For those who disagree, there is no reason for concern. Parts I and II are self-contained. If an instructor wishes to cover Part II first, he or she can easily do so; options are not a prerequisite to Part II. Part II contains a few minor references to certain topics covered in Part I, but these will in no way interfere with understanding the material.

Special Features

This text offers a number of special features.

- It emphasizes real-world practicality. The realism has been achieved by employing examples taken from options and futures price quotations during specific market environments. Thus, nearly all the concepts are illustrated not only by presenting the theory but by applying it to actual options and futures prices. The examples are presented numerically and graphically. In some cases, this realism comes with an added cost: The real world is invariably more complex, and far less perfect, than the make-believe world of many textbooks. However, I believe this will better prepare students for their careers in the financial markets.

- The emphasis on realism does not come at the expense of theory. Theory has much to teach us, especially on the subject of options and futures. In deciding when to employ theory, I have tried to keep the student audience in mind and, as just noted, made a consistent effort to illustrate the theory with real-world examples. Inevitably, some instructors will believe I have not gone far enough with the theory and others will think I have gone too far. I hope to have struck a balance, and I believe the book is sufficiently flexible that the theory can be supplemented or attenuated as needed.

- The book contains a number of boxed items that appear in the margins. Most of these items restate important theoretical principles covered in the text and provide a quick reminder of major points covered in the respective section. In addition, many key words are emphasized with italics throughout the text.

- At the end of each chapter is a set of 15 to 25 questions and problems, including a new feature called "Concept Problems" (see "Changes in the Second Edition"). In addition, each chapter provides an extensive readings list, with an emphasis on important articles and particularly practical, readable material.

- The appendices at the end of the book list the symbols used and repeat all the formulas that appear in the book. They are followed by a glossary that should facilitate learning the many esoteric terms in the world of options and futures.

- An *Instructor's Manual* contains the solutions to the end-of-chapter problems, suggestions for teaching each chapter, a test bank consisting of 15 to 25 multiple-choice and a similar number of true-false questions from each chapter, and instructions for using the software disk (see below).

- A software disk, available to instructors who adopt the text, contains Lotus 1-2-3 worksheets and a compiled program designed to facilitate computations of some of the longer problems. Instructions on the use of the software are encoded into the program and will appear on the screen when invoked. More detailed instructions are provided in the *Instructor's Manual*.

Changes in the Second Edition

A number of changes have been made to improve the second edition:

- A great deal of material has been updated to bring the book to a more current state.

- New concept questions and problems at the end of most chapters give the instructor an opportunity to challenge students to think and apply what they have learned. The number of end-of-chapter questions and problems has been increased by almost 30 percent.

- Chapter 14, new to this edition, contains some advanced material moved from earlier chapters, plus a number of new topics, including swaps, caps, floors, collars, interest rate options, primes and scores, and market-indexed securities. In addition, the chapter includes extensive discussion of several important contemporary topics in futures and options markets.

- Chapter 12 of the first edition, which covered both foreign currency futures and options as well as options on futures, has been split into two chapters. Now Chapter 12 deals with options on futures, and Chapter 13 covers foreign currency futures and options, as well as some new material on currency swaps.

- In addition to the new topics presented in Chapters 13 and 14, the second edition provides new or expanded coverage of the following topics: technology and global trading, the quality option, the turtle trade, tailing a hedge, American option pricing (including the Barone-Adesi/Whaley model and early exercise with the binomial model), convergence of the binomial model to the Black-Scholes model, implied volatility, convenience yield, backwardation/contango, the role of the clearinghouse, and the construction of stock indices.

- Chapter 3 on the foundations of option pricing has been improved and clarified.

- The sections on empirical tests, which in the first edition appeared at the end of the text material in most chapters, have been removed and the material integrated into the text.

Acknowledgments

Many individuals contributed generously to this project. I wish to thank my reviewers for the second edition: Andrew Chen, Southern Methodist University; Louis Scott, University of Georgia; Hun Park, University of Illinois; Eric Chang, University of Maryland; John Mitchell, Central Michigan University; and Majed Muhtaseb, California State Polytechnic University. In addition, the following individuals provided helpful comments on the transition between the first and second editions: Jot Yau, George Mason University; Jorge Urrutia, Loyola University; Ramon Rabinovitch, University of Houston; Nusret Cakici, Rutgers University; and Margaret Monroe, University of Illinois. Steve Nutt, Ira Kawaller, Mike Hemler, Phoebe Mix, Bridget Henneby, Joyce Blau, John MacDonald, Kuldeep Shastri, and Robert Schwitz helped by answering questions or providing unsolicited comments.

In addition, I would like to again thank those who provided reviews or comments on the first edition: Bill Welch, Mark Rzepczynski, Don Chambers, Don Taylor, Peggy Fletcher, Avraham Kamara, Ann Kremer, Jerome Duncan, Dennis Draper, Bob Klemkosky, Doug Hearth, Shanta Hegde, Hun Park, Joan Junkus, Randy Billingsley, Raman Kumar, Mary Davis, Gopi Maliwal, and Craig Ruff.

I also wish to thank the staff at The Dryden Press: acquisitions editor Ann Heath, developmental editor Millicent Treloar, and project editor Susan Jansen. Other Dryden personnel who contributed include Annette Spadoni, Bob Lange, and Cindy Lombardo.

Despite our best efforts, some errors surely remain, and I accept full responsibility. I encourage you to send me your corrections and suggestions. I can truly attest that the second edition benefited from many unsolicited comments.

Finally, I wish to thank my family, who once again endured this project. My wife, Jan, who typed the *Instructor's Manual*, and children, Kim and Ashley, each contributed in her own special way. They have continued to support my work and my frequent travels with tolerance and good humor.

Don M. Chance
Department of Finance, Insurance and Business Law
The R. B. Pamplin College of Business
Virginia Polytechnic Institute and State University
Blacksburg, Virginia

CONTENTS

part one **OPTIONS**

xi

part two **FUTURES**

part three ADVANCED TOPICS

INTRODUCTION

> *Efficiency of a practically flawless kind may be*
> *reached naturally in the struggle for bread.*
>
> JOSEPH CONRAD, The Mirror of the Sea, 1906

Few subjects command as much interest as that of making money. One way people make money is through their investments. Many people outside of the financial industry seem to know—or at least profess to know—something about stocks and bonds. Investments are a common topic at social gatherings. Investments courses are among the most popular offerings at colleges and universities. Few people, however, know much about the instruments called *options* and *futures*, which play an important but frequently misunderstood role in the investment world. This book is about options and futures. It explores their characteristics and their relationship to stocks and bonds. It also explains how to determine options and futures prices and how to use these instruments in investing.

This chapter presents some introductory concepts that will bring the role of options and futures markets into focus and lay the foundation for investigating these instruments. We begin by examining the structure of the U.S. economic system.

AN OVERVIEW OF THE U.S. ECONOMIC SYSTEM

The U.S. economic system can be characterized in many ways. One way is to organize the economy into two types of markets: the market for real assets and services and the market for financial assets.

The Market for Real Assets and Services

Real assets are tangibles; *services* are intangible. There are markets for tangibles such as food, clothing, and shelter and markets for intangibles such as haircuts, auto repairs, and financial advice. These assets are derived from the economy's natural and human resources. Individuals organize their creativity and channel their labor into the production of goods and services that society demands.

A price system governs the operations of the market for real assets and services. Society expresses its needs by its willingness to pay a price to obtain a product or service. If that good or service can be produced and sold to earn a profit, society's needs will be met.

Most of the products and services that we purchase in these markets are offered to us through business units. However, business units require *capital*—the financial resource needed to acquire the labor, machinery, and managerial talent necessary for supplying society's needs. Thousands of small businesses obtain capital from a variety of sources, including local banks, relatives, and their owners' pockets. A viable economy, however, could not exist without money and capital markets, that is, the market for financial assets.

The Market for Financial Assets

A *financial asset* is a claim on an economic unit such as a business or an individual. For example, you might borrow money from a relative by giving a promissory note. That note is a financial asset that your relative, the lender, holds and represents a claim on you, the borrower. From your perspective, the note is a financial liability or simply a liability, since all liabilities are financial.

Many financial assets, such as the stocks and bonds issued by businesses and the bonds issued by government units, trade in organized markets. After a company issues stock, the stock can, in turn, be sold by one individual to another. An active stock market makes it easier for a company to raise equity capital by assuring investors that shares purchased from the company can be sold to other investors if necessary. The purchase of shares directly from the company takes place in the *primary market*, while the trading of shares among investors occurs in the *secondary market*.

The financial markets usually are broken down into two submarkets—money markets and capital markets. The *money market* is the market for short-term debt instruments. The *capital market* is the market for long-term debt instruments and stock issued by companies.

In both the market for real goods and services and the market for financial assets, purchases and sales require that the underlying good or security be delivered either immediately or shortly thereafter. Payment usually is made immediately, although credit arrangements are sometimes used. Because of these characteristics, we refer to these markets as *cash* or *spot* markets. The sale is made, the payment is remitted, and the good or security is delivered.

In other situations, the good or security is to be delivered at a later date. Still other types of arrangements let the buyer or seller choose whether or not to go through with the sale. These types of arrangements are conducted in options, forward, and futures markets.

OPTIONS, FORWARD, AND FUTURES MARKETS

Financial markets are markets for financial assets. A *financial asset* is a claim on another person or corporation. In contrast, options, forward, and futures markets are markets for contractual instruments. A *contract* is an agreement between two parties in which each party gives something to the other. Such contracts are established by the two parties—buyer and seller—and trade in a manner similar to that of securities. Contract buyers try to buy as cheaply as possible, and contract sellers try to sell as dearly as possible. This section briefly introduces the various types of contractual instruments: options, forward, and futures contracts.

Options

An *option* is a contract between two parties—a buyer and a seller—that gives the buyer the right, but not the obligation, to purchase or sell something at a later date at a price agreed upon today.

The option buyer pays the seller a sum of money called the *price* or *premium*. The option seller stands ready to sell or buy according to the contract terms if and when the buyer so desires. An option to buy something is referred to as a *call;* an option to sell something is called a *put*.

This book focuses on options that trade in organized options markets. Most of these options are for the purchase of financial assets such as stocks or bonds. However, there are also options on futures contracts, metals, and foreign currencies. Many other types of financial arrangements, such as lines of credit, loan guaranties, and insurance, are forms of options. Moreover, stock itself is equivalent to an option on the firm's assets.

Forward Contracts

A *forward contract* is an agreement between two parties—a buyer and a seller—to purchase or sell something at a later date at a price agreed upon today. A forward contract sounds a lot like an option. However, an option carries the right, not the obligation, to go through with the transaction. If the price of the underlying good changes, the option holder may decide to forgo buying or selling at the fixed price. On the other hand, the two parties in a forward contract incur the obligation to ultimately buy and sell the good.

Although forward markets have existed in this country for a long time, they are somewhat less familiar. Unlike options markets, they have no physical facilities for trading; there is no building or formal corporate body organized as the market. Forward markets operate through informal communication channels among major financial institutions. For example, there is a healthy forward market for foreign currencies, which offers individuals or companies the opportunity to buy or sell a foreign currency at a later date at an exchange rate agreed upon today.

Because forward contracts do not trade on organized exchanges, prices and contract terms are not standardized and the extent and volume of trading are not known. Accordingly, this book devotes little space to the formal treatment of forward markets; rather, it discusses them primarily to facilitate understanding of another type of instrument: futures contracts.

Futures Contracts

A futures contract is an agreement between two parties—a buyer and a seller—to buy or sell something at a future date. The contract trades on a futures exchange and is subject to a daily settlement procedure. Futures contracts evolved out of forward contracts and possess many of the same characteristics. In essence, they are like liquid forward contracts. Unlike forward contracts, however, futures contracts trade on organized exchanges, called *futures markets*. For example, the buyer of a futures contract, who has the obligation to buy the good at the later date, can sell the contract in the futures market, which relieves him or her of the obligation to purchase the good. Likewise, the seller of the futures contract, who is obligated to sell the good at the later date, can buy the contract back in the futures market, relieving him or her of the obligation to sell the good.

Futures contracts also differ from forward contracts in that they are subject to a daily settlement procedure. In the daily settlement, investors who incur losses pay them every day to investors who make profits (we shall learn more about this in Chapter 7).

Futures prices fluctuate from day to day, and contract buyers and sellers attempt to profit from these price changes and to lower the risk of transacting in the underlying goods.

Due to their important role in the economy, futures markets comprise almost half of the material in this book.

Options on Futures

Options on futures, sometimes called *commodity options* or *futures options*, are an important synthesis of futures and options markets. An option on a futures contract gives the buyer the right to buy or sell a futures contract at a later date at a price agreed upon today.

As we shall see in this and later chapters, there are important relationships among the prices of options, futures, options on futures, and the underlying spot asset. Options on futures help establish the linkage among the prices of these instruments and offer investors many opportunities not otherwise available. Options on futures are covered in more depth in Chapter 12.

Hybrids

In recent years, there has been a proliferation of new products that do not clearly fall into the classification of options, forwards, or futures but share some of the characteristics of these instruments. For example, a corporation can borrow money with the interest rate on each payment determined by the movement of future interest rates. This type of loan, called a floating rate loan, exposes the corporation to the risk of rising interest rates. To protect itself against this risk, the corporation can arrange with another firm or bank to *cap* its interest cost at a given rate. A cap is a very common arrangement and possesses many characteristics of an option, although it is not traded in the markets like ordinary options. Other firms that borrow at floating rates can make arrangements with firms that borrow at fixed rates so that the two firms exchange interest payments. This type of arrangement, called a *swap*, has some elements of forward contracts.

These hybrid instruments represent the effects of progress in our financial system. They are examples of change and innovation that have led to improved opportunities for risk management. Swaps, caps, and several other hybrid instruments are covered in Chapter 14.

SOME IMPORTANT CONCEPTS IN FINANCIAL AND OPTIONS AND FUTURES MARKETS

Before undertaking any further study of options and futures markets, let us review some introductory concepts pertaining to investment opportunities and investors. Many of these ideas may already be familiar and usually are applied in the context of investing in stocks and bonds. These concepts also apply to options and futures.

Return and Risk

Return is the quantitative measure of investment performance. It represents the percentage increase in the investor's wealth that results from making the investment. In the case of stocks, the return is the percentage change in price plus the dividend yield. The concept of return also applies to options, but, as we shall see later, the definition of the return on a futures contract is somewhat unclear.

One fundamental characteristic of investors is their desire to increase their wealth. This translates into obtaining the highest return possible—but higher returns are accompanied by greater risk. *Risk* is the uncertainty of future returns. English author Samuel Johnson once said, "He is no wise man that will quit a certainty for an uncertainty."[1] Investors demonstrate this by avoiding risky situations when riskless ones that offer equivalent expected returns exist; however, they cannot always avoid uncertainty. Fortunately, the competitive nature of financial and speculative markets enables investors to identify investments by their degrees of risk.

For example, the stock of a company that specializes in drilling wildcat oil wells will, all other things being equal, sell for less than the stock of a company that supplies health care.[2] That is because the drilling company is engaged in a more uncertain line of business. Risk, of course, runs the spectrum from zero risk to high risk. The prices of securities will reflect the differences in the companies' risk levels. The additional return one expects to earn from assuming risk is called a *risk premium.*

What other factors influence a company's stock price and expected return? Consider a hypothetical company with no risk. Will people be willing to invest money in this company if they expect no return? Certainly not. They will require a minimum return, one sufficient to compensate them for giving up the opportunity to spend their money today. This return is called the *risk-free rate* and is the investment's opportunity cost.[3]

The return investors expect is composed of the risk-free rate and a risk premium. This relationship is illustrated in Figure 1.1, where $E(r_s)$ is the expected return on the spot asset, r is the risk-free rate, and $E(\phi)$ is the risk premium—the excess of expected return over the risk-free rate.

Note that we have not identified how risk is measured. Many readers will recall risk measures such as standard deviation and beta. At this point, we need not be concerned with the specific measure of risk. The important point is the positive relationship between risk and return known as the *risk-return trade-off.* The risk-return trade-off arises because all investors seek to maximize return subject to a minimum level of risk. If a stock moves up the line into a higher risk level, some investors will find it too risky and will sell the stock, which will drive down its price. New investors in the stock will expect to earn higher returns by virtue of paying a lower price for it.

The financial markets are very effective at discriminating among firms with different risk levels. Firms with low risk will find capital plentiful and inexpensive. Firms with high risk may have trouble raising capital and will pay dearly. Markets that do a good job of pricing the instruments trading therein are said to be *efficient.*

---

[1]Samuel Johnson, *The Idler*, 1758–1760, no. 57.

[2]In this context, "all other things being equal" means that the comparisons have not been distorted by differences in the number of shares outstanding or the amount of leverage.

[3]The concept of the risk-free rate and opportunity cost is nicely illustrated by the parable about the wealthy man who entrusted three servants to manage some of his money. Two of the servants earned 100 percent returns, while the third buried the money and returned only the principal sum. The man was infuriated that the third servant had not even earned the risk-free interest rate by putting the money in the bank, whereupon he reallocated the funds to one of the other servants' portfolios. The third servant, who was summarily discharged, evidently was not destined for a career as an investment manager.

FIGURE 1.1
Risk-Return Trade-off

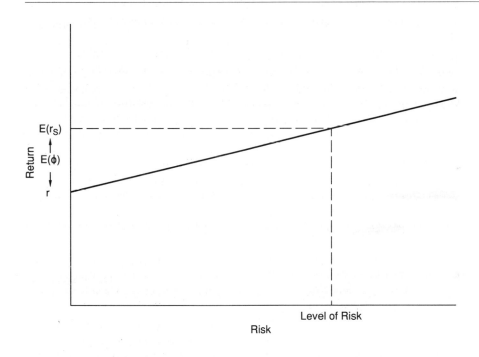

Market Efficiency

Market efficiency is the characteristic of a market in which the prices of the instruments trading therein reflect their true economic values to investors. In an efficient market, prices fluctuate randomly and investors cannot consistently earn returns above those that would compensate them for the level of risk they assume.

Considerable statistical evidence suggests that U.S. financial markets are efficient. While not all the evidence supports this proposition—and some investors do get rich in the market—most of it favors market efficiency. Market efficiency is such a natural consequence of rational investor behavior that we can accept it as a reasonable working model.

Thus, as we weave our way through the world of options and futures, we should keep in mind that by and large these markets are efficient. Although this book presents numerous strategies for buying and selling options and futures, all of them assume that the investor has already developed expectations about the direction of the market. Options and futures strategies show how to profit if those expectations prove correct and how to minimize the risk of loss if they prove wrong. These strategies are methods for managing the level of risk and thus should be considered essential tools for survival in efficient markets.

FUNDAMENTAL LINKAGES BETWEEN SPOT, OPTIONS, AND FUTURES MARKETS

So far we have not established a formal connection between spot and options and futures markets. Instruments such as options and futures are available for the purchase and sale of spot market items such as stocks and bonds. The prices of the options and futures are related to those of the underlying spot market instruments through several important mechanisms. Chapters 3, 4, 8, and 9 examine these linkages in detail; nevertheless, a general overview of the process here will be beneficial.

Arbitrage and the Law of One Price

Arbitrage is a type of transaction in which an investor seeks to profit when the same good sells for two different prices. The individual engaging in the arbitrage, called the *arbitrageur*, buys the good at the lower price and immediately sells it at the higher price. Arbitrage is an attractive strategy for investors. Thousands of individuals devote their time to looking for arbitrage opportunities. If a stock sells on one exchange at one price and on another at a different price, arbitrageurs will go to work buying at the low price and selling at the high price. The low price will be driven up and the high price driven down until the two prices are equal.

In your day-to-day life, you make many purchases and sales. Sometimes you encounter the same good selling for two different prices; for example, a stereo component system from a mail-order discount house may cost less than the same system at a local electronics store. Why is there a difference? The store may offer longer warranties, localized service, and other conveniences not available through the discounter. Likewise, a pair of running shoes purchased at a local discounter may be cheaper than the same one purchased at a sporting goods store, where you pay extra for service and product knowledge. Where real differences exist between identical goods, the prices will differ.

When you learn more about options and futures, you will see that there are many ways to create the same investment. Two seemingly different portfolios can offer the same return and risk. These portfolios must sell for identical prices, or arbitrageurs will quickly step in and their trading will drive the prices to equality. This rule is called the *Law of One Price*. The Law of One Price means that two identical goods cannot sell for different prices.

What, then, creates arbitrage opportunities? In an efficient market, they should never occur. But occasionally prices get out of line, perhaps through momentary oversight. Arbitrage is the mechanism that keeps prices in line. To make intelligent investment decisions, we need to learn how arbitrage transactions are made, which we shall do in later chapters.

The Storage Mechanism: Spreading Consumption across Time

Storage is an important linkage between spot and options and futures markets. Many types of assets can be purchased and stored. Holding a stock is a form of storage. One can also buy a commodity such as wheat or corn and store it in a grain elevator. Storage is a form of investment in which the investor defers selling the item in the hope of obtaining a higher price for it at a later date. It is also a way to spread consumption across time.

Because prices constantly fluctuate, storage entails risk. Options and futures can be used to reduce that risk by providing a means of establishing today the item's future sale price. This suggests that the risk entailed in storing the item can be removed. In that case, the overall investment should offer the risk-free rate. Therefore, it is not surprising that the prices of the storable item, the futures or options contract, and the risk-free rate will all be related.

Delivery and Settlement

Another important linkage between spot and options and futures markets is delivery and settlement. At expiration, a futures contract calls for either immediate delivery of the item or a cash payment of the same value. Thus, an expiring futures contract is equivalent to a spot transaction. The price of the expiring futures contract, therefore, must equal the spot price. Though options differ somewhat from futures at expiration, both instruments have an unambiguous value at expiration that is determined by the spot price.

Few options traders and hardly any futures traders hold their positions until the contracts expire. They use the market's liquidity to enter into offsetting transactions. Nonetheless, the fact that delivery or settlement will occur on positions open at expiration is an important consideration in pricing the spot, futures, and options instruments. For futures contracts, this mechanism is simple: Futures prices and spot prices will converge at expiration.[4]

The foregoing properties play an important role in these markets' performance. Options, futures, and spot markets are inextricably linked. Nonetheless, we have not yet determined what role options and futures markets play in the operations of spot markets.

---

[4]The price of an expiring futures contract and the spot price can differ by a small amount. This point is covered in later chapters.

THE ROLE OF OPTIONS AND FUTURES MARKETS

Risk Management

Because options and futures prices are related to the prices of the underlying spot market goods, they can be used to reduce or increase the risk of investing in the spot items. For example, buying the spot item and selling a futures contract or call option reduces the investor's risk. If the good's price falls, the price of the futures or option contract will also fall. The investor can then repurchase the contract at the lower price, effecting a gain that can at least partially offset the loss on the spot item. This type of transaction is known as a *hedge*.

Investors have different risk preferences. Some are more tolerant of risk than others. All investors, however, want to establish their investments at an acceptable risk level. Options and futures markets enable those wishing to reduce their risk to transfer it to those wishing to increase it. Because these markets are so effective at reallocating risk among investors, no one need assume an uncomfortable level of risk. Consequently, investors are willing to supply more funds to the financial markets. This benefits the economy, because it enables more firms to raise capital and keeps the cost of that capital as low as possible.

Price Discovery

Futures markets are an important means of obtaining information about investors' expectations of future prices. In fact, many people believe that the price of a futures contract is the expected future spot price. Although this issue is controversial, the consensus is that futures prices do contain at least some valuable information about future spot prices.

Information about the future normally is not cheap, nor is it necessarily accurate. Forecasting future prices is a multimillion-dollar industry. Futures markets, however, offer forecasts of future prices at virtually no cost to the general public. There is considerable evidence that these forecasts are nearly as accurate as the more expensive ones.

Options markets do not directly provide forecasts of future spot prices. They do, however, provide valuable information about the volatility and hence the risk of the underlying spot good.

Operational Advantages

Futures and options markets offer several operational advantages. First, they entail lower transaction costs. This means that commissions and other trading costs are lower for traders in these markets. This makes it easy and attractive to use these markets either in lieu of spot market investments or to complement spot positions.

Second, options and futures markets have greater liquidity than spot markets. Although stock and bond markets generally are quite liquid for the securities of major companies, they cannot always absorb some of the large dollar transactions without substantial price changes. In some cases, investors can obtain the same levels of expected return and risk by using futures or options markets, which can more easily accommodate high-volume trades. The reason for this higher liquidity is at least partly due to the smaller amount of capital required for participation in options and futures markets. Returns and risks can be adjusted to any level desired, but since less capital is required, these markets can absorb more trading.

Third, options and futures markets allow investors to sell short more easily. In stock and bond markets, investors sell short by borrowing the securities from a broker. The securities are then sold in the market and—hopefully—repurchased at a lower price later, at which time they are repaid to the broker. Securities markets impose several restrictions designed to limit or discourage short selling that are not applied to options and futures transactions. Consequently, many investors sell short in these markets in lieu of selling short the underlying securities.

Greater Market Efficiency

Stock and bond markets probably would be efficient even if there were no options and futures markets. However, a few profitable arbitrage opportunities exist even in markets that are usually efficient. The presence of these opportunities means that the prices of some assets are temporarily out of line with what they should be. Investors can earn returns that exceed what the market deems fair for the given risk level.

As noted earlier, there are important linkages among spot, futures, and options prices. The ease and low cost of transacting in these markets facilitate the arbitrage trading and rapid price adjustments that quickly eradicate these profit opportunities. Society benefits because the prices of the underlying goods more accurately reflect the goods' true economic values.

Speculation

Futures and options markets provide an alternative means of speculating. Instead of buying the underlying stocks or bonds, an investor can buy an option or futures contract. Many investors prefer to speculate with options and futures rather than with the underlying securities.

We would be remiss, however, if we left it at that. Speculation is controversial. Futures and options markets have taken much criticism from outsiders, including accusations that their activities are tantamount to legalized gambling.

CRITICISMS OF OPTIONS AND FUTURES MARKETS

As noted earlier, options and futures markets allow the transfer of risk from those wanting to remove or decrease it to those wanting to assume or increase it. These markets require the presence of speculators willing to assume risk to accommodate the hedgers wishing to reduce it. Most speculators do not actually deal in the underlying goods and sometimes are alleged to know nothing about them. In fact, futures and options markets are sometimes called *speculative markets*. Consequently, these speculators have been characterized as little more than gamblers.

This view is a bit one-sided and ignores the many benefits of futures and options markets. More important, it suggests that these markets siphon capital into wildly speculative schemes. However, nothing could be further from the truth. Unlike financial markets, futures and options markets neither create nor destroy wealth—they merely transfer it.

For example, stock markets can create wealth. Consider a firm with a new idea that offers stock to the public. Investors buy the stock, and the firm uses the capital to develop and market the idea. Customers then buy the product or service, the firm earns a profit, the stock price increases, and everyone is better off. In contrast, futures and options markets neither create nor destroy wealth. One investor's gains are another's losses. These markets put no additional risk into the economy; they merely allow risk to be passed from one investor to another. More important, they allow the risk of transacting in real goods to be transferred from those not wanting it to those willing to accept it.

An important distinction between futures and options markets and gambling is in the benefits provided to society. Gambling benefits only the participants and perhaps a few others who profit indirectly. The benefits of futures and options, however, extend far beyond the market participants. Futures and options help financial markets become more efficient and provide better opportunities for managing risk. These benefits spill over into society as a whole.

Futures and options markets probably will never escape the criticism that they foster legalized gambling. This view is voiced mostly by people who do not take the time to understand the functions of these markets. The remainder of this book is intended to convince you that these markets play an important role in modern society.

SUMMARY

This chapter presented a general overview of the U.S. financial market system. It illustrated the role that options and futures markets play in the economy and outlined their advantages and critical linkages with financial markets. This material establishes a foundation for the theme of this book: the study of options and futures.

Chapters 2 through 6 discuss options markets, and Chapters 7 through 11 cover futures markets. Parts I and II take a parallel approach. Chapters 2 and 7 discuss the characteristics of these markets; Chapters 3, 4, 8, and 9 are devoted to pricing principles; and Chapters 5, 6, 10, and 11 illustrate popular trading strategies.

Part III contains three chapters that deal with advanced topics in options and futures. Chapter 12 covers options on futures. Chapter 13 focuses on foreign currency options and futures. Chapter 14 examines a variety of applications of options and futures as well as other instruments that have characteristics of options or futures. In addition, it presents some contemporary and controversial issues that dominate the headlines in futures and options markets.

Questions and Problems

1. Distinguish between real assets and financial assets.
2. The price system works in the markets for real assets/services and financial assets. Is it likely to work in options and futures markets as well? Why or why not?
3. What is the difference between primary and secondary markets?
4. What is the difference between securities and contracts such as options and futures?
5. Explain the concept of a risk-return trade-off.
6. What are the components of the expected return?
7. What is an efficient market? Why do efficient markets benefit society?
8. Define *arbitrage* and the *Law of One Price*. What role do they play in our market system?
9. Suppose you are shopping for a new automobile. You find the same car at two dealers but at different prices. Is the Law of One Price being violated? Why or why not?
10. What is storage? Why is it risky? What role does it play in the economy?
11. Why is delivery important if so few futures contracts end in delivery?
12. What are the major functions of options and futures markets in the U.S. economy?
13. Why is speculation controversial? How does it differ from gambling?
14. Assume you have an opportunity to visit a civilization in outer space. Its society is at roughly the same stage of development as the United States is now. Its economic system is virtually identical to that of the United States, but options and futures trading is illegal. Compare and contrast this economy with the U.S. economy, emphasizing the differences due to the presence of options and futures markets in the latter.

part one
OPTIONS

THE STRUCTURE OF OPTIONS MARKETS

The cares of gain are threefold: the struggle of getting, the frenzy of increasing, the horror of losing.

ANONYMOUS, Meditations on Wall Street, 1940

An option is a contract between two parties—a buyer and a seller, or writer—in which the buyer purchases from the writer the right to buy or sell an asset at a fixed price. As in any contract, each party grants something to the other. The buyer pays the seller a fee called the *premium*, which is the option's price. The writer grants the buyer the right to buy or sell the asset at a fixed price.

An option to buy an asset is a *call option*. An option to sell an asset is a *put option*. The fixed price at which the option buyer can either buy or sell the asset is called the *exercise price* or *strike price*, or sometimes *striking price*. In addition, the option has a definite life. The right to buy or sell the asset at a fixed price exists up to a specified expiration date.

We frequently encounter some form of option in everyday life. For example, suppose your local newspaper advertises that a store has a sale scheduled for tomorrow. You notice an interesting bargain and plan to go to the store the next day and purchase the item. Unfortunately, due to unforeseen circumstances you are unable to get to the store on your lunch hour. Instead you go by after work and, not surprisingly, find that the item has been sold out. The manager offers you a rain check that allows you to come back to the store one week later and purchase the item at the sale price. You thank the manager, pocket the rain check, and leave the store with the intention of returning the following week.

You now hold a call option—the rain check—giving you the right to buy the item at a fixed price. You may or may not return to the store to buy the item. If you can find it at a cheaper price elsewhere or decide that it is not worth the cost of going back to the store, you will not use the rain check. If you return and use the rain check to purchase the item, you will have "exercised" the option.

Now suppose you are a farmer and the government announces a new program offering you a guaranteed price for a particular crop. After harvesting the crop, you determine whether the market price is higher than the government's offered price. If it is, you sell the crop in the market; if the government's price is higher, you sell the crop to the government. By selling to the government, you will have "exercised" a put option.

In both examples, the option's distinguishing feature is the right to buy or sell something at a fixed price. This right does not come free, however. With the rain check, you incur the cost and inconvenience of two trips to the store. With the government price guaranty, the cost takes the form of a burden to society in terms of potential misallocation of resources, a surplus of the good, and higher taxes.

THE DEVELOPMENT OF OPTIONS MARKETS

The rain check and price guaranty are examples of options found in everyday life. Even historians and archaeologists have discovered examples of options. While these arrangements may resemble modern options, the current system of options markets traces its origins to the nineteenth century, when puts and calls were offered on shares of stock. Little is known about the options world of the 1800s other than that it was fraught with corruption.

Then, in the early 1900s, a group of firms calling itself the Put and Call Brokers and Dealers Association created an options market. If someone wanted to buy an option, a member of the association would find a seller willing to write it. If the member firm could not find a writer, it would write the option itself. Thus, a member firm could be either a broker—one who matches buyer and seller—or a dealer—one who actually takes a position in the transaction.

Although this over-the-counter options market was viable, it suffered from several deficiencies. First, it did not provide the option holder the opportunity to sell the option to someone else before it expired. Options were designed to be held all the way to expiration, whereupon they were either exercised or allowed to expire. Thus, an option contract had little or no liquidity. Second, the writer's performance was guaranteed only by the broker-dealer firm. If the writer or the Put and Call Brokers and Dealers Association member firm went bankrupt, the option holder was simply out of luck.[1] Third, the cost of transacting was relatively high, due partly to the first two problems.

---

[1]The individual or firm could, of course, pursue costly legal remedies.

In 1973, a revolutionary change occurred in the options world. The Chicago Board of Trade, the world's oldest and largest exchange for the trading of commodity futures contracts, organized an exchange exclusively for trading options on stocks. The exchange was named the Chicago Board Options Exchange (CBOE). It opened its doors for call option trading on April 26, 1973, and the first puts were added in June 1977.

Since that time, several stock exchanges and almost all the commodity futures exchanges have begun trading options. Although activity in the over-the-counter options market had declined over the years, more recently, there has been a resurgence in the demand for over-the-counter options. However, the vast majority of options trading is done on organized exchanges.

CALL OPTIONS

A call option is an option to buy an asset at a fixed price—the exercise price. Options are available on several types of assets, but we shall concentrate on options on stock.[2] Consider the following example.

On March 6, 1991, the Chicago Board Options Exchange offered options on the stock of Federal Express. One particular call option had an exercise price of $40 and an expiration date of April 19. The Federal Express stock had a price of $39.75. The buyer of this option received the right to buy Federal Express stock any time up through April 19 at $40 per share. The writer of that option therefore was obligated to sell the stock at $40 per share through April 19 whenever the buyer wanted it. For this privilege, the buyer paid the writer the premium, or price, of $1.8125.

Why would either party have entered into the call option contract? The buyer would not have done so to immediately exercise the option, because the stock could be bought in the market for $39.75, which was less than the exercise price of $40. The buyer must have anticipated that the stock's price would rise above $40 before the option expired. Conversely, the writer expected that the stock price would not get above $40 before the option expired. The buyer and writer negotiated the premium of $1.8125, which can be viewed as the buyer's wager on the stock's price going above $40 by April 19. Alternatively, either the buyer or writer may have been using the option to protect a position in the stock—a strategy called *hedging*.

Suppose that immediately after a call is purchased the stock price increases. Because the exercise price is constant, the call option is now more valuable. New call options with the same terms will sell for higher premiums. Therefore, older call options with the same expiration date and exercise price must also sell for higher premiums. Similarly, if the stock price falls, the call's price also will decline. Clearly the buyer of a call option has bullish expectations about the stock.

[2]Options that trade on commodity futures exchanges are actually options on futures contracts and are covered in Chapter 12. Since a futures contract is not an asset, an option need not be an "option on an asset," although we shall continue to use that expression until Chapter 12.

A call in which the stock price exceeds the exercise price is said to be *in-the-money*. However, as we shall see in Chapter 3, in-the-money calls should not necessarily be exercised prior to expiration. If the stock price is less than the exercise price, the call option is said to be *out-of-the-money*. Out-of-the-money calls should never be exercised. We shall explore these points more thoroughly in Chapter 3. If the stock price equals the exercise price, the option is *at-the-money*.

PUT OPTIONS

A put option is an option to sell an asset, such as a stock. Consider the put option on Federal Express stock on March 6, 1991, with an exercise price of $40 per share and an expiration date of April 19. It allowed the put holder to sell the stock at $40 per share any time up through April 19. The stock currently was selling for $39.75. Therefore, the put holder could have elected to exercise the option, selling the stock to the writer for $40 per share. However, the put holder may have preferred to wait and see if the stock price fell further below the exercise price. The put buyer expected the stock price to fall, while the writer expected it to remain the same or rise.

The buyer and writer negotiated a premium of $2.125, which the buyer paid to the writer. The premium can be viewed as the buyer's wager that the stock price would not rise above $40 per share by April 19. The writer accepted the premium because it was deemed to be fair compensation for the willingness to buy the stock for $40 any time up through April 19. As in the case of calls, either the buyer or the writer might have been using the put to hedge a position in the stock.

Since the put allows the holder to sell the stock for a fixed price, a decrease in the stock price will make the put more valuable. Conversely, if the stock price increases, the put will be less valuable. It should be apparent that the buyer of a put has bearish expectations for the stock.

If the stock price is less than the exercise price, the put is said to be *in-the-money*. In Chapter 3, we shall see that it is sometimes, but not always, optimal to exercise an in-the-money put prior to expiration. If the stock price is more than the exercise price, the put is *out-of-the-money*. An out-of-the-money put should never be exercised. When the stock price equals the exercise price, the put is *at-the-money*.

ORGANIZED OPTIONS TRADING

As indicated earlier, most of the option trading in this country occurs on organized exchanges. In this section, we shall look at the role of the options exchanges in organized options trading.

An *exchange* is a legal corporate entity organized for the trading of securities, options, or futures. It provides a physical facility and stipulates rules and regulations governing the transactions in the instruments trading thereon. In the options markets, organized exchanges evolved in response to the lack of standardization and liquidity of over-the-counter options. Over-the-counter options were written for specific buyers by particular sellers. The terms and conditions of the contracts, such as the exercise price and expiration date, were tailored for the parties involved. Organized exchanges filled the need for standardized option contracts wherein the exchange would specify the contracts' terms and conditions. Consequently, a secondary market for the contracts was made possible.

By providing a physical trading floor, specifying rules and regulations, and standardizing contracts, options became as marketable as stocks. If an option holder wanted to sell the option before the expiration date or an option writer wished to get out of the obligation to buy or sell the stock, a closing transaction could be arranged at the options exchange. We shall examine these procedures in more detail in a later section.

The Chicago Board Options Exchange, the first organized options exchange, established the procedures that made options marketable. In addition, it paved the way for the American, Philadelphia, Pacific, and New York Stock Exchanges to begin option trading. The next several sections examine the CBOE's contract specifications.

Listing Requirements

The options exchange specifies the assets on which option trading is allowed. For stock options, the exchange's listing requirements prescribe the eligible stocks on which options can be traded. The CBOE's requirements for listing options on a stock are as follows:

1. The company must have had a profit before extraordinary items of at least $1 million for the last eight quarters and not have defaulted on any obligations in the last 12 months.

2. The company must have at least 6,000 shareholders.

3. At least 7 million shares must be owned by non-inside stockholders.

4. The stock must have sold for at least $10 a share for the previous three months.

5. The stock must have had a trading volume of at least 2.4 million shares over the last 12 months.

Although the exchange selects the stocks on which options may be traded, the Securities and Exchange Commission (SEC), the regulatory authority for stock and option trading, has had to intervene in some cases. The CBOE has argued that multiple listings—the listing of the same options on more than one exchange— are not in the public's best interest; rather, the exchanges should specialize in particular listings. However the other exchanges and the SEC contend that multiple listings encourage competition among the exchanges. While the issue is being studied, the SEC has allowed some multiple listings and assigned other listings to the exchanges by lottery. At the time of this writing, plans were in place to permit multiple listing of all options in 1991. Regardless of how this issue is resolved, it is important to note that the determination of whether to list options on a particular stock is not made by the company issuing the stock. In fact, one company— Golden Nugget—opposed the listing of options on its stock and even took legal action to prevent option trading on its stock. After more than two years in court, Golden Nugget lost its case.

The listing of options on assets other than individual stocks is decided differently. For example, if an exchange wants to create an option on an index, it drafts a proposal specifying how the index will be constructed and the terms and conditions of the contracts. It then applies to the SEC for permission to trade the option. The SEC evaluates the proposal and either grants or denies permission.

The exchange also specifies minimum requirements that a stock must meet to maintain the listing of options on it. These requirements are similar to but slightly less stringent than those for the initial listing. In all cases, however, the exchange has the authority to make exceptions to the listing and delisting requirements.

All options of a particular type—call or put—on a given stock are referred to as an option *class.* For example, the Federal Express calls are one option class and the Federal Express puts are another. An option *series* is all of the options of a given class with the same exercise price and expiration. For example, the Federal Express April 40 calls are a particular series, as are the Federal Express July 45 puts.

Contract Size

A standard option contract consists of 100 individual options. Thus, if an investor purchases one option, that option actually represents options to buy 100 shares of stock. An exception to the standard contract size occurs when either a stock splits or the company declares a stock dividend. In that case, the number of shares represented by a standard contract is adjusted to reflect the change in the company's capitalization. For example, if a company declares a 15 percent stock dividend, the number of shares represented by one contract changes from 100 to 115. In addition, the exercise price is adjusted to $1/1.15 = .8697$, rounded to the nearest eighth—.875—of its former value. However, if a stock split or stock dividend results in the new number of shares being an even multiple of 100, holders of outstanding contracts are credited with additional contracts. For example, if the stock splits two-for-one, buyers and writers are credited with two contracts for every one formerly held. In addition, the exercise price is reduced to half of its previous value.

Contract sizes for options on indices and certain other instruments are specified as a multiple. For example, an option on the S&P 100 has a multiple of 100; an investor who buys one contract actually buys 100 options.

Exercise Prices

In the old over-the-counter options market, the option's exercise price usually was the stock price at the time the option was written. In organized options markets, the exercise prices are standardized. The exchange prescribes the exercise prices at which options can be written. Investors must be willing to trade options with the specified exercise prices.

The objective in determining the exercise prices is to provide options that will attract trading volume. Most option trading is concentrated in options in which the stock price is close to the exercise price. Accordingly, exchange officials tend to list options in which the exercise prices surround but are close to the current stock price. They must use their judgment as to whether an exercise price is too far above or below the stock price to generate sufficient trading volume. If the stock price moves up or down, new exercise prices close to the stock price are added.

In establishing exercise prices of stock options, the exchange generally follows the rule that the exercise prices are in $2.50 intervals if the stock price is less than $25, in $5 intervals if the stock price is between $25 and $200, and in $10 intervals if the stock price is above $200. For index options, exercise prices are in $5 intervals. However, the exchange will waive these rules if it believes that it must to attract sufficient trading volume.

When a stock pays a dividend, the stock price falls by the amount of the dividend on the ex-dividend day, which is the day after the last day on which the purchaser of the stock is entitled to receive the upcoming dividend. Because option holders do not receive dividends and benefit from increases in the stock price, the ex-dividend decrease in the stock price would arbitrarily hurt call holders and help put holders. In the old over-the-counter options market, options were said to be dividend-protected. If the company declared a $1 dividend, the exercise price was reduced by $1. Since over-the-counter options were not meant to be traded, the frequent dividend adjustments caused no problems. For exchange-listed options, however, such dividend adjustments would have generated many nonstandard exercise prices. Thus, the exchanges elected not to adjust the exercise price when a cash dividend was paid. As we shall see in the next two chapters, this rule is an important factor in pricing options.

Expiration Dates

Expiration dates of over-the-counter options traditionally were tailored to the buyers' and writers' needs. Since the options exchanges elected to standardize expirations, each stock was classified into a particular expiration cycle. The original expiration cycles were (1) January, April, July, and October; (2) February, May, August, and November; and (3) March, June, September, and December. These were called the *January*, *February*, and *March cycles*.

Consider a stock classified into the March cycle. This means that options on the stock were offered only with expirations in March, June, September, and December. This made the longest possible expiration nine months. On any given date, only three of four expirations were available for trading. For example, in February a stock assigned to the March cycle had expirations of March, June, and September. When the March options expired, the December options were added.

The exchanges followed this procedure until 1984, when they began to modify the exercise cycles. Because of the increased demand for short maturity options, they began to add expirations consisting of the current and next several months for certain index options. These new expirations proved highly popular, and eventually equity options were placed on the new cycles.

Each stock is still classified into the January, February, or March cycle. The available expirations are the current month, the next month, and the next two months within the January, February, or March cycle to which the option is assigned. For example, in early June IBM, which is assigned to the January cycle, will have options expiring in June and July plus the next two months in the January cycle: October and the following January. When the June options expire, the August options will be added; when the July options expire, the September options will be added; and when the August options expire, the April options will be added. Although there are four possible expirations, with the longest being nine months, *The Wall Street Journal* quotations cover only the first three. In addition, in 1990 the CBOE and AMEX began offering options on individual stocks and indices with expirations of up to two years. These options, called LEAPS, for Long-Term Equity Anticipation Securities, have generated considerable interest on the part of investors.

Index options have a number of cycles. Most of the cycles offer the current month and one or more of the following consecutive months, plus one or more months from the January, February, or March cycles. Some S&P 500 Index options offer expirations as long as two years.

The expiration day is the Saturday following the third Friday of the month. The last day on which the option trades is the third Friday of the month. An investor desiring to exercise an option has until 4:30 p.m. central time for stock options and 5:30 p.m. for index options on that Friday to notify the broker. The broker has until 10:59 p.m. central time on Saturday to order the option's exercise. However, many brokerage firms impose earlier deadlines to allow them to complete the necessary paperwork in time.

Position and Exercise Limits

The options exchange also imposes *position limits* that define the maximum number of options an investor can hold on one side of the market. For example, because they are both bullish strategies, a long call and a short put on the same stock are transactions on the same side of the market. Likewise, a short call and a long put are both bearish strategies and thus are considered to be on the same side of the market. The options exchange publishes the position limit for each stock, which is either 3,000, 5,000, or 8,000 contracts, depending on the stock's trading volume and number of outstanding shares. Position limits are higher for index options. For the S&P 100 the position limit is 25,000 contracts, and an additional 75,000 contracts can be held if the investor is hedging. In addition, market makers have certain exemptions from these position limits.

TABLE 2.1
Exchanges on Which Options Trade, March 1991

Chicago Board Options Exchange
(CBOE)
400 S. LaSalle Street
Chicago, IL 60605
312-786-5600
Options on: stocks, stock
indices, Treasury bonds and
notes, interest rates

Philadelphia Stock Exchange
(PHLX)
1900 Market Street
Philadelphia, PA 19103
215-496-5357
Options on: stocks, stock
indices, foreign currencies

New York Stock Exchange
(NYSE)
11 Wall Street
New York, NY 10005
212-656-8533
Options on: stocks, stock indices

American Stock Exchange
(AMEX)
86 Trinity Place
New York, NY 10006
212-306-1000
Options on: stocks, stock
indices, Treasury bills and notes

Pacific Stock Exchange
(PSE)
301 Pine Street
San Francisco, CA 94104
415-393-4000
Options on: stocks, stock indices

Note: Exchanges on which options on futures trade are covered in Chapters 7 and 12.

Exercise limits are similar to position limits. An *exercise limit* is the maximum number of options that can be exercised on any five consecutive business days by any individual or group of individuals acting together. The figure for the exercise limit is the same as that for the position limit.

The purpose of position and exercise limits is to prevent a single individual or group from having a significant effect on the market. It is not clear, however, that such restrictions are necessary.

EXCHANGES ON WHICH OPTIONS TRADE

Options trading currently exists on several U.S. exchanges. The CBOE is the only exchange devoted solely to options trading; the other exchanges trade stocks as well as options. Table 2.1 lists the exchanges and their addresses and telephone numbers.

Options trading is not confined to these exchanges. Chapter 12 covers options on futures, which trade on virtually every commodity futures exchange in

FIGURE 2.1

Option Volume

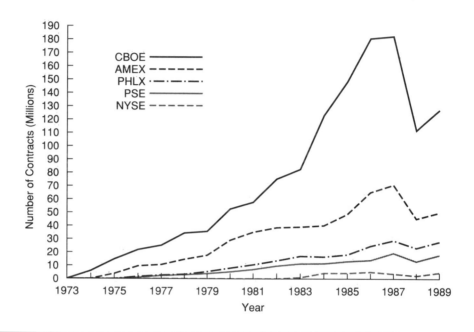

the country. We shall defer discussing those contracts and exchanges until Chapters 7 and 12.

Options are also traded on stock and futures exchanges in Sydney, São Paulo, Montreal, Toronto, Vancouver, Copenhagen, Helsinki, Osaka, Tokyo, Amsterdam, Stockholm, and London.

Figure 2.1 shows the volume of option trading on the five U.S. exchanges on which options trade. Growth in option trading had been quite phenomenal until 1988. The market crash of 1987 resulted in a reduction in volume of about 35 percent in 1988 from 1987 as many individual investors shied away from the markets. In 1989, however, volume recovered to increase about 16 percent over 1988 volume. The crash had an even greater impact on index option volume, which fell about 45 percent in 1988 over 1987 and rose only 4 percent in 1989 over 1988. However, equity option volume, which fell about 30 percent in 1988, rose about 23 percent in 1989.

The CBOE's share of stock option volume has declined over the years from about 66 percent in 1976, the first full year in which options were traded on the AMEX, to the 44 percent share it captured in 1989. However, when index, foreign currency, and bond options are included, the CBOE's share, as shown in Figure 2.2, is over 55 percent. This is because of the CBOE's share of the index option market of over 87 percent.

FIGURE 2.2
Share of Option Volume

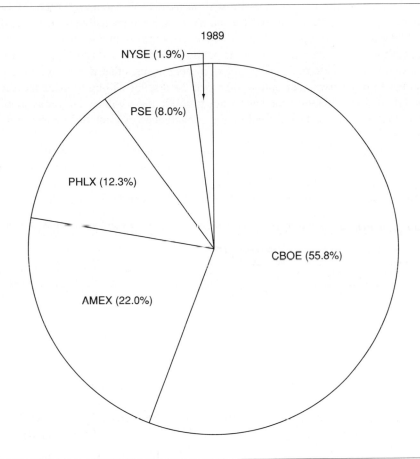

OPTION TRADERS

An exchange is a legal corporate entity whose members are individuals or firms. Each membership is referred to as a *seat*. Although the organizational structures of the various exchanges differ somewhat, membership generally entitles one to physically go onto the trading floor and trade options. The following sections discuss the types of traders who operate both on and off the exchange floor. This system of traders is based on the market maker system used by the CBOE and Pacific Stock Exchange.

The Market Maker

An individual who has purchased a seat on the CBOE can apply to be either a market maker or a floor broker.[3] The *market maker* is responsible for meeting the public's demand for options. When someone from the public wishes to buy (sell) an option and no other member of the public is willing to sell (buy) it, the market maker completes the trade. This type of system ensures that if a private investor wishes to buy a particular option, there will be a seller willing to make an offer, and if one buys an option and later wants to sell it, there will be a buyer available. The market maker offers the public the convenience of immediate execution of trades.

The market maker is essentially an entrepreneur. To survive, the market maker must profit by buying at one price and selling at a higher price. One way this is done is by quoting a bid price and an ask price. The *bid* price is the maximum price the market maker will pay for the option. The *ask* price is the minimum price the market maker will accept for the option. The ask price is set higher than the bid price. The exchange imposes upper limits on the difference between the ask and bid prices, called the *bid-ask spread*. The limits on the bid-ask spread are as follows:

Bid Price	Maximum Spread in Points
< 2	1/4
≥ 2 and ≤ 5	3/8
> 5 and ≤ 10	1/2
> 10 and ≤ 20	3/4
> 20	1

Phillips and Smith (1980) report that the median bid-ask spread on the CBOE is about one-eighth of a point compared with about one-quarter of a point for stocks on the New York Stock Exchange.

The bid-ask spread is a significant transaction cost for those who must trade with a market maker. To the market maker, however, it represents the reward for the willingness to buy when the public is selling and sell when the public is buying. Bid-ask spreads are discussed further in the section on transaction costs.

Market makers use a variety of techniques to trade options intelligently and profitably. Many look at fundamentals such as interest rates, economic conditions, and company performance. Others rely on technical analysis, which pur-

---

[3]Exchange rules allow an individual to be both a market maker and a floor broker, but not on the same day.

ports to find signals of the direction of future stock prices in the behavior of past stock prices. Still others rely simply on intuition and experience. In addition, market makers tend to employ different trading styles. Some are *scalpers*, who try to buy at the bid and sell at the ask before the price moves downward or after the price moves just slightly upward. Scalpers seldom hold positions for more than a few minutes. In contrast, *position traders* have somewhat longer holding periods. Many option traders, including some scalpers and position traders, are also *spreaders*, who buy one option and sell another in the hope of earning small profits at low risk. Option spreading strategies are covered in more detail in Chapter 6.

The Floor Broker

The *floor broker* is another type of trader on the exchange. The floor broker executes trades for members of the public. If someone wishes to buy or sell an option, that individual must first establish an account with a brokerage firm. That firm must either employ a floor broker or have an arrangement whereby it contracts with either an independent floor broker or a floor broker of a competing firm.

The floor broker executes orders for nonmembers and earns either a flat salary or a commission on each order executed. The floor broker generally need not be concerned about whether the price is expected to go up or down; however, a good broker will work diligently to obtain the best price for the customer.

The Order Book Official

A third type of trader at the CBOE is the *Order Book Official (OBO)*, an employee of the exchange. To see how an OBO works, suppose you place a *limit order*—an order specifying a maximum price to be paid on a purchase or a minimum acceptable price on a sale—to buy a call option at a maximum price of $3. The floor broker handling your order determines that the best quote offered by a market maker is 2 3/4 bid and 3 1/4 ask. This means that the lowest price at which a market maker will sell the call is 3 1/4. If your floor broker has other orders to execute, the OBO takes your limit order and enters it into the computer along with all the other public limit orders. The market makers are informed of the best public limit orders. If conditions change such that at least one market maker is willing to quote an ask price of 3 or lower, the OBO will execute your limit order.

Public limit orders are always executed before market maker orders; however, the market makers, being aware of the best public limit orders, know the maximum and minimum prices at which they can trade. For example, if your limit order to buy at 3 is the highest bid and the market maker is quoting an ask price of 3 1/4, the market maker chooses between accepting your bid and selling the call at 3 or holding out for an offer of 3 1/8 or higher. If no one bids 3 1/8 within a reasonable time period, the market maker might choose to take your bid of 3.

The options exchanges also have brought the benefits of modern technology to their order processing operations. The CBOE's Retail Automatic Execution System (RAES) fills small public orders by matching buyer and seller on a computer. Its Electronic Book (EB) expedites order processing for certain large volume options. This increased use of technology has resulted in proposals to extend option trading to hours after the exchange is closed. As we shall see in Chapter 7, the futures industry has moved more quickly than the securities and options industry toward 24-hour trading, but the securities and options exchanges are beginning to catch up in that regard.

Other Option Trading Systems

The CBOE and Pacific Stock Exchange use the system of competing market makers. The American and Philadelphia Stock Exchanges use a slightly different system. Here an individual called a *specialist* is responsible for making bids and offers on options. The specialist maintains and attempts to fill public limit orders but does not disclose them to others. In addition to the specialist are individuals called *registered option traders (ROTs)*, who buy and sell options for themselves or act as brokers for others. Unlike the CBOE market makers, ROTs are not obligated to make a market in the options; market making is the specialist's task.[4]

Clerks, runners, and exchange officials are also present on the exchange floor. Other than the traders on the floor, the most important participants in the options industry are the individuals and institutions that trade off the floor.

Off-Floor Option Traders

The investment community consists of a vast number of institutions of all sizes, many of which participate in option trading. Some of these institutions are brokerage firms that execute orders for the public. Most brokerage firms employ individuals responsible for recommending profitable option trades to their brokers. Many, however, have specialized option trading departments that search for mispriced options, trade in them, and in so doing contribute to their firms' profitability. Many large institutional investors, such as pension funds, trusts, and mutual funds, also trade options. In most cases, these types of investors write options on the stocks held in their portfolios. A growing contingent of foreign institutions also trade options.

In addition to the large institutional investors, there are numerous individuals—some wealthy and some not—who trade options. In a 1984 survey jointly commissioned by the Federal Reserve, the Commodity Futures Trading Commission, and the Securities and Exchange Commission, stock option traders reported household income as follows: 9 percent earned less than $25,000; 32 percent earned between $25,000 and $49,999; 39 percent earned between $50,000 and $99,000; 13 percent earned between $100,000 and $199,999; and 7 percent reported income in excess of $200,000. Slightly more than a third had at least an

[4]The CBOE has used a variation of the specialist system for low volume options. For a comparison of the specialist and market maker systems, see Pierog (1987).

undergraduate degree, and ages were about evenly spread between 31 and 70. About two-thirds of the respondents reported that their trading was "somewhat" or "very" successful, and about one-fourth said they had lost money overall. About 60 percent reported that they made their own decisions, and around 80 percent said they used options to speculate.

In addition to those who trade options themselves, there are many wealthy people who turn over their financial affairs to specialized managers and thus participate in the options market without being personally involved. The dollar amounts required for trading options are so small that virtually anyone can afford to participate.

Cost and Profitability of Exchange Membership

An individual who decides to purchase a seat on an exchange that has option trading can take one of several routes. The most obvious is to purchase a seat from an existing member. Figure 2.3 shows the history of the price of a seat on the CBOE.

At over $200,000, the cost of obtaining membership would seem prohibitive to most individuals. However, there are other ways to gain membership. Some seat owners lease their seats to others; rental rates run about .50 to .75 percent of the seat's price per month. Also, some members allow "trainees" to trade with their seats and charge them a percentage of the trading profits.

The *Report of the Special Study of the Options Markets* (1978), conducted by the SEC, found that in 1977 1,153 market makers reported profits totaling $38.1 million, or an average of about $33,000 each; however, 413 market makers reported losses totaling $15.9 million. Thus, the 740 profitable market makers averaged almost $73,000. Although no current figures on market maker profitability are available, it seems likely that the rewards remain high. However, the losses posted by over a third of the market makers are a subtle reminder of the risk-return trade-off.

THE MECHANICS OF TRADING

Placing an Opening Order

An individual who wants to trade options must first open an account with a brokerage firm. The individual then instructs the broker to buy or sell a particular option. The broker sends the order to the firm's floor broker on the exchange on which the option trades. All orders must be executed during the normal trading hours of 8:30 a.m. to 3:10 p.m. central time. Trading is performed within the trading pit designated for the particular option. The trading pit is a multilevel, octagonally shaped area within which the market makers and floor brokers stand.

An investor can place several types of orders. A *market order* instructs the floor broker to obtain the best price. A *limit order*, as indicated earlier, specifies a maxi-

FIGURE 2.3
CBOE Seat Prices

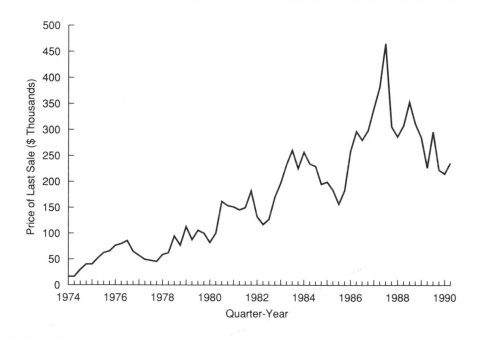

In addition to specifying the option the investor wishes to buy or sell, the order must indicate the number of contracts desired. The order might be a request to purchase ten contracts at the best possible price. The market maker's quote, however, need apply to only one contract. Therefore, if multiple contracts are needed, the market maker may offer a less favorable price. In that case, the order might be only partially filled. To avoid a partial fill, the investor can place an all or none or an all or none, same price order. An *all or none order* allows the broker to fill part of the order at one price and part at another. An *all or none, same price order* requires the broker to either fill the whole order at the same price or not fill the order at all.

mum price to pay if buying or a minimum price to accept if selling. Limit orders may be either good-till-canceled or day orders. A *good-till-canceled order* remains in effect until canceled. A *day order* stays in effect for the remainder of the day. Finally, an investor holding a particular option might place a *stop order* at a price lower than the current price. If the market price falls to the specified price, the broker is instructed to sell the option at the best available price. There are a number of other types of orders designed to handle different contingencies.

In 1989, the CBOE reported that the average number of contracts per trade was 10.2.[5] This figure has steadily increased over the years, reflecting the growing interest in options trading, particularly by large investors.

The Role of the Clearinghouse

After the trade is consummated, the clearinghouse enters the process. The *clearinghouse*, formally known as the *Options Clearing Corporation (OCC)*, is an independent corporation that guarantees the writer's performance. The OCC is the intermediary in each transaction. A buyer exercising an option looks not to the writer but to the clearinghouse. A writer exercising an option makes payment for or delivery of the stock to the clearinghouse.

Each OCC member, known as a *clearing firm*, has an account with the OCC. Each market maker must clear all trades through a member firm, as must every brokerage firm, although in some cases a brokerage firm is also a clearing firm.

We shall illustrate how the clearinghouse operates by assuming that you bought the Federal Express April 40 call we described earlier. You contacted your broker, who, through either his or her firm's floor broker or an independent floor broker, found a seller. You bought ten contracts at a price of $1.8125, which totals up to $1,812.50. The seller, whose identity you do not know, has an account with another brokerage firm.

Your brokerage firm clears its trades through XYZ Trading Company, a clearing firm that is a member of the OCC. The seller's broker clears through ABC Options, another member of the OCC. You pay your broker the $1,812.50, and your broker pays XYZ Trading Company. It pools the transactions of all of its customers and, through some predetermined formula, deposits a sum of money with the OCC.

Let us also assume that the seller does not already own the stock, so he or she will have to deposit some additional money, called *margin*, with ABC. The amount of margin required is discussed in Appendix 2A; for now, however, just assume that the amount is 20 percent of the value of the stock, which comes to $7,950. The seller gives the $7,950 to the broker, who deposits it with ABC Options, which also keeps the $1,812.50 premium. ABC, in turn, is required to deposit with the OCC an amount of money determined according to a formula that takes its oustanding contracts into account.

The OCC guarantees the performance of ABC, the seller's clearing firm. Thus, you, the buyer, need not worry about whether the money will be there if you decide to exercise your option. The OCC, in turn, will look to ABC for payment; ABC will look to the seller's brokerage firm, which will look to the seller's personal broker, who will look to the seller for payment.

The total number of option contracts outstanding at any given time is called the *open interest*. The open interest figure indicates the number of closing transac-

---

[5]CBOE, *Market Statistics 1989.*

tions that might be made before the option expires. At the end of 1989, open interest in stock options on all exchanges was over 9 million contracts.[6]

The OCC thus fulfills the important responsibility of guaranteeing option writers' performances. A call buyer need not examine the writer's credit; in fact, in the case of individuals and firms off the floor, the buyers do not even know the writers' identities.

Because the member clearing firms assume some risk, the OCC imposes minimum capital requirements on them. The OCC has a claim on their securities and margin deposits in the event of their default. As a further safeguard, the OCC maintains a special fund supported by its members. If that fund is depleted, the OCC can assess its other members to ensure its survival as well as that of the options market in general.

Placing an Offsetting Order

Suppose an investor holds a call option. The stock price recently has been increasing, and the call's price is now much higher than the original purchase price. The liquidity of the options market makes it possible for the investor to take the profit by selling the option in the market. Without the liquidity, the option would have to be held until the expiration date, at which time it would either be exercised or, if out-of-the-money, be allowed to expire.

The call holder who does not want to wait until expiration places an order to sell the option. This is called an *offsetting order* or simply an *offset*. The order is executed in the same manner as an opening order. Continuing with our example in which you bought ten contracts of the Federal Express April 40 calls, suppose the price of the calls is now $2.25. You instruct your broker to sell the calls. Your broker orders his firm's floor broker to sell the calls. The floor broker finds a buyer who agrees to the price of $2.25. The buyer pays $2,250 to her broker, who passes the funds through to his company's clearing firm, which passes the funds through to the OCC. The OCC then credits the $2,250 to the account of your broker's clearing firm, XYZ Trading Company, which credits your broker's firm, which in turn credits your account. You now have $2,250 and no outstanding position in this option. The individual who bought these options from you may have been offsetting a previously established short position in the calls or may be establishing a new, long position in them.

In 1989, the CBOE reported that about 61 percent of all opening stock option transactions were closed in this manner.[7] In some cases, however, option traders may wish to exercise the option.

---

[6]*The Wall Street Journal*, January 2, 1990.
[7]CBOE, *Market Statistics 1989*.

Exercising an Option

An American option can be exercised on any day up through the expiration date. European options (which are not necessarily traded in Europe) can be exercised only on the expiration date. Suppose you elect to exercise the Federal Express April 40 calls, which, like all options on stocks in the United States, are American options. You notify your brokerage firm, which in turn notifies the clearing firm through which the trade originally was cleared. The clearing firm then places an exercise order with the OCC, which randomly selects a clearing firm through which someone has written the same option. The clearing firm, using a procedure established and made known to its customers in advance, selects someone who has written that option.[8] The chosen writer is said to be *assigned*.

If the option is a call option on an individual stock, the writer must deliver the stock. You then pay the exercise price, which is passed on to the writer. If the option had been a put option on an individual stock, you would have to deliver the stock. The writer pays the exercise price, which is passed on to you. (Index options are exercised in a different manner, discussed in a later section.) For either type of option, however, the writer who originally wrote the contract might not be the one who is assigned the exercise.

On expiration day, if you find that the stock price is less than the exercise price or, for a put, that the stock price is greater than the exercise price, you allow the option to expire by doing nothing. When the expiration day passes, the option contract is removed from the records of the clearing firm and the OCC.

In 1989, about 11 percent of all calls and 9 percent of all puts on the CBOE were exercised and about 43 percent of the calls and 32 percent of the puts expired.[9] In some cases, options that should have been exercised at expiration were not, due to customer ignorance or oversight. Some brokerage firms have a policy of exercising options automatically when doing so is to the customer's advantage. Such a policy usually is stated in the agreement that the customer signs when opening the account. The OCC automatically exercises options owned by individuals that are in-the-money by more than three-quarters of a point (one-quarter of a point for index options) and options owned by institutions that are in-the-money by more than one-quarter of a point (one-hundredth of a point for index options).

OPTION PRICE QUOTATIONS

Option prices are available daily in *The Wall Street Journal* and in many daily newspapers in larger cities. Figure 2.4 illustrates how *The Wall Street Journal* reports options on individual stocks. At the top of the figure is a group of options on the CBOE; the remaining options shown are on the American Stock Exchange.

[8]Procedures such as first-in, first-out or random selection are commonly used.

[9]CBOE, *Market Statistics 1989*.

FIGURE 2.4

Stock Option Quotations in *The Wall Street Journal*, Trading Day of March 22, 1991

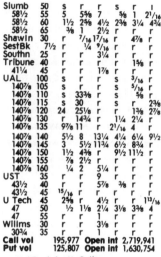

Slumb	50	s	r	r	s	r	1
58½	55	5	5⅝	7	⅝	1	2 1/16
58½	60	1½	2⅝	4½	2⅜	3¼	4¾
58½	65	⅜	1	2½	r	r	r
Shawln	30	r	7/16	1 7/16	r	4⅞	r
SestBk	7½	r	¼	9/16	r	r	r
Southn	25	r	r	3¼	r	r	r
Tribune	40	r	r	r	r	1⅝	r
41¼	45	r	r	1⅞	r	r	r
UAL	100	s	r	r	s	3/16	r
140⅞	105	s	r	r	s	5/16	r
140⅞	110	s	33⅜	r	s	⅝	r
140⅞	115	s	30	r	s	r	2⅜
140⅞	120	24	25⅛	r	r	1⅜	2⅞
140⅞	130	r	14¾	r	1¼	2¼	r
140⅞	135	9⅞	11	r	2 1/16	4	r
140⅞	140	5½	8	13¼	4¼	6¼	9½
140⅞	145	3	5½	11¾	6½	8¾	r
140⅞	150	1½	4⅜	r	9½	11½	r
140⅞	155	⅞	2½	r	r	r	r
140⅞	160	¼	2	5¼	r	r	r
UST	35	r	r	9	r	r	r
43½	40	r	r	5⅞	⅜	r	r
43½	45	15/16	r	r	r	r	r
U Tech	45	2⅝	r	4½	r	r	1 13/16
47	50	½	1⅛	2¼	3⅛	3⅜	4
47	55	r	r	1	r	r	r
Wilims	30	r	r	3⅛	r	r	r
30¾	35	r	r	1	r	r	r
Call vol		195,977	**Open int**	2,719,941			
Put vol		125,807	**Open int**	1,630,754			

r-Not Traded. s-No Option.

AMERICAN

Option & NY Close	Strike Price	Calls-Last Apr	May	Jun	Puts-Last Apr	May	Jun
Alcan	20	r	r	r	⅛	r	⅞
22	22½	r	r	r	1	r	r
22	25	r	⅛	r	3¼	r	r
Amax	25	1⅛	r	2⅛	¾	r	r
25⅜	30	⅛	r	⅜	r	r	r
AmBrnd	45	2⅛	r	r	¾	1⅜	r
46	50	r	r	1	r	r	r
Asarco	25	r	r	r	⅛	r	r
Blkbst	12½	7/16	r	r	¾	r	r
12⅛	15	r	r	½	r	r	3½
BwnFer	22½	r	r	4	r	r	½
25⅞	25	r	1⅞	2⅜	r	r	r
25⅞	30	r	r	⅝	r	r	r
Chase	12½	1¾	2	1⅞	r	½	⅝
13⅞	15	¼	7/16	11/16	1⅜	1 7/16	1⅞
ChemBk	12½	s	s	3⅜	s	s	r
15⅜	15	⅞	1⅛	1⅝	½	¾	1
15⅜	17½	3/16	⅜	⅝	2	r	2½
15⅜	20	⅛	3/16	¼	r	r	r
ChemW	17½	r	r	2 5/16	r	⅜	¾
18½	20	⅜	¾	1	1⅝	2 1/16	2
18½	22½	r	r	½	r	r	r
18½	25	r	r	⅛	6¼	r	r
18½	30	r	s	⅛	r	s	r
Chevrn	70	r	r	9	⅛	r	¾
78	75	r	r	5	¾	1½	1⅞
78	80	⅞	1½	2¼	2⅞	r	r
Circus	60	r	r	6	1	r	2½
62½	65	1⅛	r	r	3½	r	r
62½	70	r	r	2¼	r	r	r
Coastl	35	5/16	r	1¼	r	r	r
32⅝	40	r	r	¼	r	r	r
ConAg	40	r	r	4½	r	r	r
43	45	¾	r	r	r	r	r
Deere	45	r	r	r	r	r	1
50¼	50	r	r	3⅝	2	r	r
50¼	55	5/16	r	1½	r	r	r
Dover	40	1½	r	2	1	1 11/16	r
39⅞	45	r	r	⅝	r	r	r

Source: The Wall Street Journal, *March 25, 1991.*

Consider the options on Chase Manhattan Bank stock. Each line represents the closing prices of put and call options with the same exercise price. The first column shows the abbreviated name for the company—in this case, *Chase*—and immediately below it on each line is the stock's closing price, here 13 7/8. The next column shows the options' exercise prices, here 12 1/2 and 15. The next three columns give the call options' closing prices under the respective expiration months; for example, the closing price of the April 15 call was 1/4, or $0.25. The following three columns list the puts' closing prices under the corresponding expiration months.

The notation *r* indicates that the particular option did not trade during that day. The notation *s* means that options with that particular exercise price and expiration are not listed for trading. If none of the options in a given row traded during the day or none are listed for trading, the entire row is omitted. This was the case for UAL options with an exercise price of 125. It is possible that only one row will be shown for some stocks' options; in that case, the closing stock price will be omitted.

A glance over the option pages usually reveals some options in which the stock name is followed by an *o*. With those options, the terms and conditions of the contract have been modified to reflect stock splits or stock dividends.

All of the options trading on a given exchange are grouped together, as are those options with the same expiration cycles. The volume and open interest figures for calls and puts are presented at the end of the options listings for a particular exchange. In Figure 2.4, the CBOE totals for that trading day are immediately above the beginning of the listings for the American Stock Exchange.

Figure 2.5 shows a *Wall Street Journal* listing for index options. The general form is similar to that for stock option prices; however, *r*'s and *s*'s are replaced by "....", indicating that an option did not trade or is not listed. At the bottom of each listing are the volume and open interest figures for calls and puts and information on the value of the index.

The Wall Street Journal also provides a summary of the most actively traded options, as shown in Figure 2.6 on page 39. The first line of the CBOE call summary indicates that the most active call option was the April 350 S&P 100, which traded 17,142 contracts on that day. The last sale price of the day for that option was 5 7/8, which was up 1/4 from the previous day. The last column indicates that the index itself closed at 347.84.

Option prices are also reported in *Barron's*, a weekly investment newspaper. Figure 2.7 on page 40 illustrates a page of stock option quotations from *Barron's*.

Published each Monday, *Barron's* includes coverage of options that traded at least 50 contracts during the previous week; thus, not all options are covered. *Barron's* provides volume and open interest figures for the options it covers. As Figure 2.7 indicates, each option series is reported on a separate line. If the letter *p* appears directly to the right of the exercise price, the option is a put; otherwise, it is a call. The *Sales* figure is the volume of contracts traded during the previous week. The next figure is the open interest, followed by the week's high, low, and closing prices and the change in the closing price from the previous week's

FIGURE 2.5

Index Option Quotations in *The Wall Street Journal*, Trading Day of March 22, 1991

INDEX TRADING

Friday, March 22, 1991

OPTIONS

CHICAGO BOARD

S&P 100 INDEX

Strike	Calls–Last			Puts–Last		
Price	Apr	May	Jun	Apr	May	Jun
280	1/16	....	....	....	....	....
290	59	....	....	⅛	7/16	....
295	....	....	....	⅛	9/16	....
300	48¼	....	....	¼	¾	....
305	....	....	....	¼	15/16	....
310	38¼	....	....	⅜	1¼	....
315	....	35½	....	½	1 9/16	....
320	....	....	....	11/16	2	3¾
325	....	....	....	15/16	2½	5
330	21⅝	....	24¾	1⅜	3⅜	5¾
335	15⅜	17¾	....	2	4⅜	6¾
340	12¼	14¼	17¾	3	5¾	8¼
345	8⅞	11⅜	14¼	4½	7⅝	10¼
350	5⅞	8⅝	11⅛	6⅝	9½	12½
355	3¾	6½	9¼	9⅝	12⅛	15
360	2⅜	4½	7¼	13¼	15¾	18
365	1 7/16	3⅛	5¼	17½	20½	....
370	¾	2	3½	21½	23½	....
375	7/16	1⅜	....	....	....	....
380	¼	⅞	....	....	....	....

Total call volume 60,385 Total call open int. 308,840
Total put volume 58,330 Total put open int. 323,809
The index: High 348.70; Low 345.56; Close 347.84, +1.04

S&P 500 INDEX

Strike	Calls–Last			Puts–Last		
Price	Apr	May	Jun	Apr	May	Jun
305	....	....	....	1⅛	....	....
310	....	....	....	1 7/16	....	....
315	....	....	....	1⅝	....	....
320	....	....	....	1 13/16	....	....
325	....	....	....	2 5/16	....	....
330	....	....	....	....	....	2⅞
340	....	....	32¾	....	....	3⅝
345	23	....	....	15/16	....	4¾
350	19⅝	....	25⅛	1 3/16	....	5¾
355	15⅛	....	....	2	4¾	6⅝
360	11¼	....	18⅜	3⅜	6	8⅛
365	8½	11⅜	15¼	4½	7⅝	10⅛
370	6	....	11	6⅞	10⅜	11⅞
375	3¾	....	9⅞	10¾	....	14⅜
380	2¼	....	7¼	13	....	17¼
385	1⅜	....	5¾	18	....	20⅛
390	¾	....	4	....	....	....
400	....	....	2	....	....	....
425	....	....	½	....	....	....

Total call volume 8,640 Total call open int. 361,825
Total put volume 7,755 Total put open int. 392,345
The index: High 368.22; Low 365.58; Close 367.48, +0.90

LEAPS-S&P 100 INDEX

Strike	Calls–Last			Puts–Last		
Price	Dec92	Dec 93		Dec 92	Dec 93	
30	....	....	....	1 7/16	....	....
32½	....	....	....	2¼	....	....
35	....	....	....	2⅞	3¾	....
....	....	....	....	4⅜	....	....

Total call volume 0 Total call open int. 12,259
Total put volume 799 Total put open int. 49,937
The index: High 34.87; Low 34.56; Close 34.78, +0.10

LEAPS-S&P 500 INDEX

Strike	Calls–Last			Puts–Last		
Price	Dec 92	Dec 93		Dec 92	Dec 93	
30	....	....	....	1¼	....	....
35	....	6¾	....	2¼	2½	....
40	....	....	....	4	....	....

Total call volume 10 Total call open int. 12,116
Total put volume 243 Total put open int. 22,770
The index: High 36.82; Low 36.56; Close 36.75, +0.09

PHILADELPHIA

GOLD/SILVER INDEX

Strike	Calls–Last			Puts–Last		
Price	Apr	May	Jun	Apr	May	Jun
85	4¼	....	7	3	4¼	...
90	1⅞	....	....	....	....	....
100	⅜	....	....	....	....	....

Total call volume 24 Total call open int. 1,080
Total put volume 17 Total put open int. 760
The index: High 85.80; Low 85.05; Close 85.52, −0.41

VALUE LINE INDEX OPTIONS

Strike	Calls–Last			Puts–Last		
Price	Apr	May	Jun	Apr	May	Jun
255	....	....	42	....	⅜	....
260	....	....	....	....	½	¼
275	....	....	....	⅝	....	....
280	....	....	....	1	....	....
285	....	....	....	....	2⅜	....
295	4⅜	....	....	....	....	....
300	2⅜	....	....	....	....	....
305	1⅛	....	....	11⅜	....	....
320	....	⅝	....	....	....	....

Total call volume 39 Total call open int. 8,788
Total put volume 50 Total put open int. 4,293
The index: High 293.43; Low 292.50; Close 293.41, +0.16

UTILITIES INDEX

Strike	Calls–Last			Puts–Last		
Price	Apr	May	Jun	Apr	May	Jun
220	6⅞	....	....	....	....	....
235	....	1 9/16	....	....	....	....

Total call volume 6 Total call open int. 1,775
Total put volume 0 Total put open int. 8,723
The index: High 227.61; Low 224.22; Close 227.61, +3.31

PACIFIC

FINANCIAL NEWS COMPOSITE INDEX

Strike	Calls–Last			Puts–Last		
Price	Apr	May	Jun	Apr	May	Jun
200	....	....	48	....	....	....
240	8⅝	....	....	....	....	....
245	5⅝	....	....	3⅞	....	....
250	3¼	....	....	6½	....	....
255	1⅝	....	....	10¼	....	....
260	....	....	....	15⅜	....	....

Total call volume 65 Total call open int. 1,605
Total put volume 25 Total put open int. 565
The index: High 246.56; Low 244.03; Close 245.73, +0.92

NEW YORK

NYSE INDEX OPTIONS

Strike	Calls–Last			Puts–Last		
Price	Apr	May	Jun	Apr	May	Jun
190	....	....	....	11/16	....	....
192½	....	....	....	⅞	....	....
195	8⅜	....	....	1⅛	2⅝	....
197½	....	....	....	1⅞	....	....
200	4	....	7¼	2⅞	4⅞	....
202½	....	....	....	3¾	....	....
205	1⅞	....	....	6⅛	6⅞	8⅛
210	11/16	1⅞	....	9⅛	....	....

Total call volume 104 Total call open int. 3,577
Total put volume 330 Total put open int. 2,932
The index: High 201.46; Low 200.20; Close 201.13, +0.34

Source: The Wall Street Journal, *March 25, 1991.*

FIGURE 2.6

Most Active Options in *The Wall Street Journal*, Trading Day of March 22, 1991

MOST ACTIVE OPTIONS

CHICAGO BOARD

	Sales	Last	Chg	N.Y. Close
CALLS				
SP100 Apr 350	17142	5 7/8	+ 1/4	347.84
Upjohn Apr 50	15432	1 13/16	− 13/16	46 7/8
SP100 Apr 355	11547	3 3/4	+ 1/8	347.84
SP100 Apr 360	10623	2 3/8	...	347.84
Upjohn Apr 45	8870	3 5/8	− 7/8	46 7/8
SP100 Apr 345	7538	8 7/8	+ 5/8	347.84
I B M Apr 115	4248	1 15/16	− 3/16	111 1/2
N C R Apr 100	4053	1 15/16	− 1/8	98 1/4
N C R Apr 105	3434	7/16	...	98 1/4
SP100 Apr 365	3264	1 7/16	...	347.84
PUTS				
SP100 Apr 345	18085	4 1/2	− 5/8	347.84
SP100 Apr 350	12931	6 5/8	− 1	347.84
SP100 Apr 340	7918	3	− 1/2	347.84
SP100 Apr 335	4381	2	− 1/4	347.84
Upjohn Apr 45	3117	1 7/8	+ 1/4	46 7/8
I B M Apr 110	2749	2 3/16	+ 1/16	111 1/2
SP100 Apr 330	2560	1 3/8	− 1/8	347.84
SP100 Apr 355	2548	9 5/8	− 1	347.84
N C R Apr 90	2448	1 1/8	...	98 1/4
Gen El Apr 65	2380	1 1/4	− 1/8	66 1/4

AMERICAN

	Sales	Last	Chg	N.Y. Close
CALLS				
Ph Mor Apr 70	3351	2 3/16	+ 3/16	69 3/8
WellsF Apr 55	2869	16	− 2	70 7/8
WellsF Apr 50	2580	21	− 2 3/8	70 7/8
InstIdx Jun 200	2561	184	− 5/8	384.07
InstIdx Jun 450	2561	1/8	− 1/16	384.07
Ph Mor Apr 75	2501	5/8	+ 1/8	69 3/8
Lilly May 75	1971	4 1/4	− 1/4	75 3/4
AST Rs Apr 25	1452	2 3/8	+ 7/16	26
Apple Apr 55	1389	9 1/8	− 1 1/8	63 1/4
WellsF Apr 60	1358	10 7/8	− 2 5/8	70 7/8
PUTS				
InstIdx Jun 200	2561	1/16	...	384.07
InstIdx Jun 450	2561	62 1/2	+ 7/8	384.07
InstIdx Sep 330	1300	4 1/4	...	384.07
AST Rs Apr 25	1211	1 1/2	− 3/16	26
Ph Mor May 65	776	1 3/8	+ 1/16	69 3/8
Intel Apr 45	710	2 1/2	+ 5/16	43 3/4
MMIdx Apr 605	690	9 1/8	− 7/8	605.01
AST Rs Apr 22 1/2	675	13/16	...	26
MMIdx Apr 580	618	2 9/16	− 7/16	605.01
Dig Eq Apr 70	565	3 1/2	− 5/8	69 1/8

PHILADELPHIA

	Sales	Last	Chg	N.Y. Close
CALLS				
Lowes Jul 35	1490	3/4	− 1	28 1/2
Abbt L Nov 45	1483	5 5/8	...	47 1/8
Abbt L May 40	1049	7 5/8	+ 3/8	47 1/8
F N M Apr 45	779	7/8	− 5/16	42 3/4
A Hess Apr 45	620	2 7/8	− 1 1/8	47 3/4
Waste May 40	529	1 1/16	...	37 5/8
F N M Apr 40	509	3 3/8	− 1 5/8	42 3/4
GaGulf May 17 1/2	503	1 1/4	+ 1/8	15 1/8
Anheus Apr 40	500	11 5/8	+ 1 1/2	50 3/4
F N M May 45	475	1 5/8	− 3/8	42 3/4
PUTS				
Lowes Jul 25	1393	1 1/2	+ 1	28 1/2
F N M May 40	1286	1 3/8	+ 3/8	42 3/4
Abbt L May 45	1008	7/8	...	47 1/8
UniTel May 22 1/2	970	3/8	+ 1/8	24
Abbt L May 40	752	1/8	− 1/8	47 1/8
UniTel May 25	450	2	+ 9/16	24
F N M Apr 40	335	3/4	...	42 3/4
Dressr Apr 22 1/2	290	5/16	− 1/16	24 1/8
NBD Bc Apr 40	250	2 3/4	...	38 3/4
NCNB Apr 30	238	1 3/4	+ 1/2	29 1/2

PACIFIC

	Sales	Last	Chg	N.Y. Close
CALLS				
Compaq Apr 65	2434	1 1/8	− 1/2	59 5/8
SquarD Apr 80	1415	2	− 1/16	79 1/2
Compaq Apr 60	1111	2 7/8	− 1/2	59 5/8
Scher Apr 45	1010	5 1/2	+ 1/2	49
Compaq Apr 70	824	7/16	− 1/16	59 5/8
Wendy Apr 10	789	7/16	− 1/16	9 7/8
Wendy Jun 10	756	15/16	− 1/16	9 7/8
Micrsft Apr 100	692	2 3/8	− 1/4	93 3/4
A M D Apr 10	574	1 9/16	+ 5/16	11 1/4
Hilton May 45	537	1 1/8	− 1/8	40
PUTS				
Compaq Apr 60	1405	3 1/8	+ 3/4	59 5/8
Scher Apr 45	1030	3/16	+ 1/16	49
Compaq Jul 50	858	1 3/4	+ 1/8	59 5/8
Micrsft Apr 90	845	2 9/16	− 1/16	93 3/4
Compaq Apr 65	758	6 3/8	+ 1	59 5/8
TCBY Apr 7 1/2	737	1 3/16	+ 1/8	6 5/8
SquarD Apr 65	523	9/16	− 1/16	79 1/2
Conner Apr 35	501	10 1/2	− 3/4	24 1/2
Compaq Apr 70	472	10 1/8	+ 1	59 5/8
Micrsft Apr 85	471	1 3/16	...	93 3/4

NEW YORK

	Sales	Last	Chg	N.Y. Close
CALLS				
Maytag Apr 15	1313	11/16	+ 1/8	14 5/8
CSoup Apr 80	697	4 1/2	+ 2 3/8	80 3/4
Nynex Apr 80	500	1/8	− 1/16	72
Maytag Apr 17 1/2	348	1/8	+ 1/16	14 5/8
Maytag Apr 12 1/2	281	2 3/8	+ 1/2	14 5/8
Maytag May 15	255	1 1/8	+ 1/4	14 5/8
Trnsco Aug 35	234	1 3/8	− 1/4	31 1/8
Trnsco Apr 35	229	1/4	...	31 1/8
CSoup Apr 75	203	7	+ 2 7/8	80 3/4
Trnsco Apr 30	200	2	− 3/8	31 1/8
PUTS				
FtFnM Apr 30	200	2	+ 9/16	29 1/8
Maytag Apr 15	103	1 1/8	− 1/4	14 5/8
Sunstr Apr 35	103	4 1/2	...	30 3/4
GldPmp Jun 22 1/2	65	1 1/8	...	23 7/8
Nynex Apr 75	60	3 3/4	+ 5/8	72
CSoup Apr 75	58	1	− 1	80 3/4
Nynex Jul 70	55	2	+ 1/8	72
NY Idx Apr 190	53	11/16	+ 1/16	201.13
Nynex Apr 70	45	7/8	+ 1/8	72
BordCh Apr 12 1/2	40	1	+ 9/16	11 7/8

Source: The Wall Street Journal, *March 25, 1991.*

closing price (*Net Chg*.). The closing price of the underlying stock is in the last column.

Index options are reported in the same manner; however, *Barron's* also provides a summary of index option activity. An example of one week's summary is presented in Figure 2.8 on page 41. The figures for the week's range are prices of

FIGURE 2.7

Option Quotations in *Barron's,* Week Ending March 22, 1991

Expire date Strike price	Sales	Open Int.	Week's High	Week's Low	Price	Net Chg.	N.Y. Close
CBOE EQUITY OPTIONS							
AlexAl Nov25...	133	93	3⅝	2 15-16	2 15-16	....	25½
Alcoa Apr65...	285	1114	4⅛	2	2½	− 1½	65⅝
Alcoa Apr65 p..	343	1270	2¼	1 3-16	2⅛	+ ⅞	65⅝
Alcoa Apr70...	112	705	1¼	⅜	½	− 1	65⅝
Alcoa Apr70 p..	102	87	5¼	4¼	4⅞	+ 1⅜	65⅝
Alcoa Apr75 p..	130	70	10½	8¼	10½	......	65⅝
Alcoa Jul65.....	128	387	5⅛	4⅜	4½	− 2¾	65⅝
Alcoa Jul70.....	114	180	3¼	2⅜	2½	− 1	65⅝
Amdahl Apr15..	159	131	15-16	⅜	⅞	+ 1-16	14½
Amdahl Apr15 p	220	210	1¾	¾	1	+ ¼	14½
Amdahl Apr17½	125	217	⅜	1-16	⅛	− ⅜	14½
Amdahl Apr17½ p	112	73	4⅜	2¾	2¾	+ 13-16	14½
Amdahl May10 p	127	50	⅝	⅝	⅝	+ ½	14½
Amdahl May15	1300	3597	1⅜	½	1¼	+ ⅛	14½
Amdahl May15 p	152	530	2	1⅛	1⅜	+ ¼	14½
Amdahl May17½	211	654	9-16	¼	9-16	+ ⅛	14½
Amdahl May17½ p	139	4	3¼	3	3¼	+ ½	14½
Amdahl Aug12½	950	7461	3⅛	2 7-16	2 7-16	− 15-16	14½
Amdahl Nov12½ p	230	230	1½	1½	1½	......	14½
A E P May30..	253	1165	⅛	⅛	⅛	− ⅛	28¼
A E P Aug30...	100	815	⅜	⅜	⅜	......	28¼
AmGenl Apr30.	104	712	8⅛	7	8	+ ¼	37⅞
AmGenl Apr35.	179	2405	3⅜	2	3⅜	+ ⅛	37⅞
AmGenl Apr35 p	173	575	⅝	⅜	⅜	− ⅛	37⅞
AmGenl Apr40.	160	1944	⅝	¼	⅝	+ ¼	37⅞
AmGenl Jul35 p	150	250	1½	1½	1½	+ ⅜	37⅞
AmGenl Jul40..	113	545	1¾	1⅛	1¾	+ ⅛	37⅞
AlnGrp Apr90..	145	71	3¼	3	3	− 1¼	90⅝
AlnGrp Apr90 p	259	222	3⅛	2⅝	2⅝	+ ⅜	90⅝
AlnGrp May90 p	123	127	4	3¾	3¾	+ ¼	90⅝
AlnGrp May95 p	111	56	7	5¾	5⅞	+ 2½	90⅝
AlnGrp Aug85..	330	543	10⅜	9¾	9¾	− 4⅞	90⅝
AlnGrp Nov90..	719	719	9	9	9	......	90⅝
AmStr Jul75 p.	106	43	3⅜	1¾	2	− 1⅞	84⅞
AT&T Apr25....	568	20	9¾	8⅝	8⅝	− ¼	33
AT&T Apr30....	6588	4710	4⅝	3⅛	3¼	− ⅝	33
AT&T Apr30 p.	955	9079	¼	⅛	3-16	......	33
AT&T Apr35...	6720	14119	⅞	¼	5-16	− 3-16	33
AT&T Apr35 p..	1289	4805	2 9-16	1½	2¼	+ 7-16	33
AT&T Apr40....	848	3367	1-16	1-16	1-16	......	33
AT&T May30..	257	250	4⅝	3⅝	3⅝	......	33
AT&T May30 p.	279	150	7-16	⅜	⅜	......	33
AT&T May35..	5798	4154	1 5-16	9-16	¾	......	33
AT&T May35 p.	520	228	2¼	1½	2¼	......	33
AT&T Jul30....	134	2804	4⅞	4	4⅜	− ¼	33
AT&T Jul30 p..	558	2815	¾	½	11-16	......	33
AT&T Jul35.....	3955	11106	1⅞	1⅛	1 5-16	− 1-16	33
AT&T Jul35 p..	2404	6380	2⅞	2⅛	2¾	− ¼	33
AT&T Jul40....	288	978	⅜	¼	5-16	......	33
AT&T Oct30...	158	1147	5½	4½	4½	− ⅝	33
AT&T Oct30 p..	1322	825	1⅛	⅞	1⅛	+ ⅛	33
AT&T Oct35...	550	1195	2⅜	1¾	2	− ⅛	33
AT&T Oct40...	346	424	⅞	9-16	¾	+ ¼	33

Source: Barron's, *March 25, 1991.*

FIGURE 2.8

Barron's Weekly Summary of Stock Index Options, Week Ending March 22, 1991

STOCK INDEX OPTIONS: WEEKLY SUMMARY

March 22, 1991

	First	Week's Range High	Low	Last	Chg.	Call Volume	Open Interest	Put Volume	Open Interest
S&P 100	354,09	354.09	346.80	347.84	− 8.04	408,897	308,840	428,800	323,809
S&P 500	372.11	372.11	366.58	367.48	− 6.11	61,617	361,825	76,161	392,345
Leaps-S&P 100	35.41	35.41	34.68	34.78	− 0.81	619	12,259	7,102	49,937
Leaps-S&P 500	37.21	37.21	36.66	36.75	− 0.61	35	12,116	956	22,770
AMEX Major Market	619.89	619.89	603.95	605.01	− 19.49	32,817	42,865	35,160	42,875
AMEX LT-20	30.99	30.99	30.20	30.25	− 0.97	2,283	48,563	5,771	89,846
AMEX Institutional	390.07	390.07	383.27	384.07	− 7.34	15,755	37,894	11,994	46,203
AMEX Int'l Index	324.81	324.81	318.52	318.52	− 8.69	0	5	0	60
AMEX Japan Index	270.11	270.11	263.27	264.77	− 2.16	894	3,204	1,876	8,367
AMEX Comp. Tech.	122.01	122.01	112.12	112.12	− 9.13	9	1,036	5	109
AMEX Oil	248.33	250.85	248.33	250.85	− 0.79	228	255	169	314
NYSE Composite	203.31	203.31	200.66	201.10	− 2.95	1,597	3,677	3,116	2,932
Phil. Gold/Silver	85.87	86.28	85.52	85.52	− 2.71	459	1,080	113	760
Phil. Value Line	294.48	294.48	292.04	293.41	− 1.25	679	8,788	737	4,293
Phil. Nat'l O.T.C.	373.14	373.60	369.67	369.67	− 2.44	31	172	0	137
Phil. Utilities	223.33	227.61	222.70	227.61	+ 3.59	256	1,775	16,000	8,723
Pac. Fin. News Comp.	253.17	253.17	244.81	245.73	− 8.29	241	1,605	421	565

Week's High/Low range is based upon the daily closing index.

Source: Barron's, *March 25, 1991.*

the indices themselves, not the options on the indices. The volume and open interest figures, however, are for the options.

The price quotations provided in *The Wall Street Journal* and *Barron's* are useful measures of the approximate prices at which options are bought and sold. By the time they reach the public, however, those prices are already old. In addition, they are not necessarily synchronized with one another and with the stock price. The closing price of each option and of the stock reflect only the price of the last transaction. The last transaction of the day may have taken place at any time during that day. Therefore, when the last option transaction was made, the stock price may well have been something else.

Another problem with prices reported in a newspaper is that they reflect only the price of the last trade and do not indicate whether that price was a market maker's bid or ask price. For example, suppose the market maker is quoting a bid of 1 3/4 and an ask of 2. If the last trade of the day is a public order to buy, the order is filled at 2; if it is a public order to sell, the order is filled at 1 3/4. Thus, the closing price shown in the newspaper could be either 1 3/4 or 2.

Most serious option traders and certainly all institutional option traders require immediate access to bid and ask prices as well as to on-line market price information. These data are available from many commercial price reporting services, although the costs are somewhat high for individuals. With the growing use of personal computers, however, many individuals are finding that they can access option price quotes from their homes by subscribing to computerized telecommunication services.

TYPES OF OPTIONS

Stock Options

As of March 1991, there were about 750 stocks on which options traded. The CBOE had about 217, the AMEX about 206, the Philadelphia Stock Exchange about 147, the Pacific Stock Exchange about 127, and the New York Stock Exchange about 52.

Most of the stocks on which options trade are listed on the New York Stock Exchange; however, there are some over-the-counter stocks on which options are listed. On the CBOE, the most active options in 1989 were (in order) IBM, NWA, RJR Nabisco, UAL, Syntex, Avon, Paramount, General Electric, Warner Communications, and Upjohn.[10]

Index Options

The construction of stock indices is discussed in some detail in Chapter 8. For now, however, let us simply consider a stock index as a measure of the overall value of a group of stocks.

An *index option* is an option on an index of stocks. The first index option, the CBOE 100—since renamed the S&P 100—was launched on March 11, 1983. The S&P 100, commonly known by its ticker symbol, OEX, had an opening-day volume of 4,575 contracts. Soon afterward other exchanges added index options, and the success of these contracts has been phenomenal. On all exchanges combined, index option volume is approximately one-third of the total volume of all options; however, at the CBOE index option volume is about equal to stock option volume.[11]

Although index options are similar to stock options in many ways, there are several important differences. Because an index represents a portfolio of stocks, exercise of the option ordinarily would require the delivery of the stocks weighted in the same proportions as they are in the index. This would be quite difficult and inconvenient. Instead, an alternative exercise procedure called *cash settlement* is used. With this method, if an index call option is exercised, the writer pays the buyer the contract multiple times the difference between the index level and the exercise price. For example, assume you buy one index call option that has a multiple of 100. The index is at 250, and the exercise price is at 245. If you exercise the

---

[10]Ibid.

[11]CBOE, *Market Statistics 1989.*

option, the assigned writer pays you 100(250 − 245) = $500 in cash. No stock changes hands. A put option is exercised by the writer paying the buyer the multiple times the difference between the exercise price and the index level.

An order to exercise an index option during the day is executed after the close of trading. The index value *at the end of the day*, rather than the index value when the exercise was ordered, is used to determine the amount of the settlement. Thus, an investor is well advised to wait until the end of the day to order an exercise of an index option.

Table 2.2 lists the current index options. The most active index option is the CBOE's S&P 100 followed by the CBOE's S&P 500 and the AMEX's Major Market Index. Note that some of the indices are based on particular industries, such as the Utilities and Oil indices. These indices consist of stocks in the respective industries. Trading volume in these industry index options has never lived up to original expectations.

Index options have been popular for two reasons. First, the cash settlement feature enables investors to trade options without having to take or make delivery of stock. Cash settlement has, however, been both a blessing and a curse. Many institutional investors hold large portfolios of stocks that purport to replicate the index. They then write call options or sell futures against these portfolios. At other times, these investors sell short the stocks and buy call options or futures. When the options approach the expiration date, the institutional investors, not wanting to hold the stocks after the options expire, attempt to unwind their stock positions. Holders of stock sell the stock, and short sellers buy it back. As a result, many large stock transactions are made near expiration and are accompanied by increased volatility. The cash settlement feature of index options and futures has been blamed for this volatility. We shall explore this issue more thoroughly in Chapter 14.

The second reason for the popularity of index options is the fact that they are options on the market as a whole. There are over 700 stocks on which options trade, but few investors have the time to screen that many opportunities. Many prefer to analyze the market as a whole and use index options (and futures) to act on their forecasts.

Bond Options

Options on Treasury notes and bonds have been around since the early 1980s but have had little success. The AMEX has offered options on Treasury bills and Treasury notes, but volume has been quite low. The CBOE offers options on several Treasury bond issues, but their volume comprises far less than 1 percent of total volume on the CBOE.

Other Types of Options

Options on foreign currencies and futures contracts exist in this country; we shall examine these instruments later. There are also a number of other interesting types of options. For example, in 1986 the CBOE launched the first option on a

TABLE 2.2
Index Options, March, 1991

Chicago Board Options Exchange	*Philadelphia Stock Exchange*
Standard & Poor's 100 Index	Gold/Silver Index
Standard & Poor's 500 Index	Value Lines Index
American Stock Exchange	Utilities Index
Major Market Index	*Pacific Stock Exchange*
Institutional Index	Financial News Composite Index
Japan Index	*New York Stock Exchange*
Oil Index	New York Stock Exchange Index

The offerings of index options change frequently as exchanges experiment with different types of indices and terms of the contracts. For the latest information, contact the exchanges themselves. Some of these options are available with long expirations. Some are also specified as European-style exercise.

mutual fund. In 1989 the CBOE initiated options on an interest rate series. On this option, the payoff is made on the basis of an interest rate rather than the price of an underlying instrument. While this option has had very little trading volume, there is a large over-the-counter market for options on interest rates, which we shall discuss in Chapter 14.

A number of other instruments are practically identical to options. For example, many corporations issue warrants, which are long-term options to buy the companies' stock. Warrants often are issued in conjunction with a public offering of debt or equity. In early 1990, extreme uncertainty about the Japanese stock market led many financial institutions, and even the kingdom of Denmark, to issue warrants on the Japanese stock market. These warrants, called Nikkei put warrants for the Japanese market index, were put options that investors could use to speculate on the fall of the Japanese stock market. When that market fell deeply and expectations suggested that it would recover, call warrants were issued.

Many corporations issue convertible bonds, which allow the holder to convert the bond into a certain number of shares of stock. The right to convert is itself a call option. Callable bonds, which give the issuing firm the right to repay the bonds early, contain an option-like component. Finally, stock itself is equivalent to a call option on the firm's assets written by the bondholders with an exercise price equal to the amount due on the debt.

Since 1985, the financial markets have seen a number of new products that are similar to options. Instruments such as retractable and extendable bonds, market indexed securities, caps, floors, collars, and swaptions are but a few of the many new instruments that combine stocks, bonds, and options. Some of these instruments will be covered in Chapter 14. Other are too complex to cover in this book. However, after reading this book, you should be well prepared to begin study of these new instruments.

Option Funds

One of the most popular ways to invest is through mutual funds. An investor can purchase shares in a mutual fund for a small amount—often less than $1,000. The fund pools the shareholders' money and invests in stocks, bonds, or combinations thereof. The fund hires a professional portfolio manager to run the portfolio and passes the net profits through to the shareholders.

A load fund's shares usually are sold by a stockbroker, and the investor is charged a *load*—a percentage of the amount of money invested. The percentage varies and is sometimes as high as 8.5 percent. No-load funds do not charge this fee, since their shares usually are purchased directly from the funds. Both types of funds, however, entail management fees and expenses that they deduct before passing on the returns to shareholders.

Many mutual funds write call options against stocks held in their portfolios. The fund receives the option premium and is obligated to sell the stock at the exercise price if the option holder desires. A few funds, which call themselves *option funds*, specialize in writing calls against stocks held in their portfolios. While some of these funds do hold a few long positions in options, most concentrate on holding stocks and writing calls against their shares. Thus, buying an option fund is not equivalent to buying options but is more like writing options against stock already owned.[12] Table 2.3 lists some option funds and pertinent information about them.

The funds' performances have varied considerably from year to year. The strategies these funds follow are conservative and tend to do better than the market during bear markets and worse during bull markets. No single fund has consistently performed better than any other. However, comparisons among funds are somewhat biased, because their investment policies and objectives vary.

A good source of information on all mutual funds is *Wiesenberger Investment Companies Service* annual review, which contains descriptions of the funds as well as data on their historical performances. Figure 2.9 is Wiesenberger's description of the Gateway Option Index Fund.

Indices of Options Market Activity

The stock market is widely covered by various indices. Everyone has heard of the Dow Jones Industrial Average, and most are familiar with the S&P 500. Indices of options market activity are less known, because it is difficult to construct an option index. If an option were included in an index, the index's composition would change as the option approached expiration. For example, an index consisting primarily of six-month calls would consist of three-month calls three months later. As we shall see in later chapters, the behavior of three-month calls differs

[12]However, there are types of funds whose purchase is similar to actually buying options. These are called *primes, scores,* and *dual-purpose funds.* We shall discuss primes and scores in Chapter 14.

TABLE 2.3
Option Funds

	Year Started	Net Assets, 12/31/89 (Millions)
Load Funds		
American Investors Option Fund	1986	0.1
Continental Option Income Plus	1986	54.3
Dean Witter Option Income Fund	1985	263.3
Franklin Option Fund	1951	45.4
Kemper Option Income Fund	1977	347.1
Mackenzie Series Trust-Option Income	1985	241.6
Putnam Option Income II	1985	1281.7
Putnam Option Income Trust	1977	996.8
No-Load Funds		
Analytic Optioned Equity Fund	1986	102.2
Drexel Series Trust-Option Fund	1985	22.9
Gateway Option Index Fund	1977	27.3
Investment Portfolio-Option Income	1984	404.7
Prudential Bache Option Growth Fund	1983	68.1
SLH Option Income Portfolio	1985	567.3

Note: This list includes only funds listed in the 1989 edition of Wiesenberger Investment Companies Service that specifically included the word "option" in their titles. Many other funds actively use options in their investment strategies.
Source: Wiesenberger Investment Companies Service, 1989. Reprinted with permission.

substantially from that of six-month calls. Moreover, the options contained in the index eventually would expire and have to be replaced by other options. Thus, the composition of the index would constantly change.

Despite these problems, options indices have been developed by Galai (1979), Gastineau (1979), and Eckerdt and Williams (1984) and by some private firms such as *Value Line Options*, a weekly publication of Arnold Bernhard Company. The CBOE has also constructed two indices, one for puts and one for calls. The CBOE indices measure the average premium on six-month calls and puts in which the stock price is close to the exercise price. The CBOE indices are reported weekly in *Barron's* column "The Striking Price." The level of the index indicates whether option premiums are relatively high or low. Volatility of the stock market is a major factor in the size of both call and put premiums. High option premiums tend to reflect greater stock market volatility.

FIGURE 2.9
Description of an Option Fund

GATEWAY TRUST—GATEWAY OPTION INDEX FUND
(Formerly Gateway Option Income Fund)

Gateway Option Index Fund was organized in November 1977 as an open-end, diversified investment company with the primary objective of high current return at a reduced level of price volatility. In 1986 the fund was reorganized as one of two separate portfolios of Gateway Trust.

Effective March 1985, the fund's portfolio consists of the stocks in the Standard & Poors' 100-stock Index in similar weightings, as far as practical, to those of the Index. The fund will sell (write) call options on S & P Index options which are traded on the Chicago Board Options Exchange.

At the close of 1989, the fund had 100% of its assets in common stocks the majority of which was in five industries: consumer cyclical (17.3% of net assets), energy (16.3%), consumer noncyclical (16.1%), technology (15.2%) and utilities (12.5%). The five largest individual common stock holdings were Exxon (6.4%), General Electric (5.8%), IBM (5.5%), AT&T (4.9%) and Merck (3.1%). The portfolio turnover rate during the latest fiscal year was 30% of average assets. Unrealized appreciation in the portfolio at the calendar year-end was 15.1% of net assets.

Special Services: The fund offers a variety of services to shareholders. See Panorama section of this volume for details.

Statistical History

	AT YEAR-ENDS						ANNUAL DATA				
Year	Total Net Assets ($)	Number of Share-holders	Net Asset Value Per Share ($)	Yield (%)	Cash & Gov't	Bonds & Pre-ferreds	Com-mon Stocks	Income Div-idends ($)	Capital Gains Distribu-tion ($)	Expense Ratio (%)	Offering Price ($) High	Low
---	---	---	---	---	---	---	---	---	---	---	---	---
1989	31,508,700	845	15.49	2.3	—	—	100	0.37	0.43*	1.40	15.98	13.64
1988	27,338,410	1,045	13.67	1.5	(2)	—	102	0.21	—	2.08	13.71	11.41
1987	27,343,364	1,406	11.60	2.5	(5)	—	105	0.33	1.92	1.48	16.20	11.41
1986	45,319,888	1,597	14.63	2.1	—	—	100	0.34	1.46	1.49	15.32	14.08
1985	28,478,321	1,200	14.69	3.9	(2)	—	102	0.46	1.22*	1.50	15.04	13.90
1984	21,621,488	700	14.23	4.0	3	—	97	0.57	0.65*	1.18	13.19	13.04
1983	26,927,477	500	14.91	3.4	2	—	98	0.55	1.31*	1.41	15.99	14.30
1982	20,738,207	300	11.68	4.2	4	—	96	0.64	0.62*	1.45	14.76	12.45
1981	19,208,140	300	14.69	4.0	2	—	98	0.64	1.46*	1.50	16.34	13.50
1980	18,788,424	300	16.11	3.5	—	—	100	0.61	1.48*	1.50	16.16	13.61
1979	13,303,032	200	15.81	3.9	(1)	—	101	0.63	1.05**	1.62	16.20	14.78

Note: Initially offered 12/7/77 at $15.00 per share.
* All short-term capital gains.
** Includes $1.036 short-term capital gains in 1979; $0.43 in 1989.

Directors: Walter G. Sall, Pres.; Kenneth A. Drucker; Beverly S. Gordon; John F. Lebor; Walter L. Tingle, Jr.; William H. Schneebeck; Peter W. Thayer.

Investment Adviser: Gateway Investment Advisers, Inc. Compensation to the Adviser is at an annual rate of 0.9 of 1% of the first $50 million of average daily net assets, scaled down to 0.5 of 1% on assets in excess of $200 million.

Custodian: Star Bank, Cincinnati, OH.

Transfer Agent: Gateway Investment Advisers, Inc.

Distributor: None; shares sold directly by fund.

Sales Charge: None, shares are sold at net asset value.

Distribution Plan (12b-1): None.

Dividends: Income dividends are paid quarterly in March, June, September, and December. Capital gains, if any, are paid annually in December.

Shareholder Reports: Issued quarterly. Fiscal year ends December 31. The current prospectus was effective in April.

Address: P.O. Box 458167, Cincinnati, Ohio 45245.

Telephone: (513) 248-2700. Toll Free: (800) 354-6339.

An assumed investment of $10,000 in this fund, with capital gains accepted in shares and income dividends reinvested, is illustrated below. The explanation in the introduction to this section must be read in conjunction with this illustration.

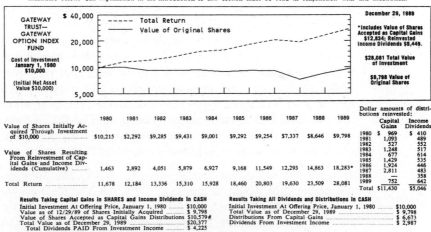

	1980	1981	1982	1983	1984	1985	1986	1987	1988	1989
Value of Shares Initially Acquired Through Investment of $10,000	$10,215	$2,292	$9,285	$9,431	$9,001	$9,292	$9,254	$7,337	$8,646	$9,798
Value of Shares Resulting From Reinvestment of Capital Gains and Income Dividends (Cumulative)	1,463	2,892	4,051	5,879	6,927	9,168	11,549	12,293	14,863	18,283*
Total Return	11,678	12,184	13,336	15,310	15,928	18,460	20,803	19,630	23,509	28,081

Dollar amounts of distributions reinvested:	Capital Gains	Income Dividends
1980	$ 969	$ 410
1981	1,093	489
1982	527	552
1983	1,248	517
1984	677	614
1985	1,429	535
1986	1,924	446
1987	2,811	483
1988	—	358
1989	752	642
Total	$11,430	$5,046

Results Taking Capital Gains in SHARES and Income Dividends in CASH
Initial Investment At Offering Price, January 1, 1980	$10,000
Value as of 12/29/89 of Shares Initially Acquired	$ 9,798
Value of Shares Accepted as Capital Gains Distributions	$10,579#
Total Value as of December 29, 1989	$20,377
Total Dividends PAID From Investment Income	$ 4,225

Results Taking All Dividends and Distributions in CASH
Initial Investment At Offering Price, January 1, 1980	$10,000
Total Value as of December 29, 1989	$ 9,798
Distributions From Capital Gains	$ 6,673
Dividends From Investment Income	$ 2,987

\# Dollar Amount of these distributions at the time shares were acquired: $9,471

TRANSACTION COSTS IN OPTION TRADING

Option trading entails certain transaction costs. The costs depend on whether the trader is a member of the exchange, a nonmember institutional investor, or a member of the public who is trading through a broker. This section discusses the different types of transaction costs.

Floor Trading and Clearing Fees

Floor trading and clearing fees are the minimum charges assessed by the exchange, the clearing corporation, and the clearing firms for handling a transaction. For trades that go through a broker, these fees are included in the broker's commission (discussed in the next section). For market makers, the fees are collected by the market maker's clearing firm.

    The clearing firm enters into a contractual arrangement with a market maker to clear trades for a fee usually stated on a per-contract basis. The amount is subject to negotiation and typically is lower the larger the number of contracts cleared. The nature of the clearing business is highly competitive, and market makers often find that lower fees are available by switching to a different clearing firm.

    Phillips and Smith (1980) report that these fees range from $.50 to $1 per contract; however, large-volume traders often obtain smaller fees.

Commissions

One of the main advantages of owning a seat on an exchange is that it lets one avoid paying commissions on each trade. The market maker pays indirectly via the opportunity cost associated with the funds tied up in the seat price, the labor involved in trading, and forgoing the earnings that would be realized in another line of work. The savings in commissions, however, are quite substantial.

    Table 2.4 is a sample commission schedule for a major discount brokerage house. Discount brokers offer the lowest commission rates, but frequent or large trades sometimes are necessary to take advantage of their prices. A discount brokerage firm does not provide the advice and research available from full-service brokers charging higher commission rates. However, one should not automatically assume that a full-service broker is more costly.

    As an example of how commission charges are determined, consider the following orders using the schedule presented in Table 2.4:

1. *One contract of an option priced at 3 1/4.* The premium is $325. The commission would be .016 ($325) + $29 = $34.20. However, the minimum charge is $37.25 plus $1.75 for one contract, for a total of $39. The maximum charge would be $40. The commission therefore would be $39.

2. *Ten contracts of an option priced at 2 3/4.* The premium is $2,750. The commission would be .008 ($2,750) + $49 = $71. The minimum charge for

TABLE 2.4
Sample Option Commission Schedule

Dollar Amount	Commission Rate
$2,500 or less	$29 + .016 of dollar amount
$2,501–$10,000	$49 + .008 of dollar amount
Over $10,000	$99 + .003 of dollar amount

Maximum charge: $40 per contract on the first two contracts, plus $4 per contract thereafter
Minimum charge: $37.25 plus $1.75 per contract

ten contracts is $37.25 and $1.75 for each contract, for a total of $37.25 + $1.75 (10) = $54.75. The maximum charge is $40 for each of the first two contracts and $4 for each of the next eight for a total of $112. Thus, the commission would still be $71.

When exercising a stock option, the investor must pay the commission for buying or selling the stock. (Stock commissions are discussed in a later section.) If an investor exercises a cash settlement option, the transaction entails only a bookkeeping entry. Some brokerage firms do not charge to exercise a cash settlement option. When any type of option expires unexercised, there normally is no commission.

Individuals pay commission rates such as those shown in Table 2.4. All commissions are subject to negotiation between the investor and the broker. Many large institutional investors trade in sufficiently large volume that they can negotiate lower commission rates from their brokers. However, they would be unable to get lower overall transaction costs than market makers, because the latter pay no commissions at all.

Bid-Ask Spread

The market maker's spread is a significant transaction cost. Suppose the market maker is quoting a bid price of 3 and an ask price of 3 1/4 on a call. An investor who buys the call immediately incurs a "cost" of the bid-ask spread, or 1/4 point; that is, if the investor immediately sold the call, it would fetch only $3, the bid price, and the investor would immediately incur a 1/4 point, or $25, loss. However, this does not mean that the investor cannot make a profit. The call price may well increase before the option is sold, but if the spread is constant, the bid price must increase by at least the amount of the bid-ask spread before a profit can be made.

The bid-ask spread is the cost of immediacy—the assurance that market makers are willing and able to buy and sell the options on demand. The cost is not explicitly observed, and the investor will not see it on the monthly statement from the broker. It is, however, a real cost and can be quite substantial. Phillips and

Smith (1980) estimate that the median bid-ask spread is 4.23 percent on calls and 3.39 percent on puts.

It may appear that market makers can avoid the bid-ask spread transaction cost. This is true in some cases. However, if the market maker must buy or sell an option, there may be no public orders of the opposite position. In that case, the market maker would have to trade with another market maker and thus would incur the cost of the bid-ask spread.

Other Transaction Costs

Option traders incur several other types of transaction costs. Some of these costs, such as margins and taxes, are discussed in Appendices 2A and 2B, respectively. Most option traders also trade stocks. Thus, the transaction costs of stock trades are a factor in option trading costs.

Stock trading commissions vary widely among brokerage firms. However, 1 to 2 percent of the stock's value for a single purchase or sale transaction is a reasonable estimate. Market makers normally obtain more favorable rates from their clearing firms. Also, large institutional investors usually can negotiate volume discounts from their brokers.

All of the transaction costs discussed here are for single transactions. If the option or stock is subsequently purchased or sold in the market, the transaction cost is incurred again.

THE REGULATION OF OPTIONS MARKETS

The options industry is regulated at several levels. While federal and state regulations predominate, the industry also regulates itself according to rules and standards established by the exchanges and the Options Clearing Corporation.

The Securities and Exchange Commission (SEC) is the primary regulator of the options market. The SEC is a federal regulatory agency created in 1934 to oversee the securities industry, which includes stocks, bonds, options, and mutual funds. The SEC's general purpose is to ensure full disclosure of all pertinent information on publicly offered investments. It has the authority to establish certain rules and procedures and to investigate possible violations of federal securities laws. If the SEC observes a violation it may seek injunctive relief, recommend that the Justice Department press charges, or impose some sanctions itself.

The exchanges establish rules and procedures that apply to all members as well as to individuals and firms participating in options transactions. Rule violations may be punishable by fines and/or suspensions. The Options Clearing Corporation also regulates its members to help ensure that all activities in the options markets are proper and do not pose a risk to the market's viability.

The regulatory authority of an individual state extends to any securities or options trading occurring within that state. States with significant option trading, such as Illinois and New York, actively enforce their own laws on the propriety of transactions conducted therein. Many important issues in the options industry as a whole are settled in state courts in Illinois and New York.

Other levels of regulation are imposed by the Federal Reserve System, which regulates the extension of margin credit; the Securities Investor Protection Corporation, which provides insurance against the failure of brokerage firms; and the National Association of Securities Dealers, of which most firms involved in options trading are members. In addition, several regional and national organizations, such as the Association for Investment Management and Research, indirectly regulate the industry by prescribing ethical standards for its members.

Many new option products were introduced in the 1980s, including options on stock indices, options on foreign currencies, and options on futures. These products created some confusion as to whether the SEC or the Commodity Futures Trading Commission (CFTC) had regulatory purview. The options on futures instrument caused the greatest confusion, because it is like an option and a futures. In an important step in resolving the matter, the then chairmen of these agencies—John Shad of the SEC and Phillip McBryde Johnson of the CFTC—reached an agreement. In what has come to be known as the *Johnson-Shad agreement* or *CFTC-SEC accord*, it was decided that the SEC would regulate options on stocks, stock indices, and foreign currencies while the CFTC would govern options on all futures contracts. Also, a CFTC-regulated contract cannot permit delivery of instruments regulated by the SEC. Although the Johnson-Shad agreement was a milestone in regulatory cooperation, continued disputes between the SEC and CFTC characterized the regulatory environment of the late 1980s. We shall hear more about these issues when we cover futures.

The primary purpose of the regulatory system is to protect the public. Over the years, many controversial issues have been raised and discussed. In an industry as large as the options industry, some abuses are certain to occur. In recent years, the options industry has been subjected to criticisms that it has manipulated the stock market and abused the public's trust by charging exorbitant prices for options. However, there is no evidence that any of these charges are true, and despite these allegations the public continues to invest heavily in options. There have even been a few defaults by writers, but, thanks to the clearinghouse, in no case has any buyer lost money because of a writer's failure to perform. The options industry works hard to maintain the public's trust by operating in an environment of self-regulation. By policing itself and punishing wrongdoers, some of the cost of having federal regulation is offset for taxpayers.

SUMMARY

This chapter provided the foundation for an understanding of the types of options, individuals, and institutions involved in the options markets. It examined contract specifications, mechanics of trading, transaction costs, and regulations. This information is a prerequisite to the study of option trading strategies and the pricing of options.

Chapters 3 and 4 focus on the principles and models that determine option prices. Chapters 5 and 6 concentrate on applying this knowledge to the implementation of option trading strategies.

Questions and Problems

1. Determine whether each of the following arrangements is an option. If so, decide whether it is a call or a put and identify the premium.

   a. You purchase homeowner's insurance for your house.

   b. You are a high school senior evaluating possible college choices. One school promises that if you enroll it will guarantee your tuition rate for the next four years.

   c. You enter into a noncancellable, long-term apartment lease.

2. Explain the difference between an American option and a European option. What do they have in common?

3. Identify and discuss some important differences between the former over-the-counter options market and the current system of organized options markets.

4. What adjustments to the contract terms of CBOE options would be made in the following situations?

   a. An option has an exercise price of 60. The company declares a 10 percent stock dividend.

   b. An option has an exercise price of 25. The company declares a two-for-one stock split.

   c. An option has an exercise price of 85. The company declares a four-for-three stock split.

   d. An option has an exercise price of 50. The company declares a cash dividend of $.75.

5. Consider the January, February, and March stock option exercise cycles discussed in the chapter. For each of the following dates, indicate which expirations in each cycle would be listed for trading in stock options.

   a. February 1

   b. July 1

   c. December 1

6. Why are short puts and long calls grouped together when considering position limits?

7. Compare and contrast the roles of market maker and floor broker. Why do you think an individual cannot be both?

8. Explain how the CBOE's Order Book Official (OBO) handles public limit orders.

9. Contrast the market maker system of the CBOE and Pacific Stock Exchange with the specialist system of the AMEX and Philadelphia Stock Exchange. What advantages and disadvantages do you see in each system?

10. Suppose the price of a seat on the CBOE is $260,000. You can lease a seat for 1 3/4 percent per month. You estimate that executing your own trades will save you $25 per trade. How many trades would you need to make to justify the lease? What do you think are the advantages of leasing a seat?

11. Compare and contrast the exercise procedure for stock options with that for index options. What major advantage does exercising an index option have over exercising a stock option?

12. Discuss the limitations of prices obtained from newspapers such as *The Wall Street Journal*.

13. How is investing in an option fund like investing in options? How is it different?

14. Why are option indices difficult to construct? Where can investors find option indices?

15. Identify and briefly discuss the various types of option transaction costs. How do these costs differ for market makers and for floor brokers?

16. Using the commission schedule in Table 2.4, determine the commissions on the following option transactions:

   a. One contract at a price of 2 7/8.

   b. Five contracts at a price of 8 1/2.

   c. Twenty contracts at a price of 4 3/4.

References

Board of Governors of the Federal Reserve System, Commodity Futures Trading Commission, and Securities and Exchange Commission. *A Survey of the Effects on the Economy of Trading in Futures and Options*. Washington, D.C., 1984.

Bookstaber, Richard M. *Option Pricing and Investment Strategies*, Chapter 1. Chicago: Probus Publishing, 1989.

Chance, Don M., and Stephen P. Ferris. "The CBOE Call Option Index: A Historical Record." *The Journal of Portfolio Management* 12 (Fall 1985): 75–83.

Characteristics and Risks of Standardized Options. The Options Clearing Corporation, September 1987.

Chicago Board Options Exchange. *Market Statistics 1989*. Chicago: Chicago Board Options Exchange, 1989.

Chicago Board Options Exchange. *Reference Manual*. Chicago: Chicago Board Options Exchange, 1982.

Chicago Board Options Exchange. *The CBOE Call Option Index: Methodology and Technical Considerations*. Chicago: Chicago Board Options Exchange, 1979.

Chicago Board Options Exchange and Options Clearing Corporation. *Constitution and Rules*. Chicago: Commerce Clearing House, 1985.

Cox, John C., and Mark Rubinstein. *Options Markets*, Chapters 1, 3, 8. Englewood Cliffs, N.J.: Prentice-Hall, 1985.

Eckerdt, Walter L., and Stephen L. Williams. "The Complete Options Indexes." *Financial Analysts Journal* 40 (July–August 1984): 48–57.

Galai, Dan. "A Proposal for Indexes for Traded Call Options." *The Journal of Finance* 34 (December 1979): 1157–1172.

Gastineau, Gary. *The Stock Options Manual*, 3d ed., Chapters 1–3, 5, 6, 9, Appendices A and E. New York: McGraw-Hill, 1988.

Gastineau, Gary L., and Albert Madansky. "Some Comments on the Chicago Board Options Exchange Call Option Index." *Financial Analysts Journal* 40 (July–August 1984): 58–67.

Hull, John. *Options, Futures, and other Derivative Securities*, Chapter 1. Englewood Cliffs, N.J.: Prentice-Hall, 1989.

Kramer, Andrea S. *Taxation of Securities, Commodities, and Options*. New York: Wiley, 1987.

Macmillan, Lawrence G. *Options as a Strategic Investment*, 2d ed., Chapters 1, 29, 35. New York: New York Institute of Finance, 1986.

NuLaw Services. *1989 Tax Facts on Investments*. Cincinnati: The National Underwriter Company, 1989.

Phillips, Susan M., and Clifford W. Smith, Jr. "Trading Costs for Listed Options: The Implications for Market Efficiency." *Journal of Financial Economics* 8 (1980): 179–201.

Pierog, Karen. "A Tale of Two Systems." *Futures* 16 (August 1987): 50.

U.S. Securities and Exchange Commission. *Report of the Special Study of the Options Markets*. Washington, D.C.: GPO, 1978.

Welch, William W. *Strategies for Put and Call Option Trading*, Chapters 1, 8. Cambridge, Mass.: Winthrop Publishers, 1982.

Wiesenberger Investment Companies. New York: Arthur Wiesenberger & Co., 1989.

---

appendix 2A

Margin Requirements

Margin is the amount of money an individual puts down when entering into an investment. The remainder is borrowed from the brokerage firm. The objective of a margin trade is to earn a higher return by virtue of investing less of one's own funds. However, this advantage is accompanied by increased risk. If the stock price does not move sufficiently in the desired direction, the profit from the investment may not be enough to pay off the loan.

Regulation T of the Federal Reserve Act authorizes the Federal Reserve to regulate the extension of credit in the United States. This authority extends to the regulation of margin credit on transactions in stocks and options.

The *initial margin* is the minimum amount of funds the investor supplies on the day of the transaction. The *maintenance margin* is the minimum amount of funds required each day thereafter. However, on any day on which a trade is executed, the initial margin requirement must be met.

The rules presented here apply to public investors. Specialists and market makers have more lenient margin requirements. Clearing firm margins deposited with the OCC are calculated differently based on a netting out of certain identical long and short positions and an additional amount based on the probabilities of customer defaults.

MARGIN REQUIREMENTS ON STOCK TRANSACTIONS

The minimum initial margin for stock purchases and short sales is 50 percent. The minimum maintenance margin is 25 percent. Many brokerage firms add an additional 5 percent or more to these requirements.

MARGIN REQUIREMENTS ON OPTION PURCHASES

All option purchases must be fully margined; that is, the investor must pay the option premium in full. This rule exists because options already contain a substantial leverage component. The additional use of margin would add leverage and thus greatly increase the risk of the investor's position.

MARGIN REQUIREMENTS ON THE UNCOVERED SALE OF OPTIONS

An *uncovered* call is a transaction in which an investor writes a call on stock not already owned. If the option is exercised, the writer must buy the stock in the market at the current price, which has no upper limit. Thus, the risk is quite high. Many brokerage firms do not allow their customers to write uncovered calls. Those that do usually restrict such trades to wealthy investors who can afford large losses; yet even these must meet the minimum margin requirements.

For an uncovered call, the investor must deposit the premium plus 20 percent of the stock's value. If the call is out-of-the-money, the requirement is reduced by the amount by which the call is out-of-the-money. The margin must be at least 10 percent of the value of the stock. Consider an investor who writes one call contract at an exercise price of $30 on a stock priced at $33 for a premium of $4.50. The required margin is .2($3,300) + $450 = $1,110. If the stock is priced at $28 and the call is at $.50, the margin is .2($2,800) + $50 − $200 = $410. These amounts are greater than 10 percent of the value of the stock. The amount by which the call is out-of-the-money reduces the required margin.

The same rules apply for puts. If a put is written at an exercise price of $30 when the stock price is $33 and the put price is $2.375, the required margin is .2 ($3,300) + $237.50 − $300 = $597.50. If the stock price is $29 and the put price is $3.25, the margin is .2($2,900) + $325 = $905. These amounts are greater than 10 percent of the value of the stock.

Index options are somewhat less volatile than options on individual stocks and, appropriately, have lower margin requirements. The required margin is 15 percent, instead of 20 percent, of the stock's value.

MARGIN REQUIREMENTS ON COVERED CALLS

A *covered* call is a transaction in which an investor writes an option against a stock already owned. If the option's exercise price is at least equal to the stock price, the investor need not deposit any additional margin beyond that required on the stock. Also, the premium on the option can be used to reduce the margin required on the stock. If, however, the exercise price is less than the stock price, the maximum amount the investor can borrow on the stock is based on the call's exercise price rather than on the stock price. For example, if the stock price is $40 and the exercise price is $35, the investor can borrow only .5($3,500) = $1,750, not .5($4,000) = $2,000, on the purchase of the stock.

Although it is possible to hold a portfolio of stocks that is identical to the index, current margin requirements do not recognize covered index call writing. Therefore, all short positions in index options must be margined according to the rules that apply to uncovered writing.

There are exceptions to many of these rules, particularly when spreads, straddles, and more complex option transactions are used. In these cases, the margin requirements often are complicated. Investors should consult a broker or some of the trade-oriented publications for additional information on margin requirements for the more complex transactions.

Questions and Problems

1. Suppose a stock is currently priced at $50. The margin requirement is 20 percent on uncovered calls and 50 percent on stocks. Calculate the required margin, in dollars, for each of the following trades:

    a.   Write 10 call contracts with an exercise price of 45 and a premium of 7.

    b.   Write 10 call contracts with an exercise price of 55 and a premium of 3.

    c.   Write 10 put contracts with an exercise price of 45 and a premium of 3.

    d.   Write 10 put contracts with an exercise price of 55 and a premium of 7.

    e.   Buy 1,000 shares of stock and write 10 call contracts with an exercise price of 45 and a premium of 7.

    f.   Buy 20 put contracts with an exercise price of 50 and a premium of 5.

appendix 2B

Taxation of Option Transactions

Determining the applicable taxation of many investment transactions is a complex process that requires the advice of highly trained specialists. The rules covered in this appendix outline most of the basic option transactions. However, there are many exceptions and loopholes, and the laws change frequently. In all cases, one should secure competent professional advice.

As of 1991, ordinary income is taxed at a maximum rate of 31 percent. Capital gains (defined as profits from positions held more than one year) are taxed at the ordinary income rate, subject to a maximum of 28 percent. Although there are some exceptions noted herein, most options profits are short term. Since most taxpayers are in the 28 percent bracket, most option profits are taxed at 28 percent.

In these examples, we ignore brokerage commissions; however, they are tax deductible. The commission on the purchase of the asset is added to the purchase price; the commission on its sale is subtracted from the sale price.

The deductibility of any losses is determined by offsetting them against other investment gains. If the losses exceed the gains, any excess up to $3,000 per year is deductible against the investor's ordinary income.

TAXATION OF LONG CALL TRANSACTIONS

If an investor purchases a call and sells it back at a later date at a higher price, the profit is taxed at the ordinary income rate. If the investor sells the call at a loss or allows it to expire, the loss is deductible as previously described.

Consider an investor in the 28 percent tax bracket who purchases a call at $3.50 on a stock priced at $36 with an exercise price of $35. Before expiration, the investor sells the call at $4.75. The profit of $1.25 is taxed at 28 percent for a tax of $1.25(.28) = $.35. If the call were sold at a loss, the loss would be deductible as described above.

If the investor exercised the call, the call price plus the exercise price would be treated as the stock's purchase price and subsequently used to determine the taxable gain on the stock. For example, if the above call were exercised when the stock price was $38, the purchase price of the stock would be considered as the $35 exercise price plus the $3.50 call price for a total of $38.50. If the investor later sold the stock for $40, the taxable gain would be $1.50 and the tax $1.50(.28) = $.42. A tax liability or deduction arises only when the stock is subsequently sold.

TAXATION OF SHORT CALL TRANSACTIONS

If an investor sells a call and later repurchases it or allows it to expire, any profit is taxable at the ordinary income rate. If the call is exercised, the exercise price plus the call price is treated as the price at which the stock is sold. Then the difference between the price at which the stock is sold and the price at which it is purchased is the taxable gain.

For example, if the above investor writes the call at a price of $3.50 and subsequently sells it at $5.25 before expiration, the profit of $1.75 will be taxed at 28 percent for a tax of $1.75(.28) = $.49. A loss would be deductible as previously described. If the call were exercised, the writer would deliver the stock. Suppose the stock price were $38 and the writer did not already own the stock. Then the writer would purchase the stock for $38 and sell it to the buyer for $35. The sum of the exercise price plus the premium, $35 + $3.50 = $38.50, would be treated as the stock's sale price. The taxable gain to the writer would be $.50 and the tax $.50(.28) = $.14. Had the writer purchased the stock at an earlier date at $30, the taxable gain would be $8.50 and the tax $8.50(.28) = $2.38.

TAXATION OF LONG PUT TRANSACTIONS

If an investor purchases a put and sells it at a later date or allows it to expire, the profit is taxed at the ordinary income rate. If the put is exercised, the exercise price minus the premium is treated as the stock's sale price. Then the profit from the stock is taxed at the ordinary income rate.

Consider an investor in the 28 percent tax bracket who purchases a put at $3 on a stock priced at $52 with an exercise price of $50. Later the investor sells the put for $4.25. The gain of $1.25 is taxed at 28 percent for a tax of $1.25(.28) = $.35. If the put is sold at a loss, the loss is deductible as previously described.

Suppose the investor exercises the put when the stock price is $46. The law would treat this as the sale of stock at $50 less the premium of $3 for a net gain of $47. If the investor purchases the stock at $46 and exercises the put, the taxable gain is $1 and the tax is $1(.28) = $.28. If the investor had previously purchased the stock at $40, the taxable gain would be $7 and the tax $7(.28) = $1.96. Had the investor purchased the stock at a price higher than $47, the loss would be deductible as described earlier.

Another possibility is that the investor uses the exercise of the put to sell short the stock. A short sale occurs when an investor borrows stock from the broker and sells it. If the stock price falls, the investor can buy back the stock at a lower price, repay the broker the shares, and capture a profit. A short sale is made in order to profit in a falling market. In our example, the stock is sold short at $47. When the investor later repurchases the stock, any gain on the stock is taxable or any loss is deductible.

TAXATION OF SHORT PUT TRANSACTIONS

If an investor writes a put and subsequently buys it back before expiration, any gain is taxed at the ordinary income rate and any loss is deductible. If the put is exercised, the put's exercise price minus the premium is considered to be the stock's purchase price. The taxable gain or loss on the stock is determined by the difference between the purchase and sale prices of the stock.

Consider the put with an exercise price of $50 written at $3 when the stock price is $52. Suppose the stock price goes to $46 and the put is exercised. The put writer is considered to have purchased the stock for $50 − $3, or $47. If the investor later sells the stock for $55, the taxable gain is $8 and the tax is $8(.28) = $2.24.

TAXATION OF NON-EQUITY OPTIONS

Index options, debt options, and foreign currency options have a special tax status. At the end of the calendar year, all realized and unrealized gains are taxed at the ordinary income rate. All losses are deductible as previously described. The profits are taxed at a blended rate in which 60 percent are taxed at the capital gains rate and 40 percent are taxed at the ordinary income rate. For an investor in the 31 percent bracket, this is an effective rate of .6(.28) + .4(.31) = .292.

For example, assume that during the year an investor in the 31 percent bracket had $1,250 of net profits (profits minus losses) on index options. At the end of the year, the investor holds 1,000 index options worth $2.25 that previously had been purchased for $1.75. The unrealized profit is thus $500. The total taxable profits are $1,250 + $500 = $1,750. The tax is $1,750(.6)(.28) + $1,750(.4)(.31) = $511.

THE WASH SALE RULE: A SPECIAL CONSIDERATION

Option traders should be aware of an important tax condition called the *wash sale rule*. A wash sale is a transaction in which an investor sells a security at a loss and replaces it with essentially the same security shortly thereafter. Tax laws disallow the deduction of the loss on the sale of the original security. The purpose of the wash sale rule is to prevent investors from taking losses at the end of a calendar year and then immediately replacing the securities. The time period within which the purchase of the security cannot occur is the 61-day period from 30 days before the sale of the stock through 30 days after.

Although, as with many tax laws, there is some murkiness, the wash sale rule usually treats a call option as being the same security as the stock. Thereafter, if the investor sells the stock at a loss and buys a call within the applicable 61-day period, the loss on the stock is not deductible.

Questions and Problems

1. Suppose a stock is priced at $30 and an eight-month call on the stock with an exercise price of $25 is priced at $6. Compute the taxable gain and tax due for each of the following cases assuming your tax bracket is 28 percent. Assume 100 shares and 100 calls.

   a. You buy the call. Four months later, the stock is at $28 and the call is at $4.50. You then sell the call.

   b. You buy the call. Three months later, the stock is at $31 and the call is at $6.50. You then sell the call.

   c. You buy the call. At expiration, the stock is at $32. You exercise the call and sell the stock a month later for $35.

   d. You buy the stock and write the call. You hold the position until expiration, whereupon the stock is at $28.

   e. You write the call. Two months later, the stock is at $28 and the call is at $3.50. You buy back the call.

2. Consider an S&P 100 index option. The index is at 280.48, and a two-month call with an exercise price of 280 is priced at $15. You are in the 31 percent tax bracket. Compute the after-tax profit for the following cases. Assume 100 calls.

   a. You buy the call. One month later, the index is at 288 and the call is at $12. You sell the call.

   b. You buy the call and hold it until expiration, whereupon the index is at 296.35. You exercise the call.

   c. You hold the call until expiration, when the index is at 277.15.

   d. How will your answers in parts a and b be affected if the option positions are not closed out by the end of the year?

3. Which of the following would be a wash sale? Explain.

   a. You buy a stock at $30. Three weeks later, you sell the stock at $26. Two weeks later, you buy a call on the stock.

   b. You buy a stock at $40. One month later, you buy a call on the stock. One week later, you sell the stock for $38.

   c. You buy a stock for $40. Three months later, you sell the stock for $42 and buy a call on the stock.

appendix 2C

Sources of Information on Options

PERIODICALS

The Wall Street Journal

The Wall Street Journal is the nation's most widely read financial newspaper. Published weekdays by Dow Jones & Company, it provides extensive coverage of all aspects of business and finance. While the *Journal* is well known for its tables of closing security prices, it also contains closing option prices on all exchanges. The *Journal* does not have a regular column devoted to options, but many articles on options appear from time to time. Subscriptions cost $129 per year and may be obtained by writing *The Wall Street Journal*, 200 Burnett Road, Chicopee, Massachusetts 01020. Discount subscriptions are available to students through many college instructors.

Barron's

Barron's is a weekly newspaper devoted almost entirely to the investment industry. Also published by Dow Jones & Company, *Barron's* provides extensive coverage of stock and option trading during the week and closing prices as of the end of that week.

    Barron's features a weekly column, "The Striking Price," that focuses on the options market. "The Striking Price" recaps activity during the past week and indicates which options had large price increases. It also gives specific strategies recommended by a panel of analysts from several brokerage firms. The column usually concludes with a section on miscellaneous topics such as regulatory issues and new contracts. "The Striking Price" is an excellent source of information on the options market and is recommended reading for all serious option followers. Figure 2C.1 presents an example of a typical column.

    Barron's subscriptions cost $99 per year and can be obtained by writing *Barron's*, 200 Burnett Road, Chicopee, Massachusetts 01020. Student discount subscriptions are also available from many college instructors.

Futures

Futures is a monthly publication that calls itself "The Magazine of Commodities and Options." *Futures* does not provide option prices, but it presents many feature articles by staff writers and outsiders covering aspects of option trading and the

FIGURE 2C.1

Barron's "The Striking Price"

March 25, 1991

Options

THE STRIKING PRICE

/ By THOMAS N. COCHRAN

Big Swingers

LAST week brought high volume and big price changes to a number of widely held shares. One was **Upjohn**, which moved 3⅝ points higher on Tuesday, adding ¾ more Thursday, each time on volume of nearly two million shares. Friday's new high of 48⅜, before the shares sold off, was the highest price in 3½ years. The action in Upjohn occurred in the face of a general market decline accompanied by weakness in drug stocks.

Upjohn, of course, has been the subject of one of the longest-standing rumors of takeover. Shearson's Brett Kellam sensibly suggested a while back that Upjohn stockholders may wish they'd had a safety net if these stories finally come to naught. In recent days, though, "the stock's been really impressive," and Kellam points out that there's been big volume in the options as well as the shares. "This time looks more for real." With the higher prices, Kellam now suggests selling the shares and buying the May 50. "I would probably only want to be an owner of the stock at this point if I felt there was a deal," he says, because otherwise the shares could fall significantly. He adds that "it shows the real value of options in being flexible" in one's ability to profit from hoped-for events while still limiting risk. Friday, pricing of the May 50 calls would give breakeven with the stock up 13%. If the big deal comes, the calls provide a fine gain, particularly at the $65 takeover value mentioned by one analyst last week. Kellam closes with a caution: "I would not be in the position until the May expiration."

IN ANOTHER sector, **IBM** led computer-stock weakness, tumbling 15½ points on the week on news that its first-quarter earnings were likely to fall to 90 cents, half analysts' estimates. How the mighty are fallen! IBM won't even earn its dividend on the projected quarterly figure. If you're an IBM stockholder, Harrison Roth of Oppenheimer guesses "you're pretty shook up about what's happened."

But Roth has a novel plan. At last week's prices, selling a round lot of IBM can provide both diversification in the industry and a long-term shot at its success, all at no out-of-pocket expense. For Roth has noted that four of the leading players in the field have long-term options expiring in July 1992: IBM, **Compaq, Digital Equipment** and **Microsoft**. Long-term calls on all four can be bought with sale proceeds from 100 shares of IBM. Roth's selections would be the IBM July 1992 85 call, trading about five points above parity, Compaq 45s (six points over), DEC 45s (five points) and Microsoft 85s, 16 points above parity. IBM is the only dividend payer in the bunch, yielding over 4%. The foregone dividends add six points to the cost of the plan, assuming the quarterly payment is not raised or (cries of Shame! Shame!) reduced to fit straightened circumstances.

"You have now used options not for leverage but for diversification," Roth points out, unable to resist adding that "you LEAP to diversification." Using the Chicago Board Options Exchange's Long-term Equity Anticipation Securities, or the similar options of other exchanges,

the former IBM shareholder of course doesn't fully participate if the market should crash in the interim. On average, a 15% decline in the underlying shares would take them down to Roth's suggested strikes, but the calls should also fall less rapidly in a market decline, and still have value if the shares are at the strikes, so the technique could be of use to those whose main concern is a modest near-term slide.

The approach might also be used by those not holding the four stocks. Buying 100 shares of each would come to about $34,000; the calls would cost $11,000. On investing the $23,-000 difference in the money market, a return of $2,100 would be a reasonable expectation over 16 months.

* * *

STEWART Winner of Prudential Securities says that "our firm is favorable toward these stocks." He's referring to waste-disposal companies, and particularly **Waste Management**, which fell three points Wednesday, to 38, on trading of
Continued on Next Page

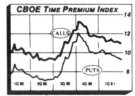

The CBOE Call Index (measuring time premiums on six-month calls) stood at 10.88% Friday, vs. 11.03% a week earlier. The Composite Put Index was 9.33%, vs. 9.45%.

options industry. Many of the articles focus on trading strategies, and a regular column features a particular strategy. *Futures* provides excellent coverage of current legal and regulatory developments and contains book and software reviews, market forecasts, and profiles on individuals involved in the industry. Subscriptions cost $39 per year and can be obtained by writing *Futures*, 219 Parkade, Cedar Falls, Iowa 50613.

Value Line Options

Value Line Options is published 48 times per year. It provides specific recommendations on option trades. Figure 2C.2 is an excerpt from a page listing a group of calls recommended by *Value Line Options*. The line describing AST Research options indicates that the stock carries a rank of 1 according to Value Line's stock rankings. Value Line ranks stocks in categories of 1 to 5, with 1 being the highest ranking. The notation *ASE* indicates that the options trade on the American Stock Exchange. The next line indicates that the options are on AST Research common stock, which has a ticker symbol of *ASQ*. The following number, 210, is the stock's volatility relative to other stocks; for example, AST Research stock is about one-and-a-half times more volatile than JWP Inc. stock, which has a volatility of 140. Immediately below the stock listing is the line for a recommended option—the July 23, with its symbol *GX*. Its volatility of 1400 is about seven times that of the stock. The next seven columns show the maximum price Value Line recommends paying for the call given a particular stock price. If the stock is at $24, Value Line recommends buying the July 23 call if the price is not more than $2.31. If the stock were at $24.50, an investor would be advised to pay no more than $2.66 for the call. These strategies are essentially limit order recommendations.

Value Line Options identifies options especially recommended for certain strategies. It also provides information on all options, whether it recommends them or not. Figure 2C.3 is a sample page from those evaluations. This feature provides a significant amount of information on the various options. Users should consult the explanations contained in each issue for information on how to interpret the data.

Value Line Options also includes a feature article that frequently covers a particular strategy. It also reports on stocks upgraded or downgraded in rank, stocks with upcoming dividends, dividend changes, and miscellaneous information on options and stock markets. Subscriptions to *Value Line Options* cost $445 per year and are available by writing to Value Line Inc., 711 Third Avenue, New York, New York 10017. New-subscriber discounts often are advertised in many financial publications.

In addition to the periodicals presented here, there are many specialized newsletters on options. Advertisements for these publications frequently appear in *Barron's* and *Futures*.

FIGURE 2C.2

Value Line Options Recommendations, June 18, 1990

SELECTED OPTIONS FOR "NAKED" CALL BUYING

Calls are recommended to buyers **at or below** prices shown in relation to the stock or index. Calls on this list tend to be underpriced on stocks or indexes expected to perform as well as or better than the market.

Cm Rank-Opt Exch / Common-Symbol / Option-Symbol	Rel Vol %	Lower Prices		Recent Market Price	Higher Prices	
AST Research - Rank 1 - ASE						
Common ASQ 210	23.00	24.00 24.50		24.88	25.00 25.50	26.50
Jul 23 GX 1400	1.87	2.31 2.66		2.94	3.03 3.43	4.30
Nov 25 KE 960	2.34	2.86 3.15		3.38	3.45 3.78	4.48
Amgen - Rank 1 - ASE						
Common AMQ 170	69.00	71.00 72.00		72.50	73.00 74.00	76.00
Jul 65 GM 1100	5.96	7.44 8.22		8.63	9.03 9.87	11.62
Jul 80 GL 820	9.58	11.37 12.29		12.75	13.22 14.16	16.09
Oct 80 JP 1450	2.61	3.30 3.68		3.86	4.08 4.51	5.45
Oct 75 JO 1200	4.07	4.99 5.49		5.75	6.02 6.57	7.75
Oct 70 JN 1000	6.12	7.30 7.93		8.25	8.58 9.25	10.66
Oct 65 JM 840	8.69	10.13 10.87		11.25	11.63 12.41	14.01
Oct 60 JL 700	11.97	13.81 14.45		14.88	15.30 16.16	17.91
Jan 80 AP 1050	4.42	5.30 5.76		6.00	6.24 6.74	7.79
Jan 75 AO 910	6.08	7.15 7.71		8.00	8.29 8.89	10.14
Jan 65 AM 700	10.77	12.24 12.99		13.38	13.76 14.53	16.11
Autodesk - Rank 1 - PAC						
Common ADQ 165	47.00	49.00 50.00		51.00	52.00 53.00	55.00
Jul 45 GI 1050	3.54	5.02 5.80		6.63	7.48 8.37	10.26
Oct 50 JJ 1050	3.05	4.08 4.65		5.25	5.89 6.56	8.01
Automatic Data Proc - Rank 1 - PHL						
Common AUD 90	54.00	56.00 57.00		57.13	58.00 59.00	61.00
Nov 60 KL 1100	1.43	2.11 2.51		2.56	2.96 3.45	4.58
Becton Dickinson & Co - Rank 1 - PHL						
Common BDX 90	68.00	70.00 71.00		71.25	72.00 73.00	75.00
Sep 65 IM 670	5.38	6.81 7.56		7.75	8.34 9.15	10.85

Cm Rank-Opt Exch / Common-Symbol / Option-Symbol	Rel Vol %	Lower Prices		Recent Market Price	Higher Prices	
JWP Inc. - Rank 1 - ASE						
Common JWP 140	36.00	37.00 37.50		38.00	38.50 39.00	40.00
Oct 40 JH 1200	1.49	1.83 2.03		2.25	2.48 2.74	3.30
Oct 35 JG 780	3.59	4.20 4.53		4.88	5.23 5.61	6.40
Johnson & Johnson - Rank 2 - CBO						
Common JNJ 70	61.00	63.00 64.00		65.00	66.00 67.00	69.00
Jan 70 AN 870	1.24	1.76 2.08		2.44	2.83 3.27	4.25
Limited Inc - Rank 1 - CBO						
Common LTD 115	45.00	47.00 48.00		48.88	49.00 50.00	52.00
Jul 45 GI 970	1.75	3.01 3.71		4.38	4.47 5.29	7.10
Nov 55 KK 1300	.77	1.20 1.48		1.75	1.79 2.15	2.98
Liz Claiborne - Rank 1 - CBO						
Common LIQ 140	30.00	31.00 31.50		31.88	32.00 32.50	33.50
Jul 30 GF 1350	1.28	1.86 2.18		2.44	2.53 2.90	3.73
Oct 35 JG 1550	.70	.96 1.12		1.25	1.30 1.49	1.93
Oct 30 JF 870	2.45	3.05 3.37		3.63	3.71 4.06	4.82
Oct 25 JE 550	5.44	6.33 6.78		7.13	7.24 7.71	8.66
Lowes Companies - Rank 1 - PHL						
Common LOW 115	45.00	47.00 48.00		48.25	49.00 50.00	52.00
Jul 45 GI 1100	1.65	2.86 3.57		3.75	4.33 5.17	7.06
Oct 50 JJ 1250	1.26	1.96 2.39		2.50	2.86 3.40	4.64
Oct 45 JI 790	3.28	4.52 5.20		5.38	5.92 6.67	8.31
Jan 45 AI 650	4.22	5.51 6.20		6.38	6.91 7.65	9.22
MAPCO Inc - Rank 2 - PAC						

ACADEMIC JOURNALS

There are no specific academic journals devoted exclusively to options. However, *The Review of Futures Markets* and *The Journal of Futures Markets* contain articles on futures markets and options on futures. More detailed information on these journals is presented in Chapter 7.

Financial Analysts Journal, published by the Association for Investment Management and Research, is devoted primarily to the stock and bond markets. In recent years, however, it has published more articles on options. Most of the articles are written by academics but are oriented toward the professional financial analyst. The journal is published bimonthly, and each issue contains six to eight articles.

L-8 VALUE LINE OPTIONS

June 18,1990

Description of each Security				Recent Mkt Price	Est. Nrml Price	Chng Per Point	Buyer Perf Rank	Relative Volatility	Leverage +10%	Leverage -10%	Writer Perf Rank	Rel. Vol.	+10%	0%	-10%
American Elec Power (8.0% yield, last ex $.60 May 3) CBO															
AEP common				30.13			4	55%							
Jul	30	GF	GG	.63	.68	52	3	2100	+405%	-100%	-	35	+2	+2	-8
Aug	35	HG	HH	.13	.02	11	-	3300	+420	-90	-	50	+10	0	-10
	30	HF	BD	.63	.85	52	3	1900	+405	-95	5↓	35	+2	+2	-8
Nov	30	KF	CD	1.00	1.23	53	3	970	+230	-85	5	30	+3	+3	-7
	25	KE	GH	5.13	5.18	99	5	280	+60	-60	-	10	0	0	0
P Jul	30	SF	HH	.63	.64	48	2	2400	-90	+370					
P Aug	30	TF	DG	.88	.88	47	3	1700	-80	+245					
P	35	TG	EH	5.13	4.91	85	3↓	320	-45	+55					
P Nov	30	WF	DE	1.00	1.30	47	1	910	-75	+210					
American Express Co (3.0% yield, last ex $.23 Apr 1) CBO,ASE															
AXP common				30.38			4	95%							
Jul	40	GH	FH	.06	.01	4	-	1600	+305%	-85%	-	95	+10	0	-10
	35	GG	CC	.06	.14	9	-	9999	+740	-90	-	75	+10	0	-10
	30	GF	AA	1.31	1.45	56	4	1950	+180	-80	4	60	+3	+3	-6
	25	GE	AA	5.50	5.46	94	4	470	+55	-50	-	15	+1	+1	+1
Oct	35	JG	BB	.50	.67	22	3	1800	+195	-70	4	75	+12	+2	-8
	30	JF	AA	2.44	2.37	59	4	860	+90	-60	4	55	+7	+7	-2
	25	JE	AA	5.88	5.90	88	4	450	+50	-45	5	20	+2	+2	+2
Jan	35	AG	BB	1.13	1.05	32	4	1000	+110	-60	4	70	+14	+4	-7
	30	AF	BB	3.13	2.89	62	4	640	+65	-50	4	50	+10	+10	0
	25	AE	FF	6.63	6.24	86	5	410	+40	-40	3	25	+5	+5	+5
P Jul	25	SE	BF	.13	.04	5	-	4500	-65	+195					
P	30	SF	AA	1.00	.84	43	3	2500	-75	+190					
P	35	SG	BB	4.63	4.69	99	2↑	490	-65	+65					
P Oct	25	VE	BB	.25	.33	9	2	2200	-55	+155					
P	30	VF	AB	1.75	1.63	41	2	1050	-50	+95					
P	35	VG	BB	5.25	5.03	76	3	480	-40	+50					
P Jan	25	NE	FE	.50	.58	12	2↑	1200	-45	+100					
P	30	NF	AA	2.25	2.04	40	2	740	-40	+65					
P	35	NG	CC	5.00	5.30	81	2	410	-45	+55					

Source: Value Line Investment Survey, June 18, 1990. Copyright © 1990 by Value Line Publishing, Inc.; used by permission.

The Journal of Portfolio Management, published by Institutional Investor, also contains many articles, most of which are written by academics but directed toward professionals. It publishes ten or more articles in each quarterly issue and usually has at least one article on options.

Many other excellent academic journals publish articles on options. Almost all the articles are written by academics for an academic audience. Some of these journals are *The Journal of Finance, Journal of Financial Economics, The Review of Financial Studies, Journal of Financial and Quantitative Analysis, The Journal of Financial Research,* and *The Financial Review.*

OTHER SOURCES OF INFORMATION

Numerous computer services provide software, analysis, and real-time option price quotations. Many brokerage houses publish information on options. Two of the best—and usually least expensive—sources of information on options are the exchanges and the Options Clearing Corporation. All publish many booklets and articles designed to educate the public about options. They also have public relations personnel available to answer questions.

PRINCIPLES OF OPTION PRICING

This chapter identifies and shows why certain factors affect an option's price. It examines option boundary conditions—rules that characterize rational option prices. Then it explores the relationship between options that differ by exercise price alone and those that differ only by time to expiration. Finally, the chapter discusses how put and call prices are related as well as several other important principles.

Most of the rules for establishing boundary conditions for option prices are products of the arbitrage process. For example, suppose a stock trades on both the New York Stock Exchange in New York and the Pacific Stock Exchange in San Francisco. Assume there are no transaction costs involved in trading stocks on either exchange. The stock is simultaneously selling for $40 in New York and $41 in San Francisco. An alert individual can buy the stock in New York, sell it in San Francisco, and capture a sure $1 profit. There is no risk, because the transactions are executed simultaneously and each offsets the other. However, other investors will quickly recognize the opportunity, and the rapid buying and selling of this stock will cause the price to converge on both markets.

Suppose an individual offers you the following proposition. You can play a game called Game I in which you draw a ball from a hat known to contain three red balls and three blue balls. If you draw a red ball, you receive nothing; if you draw a blue ball, you receive $10. Will you play? Because the individual did not mention an entry fee, of course you will play. You incur no cash outlay up front and have the opportunity to earn $10. Of course, this opportunity is too good to be true and only an irrational person would make such an offer without charging an entry fee.

Now suppose a fair fee to play this game is $4. Now consider a new game called Game II. The person offers to pay you $20 if you draw a blue ball and nothing if you draw a red ball. Will the entry fee be higher or lower? If you draw a red ball, you receive the same payoff as in Game I; if you draw a blue ball, you receive a higher payoff than in Game I. You should be willing to pay more to play Game II because these payoffs dominate those of Game I.

From these simple games and opportunities, it is easy to see some of the basic principles of how rational people behave when faced with risky situations. The collective behavior of rational investors operates in an identical manner to determine the fundamental principles of option pricing. As you read the various examples in this chapter in which arbitrage is used to establish fundamental rules about option pricing, keep in mind the similarity of the investment situation to the games just described. In so doing, the rational result should become clear to you.

In this chapter, we do not derive the exact price of an option; rather, we confine the discussion to identifying upper and lower limits and factors that influence an option's price. Chapter 4 explains how the exact option price is determined.

BASIC NOTATION AND TERMINOLOGY

The following symbols are used throughout the book:

S = stock price today

E = exercise price

T = time to expiration as defined below

r = risk-free rate as defined below

S_T = stock price at option's expiration

$C(S,T,E)$ = price of a call option in which the stock price is S, the time to expiration is T, and the exercise price is E

$P(S,T,E)$ = price of a put option in which the stock price is S, the time to expiration is T, and the exercise price is E

In some situations, we may need to distinguish an American call from a European call. If so, the call price will be denoted as either $C_a(S,T,E)$ or $C_e(S,T,E)$ for the American and European calls, respectively. If there is no a or e subscript, the call can be either an American or a European call. In the case where two options differ only by exercise price, the notations $C(S,T,E_1)$ and $C(S,T,E_2)$ will identify the prices of the calls with E_1 less than E_2. A good way to remember this is to keep in mind that the subscript of the lower exercise price is smaller than that of the higher exercise price. In the case where two options differ only by time to expiration, the times to expiration will be T(1) and T(2), where T(1) < T(2), with the values of the terms in parentheses indicating which time to expiration is longer. The options' prices will be C(S,T(1),E) and C(S,T(2),E). Identical adjustments will be made for put option prices.

We initially assume that no dividends are paid on the stock. Later we shall address the case where dividends on the stock affect the option's price. Appendix 3A shows how the principles discussed in the chapter are slightly modified by the inclusion of dividends. We assume no taxes or transaction costs except where they have special relevance.

The time to expiration is expressed as a decimal fraction of a year. For example, if the current date is April 9 and the option's expiration date is July 18, we simply count the number of days between these two dates. That would be 21 days remaining in April, 31 in May, 30 in June, and 18 in July for a total of 100 days. The time to expiration therefore would be 100/365 = .274.

The risk-free rate, r, is the rate earned on a riskless investment. An example of such an investment is a U.S. Treasury bill, or T-bill. A Treasury bill is a security issued by the U.S. government for purchase by investors. Bills with original maturities of 91 and 182 days are auctioned by the Federal Reserve each week; bills with maturities of 365 days are auctioned every four weeks. All bills mature on a Thursday.[1] Because most options expire on Fridays, there is always a Treasury bill maturing the day before expiration. The rate of return on that Treasury bill would be a proxy for the risk-free rate.

Treasury bills pay interest not through coupons but by selling at a discount. The bill is purchased at less than face value. The difference between the purchase price and the face value is called the *discount*. If the investor holds the bill to maturity, it is redeemed at face value. Therefore, the discount is the profit earned by the bill holder.

Bid and ask discounts for several T-bills for the business day of June 12 of a particular year are as follows:

Maturity	Bid	Ask
6/18	4.75	4.56
7/16	5.16	5.10
10/15	5.63	5.59

[1] If Thursday is a holiday, such as Thanksgiving, the Treasury bill matures on Wednesday of that week.

The bid and ask figures are the discounts quoted by dealers trading in Treasury bills. The *bid* is the discount if one is selling to the dealer, and the *ask* is the discount if one is buying from the dealer. Bid and ask quotes are reported daily in *The Wall Street Journal*.

Options expire on the third Friday of the month. In the above example, the third Friday of June was June 19. To find an estimate of the T-bill rate, we use the average of the bid and ask discounts, which is (4.75 + 4.56)/2 = 4.66. Then we find the discount from par value as 4.66(7/360) = .0906, which reflects the fact that the bill has 7 days until maturity. Thus, the price is

$$100 - .0906 = 99.9094.$$

Note that the price is determined by assuming a 360-day year. This is a long-standing tradition in the financial community, originating from the days before calculators, when bank loans often were for 60, 90, or 180 days. A banker could easily calculate the discount using the fraction 60/360, 90/360, or 180/360. This tradition survives today.

The yield on our T-bill is based on the assumption of buying it at 99.9094 and holding it for 7 days, at which time it will be worth 100, and repeating this transaction every 7 days for a full year. The yield is

$$\left(\frac{100}{99.9094}\right)^{365/7} - 1 = .0484,$$

which reflects the fact that there are actually 365 days in a year. Thus, we would use 4.84 percent as our proxy for the risk-free rate for options expiring on June 19.

To illustrate the principles of option pricing with real-life options, Table 3.1 presents some prices of Digital Equipment options on June 12 of a particular year. The June option expires on June 19, the July expires on July 17, and the October expires on October 16. Following the same procedure described for the June T-bill and using the Treasury bill data from the previous example gives us risk-free rates of 5.35 and 5.91 for the July and October expirations, respectively. The times to expiration are .0192 (7 days) for the June options, .0959 (35 days) for the July options, and .3452 (126 days) for the October options.

PRINCIPLES OF CALL OPTION PRICING

The Minimum Value of a Call

Because a call option need not be exercised, its minimum value is zero.

A call option is an instrument with limited liability. If the call holder sees that it is advantageous to exercise it, the call will be exercised. If exercising it will decrease the call holder's wealth, the holder will not exercise it. The option cannot have negative value, because the holder cannot be forced to exercise it. Therefore,

$$C(S,T,E) \geq 0.$$

TABLE 3.1
Digital Equipment Option Data, June 12

Exercise Price	Calls			Puts		
	Jun	**Jul**	**Oct**	**Jun**	**Jul**	**Oct**
160	4 5/8	8 5/8	15 1/4	13/16	3 7/8	8 1/8
165	1 7/8	5 3/4	13 1/4	2 15/16	6	9 3/4
170	1/2	3 3/4	10 3/4	6 1/2	8 1/2	NA
175	1/16	2 3/8	8 1/2	NA	NA	NA

Current stock price: 164
Expirations: June 19, July 17, October 16

For an American call, the statement that a call option has a minimum value of zero is dominated by a much stronger statement:

$$C_a(S,T,E) \geq Max(0, S - E).$$

The expression Max(0, S − E) means "Take the maximum value of the two arguments, zero or S − E."

The minimum value of an option is called its *intrinsic value*, sometimes referred to as *parity value*, *parity*, or *exercise value*. Intrinsic value, which is positive for in-the-money calls and zero for out-of-the-money calls, is the value the call holder receives from exercising the option and the value the call writer gives up when the option is exercised. Note that we are not concerned about the appropriateness of immediately exercising the option; we note only that one could do so if a profit opportunity such as that just described were available.

To prove the intrinsic value rule, consider the Digital Equipment July 160 call. The stock price is $164, and the exercise price is $160. Evaluating the expression gives Max(0, 164 − 160) = 4. Now consider what would happen if the call were priced at less than $4—say, $3. An option trader could buy the call for $3, exercise it—which would entail purchasing the stock for $160—and then sell the stock for $164. This arbitrage transaction would net an immediate riskless profit of $1 on each share.[2] All investors would do this, which would drive up the option's price. When the price of the option reached $4, the transaction would no longer be profitable. Thus, $4 is the minimum price of the call.

The intrinsic value of an American call is the greater of zero or the difference between the stock price and the exercise price.

---

[2]Actually, it would not be necessary to sell the stock. In the absence of transaction costs, it is immaterial whether one holds the stock—an asset valued at $164—or converts it to another asset—cash—worth $164.

What if the exercise price exceeds the stock price, as do the options with an exercise price of $165? Then Max(0, 164 – 165) = 0, and the minimum value will be zero.

Now look at all of the Digital Equipment calls. Those with an exercise price of $160 have a minimum value of Max(0, 164 – 160) = 4. All three calls with an exercise price of $160 indeed have prices of no less than $4. The calls with an exercise price of $165 have minimum values of Max(0, 164 – 165) = 0. The calls with an exercise price of 170 have minimum values of Max(0, 164 – 170) = 0. All of those options obviously have non-negative values. Thus, all of the Digital Equipment call options conform to the intrinsic value rule. In fact, extensive empirical testing has revealed that options in general conform quite closely to the rule. Bhattacharya (1983) examined over 86,000 call option prices during the period of August 24, 1976, through June 12, 1977. Only 1.3 percent violated the rule, and the average size of the violation was about one-eighth of a point. For a trader acting on the observance of such a violation, the apparent profit opportunity was eliminated by the next price 29 percent of the time. Thus, the market reacts very quickly to exploit pricing inefficiencies.

The intrinsic value concept applies only to an American call, because a European call can be exercised only on the expiration day. If the price of a European call were less than Max(0, S – E), the inability to exercise it would prevent traders from engaging in the aforementioned arbitrage that would drive up the call's price.

The price of an American call normally exceeds its intrinsic value. The difference between the price and the intrinsic value is called the *time value* or *speculative value* of the call. It reflects what traders are willing to pay for the uncertainty of the underlying stock. Table 3.2 presents the intrinsic values and time values of the Digital Equipment calls. Note that the time values increase with the time to expiration.

The Maximum Value of a Call

A call option also has a maximum value:

$$C(S,T,E) \leq S.$$

The maximum value of a call is the price of the stock.

The call is a conduit through which an investor can obtain the stock. The most one can expect to gain from the call is the stock's value less the exercise price. Even if the exercise price were zero, no one would pay more for the call than for the stock. However, one call that is worth the stock price is one with an infinite maturity. It is obvious that all of the Digital Equipment calls are worth no more than the value of the stock.

TABLE 3.2

Intrinsic Values and Time Values of Digital Equipment Calls

Exercise Price	Intrinsic Value	Time Value		
		Jun	Jul	Oct
160	4.000	0.625	4.625	11.250
165	0.000	1.875	5.750	13.250
170	0.000	0.500	3.750	10.750

The Value of a Call at Expiration

The price of a call at expiration is given as

$$C(S_T, 0, E) = Max(0, S_T - E).$$

Because no time remains in the option's life, the call price contains no time value. The prospect of future stock price increases is irrelevant to the price of the expiring option, which will be simply its intrinsic value.[3]

At expiration, an American option and a European option are identical instruments. Therefore, this rule holds for both types of options.

At expiration, a call option is worth the intrinsic value.

The Effect of Time to Expiration

Consider two American calls that differ only in their times to expiration. One has a time to expiration of T(1) and a price of $C_a(S,T(1),E)$; the other has a time to expiration of T(2) and a price of $C_a(S,T(2),E)$. Remember that T(2) is greater than T(1). Which of these two options will have the greater value?

Suppose today is the expiration day of the shorter-lived option. The stock price is $S_{T(1)}$. The value of the expiring option is $Max(0, S_{T(1)} - E)$. The second option has a time to expiration of T(2) – T(1). Its minimum value is $Max(0, S_{T(1)} - E)$. Thus, when the shorter-lived option expires, its value is the minimum value of the longer-lived option. Therefore,

$$C_a(S,T(2),E) \geq C_a(S,T(1),E).$$

Normally the longer-lived call is worth more, but if it carries no time value when the shorter-lived option expires, the two options will have the same price. This can occur if the stock price is either very high or very low. Usually the longer-lived option is worth more. Looking at the prices of the Digital Equipment calls,

A longer-lived American call must always be worth at least as much as a shorter-lived American call with the same terms.

[3]Because of the transaction cost of exercising the option, it could be worth slightly less than the intrinsic value.

FIGURE 3.1
Call Price versus Stock Price for Different Expirations

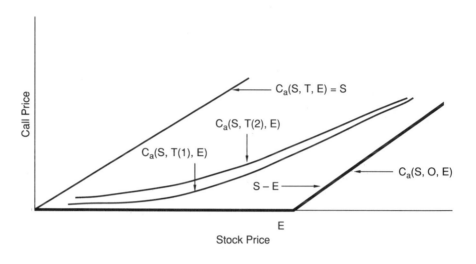

we can see that this is the case. The longer the time to expiration, the greater the call's value.

The time value of a call option varies with the time to expiration and the proximity of the stock price to the exercise price. Investors pay for the time value of the call based on the uncertainty of the future stock price. If the stock price is very high, the call is said to be *deep-in-the-money* and the time value will be low. If the stock price is very low, the call is said to be *deep-out-of-the-money* and the time value likewise will be low. The time value will be low because at these extremes, the uncertainty about the call expiring in- or out-of-the-money is lower. The uncertainty is greater when the stock price is near the exercise price, and it is at this point that the time value is higher.

Figure 3.1 illustrates these properties. Between the minimum and maximum values are curves showing the prices of two American calls with different expirations. Because we have not yet determined exactly how to find the call price, we can depict these curves only in a general sense. The graph shows the upper limit on the call price, $C_a(S,T,E)$. This would represent a call worth the stock price. The graph also shows the lower limit on the call price—the heavy, shaded line labeled $S - E$ and $C_a(S,0,E)$. This would represent a call expiring now and selling for its intrinsic value. Between these two lines lie the prices of the calls with maturities of $T(2)$ and $T(1)$.

Notice the curve representing the call with the longer time to expiration, $T(2)$. The time value is the vertical distance between this curve and the heavy, shaded line that represents the intrinsic value. Note that the time value is low when the stock price is either very high or very low and high when the stock price is close to the exercise price. The same relationships hold for the option with the shorter time to expiration, T(1). At extremely high or low stock prices, the time values of the shorter- and longer-lived calls are close, and therefore their prices are similar. Within these extreme stock prices, the time value of the longer-lived call exceeds that of the shorter-lived call.

This phenomenon is evident in the Digital Equipment calls. Note that in Table 3.2, for a given exercise price the time values increase with the time to expiration. For a given time to expiration, the time values are highest for the calls with an exercise price of 165, the exercise price closest to the stock price.

The relationship between time to expiration and option price also holds for European calls. Nevertheless, we cannot yet formally accept this as fact, because we have not yet established a minimum value for a European call. That will come a bit later.

The Effect of Exercise Price

THE EFFECT ON OPTION VALUE   Consider two European calls that are identical in all respects except that the exercise price of one is E_1 and that of the other is E_2. Recall that E_2 is greater than E_1. We want to know which price is greater— $C_e(S,T,E_1)$ or $C_e(S,T,E_2)$.

Now consider two portfolios, A and B. Portfolio A consists of a long position in the call with the exercise price of E_1 and a short position in the call with the exercise price of E_2. (This type of portfolio is called a *money spread* and is discussed further in Chapter 6.) Because we pay $C_e(S,T,E_1)$ and receive $C_e(S,T,E_2)$, this portfolio will have an initial value of $C_e(S,T,E_1) - C_e(S,T,E_2)$. We do not yet know whether the initial value is positive or negative; that will depend on which option price is higher.

Portfolio B consists simply of risk-free bonds with a face value of $E_2 - E_1$. These bonds should be considered as pure discount instruments, like Treasury bills, and as maturing at the options' expiration. Thus, the value of this portfolio is the present value of the bonds' face value, or simply $(E_2 - E_1)(1 + r)^{-T}$.

For the time being, we shall concentrate on portfolio A. First, we need to determine the portfolio's value at expiration. The value of any portfolio will be its cash flow or payoff when the options expire contingent on the stock price at expiration, S_T. The stock price at expiration has three possible ranges: (1) $S_T < E_1$; (2) $E_1 \leq S_T < E_2$; or (3) $E_1 < E_2 \leq S_T$. Table 3.3 illustrates the values of portfolios A and B at expiration.

When S_T is greater than E_1, the call option with exercise price E_1 will be worth $S_T - E_1$. If S_T exceeds E_2, the call option with exercise price E_2 will be worth $S_T - E_2$. However, we are short the option with exercise price E_2. Because the buyer receives a payoff of $S_T - E_2$ when this option expires in-the-money, the writer has a payoff of $-S_T + E_2$. Adding the payoffs from the two options shows that portfolio A will always produce a payoff of no less than zero and, in some cases, more than zero. Therefore,

$$C_e(S,T,E_1) \geq C_e(S,T,E_2).$$

TABLE 3.3

The Effect of Exercise Price on Call Value: Payoffs at Expiration of Portfolios A and B

Portfolio	Current Value	$S_T < E_1$	$E_1 \leq S_T < E_2$	$E_1 < E_2 \leq S_T$
			Payoffs from Portfolio	
			Given Stock Price at Expiration	
A	$+C_e(S,T,E_1)$	0	$S_T - E_1$	$S_T - E_1$
	$-C_e(S,T,E_2)$	0	0	$-S_T + E_2$
		0	$S_T - E_1 \geq 0$	$E_2 - E_1 > 0$
B	$(E_2 - E_1)(1+r)^{-T}$	$E_2 - E_1 > 0$	$E_2 - E_1 > 0$	$E_2 - E_1 > 0$

The price of a European call must be at least as high as the price of an otherwise identical European call with a higher exercise price.

Why is this so? The best way to understand this rule is to look at the contradiction. Suppose $C_e(S,T,E_1) < C_e(S,T,E_2)$. Since we pay $C_e(S,T,E_1)$ for the option bought and receive $C_e(S,T,E_2)$ for the option sold, we will have a net cash inflow at the beginning of the transaction. The payoffs at expiration were shown to be non-negative. Anyone would jump at the opportunity to construct a portfolio with a positive cash inflow up front and no possibility of a cash outflow at expiration. There would be no way to lose money. Everyone would try to execute this transaction, which would drive up the price of the call with exercise price E_1 and drive down the price of the call with exercise price E_2. When the call with the lower exercise price is worth at least as much as the call with the higher exercise price, the portfolio will no longer offer a positive cash flow up front.

We have proven this result only for European calls. With American calls the long call need not be exercised, so we need only consider what would happen if the short call were exercised early.

The price of an American call must be at least as high as the price of another otherwise identical American call with a higher exercise price.

Suppose the stock price prior to expiration is S_t and exceeds E_2. For whatever reason, the short call is exercised. This produces a negative cash flow, $-(S_t - E_2)$. The trader then exercises the long call, which produces a positive cash flow of $S_t - E_1$. The sum of these two cash flows is $E_2 - E_1$, which is positive because $E_2 > E_1$. Thus, early exercise will not generate a negative cash flow. Portfolio A therefore will never produce a negative cash flow at expiration even if the options are American calls. Thus, our result holds for American calls as well as for European calls.

Note that this result shows that the price of the call with the lower exercise price cannot be less than that of the call with the higher exercise price. However, the two call prices conceivably could be equal. That could occur if the stock price were very low, in which case both calls would be deep-out-of-the-money. Neither would be expected to expire in-the-money, and both would have an intrinsic value of zero. Therefore, both prices could be approximately zero. However, with a very high stock price, the call with the lower exercise price would carry a greater intrinsic value, and thus its price would be higher than that of the call with the higher exercise price.

The prices of the Digital Equipment calls adhere to the predicted relationships. The lower the exercise price, the higher the call option price.

LIMITS ON THE DIFFERENCE IN PREMIUMS Now compare the results of portfolio A with those of portfolio B. Note that in Table 3.3, portfolio B's return is never less than portfolio A's. Therefore, investors would not pay less for portfolio B than for portfolio A. The price of portfolio A is $C_e(S,T,E_1) - C_e(S,T,E_2)$, the price of the option purchased minus the price of the option sold. The price of portfolio B is $(E_2 - E_1)(1 + r)^{-T}$, the present value of the bond's face value. Thus,

$$(E_2 - E_1)(1 + r)^{-T} \geq C_e(S,T,E_1) - C_e(S,T,E_2).$$

A related and useful statement is

$$E_2 - E_1 \geq C_e(S,T,E_1) - C_e(S,T,E_2).$$

This follows because the difference in the exercise prices is greater than the present value of the difference in the exercise prices. For two options differing only in exercise price, the difference in the premiums cannot exceed the difference in the exercise prices.

The intuition behind this result is simple: The advantage of buying an option with a lower exercise price over one with a higher exercise price will not be more than the difference in the exercise prices. For example, if you own the Digital Equipment July 165 call and are considering replacing it with the July 160 call, the most you can gain by the switch is $5. Therefore, you would not pay more than an additional $5 for the 160 over the 165. This result will be useful in Chapter 6, where we discuss spread strategies.

For American calls, the call with the lower exercise price is worth at least as much as the call with the higher exercise price. However, the statement that the difference in premiums cannot exceed the present value of the difference in exercise prices does not hold for the American call. If both calls are exercised at time t before expiration and the payoff of $E_2 - E_1$ is invested in risk-free bonds, portfolio A's return will be $(E_2 - E_1)(1 + r)^{(T-t)}$, which will exceed portfolio B's return of $E_2 - E_1$. Thus, portfolio B will not always outperform or match portfolio A.

If, however, the bonds purchased for portfolio B have a face value of $(E_2 - E_1)(1 + r)^T$ and thus a present value of $E_2 - E_1$, portfolio B will always outperform portfolio A. In that case, the current value of portfolio A cannot exceed that of portfolio B. Accordingly, we can state that for American calls

$$E_2 - E_1 \geq C_a(S,T,E_1) - C_a(S,T,E_2).$$

Table 3.4 presents the appropriate calculations for examining these properties on the Digital Equipment calls. Consider the June 160 and 165 calls. The difference in their premiums is 2.75.

The present value of the difference in exercise prices is $5(1.0484)^{-.0192} = 4.996$. The remaining combinations are calculated similarly using the appropriate risk-free rates and times to expiration for those options. Since these are American

The difference in the prices of two European calls that differ only by exercise price cannot exceed the present value of the difference in their exercise prices.

The difference in the prices of two American calls that differ only by exercise price cannot exceed the difference in their exercise prices.

TABLE 3.4

The Relationship between Exercise Price and Call Price: Digital Equipment Calls

Exercise Price	Exercise Price Difference	Difference between Call Prices (Present Value of Difference between Exercise Prices in Parentheses)		
		Jun	Jul	Oct
160, 165	5	2.750	2.875	2.000
		(4.996)	(4.975)	(4.902)
160, 170	10	4.125	4.875	4.500
		(9.991)	(9.950)	(9.804)
165, 170	5	1.375	2.000	2.500
		(4.996)	(4.975)	(4.902)

Note: Risk-free rates are .0484 (Jun); .0535 (Jul); .0591 (Oct). Times to expiration are .0192 (Jun); .0959 (Jul); .3452 (Oct).

calls, the difference in their prices must be no greater than the difference in their exercise prices. As Table 3.4 shows, all of the calls conform to this condition. In addition, all of the differences in the call prices are less than the present value of the difference between the exercise prices. Remember that this result need not hold for American calls because they can be exercised early.

The Lower Bound of a European Call

We know that for an American call,

$$C_a(S,T,E) \geq Max(0, S - E).$$

Because of the requirement that immediate exercise be possible, we were unable to make such a statement for a European call. We can, however, develop a lower bound for a European call that will be higher than the intrinsic value of an American call.

Again consider two portfolios, A and B. Portfolio A consists of a single share of stock currently priced at S, while portfolio B contains a European call priced at $C_e(S,T,E)$ and risk-free bonds with a face value of E and, therefore, a present value of $E(1 + r)^{-T}$. The current value of this portfolio thus is $C_e(S,T,E) + E(1 + r)^{-T}$. The payoffs from these two portfolios are shown in Table 3.5.

As the table shows, the return on portfolio B is always at least as large as that of portfolio A and sometimes larger. Investors will recognize this fact and price portfolio B at a value at least as great as portfolio A's; that is,

$$C_e(S,T,E) + E(1 + r)^{-T} \geq S.$$

| Portfolio | Current Value | Payoffs from Portfolio Given Stock Price at Expiration | |
		$S_T \leq E$	$S_T > E$
A	S	S_T	S_T
B	$C_e(S,T,E) + E(1+r)^{-T}$	E	$(S_T - E) + E = S_T$

Rearranging this expression gives

$$C_e(S,T,E) \geq S - E(1+r)^{-T}.$$

If $S - E(1+r)^{-T}$ is negative, we invoke the rule that the minimum value of a call is zero. Combining these results gives

$$C_e(S,T,E) \geq Max[0, S - E(1+r)^{-T}].$$

The price of a European call must at least equal the stock price minus the present value of the exercise price.

Appendix 3A shows the effect of dividends on this statement.

If the call price is less than the stock price minus the present value of the exercise price, we can construct an arbitrage portfolio. We buy the call and risk-free bonds and sell short the stock.[4] This portfolio has a positive initial cash flow, because the call price plus the bond price is less than the stock price. At expiration, the payoff is $E - S_T$ if $E > S_T$ and zero otherwise. The portfolio has a positive cash flow today and either a zero or positive cash flow at expiration. Again there is no way to lose money.

When we showed that the intrinsic value of an American call is $Max(0, S - E)$, we noted that the inability to exercise early prevents this result from holding for a European call. Now we can see that this limitation is of no consequence. Because the present value of the exercise price is less than the exercise price itself, the lower bound of a European call is greater than the intrinsic value of an American call.

As expiration approaches, the present value of the exercise price approaches the value of the exercise price itself. Thus, the lower bound decreases steadily so that at expiration the call is worth only the intrinsic value. Figure 3.2 illustrates these boundary conditions for European calls.

---

[4]A short sale of stock occurs when an investor borrows stock from a broker and sells the shares in the market. If the price goes down, the investor repurchases the shares at the lower price and repays them to the broker. If the price goes up, the investor will take a loss by having to repurchase the shares at a higher price. Short sales normally are made in anticipation of a falling market.

FIGURE 3.2
Call Option Boundary Conditions

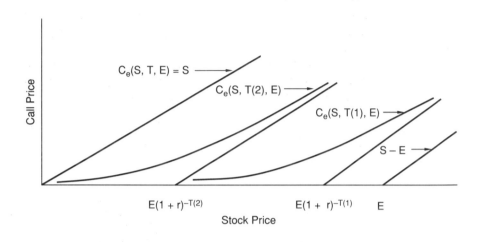

For European calls, a longer-
lived call will always be worth
at least as much as a shorter-
lived call with the same terms.

In the earlier description of how time to expiration affects the price of an American call, we could not draw the same relationship for a European call. Now we can. Consider two European calls that differ by their times to expiration, T(1) and T(2). Their prices are $C_e(S,T(1),E)$ and $C_e(S,T(2),E)$, respectively. At time T(1), the shorter-lived option expires and is worth Max $(0, S_{T(1)} - E)$. The minimum value of the longer-lived option is Max$(0, S_{T(1)} - E(1+r)^{-(T(2)-T(1))})$. Thus, the value of the shorter-lived option is less than the lower bound of the longer-lived option. Therefore, the longer-lived call must be priced at least as high as the shorter-lived call.

American Call versus European Call

Many of the results presented so far apply only to European calls. For example, we restricted the derivation of the lower bound to European calls. That is because an early exercise of an American call can negate the cash flows expected from the portfolio at expiration.

An American call will be at least
as valuable as a European call
with the same terms.

In many cases, however, American calls behave exactly like European calls. In fact, an American call can be viewed as a European call with the added feature that it can be exercised early. Since exercising an option is never mandatory,

$$C_a(S,T,E) \geq C_e(S,T,E).$$

We already proved that the minimum value of an American call is Max$(0, S - E)$ while the lower bound of a European call is Max$[0, S - E(1+r)^{-T}]$. Because $S - E(1+r)^{-T}$ is greater than $S - E$, the lower bound value of the American call must also be Max$[0, S - E(1+r)^{-T}]$.

TABLE 3.6
Lower Bounds of Digital Equipment Calls

Exercise Price	Expiration Date		
	Jun	**Jul**	**Oct**
160	4.144	4.800	7.130
165	0.000	0.000	2.230
170	0.000	0.000	0.000

Note: Risk-free rates are .0484 (Jun); .0535 (Jul); .0591 (Oct). Times to expiration are .0192 (Jun); .0959 (Jul); .3452 (Oct).

Let us now examine the Digital Equipment options to determine whether their prices exceed the lower boundary. Table 3.6 presents the lower bound of each Digital Equipment call. To see how the computations are performed, take the June 160 call. The time to expiration is .0192, and the risk-free rate is .0484. Thus,

$$\text{Max}[0, S - E(1 + r)^{-T}] = \text{Max}[0, 164 - 160(1.0484)^{-.0192}] = 4.144.$$

From Table 3.1, the price of the call is $4.625. Thus, this option does meet the boundary condition. Using Tables 3.1 and 3.6 reveals that the remaining calls also conform to the lower boundary.

In the aforementioned study by Bhattacharya (1983), the call prices were also examined to determine if they conformed to this lower bound. Violations occurred on about 7 1/2 percent of the prices, with the average violation being about one-sixteenth of a point. A trader executing a transaction at the next available price would have earned about $5 per contract. This is not sufficient to cover transaction costs. Thus, prices in general conform quite closely to the lower bound.

With the lower bound of an American call established, we can now examine whether an American call should ever be exercised early. If the stock price is S, exercising the call produces a cash flow of S – E.[5] The call's price, however, must be at least $S - E(1 + r)^{-T}$. Can the cash flow from exercising, S – E, ever exceed the call's lower bound, $S - E(1 + r)^{-T}$? Of course not. Therefore, it will always be better to sell the call in the market. When the transaction cost of exercising is added to the transaction cost of selling the call, the argument that a call should not be exercised early is strengthened.

Many people find it difficult to accept the fact that a call option should not be exercised early even when the stock price is extremely high and expected to fall. In the absence of transaction costs, exercise may well be as attractive as selling the call in the market. This would be the case if the call contained no time value. However, as long as the present value of the exercise price is less than the exercise

An American call on a non-dividend-paying stock will never be exercised early, and we can treat such a call as if it were European.

[5]We are assuming that the option is in-the-money, because no one would consider exercising it if it were out-of-the-money.

price, the call will always sell for more than its intrinsic value. Notice, however, that the call must be on a non-dividend-paying stock. If the stock pays dividends, early exercise may be justified.

The Early Exercise of American Calls on Dividend-Paying Stocks

When a company declares a dividend, it specifies that the dividend is payable to all stockholders as of a certain date, called the *holder-of-record* date. Four business days before that date is the *ex-dividend date*. To be the stockholder of record by the holder-of-record date, one must buy the stock by the ex-dividend date. The stock price tends to fall by the amount of the dividend on the ex-dividend date.

An investor who holds an in-the-money call on a stock about to go ex-dividend may be advised to exercise it just before the stock goes ex-dividend. This is because the stock price will fall by the amount of the dividend, which will cause the call's intrinsic value to fall by the dividend amount. Thus, the option will decrease in value by the amount of the dividend. By exercising the option, the call holder will avoid this loss of wealth and gain title to the stock before the ex-dividend date, thus receiving the dividend. On the other hand, the call holder will also give up the remaining time value on the call. Thus, the size of the dividend and the size of the time value are the important variables.

Consider an in-the-money American call priced at $C_a(S,T,E)$, where S is the price an instant before the stock goes ex-dividend. The dividend is D. When the stock goes ex-dividend, its price will fall to $S^* = S - D$. If the call is not exercised, the ex-dividend price will be $C_a(S^*,T,E)$. Before the stock goes ex-dividend, the time value of the call, τ, is

$$\tau = C_a(S,T,E) - (S - E).$$

If the call is exercised, the investor buys the stock at a price of E, receives a dividend of D, and owns stock that will be worth S^* when it goes ex-dividend. Because $S^* = S - D$, the ex-dividend wealth will be $-E + D + (S - D) = S - E$.

If $S - E > D$, the call will remain in-the-money on the ex-dividend date. If it is not exercised, the ex-dividend call value will be $S^* - E + \tau = S - D - E + \tau$.[6] The call should be exercised if doing so will increase the investor's wealth. Thus, to justify exercising requires that

$$S - E > S - D - E + \tau,$$

which means that

$$D > \tau.$$

---

[6]Technically the time value will be τ^*, the ex-dividend time value, but τ^* will not differ significantly from τ because so little time has elapsed.

The dividend must exceed the time value, which makes intuitive sense. The gain from exercising is the dividend; the loss from exercising is the time value given up. If the gain exceeds the loss, exercise is justified.

If $S - E \leq D$, the call is in-the-money by no more than the amount of the dividend and will be out-of-the-money when the stock goes ex-dividend. Thus, the call's ex-dividend value will consist only of its time value. The call should be exercised if

$$S - E > \tau.$$

If the option is in-the-money by less than the amount of the dividend, it should be exercised if the amount by which it is in-the-money exceeds its time value.

Combining the two cases, $S - E \leq D$ and $S - E > D$, shows that the gain from exercising is the minimum of $S - E$ and D; that is, the call will fall by the minimum of $S - E$ and D. Exercising avoids incurring this loss of wealth. The cost of exercising is the loss of the call's time value. The call should be exercised if the gain will exceed the cost.

These rules suggest that early exercise will tend to occur when dividends are high and/or time values are low. Low time values result from very high stock prices or options nearing their expirations.

The Digital Equipment stock does not pay dividends. However, for illustrative purposes, let us hold everything constant and consider how dividends might trigger an early exercise. Table 3.2 presented the calls' intrinsic values and time values. Because we are interested in exercising only the in-the-money calls, we need consider only the 160 calls. The intrinsic values and time values of those calls are as follows:

Call	Intrinsic Value	Time Value	Gain from Early Exercise
June 160	4	0.625	Min(D,4)
July 160	4	4.625	Min(D,4)
October 160	4	11.250	Min(D,4)

Assume a fairly large quarterly dividend of $2. For each option, the gain from early exercise is $2. Thus, all options with time values of less than $2 should be exercised. This means that only the June 160 call should be exercised.

The Effect of Interest Rates

Interest rates affect a call option's price. A call option can be viewed as a deferred substitute for the purchase of the stock. If the stock price is expected to increase, an investor can choose to either buy the stock or buy the call. Purchasing the call will cost far less than purchasing the stock. The difference can be invested in risk-free bonds. If interest rates increase, the combination of calls and risk-free bonds will be more attractive. This means that the call price will tend to increase with increases in interest rates.

The Effect of Stock Volatility

One of the basic principles of investor behavior is that individuals prefer less risk to more. That is indeed the case for stocks, but not for options. A call holder will prefer more stock volatility to less. Greater volatility increases the gains on the call if the stock price increases, because the stock price can then exceed the exercise price by a larger amount. On the other hand, greater volatility means that if the stock price goes down, it can be much lower than the exercise price. To a call holder, however, this does not matter because the potential loss is limited; it is said to be truncated at the exercise price. For example, consider the Digital Equipment July 165 call. Suppose the stock price is equally likely to be at 150, 160, 170, or 180 at expiration. The call, then, is equally likely to be worth 0, 0, 5, and 15 at expiration. Now suppose the stock's volatility increases so that it has an equal chance of being at 140, 160, 170, or 190. From a stockholder's point of view, the stock is far riskier, which is less desirable. From the option holder's perspective, the equally possible option prices at expiration are 0, 0, 5, and 25, which is more desirable. In fact, the option holder will not care how low the stock can go. If the possibility of lower stock prices is accompanied by the possibility of higher stock prices, the option holder will benefit, and the option will be priced higher when the volatility is higher.

Another way to understand the effect of volatility on the call price is to consider the extreme case of zero volatility. If the stock price is less than the exercise price, the absence of volatility guarantees that the option will expire out-of-the-money. No one would pay anything for this option. If the stock price exceeds the exercise price and has zero volatility, it will expire in-the-money and will be worth $S - E$ at expiration, where S is the current stock price. In this case, the call will then be worth the present value of $S - E$ and thus will simply be a risk-free asset. High stock volatility is what makes call options attractive, and investors are willing to pay higher premiums on options with greater volatility.

PRINCIPLES OF PUT OPTION PRICING

Many of the rules applicable to call options apply in a straightforward manner to put options. However, there are some significant differences.

The Minimum Value of a Put

A put is an option to sell a stock. A put holder is not obligated to exercise it and will not do so if exercising will decrease wealth. Thus, a put can never have a negative value:

$$P(S,T,E) \geq 0.$$

An American put can be exercised early. Therefore,

$$P_a(S,T,E) \geq \text{Max}(0, E-S).$$

Suppose that the Digital Equipment July 170 put sells for less than $E - S$. Let the put sell for $5. Then it would be worthwhile to buy the stock for $164, buy the put for $5, and exercise the put. This would net an immediate risk-free profit of $1. The combined actions of all investors conducting this arbitrage would force the put price up to at least $6, the difference between the exercise price and the stock price.

The value, $\text{Max}(0, E-S)$, is called the put's *intrinsic value*. An in-the-money put has a positive intrinsic value, while an out-the-money put has an intrinsic value of zero. The difference between the put price and the intrinsic value is the *time value* or *speculative value*. The time value is defined as

$$P_a(S,T,E) - \text{Max}(0, E-S).$$

The time value reflects what an investor is willing to pay to speculate in the option.

Table 3.7 presents the intrinsic values and time values of the Digital Equipment puts. Note how the time values increase with the time to expiration.

The intrinsic value specification, $\text{Max}(0, E-S)$, does not hold for European puts. That is because the option must be exercisable for an investor to execute the arbitrage transaction previously described. European puts indeed can sell for less than the intrinsic value. Later this will help us understand the early exercise of American puts.

The Maximum Value of a Put

At expiration, the payoff from a European put is $\text{Max}(0, E-S)$. The best outcome that a put holder can expect is for the company to go bankrupt. In that case, the stock will be worthless ($S = 0$) and the put holder will be able to sell the shares to the put writer for E dollars.

Thus, the present value of the exercise price is the European put's maximum possible value. Since an American put can be exercised at any time, its maximum value is the exercise price.

$$P_e(S,T,E) \leq E(1+r)^{-T},$$
$$P_a(S,T,E) \leq E.$$

Because a put option need not be exercised, its minimum value is zero.

The intrinsic value of an American put is the greater of zero or the difference between the exercise price and the stock price.

The maximum value of a European put is the present value of the exercise price. The maximum value of an American put is the exercise price.

TABLE 3.7

Intrinsic Values and Time Values of Digital Equipment Puts

Exercise Price	Intrinsic Value	Time Value		
		Jun	**Jul**	**Oct**
160	0.000	0.8125	3.8750	8.1250
165	1.000	1.9375	5.0000	8.7500
170	6.000	0.5000	2.5000	NA

The Value of a Put at Expiration

At expiration, a put option is worth the intrinsic value.

On the put's expiration date, no time value will remain. Expiring American puts therefore are the same as European puts. The value of either type of put must be the intrinsic value. Thus,

$$P(S_T, 0, E) = Max(0, E - S_T).$$

If $E > S_T$ and the put price is less than $E - S_T$, investors can buy the put and the stock and exercise the put for an immediate risk-free profit. If the put expires out-of-the-money $(E < S_T)$, it will be worthless.

The Effect of Time to Expiration

Consider two American puts, one with a time to expiration of $T(1)$ and the other with a time to expiration of $T(2)$, where $T(2) > T(1)$. Now assume today is the expiration date of the shorter-lived put. The stock price is $S_{T(1)}$. The expiring put is worth $Max(0, E - S_{T(1)})$. The other put, which has a remaining time to expiration of $T(2) - T(1)$, is worth at least $Max(0, E - S_{T(1)})$. Thus,

$$P_a(S, T(2), E) \geq P_a(S, T(1), E).$$

A longer-lived American put must always be worth at least as much as a shorter-lived American put with the same terms.

Note that the two puts could be worth the same; however, this would occur only if both puts were very deep-in- or out-of-the-money. Even then, the longer-lived would likely be worth a little more than the shorter-lived put. The longer-lived put can do everything the shorter-lived put can do and has an additional period of time in which to increase in value.

The relationship between time to expiration and put price is more complex for European puts. Think of buying a put as deferring the sale of stock at the exercise price, E. The further into the future the expiration date, the longer the put holder must wait to sell the stock and receive E dollars. This can make the longer-lived European put less valuable than the shorter-lived one. This does not hold for an American put, because the holder can always exercise it and receive E dollars today. For a European put, the longer time to expiration is both an advantage—the greater time value—and a disadvantage—the longer wait to receive the exercise price. The time value effect tends to dominate, however, and in most cases longer-lived puts will be more valuable than shorter-lived puts.

Because the Digital Equipment puts are American options, the longer-term puts should be expected to show higher prices. A check of their premiums, shown in Table 3.1, confirms this hypothesis.

The Effect of Exercise Price

THE EFFECT ON OPTION VALUE   Consider two European puts identical in all respects except exercise price. One put has an exercise price of E_1 and a premium of $P_e(S,T,E_1)$; the other has an exercise price of E_2 and a premium of $P_e(S,T,E_2)$. As before, $E_2 > E_1$. Which put will be more valuable?

Consider two portfolios. Portfolio A consists of a long position in the put priced at $P_e(S,T,E_2)$ and a short position in the put priced at $P_e(S,T,E_1)$. Portfolio B consists of a long position in risk-free bonds with a face value of $E_2 - E_1$ and a present value of $(E_2 - E_1)(1 + r)^{-T}$. Table 3.8 presents these portfolios' payoffs at expiration.

For portfolio A, all outcomes are non-negative. Because this portfolio cannot produce a cash outflow for the holder, the price of the put purchased must be no less than the price of the put sold; that is,

$$P_e(S,T,E_2) \geq P_e(S,T,E_1).$$

The price of a European put must be at least as high as the price of an otherwise identical European put with a lower exercise price.

To understand why this is so, consider what would happen if it were not. Suppose the price of the put sold were greater than the price of the put purchased. Then an investor would receive more for the put sold than would be paid for the put purchased. That would produce a net positive cash flow up front, and, from Table 3.8, there would be no possibility of having to pay out any cash at expiration. This transaction would be like a loan that need not be paid back. Obviously, this portfolio would be very attractive and would draw the attention of other investors, who would buy the put with the higher exercise price and sell the put with the lower exercise price. This would tend to drive up the price of the former and drive down the price of the latter. The transaction would cease to be attractive when the put with the higher exercise price became at least as valuable as the put with the lower exercise price.

The intuition behind why a put with a higher exercise price is worth more than one with a lower exercise price is quite simple. A put is an option to sell stock at a fixed price. The higher the price at which the put holder can sell the stock, the more attractive the put.

Suppose these were American puts. In that case, the put with the lower exercise price could be exercised early. For example, let the stock price at time t prior to expiration be S_t, where $S_t < E_1$. Let the option with exercise price E_1 be exercised. Then the investor simply exercises the option with exercise price E_2. The cash flow from these two transactions is $-(E_1 - S_t) + (E_2 - S_t) = E_2 - E_1$, which is positive.

The price of an American put must be at least as high as the price of an otherwise identical American put with a lower exercise price.

TABLE 3.8

The Effect of Exercise Price on Put Value: Payoffs at Expiration of Portfolios A and B

Portfolio	Current Value	Payoffs from Portfolio Given Stock Price at Expiration		
		$S_T < E_1$	$E_1 \le S_T < E_2$	$E_1 < E_2 \le S_T$
A	$-P_e(S,T,E_1)$	$-E_1 + S_T$	0	0
	$+P_e(S,T,E_2)$	$\underline{E_2 - S_T}$	$\underline{E_2 - S_T}$	$\underline{0}$
		$E_2 - E_1 > 0$	$E_2 - S_T > 0$	0
B	$(E_2 - E_1)(1 + r)^{-T}$	$E_2 - E_1 > 0$	$E_2 - E_1 > 0$	$E_2 - E_1 > 0$

Early exercise will not generate a negative cash flow. Thus, our result holds for American puts as well as for European puts.

LIMITS ON THE DIFFERENCE IN PREMIUMS   Now let us compare the outcomes of portfolios A and B. We see that portfolio B's outcomes are never less than portfolio A's. Therefore, no one would pay more for portfolio A than for portfolio B; that is,

$$(E_2 - E_1)(1 + r)^{-T} \ge P_e(S,T,E_2) - P_e(S,T,E_1).$$

The difference in the prices of two European puts that differ only by exercise price cannot exceed the present value of the difference in their exercise prices.

However, this result does not hold for American puts. If the puts were American and both were exercised, the investor would receive $E_2 - E_1$ dollars. This amount would be invested in risk-free bonds and would earn interest over the options' remaining lives. At expiration, the investor would have more than $E_2 - E_1$, the payoff from portfolio B.

Since the difference in exercise prices is greater than the present value of the difference in exercise prices, we can state that for European puts

$$E_2 - E_1 \ge P_e(S,T,E_2) - P_e(S,T,E_1).$$

The difference in the prices of two American puts that differ only by exercise price cannot exceed the difference in their exercise prices.

This means that the difference in premiums cannot exceed the difference in exercise prices. This result holds for American as well as European puts. To see this, let portfolio B's bonds have a face value of $(E_2 - E_1)(1 + r)^T$ and a present value of $E_2 - E_1$. If early exercise occurred at time t, the most the holder of portfolio A would have at expiration is $(E_2 - E_1)(1 + r)^{T-t}$. The holder of portfolio B would have a larger amount, $(E_2 - E_1)(1 + r)^T$. So again portfolio A would never pay more at expiration than would portfolio B. Therefore, the current value of portfolio A, $P_a(S,T,E_2) - P_a(S,T,E_1)$, could not exceed the current value of portfolio B, $E_2 - E_1$. Thus,

$$E_2 - E_1 \ge P_a(S,T,E_2) - P_a(S,T,E_1).$$

TABLE 3.9

The Relationship between Exercise Price and Put Price: Digital Equipment Puts

Exercise Price	Exercise Price Difference	Difference between Put Prices (Present Value of Difference between Exercise Prices in Parentheses)		
		Jun	Jul	Oct
160, 165	5	2.125	2.125	1.625
		(4.996)	(4.975)	(4.902)
160, 170	10	5.688	4.625	NA
		(9.991)	(9.950)	(9.804)
165, 170	5	3.563	4.625	NA
		(4.996)	(4.975)	(4.902)

Note: Risk-free rates are .0484 (Jun); .0535 (Jul); .0591 (Oct). Times to expiration are .0192 (Jun); .0959 (Jul); .3452 (Oct).

Table 3.9 shows the differences between the put premiums and exercise prices for the Digital Equipment puts. Since these are American puts, we would expect only that the difference in their put premiums will not exceed the difference in their exercise prices—which indeed is the case. In addition, the differences in premiums do not exceed the present values of the differences in exercise prices.

Lower Bound of a European Put

We showed that the minimum value of an American put is $Max(0, E - S)$. This statement does not hold for a European put, because it cannot be exercised early. However, it is possible to derive a positive lower bound for a European put.

Again consider two portfolios, A and B. Portfolio A consists of a single share of stock. Portfolio B consists of a short position in a European put priced at $P_e(S,T,E)$ and a long position in risk-free bonds with a face value of E and a present value of $E(1 + r)^{-T}$. The payoffs at expiration from these portfolios are shown in Table 3.10.

Portfolio A's outcome is always at least as favorable as portfolio B's. Therefore, no one would be willing to pay more for portfolio B than for portfolio A. Portfolio A's current value must be no less than portfolio B's; that is,

$$S \geq E(1 + r)^{-T} - P_e(S,T,E).$$

Rearranging this statement gives

$$P_e(S,T,E) \geq E(1 + r)^{-T} - S.$$

The effect of dividends on this rule is shown in Appendix 3A.

The price of a European put must at least equal the present value of the exercise price minus the stock price.

TABLE 3.10

Lower Bound of a European Put: Payoffs at Expiration of Portfolios A and B

| Portfolio | Current Value | Payoffs from Portfolio Given Stock Price at Expiration | |
		$S_T < E$	$S_T \geq E$
A	S	S_T	S_T
B	$E(1+r)^{-T} - P_e(S,T,E)$	$E - (E - S_T) = S_T$	E

If the present value of the exercise price is less than the stock price, this lower bound will be negative. Since we know that a put cannot be worth less than zero, we can say that

$$P_e(S,T,E) \geq \text{Max}[0, E(1+r)^{-T} - S].$$

Now let us compare the minimum price of the American put, its intrinsic value of $\text{Max}(0, E - S)$, with the lower bound of the European put, $\text{Max}[0, E(1+r)^{-T} - S]$. Since $E - S$ is greater than $E(1+r)^{-T} - S$, the American put's intrinsic value is higher than the European put's lower bound. Therefore, the European put's lower bound is irrelevant to the American put price because it is a lower minimum. However, $\text{Max}[0, E(1+r)^{-T} - S]$ is relevant to the European put's price.

Finally, we can use the lower bound of a European put to examine the effect of time to expiration on the option. Earlier we stated that the direction of this effect is uncertain. Consider two puts with times to expiration of $T(1)$ and $T(2)$, where $T(2) > T(1)$. Suppose we are at time $T(1)$, the stock price is $S_{T(1)}$, and the shorter-lived put is expiring and worth $\text{Max}(0, E - S_{T(1)})$. The longer-lived put has a remaining life of $T(2) - T(1)$ and a lower bound of $\text{Max}[0, E(1+r)^{-(T(2)-T(1))} - S_{T(1)}]$. Although the lower bound of the longer-lived put is less than the shorter-lived put's, the former's time value can more than make up the difference. Therefore, we cannot unambiguously tell whether a longer- or shorter-lived European put will be worth more.

American Put versus European Put

An American put will be at least as valuable as a European put with the same terms.

Everything that can be done with a European put can be done with an American put. In addition, an American put can be exercised at any time prior to expiration. Therefore, the American put price must at least equal the European put price; that is,

$$P_a(S,T,E) \geq P_e(S,T,E).$$

Put-Call Parity

The prices of European puts and calls on the same stock with identical exercise prices and expiration dates have a special relationship. The put price, call price, stock price, exercise price, and risk-free rate are all related by a formula called *put-call parity*. Let us see how this formula is derived.

Imagine a portfolio consisting of one share of stock, a European put, and a short position in a European call. Suppose the investor takes out a loan that requires repaying E dollars when the options expire. The amount received for the loan is the present value of E, $E(1 + r)^{-T}$. The current value of this portfolio is $S + P_e(S,T,E) - C_e(S,T,E) - E(1 + r)^{-T}$. Table 3.11 illustrates the payoffs at expiration from this portfolio.

The portfolio has a payoff at expiration of zero. This means that the investor is assured of not having to pay out any money at expiration. Thus, the portfolio's current value must be non-negative; that is, the statement

$$S + P_e(S,T,E) - C_e(S,T,E) - E(1 + r)^{-T} \geq 0$$

must be true. Why? The portfolio's current value represents the amount an investor must pay to execute the transaction. If this amount is positive, the investor pays a positive sum of money. But suppose it is negative, meaning that money is received up front. Table 3.11 shows that the investor need pay out no money in the future. In effect, this is like a loan that need not be paid back. Obviously anyone will take out such a loan and, as expected, quickly execute this transaction. That will tend to drive up the price of the stock and the put and drive down the price of the call. Eventually the transaction will no longer provide a cash flow today if the prices adjust until the portfolio's current value is non-negative.

Now suppose prices adjust such that $S + P_e(S,T,E) - C_e(S,T,E) - E(1 + r)^{-T} > 0$. Then an investor could sell short the stock, write the put, buy the call, and buy a risk-free bond with a face value of E. Since this portfolio is just the opposite of the other, its payoffs are found by multiplying the payoffs in Table 3.11 by –1. Thus, the overall payoff is still zero. The cash flow up front would be +S from the short sale of the stock, $+P_e(S,T,E)$ from writing the put, $-C_e(S,T,E)$ from buying the call, and $-E(1 + r)^{-T}$ from buying the bonds. If, as we assume, $S + P_e(S,T,E) - C_e(S,T,E) - E(1 + r)^{-T}$ is positive, the portfolio will generate a positive cash flow up front with no obligation to pay out anything at expiration. So again all investors would execute this transaction. Prices would adjust until $S + P_e(S,T,E) - C_e(S,T,E) - E(1 + r)^{-T} = 0$.

Rearranging this equation, we can state that the put and call prices are related by the following formula, called *put-call parity*:

$$C_e(S,T,E) = P_e(S,T,E) + S - E(1 + r)^{-T},$$

Put-call parity is the relationship among the call price, the put price, the stock price, the exercise price, the risk-free rate, and the time to expiration.

TABLE 3.11
Put-Call Parity

| Payoff From | Current Value | Payoffs from Portfolio Given Stock Price at Expiration | |
		$S_T < E$	$S_T \geq E$
Long Stock	S	S_T	S_T
Long Put	$P_e(S,T,E)$	$E - S_T$	0
Short Call	$-C_e(S,T,E)$	0	$-(S_T - E)$
Loan	$-E(1 + r)^{-T}$	$-E$	$-E$
		0	0

or

$$P_e(S,T,E) = C_e(S,T,E) - S + E(1 + r)^{-T}.$$

The effect of dividends on put-call parity is shown in Appendix 3A.

Put-call parity is a very important result in option pricing and provides many useful insights into the nature of these instruments. For example, we saw in the previous paragraph that either the call or the put price can be isolated and expressed in terms of the remaining instruments' prices. When the call price is on the left-hand side and is shown to equal the put price plus the stock price minus the present value of the exercise price, we are saying that a long position in a call is equivalent to a long position in a put, plus a long position in the stock, plus a loan in which we borrow an amount equal to the present value of the exercise price and promise to pay back an amount equal to the exercise price. When the put price is on the left-hand side, we see that a long position in a put is equivalent to a long position in a call, plus a short position in the stock, plus a loan in which we lend an amount equal to the present value of the exercise price and will be paid back an amount equal to the exercise price.[7] In rearranging the equation in this manner, we see that long and short positions in the options and the stock and positions as borrower or lender of an amount equal to the exercise price can be expressed as a variety of equivalent combinations. Thus, put-call parity can be used, as we shall do in Chapter 4, to convert a call option pricing model into a put option pricing model. In Chapter 5, we use it to examine some popular option trading strategies called *conversions* and *reversals*.

---

[7]Note that lending $E(1 + r)^{-T}$ and receiving back E is the same as holding a risk-free bond worth $E(1 + r)^{-T}$ and paying back E at maturity. Likewise, borrowing $E(1 + r)^{-T}$ and paying back E is the same as selling short a risk-free bond at a price of $E(1 + r)^{-T}$ and buying it back at a price of E when it matures.

TABLE 3.12
Put-Call Parity for Digital Equipment Options

Strike Price	Value of $P_e(S,T,E) - C_e(S,T,E) + S - E(1+r)^{-T}$		
	Jun	**Jul**	**Oct**
160	.3315	.0500	0.0110
165	.2110	.0750	−1.2660
170	.1530	−.4000	NA

Note: Risk-free rates are .0484 (Jun); .0535 (Jul); .0591 (Oct). Times to expiration are .0192 (Jun); .0959 (Jul); .3452 (Oct).

However, put-call parity does not strictly hold for American options. The possibility of early exercise makes the cash flows at expiration uncertain. However, as noted later in the chapter, put-call parity does hold reasonably well for American options. For illustrative purposes, we shall look at how it holds for the Digital Equipment calls.

Table 3.12 shows the values of portfolios constructed as in the previous example using the various Digital Equipment options. Specifically, we calculate the value of the expression $P_e(S,T,E) - C_e(S,T,E) + S - E(1+r)^{-T}$ using the actual market prices of the put and call. The value of the expression should be zero. As the table shows, put-call parity does not hold precisely. We should not expect that it would because of the possible effect of transaction costs and early exercise. Whether the factors are large enough to make up the difference in the majority of cases is a question that only empirical tests can answer. Klemkosky and Resnick (1979, 1980) examined a large sample of CBOE option transactions to determine if they conformed to the put-call parity rule. When a violation occurred, the authors executed a risk-free transaction designed to generate a profit. The test was imperfect, because the options were American and the effects of early exercise could not be completely purged from the tests. The results showed a substantial number of violations that were profitable, even after considering transaction costs. Most of these violations disappeared rather quickly. Moreover, the most significant transaction cost, the bid-ask spread, was not considered and it would have consumed their profits. Thus, options conform quite closely to the put-call parity rule, at least after considering transaction costs.

Now let us consider how to exploit a situation of mispricing. Take the June 160, which is overpriced by .3315. Note that the signs of the terms in the equation are positive (+) on the put and stock and negative (−) on the call and risk-free bonds. This means that a portfolio of long a put and stock and short a call and bonds is overpriced by .3315. The investor should reverse this transaction by selling the put, selling short the stock, and buying the call and risk-free bonds. This will generate a positive cash flow up front of .3315. If the options are not exercised early, the portfolio will have no subsequent cash flows, positive or negative. So the investor receives .3315 today and need not pay anything back later.

The Early Exercise of American Puts

Recall that an American call may be exercised early if a stock is about to go ex-dividend. It may be optimal to exercise an American put early even if the stock pays no dividends. An in-the-money American put can be exercised for a gain of $E - S$. A European put, however, can sell for less than $E - S$. The American put can be thought of as having two components: a European put and a premium paid for the privilege of exercising early. If the European put component falls below the intrinsic value, the holder should exercise the put.[8]

It is easy to see that the European put can be priced at less than the intrinsic value. Let the European put price be given by the put-call parity formula,

$$P_e(S,T,E) = C_e(S,T,E) - S + E(1 + r)^{-T}.$$

If the put could be exercised, it would pay the holder $E - S$. Could this possibly be more than $P_e(S,T,E)$? Substituting for $P_e(S,T,E)$ from put-call parity, we see that

$$E - S > C_e(S,T,E) - S + E(1 + r)^{-T}$$

if

$$C_e(S,T,E) < E\,[1 - (1 + r)^{-T}].$$

This indeed can occur if the stock price is low enough. For a very low stock price, the call will be deep-out-of-the-money and the put will be deep-in-the-money and priced at the intrinsic value. Thus, if the put were American, it would be exercised.

Another way to understand this is to consider what the holder of such a put could do. The investor could exercise the put for a gain of $E - S$ and then construct a portfolio consisting of a long call, short stock, and long risk-free bonds with a face value of E. This portfolio, called a *synthetic put*, would produce the same payoffs at expiration as a European put; that is, it would pay $E - S_T$ at expiration if $E > S_T$ and zero if $E \le S_T$. It would cost the investor $C_e(S,T,E) - S + E(1 + r)^{-T}$ to purchase this portfolio. Since $E - S > C_e(S,T,E) - S + E(1 + r)^{-T}$, the investor could exercise the put, purchase the synthetic put, and have some money left over. At expiration, the amount accumulated would be more than if the put had remained unexercised.

Figure 3.3 illustrates the boundary condition for European and American puts. Note that at a stock price of $S_e^{\ddagger}$, the European put price equals $E - S_e^{\ddagger}$. At a stock

---

[8]Strictly speaking, this is only partly true. An American put should be exercised when its price falls to its intrinsic value. Since an American put ordinarily will be priced higher than its European counterpart, it will still be priced above its intrinsic value when the European put is priced at the intrinsic value. This point will be shown in Figure 3.3.

FIGURE 3.3
Put Option Boundary Conditions

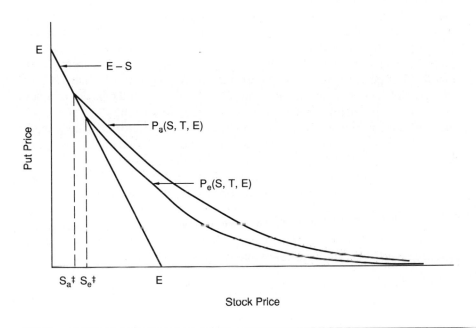

price of $S_a^{\dagger}$, the American put price equals its intrinsic value, $E - S_a^{\dagger}$. Any stock price at $S_a^{\dagger}$ or below would justify early exercise. Without an American put option pricing model, we cannot identify $S_a^{\dagger}$. However, we will identify $S_e^{\dagger}$ in Chapter 4. For now, we can accept the fact that an American put should be exercised if its price is equal to or less than its intrinsic value. For the Digital Equipment puts, this means that we should exercise the 170 puts if the price is $6 or less and the 165 puts if the price is $1 or less. As Table 3.1 indicates, currently none of these puts should be exercised. However, this could change if the stock price changed.

The Effect of Interest Rates

In contrast to call option prices, which vary directly with interest rates, put option prices vary inversely with interest rates. Purchasing a put is like deferring the sale of stock. When you finally sell the stock by exercising the put, you receive E dollars. If interest rates increase, the E dollars will have a lower present value. Thus, a put holder forgoes higher interest while waiting to exercise the option and receive the exercise price. Higher interest rates make puts less attractive to investors.

The Effect of Stock Volatility

The effect of volatility on a put's price is the same as that for a call: Higher volatility increases the possible gains for a put holder. For example, in our discussion of the effect of volatility on a call, we considered four equally likely stock prices at expiration for Digital Equipment: 150, 160, 170, and 180. The four possible put prices at expiration for a 165 put are 15, 5, 0, and 0. If the volatility increases so that the four possible stock prices at expiration are 140, 160, 170, and 180, the four possible put prices at expiration are 25, 5, 0, and 0. For the holder of a put, this increase in volatility is desirable because the put price now can rise much higher. It does not matter that the put can be even deeper out-of-the-money when it expires, because its lowest possible value is still zero. The put holder's loss thus is truncated. Therefore, the put will have a higher price if the volatility is higher.

Another approach to understanding the volatility effect is to consider a European put on a stock with zero volatility. If the put is currently in-the-money, it will be worth the present value of $E - S$, because no further changes in the stock price will be expected. If the put is out-of-the-money, it will be worthless, because it will have no chance of expiring in-the-money. Either of these cases would be like a risk-free asset and would have no speculative interest.

SUMMARY

This chapter examined the basic principles of option pricing. It identified rules that impose upper and lower limits on put and call prices and examined the variables that affect an option's price. In addition, it demonstrated how put and call prices are related to each other by the put-call parity rule. Finally, it examined the conditions that can induce an option trader to exercise an option prior to expiration.

We learned a number of principles that apply in some cases to European options only, in others to American options only, and in still others to both. Table 3.13 summarizes these principles.

An often confusing principle is the establishment of a minimum price. We started off by establishing a low minimum and then worked our way up until we could establish the highest possible minimum. First, we developed the absolute minimum price of any call, which is zero. For American calls, the intrinsic value will provide a higher minimum if the option is in-the-money. Thus, it dominates the minimum of zero. However, it does not apply to European calls, because they cannot be exercised early. Nonetheless, there is a lower bound for European calls, which is the maximum of zero or the stock price minus the present value of the exercise price. This is at least as high as the intrinsic value of the American call. Because American calls must be worth at least as much as European calls. this lower bound applies to American calls as well. Thus, the ultimate minimum for both European and American calls (on non-dividend-paying stocks) is the lower bound we established for European calls.

TABLE 3.13

Summary of the Principles of Option Pricing

	European Calls	American Calls	European Puts	American Puts
Minimum value	≥ 0	≥ 0	≥ 0	≥ 0
Intrinsic value	NA	$\text{Max}(0, S - E)$	NA	$\text{Max}(0, E - S)$
Maximum value	S	S	$E(1 + r)^{-T}$	E
Effect of time to expiration	$C_e(S,T(2),E) \geq C_e(S,T(1),E)$	$C_a(S,T(2),E) \geq C_a(S,T(1),E)$	$P_e(S,T(2),E) \gtreqless P_e(S,T(1),E)$	$P_a(S,T(2),E) \geq P_a(S,T(1),E)$
Effect of exercise price	$C_e(S,T,E_1) \geq C_e(S,T,E_2)$	$C_a(S,T,E_1) \geq C_a(S,T,E_2)$	$P_e(S,T,E_2) \geq P_e(S,T,E_1)$	$P_a(S,T,E_2) \geq P_a(S,T,E_1)$
Maximum difference in premiums	$(E_2 - E_1)(1 + r)^{-T}$	$E_2 - E_1$	$(E_2 - E_1)(1 + r)^{-T}$	$E_2 - E_1$
Lower bound	$\text{Max} = [0, S - E(1 + r)^{-T}]$	$\text{Max} = [0, S - E(1 + r)^{-T}]$	$\text{Max} = [0, E(1 + r)^{-T} - S]$	$\text{Max}(0, E - S)$

Other results:

American versus European option prices

$$C_a(S,T,E) \geq C_e(S,T,E)$$
$$P_a(S,T,E) \geq P_e(S,T,E)$$

Put-call parity

$$P_e(S,T,E) = C_e(S,T,E) - S + E(1 + r)^{-T}$$

Both American and European puts have an absolute minimum value of zero. American puts have an intrinsic value, which is the maximum of zero or the exercise price minus the stock price. This minimum does not apply to European puts, because they cannot be exercised early. European puts have a lower bound that is the maximum of zero or the present value of the exercise price minus the stock price. Because this lower bound is never greater than the intrinsic value of the American put, it does not help us raise the minimum for American puts. Thus, the lower bound is the minimum for European puts and the intrinsic value is the minimum for American puts (on non-dividend-paying stocks).

While we have identified the factors relevant to determining an option's price, we have not yet discussed how to determine the exact price. Although put-call parity appears to be a method of pricing options, it is only a relative option pricing model. To price the put, we need to know the call's price; to price the call, we must know the put's price. Therefore, we cannot use put-call parity to price one instrument without either accepting the market price of the other as correct or having a model that first gives us the price of the other.

In short, we need an option pricing model—a formula that gives the option's price as a function of the variables that should affect it. If the option pricing model is correct, it should give option prices that conform to these boundary conditions.

Most important, it should establish the theoretically correct option price. If the market price is out of line with the model price, arbitrage should force it to move toward the model price. We are now ready to look at option pricing models.

Questions and Problems

1. What would happen in the options market if the price of an American call were less than the value Max(0, S – E)? Would your answer differ if the option were European?

2. In this chapter, we did not learn how to obtain the exact price of a call without knowing the price of the put and using put-call parity. In one special case, however, we can obtain an exact price for a call. Assume the option has an infinite maturity. Then use the maximum and minimum values we learned in this chapter to obtain the prices of European and American calls.

3. Why might two calls or puts alike in all respects but time to expiration have the same price?

4. Why might two calls or puts alike in all respects but exercise price have the same price?

5. Suppose you observe a European call option that is priced at less than the value $Max[0, S - E(1 + r)^{-T}]$. What type of transaction should you execute to achieve the maximum benefit?

6. Explain the rule for early exercise of an American call.

7. Call prices are directly related to the stock's volatility, yet higher volatility means that the stock price can go lower. How would you resolve this apparent paradox?

8. The value $Max[0, E(1 + r)^{-T} - S]$ was shown to be the lowest possible value of a European put. Why is this value irrelevant for an American put?

9. Why do higher interest rates lead to higher call option prices but lower put option prices?

10. Suppose a European put price exceeds the value predicted by put-call parity. How could an investor profit?

11. Early exercise of American puts on non-dividend-paying stocks can occur. If a stock paid a dividend, what is the likely effect on the probability of early exercise?

12. Consider an option that expires in 68 days. The bid and ask discounts on the Treasury bill maturing in 67 days are 8.20 and 8.24, respectively. Find the approximate risk-free rate.

The following option prices were observed for IBM on July 6 of a particular year. Use this information to solve problems 13 through 19. Unless otherwise indicated, ignore dividends on the stock. The stock is priced at 165 1/8. The expirations are July 17, August 21, and October 16. The risk-free rates are .0516, .0550, and .0588, respectively.

	Calls			Puts		
Strike	**Jul**	**Aug**	**Oct**	**Jul**	**Aug**	**Oct**
155	10.5	11.75	14	.1875	1.25	2.75
160	6	8.125	11.125	.75	2.75	4.5
165	2.6875	5.25	8.125	2.375	4.75	6.75
170	.8125	3.25	6	5.75	7.5	9

13. Compute the intrinsic values, time values, and lower bounds of the following calls. Identify any profit opportunities that may exist.

    a.   July 160

    b.   October 155

    c.   August 170

14. Compute the intrinsic values and time values of the following puts. Identify any profit opportunities that may exist.

    a.   July 165

    b.   August 160

    c.   October 170

15. Check the following combinations of puts and calls, and determine whether they conform to the put-call parity rule. If you see any violations, suggest a strategy.

    a.   July 155

    b.   August 160

    c.   October 170

16. Assume IBM is scheduled to go ex-dividend on July 7 with a dividend of $1.10. Check each of the call options shown in the table, and determine which ones, if any, should be exercised immediately.

17. Examine the following pairs of calls, which differ only by exercise price. Determine whether any violate the rules regarding relationships between options that differ only by exercise price.

    a.   August 155 and 160

    b.   October 160 and 165

18. Examine each of the puts in the table, and determine whether any should be exercised immediately.

19. Examine the following pairs of puts, which differ only by exercise price. Determine if any violate the rules regarding relationships between options that differ only by exercise price.

    a.   August 155 and 160

    b.   October 160 and 170

20. (Concept Problem) Put-call parity is a powerful formula that can be used to create equivalent combinations of options, risk-free bonds, and stock. Suppose there are options available on the number of strikeouts Nolan Ryan will collect in his next game. For example, a call option with an exercise price of 12 would pay off Max(0, S − 12), where S is the number of strikeouts Ryan has recorded by the end of the game. Thus, if he strikes out 15, call holders receive $3 for each call. If he strikes out less than 12, call holders receive nothing. A put with an exercise price of 12 would pay off Max (0, 12 − S). If Ryan strikes out more than 12, put holders receive nothing. If he strikes out 8, put holders receive $4 for each put. Obviously there is no way to actually buy a position in the underlying asset, a strikeout. However, put-call parity shows that the underlying asset can be recreated from a combination of puts, calls, and risk-free bonds. Show how this would be done, and give the formula for the price of a strikeout.

21. (Concept Problem) In Appendix 3A, the formulas were derived for the effect of dividends on the lower bounds and put-call parity for European options. Assume a single dividend of D is paid at time t prior to expiration. Then use an arbitrage argument to prove put-call parity. Hint: Treat the dividend the same way you would treat the exercise price, that is, as a loan or a risk-free bond.

References

Cox, John C., and Mark Rubinstein. *Options Markets*, Chapters 2, 4. Englewood Cliffs, N.J.: Prentice-Hall, 1985.

Bhattacharya, Mihir. "Transaction Data Tests of Efficiency of the Chicago Board Options Exchange." *Journal of Financial Economics* 12 (1983): 161–185.

Bookstaber, Richard M. *Option Pricing and Investment Strategies*, Chapter 2. Chicago: Probus Publishing, 1987.

Evnine, Jeremy, and Andrew Rudd. "Index Options: The Early Evidence." *The Journal of Finance* 40 (1985): 743–756.

Galai, Dan. "A Convexity Test for Traded Options." *Quarterly Review of Economics and Business* 19 (Summer 1979): 83–90.

Galai, Dan. "Empirical Tests of Boundary Conditions for CBOE Options." *Journal of Financial Economics* 6 (1978): 187–211.

Gould, John P., and Dan Galai. "Transactions Costs and the Relationship between Put and Call Prices." *Journal of Financial Economics* 1 (1974): 105–129.

Hull, John. *Options, Futures, and Other Derivative Securities*, Chapters 1, 5. Englewood Cliffs, N.J.: Prentice-Hall, 1989.

Jarrow, Robert, and Andrew Rudd. *Option Pricing*, Chapters 1, 4, 5, 6. Homewood, Ill.: Irwin, 1983.

Klemkosky, Robert C., and Bruce G. Resnick. "An Ex-Ante Analysis of Put-Call Parity." *Journal of Financial Economics* 8 (1980): 363–378.

Klemkosky, Robert C., and Bruce G. Resnick. "Put-Call Parity and Market Efficiency." *The Journal of Finance* 34 (December 1979): 1141–1155.

Merton, Robert C. "The Relationship between Put and Call Option Prices: Comment." *The Journal of Finance* 28 (March 1973): 183–184.

Merton, Robert C. "Theory of Rational Option Pricing." *Bell Journal of Economics and Management Science* 4 (Spring 1973): 141–183.

Ritchken, Peter. *Options: Theory, Strategy, and Applications*, Chapter 4. Glenview, Ill.: Scott, Foresman, 1987.

Stoll, Hans R. "The Relationship between Put and Call Option Prices." *The Journal of Finance* 31 (May 1969): 319–332.

Welch, William W. *Strategies for Put and Call Option Trading*, Chapter 2. Cambridge, Mass.: Winthrop Publishers, 1982.

appendix 3A

The Effect of Dividends on Lower Bounds and Put-Call Parity

Let the stock pay a single, known dividend of D_t, where t denotes the ex-dividend date. Then the effect on the options' lower bounds and put-call parity is that the present value of the dividend is subtracted from the stock price.

Lower Bound of European Call:

$$C_e(S,T,E) \geq Max[0, S - D_t(1 + r)^{-t} - E(1 + r)^{-T}]$$

Lower Bound of European Put:

$$P_e(S,T,E) \geq Max[0, E(1 + r)^{-T} - (S - D_t(1 + r)^{-t})]$$

Put-Call Parity:

$$C_e(S,T,E) = P_e(S,T,E) + S - D_t(1 + r)^{-t} - E(1 + r)^{-T}$$

If there are several dividends, the present value of each dividend is subtracted from the stock price. The proofs of these results can be derived by following the same approach as in the no-dividend case but offsetting the dividend with a risk-free bond or loan paying D_t dollars at time t. A concept question at the end of the chapter asks you to do this.

OPTION PRICING MODELS

*What is a cynic? A man who knows the price of
everything and the value of nothing.*

OSCAR WILDE, Lady Windermere's Fan, 1892

This chapter examines option pricing models. A *model* is a simplified representation of reality that uses certain inputs to produce an output, or result. An *option pricing model* is a mathematical formula that uses the factors determining the option's price as inputs. The output is the theoretically correct option price. If the model performs as it should, the option's market price will equal the price given by the model.

In Chapter 3, we examined some basic concepts on determining option prices. However, we saw only how to price options relative to other options; for example, put-call parity demonstrates that given the price of a call, one can determine the price of a put. We also discovered relationships among the prices of options that differ by exercise prices and examined the upper and lower bounds on call and put prices. We did not, however, learn how to determine the exact option price directly from the factors that influence it.

A large body of academic literature on option pricing exists. Much of it goes far beyond the intended level of this book. The models range from the relatively simple to the extremely complex. All of the models have much in common, and it is necessary to understand the basic models before moving on to the more complex but more realistic ones.

We begin this chapter with a simple model called the *binomial option pricing model*. After taking the binomial model through several stages, we move on to the *Black-Scholes model*. Later we examine several simple modifications of the Black-Scholes model that improve its performance.

THE ONE-PERIOD BINOMIAL MODEL

First, consider what we mean by a *one-period* world. An option has a defined life, typically expressed in days. Assume the option's life is one unit of time. This time period can be as short or as long as necessary. If the time period is one day and the option has more than one day remaining, we will need a multiperiod model, which we shall examine later. For now, we will assume the option's life is a single time period.

The model is called a *binomial* model. It allows the stock price to go up or down, possibly at different rates. A binomial probability distribution is a distribution in which there are only two outcomes, or states. The probability of an up or down movement is governed by the binomial probability distribution. Because of this, the model is also called a *two-state* model.

In applying the binomial model to the stock market, however, it is immediately obvious that the range of possible outcomes is greater than the two states the binomial distribution can accommodate. However, that makes the model no less worthwhile. Its virtues are its simplicity and its ability to present the fundamental concepts of option pricing models clearly and concisely. In so doing, it establishes a foundation that facilitates an understanding of the Black-Scholes model.

Consider a world in which there is a stock priced at S on which call options are available.[1] The call has one period remaining before it expires. When the call expires, the stock can take on one of two values: It can go up by a factor of u or down by a factor of d. If it goes up the stock price will be S_u, which equals $S(1 + u)$. If it goes down it will be S_d, which equals $S(1 + d)$.

For example, suppose the stock price is currently 50 and can go either up by 10 percent or down by 8 percent. Thus, u = .10 and d = −.08. The variables u and d, therefore, are the rates of return on the stock. When the call expires, the stock will be either 50(1.10) = 55 or 50(.92) = 46.

Consider a call option on the stock with an exercise price of E and a current price of C. When the option expires, it will be worth either C_u or C_d. Because at expiration the call price is its intrinsic value,

$$C_u = Max[0, S(1 + u) - E]$$
$$C_d = Max[0, S(1 + d) - E].$$

Figure 4.1 illustrates the paths of both the stock and call prices. This tree diagram is simple, but it will become more complex when we introduce the

---

[1]The model can also price put options. We shall see how this is done in a later section and in an end-of-chapter problem.

FIGURE 4.1
The One-Period Binomial Model

(a) The Stock Price Path

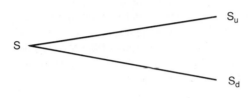

(b) The Call Price Path

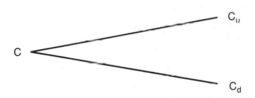

multiperiod model. The branches enable us to see more easily the paths the stock and option prices take.

If both stock prices resulted in the option expiring in-the-money, the option would not be very speculative; however, it would still be correctly priced by the model. The writer would receive a premium compensating for the future cash outflow expected upon exercising the option. To make things more interesting, however, we shall define our variables such that the option has a chance of expiring out-of-the-money. Assume $S(1 + d)$ is less than E; that is, if the stock price goes down, the option will expire out-of-the-money. Also assume $S(1 + u)$ is greater than E such that if the stock price goes up, the option will expire in-the-money.

As in previous chapters, let the risk-free rate be identified by the symbol r. The risk-free rate is the interest earned on a riskless investment over a time period equal to the option's remaining life. The risk-free rate falls between the rate of return if it goes up and the rate of return if it goes down. Thus, $d < r < u$. We shall assume all investors can borrow or lend at the risk-free rate.

The objective of this model is to derive a formula for the theoretical option price, the variable C. The theoretical price is then compared against the actual price and reveals whether the option is overpriced, underpriced, or correctly priced. The formula for C is developed by constructing a riskless portfolio of stock and options. A riskless portfolio should earn the risk-free rate. Given the stock's values and the riskless return on the portfolio, the call's value can be inferred from the other variables.

This riskless portfolio is called a *hedge portfolio* and consists of h shares of stock and a single written call. The model provides the *hedge ratio*, h. The current value of the portfolio is the value of the h shares minus the value of the short call. We subtract the call's value from the value of the h shares because the shares are assets and the short call is a liability. Thus, the portfolio value is assets minus liabilities, or simply net worth. The current portfolio value is defined as V, where $V = hS - C$.

At expiration, the portfolio value will be either V_u if the stock goes up or V_d if the stock goes down. Using the previously defined terms,

$$V_u = hS(1 + u) - C_u$$
$$V_d = hS(1 + d) - C_d.$$

If the same outcome is achieved regardless of what the stock price does, the position is riskless. We can choose a value of h that will make this happen. We simply set $V_u = V_d$ so that

$$hS(1 + u) - C_u = hS(1 + d) - C_d.$$

Solving for h,

$$h = \frac{C_u - C_d}{S(1 + u) - S(1 + d)} = \frac{C_u - C_d}{S_u - S_d}.$$

Since we know the values of S, u, and d, we can determine C_u, C_d, and h.

A riskless investment must earn a return equal to the risk-free rate. Thus, the portfolio's value one period later should equal its current value compounded for one period at the risk-free rate. If it does not, the portfolio will be incorrectly valued and represent a potential arbitrage opportunity. Later we shall see how the arbitrage would be executed.

If the portfolio's current value grows at the risk-free rate, its future value will be $(hS - C)(1 + r)$. The two values of the portfolio at expiration, V_u and V_d, are equal, so we can select either one. Choosing V_u and setting it equal to the original value of the portfolio compounded at the risk-free rate gives

$$V(1 + r) = V_u$$
$$(hS - C)(1 + r) = hS(1 + u) - C_u.$$

Substituting the formula for h and solving this equation for C gives the option pricing formula,

$$C = \frac{pC_u + (1-p)C_d}{1+r},$$

where p is defined as $(r-d)/(u-d)$. The formula gives the call option's price as a function of the variables C_u, C_d, p, and r. However, C_u and C_d are determined by the variables S, u, d, and E. Thus, the variables affecting the call option price are the current stock price, S, the exercise price, E, the risk-free rate, r, and the parameters, u and d, which define the possible future stock prices at expiration. Notice that we never specified the probabilities of the two stock price movements; they do not enter into the model. The option is priced relative to the stock. Therefore, given the stock price, one can obtain the option price. The stock, however, is priced independently of the option, and thus the probabilities of the stock price movements would be a factor in pricing the stock.

Pricing the option off of the stock in the framework used here is called *risk-neutral pricing*. The investor's feelings about risk play an important role in the pricing of securities. In the risk-neutral option pricing framework, investors' sensitivities to risk are of no consequence. However, this does not mean that the model assumes investors are risk neutral. The stock price is determined by how investors feel about risk. If investors are risk neutral and determine that a stock is worth $20, the model will use $20 and take no account of investors' feelings about risk. If investors are risk averse and determine that a stock is worth $20, the model will use $20 and disregard investors' feelings about risk. This does not mean that the stock will be priced equally by risk-averse and risk-neutral investors; rather, the model will accept the stock price as given and pay no attention to how risk was used to obtain the stock price.

An Illustrative Example

Consider a stock currently priced at $60. One period later it can go up to $69, an increase of 15 percent, or down to $48, a decrease of 20 percent. Assume a call option with an exercise price of $50. The risk-free rate is 10 percent. The inputs are summarized as follows:

S = 60
E = 50
u = .15
d = −.20
r = .10

First, find the values of C_u and C_d:

$$C_u = \text{Max}[0, S(1+u) - E]$$
$$= \text{Max}[0, 60(1.15) - 50]$$
$$= 19$$

$$C_d = \text{Max}[0, S(1+d) - E]$$
$$= \text{Max}[0, 60(.80) - 50]$$
$$= 0.$$

The hedge ratio, h, is

$$h = \frac{19 - 0}{69 - 48} = .9048.$$

The hedge requires .9048 shares of stock for each call.[2] The value of p is

$$p = \frac{r - d}{u - d} = \frac{.10 - (-.20)}{.15 - (-.20)} = .857.$$

Then

$$1 - p = 1 - .857 = .143.$$

Plugging into the formula for C gives

$$C = \frac{19(.857) + 0(.143)}{1.10} = 14.80.$$

Thus, the theoretically correct call price is $14.80.

A Hedged Portfolio

Consider a hedged portfolio consisting of a short position in 1,000 calls and a long position in 905 shares of stock. The number of shares is determined by the hedge ratio of .9048 shares per written call. The current value of this portfolio is

$$905(60) - 1,000(14.80) = 39,500.$$

Thus, you buy 905 shares at $60 per share and write 1,000 calls at $14.80. This requires a payment of 905($60) = $54,300 for the stock and takes in 1,000($14.80) = $14,800 for the calls. The net cash outlay is $54,300 − $14,800 = $39,500. This total represents the assets (the stock) minus the liabilities (the calls) and thus is the net worth.

---

[2]We assume odd lots of stock can be purchased.

If the stock goes up to $69, the call will be exercised at a value of $69 − $50 = $19. The stock will be worth 905($69) = $62,445. Thus, the portfolio will be worth 905($69) − 1,000($69 − $50) = $43,445. If the stock goes down to $48, the call will expire out-of-the-money. The portfolio will be worth 905($48) = $43,440. These two values of the portfolio at expiration are essentially equal, because the $5 difference is due only to the rounding off of the hedge ratio and call price. The return on the portfolio is

$$\left(\frac{\$43,445}{\$39,500}\right) - 1 \cong .10,$$

which is the risk-free rate. The original investment of $39,500 will have grown to $43,445—a return of about 10 percent, the risk-free rate.

If the call price were not $14.80, an arbitrage opportunity would exist. First we will consider the case where the call is overpriced.

An Overpriced Call

If the call were overpriced, a riskless hedge could generate a riskless return in excess of the risk-free rate. Suppose the market price of the call is $15.50. If you buy 905 shares and write 1,000 calls, the value of the investment today is

$$905(\$60) - 1,000(\$15.50) = \$38,800.$$

If the stock goes up to $69, at expiration the call will be priced at $19 and the portfolio will be worth 905($69) − 1,000($19) = $43,445. If the stock goes down to $48, the call will be worth nothing and the portfolio will be worth 905($48) = $43,440. In either case, the portfolio will be worth the same, the difference of $5 being due to rounding. The initial investment of $38,800 will have grown to $43,445, a return of

$$\left(\frac{\$43,445}{\$38,800}\right) - 1 \cong .12,$$

which is considerably higher than the risk-free rate.

A riskless portfolio that will earn more than the risk-free rate obviously is very attractive. All investors will recognize this opportunity and hurry to execute the transaction. This will increase the demand for the stock and the supply of the option. Consequently, the stock price will tend to increase and the option price to decrease until the option is correctly priced. For illustrative purposes, assume that the stock price stays at $60. Then the option price must fall from $15.50 to $14.80. Only at an option price of $14.80 will the portfolio offer a return equal to the risk-free rate.

Now consider what happens if the option is underpriced.

An Underpriced Call

If the option is underpriced, it is necessary to buy it. To hedge a long option position, you must sell the stock short. Suppose the call is priced at $14. Then you sell short 905 shares at $60, which generates a cash inflow of 905($60) = $54,300. Now you buy 1,000 calls at $14 each for a cost of $14,000. This produces a net cash inflow of $40,300.

If the stock goes to $69, you buy it back at 905($69) = $62,445. You exercise the calls for a gain of 1,000($69 − $50) = $19,000. The net cash flow is −$62,445 + $19,000 = −$43,445. If the stock goes down to $48, you buy it back at 905($48) = $43,440 while the calls expire worthless. The $5 difference is due solely to rounding.

In both outcomes, the returns are essentially equivalent. The overall transaction is like a loan in which you receive $40,300 up front and pay back $43,440 later. This is equivalent to an interest rate of ($43,440/$40,300) − 1 = .078. Because this transaction is the same as borrowing at a rate of 7.8 percent and the risk-free rate is 10 percent, it is an attractive borrowing opportunity. All investors will recognize this and execute the transaction. This will tend to drive up the call price (or possibly drive down the stock price) until equilibrium is reached. If the price of the stock stays at $60, equilibrium will be reached when the call price rises to $14.80.

This model considered only a single period. In the next section, we extend the model to a two-period world.

THE TWO-PERIOD BINOMIAL MODEL

In the single-period world, the stock price goes either up or down. Thus, there are only two possible future stock prices. To increase the degree of realism, we will now add another period. This will increase the number of possible outcomes at expiration.

Suppose that at the end of the first period the stock price has risen to $S(1 + u)$. During the second period it could go either up or down, in which case it would be either $S_{u^2} = S(1 + u)^2$ or $S_{ud} = S(1 + u)(1 + d)$. If the stock price has gone down in the first period to $S(1 + d)$, during the second period it will either go down again or go back up, in which case it will equal $S_{d^2} = S(1 + d)^2$ or $S_{du} = S(1 + d)(1 + u)$.

Figure 4.2 illustrates the paths of the stock price and the corresponding call prices. The option prices at expiration are

$$C_{u^2} = \text{Max}[0, S(1 + u)^2 - E]$$
$$C_{ud} = \text{Max}\,[0, S(1 + u)(1 + d) - E]$$
$$C_{d^2} = \text{Max}[0, S(1 + d)^2 - E].$$

The possible option prices at the end of the first period, C_u and C_d, initially are unknown; however, they can be found.

FIGURE 4.2
The Two-Period Binomial Model

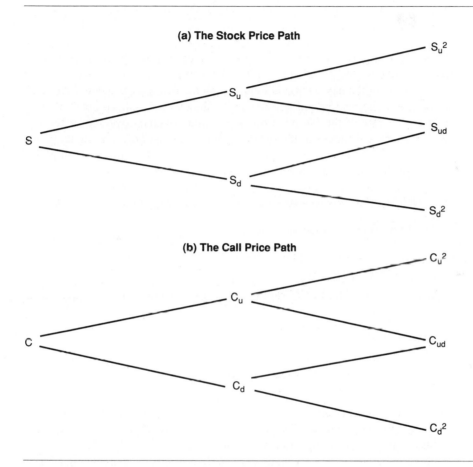

(a) The Stock Price Path

(b) The Call Price Path

Suppose that in the first period the stock price increases to S_u. Because there will be only one period remaining with two possible outcomes, the one-period binomial model is appropriate for finding the option price, C_u. If at the end of the first period the stock price decreases to S_d, we will again find ourselves facing a single-period world with two possible outcomes. Here we can use the one-period binomial model to obtain the value of C_d. Using the one-period model, the option prices C_u and C_d are

$$C_u = \frac{pC_{u^2} + (1-p)C_{ud}}{1+r}$$

and

$$C_d = \frac{pC_{ud} + (1-p)C_{d^2}}{1+r}.$$

In a single-period world, a call option's value is a weighted average of the option's two possible values at the end of the next period. The call's value if the stock goes up in the next period is weighted by the factor p; its value if the stock goes down in the next period is weighted by the factor $1-p$. To obtain the call price at the start of the period, we discount the weighted average of the two possible future call prices at the risk-free rate for one period. The single-period binomial model is thus a general formula that can be used in any multiperiod world when there is but one period remaining.

Even if the call does not expire at the end of the next period, we can use the formula to find the current call price as a weighted average of the two possible call prices in the next period; that is,

$$C = \frac{pC_u + (1-p)C_d}{1+r}.$$

First, we find the values of C_u and C_d; then we substitute these into the above formula for C.

Those who prefer a more direct approach can use

$$C = \frac{p^2 C_{u^2} + 2p(1-p)C_{ud} + (1-p)^2 C_{d^2}}{(1+r)^2}.$$

This formula illustrates that the call's value is a weighted average of its three possible values at expiration two periods later. The denominator, $(1+r)^2$, discounts this figure back two periods to the present.

Notice that we have not actually derived the formula by constructing a hedge portfolio. This is possible, however, and in a later section we shall see how the hedge portfolio works. First, note that the hedge is constructed by initially holding h shares of stock for each call written. At the end of the first period, the stock price is either S_u or S_d. At that point, we must adjust the hedge ratio. If the stock is at S_u, let the new hedge ratio be designated as h_u; if at S_d, let the new ratio be h_d. The formulas for h_u and h_d are of the same general type as that of h in the single-period model. The numerator is the call's value if the stock goes up the next period minus the call's value if the stock goes down the next period. The denominator is the price of the stock if it goes up the next period minus its price if it goes down the next period. In equation form,

$$h = \frac{C_u - C_d}{S_u - S_d}$$

$$h_u = \frac{C_{u^2} - C_{ud}}{S_{u^2} - S_{ud}}$$

$$h_d = \frac{C_{ud} - C_{d^2}}{S_{ud} - S_{d^2}}.$$

An Illustrative Example

Consider the example in a two-period world from the previous section. All input values remain the same. The possible stock prices at expiration are

$$S(1 + u)^2 = 60(1.15)^2$$
$$= 79.35$$
$$S(1 + u)(1 + d) = 60(1.15)(.80)$$
$$= 55.2$$
$$S(1 + d)^2 = 60(.80)^2$$
$$= 38.4.$$

The call prices at expiration are

$$C_{u^2} = \text{Max}[0, S(1 + u)^2 - E]$$
$$= \text{Max}(0, 79.35 - 50)$$
$$= 29.35$$
$$C_{ud} = \text{Max}[0, S(1 + u)(1 + d) - E]$$
$$= \text{Max}(0, 55.2 - 50)$$
$$= 5.2$$
$$C_{d^2} = \text{Max}[0, S(1 + d)^2 - E]$$
$$= \text{Max}(0, 38.4 - 50)$$
$$= 0.$$

The value of p is the same regardless of the number of periods in the model.

We can find the call's value by either of the two methods discussed in the previous section. Let us first compute the values of C_u and C_d:

$$C_u = \frac{(.857)(29.35) + (.143)(5.2)}{1.10} = 23.54$$

$$C_d = \frac{(.857)(5.2) + (.143)(0)}{1.10} = 4.05.$$

The value of the call today is a weighted average of the two possible call values one period later:

$$C = \frac{(.857)(23.54) + (.143)(4.05)}{1.10} = \$18.87.$$

Note that the same call analyzed in the one-period world is worth more in the two-period world. Why? Recall from Chapter 3 that a call option with a longer maturity is never worth less than one with a shorter maturity and usually is worth more. If this principle did not hold here, something would have been wrong with the model.

A Hedged Portfolio

Now consider a hedged portfolio. Let the call be trading in the market at its theoretically correct price of $18.87. The hedge will consist of 1,000 short calls. The number of shares purchased is given by the formula for h,

$$h = \frac{23.54 - 4.05}{69 - 48} = .928.$$

Thus, we buy 928 shares of stock and write 1,000 calls. The transaction can be summarized as follows:

$$
\begin{aligned}
\text{Buy 928 shares at \$60} &= \quad \$55,680 \quad \text{(assets)} \\
\text{Write 1,000 calls at \$18.87} &= -\$18,870 \quad \text{(liabilities)} \\
\text{Net investment} &= \quad \$36,810 \quad \text{(net worth)}.
\end{aligned}
$$

If the stock price goes up to $69, the portfolio will consist of 928 shares at $69 and 1,000 calls at $23.54. The value of the portfolio will be 928($69) – 1,000($23.54) = $40,492. Our investment will have grown from $36,810 to $40,492. You should be able to verify that this is a 10 percent return, the risk-free rate. Had the stock price originally gone down to $48, the portfolio would have consisted of 928 shares valued at $48 and 1,000 calls valued at $4.05. The portfolio value would have been 928($48) – 1,000($4.05) = $40,494, which differs from the outcome at a stock price of $69 only by a round-off error. Since the return is the same regardless of the change in the stock price, the portfolio is riskless.

Now suppose it is the end of the first period and the stock is at $69. To maintain a hedge through the next period, we need to revise the hedge ratio. The new hedge ratio, h_u, is

$$h_u = \frac{29.35 - 5.2}{79.35 - 55.2} = 1.$$

The new hedge ratio will be one share of stock for each call. In fact, if the call has one period remaining and there is no possibility of it expiring out-of-the-money, the hedge ratio will always be 1.[3]

---

[3]This statement can easily be verified by substituting $S(1 + u)^2 - E$ for C_{u^2} and $S(1 + u)(1 + d) - E$ for C_{ud} in the formula for h_u.

To establish the new hedge ratio, we need either 928 calls or 1,000 shares of stock. We can either buy back 72 calls, leaving us with 928, or buy 72 shares, giving us 1,000 shares. Since it is less expensive to buy the calls, we buy back 72 calls at $23.54 each for a total cost of $1,695. To avoid putting out more of our own funds, we borrow the money at the risk-free rate.

Now suppose one period later the stock goes up to $79.35. Then we sell the 928 shares at $79.35, the calls are exercised at $29.35 each, and we repay the loan of $1,695 plus 10 percent interest. The value of the portfolio will be 928($79.35) − 928($29.35) − $1,695(1.10) = $44,536. Had the stock gone down to $55.20, we would have had 928 shares valued at $55.20, 928 calls exercised at $5.20, and the repayment of the loan of $1,695 plus interest for a total portfolio value of 928($55.20) − 928($5.20) − $1,695(1.10) = $44,536. The outcome would be the same in both cases. Note also that the portfolio value would have grown from an initial value of $36,810 to $40,494 at the end of period 1 and from $40,494 to $44,536 at the end of period 2. In each period, we would have earned the risk-free rate and the outcomes would not have been affected by the stock price.

The preceding analysis covers the case where the stock price went from $60 to $69 at the end of the first period. Now consider the case where the stock price goes from $60 to $48 at the end of the first period. Recall that we had 928 shares and were short 1,000 calls. The portfolio now consists of the 928 shares valued at $48 and 1,000 short calls valued at $4.05. Thus, the portfolio is worth 928($48) − 1,000($4.05) = $40,494. This is, of course, the same value obtained when the stock rose to $69. To maintain the hedge throughout the next period, we adjust the hedge ratio to

$$h_d = \frac{5.2 - 0}{55.2 - 38.4} = .31.$$

Thus, we need 310 shares of stock for the 1,000 calls. We currently hold 928 shares, so we can sell off 618 shares at $48 and receive $29,664. Then we invest this money in riskless bonds paying the risk-free rate. At the end of the second period, the bonds will pay off $29,664 plus 10 percent interest.

Suppose that at the end of the second period the stock goes to $55.20. The portfolio will consist of 310 shares valued at $55.20, 1,000 calls exercised at $5.20, and bonds worth $29,664 plus 10 percent interest. The total value of the portfolio will be 310($55.20) − 1,000($5.20) + $29,664(1.10) = $44,542. If the stock ends up at $38.40, we will have 310 shares at $38.40, 1,000 calls expiring worthless, and principal and interest on the risk-free bonds. The value of this portfolio will be 310($38.40) + $29,664(1.10) = $44,534. This is essentially the same amount received in the case where the stock originally went up; the difference is due only to a round-off error. Thus, regardless of which path the stock takes, the hedge will produce an increase in wealth of 10 percent in each period.

Now let us consider what happens if the call is mispriced.

A Mispriced Call in the Two-Period World

If the call is mispriced at the outset, an arbitrage opportunity exists. If the call is underpriced, we should purchase it and sell short h shares of stock. If the call is overpriced, we should write it and purchase h shares of stock. Whether we earn the arbitrage return over the first period, the second period, or both periods, however, will depend on whether the call price adjusts to its theoretically correct price at the end of the first period. If it does not, we may not earn a return in excess of the risk-free rate over the first period. However, the call must be correctly priced at the end of the second period, because it expires at that time.

The two-period return will be the geometric average of the two one-period returns; that is, if 8 percent is the first-period return and 12 percent is the second-period return, the two-period return will be $\sqrt{(1.08)(1.12)} - 1 = .0998$. If one of the two returns equals the risk-free rate and the other exceeds it, the two-period return will exceed the risk-free rate. If one of the two returns is less than the risk-free rate and the other is greater, the overall return can still exceed the risk-free rate. The return earned over the full two periods will exceed the risk-free rate if the option is mispriced at the outset, the proper long or short position is taken, and the correct hedge ratio is maintained.

There are many possible outcomes of such a hedge, and it would take an entire chapter to illustrate them. We therefore shall discuss the possibilities only in general terms. In each case, we will assume the proper hedge ratio is maintained and the investor buys calls only when they are underpriced or correctly priced and sells calls only when they are overpriced or correctly priced.

Suppose the call originally was overpriced and is still overpriced at the end of the first period. Since the call has not fallen sufficiently to be correctly priced, the return over the first period actually can be less than the risk-free rate. However, because the call must be correctly priced at the end of the second period, the return earned over the second period will more than make up for it. Overall, the return earned over the two periods will exceed the risk-free rate.

If the call originally is overpriced and becomes correctly priced at the end of the first period, the return earned over that period must exceed the risk-free rate. The return earned over the second period will equal the risk-free rate, because the call was correctly priced at the beginning of the second period and is correctly priced at the end of it. Thus, the full two-period return will exceed the risk-free rate.

If the call is overpriced at the start and becomes underpriced at the end of the first period, the return earned over that period will exceed the risk-free rate. This is because the call will have fallen in price more than is justified and now is worth considerably less than it should be. At this point, we should close out the hedge and initiate a new hedge for the second period consisting of a long position in the underpriced call and a short position in the stock. We can invest the excess proceeds in risk-free bonds. The second-period return will far exceed the risk-free rate. The overall two-period return obviously will be above the risk-free rate.

TABLE 4.1

Hedge Results in the Two-Period Binomial Model

	Return from Hedge Compared to Risk-Free Rate		
	Period 1	Period 2	Two-Period
Options Overpriced at Start of Period 1 Status of option at start of period 2:			
Overpriced	indeterminate	better	better
Correctly priced	better	equal	better
Underpriced	better	better	better

Table 4.1 summarizes these results. Similar conclusions apply for an underpriced call, although the interpretation differs somewhat because the hedge portfolio is short.

It should be apparent that the binomial model can easily be extended to a three-period world. At some point, however, its usefulness would succumb to monotony and tedium. Fortunately, there is a general pricing formula for the case of n periods. This is discussed in Appendix 4A.

SOME USEFUL EXTENSIONS OF THE BINOMIAL MODEL

Pricing Put Options

We can use the binomial model to price put options just as we can for call options. We use the same formulas, but instead of specifying the call payoffs at expiration, we use the put payoffs at expiration. To see the difference, look at Figure 4.2 on p. 111. Then we simply replace every C with a P; likewise we substitute P for C in each formula; and the rest is easy. A concept problem at the end of the chapter asks you to perform some binomial put option pricing calculations.

American Options and Early Exercise

Binomial models are particularly useful in capturing the effect of early exercise. For call options on stocks without dividends, there will, of course, never be an early exercise. For put options, with or without dividends, early exercise is quite possible. The concept problem on the binomial put option pricing model will ask you to evaluate the early exercise effect on the American put. For now, let us consider how early exercise will affect American calls in the binomial model.

There are a number of ways to incorporate dividends into the model. The simplest is to assume a constant yield of δ percent per period. Thus, each time the stock price moves to a new value, it immediately declines by δ percent as it goes ex-dividend. We then use the ex-dividend stock prices in the binomial formulas. At any point, if the intrinsic value of the call exceeds the value of the call given by the binomial formula, the call should be exercised. Then the intrinsic value replaces the formula value.

Consider the same two-period problem we worked earlier in the chapter. Because we want to see a case where the call is exercised early, let us assume a fairly high dividend yield—say, 8 percent—and, of course, let the call be American. The ex-dividend stock prices become

$$S_u = 60(1.15)(1-.08) = 63.48$$
$$S_d = 60(.8)(1-.08) = 44.16$$
$$S_{u^2} = 63.48(1.15)(1-.08) = 67.16$$
$$S_{ud} = S_{du} = 63.48\,(.8)(1-.08) = 46.72$$
$$S_{d^2} = 44.16(.8)(1-.08) = 32.50.$$

The corresponding call prices at expiration are

$$C_{u^2} = \text{Max}(0, 67.16-50) = 17.16$$
$$C_{ud} = C_{du} = \text{Max}(46.72-50) = 0$$
$$C_{d^2} = \text{Max}(0, 32.50-50) = 0.$$

The call prices after one period are

$$C_u = \frac{(.857)(17.16)+(.143)(0)}{1.10} = 13.37$$

$$C_d = \frac{(.857)(0)+(.143)(0)}{1.10} = 0.$$

Note, however, that when the stock price is at $S_u = 63.48$, the intrinsic value of the call is $\text{Max}(0, 63.48-50) = 13.48$. This is slightly higher than the value of the call given by the formula, 13.37. Thus, the call is exercised and we redefine C_u to be 13.48. Then the current value of the call is

$$C = \frac{(.857)(13.48)+(.143)(0)}{1.10} = 10.50.$$

The value of the option if it were a European call would be 10.42.

A RECAP OF THE BINOMIAL OPTION PRICING MODEL

The binomial option pricing model is not necessarily meant to be realistic. The number of possible stock prices at expiration is unlimited in reality. Although the binomial model must impose some finite limits, it becomes more realistic as the number of periods increases. The model's importance, however, is not in its ability to explain real-world option prices but in its usefulness for explicating the process by which an option's price is determined.

So far we have seen that an option's price is determined by the stock price, exercise price, time to expiration, risk-free rate, and parameters defining the volatility of the stock price. The option must be priced according to the formula, or investors will engage in the type of riskless arbitrage illustrated in earlier sections. These traders' combined actions will force the option price to equal the model price. The option's price is determined without accounting for the expected future stock price or investors' feelings about risk. These particular characteristics of the manner in which option prices are determined will continue to hold as we move into our examination of a more realistic model for pricing options.

THE BLACK-SCHOLES OPTION PRICING MODEL

The year 1973 was an important one in the history of options. In that year, the Chicago Board Options Exchange was founded and became the first organized facility for options trading. Also, two professors at the Massachusetts Institute of Technology, Fischer Black and Myron Scholes, published an article in the *Journal of Political Economy* that presented a formula for pricing an option. The formula, which became known as the *Black-Scholes option pricing model*, was one of the most significant developments in the pricing of financial instruments. It has generated a long line of subsequent research attempting to test the model and improve on it. A new industry of option pricing products based on the Black-Scholes model also has developed. Even if one does not agree with everything the model says, knowing something about it is important for surviving in the options markets.

Although the Black-Scholes model did not evolve directly from the binomial model, it is a mathematical extension of it. Recall that the binomial model can be extended to any number of time periods. Suppose we let n equal infinity so that each time period is very small. The interest rate, r, is the risk-free rate over each time period. As you can imagine, the number of stock prices at expiration will be very large—in fact, infinite. Although the algebra is somewhat complex, the equation for the binomial model becomes the equation for the Black-Scholes model. Later in this chapter, we shall illustrate how the binomial price converges to the Black-Scholes price.

However, Black and Scholes did not derive their model by extending the binomial model to an infinite number of periods. The binomial model had not even been discovered when they began examining some early research on option pricing models. They supplied the intuition that an option can be priced by forming a riskless hedge portfolio consisting of stock and options. Black and Scholes applied what was to finance a new branch of mathematics called *stochastic calculus*. The mathematics of their derivation is quite complex. Interested readers can find it in the original paper, Black-Scholes (1973), and the books by Jarrow and Rudd (1983) and Ritchken (1987).

We shall omit the math here, but it is important to outline the model's assumptions:

1. The rate of return on the stock follows a *lognormal* distribution. This means that the logarithm of 1 plus the rate of return follows the normal, or bell-shaped, curve. The lognormal distribution is a convenient and realistic characterization of stock returns because it reflects stockholders' limited liability.

2. The risk-free rate and variance of the return on the stock are constant throughout the option's life.

3. There are no taxes or transaction costs.

4. The stock pays no dividends. (We shall relax this assumption later.)

5. The calls are European. As we saw in Chapter 3, this assumption is not necessary for preventing early exercise if assumption 4 holds.

Black and Scholes derived the following formula for pricing an option:

$$C = SN(d_1) - Ee^{-rT} N(d_2),$$

where

$$d_1 = \frac{\ln\left(\dfrac{S}{E}\right) + \left[r + \left(\dfrac{\sigma^2}{2}\right)\right]T}{\sigma\sqrt{T}}$$

$$d_2 = d_1 - \sigma\sqrt{T}$$

$N(d_1), N(d_2)$ = cumulative normal probabilities

σ^2 = annualized variance of the continuously compounded return on the stock

All other variables are the same ones previously used.

The Normal Distribution

It will probably be beneficial to review the normal probability distribution. Figure 4.3 illustrates the normal, or bell-shaped, curve. Recall that the curve is symmetric and everything we need to know about it is contained in the expected value, or mean, and the variance. Approximately 68 percent of the observations in a sample drawn from a normal distribution will occur within one standard deviation of the

FIGURE 4.3
The Normal Probability Distribution

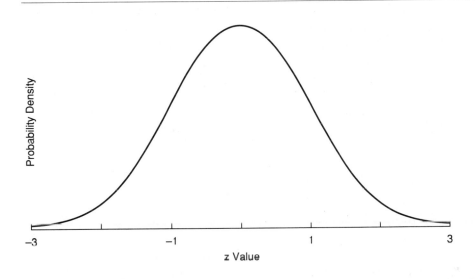

expected value. About 95 percent of the observations will lie within two standard deviations and about 99 percent within three standard deviations.

The standard normal random variable is called a *z statistic*. One can take any normally distributed random variable, convert it to a standard normal or z statistic, and use a table to determine the probability that an observed value of the random variable will be less than or equal to the value of interest.

Table 4.2 gives the cumulative probabilities of the standard normal distribution. Suppose we want to know the probability of observing a value of z less than or equal to 1.57. We go to the table and look down the first column for 1.5, then move over to the right under the column labeled 0.07; that is, the 1.5 and 0.07 add up to the z value, 1.57. The entry in the 1.5 row/0.07 column is .9418, the probability in a normal distribution of observing a value of z less than or equal to 1.57.

Suppose the value of z is less than zero—say, −1.12. We look for the appropriate value for a positive 1.12. In the 1.1 row/0.02 column is the value .8686. Then we subtract this number from 1. The answer is .1314. Because the table is symmetric, it is not necessary to show negative values. The probability of observing a value less than or equal to −1.12 is the same as that of observing a value greater than or equal to 1.12. The probability of observing a value greater than or equal to 1.12 is 1 minus the probability of observing a value less than or equal to 1.12. Note that we overlapped with the probability of observing a value exactly equal to 1.12. The probability of observing any single value is zero. This is so because we can observe an infinite number of possible values.

TABLE 4.2
Standard Normal Probabilities

z	0.00	0.01	0.02	0.03	0.04	0.05	0.06	0.07	0.08	0.09
0.0	.5000	.5040	.5080	.5120	.5160	.5199	.5239	.5279	.5319	.5359
0.1	.5398	.5438	.5478	.5517	.5557	.5596	.5636	.5675	.5714	.5753
0.2	.5793	.5832	.5871	.5910	.5948	.5987	.6026	.6064	.6103	.6141
0.3	.6179	.6217	.6255	.6293	.6331	.6368	.6406	.6443	.6480	.6517
0.4	.6554	.6591	.6628	.6664	.6700	.6736	.6772	.6808	.6844	.6879
0.5	.6915	.6950	.6985	.7019	.7054	.7088	.7123	.7157	.7190	.7224
0.6	.7257	.7291	.7324	.7357	.7389	.7422	.7454	.7486	.7517	.7549
0.7	.7580	.7611	.7642	.7673	.7704	.7734	.7764	.7794	.7823	.7852
0.8	.7881	.7910	.7939	.7967	.7995	.8023	.8051	.8078	.8106	.8133
0.9	.8159	.8186	.8212	.8238	.8264	.8289	.8315	.8340	.8365	.8389
1.0	.8413	.8438	.8461	.8485	.8508	.8531	.8554	.8577	.8599	.8621
1.1	.8643	.8665	.8686	.8708	.8729	.8749	.8770	.8790	.8810	.8830
1.2	.8849	.8860	.8888	.8907	.8925	.8943	.8962	.8980	.8997	.9015
1.3	.9032	.9049	.9066	.9082	.9099	.9115	.9131	.9147	.9162	.9177
1.4	.9192	.9207	.9222	.9236	.9251	.9265	.9279	.9292	.9306	.9319
1.5	.9332	.9345	.9357	.9370	.9382	.9394	.9406	.9418	.9429	.9441
1.6	.9452	.9463	.9474	.9484	.9495	.9505	.9515	.9525	.9535	.9545
1.7	.9554	.9564	.9573	.9582	.9591	.9599	.9608	.9616	.9625	.9633
1.8	.9641	.9649	.9656	.9664	.9671	.9678	.9686	.9693	.9699	.9706
1.9	.9713	.9719	.9726	.9732	.9738	.9744	.9750	.9756	.9761	.9767
2.0	.9772	.9778	.9783	.9788	.9793	.9798	.9803	.9808	.9812	.9817
2.1	.9821	.9826	.9830	.9834	.9838	.9842	.9846	.9850	.9854	.9857
2.2	.9861	.9864	.9868	.9871	.9875	.9878	.9881	.9884	.9887	.9890
2.3	.9893	.9896	.9898	.9901	.9904	.9906	.9909	.9911	.9913	.9916
2.4	.9918	.9920	.9922	.9925	.9927	.9929	.9931	.9932	.9934	.9936
2.5	.9938	.9940	.9941	.9943	.9945	.9946	.9948	.9949	.9951	.9952
2.6	.9953	.9955	.9956	.9957	.9959	.9960	.9961	.9962	.9963	.9964
2.7	.9965	.9966	.9967	.9968	.9969	.9970	.9971	.9972	.9973	.9974
2.8	.9974	.9975	.9976	.9977	.9977	.9978	.9979	.9979	.9980	.9981
2.9	.9981	.9982	.9982	.9983	.9984	.9984	.9985	.9985	.9986	.9986
3.0	.9987	.9987	.9987	.9988	.9988	.9989	.9989	.9989	.9990	.9990

Instead of using tables, the normal probability can be accurately approximated with a polynomial equation. There are a number of polynomial approximations, one of which is used in the Black-Scholes model spreadsheet on the software diskette that accompanies this book.

A Numerical Example

Let us use the Black-Scholes model to price the Digital Equipment July 165 call. Recall that the inputs are a stock price of $164, an exercise price of $165, and a time to expiration of .0959. We gave the risk-free rate of 5.35 percent as the Treasury bill yield that corresponds to the option's expiration. In the Black-Scholes model, however, the risk-free rate must be expressed as a continuously compounded yield. The continuously compounded equivalent of 5.35 percent is $\ln(1.0535) = .0521$. Later in this chapter, we shall take a closer look at the basis for this transformation and at how the variance or standard deviation can be determined. For now we will use .29 as the standard deviation, which corresponds to a variance of .0841.

The values of d_1 and d_2 are

$$d_1 = \frac{\ln\left(\frac{164}{165}\right) + \left[.0521 + \left(\frac{.0841}{2}\right)\right].0959}{.29\sqrt{.0959}}$$

$$= .0328$$

$$d_2 = .0328 - .29\sqrt{.0959} = -.0570.$$

Rounding off d_1 and d_2 to two digits, we obtain values of $N(.03)$ of .5120 and $N(-.06)$ of .4761 from Table 4.2. Inputting these into the Black-Scholes formula gives

$$C = 164(.5120) - 165e^{-(.0521)(.0959)}(.4761) = 5.803.$$

Thus, the theoretically correct value for the July 165 call is $5.803. The call's actual market price is $5.75. This suggests that the call is slightly underpriced. Assuming no transaction costs, an investor should buy the call. The number of calls to buy to form a riskless hedge portfolio that will outperform the risk-free rate is discussed in a later section.

The Accuracy of the Black-Scholes Model

The Black-Scholes model has undergone extensive empirical testing. It is, however, a difficult model to test because the standard deviation is not observable. Thus, an estimate based on the stock's recent history often is used. One such test employing this approach was done by Galai (1977), who used the model to identify mispriced calls and then constructed riskless hedges designed to earn risk-free arbitrage profits. The results showed a number of profitable opportunities in the options market; however, by the time the options could be bought, many of the opportunities had vanished. Moreover, transaction costs and the fact that the Black-Scholes model does not properly account for the right to exercise an American call early would have explained some of the findings. Studies by MacBeth and Merville (1979) and Rubinstein (1985) went to greater lengths to account for the early exercise problem plus other factors that might have explained the results of prior studies. They too, however, found that a number of unexplainable discrepancies between model prices and market prices remained.

Do the results of these tests cast sufficient doubt to justify a rejection of the Black-Scholes model? Not really. There is not now or ever likely to be a test that will resolve the issue of whether the Black-Scholes model exhibits biases. The various assumptions about the estimation of the standard deviation and the different data sets impose their own biases that should not be attributable to the model. It is fairly safe to say that the Black-Scholes model exhibits some biases, but that model, or a variation thereof, nonetheless is a reasonable approach to pricing options. It captures most of the important properties of options and provides otherwise unattainable insights. Thus, it is safe to proceed with our investigation of this important model.

Variables Affecting the Option's Price

The Black-Scholes formula tells us that five variables affect the option's price: (1) the stock price, (2) the exercise price, (3) the risk-free rate, (4) the time to expiration, and (5) the variance or standard deviation. Chapter 3 explained the effect of each variable on an option's price.

We can easily determine the stock price, exercise price, and time to expiration. The other two variables—the risk-free rate and the variance—are not directly observable. Later we will see how the variance and risk-free rate can be estimated and the option's sensitivity to these estimates. For now we shall look at the effects of the three observable variables. For the mathematically inclined, these comparative statics are presented more formally in Appendix 4B.

First, consider the stock price. A higher stock price should lead to a higher call price. Suppose the stock price is $168 instead of $164. Then the values of d_1 and d_2 are .3012 and .2114. This gives values of $N(.30)$ and $N(.21)$ of .6179 and .5832. Plugging into the formula gives a value of C of $8.059, which is higher than the previously obtained value, $5.803.

Now we change the exercise price to $170, which should decrease the call's value. Specifically, let us examine the July 170 call. We retain all of the other original values, including the stock price of $164. The values of d_1 and d_2 are −.2996 and −.3894. Table 4.2 gives values of $N(-.30)$ and $N(-.39)$ as .3821 and .3483, respectively. The resulting call price is $3.749, which is far less than the original $5.803.

Now consider a change in the time to expiration. This time we shall look at the October 165, which has a time to expiration of $T = .3452$. However, the October expiration will have a slightly different risk-free rate. To examine the effect of time to expiration alone, we continue to use the 5.21 percent risk-free rate associated with the July expiration. Inputting the appropriate values into the model gives a d_1 of .1551 and a d_2 of −.0153. Then $N(.16) = .5636$, $N(-.02) = .4920$, and the value of the call will be $12.697, which is considerably higher than the original value.

THE RISKLESS HEDGE IN THE BLACK-SCHOLES FRAMEWORK*

In the sections on the binomial model, we illustrated how to determine the option price by constructing a riskless hedge. The same can be done in the Black-Scholes framework, but the mathematics is slightly more complex. However, the basic concepts can be understood with a minimum of mathematics.

Consider a portfolio consisting of one short call and h shares of stock. The call is priced at C and the stock at S. The current value of the portfolio is

$$V = hS - C.$$

If the portfolio is hedged, its value will be unaffected by changes in the stock price. To construct the hedge, we solve for the value of h that will leave V unaffected by a change in S. Taking the partial derivative of V with respect to S,

$$\frac{\partial V}{\partial S} = h - \frac{\partial C}{\partial S}.$$

Setting this equal to zero and solving for h gives

$$h = \frac{\partial C}{\partial S}.$$

The hedge ratio, the number of shares for each call, is the derivative of the call price with respect to the stock price. Fortunately, this derivative is not difficult to obtain, for it is the value $N(d_1)$ from the Black-Scholes model. This value is sometimes called the option's *delta*.

Because the value of $N(d_1)$ is a probability, it must lie between 0 and 1. Therefore, the number of shares owned for each call written is between 0 and 1. This means that to construct a hedge, the number of shares must be less than the number of calls. This makes sense, because since $N(d_1)$ is less than 1, the change in the call price is never greater, and usually is less, than the change in the stock price. Thus, for the hedge to work, the number of calls must exceed the number of shares of stock.

Because the partial derivative is only the change in C for a very small change in S, a change in the call price for a change in the stock price is only approximately equal to $\partial C/\partial S$. For illustrative purposes, however, we shall assume the partial derivative is an accurate estimate of the change in the call price with respect to the change in the stock price.

---

*This section requires the use of calculus, specifically partial derivatives. These can be viewed as much like ordinary derivatives under the assumption that all other terms in the equation are constants.

A Hedging Example

For the Digital Equipment July 165 call, the value of $N(d_1)$ is .5120. Thus, the hedge ratio would be about 51 shares owned for every 100 calls written. For every $1 change in the stock price, the call price should change in the same direction by about $.51. Suppose we write 100 calls at the theoretical price of $5.803 and buy 51 shares at $164 each.

Now the stock price immediately decreases by $1. With 51 shares held, this generates a loss in value of $51. Each call will decline by about $.51. With 100 calls, the calls will lose about $51 of value. Since we are short calls, that is to our advantage. We could repurchase the calls at a cost of $51 less than what we originally received for them. Overall, the position is not influenced by the stock price change. With a change in the stock price, however, the hedge ratio, or delta, will change. As the call price increases, the delta increases; as the call price decreases, the delta decreases. The change in the delta when the stock price changes is referred to as the *gamma*. The formula for gamma is presented in Appendix 4B. The delta will also change with the passage of time, as we saw in the binomial model. As expiration approaches, the delta of an in-the-money call will approach 1 and the delta of an out-of-the-money call will approach zero. These changes in the delta will necessitate changes in the ratio of calls to stock in the hedge portfolio. In theory the changes should be made continuously, but as a practical matter no one could revise a portfolio that often.

THE BLACK-SCHOLES MODEL IN THE PRESENCE OF DIVIDENDS

The Black-Scholes model in the form we have seen so far applies to stocks that do not pay dividends, such as Digital Equipment. As we saw in Chapter 3, dividends tend to reduce the call option's price and may induce early exercise. Incorporating dividends into the Black-Scholes model for European options is not difficult. There are several suggested approaches, none of which have proven superior to the others. We shall discuss two here.

Known Discrete Dividends

Suppose a stock pays a dividend of D_t at some time during the option's life. This dividend is payable after a time period t, which is defined by the ex-dividend date. The dividend is assumed to be known with certainty. If we make a small adjustment to the stock price, the Black-Scholes model will remain applicable to the pricing of this option.

The adjustment requires that we subtract the present value of the dividend from the stock price and use the adjusted stock price in the formula. Let the stock price in the Black-Scholes formula be S_D, defined as

$$S_D = S - D_t e^{-rt}.$$

The value S_D represents the capital value of the stock. Because a stock's price is the present value of all future dividends, S_D is the present value of all the dividends expected after the option's expiration. It could be regarded as the speculative component of the stock price, because the remaining component—the upcoming dividend, D_t—is assumed to be known for certain.

As noted earlier, the Digital Equipment stock does not pay a dividend. For illustrative purposes, we will now assume that it pays a $2 dividend and has an ex-dividend date of July 15. All other variables are the same. The time to the ex-dividend date is 33 days, so $t = 33/365$, or .0904. Then the adjusted stock price is

$$S_D = 164 - 2e^{-(.0521)(.0904)} = 162.01.$$

Now we use the Black-Scholes model with a stock price of $162.01 instead of $164. All other inputs remain the same:

$$d_1 = \frac{\ln\left(\dfrac{162.01}{165}\right) + \left[.0521 + \left(\dfrac{.0841}{2}\right)\right].0959}{.29\sqrt{.0959}}$$

$$= -.1031$$

$$d_2 = -.1031 - .29\sqrt{.0959}$$

$$= -.1929.$$

Looking up $N(-.10)$ and $N(-.19)$ in Table 4.2 gives values of .4602 and .4247, respectively. The call price is

$$C = 162.01(.4602) - 165e^{-(.0521)(.0959)}(.4247) = 4.831.$$

As we would expect, the lower stock price results in a lower call price. The effect of the dividend is to render the call option less attractive, which is manifested in the lower price.

If there is more than one dividend payable during the option's life, the present value of each dividend is subtracted from the stock price. Since dividends tend to be paid at quarterly intervals and the maximum life of an option normally is nine months, the number of dividends probably is not more than three and, in the majority of cases, only one or two. An exception would be an index option. The next section suggests an approach for adjusting an index option's price for the effect of dividends.

The adjustment presented here will tend to make the model option price come closer to the actual price on a dividend-paying stock. Remember, however, that the formula still applies only to a European option. Thus, it does not reflect the flexibility afforded by the early-exercise feature of an American option. The American call option price therefore will be higher.

Continuous Dividend Yield

Another approach to the problem of adjusting the Black-Scholes formula for dividends on the stock is to assume the dividend is paid continuously at a known yield. This method assumes the dividend accrues continuously, which means that a dividend is constantly being paid. We express the annual rate as a percentage, δ. For example, let the Digital Equipment stock have an annual dividend yield of $\delta = .04$. Given the current stock price of \$164, the annual dividend is $164(.04) = \$6.56$. This dividend is not paid in four quarterly installments of \$1.64 each; rather, it accrues continuously in very small increments that are reinvested and accumulate over the year to \$6.56. Because the stock price fluctuates throughout the year, the actual dividend can change but the yield will remain constant. Thus, this model does not require the assumption that the dividend is known or is constant; it requires only that the dividend being paid at that instant be a constant percentage of the stock price.

The adjustment procedure requires substituting the value S_D for S in the Black-Scholes model, where S_D is defined as follows:

$$S_D = Se^{-\delta T}.$$

The expression $S(1 - e^{-\delta T})$ is the present value of the dividends. Subtracting this from S gives S_D as given above. The adjustment removes the present value of the dividends during the option's life from the stock price.

In this problem, S_D would be $164e^{-(.04)(.0959)} = 163.37$. Plugging this into the formulas gives a value of d_1 of $-.0100$ and a value of d_2 of $-.0998$. The values of $N(-.01)$ and $N(-.10)$ are .4960 and .4602, respectively. Plugging the appropriate values into the Black-Scholes formula gives a value of C of \$5.477. Again we see that the effect of dividends is to lower the option's price under what it would be if there were no dividends. There is, of course, no assurance that the discrete and continuous dividend adjustments will give equivalent option prices. Because the Digital Equipment stock does not pay dividends, the dividend amount and the yield are merely illustrative assumptions and are not intended to be equivalent.

The assumption of a continuous dividend is unrealistic for most options on stocks; however, the convenience of using a single yield figure in lieu of obtaining the precise dividends could justify its use. For options on stocks, however, only a few dividends are paid over the option's life; thus the discrete dividend adjustment is not especially difficult. For index options, however, the use of a yield may be preferable. The dividends on the component stocks in the index would be paid more or less continuously, and it would be difficult to obtain an accurate day-by-day figure for the dividends.[4] Since yields on the major stock indices are reported weekly in *Value Line Options*, it may be convenient and practical to use this type of adjustment when valuing index options with the Black-Scholes model.[5]

Both of the adjustments presented here assume the option is still European and thus cannot be exercised early. However, Roll (1977), Geske (1979), and Whaley (1981) have developed a variation of the Black-Scholes model that provides a formula for the price of an American call option; this variation is beyond the scope of this text. Barone-Adesi and Whaley (1987) have developed a model that provides an approximate price of an American option. That model too is rather advanced; the interested reader is referred to Appendix 4C for a discussion of it.

ESTIMATING INPUTS TO THE BLACK-SCHOLES MODEL

As we noted earlier, the five inputs to the Black-Scholes model (without dividends) are the stock price, exercise price, risk-free rate, time to expiration, and variance. The stock price, exercise price, and time to expiration are directly observable. The risk-free rate and variance must be obtained from other sources.

The Risk-Free Rate

Chapter 3 showed how to identify the risk-free rate for the purpose of examining an option's boundary conditions. In the Black-Scholes framework, the risk-free rate must be expressed as a continuously compounded rate.

A simple risk-free rate assumes only annual compounding. A continuously compounded rate assumes interest compounds continuously. A simple rate can be converted to a continuously compounded rate by taking the natural logarithm of 1 plus the simple rate.

For example, if the simple rate is 6 percent, $100 invested at 6 percent for one year becomes $106. The equivalent continuously compounded rate is ln(1.06) = .0583. Thus, $100 invested at 5.83 percent compounded continuously grows to $106 in one year. The continuously compounded rate is always less than the simple rate. To convert a continuously compounded rate to a simple rate, use the exponential function, the inverse of the logarithmic function; that is, $e^{.0583} - 1 = .06$.

In our previous problem, the risk-free rate was 5.21 percent. We obtained this as ln(1.0535), where .0535 was the yield on the Treasury bill maturing on the day before the option's expiration.

---

[4]Dividends and ex-dividend dates are available in *Moody's Dividend Record* (New York: Moody's Investor Services). However, the adjustment procedure for an index option will depend on how the index is constructed.

[5]See Chance (1986) for an examination of the validity of applying the yield-adjusted Black-Scholes model to index options. Harvey and Whaley (1990) argue that the seasonality of dividends induces some bias into yield-based pricing models. They suggest the use of a binomial model with discrete cash dividends.

So far in this book, we have used the risk-free rate to make a number of calculations that involve the present value of the exercise price. In Chapter 3, we used discrete interest rates and computed $E(1 + r)^{-T}$; in this chapter, the Black-Scholes model contains the term Ee^{-rT}. Although we shall use the same symbol for the discrete and continuous risk-free rates, it is important to remember the difference between the two cases. In the first case, the calculation uses the discrete risk-free rate; in the second, it uses the continuous risk-free rate. Because of the relationship between the two rates, the present value of the exercise price is the same regardless of how it is calculated. For example, let the exercise price be 165 and the time to expiration be .0959. The discrete risk-free rate is .0535, and the continuous risk-free rate is $\ln(1.0535) = .0521$. Performing the calculations shows that $165(1.0535)^{-.0959} = 164.18$ and $165e^{-(.0521)(.0959)} = 164.18$.

Table 4.3 presents Black-Scholes values for the Digital Equipment July 165 call option using different levels of the risk-free rate. Because the table was constructed using a computer, the numerical precision is greater and the values differ slightly from those obtained working the problems manually. The table's most striking feature is the relative insensitivity of the call price to the risk-free rate. At a risk-free rate of 6 percent, the call is priced at $5.848. Cutting that rate in half to 3 percent lowers the option price only to $5.624; doubling it to 12 percent increases the price only to $6.313.

This effect implies that estimating the risk-free rate is not particularly critical to pricing the option correctly. For example, if one forgets to convert the simple return to the continuously compounded return, the error in the call price will be very small. Even if one makes a careless error and obtains the risk-free rate for the wrong expiration date, the effect on the option price is likely to be negligible. This does not mean that one should fail to exercise care in obtaining the risk-free rate. While one should use caution at all stages of the procedure, there may be some comfort in knowing that errors in the risk-free rate do not have a significant impact on the option price.

Although the risk-free rate must be estimated, doing so is not especially difficult. Estimating the standard deviation, however, is much more complicated.

The Standard Deviation

The variance or *standard deviation* is a critical variable in the Black-Scholes model. Sometimes this variable is referred to as the *volatility*, which is the term we shall use in this text. The volatility used in the model is defined as the standard deviation of the continuously compounded return on the stock.

Obtaining a reliable estimate of the volatility is difficult. Moreover, the model is extremely sensitive to that estimate. There are two approaches to estimating the volatility: the historical volatility and the implied volatility.

HISTORICAL VOLATILITY The *historical volatility* estimate is based on the assumption that the volatility that prevailed over the recent past will continue to hold in the future. First, we take a sample of returns on the stock over a recent

TABLE 4.3
Black-Scholes Prices Using Different Risk-Free Rates—July 165 Call

S = 164	E = 165	σ = .29	T = .0959
	Risk-Free Rate	**Black-Scholes Price**	
	.01	$5.477	
	.02	5.550	
	.03	5.624	
	.04	5.698	
	.05	5.773	
	.06	5.848	
	.07	5.924	
	.08	6.001	
	.09	6.078	
	.10	6.155	
	.11	6.234	
	.12	6.313	
	.13	6.392	
	.14	6.472	

period. We convert these returns to continuously compounded returns. Then we compute the standard deviation of the continuously compounded returns.

The returns can be daily, weekly, monthly, or any desired time interval. If we use daily returns, the result will be a daily standard deviation. To obtain the annualized standard deviation the model requires, we must multiply either the variance by the number of trading days in a year, which is about 250, or the standard deviation by $\sqrt{250}$. If we use monthly returns, the result will be a monthly variance (or standard deviation) and must be multiplied by either 12 (or $\sqrt{12}$) to obtain an annualized figure.

There is no minimum number of observations; a sample size of about 60 will be adequate in most cases. The trade-off in selecting a sample size is that the more observations one uses, the further back in time one must go. The further back one goes, the more likely the volatility will change. In the example used here we do not use many historical observations, but this is primarily to keep the computations brief.

Assume we have a series of J continuously compounded returns, where each return is identified as r_t^c, which equals $\ln(1 + r_t)$ and t goes from 1 to J. First, we calculate the mean return as

$$\bar{r}^c = \sum_{t=1}^{J} r_t^c / J.$$

Then the variance is

$$\sigma^2 = \frac{\sum_{t=1}^{J}(r_t^c - \bar{r}^c)^2}{(J-1)}$$

$$= \frac{\sum_{t=1}^{J}(r_t^c)^2 - \left(\sum_{t=1}^{J}r_t^c\right)^2 / J}{(J-1)}.$$

Note that we divide the sum of the squared deviations around the mean by $J - 1$. This is the appropriate divisor if the observations are a sample taken from a larger population. This adjustment is necessary for the estimate of the sample variance to be an unbiased estimate of the population variance.

Table 4.4 illustrates this procedure for the Digital Equipment stock using weekly closing prices. The simple return, r_t, is computed and converted to a continuously compounded return, r_t^c. Then the mean and variance of the series of continuously compounded returns are calculated. The resulting variance is a weekly variance, so it must be multiplied by 52 to be converted to an annual variance. The annualized standard deviation, or volatility, thus is .3755.

IMPLIED VOLATILITY   The second approach to estimating the volatility is called the *implied volatility*. This procedure assumes the option's market price reflects the stock's current volatility. The Black-Scholes (or any other acceptable) option pricing model is used to infer a standard deviation. The implied volatility is the standard deviation that makes the Black-Scholes price equal the option's current market price.

The implied volatility approach would be simple if the Black-Scholes equation could be solved for the standard deviation. Since that cannot be done, we obtain the solution by plugging in values of σ until we find the one that makes the Black-Scholes price equal the market price. This procedure can be quite laborious, and it is helpful to use a computer to do the calculations.

Let us estimate the implied volatility for the Digital Equipment July 165 call. The input values are $S = 164$, $E = 165$, $r = .0521$, and $T = .0959$. The market price of the call is 5.75. We need to find the value of σ that will make the Black-Scholes value come to 5.75. We must also be prepared to specify a certain degree of precision in our answer; that is, how close should the model price come to the market price or how many decimal places to the right of zero do we require in our implied volatility? For illustrative purposes, we shall use two decimal places in the implied volatility and stop the trial-and-error process when we determine that the true implied volatility is within .01 of our answer.

Let us begin by trying a σ of .5. Plugging into the Black-Scholes formula gives a call price of 10.037. Obviously this is too high, so let us try a σ of .2. Plugging into the Black-Scholes formula gives a call value of 3.97, which is too low. At a σ of .4, we get 8.015, a σ of .3 gives 5.99, a σ of .29 gives 5.789, and a σ of .28 gives 5.586. Thus, our answer is between .28 and .29. We shall use .29 as the implied standard deviation and $(.29)^2 = .0841$ as the implied variance.

Week	Price	r_t	r_t^c	$(r_t^c - \bar{r}^c)^2$
12/12	106.125	—	—	—
12/19	106.375	.0024	.0024	.0002
12/26	106.750	.0035	.0035	.0002
1/2	105.750	−.0094	−.0094	.0007
1/9	113.750	.0757	.0729	.0032
1/16	138.000	.2132	.1933	.0312
1/23	143.000	.0362	.0356	.0004
1/30	145.125	.0149	.0148	.0000
2/6	152.500	.0508	.0496	.0011
2/13	151.500	−.0066	−.0066	.0005
2/20	153.875	.0157	.0156	.0000
2/27	153.250	−.0041	−.0041	.0004
3/6	169.125	.1036	.0986	.0067
3/13	163.750	−.0318	−.0323	.0024
3/20	166.500	.0168	.0167	.0000
3/27	161.125	−.0323	−.0328	.0025
4/3	169.125	.0497	.0485	.0010
4/10	166.125	−.0177	−.0179	.0012
4/16	157.000	−.0549	−.0565	.0054
4/24	162.125	.0326	.0321	.0002
5/1	172.500	.0640	.0620	.0021
5/8	167.125	−.0312	−.0317	.0023
5/15	159.500	−.0456	−.0467	.0040
5/22	155.000	−.0282	−.0286	.0021
5/29	157.375	.0153	.0152	.0000
6/5	162.000	.0294	.0290	.0001
6/12	164.000	.0123	.0123	.0000
Totals			0.4352	0.0678

$\bar{r}^c = \dfrac{0.4352}{26} = .0167.$

$\sigma^2 = \dfrac{.0678}{25} = .0027.$

Annualized $\sigma^2 = .0027(52) = .1410.$

Annualized $\sigma = \sqrt{.1410} = .3755.$

Because σ is the stock's volatility, all options on a given stock with the same expiration should give the same implied volatility. For various reasons, including the possibility that the Black-Scholes model is deficient, different options on the same stock sometimes produce different implied volatilities.

Table 4.5 presents the implied standard deviations obtained for the two options whose exercise prices surround the stock price. The implied standard devia-

TABLE 4.5

Implied Standard Deviations of Digital Equipment Calls

	Expiration		
Exercise Price	**June**	**July**	**October**
160	.21	.30	.30
165	.25	.29	.32

tions range from .21 to .32. This forces us to choose a single value for the overall implied standard deviation.

Several methods have been suggested. Some involve taking a simple arithmetic average of the various implied volatilities. Others recommend using a weighted average. Still others simply select the implied standard deviation of the option whose exercise price is closest to the current stock price.

Beckers (1981) compared the predictive power of implied and historical volatilities. Beckers found that the implied standard deviation did a better job of predicting the actual future standard deviation than did the historical standard deviation. The implied standard deviation of the option with the exercise price closest to the stock price was a better predictor of the future standard deviation than were those formed using various weighting schemes.

Becker's result is particularly useful because it turns out that the implied volatility of an at-the-money call option can be solved directly rather than through the tedious trial-and-error process just described. Brenner and Subrahmanyam (1988) have shown that an at-the-money call price is approximately given as

$$C \cong (0.398)S\sigma\sqrt{T}.$$

Thus, the implied volatility of an at-the-money call can be obtained as

$$\sigma \cong \frac{C}{(0.398)S\sqrt{T}},$$

where C is the market price of the call. For example, our Digital Equipment July 165 has $C = 5.75$, $S = 164$, and $T = .0959$. Thus,

$$\sigma \cong \frac{5.75}{(0.398)164\sqrt{.0959}} = .2845.$$

Of course, this particular call is not precisely at-the-money, but the answer is very close to its actual implied volatility, which we obtained earlier by trial and error.

S = 164	E = 165	r = .0521	T = .0959
	Standard Deviation	**Black-Scholes Price**	
	.05	$0.0927	
	.10	1.9400	
	.15	2.9530	
	.20	3.9660	
	.25	4.9780	
	.30	5.9910	
	.35	7.0030	
	.40	8.0150	
	.45	9.0270	
	.50	10.0370	
	.55	11.0480	
	.60	12.0570	
	.65	13.0660	
	.70	14.0740	
	.75	15.0820	
	.80	16.0880	
	.85	17.0930	
	.90	18.0970	
	.95	19.1010	

There is, however, an enigma in using the implied volatility. To compute an implied volatility, one must assume the option is correctly priced. This implied volatility is then used to compute a theoretical option price at a subsequent date. The theoretical price is compared to the actual option price to determine whether the option is correctly priced. Thus, it is necessary to assume that at one point in time the option is correctly priced, while at another it is incorrectly priced. When is it truly correctly priced? We do not really know.

THE SENSITIVITY OF THE CALL PRICE TO THE VOLATILITY   Table 4.6 gives the price of the July 165 call using different standard deviations. The figures suggest that the option price is very sensitive to the standard deviation. Thus, in addition to necessitating estimation of the standard deviation, the model is quite sensitive to the estimate used. This is also one of the reasons why options attract so much speculative interest. If everyone agreed on the volatility estimate, the option would always be correctly priced and there would be no reason to buy or sell. It is the ambiguity of the volatility estimation that leads to disagreement among traders. This disagreement, in turn, leads to trading among those who believe the option is incorrectly priced.[6]

THE BINOMIAL MODEL AND THE BLACK-SCHOLES MODEL

Earlier in the chapter, we briefly mentioned that the binomial model price will converge to the Black-Scholes price when n is large. Now we shall see how that is accomplished. Again let us take the Digital Equipment July 165 call. In the binomial example, we looked at a one-period call and then a two-period call. The two cases were options with different expirations. Now we compute the value of a single option when its life is divided into a greater number of periods. When we increase the number of periods, the length of each period decreases.

We start off with the inputs used in the Black-Scholes model, $S = 164$, $E = 165$, $r = .0521$, $T = .0959$, and $\sigma = .29$. To operate in the binomial framework, we must convert the continuously compounded risk-free rate to a discrete rate as we described earlier. Thus, $e^{.0521} - 1 = .0535$, which is our risk-free rate. Now let n equal the number of periods used. For a given n, the inputs in the binomial model are

Risk-free rate $= (1 + r)^{T/n} - 1$

Up parameter(u) $= e^{\sigma\sqrt{T/n}} - 1$

Down parameter(d) $= \left[\dfrac{1}{1+u}\right] - 1$

For n = 1, we have a risk-free rate of

$$(1.0535)^{.0959/1} - 1 = .0050,$$

an up parameter of

$$u = e^{.29\sqrt{.0959/1}} - 1 = .094,$$

and a down parameter of

$$\left(\frac{1}{1.094}\right) - 1 = -.0859.$$

Plugging into the binomial model gives us a call price of 7.25. This is not particularly close to the Black-Scholes value of 5.803, but we should not expect it to be

---

[6]Mark Twain in *Puddenhead Wilson* (1894) expressed this point succintly by saying, "It were not best that we should think alike; it is difference of opinion that makes horse races."

TABLE 4.7
Convergence of the Binomial Price to the Black-Scholes Price

S = 164, E = 165, r = .0535 (discrete), σ = .29, T = .0959
Black-Scholes Price = 5.803

n	u	d	r	c
1	.0940	−.0859	.0050	7.250
2	.0656	−.0615	.0025	5.350
5	.0410	−.0394	.0010	6.076
10	.0289	−.0280	.0005	5.755
25	.0181	−.0178	.0002	5.829
50	.0128	−.0126	.0001	5.796

just yet. However, in Table 4.7 notice what happens as we increase the number of time periods, n. (Of course, when n is large, these calculations must be done on a computer.) The binomial price with n = 50 is almost 5.80, the Black-Scholes price. Note that the binomial estimates bounce around the Black-Scholes price until settling down to a value close to that price.

Option pricing models have been developed primarily for call options. We now turn our attention to the pricing of put options.

PUT OPTION PRICING MODELS

Chapter 3 showed that regardless of whether the stock pays dividends, it may be optimal to exercise an American put option early. Because the time at which this will occur is unpredictable, a put option is more difficult to price. There has been some progress, however. Approximations by Barone-Adesi and Whaley (1987), Brennan and Schwartz (1977), Johnson (1983), and Blomeyer (1986) and exact but more complex solutions by Geske and Johnson (1984) and Parkinson (1977) have provided formulas for the pricing of puts.

Because of the mathematics involved in those papers, the models are beyond the scope of this text.[7] Fortunately, however, we can gain some insights simply by using the Black-Scholes call option pricing model and put-call parity.

Recall that the put-call parity formula gives the relationship between a put price and a call price. Expressing the put price as a function of the call price, we have

$$P_e(S,T,E) = C_e(S,T,E) - S + E(1+r)^{-T}.$$

[7]However, the Barone-Adesi/Whaley model is presented in Appendix 4C.

In the Black-Scholes world, it is necessary to use continuous compounding and discounting. Restating put-call parity so that the present value of the exercise price is computed using continuous discounting gives

$$P_e(S,T,E) = C_e(S,T,E) - S + Ee^{-rT},$$

where, as discussed earlier, r is expressed as a continuously compounded rate. Then we can substitute the Black-Scholes value for the call price. Letting P stand for $P_e(S,T,E)$ gives the Black-Scholes European put option pricing model:

$$P = Ee^{-rT}[1 - N(d_2)] - S[1 - N(d_1)],$$

where d_1 and d_2 are the same as in the call option pricing model.

In the example of the July 165 call, the values of $N(d_1)$ and $N(d_2)$ were .5120 and .4761, respectively. Plugging into the formula, we get

$$P = 165e^{-(.0521)(.0959)}(1 - .4761) - 164(1 - .5120)$$
$$= 5.981.$$

The actual market price of the July 165 put was 6. Because this price must also include a premium for the additional benefit of early exercise, the difference between the market and model prices could be the effect of early exercise. In other words, if the put option pricing model reflected the early exercise premium, it would produce a higher theoretical price.

A Riskless Hedge with Puts[*]

Earlier in the chapter, we constructed a riskless hedge with calls. The number of shares for each call was the value $\partial C/\partial S$, which is $N(d_1)$. We can do the same for puts, but the optimal hedge ratio will differ.

Consider a portfolio consisting of h units of stock and one put. The portfolio initially is worth the amount V, where V is

$$V = hS + P.$$

If we are hedged, this portfolio's value will not change as the stock price changes. To achieve this objective, we set $\partial V/\partial S = 0$:

$$\frac{\partial V}{\partial S} = h + \frac{\partial P}{\partial S} = 0.$$

[*]This section requires the use of calculus.

Solving for h gives

$$h = -\frac{\partial P}{\partial S}.$$

Now we need to know the value of $\partial P/\partial S$. To find this, we simply differentiate the right-hand side of the put-call parity formula:

$$\frac{\partial P}{\partial S} = \frac{\partial C}{\partial S} - 1.$$

Thus, the hedge ratio is $-[N(d_1) - 1]$.

Because the value of $N(d_1) - 1$ is negative, the minus sign in front makes the overall hedge ratio positive. This indicates that if one takes a long position in stock, one must also be long in puts.

In this example, the value of $\partial C/\partial S$ was .5120, so $\partial P/\partial S$ is $-.4880$. For each dollar change in the stock price, the put changes by .4880 in the opposite direction. In this problem, the hedge ratio will be .4880 shares for each put; therefore, if we buy 1,000 puts, we should also buy 488 shares. If the stock price increases by $1, we will gain $488 on the stock and lose $488 on the puts. This result, of course, is only an approximation, because the partial derivative reflects the change in the put price for a very small change in the stock price.

Early Exercise of a Put

Chapter 3 showed that at a very low stock price, a put will lose all of its time value. Any stock price below that will trigger an early exercise if the put is exercisable. The critical stock price, $S_e^\ddagger$, was shown to be the one that results in

$$P = E - S_e^\ddagger,$$

which occurs if $C = E(1 - e^{-rT})$;[8] that is, we need to know what stock price will cause this relationship to hold. Using the Black-Scholes European put option pricing formula, we can solve iteratively for $S_e^\ddagger$.

To illustrate this procedure, consider the Digital Equipment October 170 put, which has a time to expiration of .3452. Using the risk-free rate of .0574, the critical value of interest is

$$E(1 - e^{-rT}) = 170(1 - e^{-(.0574)(.3452)}) = 3.3353.$$

---

[8]The value of $S_e^\ddagger$ is only a rough approximation of the stock price at which early exercise should occur. This is because $S_e^\ddagger$ can be derived only with the European put option pricing model. The actual critical price, $S_a^\ddagger$, can be much lower. Our interest in the value of $S_e^\ddagger$ is in tracking its path as it moves upward toward the exercise price. This path is similar to that of the actual critical stock price, $S_a^\ddagger$.

TABLE 4.8

Critical Stock Price for Early Exercise of Digital Equipment October 170 Put

Date	Days to Expiration	Time to Expiration	$E(1 - e^{-rT})$	Critical Stock Price ($S_e^{\ddagger}$)
6/12	126	.3452	3.3353	146.1
6/19	119	.3260	3.1518	146.4
6/26	112	.3068	2.9675	146.7
7/3	105	.2877	2.7843	147.0
7/10	98	.2685	2.5999	147.4
7/17	91	.2493	2.4153	147.8
7/24	84	.2301	2.2306	148.2
7/31	77	.2110	2.0465	148.6
8/7	70	.1918	1.8613	149.2
8/14	63	.1726	1.6759	149.7
8/21	56	.1534	1.4903	150.3
8/28	49	.1342	1.3045	151.0
9/4	42	.1151	1.1194	151.8
9/11	35	.0959	0.9332	152.8
9/18	28	.0767	0.7468	153.9
9/25	21	.0575	0.5602	155.3
10/2	14	.0384	0.3743	157.0
10/9	7	.0192	0.1873	159.8
10/16	0	.0000	0.0000	170.0

We need to find the stock price that will cause the call price to equal 3.3353. At that stock price, the put will be worth the intrinsic value.

Note that the current stock price is not a factor in identifying the critical stock price; however, the two prices will be compared to determine if early exercise currently is justified. The critical stock price will change through time. The value of T will vary, and a path of critical stock prices can be found that will indicate the critical stock price at different times in the put's life.

Because the solution is derived by plugging in values of the stock price until the correct one is found, it is helpful to work it out on a computer. Table 4.8 and Figure 4.4 indicate the critical stock prices for the October 170 put.

Take the first entry in the table. On June 12, the October 170 put option has 126 days remaining until expiration. The time to expiration is .3452. At a stock price of about 146.1, the put will be worth $E - S$, because the call will be worth $E(1 - e^{-rT})$. Seven days later, the time to expiration is .3260 and the critical stock price is about 146.4. As we move closer and closer to expiration, the critical stock price slowly rises. Then, in the last two weeks, the critical stock price rises steeply. At expiration, the critical stock price is, of course, the exercise price.

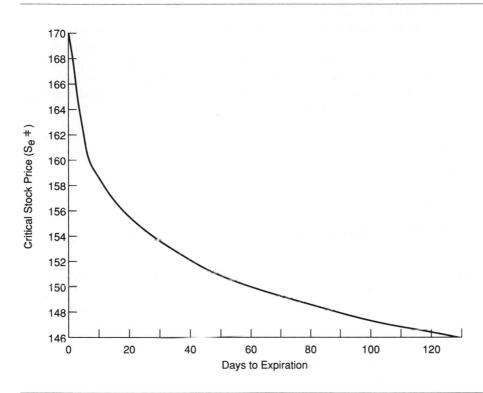

SUMMARY

This chapter examined option pricing models. Starting with the simple one-period binomial option pricing model, it developed the formula and illustrated why investors' actions would force it to hold. Then it extended the one-period model to a two-period world. Here the model was shown to be only slightly more complex but more realistic.

One reason for presenting the binomial model was to provide a foundation for the Black-Scholes model. One can avoid the mathematics necessary for deriving the Black-Scholes model if one can grasp the intuition behind the binomial model.

The Black-Scholes model was shown to be a practical method for obtaining a theoretical price for a call option. The chapter reviewed the effects of changing the various inputs and observed the difficulty of obtaining certain inputs, such as the volatility of the underlying stock. The volatility was shown to be the most critical item because it must be estimated. Moreover, the model was found to be highly sensitive to the volatility.

By using put-call parity, the Black-Scholes model can also be applied to European puts. This makes it possible to determine the approximate stock price below which a put should be exercised early.

Chapters 3 and 4 examined option pricing theory and the economic rationale behind the pricing of options. Chapters 5 and 6 examine some of the popular practical option trading strategies. However, we should not lose sight of the theoretical underpinnings of options. In fact, the basic principles of pricing options will remain with us for the next two chapters and will help us understand and evaluate trading strategies.

Questions and Problems

1. Explain the similarities and differences between pricing an option by its boundary conditions and using an exact option pricing formula.

2. Explain how an n-period binomial option pricing model is similar to the Black-Scholes model.

3. What is the principal benefit of studying binomial option pricing models?

4. Discuss each assumption of the Black-Scholes model, and comment on the extent to which it is violated in the real world.

5. What is the most critical variable in the Black-Scholes model? Explain.

6. Consider the various versions of the Black-Scholes model presented here that allow for the inclusion of dividends. Why are these models not strictly appropriate for pricing most options?

7. Explain why it is much more difficult to derive an exact formula for pricing an American put option than for a call option.

8. Suppose you are planning to use the Black-Scholes model to price a call option. Unfortunately, you have no access to any information on Treasury bill yields. You elect to substitute the yield on high-grade commercial paper. Assess the likely implications of this substitution.

9. Suppose you subscribe to a service that gives you estimates of the theoretically correct standard deviations of stocks. You note that the implied standard deviation of a particular option is substantially higher than the theoretical standard deviation. What action should you take?

10. Consider a two-period, two-state world. Let the current stock price be 45 and the risk-free rate be 5 percent. Each period the stock price can go either up by 10 percent or down by 10 percent. A call option expiring at the end of the second period has an exercise price of 40.

    a. Find the stock price sequence.

    b. Determine the possible prices of the call at expiration.

    c. Find the possible prices of the call at the end of the first period.

    d. What is the current price of the call?

    e. What is the initial hedge ratio?

f.   What are the two possible hedge ratios at the end of the first period?

g.   Construct an example showing that the hedge works. Make sure the example illustrates how the hedge portfolio earns the risk-free rate over both periods.

h.   What would an investor do if the call were overpriced? If it were underpriced?

11. Consider the following binomial option pricing problem involving an American call. This call has two periods to go before expiring. Its stock price is 30, and its exercise price is 25. The risk-free rate is .05. The value of u is .15, and the value of d is –.1. The dividend yield is .06. Find the value of the call.

The following option prices were observed for calls and puts on IBM for the trading day of July 6 of a particular year. Use this information in problems 12 through 20. The stock was priced at 165 1/8. The expirations were July 17, August 21, and October 16. The risk-free rates associated with the three expirations were .0503, .0535, and .0571, respectively.

	Calls			Puts		
Strike	**Jul**	**Aug**	**Oct**	**Jul**	**Aug**	**Oct**
155	10.5	11.75	14	.1875	1.25	2.75
160	6	8.125	11.125	.75	2.75	4.5
165	2.6875	5.25	8.125	2.375	4.75	6.75
170	.8125	3.25	6	5.750	7.5	9

12. Let the standard deviation of the continuously compounded return on the stock be .21. Ignore dividends. Answer the following:

a.   What is the theoretically correct price of the October 165 call?

b.   Based on your answer in part a, recommend a riskless strategy.

c.   If the stock price decreases by $1, how will the option position offset the loss on the stock?

13. Use the Black-Scholes European put option pricing formula for the October 165 put option. Repeat parts a, b, and c of question 12 with respect to the put.

14. IBM pays a $1.10 dividend with an ex-dividend date of September 10. Rework part a of problem 12 using an appropriate dividend-adjusted procedure. What assumption does this procedure make that is not strictly correct?

15. On July 6, the dividend yield on IBM stock is 2.7 percent. Rework part a of problem 12 using the yield-based dividend adjustment procedure.

16. Determine when the following put options should be exercised early:

    a.   August 165

    b.   July 170

17. Following is the sequence of daily stock prices on IBM for the preceding month of June:

Date	Price	Date	Price
6/1	159.875	6/16	162.000
6/2	157.250	6/17	161.375
6/3	160.250	6/18	160.875
6/4	161.375	6/19	161.375
6/5	160.000	6/22	163.250
6/8	161.250	6/23	164.875
6/9	159.875	6/24	166.125
6/10	157.750	6/25	167.875
6/11	157.625	6/26	166.500
6/12	156.625	6/29	165.375
6/15	159.625	6/30	162.500

Estimate the historical standard deviation of the IBM stock for use in the Black-Scholes model. (Ignore dividends on the stock.)

18. Estimate the implied volatility of the August 165 call. Compare your answer with that obtained in problem 17. Use trial and error. Stop when your answer is within .01 of the true implied volatility.

19. Repeat problem 18 using the approximation for an at-the-money call. Compare your answer with the one you obtained in problem 18. Is the approximation worthwhile?

20. In problem 12, you estimated the value of the October 165 call using the Black-Scholes model. Now estimate the value of that option using the binomial model for 1, 5, 10, 25, and 50 time periods. Be sure to make the appropriate adjustments to the risk-free rate and the up and down parameters. You will need to use the binomial program on the software diskette.

21. (Concept Problem) Find the value of an American put option using the binomial option pricing model. The parameters are $S = 62$, $E = 70$, $r = .08$, $u = .1$, and $d = -.05$. There are no dividends. Use $n = 2$ periods.

22. (Concept Problem) Find the value of a European call option using the Black-Scholes option pricing model. The parameters are $S = 80$, $E = 80$, $r = .05$, $\sigma = .35$, and $T = .25$. Determine the delta and estimate the change in the call price if the stock goes to the following prices: 70, 75, 78, 79, 81, 82, 85, 90. Then

compute the Black-Scholes values for each of these new stock prices. Compare your estimates with the actual prices, and comment on the differences. Note: You may wish to use the Black-Scholes spreadsheet on the software diskette.

References

Barone-Adesi, Giovanni, and Robert E. Whaley. "Efficient Analytic Approximation of American Option Values." *The Journal of Finance* 42 (June, 1987): 301–320.

Beckers, Stan. "Standard Deviations Implied in Option Prices as Predictors of Future Stock Price Variability." *Journal of Banking and Finance* 5 (September 1981): 363–382.

Black, Fischer. "Fact and Fantasy in the Use of Options." *Financial Analysts Journal* 31 (July–August 1975): 36–41, 61–72.

Black, Fischer, and Myron Scholes. "The Pricing of Options and Corporate Liabilities." *Journal of Political Economy* 81 (May–June 1973): 637–659.

Black, Fischer, and Myron Scholes. "The Valuation of Option Contracts and a Test of Market Efficiency." *The Journal of Finance* 27 (May 1972): 399–418.

Blomeyer, Edward C. "An Analytic Approximation for the American Put Price for Options on Stocks with Dividends." *Journal of Financial and Quantitative Analysis* 21 (June 1986): 229–233.

Blomeyer, Edward C., and Robert C. Klemkosky. "Tests of Market Efficiency of American Call Options." In *Option Pricing*, edited by Menachem Brenner. Lexington, Mass.: Heath, 1983.

Bookstaber, Richard M. *Option Pricing and Investment Strategies*, Chapters 3, 4, 5. Chicago: Probus Publishing, 1987.

Brennan, Michael J., and Eduardo S. Schwartz. "The Valuation of American Put Options." *The Journal of Finance* 32 (May 1977): 449–462.

Brenner, Menachem, and Marti G. Subrahmanyam. "A Simple Formula to Compute the Implied Volatility." *Financial Analysts Journal* 45 (September–October 1988): 80–83.

Chance, Don M. "Empirical Tests of the Pricing of Index Call Options." *Advances in Futures and Options Research* 1, part A (1986): 141–166.

Chiras, Donald P., and Steven Manaster. "The Information Content of Option Prices and a Test of Market Efficiency." *Journal of Financial Economics* 6 (June–September 1978): 213–234.

Cornell, Bradford. "Using the Option Pricing Model to Measure the Uncertainty Producing Effect of Major Announcements." *Financial Management* 7 (Spring 1978): 54–59.

Cornell, Bradford, and Dhafrallah Hammani. "Option Pricing in Bull and Bear Markets." *The Journal of Portfolio Management* 5 (Summer 1979): 30–32.

Cox, John C., Stephen A. Ross, and Mark Rubinstein. "Option Pricing: A Simplified Approach." *Journal of Financial Economics* 7 (September 1979): 229–263.

Cox, John C., and Mark Rubinstein. *Options Markets*, Chapters 5, 6. Englewood Cliffs, N.J.: Prentice-Hall, 1985.

Cox, John C., and Mark Rubinstein. "A Survey of Alternative Option Pricing Models." In *Option Pricing*, edited by Menachem Brenner. Lexington, Mass.: Heath, 1983.

Evnine, Jeremy, and Andrew Rudd. "Index Options: The Early Evidence." *The Journal of Finance* 40 (1985): 743–756.

Farkas, Karen L., and Robert E. Hoskin. "Testing a Valuation Model for American Puts." *Financial Management* 8 (Autumn 1979): 51–56.

Finnerty, Joseph E. "The CBOE and Market Efficiency." *Journal of Financial and Quantitative Analysis* 13 (March 1978): 29–38.

Galai, Dan. "Tests of Market Efficiency of the Chicago Board Options Exchange." *Journal of Business* 50 (April 1977): 167–197.

Geske, Robert. "A Note on an Analytic Formula for Unprotected American Call Options on Stocks with Known Dividends." *Journal of Financial Economics* 7 (December 1979): 375–380.

Geske, Robert, and H. E. Johnson. "The American Put Option Valued Analytically." *The Journal of Finance* 39 (December 1984): 1511–1524.

Gultekin, N. Bulent, Richard J. Rogalski, and Seha M. Tinic. "Option Pricing Model Estimates: Some Empirical Results." *Financial Management* 12 (Spring 1982): 58–69.

Hart, James F. "The Riskless Option Hedge: An Incomplete Guide." *The Journal of Portfolio Management* 4 (Winter 1978): 58–63.

Harvey, Campbell R., and Robert E. Whaley. "The Impact of Discrete Cash Dividends on the Valuation of S&P 100 Index Options." Working paper, Fuqua School of Business, Duke University, 1990.

Hsia, Chi-Cheng. "On Binomial Option Pricing." *The Journal of Financial Research* 6 (Spring 1983): 41–50.

Hull, John. *Options, Futures, and Other Derivative Securities*, Chapters 4, 8. Englewood Cliffs, N.J.: Prentice-Hall, 1989.

Jarrow, Robert, and Andrew Rudd. *Option Pricing*, Chapters 7–13. Homewood, Ill.: Irwin, 1983.

Johnson, H. E. "An Analytic Approximation of the American Put Price." *Journal of Financial and Quantitative Analysis* 18 (March 1983): 141–148.

Latané, Henry A., and Richard J. Rendleman, Jr. "Standard Deviations of Stock Price Ratios Implied in Option Prices." *The Journal of Finance* 31 (May 1976): 369–382.

Macbeth, James D., and Larry J. Merville. "Tests of the Black-Scholes and Cox Call Option Valuation Models." *The Journal of Finance* 35 (May 1980): 285–300.

Macbeth, James D., and Larry J. Merville. "An Empirical Examination of the Black-Scholes Call Option Pricing Model." *The Journal of Finance* 34 (December 1979): 1173–1186.

Manaster, Steven, and Gary Koehler. "The Calculation of Implied Variances from the Black-Scholes Model: A Note." *The Journal of Finance* 37 (March 1982): 227–230.

Parkinson, Michael. "Option Pricing: The American Put." *Journal of Business* 50 (January 1977): 21–36.

Rao, Ramesh K. S. "Modern Option Pricing Models: A Dichotomous Classification." *The Journal of Financial Research* 4 (Spring 1981): 33–44.

Rendleman, Richard J., Jr., and Brit J. Bartter. "Two-State Option Pricing." *The Journal of Finance* 34 (December 1979): 1093–1110.

Ritchken, Peter. *Options: Theory, Strategy, and Applications*, Chapters 8–10. Glenview, Ill.: Scott, Foresman, 1987.

Roll, Richard. "An Analytic Valuation Formula for Unprotected American Call Options on Stocks with Known Dividends." *Journal of Financial Economics* 5 (November 1977): 251–258.

Rubinstein, Mark. "Nonparametric Tests of Alternative Option Pricing Models Using All Reported Trades and Quotes on the 30 Most Active CBOE Option Classes from August 23, 1976 through August 31, 1978." *The Journal of Finance* 40 (June 1985): 455–480.

Smith, Clifford W., Jr. "Option Pricing: A Review." *Journal of Financial Economics* 3 (January–March 1976): 3–51.

Sterk, William. "Comparative Performance of the Black-Scholes and Roll-Geske-Whaley Option Pricing Models." *Journal of Financial and Quantitative Analysis* 18 (September 1983a): 345–354.

Sterk, William. "Option Pricing and the In- and Out-of-the-Money Bias." *Financial Management* 12 (Winter 1983b): 47–53.

Sterk, William. "Tests of Two Models for Valuing Call Options on Stocks with Dividends." *The Journal of Finance* 37 (December 1982): 88–99.

Trennepohl, Gary. "A Comparison of Listed Option Premiums and Black-Scholes Model Prices: 1973–1979." *Journal of Financial Research* 4 (Spring 1981): 11–20.

Trippi, Robert R. "A Test of Option Market Efficiency Using a Random-Walk Valuation Model." *Journal of Economics and Business* 29 (Winter 1977): 93–98.

Whaley, Robert E. "Valuation of American Call Options on Dividend Paying Stocks: Empirical Tests." *Journal of Financial Economics* 19 (March 1982): 29–58.

Whaley, Robert E. "On the Valuation of American Call Options on Stocks with Known Dividends." *Journal of Financial Economics* 9 (June 1981): 207–212.

---

appendix 4A

The n-Period Binomial Model

With n periods remaining until the option expires, the call price is given by the formula

$$C = \frac{\sum_{j=0}^{n} \frac{n!}{j!(n-j)!} p^j (1-p)^{n-j} \text{Max}[0, S(1+u)^j(1+d)^{n-j} - E]}{(1+r)^n}.$$

This ominous formula actually is not nearly as complex as it seems. It simply captures all of the possible stock price paths over the n periods until the option expires. Consider the example from the text in a three-period world where j will go from 0 to 3. First, we find the summation of the following terms.

For $j = 0$,

$$\frac{3!}{0!3!}(.857)^0(.143)^3 \text{Max}[0, 60(1.15)^0(.80)^3 - 50] = 0.$$

For $j = 1$,

$$\frac{3!}{1!2!}(.857)^1(.143)^2 \text{Max}[0, 60(1.15)^1(.80)^2 - 50] = 0.$$

For $j = 2$,

$$\frac{3!}{2!1!}(.857)^2(.143)^1 \text{Max}[0, 60(1.15)^2(.80)^1 - 50] = 4.2473.$$

For $j = 3$,

$$\frac{3!}{3!0!}(.857)^3(.143)^0 \text{Max}[0, 60(1.15)^3(.80)^0 - 50] = 25.9653.$$

Adding these and dividing by $(1.10)^3$ gives

$$\frac{0+0+4.2473+25.9653}{(1.10)^3} = 22.70.$$

The value of the call is higher in the three-period world than in the two-period world. This reflects the effect of a longer time to expiration.

The n-period binomial formula works because the factorial term, $n!/j!(n-j)!$, counts the number of ways a stock price could end up at a certain level. For example, when $n = 3$, the stock price at the end of the third period could be either S_{d^3}, S_{ud^2}, S_{u^2d}, or S_{u^3}. There is only one path the stock could have taken for it to end up at S_{d^3}: to go down three straight periods. There is only one path it could have taken for it to end up at S_{u^3}: to go up three straight periods. For the stock price to end up at S_{ud^2}, there are three possible routes: (1) up, down, down; (2) down, down, up; or (3) down, up, down. For the stock to end up at S_{u^2d}, there are three paths: (1) up, down, up; (2) down, up, up; and (3) up, up, down. The factorial expression enumerates the routes that a stock can take to reach a certain level. The remaining terms in the formula then apply exactly as we have seen in the one- and two-period cases.

---

appendix 4B

Comparative Statics of the Black-Scholes Model*

The Black-Scholes model is

$$C = SN(d_1) - Ee^{-rT}N(d_2),$$

where

$$d_1 = \frac{\ln(S/E) + [r + (\sigma^2/2)]T}{\sigma\sqrt{T}}$$

$$d_2 = d_1 - \sigma\sqrt{T}$$

*This appendix requires the use of calculus.

The analysis of changes in the call price for an infinitesimally small change in the underlying variables is called the *comparative statics*. These effects are characterized by the derivatives of C with respect to S, E, r, T, and σ:

$$\frac{\partial C}{\partial S} = N(d_1) > 0. \text{ This is called the } \textit{delta}.$$

$$\frac{\partial C}{\partial E} = -e^{-rT}N(d_2) < 0.$$

$$\frac{\partial C}{\partial r} = ETN(d_2)e^{-rT} > 0. \text{ This is called the } \textit{rho}.$$

$$\frac{\partial C}{\partial T} = \left[\left(\frac{S\sigma}{2\sqrt{T}}\right)\left(\frac{\partial N(d_1)}{\partial d_1}\right)\right] + re^{-rT}EN(d_2) > 0. \text{ The value}$$

$$-(\partial C/\partial T) \text{ is called the } \textit{theta}.$$

$$\frac{\partial C}{\partial \sigma} = S\sqrt{T}\left(\frac{\partial N(d_1)}{\partial d_1}\right) > 0. \text{ This is called the } \textit{vega}, \textit{lambda}, \text{ or}$$

$$\textit{kappa}.$$

$$\frac{\partial}{\partial S}\left(\frac{\partial C}{\partial S}\right) = \frac{\left(\dfrac{\partial N(d_1)}{\partial d_1}\right)}{S\sigma\sqrt{T}} > 0. \text{ This is called the } \textit{gamma}.$$

These values are useful in understanding why call option prices change. As discussed in the text, delta measures the approximate change in the call price for a $1 change in the stock price. Gamma measures the approximate change in the delta for a $1 change in the stock price. Gamma is always positive, meaning that the delta increases as the stock price increases. The magnitude of the gamma can be useful in determining how often the hedge ratio needs to be revised. The gamma is positive but fairly small when the call is deep-in- or deep-out-of-the-money and is fairly large when the call is at-the-money.

Rho measures the effect of a change in the risk-free rate on the value of the call. As we observed in the chapter, the risk-free rate has only a small impact on the call price. Theta is negative and measures the effect on the call price of moving closer to expiration. The call price, of course, declines as it moves toward expiration, but the rate of that decline varies, as we shall see in Chapter 6. Finally, vega, which is sometimes called *lambda* or *kappa*, measures the impact of changes in volatility on the call price. As we observed in the chapter, the call price is rather sensitive to changes in the volatility, and this measure can be used to compare the sensitivities of different calls.

appendix 4C

An Approximate American Option Pricing Model

In the chapter, the only American option pricing model we covered was the binomial model. This is because the mathematics requires the computation of some very complex probabilities and thus is beyond the scope of this text. There is, however, an American option pricing model that, although somewhat advanced, can be understood without resorting to advanced mathematics. This model was developed by Barone-Adesi and Whaley (1987) and we shall call it the *BAW model*.

It should be emphasized that this model is not an exact formula; it provides only an approximate price. However, the approximation is quite good and serves a useful purpose in distinguishing American from European options.

The BAW model incorporates a mathematical formula that behaves like the early exercise premium, which is the difference between the American and European option prices. The early exercise premium should be small when the option is deep-out-of-the-money and deep-in-the-money and should decline as expiration approaches. When the option is deep-in-the-money, it should sell for its intrinsic value. This early exercise premium is then added to the European option price given by the Black-Scholes formula, and the result is the American option price. The formula provides a critical stock price, above which an American call should be exercised and below which an American put should be exercised.

The formula for calls is

$$C_a = C_e + A_2 \left(\frac{S}{S^*} \right)^{q_2} \quad \text{when } S < S^*$$

$$C_e = S - E \qquad\qquad \text{when } S \geq S^*.$$

In this formula,

C_a = American call price

C_e = European call price given by the Black-Scholes formula in which S, E, r, T, σ, and δ are the parameters and were defined in the chapter

$$A_2 = \left(\frac{S^*}{q_2} \right) \left[1 - e^{-\delta T} N(d_1^*) \right]$$

$$q_2 = \frac{\left[-(N-1)+\sqrt{(N-1)^2+\dfrac{4M}{K}}\right]}{2}$$

$$K = 1 - e^{-rT}$$

$$N = \frac{2(r-\delta)}{\sigma^2}$$

$$M = \frac{2r}{\sigma^2}$$

S* is the critical stock price, above which the call would be exercised and would be worth S* − E. S* must be found implicitly by solving the following equation:

$$S^* - E = C_e^* + \frac{\left[1-e^{-\delta T}N(d_1^*)\right]S^*}{q_2},$$

where C_e^* is the Black-Scholes value when S* is the stock price and $N(d_1^*)$ is the cumulative normal probability when d_1 is computed using S*.

Consider the following example: S = 100, E = 100, r = .05, T = .25, σ = .3, and δ = .08. We choose a relatively high dividend yield to ensure the existence of an early exercise premium. First, we calculate

$$M = \frac{2(.05)}{(.3)^2} = 1.1111$$

$$N = \frac{2(.05-.08)}{(.3)^2} = -0.6667$$

$$K = 1 - e^{-.05(.25)} = 0.0124$$

$$q_2 = \frac{\left[-(-0.6667-1)+\sqrt{(-0.6667-1)^2+\left(\dfrac{4(1.1111)}{0.0124}\right)}\right]}{2}$$

$$= 10.3275.$$

Now we must solve for S*. This is a tedious procedure and should be done with a computer. The solution is S* = 127.3603. Let us check this out.

- *Left-hand side*: S* − E = 127.3603 − 100 = 27.3603.
- *Right-hand side*: Using 127.3603 in the Black-Scholes formula (don't forget δ = .08) gives a value of d_1 = 1.637 and N(1.637) = .9492 (using a computer

algorithm). The Black-Scholes value is $^*C_e = 26.5025$. Thus, the right-hand side is

$$26.5025 + \frac{\left[1 - e^{-.08(.25)}(.9492)\right](127.3603)}{10.3275} = 27.3608,$$

which is close enough.

Then

$$A_2 = \left(\frac{127.3603}{10.3275}\right)\left[1 - e^{-.08(.25)}(.9492)\right]$$

$$= .8583,$$

and, because $S < S^*(100 < 127.3603)$, we use the formula

$$C_a = 5.5206 + .8583\left(\frac{100}{127.3603}\right)^{10.3275} = 5.59,$$

where 5.5206 was obtained by using the Black-Scholes formula with $S = 100$. The early exercise premium thus is .07.

The formula for puts is

$$P_a = P_e + A_1\left(\frac{S}{S^{**}}\right)^{q_1} \quad \text{when } S > S^{**}$$

$$P_a = E - S \qquad \qquad \text{when } S \leq S^{**},$$

where

P_a = American put price

P_e = European put price given by the Black-Scholes formula

$$A_1 = \left(-\frac{S^{**}}{q_1}\right)\left[1 - e^{-\delta T}N(-d_1^{**})\right]$$

$$q_1 = \frac{\left[-(N-1) - \sqrt{(N-1)^2 + \frac{4M}{K}}\right]}{2}$$

K, N, and M are defined as before

S^{**} is the critical stock price, below which the put would be exercised and would be worth $E - S^{**}$. S^{**} must be found implicitly by solving the following equation:

$$E - S^{**} = P_e^{**} - \frac{\left[1 - e^{-\delta T}N\left(-d_1^{**}\right)\right]S^{**}}{q_1},$$

where P_e^{**} is the Black-Scholes put value using S^{**} as the stock price and $N(-d_1^{**})$ is the cumulative normal probability when d_1 is computed using S^{**} and then multiplied by -1.

Working the same problem that we worked with calls,

$$q_1 = \frac{-(-0.6667 - 1) - \sqrt{(-0.6667 - 1)^2 + \left(\frac{4(1.1111)}{0.0124}\right)}}{2}$$

$$= -8.6609.$$

The value of S^{**} is 56.2158. As a check,

- *Left-hand side*: $E - S^{**} = 100 - 56.2158 = 43.7842$
- *Right-hand side*: Using 56.2158 in the Black-Scholes formula gives a value of d_1 of -3.8148. Then $-d_1^{**} = 3.8148$, so $N(3.8148) = .9999$. The Black-Scholes value is $P_e^{**} = 43.6552$. Thus, the right-hand side is

$$43.6552 - \frac{\left[1 - e^{-.08(.25)}(.9999)\right](56.2158)}{-8.6609} = 43.7843,$$

which is close enough.

Then

$$A_1 = -\left(\frac{56.2158}{-8.6609}\right)\left[1 - e^{-.08(.25)}(.9999)\right] = 0.1292,$$

and, because $S > S^{**}$ ($100 > 56.2158$), we use the formula

$$P_a = 6.2585 + (0.1292)\left(\frac{100}{56.2158}\right)^{-8.6609} = 6.2594,$$

where 6.2585 is the Black-Scholes value using $S = 100$. At less than .01, the early exercise premium is very low.

The software diskette that accompanies the text contains a spreadsheet that performs all of the model's calculations.

appendix 4D

A Shortcut to the Calculation of Implied Volatility

Solving for the implied volatility can be a tedious trial-and-error process. However, Manaster and Koehler (1982) provide a shortcut that can quickly lead to the solution. The technique employs a Newton-Raphson search procedure.

Suppose that for a given standard deviation, σ^*, the Black-Scholes formula gives the call price as $C(\sigma^*)$. The true market price, however, is $C(\sigma)$, where σ is the true volatility. Manaster and Koehler recommend an initial guess of σ_1^*, where

$$\sigma_1^* = \sqrt{\left|\ln\left(\frac{S}{E}\right) + rT\right|\left(\frac{2}{T}\right)}.$$

Then compute the value of $C(\sigma_1^*)$ and compare it to the market price, $C(\sigma)$. If this is not close enough, the next guess should be

$$\sigma_2^* = \sigma_1^* - \frac{\left[C(\sigma_1^*) - C(\sigma)\right]e^{d_1^2/2}\sqrt{2\pi}}{S\sqrt{T}},$$

where d_1 is computed using σ_1^*. Then compute the value $C(\sigma_2^*)$ and compare it to the market price, $C(\sigma)$. If it is not close enough, the next guess should be

$$\sigma_3^* = \sigma_2^* - \frac{\left[C(\sigma_2^*) - C(\sigma)\right]e^{d_1^2/2}\sqrt{2\pi}}{S\sqrt{T}},$$

with d_1 computed using σ_2^*. Repeat the process until the model price is sufficiently close to the market price. In other words, given the ith guess of the implied volatility, the $(i + 1)$th guess should be

$$\sigma_{i+1}^* = \sigma_i^* - \frac{\left[C(\sigma_i^*) - C(\sigma)\right]e^{d_1^2/2}\sqrt{2\pi}}{S\sqrt{T}},$$

where d_1 is computed using σ_i^*.

Let us apply this procedure to the problem in the text. We have $S = 164$, $E = 165$, $T = .0959$, $r = .0521$, and $C(\sigma) = 5.75$. The initial guess for the implied volatility is

$$\sigma_1^* = \sqrt{\left|\ln\left(\frac{164}{165}\right) + .0521(.0959)\right|\left(\frac{2}{.0959}\right)} = .1503.$$

At a volatility of .1503, the Black-Scholes value is 2.959. The next guess should be

$$\sigma_2^* = .1503 - \frac{[2.959 - 5.75]e^{(.000012)^2/2}(2.5066)}{164\sqrt{.0959}} = .2881,$$

where .000012 is the value of d_1 computed from the Black-Scholes model using .1503 as the standard deviation. The value 2.5066 is $\sqrt{2\pi}$. The Black-Scholes price using .2881 as the volatility is 5.75.

Thus, we have found the solution in only two steps. In the chapter we noted that the implied volatility was .29, with the slight difference being due to rounding off our answer.

BASIC OPTION STRATEGIES

> *Strategy is a fancy word for a road map for getting from here to there,*
> *from the situation at hand to the situation one wishes to attain.*
>
> PAUL SEABURY and ANGELO CODEVILLA, War, 1989

One of the most interesting characteristics of an option is that it can be combined with stock or other options to produce a wide variety of alternative strategies. The profit possibilities are so diverse that virtually any investor can find an option strategy to suit his or her risk preference and market forecast.

In a world without options, the available strategies would be quite limited. If the market were expected to go up, one would buy stock; if it were expected to go down, one would sell short stock. Unfortunately, selling short stock requires an investor to meet certain requirements, such as having a minimum amount of capital to risk, selling short on an uptick or zero-plus tick,[1] and maintaining minimum margins. Options make it simple to convert one's forecast into a plan of action that will reward one if correct. Of course, any strategy will penalize one if one is wrong. With the judicious use of options, however, the penalties can be relatively small and known in advance.

---

[1]An *uptick* occurs when the price at which the stock is sold short is higher than the last price at which a transaction took place. A *zero-plus tick* occurs when the stock is sold short at the same price as that at which the last transaction took place but the last price change was an increase.

This and the next chapter examine some of the more popular option strategies. It is not possible to cover all the strategies option traders could use. The ones we examine here should provide a basic understanding of the process of analyzing option strategies. Further study and analysis of the more advanced and complex strategies can be done using the framework presented here.

This chapter presents the basic option strategies. These strategies are the easiest to understand and involve the fewest transactions. Specifically, we shall cover the strategies of calls, puts, and stock and combining calls with stock and puts with stock. We shall see how calls and stock can be combined to form puts and how puts and stock can be combined to form calls. Chapter 6 will look at spread strategies, which involve one short option and one long option, and combination strategies, which entail both puts and calls.

The approach we use here to analyze option strategies is to determine the profit a strategy will produce for a broad range of stock prices when the position is closed. This methodology is simple yet powerful enough to demonstrate its strengths. One attractive feature is that there are actually three ways to present the process. Because reinforcement enhances learning, we shall utilize all three presentations.

The first method is to determine an equation that gives the profit from the strategy as a function of the stock price when the position is closed. You will find that the equations are quite simple and build on skills covered in Chapters 3 and 4. The second method is a graphical analysis that uses the equations to construct graphs of the profit as a function of the stock price when the position is closed. The third approach is to use a specific numerical example to illustrate how the equations and graphs apply to real-world options. This is consistent with the approaches we took in previous chapters. We continue with the same Digital Equipment options previously examined.

As with our earlier analyses of options, we require several symbols. For convenience and because there are a few new notations, the following section presents the complete set of symbols.

TERMINOLOGY AND NOTATION

C = current call price
P = current put price
S = current stock price
T = time to expiration as a fraction of a year
E = exercise price
S_T = stock price at option's expiration
Π = profit from the strategy

The following symbols indicate the number of calls, puts, or shares of stock:

N_C = number of calls
N_P = number of puts
N_S = number of shares of stock

As indicated in Chapter 2, the standard number of calls, puts, and shares is 100. For our purposes, it will not matter if we use a simple number such as 1 or 2. When working with the numerical data, however, we shall assume a standard contract of options or block of stock, which, of course, means 100 options or shares.

The Profit Equations

One of the powerful features of the N_C, N_P, and N_S notation is that these numbers' signs indicate whether the position is long or short. For example,

> If $N_C > (<) 0$, the investor is buying (writing) calls
> If $N_P > (<) 0$, the investor is buying (writing) puts
> If $N_S > (<) 0$, the investor is buying (selling short) stock.

To determine the profit from a particular strategy, we need only know how many calls, puts, and shares of stock are involved, whether the position is long or short, the prices at which the options or stock were purchased or written, and the prices at which the positions were closed. With calls held to the expiration date, we already know that the call will be worth its intrinsic value at expiration. Thus, the profit can be written as

$$\Pi = N_C[\text{Max}(0, S_T - E) - C].$$

Notice how the sign of N_C allows the profit equation to give the profit for both the call buyer and the call writer. For example, a buyer with one call, $N_C = 1$, has a profit of

$$\Pi = \text{Max}(0, S_T - E) - C.$$

For the writer with one call, $N_C = -1$, profit is

$$\Pi = -\text{Max}(0, S_T - E) + C.$$

For a put option, the profit can be written as

$$\Pi = N_P[\text{Max}(0, E - S_T) - P].$$

For a buyer with one put, $N_P = 1$,

$$\Pi = \text{Max}(0, E - S_T) - P.$$

For a writer with one put, $N_P = -1$,

$$\Pi = -\text{Max}(0, E - S_T) + P.$$

For a transaction involving only stock, the profit equation is simply

$$\Pi = N_S(S_T - S).$$

For a buyer of one share of stock, $N_S = 1$, profit is

$$\Pi = S_T - S.$$

For a short seller of one share of stock, $N_S = -1$, profit is

$$\Pi = -S_T + S.$$

These profit equations make it simple to determine the profit from any transaction. Take, for example, the equations for the call buyer and the put buyer. In both cases, the profit is simply the dollar amount received from exercising the option minus the dollar amount paid for the option. This figure is then multiplied by the number of options. For the call writer and put writer, the profit is the amount received as the premium minus the amount paid out from exercising the option. This figure is then multiplied by the number of options written. Similarly, the profit for a stock buyer is simply the price at which the stock is sold minus the price paid for the stock. This figure is then multiplied by the number of shares. For the short seller, the profit is the price received from the short sale minus the price paid for repurchasing the stock. This figure is then multiplied by the number of shares sold short.

Different Holding Periods

The cases described in the previous section are strategies in which the position is held until the option expires. Because the option has no time value remaining and sells for its intrinsic value, the profit is easy to determine. It is not necessary, however, that an option trader hold the position open until the option expires. The length of the investor's holding period can be any time interval desired. In the case of a position closed out prior to the option's expiration, it is necessary to determine at what price the option would sell. How would we go about doing this?

Remember that the available information would be the exercise price and the time remaining on the option. We would want to know at what price the option would sell given a certain stock price. If the risk-free rate and an estimate of the variance of the return on the stock were available, we could use the Black-Scholes model. Here we shall assume this information is available, and we shall use the model to estimate the option's remaining time value to determine the profit from the strategy.

For expository purposes, we define three points in time: T(1), T(2), and T. We allow the investor to hold the position until either T(1), T(2), or all the way to expiration, T. The holding period from today until T(1) is the shortest. If an investor closes out the position at time T(1), the option will have a remaining time to expiration of $T - T(1)$. The holding period from today until T(2) is of intermediate

TABLE 5.1
Digital Equipment Option Data, June 12

Exercise Price	Calls			Puts		
	Jun	**Jul**	**Oct**	**Jun**	**Jul**	**Oct**
160	4 5/8	8 5/8	15 1/4	13/16	3 7/8	8 1/8
165	1 7/8	5 3/4	13 1/4	2 15/16	6	9 3/4
170	1/2	3 3/4	10 3/4	6 1/2	8 1/2	NA
175	1/16	2 3/8	8 1/2	NA	NA	NA

Current stock price: 164
Expirations: June 19, July 17, October 16
Risk-free rates: .0473 (Jun); .0521 (Jul); .0574 (Oct)

length. The investor who chooses it closes the option position with a remaining time to expiration of $T - T(2)$. If the investor holds the position until expiration, the remaining time is $T - T = 0$.

Thus, the profit from a call position, if terminated at time $T(1)$ before expiration and when the stock price is $S_{T(1)}$, is

$$\Pi = N_c[C(S_{T(1)}, T - T(1), E) - C],$$

where $C(S_{T(1)}, T - T(1), E)$ is the value obtained from the Black-Scholes or any other appropriate call option pricing model using a stock price of $S_{T(1)}$. C is, of course, the original price of the call. The expression for puts is the same except that we use a P instead of a C and employ the Black-Scholes or any other appropriate put option pricing model to calculate $P(S_{T(1)}, T - T(1), E)$. Similar expressions obviously apply when the position is closed at $T(2)$.

Assumptions

Several important assumptions underlie the analysis of option strategies.

First, we assume the stock pays no dividends. As we saw in Chapters 3 and 4, dividends can complicate option decisions. While including them here would not be especially difficult, we will intentionally omit them to keep the analysis simple. Where it is especially important, we will discuss the effect of dividends.

Second, we assume no taxes or transaction costs. These already have been covered and certainly are a consideration in option decisions, but they would add little to the analysis here. Where there are special tax and transaction cost factors, we provide an interpretation of their effects.

Recall that we have been analyzing the Digital Equipment options in previous chapters. For convenience, Table 5.1 repeats those data.

FIGURE 5.1
Buy Stock

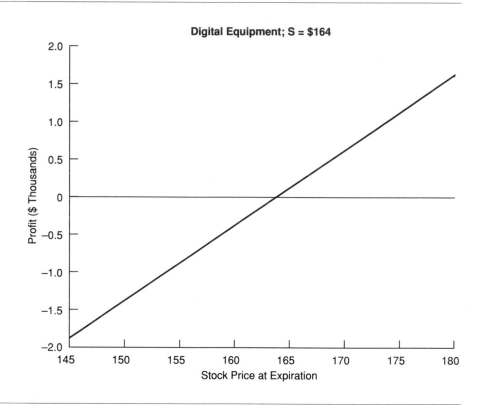

Now let us move on to analyzing the strategies. The first group of strategies we shall examine are transactions involving stock.

STOCK TRANSACTIONS

Buy Stock

The simplest transaction is the purchase of stock. The profit equation is

$$\Pi = N_S(S_T - S) \text{ given that } N_S > 0.$$

For illustrative purposes, let $N_S = 100$, a single round lot of stock. Figure 5.1 shows how the profit from this transaction varies with the stock price when the position is closed. The transaction is profitable if the Digital Equipment stock ultimately is sold at a price higher than $164, the price paid for the stock. Dividends would

FIGURE 5.2
Sell Short Stock

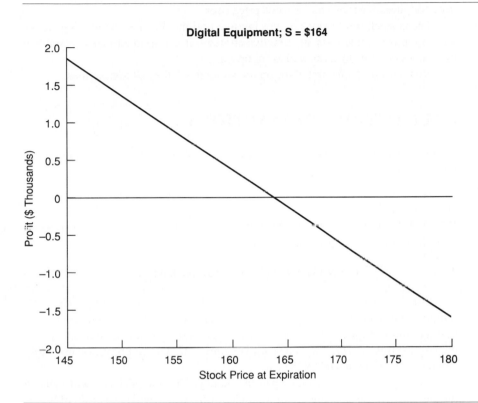

Digital Equipment; S = $164

lower this breakeven by the amount of the dividend, while transaction costs would raise it by the amount of those costs.

Sell Short Stock

The short sale of stock is the mirror image of the purchase of stock. The profit equation is

$$\Pi = N_S(S_T - S) \text{ given that } N_S < 0.$$

In this example, let $N_S = -100$, which means that 100 shares have been sold short. Figure 5.2 shows how the profit from the short sale varies with the price of the Digital Equipment stock at the end of the investor's holding period. Short selling is a strategy undertaken in anticipation of a bear market. The investor borrows the stock from the broker, sells it at $164, and repurchases at—hopefully—a lower price.[2] If the shares are repurchased at less than $164, the transaction earns a profit. As Figure 5.2 shows, selling short has the potential for unlimited losses if the investor guesses wrong and the stock price rises.

These stock transactions do not involve options. Because combining stocks with options is sometimes an attractive strategy, it is important that we establish the framework for stocks as well as for options.

Now we turn to the first of the option strategies—the call transactions.

CALL OPTION TRANSACTIONS

There are two types of call option transactions. We first examine the strategy of buying a call.

Buy a Call

The profit from a call option purchase is

$$\Pi = N_C[Max(0, S_T - E) - C] \text{ given that } N_C > 0.$$

Consider the case where the number of calls purchased is simply 1 ($N_C = 1$). Suppose the stock price at expiration is less than or equal to the exercise price so that the option expires out-of-the-money. What is the profit from the call? Since the call expires unexercised, the profit is simply $-C$. The call buyer incurs a loss equal to the premium paid for the call.

Suppose the call option ends up in-the-money. Then the call buyer will exercise the call, buying the stock for E and selling it for S_T, which will net a profit of $S_T - E - C$.[3] These results are summarized as follows:

$$\Pi = S_T - E - C \qquad \text{if } S_T > E$$
$$\Pi = -C \qquad \text{if } S_T \le E.$$

Figure 5.3 illustrates this transaction for the Digital Equipment July 165 call, which sells for $5.75. The call has limited downside risk. The maximum possible loss for a single contract is $575, which is the premium times 100. At any stock price at expiration less than the exercise price of 165, the call buyer loses the maximum amount. If the stock price is above 165, the loss will be less than $575. Losses, however, are incurred if the stock price is below a critical stock price, which we shall call the *breakeven stock price* at expiration.

---

[2]Any dividends paid while the stock is sold short go to whoever purchased the stock from the short seller. In addition, the short seller must pay the broker the amount of the dividends.

[3]The stock need not be sold for this result to hold. The call buyer can retain the stock worth S_T or convert it to cash. An even better strategy would be to sell the call an instant before it expires. At that time it should have little, if any, time value left. This would avoid the high transaction cost of taking delivery of the stock.

FIGURE 5.3
Buy Call

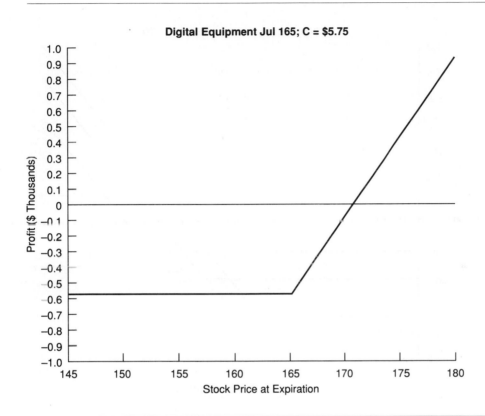

Notice in Figure 5.3 that the breakeven stock price is above the exercise price and between $170 and $175. We can find the breakeven stock price at expiration by simply setting to zero the profit for the case where stock price exceeds exercise price. We then solve for the breakeven stock price, S_T^*. Thus,

$$\Pi = S_T^* - E - C = 0.$$

Solving for S_T^* gives

$$S_T^* = E + C.$$

The breakeven stock price at expiration, then, is the exercise price plus the call price. The call premium, C, is the amount already paid for the call. To break even, the call buyer must exercise the option at a price high enough to recover the option's cost. For every dollar by which the stock price at expiration exceeds the exercise price, the call buyer gains a dollar. Therefore, the stock price must

FIGURE 5.4
Buy Call: Different Strike Prices

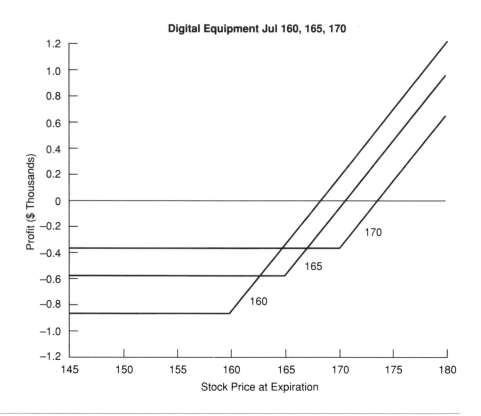

Digital Equipment Jul 160, 165, 170

exceed the exercise price by C dollars for the call buyer to recover the cost of the option. In this problem, the breakeven stock price at expiration is $165 + $5.75 = $170.75.

Notice how the call option offers the buyer a potentially unlimited profit while restricting the loss to the amount paid for the option. Although the likelihood of abnormally large profits is minimal, it is comforting to know that the potential loss is small. This makes the purchase of a call a particularly attractive strategy for students and others with limited budgets who wish to "play the market" while limiting their losses to a level that will not wipe them out.

THE CHOICE OF EXERCISE PRICE   Usually several options with the same expirations but different strike prices are available. Which option should we buy? There is no unambiguous answer.

Figure 5.4 compares the profit graphs for the three Digital Equipment July calls with strike prices of 160, 165, and 170. There are advantages and disadvantages to each. First, compare the 165, which we previously examined, with the

170. If we choose a higher strike price, the gain if the stock price rises will be less. However, because the call with the higher exercise price commands a lower premium, the loss if the stock price falls will be smaller. The breakeven for the 170 is $E + C = 170 + 3.75 = 173.75$, which is higher than that for the 165.

If we choose the 160 over the 165, we have the potential for a greater profit if the stock price at expiration is higher. Also, the breakeven is $E + C = 160 + 8.625 = 168.625$. If the market is down, however, the loss will be greater. The potential loss is the full premium of $862.50. This is because the call with the lower exercise price will command a greater premium.

Thus, the choice of which option to purchase is not easy and depends on how confident the call buyer is about the market outlook. If one feels strongly that the stock price will increase, the call with the lowest exercise price is preferable. Otherwise, a higher exercise price will minimize the potential loss.

THE CHOICE OF HOLDING PERIOD The strategies previously examined assume the investor holds the option until the expiration date. Alternatively, the call buyer could sell the option prior to expiration. Let us look at what happens if a shorter holding period is chosen.

Recall that we plan to examine three holding periods. The shortest holding period involves the sale of the call at time $T(1)$. The intermediate-length holding period is that in which the call is sold at time $T(2)$. The longest holding period is that in which the option is held until expiration. If the option is sold at time $T(1)$, the profit is the call price at the time of the sale minus the price originally paid for it. We can use the Black-Scholes model with a time to expiration of $T - T(1)$ to estimate the price of the call for a broad range of possible stock prices and, thereby, determine the profit graph. Using the October 165 call, the three holding periods are (1) sell the call on July 24, $T(1)$; (2) sell the call on September 4, $T(2)$; and (3) hold the call until it expires on October 16, T.

For the shortest holding period, in which the position is closed on July 24, the time remaining is 84 days; that is, there are 84 days between July 24 and October 16. Thus, the call price will be based on a remaining time to expiration of $84/365 = .2301$. The call's time to expiration is $T - T(1) = .2301$. For the intermediate-length holding period, in which the position is held until September 4, the time remaining to expiration is 42 days. Thus, the time to expiration is $42/365 = .1151$ and $T - T(2) = .1151$. For the longest holding period, the time remaining is, of course, zero. The parameters used in the model are $E = 165$, $\sigma = .29$, and $r = .0574$.

The results are shown in Table 5.2. Take the first entry. On July 24, at a stock price of $145, the call would have a Black-Scholes value of $2.4160. Since the investor paid $13.25 for the call, the profit per contract is $100(\$2.4160 - \$13.25) = -\$1,083.40$. If the stock price were $150, the call would be worth $3.7210 and the profit would be $100(\$3.7210 - \$13.25) = -\$952.90$. On September 4, at a stock price of $145, the call would be worth $.7728 and the profit would be $100(\$.7728 - \$13.25) = -\$1,247.72$. The remaining entries are computed in the same manner.

In Figure 5.5, the profit per contract is graphed as the dependent variable and the stock price at the end of the holding period is graphed as the independent variable. The graph indicates that the shortest holding period provides a higher

TABLE 5.2

Estimation of Black-Scholes Prices and Profits for Digital Equipment Oct 165 Calls

Position Closed at: Time to Expiration:	7/24 .2301		9/4 .1151	
Stock Price at End of Holding Period	Black-Scholes Call Price	Profit Per Contract	Black-Scholes Call Price	Profit Per Contract
145	$2.4160	−$1,083.40	$0.7728	−$1,247.72
150	3.7210	−952.90	1.5437	−1,170.63
155	5.4417	−780.83	2.7823	−1,046.77
160	7.6045	−564.55	4.5881	−866.19
165	10.2129	−303.71	7.0102	−623.98
170	13.2485	−.15	10.0380	−321.20
175	16.6756	342.56	13.6091	35.91
180	20.4470	719.70	17.6282	437.82

profit for all stock prices at expiration. It would appear that the shorter the holding period, the greater the potential profit. This is because with a shorter holding period, the call can be sold to recover some of its remaining time value. The longer the call is held, the greater is the time value lost.

This seems to present a paradox: It suggests that to maximize profits, one should hold the option for the shortest time possible. Obviously option traders do not always use such short holding periods. What is missing from the explanation?

The answer is that the shorter holding period provides superior profits *for a given stock price*. The profit graph does not indicate the likelihood that the stock price will end up high or low. In fact, with a shorter holding period, the possible range of stock prices is much lower because there is less time for the stock price to move. The longer holding period, on the other hand, gives the stock price more time to increase.

This completes our discussion of the strategy of buying a call. We now turn to the strategy of writing a call.

Write a Call

An option trader who writes a call without concurrently owning the stock is said to be writing an *uncovered* or *naked* call. The reason for this nomenclature is that the position is a high-risk strategy, one with the potential for unlimited losses. The uncovered call writer undertakes the obligation to sell stock not currently owned to the call buyer at the latter's request. The writer therefore may have to buy the stock at an unfavorable price. As a result, writing an uncovered call is a privilege restricted to those few traders with sufficient capital to risk. Since the brokerage

FIGURE 5.5
Buy Call: Different Holding Periods

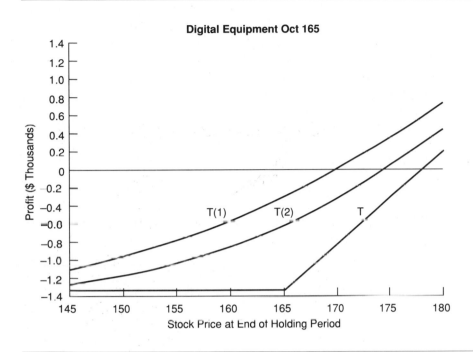

Digital Equipment Oct 165

firm must make up losses to the clearinghouse, it too is at risk. Therefore, a trader's broker must agree to handle the transaction—and that is likely to be done only for the best and wealthiest customers. Of course, traders owning seats on the exchange are less restricted and can more easily write uncovered calls, but because of the high risk even they do so infrequently. Moreover, with stocks that pay dividends, the writer faces the risk of early exercise, as discussed in Chapter 3.

If writing an uncovered call is such a risky strategy, why should we examine it? The reason is that writing an uncovered call can be combined with other strategies, such as buying stock or another option, to produce a strategy with very low risk. Therefore, it is necessary to establish the results for the short call before combining it with other strategies.

Because the buyer's and writer's profits are the mirror images of each other, the profit equations and graphs are already familiar. The writer's profit is

$$\Pi = N_C[\text{Max}(0, S_T - E) - C] \text{ given that } N_C < 0.$$

Assume one call, $N_C = -1$. Then the profit is

$$\Pi = C \qquad\qquad \text{if } S_T \leq E$$
$$\Pi = -S_T + E + C \quad \text{if } S_T > E.$$

FIGURE 5.6

Write Call

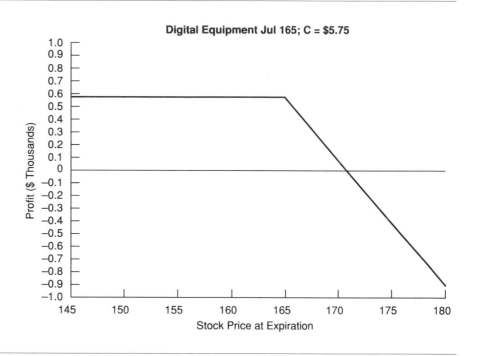

Figure 5.6 illustrates the profit graph for the writer of 100 Digital Equipment July 165 calls at a price of $5.75. Note that the breakeven stock price for the writer must be the breakeven stock price for the buyer, E + C = $170.75. The maximum loss for the buyer is also the maximum gain for the writer, $575. If the stock price ends up above the exercise price, the loss to the writer can be substantial—and, as is obvious from the graph, there is no limit to the possible loss in a bull market.

THE CHOICE OF EXERCISE PRICE   Figure 5.7 compares the strategy of writing calls at different strike prices by showing the 160, 165, and 170 calls. Figure 5.7 is the mirror image of Figure 5.4. The greatest profit potential is in the 160, which has the highest premium, $862.50, but is accompanied by the greatest loss potential and the lowest breakeven, E + C = 160 + 8.625 = 168.625. This would be the highest-risk strategy. The 170 would have the lowest risk of the three with the highest breakeven, E + C = 170 + 3.75 = 173.75, but also the lowest profit potential, the $375 premium.

THE CHOICE OF HOLDING PERIOD   Figure 5.8 illustrates the profit for the three possible holding periods previously described. These are the October 165 calls in which the holding period T(1) involves the repurchase of the call on July

FIGURE 5.7
Write Call: Different Strike Prices

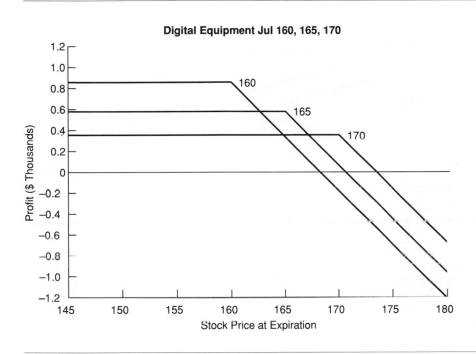

Digital Equipment Jul 160, 165, 170

24; T(2) assumes the call is repurchased on September 4; and T allows the call to be held until expiration, when it either is exercised or expires out-of-the-money.

Figure 5.8 is the mirror image of Figure 5.5. A writer repurchasing the call prior to expiration will have to pay for some of the remaining time value. Therefore, for the call writer, the profit is lowest with the shortest holding period *for a given stock price*. This is because the time value repurchased is greater with the shorter holding period. However, with a shorter holding period, the stock price is less likely to move substantially; thus, the range of possible profits is far smaller. If the investor holds the position until expiration, the profit may be greater but the stock will have had more time to move—perhaps unfavorably.

This completes our discussion of call buying and writing, which we see are mirror images of each other. We next turn to put option transactions.

FIGURE 5.8

Write Call: Different Holding Periods

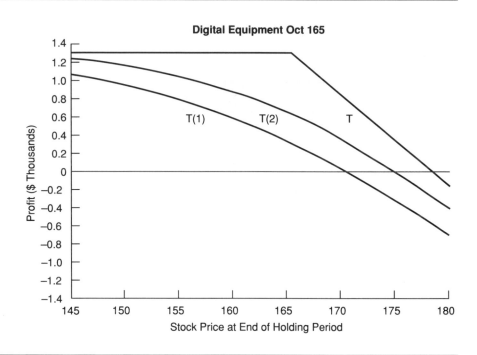

Digital Equipment Oct 165

PUT OPTION TRANSACTIONS

Buy a Put

Buying a put is a strategy for a bear market. The potential loss is limited to the premium paid. The gain is also limited but can still be quite substantial. The profit from the purchase of a put is given by the equation

$$\Pi = N_p[Max(0, E - S_T) - P] \text{ given that } N_p > 0.$$

As in the example for calls, assume the purchase of a single put, $N_p = 1$. If the stock price at expiration ends up less than the exercise price, the put is in-the-money and is exercised. If the stock price at expiration is greater than or equal to the exercise price, the put ends up out-of-the-money. The profits are

$$\Pi = E - S_T - P \quad \text{if } S_T < E$$
$$\Pi = -P \quad\quad\quad \text{if } S_T \geq E.$$

FIGURE 5.9
Buy Put

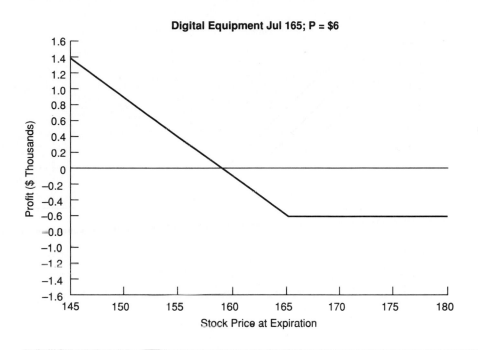

Digital Equipment Jul 165; P = $6

Figure 5.9 illustrates the profits from the put-buying strategy for the Digital Equipment July 165 put with a premium of $6. The potential loss is limited to the premium paid, which in this case is $600. The profit is also limited, because there is a limit to how low the stock price can fall. The best outcome for a put buyer is for the company to go bankrupt. In that case, the stock would be worthless, $S_T = 0$, and the profit would be $E - P$. In this example, that would be $100(165 - 6) = 15,900$.

Notice that the breakeven occurs where the stock price is below the exercise price. Setting the profit equation for this case equal to zero gives

$$\Pi = E - S_T^* - P = 0.$$

Solving for the breakeven stock price, S_T^*, at expiration reveals that

$$S_T^* = E - P.$$

The put buyer must recover enough from the option's exercise to cover the premium already paid. For every dollar by which the option is in-the-money, the put buyer gains a dollar. Therefore, the stock price must fall below the exercise price by the amount of the premium. In this instance, this is $165 - 6 = 159$. For the investor to profit from this put, the stock price must fall to $159 or less by the expiration date.

FIGURE 5.10
Buy Put: Different Strike Prices

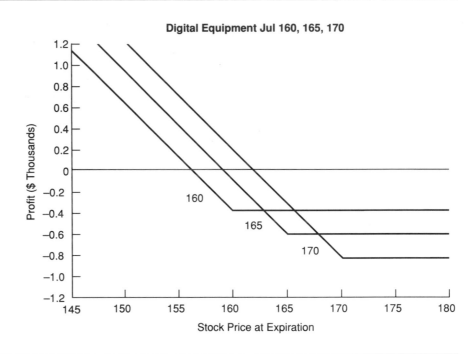

Buying a put is an appropriate strategy when anticipating a bear market. The loss is limited to the premium paid, and the potential gain is quite high. Moreover, it is easier to execute a put transaction than a short sale. Puts need not be bought when the stock is on an uptick or zero-plus tick, and the amount paid for the put is far less than the margin on a short sale. More important, a put limits the loss while a short sale has an unlimited loss.

THE CHOICE OF EXERCISE PRICE   Figure 5.10 compares the profit graphs for puts with different strike prices using the July 160, 165, and 170 puts. The highest exercise price, the 170, has a higher premium; thus, the potential loss is greatest—in this case, $850. Its profit potential is highest, however, with a maximum possible profit of $100(170 - 8.50) = 16,150$ if the stock price at expiration is zero. The breakeven is $170 - 8.50 = 161.50$. The 160 has the lowest potential profit, $100(160 - 3.875) = 15,612.50$, and the lowest breakeven stock price, $160 - 3.875 = 156.125$. However, it also has the lowest loss potential, its premium of $387.50. The put chosen will be determined by the risk the option trader is willing to take. The more aggressive trader will go for the maximum profit potential and choose the highest exercise price. The more conservative trader will choose a lower exercise price to limit the potential loss.

FIGURE 5.11
Buy Put: Different Holding Periods

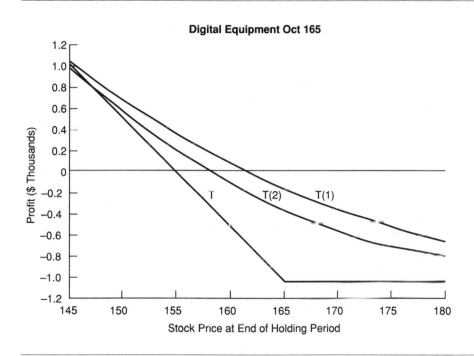

THE CHOICE OF HOLDING PERIOD   Figure 5.11 compares the profit potential of the three holding periods for the October 165 put. The Black-Scholes option pricing model for European puts was used to estimate the put prices for the shorter holding periods.

By electing a shorter holding period—say, T(1)—the put buyer can sell the put back for some of the time value originally purchased. If the put buyer holds until T(2), less time value will be recovered. If held until expiration, no remaining time value will be recaptured. As with the case for calls, the shorter holding periods show greater potential profit *for a given stock price*. However, they allow less time for the stock price to go down. Therefore, shorter holding periods are not necessarily inferior or superior to longer ones. The choice depends on the trader's forecast for the stock price, specifically how much it is expected to move, the direction, and in how much time.

With an understanding of the put buyer's profit potential, it should be simple to examine the case for the put writer. As you probably expect, the put writer's position is the mirror image of the put buyer's.

FIGURE 5.12

Write Put

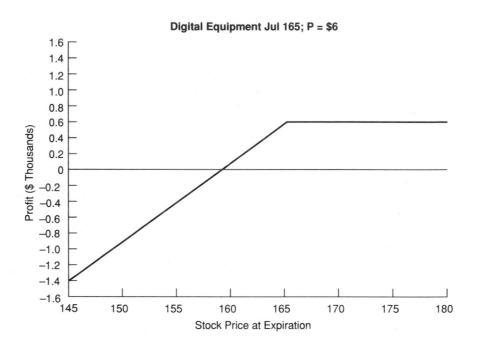

Digital Equipment Jul 165; P = $6

Profit ($ Thousands)

Stock Price at Expiration

Write a Put

The put writer is obligated to buy the stock from the put buyer at the exercise price. The put writer profits if the stock price goes up and the put therefore is not exercised, in which case the writer keeps the premium. If the stock price falls such that the put is exercised, the put writer is forced to buy the stock at a price greater than its market worth. For an American put this can, of course, occur prior to as well as at expiration.

The profit equation for the put writer is

$$\Pi = N_P[\text{Max}(0, E - S_T) - P] \text{ given that } N_P < 0.$$

Assume the simple case of a single short put, $N_P = -1$. The writer's profits are the mirror images of the buyer's:

$$\Pi = -E + S_T + P \text{ if } S_T < E$$
$$\Pi = P \qquad\qquad \text{ if } S_T \geq E.$$

Figure 5.12 illustrates the put writer's profits using the July 165 put written at a premium of $6. The writer's maximum potential profit is the buyer's maximum

FIGURE 5.13
Write Put: Different Strike Prices

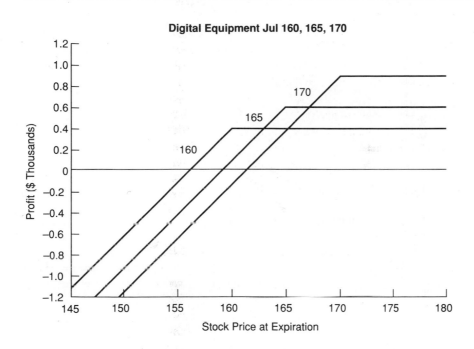

Digital Equipment Jul 160, 165, 170

potential loss—the amount of the premium, $600. The maximum potential loss for the writer is limited, but, like the buyer's maximum potential gain, is a very large amount—here, $15,900. The breakeven stock price at expiration is the same as that for the buyer—E – P, or $159.

THE CHOICE OF EXERCISE PRICE   Figure 5.13 compares the put writer's profits for different strike prices using the July puts. The highest strike price, 170, offers the greatest premium income and therefore the greatest profit potential. The maximum profit is $850, and the breakeven is 170 – 8.50 = 161.50. The risk, however, is greatest, since any losses will be larger in a bear market. The lowest strike price offers the lowest maximum profit—the premium income of $387.50—but also has the lowest breakeven—160 – 3.875 = 156.125—and the lowest loss if the market is down. Once again the range of exercise prices offers the put writer several choices for assuming various degrees of risk and expected reward.

THE CHOICE OF HOLDING PERIOD   Figure 5.14 compares the put writer's profits for different holding periods. Like the call writer, the put writer who chooses a shorter holding period makes a smaller profit or incurs a greater loss *for a given stock price*. This is because the writer buying back the put before expiration

FIGURE 5.14
Write Put: Different Holding Periods

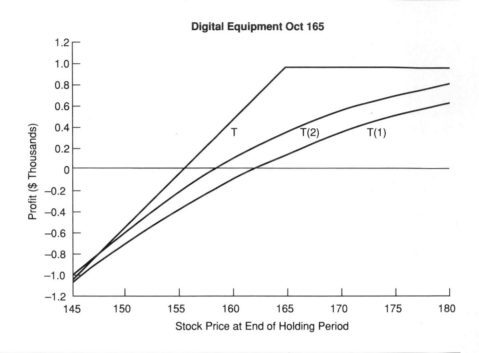

must pay for some of the remaining time value. The advantage to the writer, however, is that with a short holding period there is a much smaller probability of a large, unfavorable stock price move. Again the choice of holding period depends on the forecast for the market price and the time frame over which the writer expects that forecast to hold.

The put writer must also be aware of the possibility of early exercise of a deep-in-the-money put. Since the stock price at which early exercise occurs can be approximated, as shown in Chapter 4, the put writer can consider rolling into a lower exercise price when the threat of early exercise increases.

We now have covered all of the simple strategies of buying stock, selling short stock, buying calls, writing calls, buying puts, and writing puts. Figure 5.15 summarizes the profit graphs of these strategies. They can be viewed as building blocks that are combined to produce other strategies. In fact, all of the remaining strategies are but combinations of these simple ones. The remainder of this chapter examines the strategies of combining calls with stock, combining puts with stock, replicating puts with calls and stock, and replicating calls with puts and stock.

FIGURE 5.15
Summary of Profit Graphs for Positions Held to Expiration

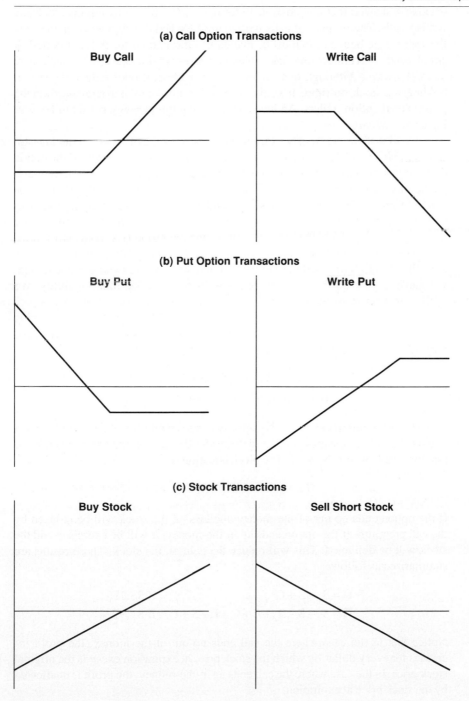

CALLS AND STOCK: THE COVERED CALL

Chapter 4 showed that it is possible to form a riskless hedge by buying stock and writing calls. The number of calls written must exceed the number of shares, and the appropriate hedge ratio must be maintained throughout the holding period. A simpler but nevertheless low-risk strategy involves writing one call for each share of stock owned. Although this strategy is not riskless, it does reduce the risk of holding the stock outright. It is also one of the most popular strategies among professional option traders. An investor executing this strategy is said to be writing a *covered call*.

Recall that we previously examined the uncovered call in which the investor writes a call on a stock not owned. We found the risk to be unlimited. If the option trader owns the stock, however, there is no risk of buying it in the market at a potentially high price. If the call is exercised, the investor simply delivers the stock. From another point of view, the holder of stock with no options written thereon is exposed to substantial risk of the stock price moving down. By writing a call against that stock, the investor reduces the downside risk. If the stock price falls substantially, the loss will be cushioned by the premium received for writing the call. Although in a bull market the call may be exercised and the stockholder will have to give up the stock, there are ways to minimize this possibility. We shall consider how to do this later.

Because we already examined the strategies of buying stock and writing calls, determining the profits from the covered call strategy is simple: We need only add the profit equations from these two strategies. Thus,

$$\Pi = N_S(S_T - S) + N_C[\text{Max}(0, S_T - E) - C]$$
$$\text{given that } N_S > 0, N_C < 0, \text{ and } N_S = -N_C.$$

The last requirement, $N_S = -N_C$, specifies that the number of calls written must equal the number of shares purchased. Consider the case of one share of stock and one short call, $N_S = 1$, $N_C = -1$. The profit equation is

$$\Pi = S_T - S - \text{Max}[0, S_T - E] + C.$$

If the option ends up out-of-the-money, the loss on the stock will be reduced by the call premium. If the option ends up in-the-money, it will be exercised and the stock will be delivered. This will reduce the gain on the stock. These results are summarized as follows:

$$\Pi = S_T - S + C \qquad\qquad\qquad\quad \text{if } S_T \le E$$
$$\Pi = S_T - S - S_T + E + C = E - S + C \quad \text{if } S_T > E.$$

Notice that in the case where the call ends up out-of-the-money, the profit increases for every dollar by which the stock price at expiration exceeds the original stock price. In the case where the call ends up in-the-money, the profit is unaffected by the stock price at expiration.

FIGURE 5.16
Covered Call

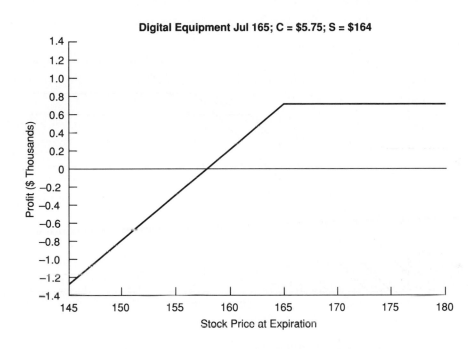

Digital Equipment Jul 165; C = $5.75; S = $164

These results are illustrated in Figure 5.16 for the Digital Equipment July 165 call written at a premium of $5.75. The maximum profit occurs when the stock price exceeds the exercise price; this profit is E − S + C, which in this example is $100(165 − 164 + 5.75) = 675$. The maximum loss occurs if the stock price at expiration goes to zero. In that case, the profit will simply be −S + C, which is $100(−164 + 5.75) = −15,825$.

The breakeven stock price occurs where the profit is zero. This happens when the call ends up out-of-the-money. Setting the profit equal to zero for the case where the call is out-of-the-money,

$$\Pi = S_T^* - S + C = 0,$$

and solving for S_T^* gives a breakeven of

$$S_T^* = S - C.$$

Here the breakeven is $164 − 5.75 = 158.25$. At any stock price above $158.25, this covered call is profitable. Another way to view this is that the covered call provides a profit at any stock price at expiration down to $158.25. Ownership of the stock without the protection of the call provides a profit only at a stock price above $164, the current stock price.

FIGURE 5.17

Covered Call: Different Strike Prices

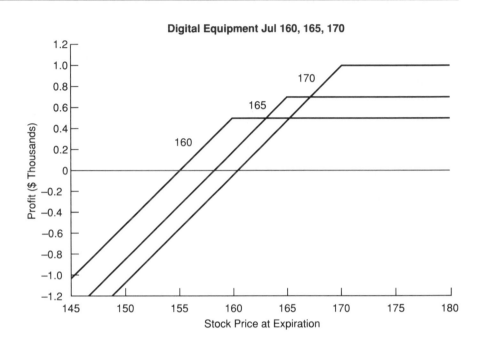

THE CHOICE OF EXERCISE PRICE   The covered call writer has a choice of calls at different strike prices. Figure 5.17 illustrates the profit graphs for the covered call using the Digital Equipment July calls with strike prices of 160, 165, and 170. Because the highest strike price, the 170, has the lowest premium with which to cushion a stock price decrease, it offers the least amount of protection for the covered call writer. It offers the maximum profit potential, however, because the high strike price allows the writer to receive a greater amount for the stock if the call is exercised. In this example, the 170 call has a maximum profit of $100(170 - 164 + 3.75) = 975$. The breakeven is $164 - 3.75 = 160.25$. The minimum profit, which occurs if the stock price at expiration is zero, is $100 (-164 + 3.75) = -16,025$.

In contrast, the lowest exercise price, the 160, offers the most protection. Because it has the highest premium, the cushion on the downside is greater. However, if the stock moves up and the call is exercised, the writer will receive a lower price for the stock. The maximum profit is $100(160 - 164 + 8.625) = 462.50$. The breakeven stock price is $164 - 8.625 = 155.375$. The minimum profit, which occurs at a stock price at expiration of zero, is $100(-164 + 8.625) = -15,537.50$.

FIGURE 5.18
Covered Call: Different Holding Periods

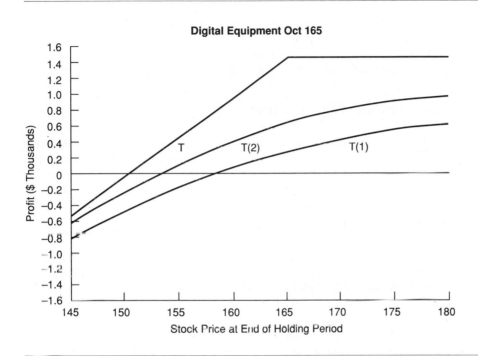

Digital Equipment Oct 165

Writing a covered call at the lowest exercise price is the most conservative choice, because the loss on the downside is lower; however, the gain on the upside is also lower. Writing a covered call at the highest exercise price is a riskier strategy, because the upside profit potential is greater but the downside protection is less. Regardless of the exercise price chosen, writing a covered call is far less risky than owning the stock outright. The premium on the call, no matter how large or small, cushions the stockholder against a loss on the stock in a falling market.

THE CHOICE OF HOLDING PERIOD Figure 5.18 illustrates the October 165 covered call in which the position is closed out prior to expiration. Again the Black-Scholes model was used to estimate the call's value in the manner described earlier in the chapter. The shortest holding period, T(1), which corresponds to closing out the position on July 24, gives the smallest profit *for a given stock price*. This is because the writer closes out the position by buying back the call. If there is time remaining, the writer must buy back some of the remaining time value. If a longer holding period is used, the remaining time value, which must be bought back, is less. If held to expiration, there is no time value remaining for repurchase.

Does this suggest that covered call writers should use short holding periods? Not necessarily. Again it depends on the covered call writer's forecast for the stock price and the time frame over which it applies. The investor might earn a larger profit by holding the position until expiration, but such a long holding period will also give the stock price more time to move down. A shorter holding period increases the likelihood that the stock price will not move much, and this could be more profitable for the covered call writer.

Some General Considerations

As indicated earlier, covered call writing is a very popular strategy among professional option traders. This is because it is a low-risk strategy—much less risky than buying stock or options outright.

Two studies have compared the performances of covered call writing strategies with those of call buying strategies. Trennepohl and Dukes (1979) examined the performance of a number of these strategies over the 1973–1976 period for the first options listed on the CBOE. Covered call writing strategies offered higher returns and lower risk than buying the stock outright. Buying calls proved a very poor strategy. Yates and Kopprasch (1980) compared the performance of an index of covered call writing with that resulting from owning the S&P 500 stocks. The covered call writing strategy was far superior.

These results should make one wonder why everyone does not simply write covered calls. Obviously, if that occurred the prices of the calls would fall so low that the strategy would no longer be attractive. This superior performance of covered call writing is most likely attributable to the fact that the studies covered years in which listed options were new. Veterans of those early years widely agree that the public avidly purchased these new instruments as a cheap and exciting way to play the market. Little regard was paid to whether the calls were fairly priced. In fact, option pricing theory itself was in its infancy, and little was known about pricing options. Public demand, coupled with ignorance, most likely kept call prices artifically high and led to substantial profits for clever call writers in those years. Although there have been no similar studies recently, it seems unlikely that such superior performance could be sustained.

It is commonly believed that writing covered calls is a way to pick up extra income from a stock. However, writing a call imposes on the stockholder the possibility of having to sell the stock at an inconvenient or unsuitable time. If the stock price goes up, the covered call writer will be unable to participate in the resulting gains and the stock will likely be called away by exercise. If, however, the call is exercised early, the writer will be no worse off from a financial perspective. The profit will still be $E - S + C$, the maximum expected profit at expiration. In fact, the writer actually will be better off, because this amount will be available before expiration.

Suppose the covered writer does not want to lose the stock by exercise. One way to minimize the likelihood of exercise is to write calls at a high exercise price so that the call is deep-out-of-the-money. This reduces the chance of the call ending up in-the-money. Suppose the stock price starts upward and it appears that the out-of-the-money call will move in-the-money and thus increase the chance of exercise. The writer can then buy the call back and write a new call at a higher exercise price. If the stock price continues to rise, the writer can buy back the new call and write another one at an even higher exercise price. In this manner, the covered call writer establishes a position in which the exercise price will always stay well ahead of the stock price. The purpose of this rollover strategy is to avoid exercise and keep the stock in the portfolio. This may be important to someone who likes to hold on to certain stocks for various reasons. The disadvantage of this strategy is that the high exercise price means a lower premium and less downside protection. Also, transaction costs from the frequent rollovers will be higher. These factors can be weighed against the inconvenience of exercise and the investor's willingness to give up the stock.

Many institutional investors also use a covered call writing strategy. Those holding large portfolios of stocks that are expected to gain little value often believe that their portfolios' performances will improve if they write calls against the stock they own. But covered call writing—or any other strategy—cannot be the gate to unlimited wealth. In fact, it is more likely to *reduce* the portfolio's return, because it decreases its risk. It therefore should be viewed as a risk-reducing rather than return-enhancing strategy.

As one might imagine, the opposite of a long stock–short call position is to buy a call to protect a short stock position. The results obtained from this strategy are the mirror image of the covered call results. We explore this strategy in an end-of-chapter problem.

Another option strategy that can be used to reduce the risk of holding stock is the protective put—the topic of the next section.

PUTS AND STOCK: THE PROTECTIVE PUT

As discussed in the previous section, a stockholder who wants protection against falling stock prices may elect to write a call. In a strong bull market, the stock is likely to be called away by exercise. One way to obtain protection against a bear market and still be able to participate in a bull market is to buy a *protective put*; that is, the investor simply buys stock and buys a put. The put provides a guaranteed selling price for the stock.

The profit equation for the protective put is found by simply adding the profit equations for the strategies of buying stock and buying a put. From this we get

$$\Pi = N_S(S_T - S) + N_P[\text{Max}(0, E - S_T) - P]$$
$$\text{given that } N_S > 0, N_P > 0, \text{ and } N_S = N_P.$$

As in previous examples, assume one share of stock and one put, $N_S = 1$, $N_P = 1$. If the stock price ends up above the exercise price, the put will expire out-of-the-

FIGURE 5.19

Protective Put

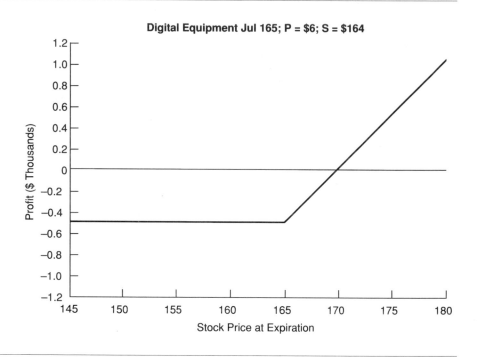

Digital Equipment Jul 165; P = $6; S = $164

Profit ($ Thousands) vs _Stock Price at Expiration_

money. If the stock price ends up less than the exercise price, the put will be exercised. The results are as follows:

$$\Pi = S_T - S - P \qquad\qquad\qquad \text{if } S_T \geq E$$
$$\Pi = S_T - S + E - S_T - P = E - S - P \quad \text{if } S_T < E.$$

The protective put works like an insurance policy. When you buy insurance for an asset such as a house, you pay a premium that assures you that in the event of a loss, the insurance policy will cover at least some of the loss. If the loss does not occur during the policy's life, you simply lose the premium. Similarly, the protective put is insurance for a stock. In a bear market, a loss on the stock is somewhat offset by the put's exercise. This is like filing a claim on the insurance policy. In a bull market, the insurance is not needed and the gain on the upside is reduced by the premium paid.

From the above equations, it is clear that the profit in a bull market varies directly with the stock price at expiration. The higher S_T is, the higher is the profit, Π. In a bear market, the profit is not affected by the stock price at expiration. Whatever losses are incurred on the stock are offset by gains on the put. The profit graph for a protective put is illustrated in Figure 5.19 for the Digital Equipment July 165 put purchased at a premium of $6.

The maximum loss on a protective put is found as the profit if the stock price at expiration ends up below the exercise price. Since the profit equation shows that this is $E - S - P$, the Digital Equipment protective put has a minimum profit of $100(165 - 164 - 6) = -500$. Clearly there is no maximum gain, because the investor profits dollar for dollar with the excess of the stock price over the exercise price. Notice how the graph of the protective put is the same shape as that of a long call.

The breakeven stock price at expiration occurs when the stock price at expiration exceeds the exercise price. Setting this profit to zero and solving for the breakeven stock price, S_T^*, gives

$$\Pi = S_T^* - S - P = 0$$
$$S_T^* = P + S.$$

Thus, breakeven occurs at a stock price at expiration equal to the original stock price plus the premium. This should be apparent, since the stock price must rise above the original stock price by an amount sufficient to cover the premium paid for the put. In this example, the breakeven stock price at expiration is $6 + 164 = 170$.

THE CHOICE OF EXERCISE PRICE: THE DEDUCTIBLE DECISION   The amount of coverage the protective put provides is affected by the chosen exercise price. This is equivalent to the insurance problem of deciding on the deductible. A higher deductible means that the insured bears more of the risk and thus pays a lower premium. With a lower deductible, the insurer bears more of the risk and charges a higher premium. With a protective put, a higher exercise price is equivalent to a lower deductible.

Figure 5.20 illustrates the comparative performances of Digital Equipment protective puts at different exercise prices. The 170 put gives the stockholder the right to sell the stock at $170 per share. The breakeven on this strategy is $164 + 8.5 = 172.5$. This will be the most expensive insurance but will provide the greatest coverage, with a minimum profit of $100(170 - 164 - 8.5) = -250$. If the stock price rises and the put is not needed, the gain from the stock will be lower than it would be with a lower exercise price. This is because the more expensive premium was paid but the insurance was not needed.

The lowest exercise price, the 160, provides the least coverage. The breakeven is $164 + 3.875 = 167.875$. The minimum profit is $100(160 - 164 - 3.875) = -787.50$. If the market rises, the less expensive insurance will reduce the gain by a smaller amount.

As you can see, selecting an exercise price is like choosing a deductible: The investor must balance the willingness to assume some of the risk against the ability to pay for the coverage.

THE CHOICE OF HOLDING PERIOD   Figure 5.21 illustrates the profit for different holding periods for the Digital Equipment October 165 protective put. The shorter holding period provides more coverage *for a given stock price*. This is be-

FIGURE 5.20
Protective Put: Different Strike Prices

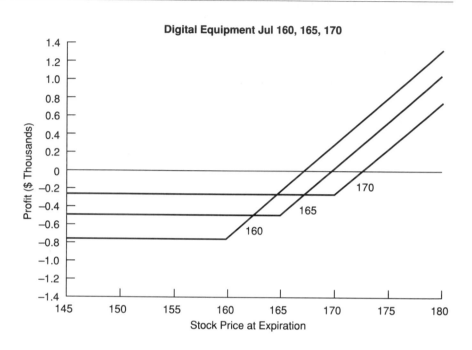

cause with a shorter holding period, the investor can sell back the put before expiration and recover some of the time value previously purchased. With a longer holding period, there will be less time value to recover. By holding all the way to expiration, there will be no time value to recover.

The choice of holding period depends on the investor's view of the probable stock price moves and the period over which they are likely to occur. If a large stock price move is needed to provide a profit, a longer holding period will allow more time for the stock price to move. A shorter holding period is preferable if the stock price is not expected to move much. However, the stock price must increase by at least the amount of the premium for the investor to break even. Therefore, the investor must weigh the likelihood of this occurring over the holding period.

The protective put strategy can also be turned around so that a short sale of stock is protected by a short put, or vice versa. The results would be the mirror image of those presented here. We examine this strategy as an end-of-chapter problem.

We have seen that investors holding stock can use both the covered call and the protective put to reduce risk. Which strategy is preferable? The answer de-

FIGURE 5.21
Protective Put: Different Holding Periods

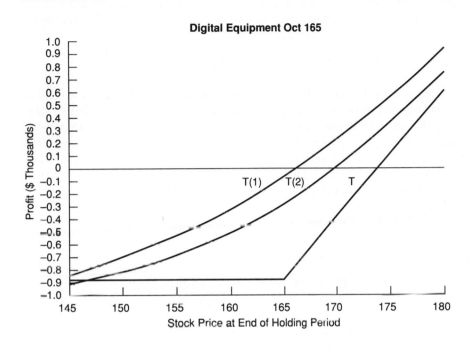

pends on the investor's outlook for the market. If a bull market is believed more likely to occur, the protective put will allow the investor to participate in it. However, the protective put will be more expensive, because the investor must pay for it. The covered call writer actually receives money for writing the call. Thus, there are advantages and disadvantages to each strategy that one must carefully weigh before making a decision.

The role of put options in providing insurance is explored more thoroughly in Chapter 14. That material will show how puts, calls, Treasury bills, and futures can be used to create *portfolio insurance*.

The following section examines some strategies in which puts can be created from calls and calls created from puts. For obvious reasons, these are called *synthetic puts* and *calls*.

SYNTHETIC PUTS AND CALLS

Chapter 3 covered put-call parity, the relationship between call prices and put prices:

$$C = P + S - Ee^{-rT}.$$

The left-hand side of the equation is the price of a call; the right-hand side is the value of a portfolio that behaves like a call. In Chapter 3, we derived put-call parity with a simple arbitrage argument. The portfolio on the right-hand side is a long put, a long stock, and a loan with a face value equal to the exercise price. Similarly, we can turn put-call parity around,

$$P = C - S + Ee^{-rT},$$

where the left-hand side is the price of a put and the right-hand side is the value of a portfolio that behaves like a put. That portfolio consists of a long call, a short sale of stock, and the purchase of a pure discount bond (or making of a loan) with a face value equal to the exercise price. Note that the signs in front of the prices in the equations indicate whether we are long or short in puts, calls, or stocks. Long positions are represented by plus (+) signs and short positions by minus (−) signs.

We actually need not borrow money to replicate a call or buy a bond to replicate a put. The term representing the present value of the exercise price is simply a constant value that does not affect the shape of the profit graph. For example, consider a *synthetic put*, which consists of long calls and the short sale of an equal number of shares of stock. The profit is simply

$$\Pi = N_c[\text{Max}(0, S_T - E) - C] + N_s(S_T - S)$$
$$\text{given that } N_c > 0, N_s < 0, \text{ and } N_c = -N_s.$$

Letting the number of shares and the number of calls both be 1, the profits for the two possible ranges of stock prices at expiration are

$$\Pi = -C - S_T + S \qquad\qquad \text{if } S_T \leq E$$
$$\Pi = S_T - E - C - S_T + S = S - E - C \quad \text{if } S_T > E.$$

If the stock price at expiration is equal to or below the exercise price, the profit will vary inversely with the stock price at expiration. If the stock price at expiration is above the exercise price, the profit will not be affected by the stock price at expiration. This is the same general outcome provided by a put, hence the name *synthetic put*.

We can see the difference between the actual put and the synthetic put from the put-call parity formula. In put-call parity, one replicates the put by buying a call, selling short a stock, and buying a pure discount bond with a face value equal to the exercise price. To replicate a put precisely, we need to buy that pure discount bond. In practice, however, most traders simply buy the call and sell short the stock.

Figure 5.22 compares the synthetic put and its actual counterpart using the Digital Equipment July 165 options. The synthetic put has a profit of

$$-C - S_T + S \quad \text{if } S_T \leq E$$
$$S - E - C \quad \text{if } S_T > E.$$

FIGURE 5.22
Synthetic and Actual Put

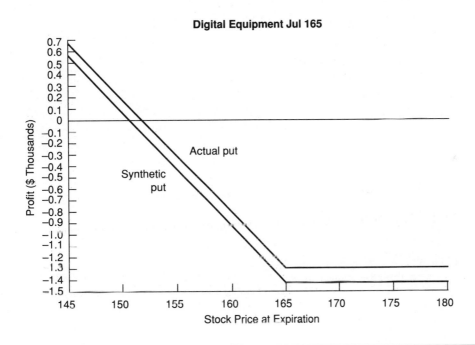

The actual put has a profit of

$$E - S_T - P \quad \text{if } S_T \leq E$$
$$-P \quad \text{if } S_T > E.$$

The difference is the profit of the actual put minus the profit of the synthetic put, $E - P + C - S$, in either case. From put-call parity, we can substitute $C - S + Ee^{-rT}$ for P. The difference is then

$$E(1 - e^{-rT}),$$

which is the interest lost by not buying the pure discount bond.

There are two reasons why someone would want to use a synthetic put. First, there once were restrictions on the listing of puts on the exchanges; puts were phased in slowly. There was also a moratorium on new option listings that started soon after the first few puts were listed in 1977. This prevented more puts from being listed until the moratorium was lifted in 1980. During that period, an investor could have created a synthetic put to use in lieu of the actual put.

Second, one can use a synthetic put to take advantage of mispricing in the relationship between puts and calls. For example, the difference between the

TABLE 5.3
Payoffs from Reverse Conversion

Position	$S_T \leq E$	$S_T > E$
Long call	0	$S_T - E$
Short stock	$-S_T$	$-S_T$
Short put	$-E + S_T$	0
	$-E$	$-E$

actual put price, P, and the value of the synthetic put, C – S, should be Ee^{-rT}; however, if $P - (C - S)$ is greater than Ee^{-rT}, either the actual put is overpriced or the synthetic put is underpriced. The investor should sell the actual put and buy the synthetic put by purchasing the call and selling short the stock. This strategy often is called a *reverse conversion* or simply *reversal*. It will generate a cash outflow at expiration of E, as shown in Table 5.3.

This property makes the reverse conversion resemble a risk-free loan. The money received when the position is opened is (1) S (from the short sale of the stock), (2) P (from the sale of the put), and (3) –C (from the purchase of the call). If, as we assumed, this exceeds the present value of the exercise price, we can invest the amount S + P – C at the risk-free rate, r, until the options expire. The accumulated future value of this investment will then exceed E. This means that we can repay the loan with money left over.[4] Of course, investing this money at the risk-free rate is equivalent to buying the risk-free bonds.

We can also create *synthetic calls* by buying stock and an equal number of puts. It should be apparent that this strategy is like a call, because it is nothing more than a protective put. The graph for the protective put is, as we saw earlier, the same type of graph as that for a call.

Many investors buy the synthetic call and write the actual call when the latter is overpriced. This strategy is called a *conversion* and is used to exploit mispricing in the relationship between put and call prices.

SUMMARY

This chapter examined the basic option strategies. Designing the profit equations and graphs is a simple extension of material learned in previous chapters. For positions held to expiration, it is necessary only to determine the intrinsic values

---

[4]If the options are American and the short put is exercised early, however, we will have to pay out E dollars prior to expiration. Thus, it is possible that the interest earned on the cash inflow will be insufficient to make the required payout.

of puts and calls. If we elect not to hold the options until expiration, we can use the Black-Scholes model to estimate their prices. The material in this chapter, however, is basic. Option investors should always be aware of the factors that lead to early exercise, as well as tax and dividend implications. Moreover, transaction costs will lower profits, increase losses, and make breakevens higher for bullish strategies and lower for bearish strategies. The more options and stocks employed, the greater will be the transaction costs. Understanding how option transactions produce payoffs is only the first step toward using options. Unfortunately, there are no simple (or even complex) formulas for predicting the future. We have seen, however, that options can be used to modify risk—to increase or decrease it as needed.

The strategies examined here form the building blocks for exploring more exotic strategies. Chapter 6 looks at these advanced strategies, which combine many of those discussed here to produce a much more diverse set of opportunities.

Questions and Problems

1. Explain the advantages and disadvantages to a call buyer of closing out a position prior to expiration rather than holding all the way until expiration.

2. Suppose one is considering buying a call at a particular exercise price. What reasons could be given for the alternative of buying a call at a higher exercise price? At a lower exercise price?

3. Explain how a protective put is like purchasing insurance on a stock.

4. Why is the choice of exercise price on a protective put like the decision on which deductible to take on an insurance policy?

5. Discuss and compare the two bullish strategies of buying a call and writing a put. Why would one strategy be preferable to the other?

6. Suppose you wish to buy stock and protect yourself against a downside movement in its price. You consider both a covered call and a protective put. What factors will affect your decision?

7. You have inherited some stock from a rich relative. The stock has had poor performance recently, and analysts believe it has little growth potential. You would like to write calls against the stock; however, the will stipulates that you must agree not to sell it unless you need the funds for a personal financial emergency. How can you write covered calls and minimize the likelihood of exercise?

8. We briefly mentioned the synthetic call, which consists of stock and an equal number of puts. Assume the combined value of the puts and stock exceeds the value of the actual call by less than the present value of the exercise price. Show how an arbitrage profit can be made. (Note: Do not use the data from the chapter. Show your point as it was illustrated in the text for the synthetic put.)

9. A short position in stock can be protected by holding a call option. Determine the profit equations for this position, and identify the breakeven stock price at expiration and maximum and minimum profits.

10. A short stock can be protected by selling a put. Determine the profit equations for this position, and identify the breakeven stock price at expiration and maximum and minimum profits.

11. Explain the advantages and disadvantages to a covered call writer of closing out the position prior to expiration.

12. Explain the considerations facing a covered call writer regarding the choice of exercise prices.

The following option prices were observed for IBM for July 6 of a particular year. Use this information in problems 13 through 18. Ignore dividends on the stock. The stock is priced at 165 1/8. The expirations are July 17, August 21, and October 16. The continuously compounded risk-free rates are .0503, .0535, and .0571, respectively. The standard deviation is .21.

	Calls			Puts		
Strike	**Jul**	**Aug**	**Oct**	**Jul**	**Aug**	**Oct**
165	2 11/16	5 1/4	8 1/8	2 3/8	4 3/4	6 3/4
170	13/16	3 1/4	6	5 3/4	7 1/2	9

In problems 13 through 18, determine the profits for the following stock prices: 155, 160, 165, 170, 175, and 180. Answer any other questions as requested.

13. Buy one August 165 call contract. Hold until the options expire. Determine the profits and graph the results. Then identify the breakeven stock price at expiration. What is the maximum possible loss on this transaction?

14. Repeat problem 13, but close the position on August 1. Use your graph to identify the approximate breakeven stock price.

15. Buy one October 165 put contract. Hold until the options expire. Determine the profits and graph the results. Identify the breakeven stock price at expiration. What are the maximum possible gain and loss on this transaction?

16. Buy 100 shares of stock and write one October 170 call contract. Hold the position until expiration. Determine the profits and graph the results. Identify the breakeven stock price at expiration, the maximum profit, and the maximum loss.

17. Repeat problem 16, but close the position on September 1. Use your graph to approximate the breakeven stock price.

18. Buy 100 shares of stock and buy one August 165 put contract. Hold the position until expiration. Determine the profits and graph the results. Determine the breakeven stock price at expiration, the maximum profit, and the maximum loss.

19. (Concept Problem) In each case examined in the chapter and in the preceding problems, we did not account for the interest on funds invested. One useful way to observe the effect of interest is to look at a conversion or a reverse conversion. Evaluate the August 165 puts and calls, and recommend a conversion or a reverse conversion. Determine the profit from the transaction if the options are held to expiration. Make sure the profit properly accounts for the interest that accrues over the holding period.

20. (Concept Problem) Another consideration in evaluating option strategies is the effect of transaction costs. Suppose purchases and sales of options incur a brokerage commission of 1 percent of the option's value. Purchases and sales of shares of stock incur a brokerage commission of .5 percent of the stock's value. If the option is exercised, there is a transaction cost on the purchase or sale of the stock. Determine the profit equations for the following strategies assuming the options are held to expiration and exercised if in-the-money rather than sold back. Assume that one option and/or share is used and that any shares left in the portfolio are sold.

    a. Long call

    b. Long put

    c. Covered call

    d. Protective put

References

Bookstaber, Richard M. *Option Pricing and Investment Strategies*, Chapter 4. Chicago: Probus Publishing, 1987.

Dawson, Frederic S. "Risks and Returns in Continuous Option Writing." *The Journal of Portfolio Management* 5 (Winter 1979): 58–63.

Galai, Dan. "Characterization of Options." *Journal of Banking and Finance* 1 (December 1977): 373–385.

Gastineau, Gary. *The Options Manual*, 3d ed., Chapter 4. New York: McGraw-Hill, 1988.

Grube, R. Corwin, Don B. Panton, and J. Michael Terrell. "Risks and Rewards in Covered Call Positions." *The Journal of Portfolio Management* 5 (Winter 1979): 64–68.

Hull, John. *Options, Futures and Other Derivative Securities*, Chapter 1. Englewood Cliffs, N.J.: Prentice-Hall, 1989.

Malkiel, Burton G., and Richard E. Quandt. *Strategies and Rational Decisions in the Securities Options Market*, Chapter 2. Cambridge, Mass.: M.I.T. Press, 1969.

McMillan, Lawrence G. *Options as a Strategic Investment*, 2d ed., Chapters 1–5, 15–17. New York: New York Institute of Finance, 1986.

Mueller, Paul A. "Covered Call Options: An Alternative Investment Strategy." *Financial Management* 10 (Winter 1981): 64–71.

Pounds, Henry M. "Covered Call Option Writing: Strategies and Results." *The Journal of Portfolio Management* 5 (Winter 1978): 31–42.

Pozen, Robert. "The Purchase of Protective Puts by Financial Institutions." *Financial Analysts Journal* 34 (July-August 1978): 47–60.

Ritchken, Peter. *Options: Theory, Strategy, and Applications*, Chapter 3. Glenview, Ill.: Scott, Foresman, 1987.

Singleton, J. Clay, and Robin Grieves. "Synthetic Puts and Portfolio Insurance Strategies." *The Journal of Portfolio Management* 10 (Spring 1984): 63–69.

Slivka, Ronald T. "Risk and Return for Option Investment Strategies." *Financial Analysts Journal* 36 (September–October 1980): 67–73.

Trennepohl, Gary L., and William P. Dukes. "Return and Risk from Listed Option Investments." *The Journal of Financial Research* 2 (Spring 1979): 37–49.

Welch, William W. *Strategies for Put and Call Option Trading*, Chapter 4. Cambridge, Mass.: Winthrop Publishers, 1982.

Yates, James W., Jr., and Robert W. Kopprasch, Jr. "Writing Covered Call Options: Profits and Risks." *The Journal of Portfolio Management* 6 (Fall 1980): 74–80.

ADVANCED OPTION STRATEGIES

Chapter 5 provided a foundation for the basic option strategies. We can now move on to some of the more advanced strategies. As often noted, options can be combined in some interesting and unusual ways. In this chapter, we look at two types of advanced option strategies: *spreads* and *combinations*.

OPTION SPREADS: BASIC CONCEPTS

A *spread* is the purchase of one option and the sale of another. There are two general types of spread. One is the *vertical*, *strike*, or *money* spread. This strategy involves the purchase of an option with a particular exercise price and the sale of another option differing only by exercise price. For example, one might purchase an option on IBM expiring in October with an exercise price of 150 and sell an option on IBM also expiring in October but with an exercise price of 155; hence the terms *strike* and *money spread*. Because exercise prices are arranged vertically in the option pages of newspapers, this is also called a *vertical spread*.

Another type of spread is a *horizontal*, *time*, or *calendar spread*. In this spread, the investor purchases an option with an expiration of a given month and sells an otherwise identical option with a different expiration month. For example, one might purchase an IBM October 150 call and sell an IBM January 150 call. The term *horizontal spread* is due to the horizontal arrangement of expiration months in newspaper option pages.

Sometimes spreads are identified by a special notation. The aforementioned IBM money spread is referred to as the October 150/155 spread. The month is given first; the exercise price before the slash (/) is the option purchased; and the exercise price after the slash is the option sold. If the investor buys the October 155 and sells the October 150, the result is an October 155/150 spread. The calendar spread described in the previous paragraph is identified as the October/ January 150 spread. The month preceding the slash is the option purchased, while the month following the slash identifies the option sold.

Spreads can be executed using either calls or puts. An October 150/155 call spread is a net long position. This is because the 150 call costs more than the 155 call; that is, the cash outflow from buying the 150 exceeds the inflow received for selling the 155. This transaction is called *buying the spread*. In the October 150/ 155 put spread, the cash inflow received from selling the 155 put is more than the cash outflow paid in buying the 150 put. This transaction is known as *selling the spread* and results in a net short position.

For calendar spreads, the October/January 150 call spread would be net short and selling the spread, because an investor would receive more for the January call than he or she would pay for the October call. The January/October 150 call spread would be net long and buying the spread, because the January call would cost more than the October call. With calendar spreads these rules similarly hold for both calls and puts, because the premiums for both are greater the longer the time to expiration.

Why Investors Use Spreads

Spreads offer the potential for a small profit while limiting the risk. They are not, of course, the sure route to riches; we already have seen that no such strategy is. But spreads can be very useful in modifying risk while allowing profits if market forecasts prove accurate.

Risk reduction is achieved by being long in one option and short in another. If the stock price decreases, the loss on a long call will be somewhat offset by a gain on a short call. Whether the gain outweighs the loss depends on the volatility of each call. We shall illustrate this effect later. For now, consider a money spread held to expiration. Assume we buy the call with the low strike price and sell the call with the high strike price. In a bull market we will make money, because the low-exercise-price call will bring a higher payoff at expiration than will the high-exercise-price call. In a bear market, both calls will probably expire worthless and we will lose money. For that reason, the spread involving the purchase of the low-exercise-price call is referred to as a *bull spread*. Similarly, in a bear market we make money if we are long the high-exercise-price call and short the low-exercise-price call. This is called a *bear spread*. Opposite rules apply for puts. A position of long (short) the low-exercise-price put and short (long) the high-exercise-price put is a bull (bear) spread. In general, a bull spread should profit in a bull market and a bear spread should profit in a bear market.

Time spreads are not classified into bull and bear spreads. They profit by either increased or decreased volatility. We shall reserve further discussion of time spreads for a later section.

Transaction costs are an important practical consideration in spread trading. These costs can represent a significant portion of invested funds, especially for small traders. Spreads involve several option positions, and the transaction costs can quickly become prohibitive for all but floor traders and large institutional investors. As in Chapter 5, we will not build transaction costs directly into the analyses here but will discuss their special relevance where appropriate.

Notation

The notation here is the same as that used in previous chapters. However, we must add some distinguishing symbols for the spreads' different strike prices and expirations. For a money spread, we will use subscripts to distinguish options differing by strike price. For example,

$$E_1, E_2, E_3 = \text{exercise prices of calls where } E_1 < E_2 < E_3$$
$$C_1, C_2, C_3 = \text{prices of calls with exercise prices } E_1, E_2, E_3$$
$$N_1, N_2, N_3 = \text{quantity held of each option.}$$

The N notation indicates the number of options where a positive N is a long position and a negative N is a short position.

In time spreads,

$$T(1), T(2) = \text{times to expiration where } T(1) < T(2)$$
$$C_1, C_2 = \text{prices of calls with times to expiration of } T(1), T(2)$$
$$N_1, N_2 = \text{quantity held of each option.}$$

The numerical illustrations will use the Digital Equipment options presented in earlier chapters. For convenience, Table 6.1 repeats the data. Unless otherwise stated, assume 100 options are employed.

Because the analyses of call and put spreads are so similar, we shall spend little time on put spreads. We will cover any important considerations but reserve treatment of put spreads mainly for end-of-chapter problems. This will give readers an opportunity to determine whether they understand the concepts well enough to apply them to slightly different situations.

TABLE 6.1

Digital Equipment Option Data, June 12

Exercise	Calls			Puts		
Price	**Jun**	**Jul**	**Oct**	**Jun**	**Jul**	**Oct**
160	4 5/8	8 5/8	15 1/4	13/16	3 7/8	8 1/8
165	1 7/8	5 3/4	13 1/4	2 15/16	6	9 3/4
170	1/2	3 3/4	10 3/4	6 1/2	8 1/2	NA
175	1/16	2 3/8	8 1/2	NA	NA	NA

Current stock price: 164
Expirations: June 19, July 17, October 16
Risk-free rates: .0473 (Jun); .0521 (Jul); .0574 (Oct)

MONEY SPREADS

As indicated earlier, *money spreads* can be designed to profit in either a bull market or a bear market. The former is called a *bull spread*.

Bull Spreads

Consider two call options differing only by exercise price, E_1 and E_2, where $E_1 < E_2$. Their premiums are C_1 and C_2, and we know that $C_1 > C_2$. A bull spread consists of the purchase of the option with the lower exercise price and the sale of the option with the higher exercise price. Assuming one option of each, $N_1 = 1$ and $N_2 = -1$, the profit equations are

$$\Pi = Max(0, S_T - E_1) - C_1 - Max(0, S_T - E_2) + C_2 .$$

The stock price at expiration can fall in one of three ranges: less than or equal to E_1, greater than E_1 but less than or equal to E_2, or greater than E_2. The profits for these three ranges are as follows:

$$\Pi = -C_1 + C_2 \qquad\qquad \text{if } S_T \le E_1 < E_2$$
$$\Pi = S_T - E_1 - C_1 + C_2 \qquad \text{if } E_1 < S_T \le E_2$$
$$\Pi = S_T - E_1 - C_1 - S_T + E_2 + C_2$$
$$= E_2 - E_1 - C_1 + C_2 \qquad \text{if } E_1 < E_2 < S_T.$$

In the case where the stock price ends up equal to or below the lower exercise price, both options expire out-of-the-money. The spreader loses the premium on the long call and retains the premium on the short call. The profit is the same regardless of how far below the lower exercise price the stock price is. However, because the premium on the long call is greater than the premium on the short call, this profit is actually a loss.

In the third case, where both options end up in-the-money, the short call is exercised on the spreader, who exercises the long call and then delivers the stock. The effect of the stock price cancels and the profit is constant for any stock price above the higher exercise price. Is this profit positive? The profit is $(E_2 - E_1) - (C_1 - C_2)$, or the difference between the exercise prices minus the difference between the premiums. Recall from Chapter 3 that the difference in premiums cannot exceed the difference in exercise prices. The spreader paid a premium of C_1, received a premium of C_2, and thus obtained the spread for a net investment of $C_1 - C_2$. The maximum payoff from the spread is $E_2 - E_1$. No one would pay more than the maximum payoff from an investment. Therefore, the profit is positive.

Only in the second case, where the long call ends up in-the-money and the short call is out-of-the-money, is there any uncertainty. The equation shows that the profit increases dollar for dollar with the stock price at expiration.

Figure 6.1 illustrates the profits from the bull spread strategy for the Digital Equipment July 165 and 170 calls with premiums of $5.75 and $3.75, respectively. The maximum loss is the net premium of $575 - $375, or $200, which occurs at any stock price at expiration at or below 165. The maximum gain is the difference in strike prices minus the difference in premiums, $100(170 - 165 - 2) = 300$, which occurs at any stock price at expiration above 170.

From the graph, it is apparent that the breakeven stock price at expiration is between the two exercise prices. To find this breakeven—call it S_T^*—take the profit equation for the second case, where the stock price is between both exercise prices, and set it equal to zero:

$$\Pi = S_T^* - E_1 - C_1 + C_2 = 0.$$

Then solve for S_T^*:

$$S_T^* = E_1 + C_1 - C_2.$$

The stock price must exceed the lower exercise price by the difference in the premiums. This makes sense. The spreader exercises the call with exercise price E_1. The higher the stock price, the greater the amount received from the exercise. To break even, the spreader must receive enough to recover the net premium, $C_1 - C_2$. In this problem, the breakeven stock price at expiration is $165 + 5.75 - 3.75 = 167$.

THE SPREAD DELTA   As Figure 6.1 shows, this spread will profit in a bull market and lose in a bear market. The reason is that the low-exercise-price call—the option bought—is more sensitive to stock price changes than the high-exercise-price call—the option written. Recall from Chapter 4 that a call's sensitivity to stock price changes is referred to as its *delta*. The Black-Scholes model provides a means for estimating the delta. The delta is simply the value of $N(d_1)$, the approximate change in the call price for a $1 change in the stock price. The spread's delta

FIGURE 6.1

Call Bull Spread

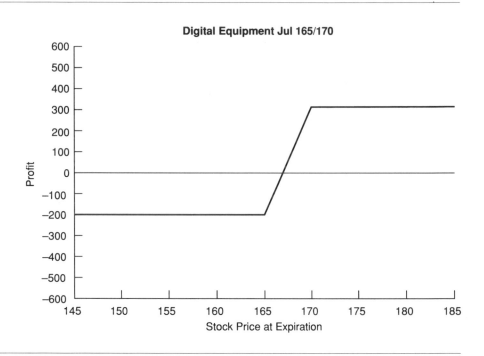

is its overall sensitivity to a $1 change in the stock price. It is computed as the long call's delta minus the short call's delta. Table 6.2 illustrates the deltas for these two options.

As indicated, each call's delta increases with the stock price, but the delta of the low-exercise-price call is always larger than that of the high-exercise-price call. Because we are long the low-exercise-price call and short the high-exercise-price call, the spread's delta is positive. Because the low-exercise-price call will increase more than the high-exercise-price call, the spread will increase in value with any rise in stock price. If the stock price falls the spread will lose value, because the low-exercise-price call will fall more than the high-exercise-price call.

THE CHOICE OF HOLDING PERIOD As with any option strategy, it is possible to hold the position for a period shorter than the option's entire life. Recall that in Chapter 5 we made assumptions about closing out the option positions prior to expiration. We used short holding periods of T(1), which meant closing the position on July 24, and T(2), in which we closed the position on September 4. When a position is closed prior to expiration, we estimate the option price for a range of stock prices and use those estimates to generate the profit graph. We illustrated

TABLE 6.2
Call Spread Deltas, July 165 and 170 Calls

Stock Price	Jul 165	Jul 170	Spread
145	.090	.047	.043
150	.168	.098	.070
155	.276	.177	.099
160	.404	.283	.121
165	.540	.408	.132
170	.667	.540	.127
175	.775	.664	.111
180	.858	.769	.089

Notes: $\sigma = .29$, $T = .0959$, $r = .0521$.
The spread's delta is the delta of the long call, the 165, minus the delta of the short call, the 170.

the general procedure in Chapter 5. Using the same methodology here, we obtain Figure 6.2, the bull spread under the assumption of three different holding periods.

Recall that $T(1)$ is the shortest holding period, $T(2)$ is slightly longer, and T represents holding all the way to expiration. The graph indicates that the short holding period has the lowest range of profits. If the stock price is low, the shortest holding period produces the smallest loss while the longest holding period produces the largest loss. If the stock price is high, the shortest holding period produces the smallest gain and the longest holding period the largest gain.

The logic behind this graph is simple. First, recall that the low-exercise-price call will always be worth more than the high-exercise-price call; however, their relative time values will differ. An option's time value is greatest when the stock price is near the exercise price. Therefore, when stock prices are high, the high-exercise-price call will have the greater time value and when they are low, the low-exercise-price call will have the greater time value.

When we close out the spread prior to expiration, we can always expect the long call to sell for more than the short call because the long call has the lower exercise price. However, the excess of the long call's price over the short call's price will decrease at high stock prices. This is because the time value will be greater on the short call, because the stock price is closer to the exercise price. The long call will still sell for a higher price because it has more intrinsic value, but the difference will be smaller at high stock prices. Conversely, at low stock prices the long call will have a greater time value because its exercise price is closer to the stock price.

The result of all this is that when we close the bull spread well before expiration, the profit will be lower at high stock prices and higher at low stock prices than if we did so closer to expiration. If we hold the position longer but not all the

FIGURE 6.2
Call Bull Spread: Different Holding Periods

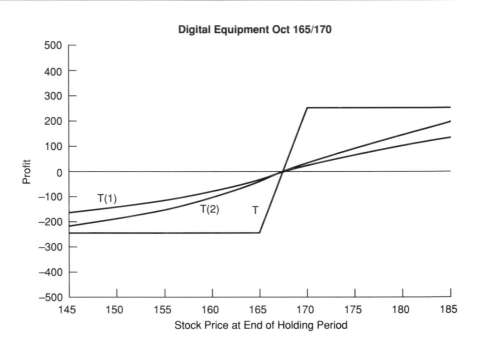

Digital Equipment Oct 165/170

way to expiration, we will obtain the same effect, but the impact will be smaller because the time value will be less.

Which holding period should an investor choose? There is no consistently right or wrong answer. An investor who is strongly bullish should realize that the longer the position is held, the greater the profit that can be made if the forecast is correct. In addition, a long holding period allows more time for the stock price to move upward. If the forecast proves incorrect, the loss will be lower the shorter the holding period. With short holding periods, however, there is less time for a large stock price change.

THE TIME VALUE DECAY   What about an investor who expects little, if any, change in the stock price over the option's life? As we shall see later, there are some better strategies to use in this situation. For now, consider how one could construct a money spread to take maximum advantage of this scenario.

Because both calls expire at the same time, both will lose their time values by the expiration date. However, they will not lose their time values at the same rate. Because both options must lose their time values over the same time period, the option with the greater time value must lose it more rapidly. Therefore, it would make sense to write the option that will lose its time value more rapidly and buy the option that will lose it more slowly. The trader could hold this position for as long as the stock price is expected to show little or no change.

Which option will lose its time value more rapidly? Recall that time value is greatest when the stock price is closest to the exercise price. Therefore, the option with the stock price closest to the exercise price can be counted on to lose its time value more rapidly. For example, in the case of the Digital Equipment 165 and 170 calls, the 165 will lose its time value more quickly if the stock price is no more than $167.50. For any stock price in the range of $0 to $167.50, the stock price is closer to $165 than to $170. For any stock price more than $167.50, the stock price is closer to $170. In that case, the 170 call will lose its time value more rapidly. If the stock price is less than $167.50 and expected to be stable, the trader should write the 165 and buy the 170. If the stock price is higher than $167.50 and expected to hold, the trader should write the 170 and buy the 165.[1]

Early exercise poses no problem with the bull spread. Suppose the stock price prior to expiration is S_t. If the short call is exercised, the stock price must be greater than E_2. This means that the stock price is also greater than E_1, and the long call can be exercised for a net payoff of $(S_t - E_1) - (S_t - E_2) = E_2 - E_1$. This is the best outcome one could obtain by holding the spread all the way to expiration.

The following section examines a call bear spread. We shall see that a bear spread is, in many respects, the opposite of a bull spread but does not carry the same risk of early exercise.

Bear Spreads

A bear spread is the mirror image of a bull spread: The trader is long the high-exercise-price call and short the low-exercise-price call. Since $N_1 = -1$ and $N_2 = 1$, the profit equation is simply

$$\Pi = -\text{Max}(0, S_T - E_1) + C_1 + \text{Max}(0, S_T - E_2) - C_2.$$

The outcomes are as follows:

$$\Pi = C_1 - C_2 \qquad\qquad \text{if } S_T \le E_1 < E_2$$
$$\Pi = -S_T + E_1 + C_1 - C_2 \qquad\qquad \text{if } E_1 < S_T \le E_2$$
$$\Pi = -S_T + E_1 + C_1 + S_T - E_2 - C_2$$
$$= E_1 - E_2 + C_1 - C_2 \qquad\qquad \text{if } E_1 < E_2 < S_T.$$

Figure 6.3 illustrates the bear spread with the Digital Equipment July 165 and 170 calls. The spread is profitable if the stock price is low and loses money if the stock price is high. Because a bear spread is the opposite of a bull spread, the formula for the breakeven stock price is still $E_1 + C_1 - C_2$. In this example, the

---

[1]The crossover stock price is not exactly $167.50 but somewhat lower. One could use a computer search routine with the Black-Scholes model to find the exact price.

FIGURE 6.3
Call Bear Spread

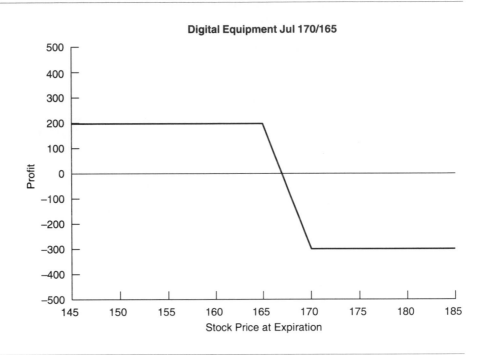

Digital Equipment Jul 170/165

breakeven stock price is $165 + 5.75 - 3.75 = 167$. The maximum and minimum profits are

$$\text{Maximum: } C_1 - C_2 = 100(5.75 - 3.75) = 200$$
$$\text{Minimum: } E_1 - E_2 + C_1 - C_2 = 100(165 - 170 + 5.75 - 3.75) = -300.$$

THE SPREAD DELTA   The bear spread is effective in a bear market, because the short call's delta is greater than the long call's. Referring back to Table 6.2, we can see the effects by simply reversing the sign of the spread delta. The spread delta is the delta of the long call, the 170, minus the delta of the short call, the 165. This gives a negative delta, because the short call is more volatile than the long call. The negative spread delta means that the bear spread will decrease in value in a bull market and increase in value in a bear market.

THE CHOICE OF HOLDING PERIODS   Figure 6.4 illustrates the bear spread when different holding periods are used. The longer holding period produces higher profits in a bear market and larger losses in a bull market. Again this is because of the time value effect. The spread trader closing the position prior to expiration buys back the time value of the short call and sells the long call's remaining time

FIGURE 6.4
Call Bear Spread: Different Holding Periods

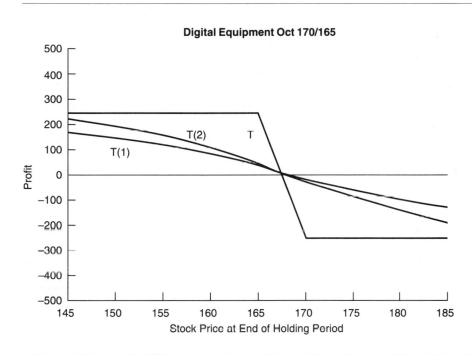

value. For high stock prices, there will be more time value on the high-exercise-price call than on the low-exercise-price call. That means that more time value can be captured on the resale of the long call than must be paid for on the repurchase of the short call. However, both calls are in-the-money; thus, the short call has more intrinsic value to be repurchased. Therefore, the short holding period produces a loss at high stock prices. This loss increases with longer holding periods, because the long call's time value advantage is diminished. With low stock prices, the opposite effect prevails: The profit is greater for longer holding periods and is maximized when holding all the way to expiration.

We should repeat, however, that these statements do not advocate a short or long holding period, because the length of the holding period affects the range of possible stock prices.

Gombola, Roenfeldt, and Cooley (1978) examined the performance of bull and bear spreads over three-, six-, and nine-month holding periods for CBOE calls during the period of April 1973 through July 1976. Before considering commissions, bull spreads provided very attractive returns with lower risk than did outright long positions in calls. However, commission costs consumed much of the advantage. Returns from longer holding periods were much higher, as would be expected. Returns from bear call spreads were inferior to those from bull spreads as well as from uncovered call positions. As we noted in Chapter 5, however, these results reflected the early years of listed options, and the favorable performance may have deteriorated as investors gained knowledge about pricing options.

EARLY EXERCISE   The risk of early exercise for bear spreads is a special problem. The short call can be sufficiently in-the-money to justify early exercise while the long call is still out-of-the-money. Even if the long call is in-the-money, the cash flow from early exercise will be negative.

For example, suppose S_t is the stock price prior to expiration. The cash flow from the exercise of the short call is $-(S_t - E_1)$, while the cash flow from the exercise of the long call is $S_t - E_2$. This gives a total cash flow of $E_1 - E_2$, which is negative. Early exercise ensures that the bear spreader will incur a cash outflow. Because the loss occurs prior to expiration, it is greater in present value terms than if it had occurred at expiration. Thus, the call bear spread entails a risk not associated with the bull spread. To profit in a bear market, it may be better to execute a put spread.

A Word about Put Money Spreads

As we have seen, it is possible to design call money spreads that will profit in either a bull market or a bear market. It is also possible to construct put money spreads. Like a call spread, a put spread is considered a bull spread if designed to make money in a bull market and a bear spread if designed to make money in a bear market.

Given that both bull and bear spreads can be constructed from calls, put spreads would seem unnecessary. For illustrative purposes, this is probably true. As a practical matter, however, put spreads occasionally offer opportunities unavailable with call spreads. As we saw in Chapter 4, the Black-Scholes model provides a method of determining if an option is correctly priced. If a put is incorrectly priced, the investor can execute a spread to profit from the mispricing. Also, the put bear spread does not run the same risk of early exercise as the call bear spread. This is because the put bear spread will have the long put in-the-money whenever the short put is in-the-money. If the short put is exercised, the long put can be exercised for an overall cash flow of $E_2 - E_1$, which is the maximum payoff obtainable if held to expiration.

For illustrative purposes, however, we can analyze put spreads in the same manner as call spreads. We need only change the intrinsic values to reflect the use of puts. This we will leave as an end-of-chapter problem. For now, we will turn to a variation of the money spread: the butterfly spread.

Butterfly Spreads

A *butterfly spread*, sometimes called a *sandwich spread*, is a combination of a bull spread and a bear spread. However, this transaction involves three exercise prices: E_1, E_2, and E_3. Suppose we construct a call bull spread by purchasing the call with the low exercise price, E_1, and writing the call with the middle exercise price, E_2. Then we also construct a call bear spread by purchasing the call with the high exercise price, E_3, and writing the call with the middle exercise price, E_2. Combining these positions shows that we are long one each of the low- and high-exercise-price options and short two middle-exercise-price options. Since $N_1 = 1$, $N_2 = -2$, and $N_3 = 1$, the profit equation is

$$\Pi = \text{Max}(0, S_T - E_1) - C_1 - 2\text{Max}(0, S_T - E_2) + 2C_2 + \text{Max}(0, S_T - E_3) - C_3.$$

To analyze the behavior of the profit equation, we must examine four ranges of the stock price at expiration:

$$\Pi = -C_1 + 2C_2 - C_3 \qquad\qquad\qquad \text{if } S_T \le E_1 < E_2 < E_3$$

$$\Pi = S_T - E_1 - C_1 + 2C_2 - C_3 \qquad\qquad \text{if } E_1 < S_T \le E_2 < E_3$$

$$\Pi = S_T - E_1 - C_1 - 2S_T + 2E_2 + 2C_2 - C_3$$
$$= -S_T + 2E_2 - E_1 - C_1 + 2C_2 - C_3 \qquad \text{if } E_1 < E_2 < S_T \le E_3$$

$$\Pi = S_T - E_1 - C_1 - 2S_T + 2E_2 + 2C_2 + S_T - E_3 - C_3$$
$$= -E_1 + 2E_2 - E_3 - C_1 + 2C_2 - C_3 \qquad \text{if } E_1 < E_2 < E_3 < S_T.$$

Now look at the first profit equation, $-C_1 + 2C_2 - C_3$. This can be separated into $-C_1 + C_2$ and $C_2 - C_3$. We already know that a low-exercise-price call is worth more than a high-exercise-price call. Thus, the first pair of terms is negative and the second pair is positive. Which pair will be greater in an absolute sense? The first pair will. The advantage of a low-exercise-price call over a high-exercise-price call is smaller at higher exercise prices, because there the likelihood of both calls expiring out-of-the-money is greater. If that happens, neither call will be of any value to the trader. Because $-C_1 + C_2$ is larger in an absolute sense than $C_2 - C_3$, the profit for the lowest range of stock prices at expiration is negative.

For the second range, the profit is $S_T - E_1 - C_1 + 2C_2 - C_3$. The last three terms, $-C_1 + 2C_2 - C_3$, represent the net price paid for the butterfly spread. Because the stock price at expiration has a direct effect on the profit, a graph would show the profit varying dollar for dollar and in a positive manner with the stock price at expiration. However, the profit in this range of stock prices can be either positive or negative. This implies that there is a breakeven stock price at expiration. To find that stock price, S_T^*, set this profit equal to zero:

$$S_T^* - E_1 - C_1 + 2C_2 - C_3 = 0.$$

Solving for S_T^* gives

$$S_T^* = E_1 + C_1 - 2C_2 + C_3.$$

The breakeven equation indicates that a butterfly spread is profitable if the stock price at expiration exceeds the low exercise price by an amount large enough to cover the net price paid for the spread.

Now look at the third profit equation. Since the profit varies inversely dollar for dollar with the stock price at expiration, a graph would show the profit decreasing one for one with the stock price at expiration. The profit can be either positive or negative; hence, there is a second breakeven stock price. To find it, set the profit equal to zero:

$$-S_T^* + 2E_2 - E_1 - C_1 + 2C_2 - C_3 = 0.$$

Solving for S_T^* gives

$$S_T^* = 2E_2 - E_1 - C_1 + 2C_2 - C_3.$$

Recall that in this range of stock prices, the profit declines with higher stock prices. Profit will disappear completely if the stock price is so high that it exceeds the cash flow received from the exercise of the middle-exercise-price call, $2E_2$, minus the cash flow paid for the exercise of the low-exercise-price call, E_1, minus the net premiums on the calls.

In the final range of the stock price at expiration, profit is the net premiums paid plus the difference in the exercise prices. However, in a butterfly spread, the exercise prices are equally spaced; that is, $E_2 - E_1$ is the same as $E_3 - E_2$. Therefore, $-E_1 + 2E_2 - E_3 = 0$. This means that the profit in this range is the same as that in the first range and is simply the difference in the premiums.

Now we have a good idea of what a butterfly spread looks like. Figure 6.5 illustrates the butterfly spread for the Digital Equipment July 160, 165, and 170 calls. The minimum profit is simply the net premiums, or $100[-8.625 + 2(5.75) - 3.75] = -87.50$. This is obtained for any stock price less than \$160 or greater than \$170. The maximum profit is obtained when the stock price at expiration is at the middle exercise price. Using the second profit equation and letting $S_T = E_2$, the maximum profit is

$$\Pi = E_2 - E_1 - C_1 + 2C_2 - C_3,$$

which in this example is $100[165 - 160 - 8.625 + 2(5.75) - 3.75] = 412.50$. The lower breakeven is $E_1 + C_1 - 2C_2 + C_3$, which in this case is $160 + 8.625 - 2(5.75) + 3.75 = 160.875$. The upper breakeven is $2E_2 - E_1 - C_1 + 2C_2 - C_3$, which in this example is $2(165) - 160 - 8.625 + 2(5.75) - 3.75 = 169.125$.

The butterfly spread strategy assumes the stock price will fluctuate very little. In this example, the trader is betting that the stock price will stay within the range of \$160.875 to \$169.125. However, if this prediction of low stock price volatility proves incorrect, the potential loss will be limited—in this case, to \$87.50. Thus, the butterfly spread is a low-risk transaction.

A trader who believes the stock price will be extremely volatile and will fall outside of the two breakeven stock prices can write a butterfly spread. This will involve one short position in each of the E_1 and E_3 calls and two long positions in the E_2 call. We shall leave it as an end-of-chapter problem to explore the short butterfly spread.

FIGURE 6.5
Call Butterfly Spread

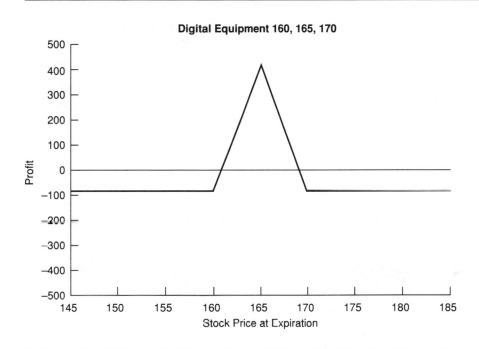

THE CHOICE OF HOLDING PERIOD   As with any option strategy, the investor might wish to close the position prior to expiration. Consider the July 160, 165, and 170 calls. Let holding period T(1) involve closing the position on July 1 and holding period T(2) on July 10.[2]

In this example, a plot of the results would reveal that the shortest holding period would not profit at any stock price. That would create an arbitrage opportunity. If the transaction were reversed, the shortest holding period would have no loss at any stock price. Thus, the general results of this example are quite sensitive to the options' prices. The reason is that the butterfly spread involves more options than most of the other strategies we have covered. That means that the strategy is sensitive to the possibility of option mispricing. Also, the short holding periods imply that the investor has little time to recapture the original cost of the options. If that cost is incorrectly estimated, the results will be greatly affected. To remove this bias, let us use the three calls' Black-Scholes prices instead of their market prices. The Black-Scholes prices are 8.5 for the 160, 5.79 for the 165, and 3.74 for the 170. The graph is shown in Figure 6.6.

[2]The holding period was changed in this example because the time value decay does not show up as clearly for the holding periods we have previously used.

FIGURE 6.6

Call Butterfly Spread: Different Holding Periods

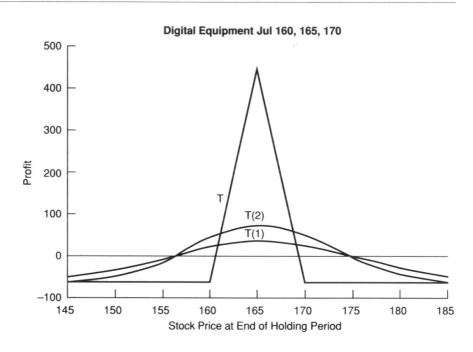

At high stock prices, time value will be greatest on the call with the highest exercise price. Since we are long that call, we gain the advantage of being able to sell it back early and recapture some of the time value. This advantage, however, erodes with a longer holding period because the time value decreases.

At low stock prices, the time value will be greatest on the call with the lowest exercise price. Since we are also long that call, we can sell it back early and recapture some of its remaining time value. However, this advantage also decreases as we hold the position longer and time value decays.

In the middle range of stock prices, the time value will be very high on the two short calls. For short holding periods, this is a disadvantage because we have to buy back these calls, which means that we must pay for the remaining time value. However, this disadvantage turns to an advantage as the holding period lengthens and time value begins to disappear. At expiration, no time value remains; thus, profit is maximized in this range.

The breakeven stock prices are substantially further away with shorter holding periods and are highest with the shortest. This is advantageous, because it will then take a much larger stock price change to produce a loss.

As always, we cannot specifically identify an optimal holding period. Because the butterfly spread is one in which the trader expects the stock price to stay within a narrow range, profit is maximized with a long holding period. The disadvantage of a long holding period, however, is that it gives the stock price more time to move outside of the profitable range.

EARLY EXERCISE   Suppose the stock price prior to expiration is S_t, where S_t is greater than or equal to E_2 and less than or equal to E_3. Assume the short calls are exercised shortly before the stock goes ex-dividend. The spreader then exercises the long call with exercise price E_1. The cash flow from the short calls is $-(2S_t - 2E_2)$, and the cash flow from the long call is $S_t - E_1$. This gives a total cash flow of $-S_t + E_2 + E_2 - E_1$. The minimum value of this expression is $-E_3 + E_2 + E_2 - E_1$, which occurs if $S_t = E_3$. Since the exercise prices are equally spaced, this equals zero. The maximum value occurs when $S_t = E_2$ and is $-E_2 + E_2 + E_2 - E_1 = E_2 - E_1$, which is positive. If S_t exceeds E_3 and the two short calls are exercised, they will be offset by the exercise of both long calls, and the overall cash flow will be zero.

Thus, early exercise does not result in a cash outflow, but that does not mean that it poses no risk. If the options are exercised early, there is no possibility of achieving the maximum profit obtainable at expiration when $S_T = E_2$. If the spread were reversed and the E_1 and E_3 calls were sold while two of the E_2 calls were bought, early exercise could generate a negative cash flow.

All of the above spreads are money spreads. We now turn to an examination of calendar spreads.

CALENDAR SPREADS

A *calendar spread*, also known as a *time* or *horizontal spread,* involves the purchase of an option with one expiration date and the sale of an otherwise identical option with a different expiration date. Because it is not possible to hold both options until expiration, analyzing a calendar spread is more complicated than analyzing a money spread. Since one option expires before the other, the longest possible holding period would be to hold the position until the shorter-maturity option's expiration. Then the other option would have some remaining time value that must be estimated.

Because both options have the same exercise prices, they will have the same intrinsic values; thus, the profitability of the calendar spread will be determined solely by the difference in their time values. The longer-term call will have more time value. However, this does not necessarily mean that one should always buy the longer-term call and sell the shorter-term call. As with most option strategies, which option is purchased and which one is sold depends on the investor's outlook for the stock.

To best understand the calendar spread, we will again illustrate with the Digital Equipment calls. This spread consists of the purchase of the October 160 call at $15.25 and the sale of the July 160 call at $8.625. Consider two possible holding periods. One, T(1), will involve the spread's termination on July 1; the

FIGURE 6.7
Call Calendar Spread

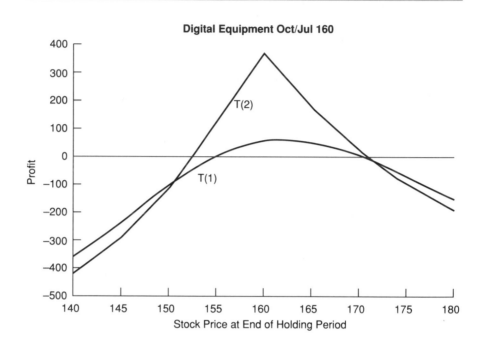

other, T(2), will have the spread held until July 17, the date of the July call's expiration. Using the Black-Scholes model to estimate the remaining time values produced the graph in Figure 6.7.

Like the butterfly spread, the calendar spread is one in which the stock's volatility is a major factor in its performance. The investor obtains the greatest profit if the stock has low volatility and thus trades within a narrow range. If the stock price moves substantially, the investor will likely incur a loss.

How does the calendar spread work? Recall that we are short the July call and long the October call. When closing out the position, we buy back the July call and sell the October call. If the stock price is around the exercise price, both calls will have more time value remaining than if the stock price were at the extremes. However, the July call will always have less time value than the October call on any given date. Thus, when we close out the position, the time value repurchased on the July call will be low relative to the remaining time value received from the sale of the October call. As we hold the position closer and closer to the July call's expiration, the remaining time value we must repurchase on that option will get lower and lower.

If the stock price is at the high or low extreme, the time values of both options will be low. If the stock price is high enough or low enough, there may be little, if any, time value on either option. Thus, when closing out the position there may be

TABLE 6.3
Time Value Decay Pattern, July and October 165

| Date | Jul 165 | | Oct 165 | | Spread Time Value |
	Time	Time Value	Time	Time Value	
6/12	.0959	5.789	.3452	12.066	6.277
6/19	.0767	5.090	.3260	11.675	6.585
6/26	.0575	4.307	.3068	11.275	6.968
7/3	.0384	3.400	.2877	10.866	7.466
7/10	.0192	2.239	.2685	10.443	8.204
7/17	.0000	0.000	.2493	10.008	10.008

Notes: $\sigma = .29$, $S = 164$, r (July) $= .0521$, r (October) $= .0574$.
The spread time value equals the time value on the long call minus the time value on the short call.

little time value to recover from the October option. Since the October call is more expensive, we will end up losing money on the overall transaction.

The breakeven stock prices can be obtained only by visual examination.[3] In this example, the shortest holding period has a tighter range between its two breakeven stock prices, about $154 and $170. For the longer holding period, the lower breakeven is about $152 and the higher breakeven is around $171.

An investor who expected the stock price to move into the extremes could execute a reverse calendar spread. This would require purchasing the July call and selling the October call. If the stock price became extremely low or high, there would be little time value remaining to be repurchased on the October call. Since the spreader received more money from the sale of the October call than was paid for the purchase of the July call, a profit would be made. However, if the stock price ended up around the exercise price, the trader could incur a potentially large loss. This is because the October call would possibly have a large time value that would have to be repurchased.

THE TIME VALUE DECAY   Because a calendar spread is completely influenced by the behavior of the two calls' time value decay, it provides a good opportunity to examine how time values decay. Using the Black-Scholes model, we can compute the week-by-week time values for each call during the spread's life, holding the stock price constant at $164. Keep in mind, of course, that time values will change if the stock price changes. Because time values are greatest in at-the-money options, we use the July and October 165 calls. The pattern of time values at various points during the options' lives is presented in Table 6.3.

---

[3]However, it is possible to use a computer search routine with the Black-Scholes model to find the precise breakeven.

FIGURE 6.8

Time Value Decay

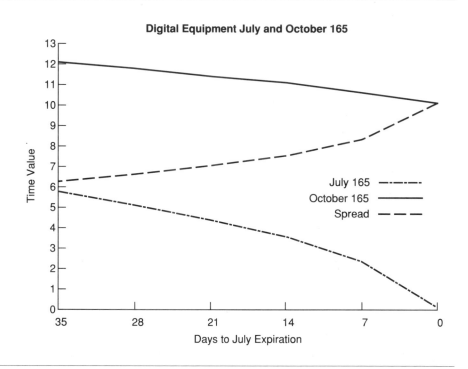

Notice how the time value decays as expiration approaches. Because of the July call's earlier expiration, its time value decays more rapidly than does that of the October call. Since we are long the October call and short the July call, the spread's time value—the time value of the long call minus the time value of the short call—increases.

Figure 6.8 illustrates the time value decay. As expiration approaches, the time value of the July call rapidly decreases and the overall time value of the spread greatly increases. At expiration of the July call, the spread's time value is composed entirely of the October call's time value.

The time value decay would appear to make it easy to profit with a time spread. One would simply buy the longer-term option and write the shorter-term option. As the time values decayed, the spread would gain value. In reality, however, it seldom works out like this. The pattern of time value decay illustrated here was obtained by holding the stock price constant. In the real world, the stock price probably will not remain constant. Thus, there is indeed risk to a calendar spread. However, this risk is mitigated somewhat by the fact that the investor is long one option and short the other. Nonetheless, the calendar spread, in which one buys the long-term option and writes the short-term option, is a good strategy if one expects the stock price to remain fairly stable.

EARLY EXERCISE   The degree of risk of early exercise on a calendar spread depends on which call is bought and which is sold. Since both calls have the same exercise price, the extent to which they are in-the-money is the same. However, as discussed in Chapter 3, the time to expiration is a factor in encouraging early exercise. We saw that if everything else is equal, the shorter-term option is the one more likely to be exercised early. Thus, if we write the shorter-term option, it could be exercised early. However, we always have the choice of exercising the longer-term option early. It will certainly be in-the-money if the shorter-term option is in-the-money. If S_t is the stock price prior to expiration and the shorter-term call is exercised, the cash flow will be $-(S_t - E)$ while the cash flow from exercising the longer-term option will be $S_t - E$. Thus, the total cash flow will be zero. This means that in the event of early exercise there will be no negative cash flow. However, it does not mean that there will be no overall loss on the transaction. The longer-term call is more expensive than the shorter-term call. This means that early exercise would ensure a loss by preventing us from waiting to capture the time value decay.

Calendar spreads can also be constructed with puts. By using the Black-Scholes model to price the time value on the puts, similar results can be obtained. Like money spreads, put calendar spreads should not be overlooked. The puts could be mispriced, in which case a spread might offer the most profitable opportunity.

In the aforementioned study by Gombola, Roenfeldt, and Cooley (1978), calendar spreads involving the purchase of a six-month call and the sale of a three-month call were formed and held until the three-month call expired. The results were superior to those of simple long call positions before deducting commissions; however, after commissions the spreads lost money. Although this raises questions about the value of calendar spreads, it should be noted that this study was done under the old system in which commissions were fixed. Since that time commissions have been negotiable, and for institutional investors this generally has led to lower commissions. In addition, the study was conducted during the early years of listed options, when few people knew how to price them. Unfortunately, there have been no subsequent studies using recent actual option prices.

All of the strategies covered so far are risky. Some option traders, however, prefer riskless strategies because if the options are mispriced, it may be possible to construct a riskless portfolio that will earn a return in excess of the risk-free rate.

RATIO SPREADS[*]

Chapter 4 examined the Black-Scholes model. It showed that when an option is mispriced, an investor can construct a riskless hedge by buying an underpriced call and selling short the stock or by buying stock and selling an overpriced call. Because of margin requirements and the uptick rule, selling short stock can be

[*]This section requires the use of calculus.

undesirable. By using spreads, however, the investor can buy an underpriced call and sell an over-priced or correctly priced call, producing a ratio of one call to the other that creates a riskless position. This transaction is called a *ratio spread*.

The ratio spread can be either a money spread or a calendar spread. Consider two calls priced at C_1 and C_2. Initially we need not be concerned with which one is purchased and which one is sold, nor do we need to determine whether the two calls differ by time to expiration or by exercise price. The model presented here can accommodate all cases.

Let the investor hold N_1 units of the call priced at C_1 and N_2 units of the call priced at C_2. The value of the portfolio is

$$V = N_1 C_1 + N_2 C_2.$$

If the stock price changes, the spread's value will change. The change in the spread's value for a small change in the stock price is the partial derivative of V with respect to S:

$$\frac{\partial V}{\partial S} = N_1 \left(\frac{\partial C_1}{\partial S} \right) + N_2 \left(\frac{\partial C_2}{\partial S} \right).$$

A hedged position is one in which the portfolio's value is not influenced by a change in the stock price. Set this partial derivative equal to zero, then solve for the ratio N_1/N_2:

$$\frac{N_1}{N_2} = -\frac{\partial C_2 / \partial S}{\partial C_1 / \partial S}.$$

Thus, a riskless position is established if the ratio of the quantity of the first call to the quantity of the second call equals the ratio of their partial derivatives with respect to the stock price. Recall from the discussion of the Black-Scholes model that the partial derivative of the call price with respect to the stock price is the value $N(d_1)$.

Consider an example using the Digital Equipment July 160 and July 165 calls. Using $S = 164$, $r = .0521$, and $T = .0959$ in the Black-Scholes model gives a value of $N(d_1)$ of .646 for the July 160 and .513 for the July 165. Thus, the ratio of the number of July 160s to July 165s should be $-(.513/.646) = -.794$. Hence, the investor would buy 794 of the July 160s and sell 1,000 of the July 165s.

Note that the investor could have purchased 1,000 of the July 165s and sold 794 of the July 160s. The minus sign in the formula is a reminder to be long one option and short the other. An investor should, of course, always buy underpriced or correctly priced calls and sell overpriced or correctly priced calls.

The values of $N(d_1)$ are simply approximations of the change in the call price for a change in the stock price. They are partial derivatives and, therefore, assume only very small changes in the stock price. However, they can be used to approximate the change in the call price for a given change in the stock price.

If the stock price decreases by \$1, the July 160 should decrease by .646 and the July 165 by .513. The investor is long 794 of the July 160s and therefore loses $.646(794) \cong 513$. Likewise, the investor is short 1,000 of the July 165s and thus gains $.513(1,000) \cong 513$. The gain on one call offsets the loss on the other.

The ratio spread, of course, does not remain riskless unless the ratio is continuously adjusted. Because this is somewhat impractical, no truly riskless hedge can be constructed. Nonetheless, spreads of this type are frequently done by option traders attempting to simulate riskless positions. Although the positions are not exactly riskless, they will come very close to being so as long as the ratio does not deviate too far from the optimum.

This completes our coverage of option spread strategies. The next group of strategies are called *combinations*, because they involve combined positions in puts and calls. We previously covered some combination strategies, namely conversions and reversals, which we used to illustrate put-call parity. The strategies covered in the remainder of this chapter are straddles, straps, strips, and box spreads. We will use the same approach as before; the notation should be quite familiar by now.

STRADDLES

A *straddle* is the purchase of a call and a put that have the same exercise price and expiration date. By holding both a call and a put, the trader can capitalize on stock price movements in either direction.

Consider the purchase of a straddle with the call and put having an exercise price of E and an expiration of T. Then $N_C = 1$ and $N_P = 1$, and the profit from this transaction if held to expiration is

$$\Pi = Max(0, S_T - E) - C + Max(0, E - S_T) - P.$$

Since there is only one exercise price involved, there are only two ranges of the stock price at expiration. The profits are as follows:

$$\Pi = S_T - E - C - P \quad \text{if } S_T \geq E$$
$$\Pi = E - S_T - C - P \quad \text{if } S_T < E.$$

For the first case, in which the stock price equals or exceeds the exercise price, the call expires in-the-money.[4] It is exercised for a gain of $S_T - E$, while the put expires out-of-the-money. The profit is the gain on the call minus the premiums paid on the call and the put. For the second case, in which the stock price is less than the exercise price, the put expires in-the-money and is exercised for a gain of $E - S_T$. The profit is the gain on the put minus the premiums paid for the put and the call.

---

[4]The case in which $S_T = E$ is included in this range. Even though $S_T = E$ means that the call is at-the-money, it can still be exercised for a gain of $S_T - E = 0$.

FIGURE 6.9

Straddle

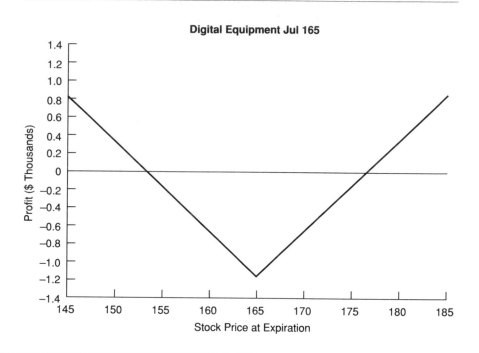

Digital Equipment Jul 165

For the range of stock prices above the exercise price, the profit increases dollar for dollar with the stock price at expiration. For the range of stock prices below the exercise price, the profit decreases dollar for dollar with the stock price at expiration. When the options expire with the stock price at the exercise price, both options are at-the-money and essentially expire worthless. The profit then equals the premiums paid, which, of course, makes it a loss. These results suggest that the graph is V shaped. Figure 6.9 illustrates the straddle for the Digital Equipment July 165 options.

The straddle strategy is designed to capitalize on high stock price volatility. To create a profit, the stock price must move substantially in either direction. It is not necessary to know which way the stock will go; it is necessary only that it make a significant move. How much must it move? Look at the two breakeven points.

For the case in which the stock price exceeds the exercise price, set the profit equal to zero:

$$S_T^* - E - C - P = 0.$$

Solving for S_T^* gives a breakeven of

$$S_T^* = E + C + P.$$

The upside breakeven is simply the exercise price plus the premiums paid for the options.

For the case in which the stock price is below the exercise price, set the profit equal to zero:

$$E - S_T^* - C - P = 0.$$

Solving for S_T^* gives a breakeven of

$$S_T^* = E - C - P.$$

The downside breakeven is the exercise price minus the premiums paid on the options.

Thus, the breakeven stock prices are simply the exercise price plus or minus the premiums paid for the call and the put. This makes sense. On the upside, the call is exercised for a gain equal to the difference between the stock price and the exercise price. For the investor to profit, the stock price must exceed the exercise price by enough that the gain from exercising the call will cover the premiums paid for the call and the put. On the downside, the put is exercised for a gain equal to the difference between the exercise price and the stock price. To create a profit, the stock price must be sufficiently below the exercise price that the gain on the put will cover the premiums on the call and the put.

In this example, the premiums are $5.75 for the call and $6 for the put for a total of $11.75. Thus, the breakeven stock prices at expiration are $165 plus or minus $11.75, or $153.25 and $176.75. The stock price currently is at $164. To create a profit, the stock price must increase by $12.75 or decrease by $10.75 in the remaining 35 days until the options expire.

The worst-case outcome for a straddle is for the stock price to end up equal to the exercise price where neither the call nor the put can be exercised for a gain.[5] The option trader will lose the premiums on the call and the put, which in this example total $100(5.75 + 6) = 1,175$.

The profit potential on a straddle is unlimited. The stock price can rise infinitely, and the straddle will earn profits dollar for dollar with the stock price in excess of the exercise price. On the downside, the profit is limited simply because the stock price can go no lower than zero. The downside maximum profit is found by setting the stock price at expiration equal to zero for the case in which the stock price is below the exercise price. This gives a profit of $E - C - P$, which here is $100(165 - 5.75 - 6) = 15,325$.

---

[5]Either the put, the call, or both could be exercised, but the gain on either would be zero. Transaction costs associated with exercise would suggest that neither the call nor the put would be exercised when $S_T = E$.

The potentially large profits on a straddle can be a temptation too hard to resist. One should be aware that the straddle normally requires a fairly large stock price move to be profitable. Even to a novice investor stock prices always seem highly volatile, but that volatility may be misleading.

For example, consider a two-month straddle on a market index. A reasonable estimate of the market's annualized standard deviation would be about .14. For a two-month holding period, the standard deviation would be about $\sqrt{(2/12)(.14)^2}$ = .0572. Assuming a normal distribution of returns, the stock price would be expected to fluctuate within 5.72 percent up or down about two-thirds of the time. This is a fairly small stock price change and would result in a loss in many straddle transactions. In this example, it would require about an 8 percent increase or a 7 percent decrease in the stock price to make a profit. An investor considering a straddle is advised to carefully assess the probability that the stock price will move into the profitable range.

Because both the call and the put are owned, the problem of early exercise does not exist with a straddle. The early-exercise decision is up to the straddle holder. However, transaction costs are an important consideration.

When the straddle is established, there is a commission on both the call and the put. At exercise there will be a commission only on either the call or the put, whichever is in-the-money. Suppose the stock price ends up slightly higher than the exercise price. Because of the commission on the exercise of the call, it might be inadvisable to exercise the call even though it is in-the-money. A similar argument can be made for the case against exercising the put when the stock price ends up slightly less than the exercise price. This means that, as with any option strategy, the maximum loss is slightly more than the analysis indicates because of the commission. Moreover, the stock price at which such a loss occurs is actually a range around the exercise price.

THE CHOICE OF HOLDING PERIOD   Now consider what happens upon closing the position prior to expiration. Figure 6.10 illustrates the outcomes for the Digital Equipment October 165 straddle using the same three holding periods employed in examining the other strategies;[6] that is, the shortest holding period involves closing the position on July 24, the intermediate-length holding period on September 4, and the long holding period at expiration. The profit graphs are curves that collapse onto the straight line for the case in which the position is held to expiration. The highest curve is the shortest holding period.

We should keep in mind that this graph does not imply that the shortest holding period is the best strategy. For a given stock price, the shortest holding period indeed provides the highest profit. The uncertainty of the stock price at expiration prevents the short holding period from dominating the longer holding periods. Because a straddle is designed to permit profiting from large stock price

---

[6]Specifically, the holding period T(1) means that the remaining maturity is .2301 based on 84 days remaining, T(2) means that the remaining maturity is .1151 based on 42 days remaining, and T = 0 assumes holding all the way to expiration.

FIGURE 6.10
Straddle: Different Holding Periods

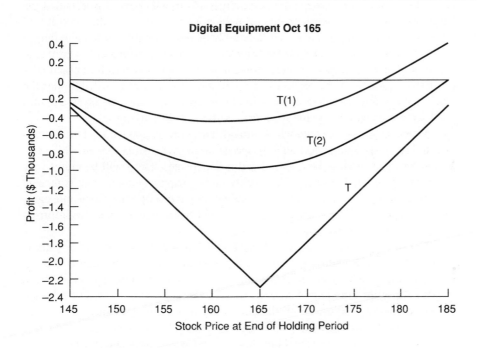

Digital Equipment Oct 165

fluctuations, the short holding period leaves less time for the stock price to make a significant move.

When the straddle is closed out prior to expiration, both the call and the put will contain some remaining time value. If the stock price is extremely high or low, neither option will have much time value, but either the call or the put will have a high intrinsic value. If the stock price is close to the exercise price, both options will have a fair amount of time value. When closing out the position, the investor sells the options back and recovers this time value. As the holding period is extended closer to the expiration date, there is less time value to recover and the profit declines. The profit curve gradually decreases until at expiration it becomes the curve for the case in which the straddle is held to expiration. Thus, the higher profits from shorter holding periods come from recapturing the time value of the put and the call.

Figure 6.10 shows that the shorter holding period leads to a lower upside and higher downside breakeven. This reduces the risk to the trader, because the range of stock prices in which a loss can be incurred is smaller. In this example, the shortest holding period has breakeven stock prices of about $145 and $177 and the intermediate-term holding period has breakeven stock prices of about $143 and $185.

Applications of Straddles

A straddle is an appropriate strategy for situations in which one suspects that the stock price will move substantially but does not know in which direction it will go. An example of this occurs when a major bank or corporation is about to fail.

Suppose a failing bank applies for a bailout from the government.[7] During the period in which the request is under consideration, a straddle will be a potentially profitable strategy. If the request is denied, the bank probably will fail and the stock will become worthless. If the bailout is granted, the bank may be able to turn itself around, in which case the stock price will rise substantially.

A similar scenario exists when a major corporation applies for federal loan guaranties. A straddle is also an appropriate strategy for situations in which important news is about to be released and it is expected that it will be either very favorable or very unfavorable. The weekly money supply announcements present opportunities that possibly could be exploited with index options. Corporate earnings announcements are other examples of situations in which uncertain information will be released on a specific date.

The straddle certainly is not without risk, however. If investors already know or expect the information, the stock price may move very little when the announcement is made. If this happens, the investor might be tempted to hold on to the straddle in the faint hope that some other, unanticipated news will be released before the options expire. In all likelihood, however, the stock price will move very little and the straddle will produce a loss. The trader might wish to cut the loss quickly by closing the position if the expected move does not materialize.

A Short Straddle

An investor who expects the market to stay within a narrow trading range might consider writing a straddle. This would involve the sale of a put and a call with the same exercise price and expiration date. From the previous analysis, it should be obvious that the profit graph would be an inverted V. A short straddle would be a high-risk strategy because of the potential for large losses if the stock price moved substantially, particularly upward. Also, there would be the risk of early exercise of either the put or the call.

There are two popular variations of the straddle: the strap and the strip.

---

[7]Bailouts frequently take the form of loan guaranties, sale of unproductive assets, or sale of new equity or hybrid securities.

VARIATIONS OF STRADDLES

Straps

A *strap* can be more easily understood by comparing it to a straddle. Suppose an investor expects the stock price to make a large move but does not know the direction. If the stock is as likely to increase as it is to decrease, a straddle will be appropriate because it has a symmetric payoff. Large stock price increases are as profitable as equivalent stock price decreases. A straddle can be viewed as a wager in which the trader places equal bets on a bull and bear market.

Now suppose an investor is feeling slightly more bullish than bearish. He or she expects a large stock price movement, but it is more likely that the stock price will increase than decrease. It would make sense to increase the number of calls relative to the number of puts. The more calls used, the more bullish is the investor. A strap, then, is the special case in which two calls are purchased for each put.

In a strap, $N_C = 2$ and $N_P = 1$. The profit is

$$\Pi = 2\text{Max}(0, S_T - E) - 2C + \text{Max}(0, E - S_T) - P.$$

The profits for the two ranges of stock price at expiration are as follows:

$$\Pi = 2S_T - 2E - 2C - P \quad \text{if } S_T \geq E$$
$$\Pi = -2C + E - S_T - P \quad \text{if } S_T < E.$$

For the case in which the stock price equals or exceeds the exercise price, the strap's profit is greater than the straddle's by the amount $S_T - E - C$. For the case in which the stock price is less than the exercise price, the strap's profit is lower than the straddle's by the amount C, the premium on the additional call. The second call was purchased, but with this outcome it expires worthless.

Figure 6.11 illustrates the strap overlaid with the straddle for the Digital Equipment July 165 options. Notice how the maximum loss still occurs if the stock price ends up at the exercise price of 165. In this case, neither the two calls nor the one put end up in-the-money. The strap is a slightly "tilted" version of the straddle. The upside profit of a strap can be greater than the straddle's if the stock price is sufficiently high. On the downside, however, the strap will always do worse than the straddle. This is because of the lost premium on the second call if the stock price ends up below the exercise price.

The two breakeven stock prices at expiration are found by setting the two profit equations to zero and solving for the stock price at expiration, S_T^*. For the case in which the stock price exceeds the exercise price,

$$2S_T^* - 2E - 2C - P = 0.$$

FIGURE 6.11
Strap versus Straddle

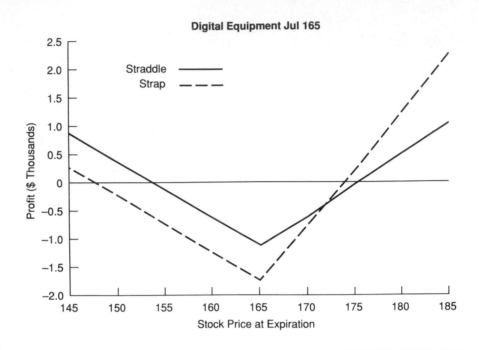

Solving for S_T^* gives

$$S_T^* = E + C + \frac{P}{2}.$$

For the case in which the stock price is less than the exercise price,

$$-2C + E - S_T^* - P = 0.$$

Solving for S_T^* gives

$$S_T^* = E - P - 2C.$$

The upside breakeven stock price is lower by one-half of the put premium. The downside breakeven is lower by the call premium. This means that the upside breakeven stock price is easier to reach and the downside breakeven stock price is harder. This is the price one pays with such a strategy. By increasing the "bet" on a bull market, the payoff in a bull market is higher but the payoff in a bear market is lower.

In this example, the upside breakeven is 165 + 5.75 + 6/2 = 173.75 as opposed to $176.75 for the straddle. The downside breakeven is 165 – 6 – 2(5.75) = 147.50 as opposed to $153.25 for the straddle.

The minimum profit is the profit at a stock price at expiration equal to the exercise price. This is 100[– 2(5.75) – 6] = –1,750. In this straddle, the minimum profit is a loss of $1,175.

Strips

A *strip* is simply a long position in two puts and one call. Compared to the straddle, the strip involves increasing one's bet that the market will go down. The investor is still uncertain which way the market will go but is feeling slightly more bearish than bullish. If the market goes down, there will be two puts to exercise. If the market goes up, the cost of the second put will cut into the profit.

In a strip, $N_C = 1$ and $N_P = 2$. The profit equation is

$$\Pi = \text{Max}(0, S_T - E) - C + 2\text{Max}(0, E - S_T) - 2P.$$

The profit equations for the two possible ranges of stock price at expiration are as follows:

$$\Pi = S_T - E - C - 2P \qquad \text{if } S_T \geq E$$
$$\Pi = -C + 2E - 2S_T - 2P \quad \text{if } S_T < E.$$

When the stock price at expiration is below the exercise price, the extra put adds the amount $E - S_T - P$ to the profit. If the stock price ends up above the exercise price, the profit from the strip falls below the profit from a straddle by the amount of the second put premium.

Figure 6.12 illustrates the strip overlaid with the straddle for the Digital Equipment July 165 options. The strip "tilts" the straddle up from the left. The worst case is still when the stock price ends up at the exercise price, because with that outcome neither the puts nor the call are worth anything. The profit in this case is $-2P - C$, which here equals $-100[5.75 + 2(6)] = -1,775$.

The upside breakeven is found by setting to zero the profit for the case in which the stock price at expiration exceeds the exercise price:

$$S_T^* - E - C - 2P = 0.$$

Solving for S_T^* gives

$$S_T^* = E + C + 2P.$$

The downside breakeven is found by setting to zero the profit for the case in which the stock price at expiration is less than the exercise price:

$$-C + 2E - 2S_T^* - 2P = 0.$$

FIGURE 6.12

Strip versus Straddle

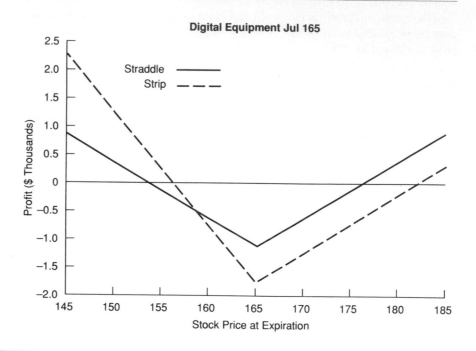

Solving for S_T^* gives

$$S_T^* = E - P - \left(\frac{C}{2}\right).$$

The upside breakeven reflects the fact that the stock price must exceed the exercise price by the premiums on the one call and the two puts. On the downside, the breakeven is reduced by one-half of the premium on the call. In this example, the upside breakeven is $165 + 5.75 + 2(6) = 182.75$ and the downside breakeven is $165 - 6 - 5.75/2 = 156.125$. Recall that for the straddle the breakevens were $153.125 and $176.75. The downside breakeven on the strip is higher, meaning that the stock price need not fall as much to create a profit. On the upside, however, the stock price must increase more with the strip than with the straddle to generate a profit.

Some Additional Considerations with Straps and Strips

Figures 6.11 and 6.12 show that there are crossover stock prices at which the strap and the straddle have equal profits and the strip and the straddle have equal profits. These can be found by setting the profit equations for the strap and straddle equal and those for the strip and straddle equal.

For the strap, the crossover stock price, $S_T^\dagger$, is found as

$$S_T^\dagger - E - C - P = 2S_T^\dagger - 2E - 2C - P.$$

Therefore,

$$S_T^\dagger = E + C.$$

For the strip,

$$-C + 2E - 2S_T^\dagger - 2P = -C + E - S_T^\dagger - P.$$

Therefore,

$$S_T^\dagger = E - P.$$

In this example, the crossover stock price for the strap is $165 + 5.75 = 170.75$ and for the strip it is $165 - 6 = 159$. These prices can be used to assess the attractiveness of a strap or a strip over a straddle. For example, the strap would be preferable to a straddle if the investor were confident that the stock price would be above \$170.75. If the investor expected the stock price to fall below \$159, a strip would be preferable to a straddle.

Early exercise does not pose a problem for holders of straps and strips, since all of the options are owned. One should keep in mind the conditions that trigger early exercise so that one can exercise the options early if that is optimal.

Because of the number of options involved, commissions are a major consideration with straps and strips. For many individuals, commissions make straps and strips prohibitive.

As with any other option strategy, the investor can choose to close the position prior to expiration. The considerations are much the same as for the straddle. A portion of the time values can be recovered on the resale of the options if the position is closed prior to expiration. Time values will be greatest if the stock price is near the exercise price.

An investor can also do short straps and strips. A short strap would be a bearish strategy and a short strip a bullish strategy. Short straps and strips would have unlimited loss potential and would carry the risk of early exercise.

BOX SPREADS

A *box spread* is a combination of a bull call money spread and a bear put money spread. Such a combination creates a low-risk—in fact, riskless—strategy.

Consider a group of options with two exercise prices, E_1 and E_2, and the same expiration. A bull call spread would involve the purchase of the call with exercise price E_1 at a premium of C_1 and the sale of the call with exercise price E_2 at a premium of C_2. A bear put spread would require the purchase of the put with exercise price E_2 at a premium of P_2 and the sale of the put with exercise price E_1 at a premium of P_1. Under the rules for the effect of exercise price on put and call prices, both the call and put spread would involve an initial cash outflow, because $C_1 > C_2$ and $P_2 > P_1$. Thus, the box spread would have a net cash outflow at the initiation of the strategy.

The profit at expiration is

$$\Pi = \text{Max}(0, S_T - E_1) - C_1 - \text{Max}(0, S_T - E_2) + C_2$$
$$+ \text{Max}(0, E_2 - S_T) - P_2 - \text{Max}(0, E_1 - S_T) + P_1.$$

Because there are two exercise prices, we must examine three ranges of the stock price at expiration. The profits are

$$\Pi = -C_1 + C_2 + E_2 - S_T - P_2 - E_1 + S_T + P_1$$
$$= E_2 - E_1 - C_1 + C_2 - P_2 + P_1 \qquad \text{if } S_T \leq E_1 < E_2$$
$$\Pi = S_T - E_1 - C_1 + C_2 + E_2 - S_T - P_2 + P_1$$
$$= E_2 - E_1 - C_1 + C_2 - P_2 + P_1 \qquad \text{if } E_1 < S_T \leq E_2$$
$$\Pi = S_T - E_1 - C_1 + E_2 - S_T + C_2 - P_2 + P_1$$
$$= E_2 - E_1 - C_1 + C_2 - P_2 + P_1 \qquad \text{if } E_1 < E_2 < S_T.$$

Notice that the profit is the same in each case: The box spread will be worth $E_2 - E_1$ at expiration, and the profit will be $E_2 - E_1$ minus the premiums paid, $C_1 - C_2 + P_2 - P_1$. The box spread is thus a riskless strategy. Why would anyone want to execute a box spread if one can more easily earn the risk-free rate by purchasing Treasury bills? The reason is that the box spread may prove to be incorrectly priced, as a valuation analysis can reveal.

Valuation of Box Spreads

Because the box spread is a riskless transaction that pays off the difference in the exercise prices at expiration, it should be easy to determine whether it is correctly priced. The payoff can be discounted at the risk-free rate. The present value of this amount is then compared to the cost of obtaining the box spread, which is the net premiums paid. This procedure is like analyzing a capital budgeting problem. The present value of the payoff at expiration minus the net premiums is a net present value (NPV). Since the objective of any investment decision is to maximize NPV, an investor should undertake all box spreads in which the NPV is positive. On those spreads with a negative NPV, one should execute a reverse box spread.

The net present value of a box spread is

$$NPV = (E_2 - E_1)(1 + r)^{-T} - C_1 + C_2 - P_2 + P_1,$$

where r is the risk-free rate and T is the time to expiration.[8] If NPV is positive, the present value of the payoff at expiration will exceed the net premiums paid. If NPV is negative, the total amount of the premiums paid will exceed the present value of the payoff at expiration.

An alternative way to view the box spread is as the difference between two put-call parities. For example, for the options with exercise price E_1, put-call parity is

$$P_1 = C_1 - S + E_1(1 + r)^{-T},$$

and for the options with exercise price E_2, put-call parity is

$$P_2 = C_2 - S + E_2(1 + r)^{-T}.$$

Rearranging both equations to isolate the stock price gives

$$S = C_1 - P_1 + E_1(1 + r)^{-T}$$
$$S = C_2 - P_2 + E_2(1 + r)^{-T}.$$

Since the left-hand sides are equal, the right-hand sides must also be equal; therefore,

$$C_1 - P_1 + E_1(1 + r)^{-T} = C_2 - P_2 + E_2(1 + r)^{-T}.$$

Rearranging this equation gives

$$0 = (E_2 - E_1)(1 + r)^{-T} - C_1 + C_2 - P_2 + P_1.$$

This is our put-call parity equation when the NPV is zero, which results if all puts and calls are correctly priced relative to one another.

Let us examine the Digital Equipment July box spread using the 165 and 170 options. Consider the following transaction: Buy the 165 call at $5.75, buy the 170 put at $8.50, write the 170 call at $3.75, and write the 165 put at $6.00. The premiums paid for the 165 call and 170 put minus the premiums received for the 170 call and 165 put net out to $4.50. Thus, it will cost $450 to buy the box spread.

The payoff at expiration is $E_2 - E_1$. The net present value is

$$NPV = (100)[(170 - 165)(1.0535)^{-.0959} - 4.50] = \$47.51,$$

where .0535 is the discrete risk-free rate for July as determined in Chapter 3 and .0959 is the time to expiration from June 12 to July 17. Thus, the spread is

---

[8]Of course, one should remember to use the discrete risk-free rate in the above formula. Alternatively, one could compute $(E_2 - E_1)e^{-rT}$ using the continuous risk-free rate and obtain the same result.

underpriced and should be purchased. Had the NPV been negative, the box spread would have been overpriced and should be sold. In that case, an investor would buy the 170 call and 165 put and sell the 165 call and 170 put. This would generate a positive cash flow up front that exceeded the present value of the cash outflow of $E_2 - E_1$ at expiration.

If the investor is holding a long box spread, the risk of early exercise is unimportant. Suppose the short call is exercised. Because the short call is in-the-money, the long call will be even deeper in-the-money. The investor can then exercise the long call. If the short put is exercised, the investor can in turn exercise the long put, which will be even deeper in-the-money than the short put. The net effect is a cash inflow of $E_2 - E_1$, the maximum payoff at expiration. For the short box spread, however, early exercise will result in a cash outflow of $E_2 - E_1$. Thus, the early exercise problem is an important consideration for short box spreads.

Transaction costs on a box spread will be high because four options are involved. However, at least two of the four options will expire out-of-the-money. Nonetheless, the high transaction costs will make the box spread costly to execute for all but those who own seats on the exchange.

The performance of box spreads has been studied by Billingsley and Chance (1985), Chance (1987), and Ronn and Ronn (1989). All three studies revealed that profitable opportunities in box spreads are quite rare except for investors who have the lowest transaction costs. This result is consistent with our conclusion in Chapter 3 that options are nearly always priced to conform with put-call parity.

SUMMARY

This chapter showed how some of the basic option strategies introduced in Chapter 5 can be combined to produce more complex strategies such as spreads and combinations. Spreads were shown to be relatively low-risk strategies. Money spreads can be designed to profit in both a bull and a bear market. Calendar spreads and butterfly spreads are used to profit in either the presence or absence of high stock price volatility. Straddles, straps, and strips were also shown to be attractive in periods of high or low volatility. Straps and strips are variations of the straddle in which a trader can increase a bet on the direction of the market. Finally, the chapter introduced the box spread, a riskless transaction that lends itself to a variation of a standard capital budgeting analysis with the end result being a net present value, a concept often encountered in other finance courses.

The strategies covered in this and the preceding chapter are but a few of the many possible option strategies. Those interested in furthering their knowledge of options can explore the many excellent books cited in the references in this and other chapters. The framework developed here should be sufficient to get you started. At this point, you should be capable of assessing the risks and rewards of a few simple option strategies. This book is an introduction and hopefully will encourage you to explore the world of options in more depth.

At one time, options and futures markets existed almost independently of each other. Now it is sometimes difficult to tell where one market ends and the other begins. Although we shall leave the world of options for awhile, we will return to it in Chapter 12, where we introduce options on futures.

Questions and Problems

1. Explain why option traders often use spreads instead of simple long or short options and combined positions of options and stock.

2. Suppose an option trader has a bull call spread. The stock price has risen substantially, and the trader is considering closing the position early. What factors should the trader consider with regard to closing the transaction before the options expire?

3. Suppose you are following the stock of a firm that has been experiencing severe problems. Failure is imminent unless the firm is granted government-guaranteed loans. If the firm fails, its stock will, of course, fall substantially. If the loans are granted, it is expected that the stock price will rise substantially. Identify two strategies that would be appropriate for this situation. Justify your answers.

4. Explain why in some situations a bear put money spread could offer an advantage over a similar bear call money spread.

5. Derive the profit equations for a bull put money spread. Determine the maximum and minimum profits and the breakeven stock price at expiration.

6. Explain the process by which the profit of a short straddle closed out prior to expiration is influenced by the time values of the put and call.

7. Explain why selecting a strap over a straddle is like increasing one's bet on a bull market.

8. The chapter showed how analyzing a box spread is like a capital budgeting problem using the net present value approach. Consider the internal rate of return method of examining capital budgeting problems, and analyze the box spread in that context.

The following option prices were observed for calls and puts on IBM on July 6 of a particular year. Use this information for problems 9 through 21. The stock was priced at 165 1/8. The expirations are July 17, August 21, and October 16. The continuously compounded risk-free rates associated with the three expirations are .0503, .0535, and .0571, respectively. The standard deviation is .21.

Strike	Calls			Puts		
	Jul	Aug	Oct	Jul	Aug	Oct
160	6	8 1/8	11 1/8	3/4	2 3/4	4 1/2
165	2 11/16	5 1/4	8 1/8	2 3/8	4 3/4	6 3/4
170	13/16	3 1/4	6	5 3/4	7 1/2	9

For problems 9 through 12 and 15 through 18, determine the profits for the holding period indicated for stock prices of 155, 160, 165, 170, 175, and 180 at the end of the holding period. Answer any other questions as indicated.

9. Construct a bear money spread using the October 165 and 170 calls. Hold until the options expire. Determine the profits and graph the results. Identify the breakeven stock price at expiration and the maximum and minimum profits.

10. Repeat problem 9, but close the position on September 20. Use the graph to identify the approximate breakeven stock price.

11. Suppose you are expecting the stock price to move substantially over the next three months. You are considering a butterfly spread. Construct an appropriate butterfly spread using the October 160, 165, and 170 calls. Hold the position until expiration. Determine the profits and graph the results. Identify the two breakeven stock prices and the maximum and minimum profits.

12. Construct a calendar spread using the August and October 170 calls that will profit from high volatility. Close the position on August 1. Graph the results and use the graph to estimate the maximum and minimum profits and the breakeven stock prices.

13. Using the Black-Scholes model, compute and graph the time value decay of the October 165 call on the following dates: July 15, July 31, August 15, August 31, September 15, September 30, and October 16. Assume the stock price remains constant. Note: You may wish to use the Black-Scholes spreadsheet on the software diskette.

14. Consider a riskless spread with a long position in the August 160 call and a short position in the October 160 call. Determine the appropriate hedge ratio. Then show how a $1 stock price increase would have a neutral effect on the spread value.

15. Construct a long straddle using the October 165 options. Hold until the options expire. Determine the profits and graph the results. Identify the breakeven stock prices at expiration and the minimum profit.

16. Repeat problem 15, but close the positions on September 20. Use the graph to identify the approximate breakeven stock prices.

17. Construct a long strap using the October 165 options. Hold the position until expiration. Determine the profits and graph the results. Identify the breakeven stock prices at expiration and the minimum profit. Compare the results with the October 165 straddle. Determine the stock price above which the strap outperforms the straddle.

18. Construct a short strip using the August 170 options. Hold the position until the options expire. Determine the profits and graph the results. Identify the breakeven stock prices at expiration and the minimum profit.

19. Analyze the August 160/170 box spread. Determine whether a profit opportunity exists and, if so, how one should exploit it.

20. (Concept Problem) The chapter presented two variations of the straddle, straps and strips. Another variation of the straddle is called a *strangle*. A strangle is the purchase of a call with a higher exercise price and a put with a lower exercise price. Evaluate the strangle strategy by examining the purchase of the IBM August 165 put and 170 call. As in the problems above, determine the profits for stock prices of 155, 160, 165, 170, 175, and 180. Hold the position until expiration and graph the results. Find the breakeven stock prices at expiration. Explain why one would want to use a strangle.

21. (Concept Problem) Many option traders use a combination of a money spread and a calender spread called a *diagonal spread*. This transaction involves the purchase of a call with a lower exercise price and longer time to expiration and the sale of a call with a higher exercise price and shorter time to expiration. Evaluate the diagonal spread that involves the purchase of the IBM October 165 call and the sale of the August 170 call. Determine the profits for the same stock prices you previously examined under the assumption that the position is closed on August 1. Graph the results. Estimate the breakeven stock price at the end of the holding period. Then explain why you think someone would want to use a diagonal spread.

References

Billingsley, Randall S., and Don M. Chance. "Options Market Efficiency and the Box Spread Strategy." *The Financial Review* 20 (November 1985): 287–301.

Bookstaber, Richard M. *Option Pricing and Investment Strategies*, Chapter 5. Chicago: Probus Publishing, 1987.

Chance, Don M. "Parity Tests of Index Options." *Advances in Futures and Options Research* 2 (1987): 47–64.

Frankfurter, George, Richard Stevenson, and Allan Young. "Option Spreading: Theory and Illustration." *The Journal of Portfolio Management* 5 (Summer 1979): 59–63.

Gastineau, Gary. *The Options Manual*, 3d ed., Chapter 4. New York: McGraw-Hill, 1988.

Gombola, Michael J., Rodney L. Roenfeldt, and Philip L. Cooley. "Spreading Strategies in CBOE Options: Evidence on Market Performance." *The Journal of Financial Research* 1 (Winter 1978): 35–44.

Hull, John. *Options, Futures and Other Derivative Instruments*, Chapter 1. Englewood Cliffs, N.J.: Prentice-Hall, 1989.

Malkiel, Burton G., and Richard E. Quandt. *Strategies and Rational Decisions in the Securities Options Market*, Chapter 2. Cambridge, Mass.: M.I.T. Press, 1969.

McMillan, Lawrence G. *Options as a Strategic Investment*, 2d ed., Chapters 7–14, 18, 20, 22–24, 27. New York: New York Institute of Finance, 1986.

Ritchken, Peter. *Options: Theory, Strategy, and Applications*, Chapter 3. Glenview, Ill.: Scott, Foresman, 1987.

Ritchken, Peter H., and Harvey M. Salkin. "Safety First Selection Techniques for Option Spreads." *The Journal of Portfolio Management* 9 (1981): 61–67.

Ronn, Aimée Gerbarg, and Ehud I. Ronn. "The Box Spread Arbitrage Conditions: Theory, Tests, and Investment Strategies." *The Review of Financial Studies* 2 (1989): 91–108.

Slivka, Ron. "Call Option Spreading." *The Journal of Portfolio Management* 7 (Spring 1981): 71–76.

Welch, William W. *Strategies for Put and Call Option Trading*, Chapters 5, 6, 7. Cambridge, Mass.: Winthrop Publishers, 1982.

part two
FUTURES

THE STRUCTURE OF FUTURES MARKETS

> *Speculation is the romance of trade, and casts contempt*
> *upon all its sober realities. It renders the stock-jobber a*
> *magician, and the exchange a region of enchantment.*
>
> WASHINGTON IRVING, Wolfert's Roost, 1855

Part One explored the world of options. The next four chapters look at futures. Before defining a futures contract, however, we must examine a forward contract. A *forward contract* is an agreement between two parties, a buyer and a seller, that calls for the delivery of a commodity at a future point in time with a price agreed upon today. A *futures contract* is a forward contract that has standardized terms, is traded on an organized exchange, and follows a daily settlement procedure in which the losses of one party to the contract are paid to the other party.

Futures contracts have many of the characteristics of option contracts. Both provide for the sale and delivery of a commodity on a later date at a price agreed upon today. An option—more specifically, a call option—gives the holder the right to forgo the future purchase of the good. This is done, as we have seen, if the good's price is below the exercise price. A futures contract does not offer the right to forgo purchase of the good. However, like an exchange-listed option, a futures contract can be sold in the market prior to expiration.

Futures contracts, as noted, are very similar to forward contracts, and many of their essential ingredients can be understood by examining forward contracts. Forward contracts, sometimes called *forward commitments*, are very common in everyday life. For example, an apartment lease is a forward commitment. By signing a one-year lease, the tenant agrees to purchase the service—use of the apartment—each month for the next twelve months at a predetermined rate. Likewise, the landlord agrees to provide the service each month for the next twelve months at the agreed-upon rate. Now suppose that six months later the tenant finds a better apartment and decides to move out. The forward commitment remains in effect, and the only way the tenant can get out of the contract is to sublease the apartment. Because there is usually a market for subleases, the lease is even more like a futures contract than a forward contract.

Any type of contractual arrangement that calls for the future purchase of a good or service at a price agreed upon today and without the right of cancellation is a forward contract. Because arrangements such as apartment leases and noncancellable subscriptions are so commonplace, it is not surprising that the financial world is replete with forward commitments. When these contracts trade in organized markets and are subject to a daily settlement procedure, we call them *futures contracts*.

THE DEVELOPMENT OF FUTURES MARKETS

Futures markets evolved from forward markets, whose origins go back to medieval trade fairs. In these arrangements, merchants often contracted for deferred delivery of goods at a price agreed to in advance. Over the next few hundred years, organized spot markets for commodities began to develop in major European cities. Meanwhile, a market for rice futures developed in Japan. The characteristics of these markets were very similar to those of today's futures markets. Modern futures markets, however, generally trace back to the formation of the Chicago Board of Trade in 1848.

Chicago Futures Markets

In the 1840s, Chicago was rapidly becoming the transportation and distribution center of the Midwest. Farmers shipped their grain from the farm belt to Chicago for sale and subsequent distribution eastward along rail lines and the Great Lakes. However, due to the seasonal nature of grain production, large quantities of grain were shipped to Chicago in the late summer and fall. The city's storage facilities were inadequate for accommodating this temporary increase in supply. Prices fell drastically at harvest time as supplies increased and then rose steadily as supplies were consumed.

In 1848, a group of businessmen took the first step toward alleviating this problem by forming the Chicago Board of Trade (CBOT). The CBOT initially was organized for the purpose of standardizing the quantities and qualities of the grains. A few years later, the first forward contract was developed. Called a *to-arrive* contract, it provided that a farmer could agree to deliver the grain at a future date at a price determined in advance. This meant that the farmer would not ship the grain to Chicago at harvest time but could fix the price and date at which the grain subsequently would be sold.

These to-arrive contracts proved to be a curious instrument. Speculators soon found that rather than buy and sell the grain itself they could buy and sell the contracts. In that way, they could speculate on the price of grain to be delivered at a future date and not have to worry about taking delivery of and storing the grain. Soon thereafter, the exchange established a set of rules and regulations for governing these transactions. In the 1920s, the Clearinghouse was established. By that time, most of the essential ingredients of futures contracts were in place.

In 1874 the Chicago Produce Exchange was formed and later became the Chicago Butter and Egg Board. In 1898 it was reorganized as the Chicago Mercantile Exchange, which is now the world's second largest futures exchange. Over the years many new exchanges were formed, including the New York Futures Exchange, started in 1979 as a subsidiary of the New York Stock Exchange.

The Development of Financial Futures

For the first 120 years, futures exchanges offered trading in contracts on commodities such as agricultural goods and metals. Then, in 1971, the major Western economies began to allow their currency exchange rates to fluctuate. This opened the way for the formation in 1972 of the International Monetary Market (IMM), a subsidiary of the Chicago Mercantile Exchange that specializes in the trading of futures contracts on foreign currencies. These were the first futures contracts that could be called *financial futures*. The first interest rate futures contract appeared in 1975, when the Chicago Board of Trade originated its GNMA futures, a contract on Government National Mortgage Association pass-through certificates, whose yields reflect mortgage interest rates.

In 1976, the International Monetary Market introduced the first futures contract on a government security and a short-term financial instrument—90-day U.S. Treasury bills. This contract was actively traded for many years, but its popularity has declined somewhat, at least partly due to the remarkable success of a competing contract, the Eurodollar futures.

In 1977, the Chicago Board of Trade launched what became the most successful contract of all time—U.S. Treasury bond futures. In just a few years, this instrument became the most actively traded contract, surpassing many grain futures that had traded for more than 100 years.

The 1980s brought the highly successful stock index futures contract. This instrument, sometimes referred to as "pin-stripe pork bellies," has helped bridge the long-standing gap between New York's stock traders and Chicago's futures traders. Interestingly, however, the first stock index futures contract appeared not in New York or Chicago but in Kansas City. The Kansas City Board of Trade completed the formal registration process ahead of its New York and Chicago counterparts and on February 16, 1982, launched the Value Line Index futures. The Index and Option Market, a division of the Chicago Mercantile Exchange, followed on April 21 with its S&P 500 futures contract, the second most active of all futures contracts. The New York Futures Exchange entered the game on May 6 with its New York Stock Exchange Index futures.

The entire decade of the 1980s was characterized by enormous growth in futures markets. However, a parallel growth of similar contracts occurred in over-the-counter markets. In Chapter 14, we shall look at some of these instruments—which include swaps, caps, floors, and interest rate options—that have posed a competitive threat to the futures markets. Because so far the 1990s show no likelihood of a reduction in the use of these specialized instruments, the futures markets again will be challenged to develop new contracts and improve existing ones.

FUTURES CONTRACTS, FORWARD CONTRACTS, AND RELATED INSTRUMENTS

The similarity between forward and futures contracts is obvious, but their differences are substantial. Despite the somewhat informal nature of forward contracts, forward markets do exist in this country. For example, there is a healthy, viable forward market for foreign currency called the *interbank market*. Therein firms and institutions arrange to purchase and sell foreign currencies at future dates. There is no organized, centralized marketplace, nor do any formal rules and regulations govern trading; rather, the structure exists somewhat loosely, with participants trading informally among one another. The foreign exchange spot market operates in the same manner.

In addition to the interbank market in foreign currencies, there is a growing market for customized forward contracts to lend money to corporations. However, forward markets are less developed than futures markets in this and other countries. This is no doubt due to the many advantages futures markets offer over forward markets. For example, futures markets provide for trading in standardized instruments. The exchange specifies the contracts that will trade as well as the underlying terms and conditions. Consequently, futures contracts are marketable. An investor who holds a futures contract can sell it in the market before expiration and avoid having to make or take delivery of the commodity. Futures markets also offer the convenience of a clearinghouse that guarantees the performance of both parties to a contract. This frees the participants from having to check each other's creditworthiness. The clearinghouse requires the deposit and maintenance of margin that assure participants that losses will be paid and profits received on a daily basis rather than when the contract expires.

One attractive feature of futures contracts is their substantial leverage component. The margin requirements usually are less than 10 percent of the contract's face value. Thus, for a small deposit a trader can control a large market position. We shall see how this works later in the chapter, when we look at the daily settlement procedure. We should also note that forward contracts may require a small margin deposit and thus can have a substantial leverage component as well.

Leverage contracts are similar to forward and futures contracts and often are used in transactions in precious metals. A customer who wishes to purchase a metal such as gold makes a down payment—usually about 20 percent—and pays the balance later, whereupon the commodity is delivered. Unlike futures contracts, leverage contracts usually end in delivery of the underlying commodity. Leverage contracts meet the specialized needs of customers that are not met by standardized exchange-traded contracts.

At this point, we have a general overview of futures markets. In the next section, we look more closely at how futures trading is organized.

ORGANIZED FUTURES TRADING

Futures trading is organized around the concept of a futures exchange. The exchange is probably the most important component of a futures market and distinguishes it from forward markets.

A *futures exchange* is a corporate entity composed of members. Although some exchanges allow corporate memberships, most members are individuals. The members elect a board of directors, which in turn selects individuals to manage the exchange. The exchange has a corporate hierarchy consisting of officers, employees, and committees. The exchange establishes rules for its members and may impose sanctions on violators.

Contract Development

One of the exchange's important ongoing activities is identifying new and useful futures contracts. Most exchanges maintain research staffs that continuously examine the feasibility of new contracts. When the exchange determines that a contract is likely to be successful, it writes a proposal specifying the terms and conditions and applies to the Commodity Futures Trading Commission (CFTC), the regulatory authority, for permission to initiate trading.[1]

It has long been said that a few key characteristics make a commodity attractive for futures trading: The commodity should be homogeneous, be easily identifiable, have a spot market with uncertain demand and supply, and have at least limited storage capability.[2] In recent years the initiation of futures contracts on the Consumer Price Index, an index of the dollar against other foreign currencies, and ocean freight rates seems to have made these requirements somewhat outdated. It is now conceivable that virtually anything can have a futures contract traded on it. Whether the contract will be actively traded will depend on whether it fills the needs of hedgers and whether speculators are interested enough to take risks in it.

---

[1] The CFTC's responsibility is discussed later in the chapter.
[2] Loosigian (1980), pp. 20–22.

Contract Terms and Conditions

The contract's terms and conditions are determined by the exchange subject to CFTC approval. The specifications for each contract are the size, quotation unit, minimum price fluctuation, grade, and trading hours. In addition, the contract specifies delivery terms and daily price limits as well as delivery procedures, which are discussed in separate sections. Complete contract terms on selected financial futures contracts are provided in Appendix 7A.

Contract size means that one contract covers a specific number of units of the commodity. This might be a designated number of bushels of a grain or dollars of face value of a financial instrument. Contract size is an important decision. If too small, speculators will find it more costly to trade because there is a cost for trading each contract. The contracts are not divisible; thus, if they are too large, hedgers may be unable to get a matching number of contracts. For example, if the Chicago Board of Trade established $1 million as the Treasury bond contract, a hedger with $500,000 of bonds to hedge probably would be unable to use it.[3]

The quotation unit is simply the unit in which the price is specified. For example, corn is quoted in fourths of a cent and Treasury bonds in percentage points and thirty-seconds of a point of par value. The quotation unit chosen is not necessarily critical, but it should be one that is easily understandable. In most cases, the spot market quotation unit is used.

Closely related to the quotation unit is the minimum price fluctuation. This is usually the smallest unit of quotation. For example, Treasury bonds are quoted in a minimum unit of thirty-seconds. Thus, the minimum price change on a Treasury bond futures contract is 1/32 of 1 percent of the contract price, or .0003125. Since the contract has a face value (contract size) of $100,000, the minimum price change is .0003125 ($100,000) = $31.25.

The exchange also establishes the contract grade. In the case of agricultural commodities there may be numerous grades, each of which would command a quality price differential in the spot market. The contract must specify the grades that are acceptable for delivery. Financial futures contracts must indicate exactly which financial instrument or instruments are eligible for delivery.

The exchange also specifies the hours during which the contract trades. Most agricultural futures trade for four to five hours during the day. Most financial futures trade for about six hours. In addition, a few financial futures have night trading sessions. For example, the Chicago Board of Trade's Treasury bond contract trades from 7:20 a.m. to 2:00 p.m. central time on Monday through Friday and from 5:00 p.m. to 8:30 p.m. each evening on Sunday through Thursday. The night session officially begins the next day's session and has active participation by investors in Asia.

---

[3]We say *probably* because if the bonds being hedged were twice as volatile as the futures contract, one contract would be the correct number. Chapter 10 explains this point.

Delivery Terms

The contract must also indicate a specific delivery date or dates, delivery procedure, and a set of expiration months. In the case of harvestable commodities, the exchange usually establishes expiration months to correspond with harvest months. In nonharvestable commodities such as financial futures, the exchange usually has followed the pattern of allowing expirations in March, June, September, and December. There are some exceptions, however—most notably the Chicago Board of Trade's Major Market stock index futures contract, which has expirations in several months.

The exchange also decides how far into the future the expiration dates will be set. For some contracts, the expirations extend as far as two to three years.

Once the expiration month has been set, the exchange determines a final trading day. This may be any day in the month, but the most common ones are the third Friday of the month and the business day prior to the last business day of the month. The first delivery day also must be set. Most contracts allow delivery on any day of the month following a particular day. Usually the first eligible delivery day is the first business day of the month, but for certain contracts other days may be specified. In the case of stock index futures and other cash-settled contracts, the settlement occurs on the last trading day or on the day after the last trading day.

For non-cash-settled contracts, the delivery procedure must be specified. The deliverable spot commodity must be sent to any of several eligible locations. Financial adjustments to the price received upon delivery are required when an acceptable but lower-grade commodity is delivered. We shall say more about the delivery procedure later.

Daily Price Limits and Trading Halts

During the course of a trading day prices fluctuate continuously, but many contracts have limits on the maximum daily price change. If a contract price hits the upper limit, the market is said to be *limit up*. If the price moves to the lower limit, the market is said to be *limit down*. Any such move, up or down, is called a *limit move*. Normally no transactions above or below the limit price are allowed. Some contracts have limits only during the opening minutes; others have limits that can be expanded according to prescribed rules if prices remain at the limits for extended periods.

In conjunction with price limits, some futures contracts—notably stock index futures—contain built-in trading halts sometimes called *circuit breakers*. When prices move rapidly, trading can be stopped for predetermined periods. These halts can be accompanied by similar halts in the spot market. Such cessations of trading were installed after the stock market crash of 1987 in response to concern that extremely volatile markets might need a cooling-off period. While it is not clear that trading halts are necessarily effective, it seems likely that they will continue to be used in futures markets.

Other Exchange Responsibilities

The exchange also specifies that members meet minimum financial responsibility requirements. In some contracts it may establish position limits, which, like those in options markets, restrict the number of contracts that an individual trader can hold. The exchange establishes rules governing activities on the trading floor and maintains a department responsible for monitoring trading to determine whether anyone is attempting to manipulate the market. In some extreme cases, the exchange may elect to suspend trading if unusual events occur.[4]

FUTURES EXCHANGES

Futures trading takes place on 12 futures exchanges in the United States. Table 7.1 lists the exchanges and provides pertinent information about each.

There are also several futures exchanges in other countries. The number has grown rapidly, and today almost every large country—and even a few small ones—has a futures exchange. Some of the more active futures exchanges are in Sydney, Hong Kong, Tokyo, Osaka, Paris, London, Singapore, and Toronto. Several of the foreign futures exchanges are fully automated, meaning that there is no trading floor with buyers and sellers calling out bids and offers; rather, everyone trades through computers.

One advantage of such global futures trading, particularly when it is fully automated, is the potential it offers for linkages between exchanges. For example, the Chicago Mercantile Exchange and the Singapore International Monetary Exchange (SIMEX) are linked so that a trader opening a position in Eurodollars or certain foreign currencies on one exchange can close the position on the other. Linkages also exist between the London International Financial Futures Exchange (LIFFE) and the Sydney Futures Exchange and between the latter and the COMEX in New York.

In addition, some of the foreign futures exchanges trade contracts on assets primarily from outside their countries. For example, LIFFE began trading a contract on the German government bond well before Germany even had a futures market.

The trading of futures on foreign products also creates the opportunity for near 24-hour trading of certain contracts. For example, U.S. Treasury bond futures trade on LIFFE, the Chicago Board of Trade, the MidAmerica Commodity Exchange in Chicago, and the Sydney Futures Exchange. The exchanges are not linked and the contracts are not necessarily identical and cannot be bought in one market and sold in another. Nonetheless, there is only a 30-minute period—which occurs during the middle of the night in the United States—in which a futures on a U.S. Treasury bond does not trade.

---

[4]The 1980 grain embargo against the Soviet Union and the 1987 stock market crash were two such cases.

TABLE 7.1
U.S. Futures Exchanges

AMEX Commodities Corporation
(an affiliate of the American Stock Exchange)
86 Trinity Place
New York, NY 10006
212-306-8940
Financials

Chicago Board of Trade (CBOT)
141 W. Jackson Boulevard
Chicago, IL 60604
312-435-3500
Grains and oilseeds, metals, financials

Chicago Mercantile Exchange (CME)
30 S. Wacker Drive
Chicago, IL 60606
312-930-1000
Divisions: International Monetary Market
(IMM), Index and Option Market (IOM)
Livestock, meat, financials, wood

Coffee, Sugar, and Cocoa Exchange (CSCE)
4 World Trade Center
New York, NY 10048
212-938-2800
Food and fiber, financial

Commodity Exchange, Inc. (COMEX)
4 World Trade Center
New York, NY 10048
212-938-2900
Metals, financials

New York Futures Exchange (NYFE)
4 World Trade Center
New York, NY 10048
212-656-4949
Financials

New York Mercantile Exchange (NYMEX)
4 World Trade Center
New York, NY 10048
212-938-2222
Metals, petroleum, food and fiber

Kansas City Board of Trade (KCBT)
4800 Main Street, Suite 303
Kansas City, MO 64112
816-753-7500
Grains, financials

MidAmerica Commodity Exchange (MCE)
(an affiliate of the CBOT)
141 W. Jackson Boulevard
Chicago, IL 60604
312-341-3000
Grains and oilseeds, livestock, meat, metals, financials

Minneapolis Grain Exchange (MGE)
400 S. Fourth Street
Minneapolis, MN 55415
612-338-6212
Grains

New York Cotton Exchange (CTN)
(an affiliate of the New York Stock Exchange)
4 World Trade Center
New York, NY 10048
212-938-2650
Divisions: Financial Instruments Exchange (FINEX),
Citrus Associates
Food and fiber, financials

Chicago Rice and Cotton Exchange (CRCE)
(an affiliate of the MCE)
141 W. Jackson Boulevard
Chicago, IL 60604
312-341-3078
Food and fiber

Philadelphia Board of Trade (PBT)
(an affiliate of the Philadelphia Stock Exchange)
1900 Market Street
Philadelphia, PA 19103
215-496-5357
Financials

FIGURE 7.1

Volume of Futures Contracts Traded, 1977–1989

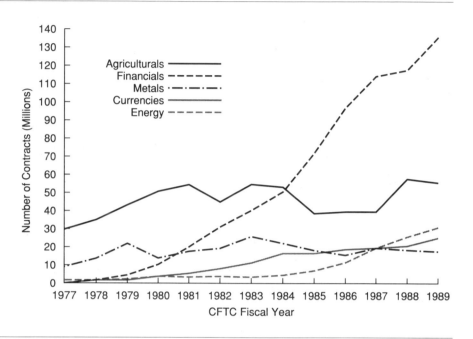

In recent years, Japan has become a major world economic power. Because it has the largest trade surplus, it is no surprise that the ten largest banks in the world are Japanese. Japan has also become a major player in the futures markets. Japanese futures markets began in October 1985 with the introduction of a contract on Japan's yen bond. However, the Japanese were not allowed to trade in foreign markets until June 1987. In the fall of that year, the Japanese began trading stock index futures contracts on indices of Japanese stocks. They have since added several contracts and now generate extensive volume both domestically and in the U.S. futures markets. In the fall of 1990 both the Chicago Board of Trade and the Chicago Mercantile Exchange began trading futures contracts on Japanese stock indices and bonds. However, volume has been very low. The interest and participation of the Japanese is also a major (if not the primary) reason why the Chicago Board of Trade has a night session in its Treasury bond and note contracts.

Figure 7.1 illustrates the volume of trading in futures contracts on domestic futures exchanges since 1977. As can be seen, the growth of trading volume has been quite phenomenal. Most of the growth has come from financial futures contracts. Many futures traders who formerly traded in porkbellies and corn have switched to various financial contracts. In addition, the remarkable success of stock index futures has brought many investors and institutions that formerly traded only in stocks and bonds to the arena of futures trading.

TABLE 7.2
Trading Volume by Exchange, 1990

Exchange	1,000 Contracts
Chicago Board of Trade	120,777
Chicago Mercantile Exchange	84,838
New York Mercantile Exchange	36,358
Commodity Exchange	15,497
Coffee, Sugar, and Cocoa Exchange	8,974
MidAmerica Commodity Exchange	3,976
New York Cotton Exchange	2,746
New York Futures Exchange	1,657
Kansas City Board of Trade	1,187
Minneapolis Grain Exchange	478
Chicago Rice and Cotton Exchange	55
	276,535

Source: Consensus, *January 18, 1991*

The Chicago Board of Trade remains the largest futures exchange. Table 7.2 indicates that the CBOT's 1990 market share was about 44 percent. The Chicago Mercantile Exchange is the second largest exchange, capturing about a third of the market. The New York Mercantile Exchange ranks third, a result of its increasingly popular energy futures contracts. COMEX, the United States' leading market for precious metal futures, is fourth. The CBOT and CME, however, clearly are the industry leaders, with the other exchanges dividing among themselves the remainder of a very large pie.

FUTURES TRADERS

The members of the exchange are individuals who physically go on the exchange floor and trade futures contracts. There are several ways to characterize these futures traders.

General Classes of Futures Traders

All traders on the floor of the futures exchange are either commission brokers or locals.

Commission brokers simply execute transactions for other people. A commission broker can be an independent businessperson who executes trades for individuals or institutions or a representative of a major brokerage firm. In the futures industry, these brokerage firms are called *futures commission merchants (FCM)*. The commission broker simply executes trades for the FCM's customers. Commission brokers make their money by charging a commission for each trade.

Locals are individuals in business for themselves who trade from their own accounts. They attempt to profit by buying contracts at a given price and selling them at a higher price. Their trading provides liquidity for the public. Locals assume the risk and reap the rewards from their skill at futures trading. It has been said that locals represent the purest form of capitalism and entrepreneurship.

Because a futures trader can be a local or an FCM, a conflict occasionally arises between traders' loyalty to themselves and their customers' interests. For example, some traders engage in *dual trading*, in which they trade for themselves and also trade as brokers for someone else. Dual trading has become very controversial in recent years. To illustrate the conflict that might arise, suppose a trader holds a set of orders that includes a large order for a customer. Knowing that the price may move substantially when the customer's order is placed, the trader executes a purchase for his or her own account prior to placing the customer's order. There are a number of other ways in which dual trading can be profitable to the trader at the expense of the customer. However, for this to occur the trader must act unscrupulously. The exchanges argue that abuses of dual trading are rare. Moreover, they claim that dual trading provides liquidity to the market. As of mid-1990 the issue was still being debated, and some limitations on dual trading already have been enacted.

Classification by Trading Strategy

Futures traders can be further classified by the strategies they employ.

A *hedger* holds a position in the spot market. This might involve owning a commodity, or it may simply mean that the individual plans or is committed to the future purchase or sale of the commodity. Taking a futures contract that is opposite to the position in the spot market reduces the risk. For example, if you hold a portfolio of stocks, you can hedge that portfolio's value by selling a stock index futures contract. If the stocks' prices fall, the portfolio will lose value, but the price of the futures contract is also likely to fall. Since you are short the futures contract, you can repurchase it at a lower price, thus making a profit. The gain from the futures position will at least partially offset the loss on the portfolio.

Hedging is an important activity in any futures market. This section has given only a cursory overview of it. Chapter 10 is devoted exclusively to hedging.

Speculators attempt to profit from guessing the direction of the market. Speculators include locals as well as the thousands of individuals and institutions off the exchange floor. They play an important role in the market by providing the liquidity that makes hedging possible and assuming the risk that hedgers are trying to eliminate. Speculating is discussed in more detail in Chapter 11.

Spreaders use futures spreads to speculate at a low level of risk. Like an option spread, a futures spread involves a long position in one contract and a short position in another. Spreads may be intracommodity or intercommodity. An *intracommodity* spread is like a time spread in options. The spreader buys a contract with one expiration month and sells an otherwise identical contract with a different expiration month. An *intercommodity* spread, which normally is not used in options, consists of a long position in a futures contract on one commodity and a short position in a contract on another. In some cases, the two commodities even trade on different exchanges. The rationale for this type of spread rests on a perceived "normal" difference between the prices of the two futures contracts. When the prices move out of line, traders employ intercommodity spreads to take advantage of the expected price realignment.

Futures spreads work much like option time spreads in that the long position in one contract is somewhat offset by the short position in the other. There actually is no real difference between this type of spread and a hedge. For example, suppose the commodity is Treasury bills, the current month is October, and the available futures expirations are December, March, and June. A hedger holds Treasury bills and sells a December contract. A spreader holds a December contract and sells a March contract. Each holds a long position in a spot or nearby futures contract and a short position in a deferred futures contract. Each is attempting to profit from one position while expecting a loss on the other. Neither knows which position will make a profit and which will create a loss.

Arbitrageurs attempt to profit from differences in the prices of otherwise identical spot and futures positions. An analogous type of arbitrage that we already covered is the execution of conversions and reversals to take advantage of option prices that fail to conform to put-call parity. In futures markets there are some important theoretical relationships, which we shall study in Chapters 9 and 11. When prices get out of line with these theoretical predictions, arbitrageurs enter the market and execute trades that bring prices back in line. Because arbitrage is designed to be riskless, it resembles hedging and spreading. In many cases, however, it is difficult to determine whether a given strategy is arbitrage, hedging, or spreading.

Classification by Trading Style

Futures traders can also be classified by the style of trading they practice. There are three distinct trading styles: scalping, day trading, and position trading.

Scalpers attempt to profit from small changes in the contract price. Scalpers seldom hold their positions for more than a few minutes. They trade by using their skill at sensing the market's short-term direction and by buying from the public at the bid price and selling to the public at the ask price. They are constantly alert for large inflows of orders and short-term trends. Because they operate with very low transaction costs, they can profit from small moves in contract prices. The practice of making a large number of quick, small profits is referred to as *scalping*.

Day traders hold their positions for no longer than the duration of the trading day. Like scalpers, they attempt to profit from short-term market movements; however, they hold their positions much longer than do scalpers. Nonetheless, they are unwilling to assume the risk of adverse news that might occur overnight or on weekends.

Position traders hold their transactions open for much longer periods than do scalpers and day traders. Position traders believe they can make profits by waiting for a major market movement. This may take as much as several weeks or may not come at all.

Scalpers, day traders, and position traders are not mutually exclusive. A speculator may employ any or all of these techniques in transactions.

In addition to those who trade on the floor of the exchange, there are many individuals who trade off the exchange floor and employ some of the same techniques.

Off-Floor Futures Traders

Participants in the futures markets also include thousands of individuals and institutions. Institutions include banks and financial intermediaries, investment banking firms, mutual funds, pension funds, and other corporations. In addition, some farmers and numerous individuals actively trade futures contracts. As noted earlier, foreign institutions are becoming increasingly active in U.S. futures markets. The extent of this off-floor participation in futures markets has greatly increased in recent years, due in part to the popularity of stock index futures but also to the contracts on U.S. Treasury securities, foreign currencies, and Eurodollars.

In addition to those who directly participate in trading, federal law recognizes and regulates certain other participants. An *introducing broker (IB)* is an individual who solicits orders from public customers to trade futures contracts. IBs do not execute orders themselves, nor do their firms; rather, they subcontract with FCMs to do this. The IB and the FCM divide the commission.

A *commodity trading advisor (CTA)* is an individual or firm that analyzes futures markets and issues reports, gives advice, and makes recommendations on the purchase and sale of contracts. CTAs earn fees for their services but do not necessarily trade contracts themselves.

A *commodity pool operator (CPO)* is an individual or firm that solicits funds from the public, pools them, and uses them to trade futures contracts. The CPO profits by collecting a percentage of the assets in the fund and sometimes through sales charges deducted from deposits. A CPO essentially is the operator of a futures fund, a topic discussed later in this chapter. However, some commodity pools are privately operated and not open for public participation.

An *associated person (AP)* is an individual associated with any of the above individuals or institutions or any other firm engaged in the futures business. APs include directors, partners, officers, and employees but not clerical personnel. We mention APs here because, as we shall discuss later, they are required to register with regulatory authorities.

The Cost and Profitability of Exchange Membership

Most futures exchanges have a limited number of full memberships, called *seats*. There usually is a market for seats, with the highest and lowest bids publicly reported. Seat prices tend to fluctuate with the amount of trading activity in the market and the number of new contracts introduced. Figure 7.2 illustrates the history of seat

FIGURE 7.2

Seat Prices on Chicago Board of Trade, 1974–1990

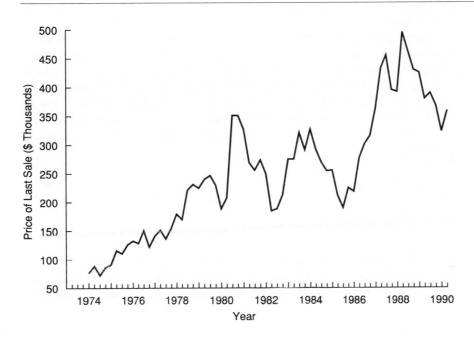

prices since 1974 for a full membership on the Chicago Board of Trade. The price has been as high as nearly $500,000 and as low as about $70,000.

Seats can also be leased, and some exchanges have different levels of membership. For example, the Chicago Board of Trade has 1,402 full members and a lesser number of Associate Members, Government Instrument Market Membership Interests, Index, Debt, and Energy Membership Interests, and Commodity Options Membership Interests. Associate Members can trade in all markets except agricultural futures. Government Instrument Market Memberships allow trading in futures contracts on government securities. Index, Debt, and Energy Membership Interests allow trading in futures on stock indices, bonds, and any energy-related contracts as well as options on those futures. Commodity option memberships allow trading in any options on futures contracts; these are covered in Chapter 12. There are also special trading permits that allow trading in only one futures, such as the Major Market Index. These are frequently offered when a new contract is introduced. There are markets for futures exchange seats, and their prices are in proportion to the extent of trading permitted by the membership.

Like options markets, futures markets do not create or destroy wealth. Therefore, one trader's gains are another's losses subject to some slippage due to commissions and taxes. It has been said, however, that the vast majority of futures traders lose money. It is not surprising that a small number of individuals probably earn large profits while assuming high risks. Some are lucky and, of course, some are unlucky. There have been several studies of the speculators' performances. Unfortunately, most of those studies are somewhat dated, but we shall look at two of them here.

Hieronymous (1977) examined all trades executed in 1969 by an unnamed futures commission merchant.[5] A total of 462 accounts were examined, of which 164 earned a profit and 298 incurred a loss. The average profit for profitable accounts was $2,819, while the average loss for unprofitable accounts was $3,783. For the 462 accounts taken as a whole, the average performance was a loss of $1,439. These figures included commissions. The average performance before commissions was a loss of $560. These results suggest that the average public trader does poorly in futures trading.

While the Hieronymous study looked at public traders, Silber (1984) examined the trading of an unidentified scalper on the New York Futures Exchange who traded the NYSE Index futures. The time period covered was December 1982 through January 1983. Silber analyzed a total of 2,106 transactions. The average profit per trade was $10.56, the average length of time a position was held was only 77 seconds, and the average number of contracts traded was 2.9. Of the total number of trades, 48 percent were profitable, 22 percent were unprofitable, and 30 percent were scratch trades.[6] As these figures reveal, the scalper makes profits less than half the time but makes money overall. In an efficient market, this probably is a normal return earned for incurring the risk that this type of trading entails.

THE MECHANICS OF FUTURES TRADING

Before placing an order to trade futures contracts, an individual must open an account with a broker. Because the risk of futures trading can be quite high, the individual must make a minimum deposit—usually at least $5,000—and sign a disclosure statement acknowledging the possible risks.

Placing an Order

One can place several types of orders. These are essentially the same as the option orders covered in Chapter 2. Stop orders and limit orders are used as well as good-till-canceled and day orders.

When an investor places an order, the broker phones the firm's trading desk on the exchange floor and relays the order to the firm's floor broker. The floor broker goes to the pit in which the contract trades. The *pit* is an octagonal- or po-

---

[5]This and several other, similar studies are discussed in Teweles and Jones (1987).

[6]A *scratch trade* essentially is a breakeven trade. For example, suppose a trader wants to buy two contracts but gets an offer for four contracts. The trader might take the offer, buy the four contracts, and immediately sell two of the contracts at the same price at which they were purchased.

lygonal-shaped ring with steps descending to the center. Hand signals and a considerable amount of verbal activity are used to place bids and make offers. This process is called *open outcry*. When the order is filled, the information is relayed back, ultimately to the broker's office, whereupon the broker telephones the customer to confirm the trade.

The process of placing and executing an order through the open-outcry system is a 140-year tradition. However, it may become a thing of the past. As noted earlier, several new futures exchanges in foreign countries are fully automated so that bids and offers are submitted through a computer and trades are executed off the floor. Some systems will even match buyer and seller. As we noted in Chapter 2, the CBOE has made some progress in automating its option orders, but it too remains essentially an open-outcry market. This primarily reflects the desire of the exchange members to preserve the open-outcry system, in which they participate and indeed enjoy each day.

However, the Chicago Mercantile Exchange and Chicago Board of Trade, recognizing the growing demand for automated systems, have begun developing automated systems of their own. The CME's system, called GLOBEX, matches buyer and seller; the CBOT's AURORA system allows buyer and seller to choose each other. In 1990 the CBOT and CME agreed to work together toward a single system, which will apparently be essentially the GLOBEX system. The system is intended for use only during hours when the exchanges are closed; nonetheless, it seems likely that competitive pressures will force the system to be available during regular trading hours. As of mid-1991, however, GLOBEX had not begun operating.

The Role of the Clearinghouse

At this point in the process, the clearinghouse intervenes. Each futures exchange operates its own independent clearinghouse. The clearinghouse in futures markets works like that in options markets, so its basic operations should be familiar to you from Chapter 2.

The concept of a clearinghouse as an intermediary and guarantor to every trade is not nearly as old as the futures markets themselves. The first such clearinghouse was organized in 1925 at the Chicago Board of Trade. The clearinghouse is an independent corporation, and its stockholders are its member clearing firms. Each firm maintains a margin account with the clearinghouse and must meet minimum standards of financial responsibility.

For each transaction, obviously, there is both a buyer, usually called the *long*, and a seller, typically called the *short*. In the absence of a clearinghouse, each party would be responsible to the other. If one party defaulted, the other would be left with a worthless claim. The clearinghouse assumes the role of intermediary to each transaction. It guarantees the buyer that the seller will perform and guarantees the seller that the buyer will perform. The clearinghouse's financial accounts contain separate records of contracts owned and the respective clearing firms and contracts sold and the respective clearing firms. Note that the clearinghouse keeps track only of its member firms. The clearing firms, in turn, monitor the long and short positions of individual traders and firms. All parties to futures transactions must have an account with a clearing firm or with a firm that has an account with a clearing firm.

Let us illustrate how the clearinghouse operates by assuming you sell a U.S. Treasury bond futures contract at a price of 97 27/32, which is $97,843.75. You have contacted your broker, who either is a futures commission merchant (FCM) or contracts with an FCM, who finds a buyer in the U.S. Treasury bond futures pit of the Chicago Board of Trade. The buyer might be a local or an FCM, representing a customer off the floor.

Your brokerage firm clears its trades through ABC Futures, a member firm of the Chicago Board of Trade Clearing Corporation (BOTCC). The buyer's FCM clears through ACME Trading Company, a clearing firm that is also a member of the BOTCC. The required margin changes often on these contracts; we shall assume it is $2,500. You deposit this amount with ABC. ABC pools the transactions of all of its customers and deposits an amount required in its account with the BOTCC. The buyer deposits the same amount with ACME, which also deposits a sum of money, based on its customers' open positions, with the BOTCC.

The BOTCC guarantees the performance of you and the buyer. Thus, neither of you has to worry about whether the other will be able to make up the losses. The BOTCC will look to the clearing firms, ABC and ACME, for payment, and they in turn will look to their customers.

Daily Settlement

One way in which the clearinghouse helps ensure its survival is by using margins and the daily settlement of accounts. For each contract there is both an *initial* margin, the amount that must be deposited on the day the transaction is opened, and a *maintenance margin*, the amount that must be maintained every day thereafter. There are also initial and maintenance margins for spread and hedge transactions, which usually are lower than those for purely speculative positions.

The margin deposit is not quite like the margin on a stock trade. In stock trading, the investor deposits margin money and borrows the remainder of the stock price from the broker. In futures trading, not only is the margin requirement much smaller, but the remainder of the funds are not borrowed. The margin deposit is more like a good-faith security deposit. Some large and actively trading investors are able to deposit Treasury bills for margins. Others are required to deposit cash.

At the end of each day, a committee composed of clearinghouse officials establishes a *settlement price*. This usually is an average of the prices of the last few trades of the day. Using the settlement price, each account is *marked to market*. The difference in the current settlement price and the previous day's settlement price is determined. If the difference is positive because the settlement price increased, the dollar amount is credited to the margin accounts of those holding long positions. Where does the money come from? It is charged to the accounts of those holding short positions. If the difference is negative because the settlement price decreased, the dollar amount is credited to the holders of short positions and charged to those holding long positions.

This process, sometimes called the *daily settlement*, is an important feature of futures markets and a major difference between futures and forward markets. In forward markets, the gains and losses are incurred at the end of the contract's life, when delivery is made. Futures markets credit and charge the price changes on a daily basis. This helps ensure the markets' integrity, because large losses are covered a little at a time rather than all at the end, by which time the holder of the losing position may be unable to cover the loss.

To illustrate the daily settlement procedure, let us consider the transaction we previously described. We assume it was initiated on Friday, August 1. You sold one Treasury bond futures contract on the Chicago Board of Trade at that day's opening price of 97 27/32. One such contract is for a face value of $100,000, so the price is .9784375($100,000) = $97,843.75. The initial margin requirement was $2,500, and the maintenance margin requirement was $2,000. You maintain the position until repurchasing the contract on August 18 at the opening price of 100 16/32, or $100,500. Table 7.3 illustrates the transactions to the account while the position was open.

Note that the account is first marked to market on the day of the trade and you made a profit of $437.50 on the first day. Each day thereafter, you must maintain $2,000 in the account so that on any given day when the balance is greater than $2,000, the excess over the initial margin can be withdrawn. However, we shall assume you do not withdraw the excess. If the balance falls below the $2,000 maintenance margin requirement, you receive a margin call and must deposit enough funds to bring the balance back up to the initial margin requirement. The additional funds deposited are called the *variation margin*. They are officially due within a few days but usually are required to be deposited immediately; we shall assume the money is deposited before trading begins on the day you receive the margin call. By the end of the day on Friday, August 8, the account shows a balance of $1,250. On Monday morning you receive a margin call for $1,250, which is immediately deposited. Another margin call, for $1,937.50, follows the next morning. Undaunted and still confident of ultimately turning things around, you make the deposit on August 12. When you finally buy back the contract on August 18, the account balance withdrawn is $3,031.25. In all, you have made deposits of $2,500, $1,250, and $1,937.50 for a total of $5,687.50. Thus, the overall loss on the trade is $2,656.25.

The above example is not at all unusual. It was selected at random. You, the seller of this contract, quickly incurred a substantial loss. However, for every dollar lost, there is a dollar gained by someone else. Traders who were bullish on Treasury bond futures from August 1 to 18 did quite well. Nonetheless, the large dollar flows from day to day serve as a stern reminder of the substantial leverage component futures contracts offer.

It is also important to note that with futures contracts it is possible to lose more money than one has invested. For example, assume the market makes a substantial move against the investor. The account balance is depleted, and the

TABLE 7.3

Daily Settlement Example

Assume that on Friday, August 1, you sell one Chicago Board of Trade September Treasury bond futures contract at the opening price of 97 27/32 ($97,843.75). The initial margin is $2,500, and the maintenance margin is $2,000. You maintain your position every day through Friday, August 15, and then buy back the contract at the opening price on Monday, August 18.

Date	Settlement Price	Settlement Price (Dollars)	Mark-to-Market	Other Entries	Account Balance
8/1	97-13	$97,406.25	+$437.50	+2,500.00[a]	$2,937.50
8/4	97-25	97,781.25	-375.00		2,562.50
8/5	96-18	96,562.50	+1,218.75		3,781.25
8/6	96-07	96,218.75	+343.75		4,125.00
8/7	97-05	97,156.25	-937.50		3,187.50
8/8	99-03	99,093.75	-1,937.50		1,250.00
8/11	101-01	101,031.25	-1,937.50	+1,250.00[b]	562.50
8/12	99-25	99,781.25	+1,250.00	+1,937.50[c]	3,750.00
8/13	101-01	101,031.25	-1,250.00		2,500.00
8/14	100-25	100,781.25	+250.00		2,750.00
8/15	100-25	100,781.25	0.00		2,750.00
8/18	100-16[d]	100,500.00	+281.25	-3,031.25[e]	0.00

[a]Initial margin deposit of $2,500.
[b]Deposits $1,250 to meet margin call.
[c]Deposits $1,937.50 to meet margin call.
[d]Indicates opening price at which contract is purchased.
[e]After purchasing contract, account balance is $3,031.25. Entire amount is withdrawn.

broker asks the investor to deposit additional funds. If the investor does not have the funds, the broker will attempt to close out the position. Now assume the market moves quickly before the contracts can be closed. Ultimately the contracts are sold out, but not before the investor has incurred additional losses. Those losses must be covered in cash. In the limit, a long position can ultimately lose the full price of the contract. This would occur if the price went to zero. On a short position, however, there is no upper limit on the price. Therefore, the loss theoretically is infinite.

One method futures exchanges use to limit the losses incurred on any given day is the daily price limit, which we briefly discussed earlier. The maximum upward and downward move corresponds somewhat to the margin requirement. The maximum loss in an account on a given day usually will not exceed the margin balance at the beginning of that day. However, under some conditions, the limits are relaxed. The clearinghouse can request that additional margin funds be deposited during a trading session rather than waiting until the end of the day.

The total number of contracts outstanding at any one time is called the *open interest*. The concept is the same as it is for options markets. Each contract has both a long and a short position and counts as one contract of open interest. As an example of the potential size of open interest, the average month-ending open interest in the CFTC's 1989 fiscal year was about 3.2 million contracts, with financial and currency futures contracts accounting for slightly less than half of the total.[7]

The clearinghouse has fulfilled quite well its mission to protect the market. In March 1985, Volume Investors, a COMEX clearing firm, failed to meet a margin call due to a default by several of its customers who were carrying large short positions in options on gold futures. The potential damage to the market never materialized, as the COMEX Clearing Association handled the affair with a barely discernable ripple.

Most futures traders do not hold their positions to expiration; rather, they simply re-enter the market and execute an offsetting transaction. In other words, if one held a long position in a contract, one might elect to simply sell that contract in the market. The clearinghouse would properly note that the trader's positions were offsetting. If the position were not offset before the expiration month, delivery would become likely.

Delivery and Cash Settlement

All contracts eventually expire. As noted earlier, each contract has a delivery month. The delivery procedure varies among contracts. Some contracts can be delivered on any business day of the delivery month. Others permit delivery only after the contract has traded for the last day—a day that also varies from contract to contract. Still others are cash settled; thus, there is no delivery at all.

Most non-cash-settled financial futures contracts permit delivery any day of the delivery month. Delivery usually is a three-day sequence beginning two days prior to the first possible delivery day. The clearing member firms report to the clearinghouse those of their customers who hold long positions. Two days before the intended delivery day, the holder of a short position who intends to make delivery notifies the clearinghouse of desire to deliver. This day is called the *notice of intention day*. On the next business day, called the *position day*, the exchange selects the oldest long position to receive delivery. On the third day, the *delivery day*, delivery takes place and the long pays the short. For most financial futures, delivery is consummated by wire transfer.

Most futures contracts allow for more than one deliverable instrument. The contract usually specifies that the price paid by the long to the short be adjusted to reflect a difference in the quality of the deliverable good. We shall look at this more closely in Chapter 11.

On cash-settled contracts, such as stock index futures, the settlement price on the last trading day is fixed at the closing spot price of the underlying instrument,

---

[7]Commodity Futures Trading Commission, *Annual Report*, 1989.

such as the stock index. All contracts are marked to market on that day, and the positions are deemed to be closed. One exception to this procedure is the S&P 500 futures contract, which closes trading on the Thursday before the third Friday of the expiration month but bases the final settlement price on the opening stock price on Friday morning. This procedure was installed to avoid some problems created when a contract settles at the closing prices. These problems are discussed in Chapter 14.

The fact that all futures contracts can be delivered or cash settled is critical to their pricing. However, most contracts are not delivered. In the CFTC's fiscal year 1989, 267 million contracts were traded, but only 1.7 million—fewer than 1 percent—ended in delivery; this figures includes cash-settled contracts. Of over 50 million cash-settled contracts traded in all, fewer than 700,000 were held to the final trading day.[8] Thus, delivery, albeit an important feature of futures contracts, seldom takes place. Most traders close out their positions prior to expiration, a process called *offsetting*. The futures market is not the best route to acquiring a commodity, because the long contract holder is at the mercy of the short contract holder. The short can deliver on any of several delivery days and can choose to deliver any of several related but slightly different commodities. The long must accept whatever the short offers. Thus, the long usually closes out the position early. Therefore, if one needs the commodity, one often will do better to purchase it in the spot market.

Despite the flexibility sellers have in determining the delivery terms, some contracts actually are delivered through a process called *exchange for physicals (EFP)*, also known as *against actuals* or *versus cash*. This is, in fact, the only type of permissable futures transaction that occurs off the floor of the exchange. In an EFP transaction, the holders of long and short positions get together and agree on a cash transaction that would close out their futures positions. For example, farmer A holds a short position in a wheat contract and firm B holds a long position in the same contract. Firm B wants to buy farmer A's wheat, but either the wheat is not one of the grades acceptable for delivery on the contract or the farmer would find it prohibitively expensive to deliver at Chicago or Toledo as the contract requires. In either case, farmer A and firm B could arrange for A to deliver the wheat at some other acceptable location and B to pay A for the wheat at an agreed-upon price. Then A and B would be permitted to report this transaction to the CBOT as though each had offset its futures contract with a trade with the other party. Thus, the EFP market simply gives the parties additional flexibility in making delivery, choosing the terms, and conducting such business when the exchanges are closed. EFPs can also be used in cash settlement contracts. EFPs are used in several futures markets and comprise almost 100 percent of deliveries made in oil futures markets.

[8]Ibid.

FUTURES PRICE QUOTATIONS

The best source of daily futures prices is *The Wall Street Journal*. Figure 7.3 illustrates how *The Wall Street Journal* reports futures prices. Contracts are grouped into categories: grains and oilseeds, livestock and meat, food and fiber, wood, and financials. The financial contracts appear on different pages, grouped with the options on the underlying instruments and the options on futures. Figure 7.3 shows the prices of some grains/oilseeds and financials.

At the top of the column are headings. For the grains and oilseeds, we have the day's opening, high, low, and settlement price, followed by the change in the settlement price from the previous day. The next two columns give the high and low over the contract's life. The final column is the open interest.

The first line indicates the name of the commodity and the abbreviation for the exchange, followed by the contract size and the units of quotation. For example, the corn contract is traded at the Chicago Board of Trade, which is abbreviated here as CBT. One contract is for 5,000 bushels, and the prices are in cents per bushel.

Each line in the quotes indicates a particular contract. For corn we see the May 91 contract, followed by the July 91, September, December, March 92, and May contracts. The May 91 contract had a settlement price of 253 3/4 cents, or $2.5375, per bushel.

At the end of each contract's quotes are estimates of that day's volume—here 50,000 contracts—volume the previous day (46,186), total open interest (222,705)—which is the total as of the beginning of the trading session—and the change in open interest from the previous day (+2,462). The total open interest figure normally equals the total of the open interest figures for each contract; however, the markets move so quickly that sometimes this information is not completely accurate.

At the bottom of the first column are the stock index futures prices. The headings are the same as those for the grains and oilseeds. Below the volume and open interest figures are information on the spot index. The second column of quotations contains some other financial futures. The headings vary slightly. Look at the Treasury bond futures prices. The contract is at the CBOT, is for $100,000 face value, and is quoted in points and thirty-seconds of 100 percent. Thus, we can interpret the settlement price of the June 91 contract as 94 14/32 (94.4375) or $94,437.50. The change in the settlement price is an increase of one point. The next column, "Yield," shows 8.587. To understand this figure, it is necessary to know some of the contract terms and conditions.

The contract permits delivery of any Treasury bond that will not mature or be called for 15 years. The coupon rate on the deliverable bond is supposed to be 8 percent; however, any coupon bond is acceptable subject to an adjustment to the price paid at delivery.[9] The yield of 8.587 percent is the yield on a hypothetical 20-year bond with an 8 percent coupon and a price equal to the settlement price of

---

[9]We shall examine this adjustment in Chapter 10.

FIGURE 7.3

Futures Quotations in *The Wall Street Journal*, Trading Day of March 22, 1991

—GRAINS AND OILSEEDS—

CORN (CBT) 5,000 bu.; cents per bu.

	Open	High	Low	Settle	Change	Lifetime High	Lifetime Low	Open Interest
May	253¾	254¼	252	253¾	+ 1	306½	235	73,799
July	259½	260½	258¾	260½	+ 1½	308¼	241½	81,327
Sept	258½	259½	257¾	258¾	+ 1½	287½	240¼	14,772
Dec	257¾	259	257¼	258½	+ 1¾	275	242½	46,907
Mr92	265½	266	264½	265½	+ 1¼	275¼	249	5,627
May	271	271	269½	270¼	+ 1	279½	258¼	260

Est vol 50,000; vol Thur 46,186; open int 222,705, +2,462.

OATS (CBT) 5,000 bu.; cents per bu.

	Open	High	Low	Settle	Change	Lifetime High	Lifetime Low	Open Interest
May	123¼	124¾	121½	123½	+ 1¼	183¾	111¼	6,782
July	129¼	130¼	127½	129½	+ 1¼	164¾	117	6,457
Sept	134	134¾	132	134¼	+ 1¼	153	122½	478
Dec	140¾	140¾	138½	140¼	+ 1	149	131	533

Est vol 1,700; vol Thur 1,351; open int 14,260, +152.

SOYBEANS (CBT) 5,000 bu.; cents per bu.

	Open	High	Low	Settle	Change	Lifetime High	Lifetime Low	Open Interest
May	580	580¾	575	575½	− 2½	711	561	37,234
July	591½	593¾	587¾	588½	− 2	718	576	37,914
Aug	598	599¼	593½	593½	− 2¾	695	582	5,014
Sept	602½	603¼	597¾	598	− 2¼	670	583½	5,212
Nov	613	613¾	607½	608	− 2½	674	590½	16,891
Ja92	624	624	619	619	− 2	649½	602½	3,230
Mar	635	635	630½	630	− 2	660	615	502

Est vol 40,000; vol Thur 33,361; open int 106,102, −1,433.

SOYBEAN MEAL (CBT) 100 tons; $ per ton.

	Open	High	Low	Settle	Change	Lifetime High	Lifetime Low	Open Interest
May	166.70	166.90	165.60	166.00	− .20	208.00	164.10	25,899
July	170.00	170.50	169.50	169.70	....	209.00	168.00	15,630
Aug	172.20	172.20	171.50	171.50	− .40	199.00	170.00	4,507
Sept	175.80	174.00	173.50	173.60	+ .10	193.50	171.80	4,142
Oct	175.80	175.80	175.30	175.40	− .30	190.00	172.50	2,552
Dec	179.00	179.00	178.20	178.60	....	191.50	174.00	3,720
Ja92	....	....	....	179.50	....	190.50	177.50	598

Est vol 12,000; vol Thur 11,892; open int 57,018, +4.

S&P 500 INDEX (CME) 500 times index

	Open	High	Low	Settle	Chg	High	Low	Open Interest
June	369.10	371.50	368.10	371.20	+ 1.55	386.00	300.90	138,607
Sept	371.70	374.25	371.00	373.95	+ 1.60	386.90	304.00	2,469
Dec	376.65	376.80	374.00	376.85	+ 1.45	388.90	316.50	1,219

Est vol 41,368; vol Thur 39,736; open int 142,295, +497.
Indx prelim High 368.22; Low 365.58; Close 367.48 +.90

NIKKEI 225 Stock Average (CME) −$5 times NSA

	Open	High	Low	Settle	Chg	High	Low	Open Interest
June	27395.	27425.	27255.	27335.	− 75.0	27800.	21765.	4,930

Est vol 397; vol Thur 680; open int 4,939, +73.
The index: High 26782.72; Low 26513.75; Close 26613.19 +163.84

NYSE COMPOSITE INDEX (NYFE) 500 times index

	Open	High	Low	Settle	Chg	High	Low	Open Interest
June	201.90	203.25	201.25	203.00	+ .80	209.60	165.85	4,139
Sept	203.15	204.25	203.00	204.35	+ .85	210.50	173.10	366

Est vol 5,822; vol Thur 5,786; open int 4,551, +45.
The index: High 201.46; Low 200.20; Close 201.13 +.34

MAJOR MKT INDEX (CBT) $250 times index

	Open	High	Low	Settle	Chg	High	Low	Open Interest
Apr	605.50	609.30	604.20	608.25	+ 2.05	634.50	547.75	5,902
May	607.25	608.75	604.75	608.40	+ 2.15	634.50	604.75	294
June	607.25	610.75	607.00	610.40	+ 2.15	636.50	607.00	154

Est vol 2,500; vol Thur 2,354; open int 6,350, +31.
The index: High 606.69; Low 601.77; Close 605.01 +1.06

TREASURY BONDS (CBT)−$100,000; pts. 32nds of 100%

	Open	High	Low	Settle	Chg	Yield Settle	Chg	Open Interest
June	94-10	94-15	94-01	94-14	+ 4	8.587	− .014	235,344
Sept	93-21	93-25	93-12	93-24	+ 4	8.663	− .014	12,679
Dec	92-27	93-04	92-24	93-04	+ 4	8.733	− .014	4,654
Mr92	92-10	92-19	92-10	92-19	+ 4	8.793	− .014	1,069
June	....	....	....	92-03	+ 4	8.850	− .014	516
Sept	....	....	....	91-20	+ 4	8.904	− .014	268
Dec	....	....	....	91-06	+ 4	8.955	− .014	153

Est vol 180,000; vol Thur 263,369; op int 259,797, +3,097.

TREASURY BONDS (MCE)−$50,000; pts. 32nds of 100%

	Open	High	Low	Settle	Chg	Yield Settle	Chg	Open Interest
June	94-11	94-20	94-01	94-19	+ 8	8.570	− .027	10,159

Est vol 4,300; vol Thur 5,944; open int 10,216, +508.

T−BONDS (LIFFE) U.S. $100,000; pts of 100%

	Open	High	Low	Settle	Chg		Open Interest
June	94-10	94-13	94-03	94-07	− 0-03	96-29 94-03	5,827

Est vol 1,321; vol Thur 1,860; open int 5,827, −269.

GERMAN GOV'T. BOND (LIFFE)
250,000 marks; $ per mark (.01)

	Open	High	Low	Settle	Chg		Open Interest
June	84.80	84.99	84.75	84.84	− .07	86.80 81.33	69,739
Sept	85.23	85.26	85.07	85.15	− .08	86.52 85.79	1,861

Est vol 24,759; vol Thur 41,744; open int 71,600, +147.

TREASURY NOTES (CBT)−$100,000; pts. 32nds of 100%

	Open	High	Low	Settle	Chg	Yield Settle	Chg	Open Interest
June	97-30	98-01	97-25	98-00	+ 2	8.298	− .010	65,059
Sept	97-13	97-15	97-09	97-15	+ 1	8.379	− .005	607

Est vol 8,000; vol Thur 15,706; open int 76,367, −748.

5 YR TREAS NOTES (CBT)−$100,000; pts. 32nds of 100%

	Open	High	Low	Settle	Chg	Yield Settle	Chg	Open Interest
June	100-03	100-04	100-00	00-035	+ 1	7.97	− .01	74,489

Est vol 4,500; vol Thur 6,298; open int 81,014, −414.

TREASURY BILLS (IMM)−$1 mil.; pts. of 100%

	Open	High	Low	Settle	Chg	Discount Settle	Chg	Open Interest
June	94.26	94.28	94.23	94.27	+ .01	5.73	− .01	32,241
Sept	93.99	94.00	93.95	93.99	+ .02	6.01	− .02	6,817
Dec	93.53	93.53	93.50	93.50	− .01	6.50	+ .01	659

Est vol 4,393; vol Thur 5,812; open int 39,768, +641.

LIBOR-1 MO. (IMM)−$3,000,000; points of 100%

	Open	High	Low	Settle	Chg	Yield Settle	Chg	Open Interest
Apr	93.63	93.67	93.62	93.65	+ .02	6.35	− .02	4,130
May	93.62	93.65	93.62	93.63	....	6.37	....	1,584
June	93.63	93.43	93.57	93.57	+ .01	6.43	− .01	1,981
July	93.40	93.40	93.40	93.40	− .02	6.60	+ .02	244

Est vol 2,005; vol Thur 1,678; open int 8,032, −330.

MUNI BOND INDEX (CBT)−$1,000; times Bond Buyer MBI

	Open	High	Low	Settle	Chg		Open Interest
June	90-07	99-10	90-04	90-09	....	93-02 84-26	8,520

Est vol 500; vol Thur 1,908; open int 8,561, +284.
The index: Close 91-13; Yield 7.43.

EURODOLLAR (IMM)−$1 million; pts of 100%

	Open	High	Low	Settle	Chg	Yield Settle	Chg	Open Interest
June	93.37	93.38	93.33	93.37	+ .01	6.63	− .01	269,327
Sept	93.06	93.07	93.01	93.06	+ .02	6.94	− .02	122,634
Dec	92.58	92.58	92.51	92.55	− .02	7.45	+ .02	83,076
Mr92	92.38	92.39	92.32	92.36	− .01	7.64	+ .01	54,203
June	92.07	92.08	92.03	92.06	....	7.94	....	37,342
Sept	91.81	91.83	91.77	91.82	+ .02	8.18	− .02	31,227
Dec	91.54	91.55	91.50	91.55	+ .02	8.45	− .02	24,685
Mr93	91.47	91.49	91.44	91.49	+ .02	8.51	− .02	20,089
June	91.38	91.41	91.36	91.40	+ .03	8.60	− .03	15,070
Sept	91.29	91.32	91.27	91.32	+ .04	8.68	− .04	12,192
Dec	91.12	91.15	91.10	91.14	+ .03	8.86	− .03	8,305
Mr94	91.08	91.11	91.06	91.11	+ .03	8.89	− .03	5,219
June	90.99	91.03	90.98	91.02	+ .03	8.98	− .03	4,152
Sept	90.93	90.98	90.92	90.96	+ .03	9.04	− .03	2,824
Dec	90.82	90.85	90.81	90.85	+ .03	9.15	− .03	2,659
Mr95	90.78	90.79	90.77	90.81	+ .03	9.19	− .03	327

Est vol 110,679; vol Thur 183,286; open int 693,331, −1,935.

EURODOLLAR (LIFFE)−$1 million; pts of 100%

Source: The Wall Street Journal, *March 25, 1991.*

FIGURE 7.4

Futures Quotations in *Barron's*, Week Ending March 22, 1991

SOYBEAN MEAL
100 tons; dollars per ton

208.00	164.00	May	167.00	164.00	166.00	+.70	25,899
209.00	168.00	Jul	170.70	168.00	169.70	+.60	15,630
195.50	170.00	Aug	172.30	170.00	171.50	+.30	4,507
193.50	171.80	Sep	174.20	171.80	173.60	+.90	4,142
189.00	172.50	Oct	176.00	173.60	175.40	+.60	2,522
191.50	174.00	Dec	179.00	176.70	178.60	+.80	3,720
190.50	177.50	Jan	178.10	177.50	179.50	+1.30	598
.....	.....	May	.....	.....	183.20	......	......

Fri. to Thurs. sales 80,144.
Total open interest 57,018.

US TREASURY BONDS
(8 pct-$100,000;pts & 32nds of 100 pct)

99-4	82-18	Jun	94-24	93-4	94-14	− 06	235,344
99-5	85-29	Sep	94	92-16	93-24	− 05	12,679
98-20	85-19	Dec	93-13	91-29	93-4	− 05	4,654
98-13	85-14	Mar	92-24	91-14	92-19	− 04	1,069
97-19	85-3	Jun	92-10	90-30	92-3	− 04	516
95-8	87-14	Sep	91-17	91-16	91-20	− 04	268
94-11	85-6	Dec	91-2	90-4	91-6	− 05	153

Fri. to Thurs. sales 1,473,384.
Total open interest 259,797.

MUNICIPAL BONDS
$1000x index;pts & 32nds of 100 pct

93-2	84-26	Jun	90-20	89-18	90-9	− 07	8,520
92-11	84-7	Sep	90	89-16	89-25	− 06	37
89-28	89-28	Dec	.....	.....	89-9	− 06	4

Last index 91-13, off 07.
Fri. to Thurs. sales 15,526.
Total open interest 8,561.

EURODOLLARS
$1 million;pts of 100 pct.

93.55	89.91	Jun	93.43	93.16	93.37	−.07	269,327
93.35	90.04	Sep	93.12	92.79	93.06	−.06	122,634
93.03	90.04	Dec	92.64	92.33	92.55	−.11	83,076
92.89	90.09	Mar	92.45	92.15	92.36	−.10	54,203
92.62	90.35	Jun	92.17	91.90	92.06	−.12	37,342
92.35	90.32	Sep	91.94	91.67	91.82	−.11	31,227
92.04	90.24	Dec	91.67	91.41	91.55	−.12	24,685
91.99	90.28	Mar	91.62	91.36	91.49	−.13	20,089
91.89	90.27	Jun	91.51	91.25	91.40	.10	15,070
91.81	90.27	Sep	91.40	91.14	91.32	−.08	12,192
91.66	90.22	Dec	91.23	90.99	91.14	−.09	8,305
91.66	90.24	Mar	91.20	90.96	91.11	−.09	5,219
91.57	90.40	Jun	91.11	90.88	91.02	−.09	4,152
91.52	90.36	Sep	91.05	90.82	90.96	−.09	2,824
91.44	90.71	Dec	90.94	90.71	90.85	−.09	2,659
90.79	90.76	Mar	90.79	90.76	90.81	......	327

Fri. to Thurs. sales 983,168.
Total open interest 693,331.

S&P 500

points and cents

383.20	298.00	Mar	378.00	378.00	379.70	+6.10	......
383.90	300.90	Jun	377.75	368.00	371.20	−4.35	138,607
386.30	304.00	Sep	380.30	371.10	373.95	−4.30	2,469
387.60	321.75	Dec	378.90	374.90	376.85	−4.30	1,219

Last index 367.48, off 6.11.
Fri. to Thurs. sales 223,241.
Total open interest 142,295.

Source: Barron's, *March 25, 1991.*

94.4375. There is no "yield" on a futures contract; the figure shown is primarily for the convenience of bond traders, who might find it useful. For example, most bond traders think in terms of yields rather than prices. A price of 94.4375 can be understood as if it were the price of a bond with a yield of 8.587 percent, maturity of 20 years, and coupon of 8 percent.

The next column gives the change in the yield, and the final column gives the open interest. Summary figures for volume and open interest appear at the end of the list of contracts.

The quotes for the Eurodollar and Treasury bill contracts differ slightly, but that is due primarily to the manner in which their prices are quoted. We shall take a closer look at those contracts in later chapters. All of the remaining price quotations should be easily understandable.

Figure 7.4 presents a page from the price quotations from *Barron's*. Recall that *Barron's* is a weekly publication; therefore, the prices reflect the previous Friday's trades. *Barron's* groups all non-index futures by exchange rather than by type of contract. Index futures are presented together by exchange. At this point, you should be able to interpret the quotations quite easily.

As you might expect, these prices will be dated by the time you read them. Futures markets move very quickly, and serious traders will wish to acquire real-time quotes from a commercial vendor.

TYPES OF FUTURES CONTRACTS

Almost 100 types of futures contracts trade on U.S. futures exchanges. Some of these contracts are essentially the same underlying commodity. Many of those listed are not actively traded; some have not been traded at all for some time. Table 7.4 lists all registered contracts on U.S. futures exchanges covered in *The Wall Street Journal*, the exchanges that list them, and contract sizes. A brief discussion of some of the characteristics of each major group of contracts follows.

Grains and Oilseeds

Grains and oilseeds comprise the oldest category of futures contracts. For many years, these contracts were the most actively traded futures; however, in recent years their volume has been surpassed by the financials. The primary trading interest comes from speculative activity and hedging by farmers, food processors, grain storage firms, exporters, and an increasing number of foreign countries that import grain. These futures prices are heavily influenced by agricultural production, weather, government farm policies, and international trade, among other factors.

Livestock and Meat

In the livestock-and-meat category of futures contracts are the celebrated pork bellies, so often acclaimed as the quintessential speculative instrument. In reality, however, pork bellies are no more speculative than most other futures contracts; neither are hogs, live cattle, or feeder cattle, the other contracts in this category. Prices of livestock and meat futures are influenced not only by the obvious—domestic and worldwide demand for beef—but by the not so obvious—prices of grains used as feed, as well as government policies, demographic trends, and international trade. Traders in this category include farmers, slaughterhouses, meat packers, and major users of beef and pork, such as fast-food restaurant chains.

Food and Fiber

Food and fiber is a diverse category that includes coffee, cocoa, cotton, orange juice, and sugar. Prices are influenced by many of the same factors cited for the previous categories. Other factors include weather in central Florida (orange juice), Africa (cocoa and coffee), and Central and South America (coffee). Because most of these commodities are imported, international economic and political conditions also are major considerations.

Metals and Petroleum

The metal and petroleum category includes metals used in jewelry and industry and in energy-related products. Each of these commodities is considered a nonrenewable natural resource. Many are produced in politically unstable foreign countries. A considerable volume of spot and futures trading in these commodities takes place in foreign cities such as London, Paris, Amsterdam, and Zurich. Without question, international economic and political factors are critical influences in these markets. The risks, particularly political, are quite high, as are the stakes.

Wood

Wood is a relatively small and less actively traded group; it includes only the Chicago Mercantile Exchange's lumber futures contract. It has declined in usage in recent years.

Foreign Currency/Eurodollar

Foreign currency futures were introduced in 1972 and were the forerunners of the pure interest rate futures contracts. Over the years their popularity has increased, but trading has concentrated in British pounds, Japanese yen, Swiss francs, and deutsche marks. French francs have never been widely traded, and the Mexican peso, Belgian franc, and Dutch guilder have since been delisted. The active contracts remain an amazing success story in light of the large size of the interbank foreign currency forward market.

The Eurodollar contract is the most successful of the several short-term interest rate futures contracts. A *Eurodollar* is a dollar deposited in a foreign bank or foreign branch of a U.S. bank. The deposit is denominated in dollars rather than in the country's currency. Eurodollars avoid U.S. reserve requirements and many other regulations, and in recent years their use by U.S. corporations and banks has greatly increased. The Eurodollar interest rate, called *LIBOR* for *London Interbank Offer Rate*, is considered one of the best indicators of the cost of short-term borrowing. The Eurodollar futures contract has achieved great success, quickly surpassing in volume the Treasury bill futures contract, the first short-term interest rate futures contract. The Eurodollar contract's success is at least partly due to its cash settlement feature.

In addition to Eurodollar deposits are other, similar deposits such as Euroyen, Euromarks, and Europounds. These are deposits in one foreign country denominated in the currency of another such as yen, marks, and pounds. There are no futures contracts on U.S. exchanges on Euroyen, Euromarks, and Europounds. In 1989, however, the International Monetary Market experimented with futures contracts on the difference between the Eurodollar rate and the rates on these other deposits. These contracts, called *diffs*, were highly publicized and appeared to offer many hedging, arbitrage, and speculative opportunities. However, they did not trade sufficiently to remain listed.

TABLE 7.4

Registered Futures Contracts on U.S. Futures Exchanges Covered in *The Wall Street Journal* (as of February 15, 1991)

Contract	Exchange	Contract Size	
Grains and Oilseeds			
Corn	CBOT	5,000	bu.
Corn	MCE	1,000	bu.
Oats	CBOT	5,000	bu.
Soybeans	CBOT	5,000	bu.
Soybeans	MCE	1,000	bu.
Soybean meal	CBOT	100	tons
Soybean meal	MCE	20	tons
Soybean oil	CBOT	60,000	lbs.
Wheat	CBOT	5,000	bu.
Wheat	KCBT	5,000	bu.
Wheat	MCE	1,000	bu.
Wheat	MGE	5,000	bu.
Livestock and Meat			
Feeder cattle	CME	44,000	lbs.
Hogs	CME	30,000	lbs.
Hogs	MCE	15,000	lbs.
Live cattle	CME	40,000	lbs.
Live cattle	MCE	20,000	lbs.
Pork bellies	CME	40,000	lbs.
Food and Fiber			
Cocoa	CSCE	10	metric tons
Coffee	CSCE	37,500	lbs.
Cotton	NYCTN	50,000	lbs.
Domestic sugar	CSCE	112,000	lbs.
Orange juice	NYCTN	15,000	lbs.
Rough rice	CRCE	200,000	lbs.
World sugar	CSCE	112,000	lbs.
Metals and Petroleum			
Copper	COMEX	25,000	lbs.
Crude oil	NYMEX	1,000	bbls.
Gold—1 kilo	CBOT	32.15	troy ozs.
Gold	COMEX	100	troy ozs.
Heating oil—no. 2	NYMEX	42,000	gals.
Natural gas	NYMEX	10	ct. per million BTU
Palladium	NYMEX	100	troy ozs.
Platinum	NYMEX	50	troy ozs.
Propane	NYMEX	42,000	gals.
Silver	CBOT	1,000	troy ozs.
Silver	COMEX	5,000	troy ozs.
Silver	MCE	1,000	troy ozs.
Unleaded gasoline	NYMEX	42,000	gals.
Wood			
Lumber	CME	150,000	board ft.

Contract	Exchange	Contract Size	
Foreign Currency/Eurodollar			
Australian dollar	IMM	100,000	$A
British pound	IMM	62,500	£
British pound	MCE	12,500	£
Canadian dollar	IMM	100,000	CD
Deutsche mark	IMM	125,000	DM
Deutsche mark	MCE	62,500	DM
Eurodollar—90-day	IMM	1,000,000	$
Eurodollar—30-day	IMM	3,000,000	$
Japanese yen	IMM	12,500,000	JY
Japanese yen	MCE	6,250,000	JY
Swiss franc	IMM	125,000	SFr
Swiss franc	MCE	62,500	SFr
U.S. Dollar Index	FINEX	$500	× Index
Economic Indices			
Commodity Research Bureau	NYFE	$250	× Index
Stock Indices			
Nikkei 225 Index	IOM	$5	× Index
Major Market Index	CBOT	$250	× Index
Mini Value Line Index	KCBT	$100	× Index
New York Stock Exchange Index	NYFE	$500	× Index
S&P 500 Index	IOM	$500	× Index
Value Line Index	KCBT	$500	× Index
Interest Rates			
Mortgage-backed securities	CBOT	$100,000	
Municipal Bond Index	CBOT	$1,000	× Index
30-day interest rates	CBOT	$5,000,000	
Treasury bills	IMM	$1,000,000	
Treasury bonds	CBOT	$100,000	
Treasury bonds	MCE	$50,000	
Treasury notes (6 1/2–10 yr.)	CBOT	$100,000	
Treasury notes (5 yr.)	FINEX	$100,000	
Treasury notes (5 yr.)	CBOT	$100,000	
Treasury notes (2 yr.)	CBOT	$200,000	

Exchange symbols:
Chicago Board of Trade (CBOT)
Chicago Mercantile Exchange (CME)
Chicago Rice and Cotton Exchange (CRCE)
Commodity Exchange (COMEX)
Financial Instruments Exchange (FINEX)
Index and Option Market (IOM)
International Monetary Market (IMM)
Kansas City Board of Trade (KCBT)
MidAmerica Commodity Exchange (MCE)
Minneapolis Grain Exchange (MGE)
New York Cotton Exchange (NYCTN)
New York Futures Exchange (NYFE)
New York Mercantile Exchange (NYMEX)

The European Currency Unit (ECU), a composite measure of several European foreign currencies, and the U.S. Dollar Index, a similar measure of the dollar's composite value against foreign currencies, also have had futures contracts in this category. The ECU contract has not been actively traded, but the Dollar Index contract has been successful in generating trading volume.

Domestic and international economics and politics are the primary factors determining these futures prices. Chapter 13 looks more closely at foreign currency futures.

Economic Indices

The first economic index futures contract, the Consumer Price Index futures, was launched with much fanfare in June 1985. Although promoted as a means of hedging the uncertainty of inflation, the contract never generated much trading volume. Exchange officials attributed this to the relatively low and stable inflation rate since the contract's initiation, although the lack of a clearly defined spot market and the unavailability of continuous information on the true spot price probably were more serious impediments.

This category also includes the Commodity Research Bureau Index, an index of the prices over the last nine months of 21 commodity futures contracts. This contract, which trades on the New York Futures Exchange, is a futures contract on an index of futures contracts. So far, it has drawn little trading volume.

Stock Indices

Stock index futures have been one of the spectacular success stories of the financial markets in recent years. These cash-settled contracts are indices of combinations of stocks. Investors use them to hedge positions in stock, speculate on the direction of the stock market in general, and arbitrage the contracts against comparable combinations of stocks. Stock index futures have not been without controversy, however; we shall say more about this in Chapter 14.

In the spring of 1989, the Philadelphia Stock Exchange, American Stock Exchange, and Chicago Board Options Exchange each began trading a new type of stock index instrument. These devices, called *index participations*, were essentially spot positions in a stock index. In other words, the buyer of an index participation would receive a spot position in the value of the index but not actually gain possession of the stocks. The dividends were paid and in most respects, the instrument was a spot market security. However, the futures exchanges argued that it was a futures contract with an immediate maturity and, thus, could only be traded on a futures exchange. Soon thereafter the futures industry obtained an injunction against further trading of index participations. However, it is unlikely we have heard the last of these instruments.

Interest Rates

Interest rate futures have been a remarkable success. Their popularity is due to the increased volatility of interest rates over the last ten years. Their volume has also increased because individuals and firms that formerly traded only in the spot bond market have begun trading futures contracts as well.

The most successful of all futures contracts, the Chicago Board of Trade's Treasury bond contract, continues to grow in volume; however, some of the contracts introduced in earlier years have declined in popularity. The Treasury bill contract has been surpassed by the Eurodollar contract for the lead in the short-term interest rate futures race. The GNMA contract has had a strange history. Launched in 1975, it was the first interest rate futures contract. Hailed as a means of hedging mortgage interest rate risk, it grew in popularity but in recent years has diminished and now is inactive. There have been several other GNMA-related contracts, all designed to attract trading volume, but each has died quietly. Efforts to offer futures contracts on corporate bond indices and short-term interest rate indices have also been largely unsuccessful.

A recent successful contract has been the Chicago Board of Trade's Municipal Bond Index futures contract. Based on an index of municipal bond prices, it is used for speculating on the large municipal bond market and allows holders of municipal bonds to hedge their portfolios.

Table 7.5 lists the most active futures contracts. As can be seen, financial futures contracts are among the most popular. Appendix 7A provides a detailed list of contract specifications for the actively traded financial futures contracts.

Futures Funds

A *futures fund* is a type of mutual fund that pools investors' money and trades futures contracts. Most futures funds invest only about 20 percent of their funds in futures contracts. The remaining funds are kept as cash reserves and in interest-bearing money market instruments. Futures funds usually offer the public a means of participating in the futures markets without the risk of margin calls that they would face by trading futures contracts directly. The fund meets all margin calls with its excess cash. Most funds also guarantee participants that they cannot lose more than they have invested.

The performance of futures funds has been a subject of much interest. Each month *Futures* magazine provides a report on each fund's returns over the last month. Irwin and Brorsen (1985) and Elton, Gruber, and Rentzler (1987, 1990) examined the performance of futures funds and concluded that it has been far from spectacular. Their returns exhibit extremely high variability, and losses are common for a very large number of them. Much of the poor performance can be attributed to the expenses. The funds show little consistency from year to year. With all of these negative results, it seems questionable why anyone would bother to buy commodity funds. They had been found to have a low correlation with stocks and bonds and thus could provide diversification benefits, but even that has

TABLE 7.5
Most Active Futures Contracts, 1990

Contract (Exchange)	Volume (Number of Contracts)
All Futures:	
Treasury bonds (CBOT)	75,499,257
Eurodollars (IMM)	34,695,625
Crude Oil (NYMEX)	23,686,897
S&P 500 (IOM)	12,139,209
Corn (CBOT)	11,423,027
Soybeans (CBOT)	10,301,905
Gold (COMEX)	9,730,041
Deutsche mark (IMM)	9,169,230
Japanese Yen (IMM)	7,437,235
Swiss Franc (IMM)	6,524,893
Financials (Excluding Currencies)	
Treasury Bonds (CBOT)	75,499,257
Eurodollars (IMM)	34,695,625
S&P 500 (IOM)	12,139,209
Treasury Notes, 6 1/2–10 years (CBOT)	6,054,222
Treasury Notes, 5 years (CBOT)	2,532,828

Source: Consensus, *January 18, 1991*

been challenged in the more recent Elton, Gruber, and Rentzler study. Moreover, there are many ways to achieve diversification, and futures funds seem a very costly way to do it.

Indices of Futures Market Activity

In Chapter 2, we noted that indices of options market activity are relatively rare and difficult to construct. This is also true of futures market indices. There are so many diverse futures contracts with different expirations and quotations in different units that futures indices never have attracted much attention. Two indices, however, are reported regularly.

The Dow Jones Index of Futures Prices was introduced in 1982. Separate spot and futures price indices include 12 equally weighted commodities from the agricultural, metal, animal, and wood futures markets. Two contract months, a near-term and a far-term, are used. No financial futures are included. The index has a base date of December 31, 1974, and is reported daily on the commodities page of *The Wall Street Journal*.

We noted earlier that the Commodity Research Bureau Index has a futures contract trading on it at the New York Futures Exchange. The CRB index is also reported on the commodities page of *The Wall Street Journal*.

Barron's also publishes meat, metals, and grain indices prepared by a private firm. Nonetheless, there is no index of financial futures prices. As a substitute, one can simply follow the prices of the nearby Treasury bond and Eurodollar contracts. These fairly accurately reflect the behavior of long- and short-term interest rate futures prices. However, futures prices move so closely in tandem with spot prices that futures indices may be unnecessary because the spot market is so well covered with indices.

TRANSACTION COSTS IN FUTURES TRADING

In Chapter 2, we discussed the different types of option trading costs that the public and professional traders incur. In this section, we shall do the same for futures. However, there is less material available on the trading costs in futures markets. One reason is that futures markets have very low trading costs—indeed, that is one of their major advantages. In addition, the costs of trading futures contracts are less documented than the cost of trading options and stocks.

Commissions

Commissions paid by the public to brokers are assessed on the basis of a dollar charge per contract. The commission is paid at the order's initiation and includes both the opening and closing commissions; that is, a round-trip commission is charged regardless of whether the trader ultimately closes out the contract, makes or takes delivery, or makes a cash settlement. There is no typical commission rate. Investors can negotiate with brokers for whatever deals they can get. Many brokerage firms advertise specials for new customers, offering rates as low as $10 per contract. Some even do a few contracts free. Active traders can trade at the CBOT for about $12.

All traders, whether on or off the exchange floor, incur a minimum charge that is paid to the clearing firm and includes the exchange fee. For floor traders, this charge is $.25 to $.50 per contract. As in options trading, this fee is negotiable between trader and clearing firm. For public traders who pay commissions, this figure usually is included in the commission.[10]

Bid-Ask Spread

A second type of trading cost is the bid-ask spread. Chapter 2 explained the concept of the spread for options. Unlike for options and stock markets, however, there is no real market maker. Many floor traders, particularly spreaders and scalpers, quote prices at which they are willing to simultaneously buy at the bid

[10]These figures and the $12 CBOT rate are taken from Lane (1989), which contains an excellent comparison of the costs of trading on an open-outcry system with the costs of automated systems like GLOBEX and AURORA.

price and sell at the ask price. The bid-ask spread is the cost to the public of liquidity—the ability to buy and sell quickly without a large price concession. Because the spread is not captured and reported electronically, there is little statistical evidence on its size. Traders claim that the spread usually is the value of a minimum price fluctuation, called a *tick*, but occasionally equals two ticks.

Delivery Costs

A futures trader who holds a position to delivery faces the potential for incurring a substantial delivery cost. In the case of most financial instruments, this cost is rather small. For commodities, however, it is necessary to arrange for the commodity's physical transportation, delivery, and storage. While the proverbial story of the careless futures trader who woke up to find thousands of pounds of pork bellies dumped on the front lawn certainly is an exaggeration, anyone holding a long position in the delivery month must be aware of the delivery possibility. This no doubt explains part of the popularity of cash settlement contracts.

THE REGULATION OF FUTURES MARKETS

Futures contracts have always been somewhat controversial. Many regulators and legislators have taken a dim view of futures trading, likening it to gambling. In the nineteenth century, there were numerous attempts to outlaw futures trading. As a result, there probably is no industry more regulated than the futures industry. Most of the early regulation was at the state and local level.

Early Federal Regulation

The first attempt at federal regulation was the 1914 Cotton Futures Act, which was a relatively weak law. It was followed in 1922 by the Grain Futures Act, but that too was weak and prohibited only "excessive speculation," which was difficult to define. In 1936 the Commodity Exchange Act created the Commodity Exchange Authority (CEA), a division of the Department of Agriculture. The first federal futures regulatory agency, the CEA was authorized to regulate specific futures contracts. As new contracts were added, various amendments expanded the CEA's coverage. With the introduction of currency futures and the anticipated birth of financial futures, Congress decided that a major new law was needed. It passed the Commodity Futures Trading Commission Act of 1974, which created the Commodity Futures Trading Commission (CFTC).

The Commodity Futures Trading Commission

The Commodity Futures Trading Commission (CFTC) is a federal agency that regulates futures markets. The CFTC is responsible for licensing futures exchanges and contracts. It approves all terms and conditions of each proposed contract as well as modifications of the terms of existing contracts. To be approved by the CFTC, a contract must have an economic purpose and not be contrary to the "public interest." An "economic purpose" generally is construed to mean that it can be used for hedging.

The CFTC is responsible for ensuring that the exchanges make price information available to the public. It also establishes requirements for *reportable positions*, stipulating that futures traders report their outstanding positions if they exceed certain levels, which vary from contract to contract.

The commission is responsible for the authorization or licensing of individuals offering their services to the public. This includes floor brokers, FCMs, APs, CTAs, and CPOs as discussed earlier. These individuals must meet minimum capital requirements, and their backgrounds must be investigated.

The CFTC has the authority to require exchanges to establish and enforce disciplinary actions against members found to be in violation of the exchange's rules. The CFTC can also seek court injunctions and impose certain disciplinary actions itself.

The CFTC is also authorized to establish a system of addressing complaints brought by the public against brokers, traders, and other licensed futures professionals. As we shall see shortly, much of this authority has been turned over to the National Futures Association.

One of the CFTC's primary responsibilities is market surveillance. Federal law makes it a felony to attempt to manipulate the futures market. The CFTC monitors trading for indications of possible manipulation.

As part of the requirements of the 1974 law, the CFTC was formally reviewed and reauthorized in 1978 and again in 1982, when several changes were instituted into law. The CFTC's registration requirements for individuals were expanded, and authority was granted for a test program in agricultural options, which until that time had been banned. The 1982 amendment also confirmed the Johnson-Shad agreement, discussed in Chapter 2, which helped establish the lines of regulatory authority over options and options on futures.

In 1986 Congress passed the Futures Trading Act, which reauthorized the CFTC for three more years. The act extended the agency's powers to include regulation of any futures transaction, whether conducted on or off an exchange. As of spring 1991, the CFTC's latest reauthorization bill was still being debated by Congress.

Over the years, the states have been restricted from regulating futures trading. That too changed in 1982, when the states were given some limited regulatory authority. Also, individuals were allowed to pursue private lawsuits against brokers and firms involved in futures trading. However, the most significant recent regulatory development was the authorization of the National Futures Association.

The National Futures Association

The National Futures Association (NFA) is an organization of individuals and firms that participate in the futures industry. The NFA is an industry self-regulatory agency. The 1974 law had encouraged the development of such an organization, and in 1982 the NFA was formally chartered.

All FCMs, CPOs, IBs, APs, and CTAs are required to join the NFA, and no NFA member may accept a transaction from anyone other than an NFA member. Floor traders, floor brokers, and exchanges are not required to join; they are regulated solely by the CFTC.

The NFA's objective is to prevent fraud and manipulation, protect the public interest, and encourage free markets. The NFA requires registration of its members, who must meet strict requirements and pass an examination. Like the CFTC, the NFA is authorized to monitor trading and identify rule violations as well as impose disciplinary action. Thus, it relieves the CFTC of some of this responsibility and turns the regulatory authority over to the market participants themselves.

The NFA has established a system of arbitrating disputes between individuals and registered futures markets participants. The system is designed so that individuals can obtain faster and more efficient settlements of claims than would be possible with the CFTC or through the legal system.

SUMMARY

This chapter provided the descriptive material necessary for understanding how the futures markets operate. We learned what a futures contract is, which contracts trade in U.S. markets, the characteristics of the markets and traders, the role of the exchange, and the mechanics of trading. We also examined the nature of transaction costs and the structure of regulation.

The next four chapters deal with specific aspects of futures trading. Chapters 8 and 9 explain the concepts of pricing spot transactions and the related futures contracts. Chapter 10 examines futures hedging strategies and provides illustrations of hedge transactions. Chapter 11 looks at more futures strategies, including arbitrage, speculation, and spread transactions.

Questions and Problems

1. Explain the difference between a forward contract and an option.

2. What factors distinguish a forward contract from a futures contract? What do forward and futures contracts have in common? How do leverage contracts differ from futures contracts?

3. Identify the most actively traded contract from each of the following groups of futures contracts: (a) financial futures, (b) foreign currency futures, and (c) agricultural futures.

4. The open interest in a futures contract changes from day to day. Suppose investors holding long positions are divided into two groups: A is an individual investor and OL represents other investors. Investors holding short positions are denoted as S. Currently A holds 1,000 contracts and OL holds 4,200; thus, S is short 5,200 contracts. Determine the holdings of A, OL, and S after each of the following transactions.

   a. A sells 500 contracts, OL buys 500 contracts.

   b. A buys 700 contracts, OL sells 700 contracts.

   c. A buys 200 contracts, S sells 200 contracts.

   d. A sells 800 contracts, S buys 800 contracts.

   What can you conclude determines whether volume increases or decreases open interest?

5. List and briefly explain the important contributions provided by futures exchanges.

6. How do locals differ from commission brokers? How do the latter differ from futures commission merchants?

7. Explain the basic differences between open outcry and electronic trading systems.

8. One of the more controversial floor trading practices is dual trading. Explain what dual trading is, and give an example of how a dual trader could profit at the expense of a customer. (Hint: Consider the types of orders public customers can place. These are briefly mentioned in this chapter and discussed in more detail in Chapter 2.) What benefit is associated with dual trading?

9. What factors would determine whether a particular strategy is a hedge or a speculative strategy?

10. How are spread and arbitrage strategies forms of speculation? How can they be interpreted as hedges?

11. What are the differences among scalpers, day traders, and position traders?

12. What are the various ways in which an individual may obtain the right to go on to the floor of an exchange and trade futures?

13. What are daily price limits, and why are they used?

14. What are circuit breakers? What are their advantages and disadvantages?

15. Explain how the clearinghouse operates to protect the futures market.

16. Explain the differences among the three means of terminating a futures contract: an offsetting trade, cash settlement, and delivery.

17. Suppose you buy a stock index futures contract at the opening price of 252.25 on July 1. The multiplier on the contract is 500, so the price is $500(252.25) = $126,125. You hold the position open until selling it on July 16 at the opening price of 235.50. The initial margin requirement is $6,000, and the maintenance margin requirement is $2,500. Assume you deposit the initial margin and do not withdraw the excess on any given day. Construct a table

showing the charges and credits to the margin account. The daily prices on the intervening days are as follows:

Day	Settlement Price
7/1	253.95
7/2	254.50
7/3	252.00
7/7	243.55
7/8	241.65
7/9	242.85
7/10	244.15
7/11	242.25
7/14	238.30
7/15	235.05
7/16	235.50

18. Why are futures indices difficult to construct? What are some of the available futures indices?

19. Explain in general terms the responsibility of the CFTC.

20. What role does the National Futures Association play in regulating the futures industry?

21. What are some advantages and disadvantages to the United States of the increasing use of futures by foreign investors?

References

Chicago Board of Trade. *Rules and Regulations*. Chicago: Board of Trade of the City of Chicago, 1986.

Chicago Board of Trade. *Commodity Trading Manual*. Chicago: Board of Trade of the City of Chicago, 1989.

Chicago Mercantile Exchange. *The Regulatory Environment*. Chicago: Chicago Mercantile Exchange, 1982.

Commodity Futures Trading Commission. *Annual Report*, 1989.

Duffie, Darrell. *Futures Markets*, Chapters 1, 2, 3. Englewood Cliffs, N.J.: Prentice-Hall, 1989.

Elton, Edwin J., Martin J. Gruber, and Joel C. Rentzler. "Professionally Managed Publicly Traded Commodity Funds." *Journal of Business* 60 (1987): 175–200.

Elton, Edwin J., Martin J. Gruber, and Joel C. Rentzler. "The Performance of Publicly Offered Commodity Funds." *Financial Analysts Journal* 46 (July–August 1990): 23–30.

Hieronymous, Thomas A. *The Economics of Futures Trading*. New York: Commodity Research Bureau, 1977.

Hore, John. *Trading on Canadian Futures Markets*, 2d ed., Chapters 1–5. Toronto: Canadian Securities Institute, 1984.

Hull, John. *Options, Futures, and Other Derivation Securities*, Chapter 1. Englewood Cliffs, N.J.: Prentice-Hall, 1989.

Irwin, Scott H., and B. Wade Brorsen. "Public Futures Funds." *The Journal of Futures Markets* 5 (1985): 463–485.

Kaufman, Perry J. *Handbook of Futures Markets*, Chapters 1–6, 10. New York: Wiley, 1984.

Kramer, Andrea S. *Taxation of Securities, Commodities, and Options*. New York: Wiley, 1987.

Lane, Morton. "TIFFE, APT, DTB, GLOBEX, AURORA, . . . and All That." Discount Corporation of New York Futures, unpublished newsletter, November 20, 1989.

Leuthold, Raymond M., Joan C. Junkus, and Jean E. Cordier. *The Theory and Practice of Futures Markets*, Chapters 1, 2. Englewood Cliffs, N.J.: Prentice-Hall, 1989.

Loosigian, Allan M. *Interest Rate Futures*, Chapters 1–4. Homewood, Ill.: Dow Jones–Irwin, 1980.

National Futures Association. *An Introduction to the National Futures Association*. Chicago: National Futures Association, n.d.

Powers, Mark J. *Inside the Financial Futures Market*, 2d ed., Chapters 1–4. New York: Wiley, 1984.

Rothstein, Nancy H., ed. *The Handbook of Financial Futures*, Chapters 1–4, 19–20, 22. New York: McGraw-Hill, 1984.

Schwarz, Edward W. *How to Use Interest Rate Futures Contracts*, Chapters 1–3. Homewood, Ill.: Dow Jones–Irwin, 1979.

Schwarz, Edward W., Joanne M. Hill, and Thomas Schneeweis. *Financial Futures: Fundamentals, Strategies, and Applications*, Chapters 1–2. Homewood, Ill.: Irwin, 1986.

Siegel, Daniel R., and Diane F. Siegel. *Futures Markets*, Chapter 1. Hinsdale, Ill.: Dryden Press, 1990.

Silber, William L. "Marketmaker Behavior in an Auction Market: An Analysis of Scalpers in Futures Markets." *The Journal of Finance* 39 (September 1984): 937–953.

Teweles, Richard, and Frank J. Jones. *The Futures Game: Who Wins? Who Loses? Why?*, 2d ed., Chapters 1–3, 17. New York: McGraw-Hill, 1987.

Selected Financial Futures Contract Specifications[1]

Contract	Exchange	Trading[a] Hours	Delivery Months	Contract Size	Minimum Price Change	Daily Price Limits	Last Trading Day	First Delivery Day	Margin[b]
U.S. Treasury bonds	CBOT	7:20–2:00 (M–F) 5:00–8:30 (S–Th)	M, J, S, D	$100,000	1/32 = $31.25	96/32 = $3,000	Business day prior to last seven days	First business day of month	$2,700 (I), $2,000 (M)
U.S. Treasury notes (6 1/2–10 yr.)	CBOT	7:20–2:00 (M–F) 5:00–8:30 (S–Th)	M, J, S, D	$100,000	1/32 = $31.25	96/32 = $3,000	Business day prior to last seven days	First business day of month	$1,350 (I), $1,000 (M)
U.S. Treasury notes (5 yr.)	CBOT	7:20–2:00	M, J, S, D	$100,000	1/64 = $15.625	192/64 = $3,000	Business day prior to last seven days	First business day of month	$1,350 (I), $1,000 (M)
Eurodollars	IMM	7:20–2:00	M, J, S, D	$1,000,000	.01 = $25	None	Second London business day prior to third Wednesday of month	Cash settled on last trading day	$810 (I), $600 (M)
U.S. Treasury bills	IMM	7:20–2:00	M, J, S, D	$1,000,000	.01 = $25	None	Varies according to maturity date of 365 day bill	Business day after last trading day	$810 (I), $600 (M)
S&P 500 Index	IOM	8:30–3:15	M, J, S, D	$500 x Index	.05 = $25	Varies (contact exchange)	Thursday before third Friday of month	Cash settled on Friday opening after last trading day	$22,000 (I), $10,000 (M)
Major Market Index	CBOT	8:15–3:15	March cycle plus next 3 consecutive months	$250 x Index	.05 = $12.50	None	Third Friday of month	Cash settled on last trading day	$21,000 (I), $6,700 (M)
NYSE Index	NYFE	9:30–4:15	M, J, S, D	$500 x Index	.05 = $25	Varies (contact exchange)	Third Friday of month	Cash settled on Friday opening after last trading day	$10,00 (I), $7,000 (M)
Municipal Bond Index	CBOT	7:20–2:00	M, J, S, D	$1,000 x Index	1/32 = $31.25	96/32 = $3,000	Business day prior to last seven business days	Cash settled on last trading day	$1,350 (I), $1,000 (M)

[a]All times are local. All trading days are Monday through Friday unless otherwise indicated. Evening trading hours for CBOT are 6:30–9:30 during DST.
[b]Margins shown are initial (I) and maintenance (M). These are for speculators. Hedge and spread margins usually are lower.
Source: Futures 1991 Reference Guide (1991), Consensus (any issue), and exchanges.

[1]This material is believed to be current as of January 1991. Contract specifications frequently change, especially margins and daily price limits. Investors should consult the exchanges and their clearinghouses for the latest information. Currency contract specifications are presented in Appendix 13A.

appendix 7B

Taxation of Futures Transactions

Profits from futures contracts, as well as index options, are considered to be 60 percent capital gains and 40 percent ordinary income. This rule has been in effect since 1981. However, from 1988 to 1990 the tax laws required equal taxation of ordinary income and capital gains. This meant that futures profits were subject to a tax rate equal to the investor's ordinary income tax rate. New tax legislation, effective in 1991, provided for a more favorable treatment of capital gains. The maximum ordinary income tax rate was established at 31 percent. Capital gains are taxed at the ordinary income rate, but subject to a maximum of 28 percent. Thus, an investor in the 31 percent tax bracket would have futures profits taxed at a blended rate of $.6(.28) + .4(.31) = .292$.

In addition, all futures and index options profits are subject to a mark to market rule in which accumulated profits are taxable in the current year even if the contract has not been closed out. For example, assume you bought a futures contract on October 15 at a price of $1,000. Your account was, of course, marked to market daily. At the end of the year, the accumulated profit in the account was $400, meaning that the futures price at the end of the year was $1,400. Then you would have to pay the tax that year on $400 even though you had not closed out the contract. In other words, realized and unrealized profits are taxed.

These rules apply only to speculative transactions; hedges are considered to be the protection of ordinary income. All profits from hedges are taxed at the ordinary income rate and are exempt from the year-end mark to market rule. As with most tax rules, there are some exceptions to all of these requirements.

Consider the following example. Suppose an investor in the 31 percent tax bracket purchased a futures contract at $1,000 on October 15 and ultimately sells it at $1,300 on January 20 of the next year. Assume the contract price was $1,400 at the end of the year. The first year the tax liability is on $400, so the tax is $400(.6)(.28) + $400(.4)(.31) = 116.80, an effective rate of 29.2%. In the second year, there is a taxable loss of $1,400 - $1,300 = 100. This can be used to offset taxable gains; thus, it will save the trader $.292($100) = 29.20 in taxes on profitable futures trades in that year. Losses can be used to offset gains, but not more than the total amount of taxable gains. Any losses not used can be carried back to offset prior trading profits for up to three years.

Suppose the contract expired in February and the investor took delivery of the commodity. Then it would be assumed that the commodity was purchased at $1,400, the year-end settlement price. The investor would have paid tax on the $400 profit at the end of the year in which the contract was bought; however, no additional tax would have been due until the commodity was sold.

Although recent tax laws have greatly simplified the taxation of futures con-tracts, many complexities remain. Competent tax advice is necessary to keep up with the many changes and ensure compliance with the various rules.

Questions and Problems

1. On October 1, you purchase one March stock index futures contract at the opening price of 110.30. The contract multiplier is $500, so the price of 110.30 is really $500(110.30) = $55,150. You hold the position open until February 20, whereupon you sell the contract at the opening price of 127.30. The settlement price on December 31 was 122.40. You are in the 31 percent tax bracket. Compute your tax liability.

2. In November you buy a futures contract on a commodity at a price of $10,000. At the end of the year, the futures price is $10,500. You hold your position open until January 20, at which time the contract expires and you take delivery. On March 1 you sell the commodity at $12,200. You are in the 31 percent tax bracket. Compute your tax liability in both years.

3. On September 15, you buy a commodity at $5,000 and sell a futures contract on that commodity at $4,500. On December 31, the spot price is $5,750 and the futures price is $5,600. On February 1, you sell the commodity at $5,875 and buy back the futures contract at $5,690. You are in the 31 percent tax bracket. Compute your taxable gains in both years.

---

appendix 7C

Sources of Information on Futures

Appendix 2C reviewed some sources of information on options. Several of these also provide information on futures. Therefore, some of the information about these publications is omitted here; the reader should refer to the appropriate section of Appendix 2C.

PERIODICALS

The Wall Street Journal

As noted in the chapter, *The Wall Street Journal* provides daily price information on futures markets. It also contains a daily column called "Commodities" that recaps the day's events in the commodity futures markets. The article usually contains a short feature story and is divided into sections, each of which provides information about a particular futures contract or group of contracts. It also provides daily spot prices of commodities. Coverage of financial and currency futures is included in its general coverage of stock, bond, and international markets.

Barron's

Barron's provides coverage of week-ending futures prices as well as spot prices of securities. It contains a weekly article called "Commodities Corner"; however, this article is devoted almost exclusively to agricultural and metallurgical futures. Coverage of interest rate futures usually appears in the options column, "The Striking Price" (see Appendix 2C), and in the bond markets column, "The Current Yield."

Futures

Appendix 2C briefly covered *Futures* magazine. While this periodical provides coverage of options, its emphasis is clearly on futures. *Futures* contains several feature articles on contemporary issues and trading strategies. It also has regular columns featuring individuals in the industry, recent news, key upcoming dates, forthcoming seminars, regulatory issues, software and book reviews, and the outlook for each contract group. *Futures* publishes two special issues: a reference guide to the futures and options industry and an issue devoted to the annual trade show held by the futures industry.

Futures also publishes a sister magazine called *Corporate Risk Management*, which is aimed at financial managers of corporations. It contains numerous articles that deal primarily with hedging from the corporate perspective. It also includes articles on the use of swaps, forwards, and various other over-the-counter hedging instruments. Subscriptions cost $60 per year and can be obtained by writing *Corporate Risk Management*, 219 Parkade, Cedar Falls, IA 50613.

Consensus

Consensus is a weekly newspaper that covers the futures industry. It contains a vast amount of reference material and trade statistics as well as articles and commentaries on the current and expected future behavior of the futures market. *Consensus* usually contains numerous charts showing the recent price history of futures contracts. Subscriptions cost $365 per year and are available by writing to *Consensus*, P.O. Box 411128, Kansas City, Missouri 64141.

ACADEMIC JOURNALS

All of the academic journals covering options that were mentioned in Appendix 2C also publish articles dealing with futures. In addition, there are several specialized journals on futures.

The Journal of Futures Markets is published bimonthly and contains academic studies on futures markets. Each issue contains 10 to 12 full-length articles and sometimes several short comments and notes. In addition, there usually are columns on legal issues and a bibliography of articles on futures. The *Journal* is cosponsored by John Wiley & Sons and the Center for the Study of Futures Markets at Columbia University.

The Review of Futures Markets is published by the Chicago Board of Trade. The CBOT has been actively encouraging and sponsoring academic research on futures markets for many years. As part of its efforts, it regularly sponsors research seminars at which academics, practitioners, and regulators assemble and discuss research papers and issues. The *Review* publishes the complete papers as well as the contents of the discussions. Each issue contains four to six papers, and there are three to four issues per year.

OTHER SOURCES OF INFORMATION

There is a large industry that provides information on futures markets in the form of online computer services and printed matter. The annual reference guide published by *Futures* magazine contains information on these suppliers.

Owing to its stigma of legalized gambling, the futures industry has had to overcome a controversial and sometimes unfavorable public image. Because of this, the industry has devoted considerable resources to publishing information to inform the public about the role of futures markets. Some of their educational efforts are directed at high schools and 4-H clubs. The industry has published many materials, most of which are available free to the public. The exchanges and the CFTC are excellent sources of low-cost, easy-to-read, and informative publications.

PRINCIPLES OF FUTURES PRICING I: SPOT MARKET PRICING

A sound foundation in the principles of pricing the underlying spot instruments is important to understanding how futures contracts are priced. Since this book is devoted primarily to financial futures and options, we need to understand how stocks and bonds are priced. Accordingly, in this chapter we deal with the basic principles of pricing these instruments. In addition, we look at a simple approach to pricing all risky instruments. We will use these models in Chapter 9, when we examine the pricing of futures contracts.

PRICING FIXED-INCOME SECURITIES

Fixed-income securities, commonly known as *bonds*, are priced according to the size and timing of the cash flows promised by the issuer and the interest rates available in the market. The market-determined interest rates are defined by the term structure of interest rates. The *term structure of interest rates*, sometimes called simply the *term structure*, is the relationship among interest rates on bonds of different maturities. To understand the term structure, we must first comprehend the difference between spot and forward rates.

283

The Concept of Spot and Forward Rates

The interest rate on a loan made immediately is called the *spot rate* or, in the parlance of futures markets, the *cash rate*. Sometimes, however, a loan is to be made at a future point in time but the terms and conditions, such as the rate and maturity, are established today. This type of transaction is a forward loan, and the agreement is a forward contract or forward rate commitment, as discussed in Chapter 7. The agreed-upon interest rate is called the *forward rate*.

Let us consider some notation for spot and forward rates. Let r(a,b) be the interest rate on a loan made at time a and paid back at time b. The loan has a maturity of b − a. It is a *pure-discount loan*, meaning that the interest is taken out in advance. If a = 0, r(0,b) is a spot rate; if a > 0, r(a,b) is a forward rate. Note that b must always exceed a.[1]

Suppose that today you take out a $1,000 loan with the promise to pay it back in one year at a rate of 10 percent. Then r(0,1) = .10. The price of the loan, which is the amount of money you receive today, is $1,000(1.10)^{-1} = 909.09$. Now suppose you find you will not need the money until one year from now. The lender quotes you a forward rate of 12 percent. Then r(1,2) = .12. The forward price is $1,000(1.12)^{-1} = 892.86$. This is the amount you will receive in one year. A year after that, or two years from today, you will pay back $1,000.

The Relationship between Spot and Forward Rates

Assume all loans are free of default risk. Then we can examine the relationship between spot and forward rates by observing the term structure. The term structure defines the spot rates for various maturities. Although the forward rates are not explicitly defined by the term structure, they can be inferred.

Consider the following term structure:

$$r(0,1)= .06$$
$$r(0,2)= .08$$
$$r(0,3)= .09$$
$$r(0,4)= .10.$$

These are rates on loans of one to four years. As you can see, the rates increase with maturity. The term structure thus is said to be increasing, or upward sloping.

For a given set of Z spot rates, there are $Z(Z − 1)/2$ forward rates. For example, the rates r(1,2), r(1,3), r(1,4), r(2,3), r(2,4), and r(3,4) are six forward rates that can be derived from these four spot rates; that is, $4(4 − 1)/2 = 6$.[2] Figure 8.1 indicates the spot and forward rates for this term structure. Each rate is positioned

---

[1]After all, a loan cannot be paid off before it is taken out.

[2]Actually, there are an infinite number of forward rates. For example, r(1,2.5), r(2,3.7), and so forth are forward rates. When we say there are $Z(Z − 1)/2$ forward rates, we are considering only integer time intervals.

FIGURE 8.1
The Spot Rate–Forward Rate Structure

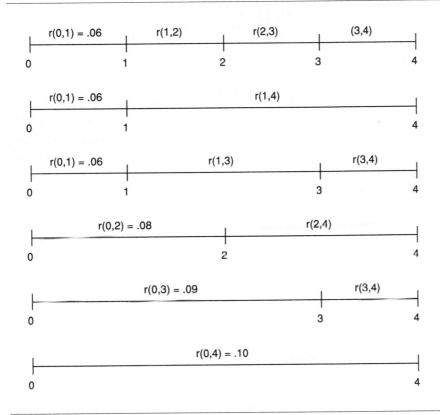

in the time interval to which it applies. We know the value of each spot rate, so we can derive the values of the forward rates.

Assume you need to borrow $1 today for two years, after which you will pay back $[1 + r(0,2)]^2$ dollars. Alternatively, you take out a one-year loan today and simultaneously enter into a forward contract with a lender that will let you borrow one year from now at the rate $r(1,2)$, with that loan to be repaid a year later. In other words, you make a one-year loan, followed by a one-year loan; however, the rate on the second loan is agreed upon today. At the end of the first year, you will owe $[1 + r(0,1)]$. You then take out the second loan. At the end of the second year, you will owe $[1 + r(0,1)][1 + r(1,2)]$. Assuming you and the lender are indifferent between the one two-year loan and the two one-year loans, the amount ultimately paid back under the two arrangements should be equal; that is,

$$[1 + r(0,2)]^2 = [1 + r(0,1)][1 + r(1,2)].$$

Knowing the values r(0,2) and r(0,1), you can solve for r(1,2):

$$r(1,2) = \frac{\left[1+r(0,2)\right]^2}{\left[1+r(0,1)\right]} - 1.$$

In this example,

$$r(1,2) = \frac{(1.08)^2}{1.06} - 1 = .1004.$$

We can derive any forward rate from our knowledge of two overlapping spot rates. Look again at Figure 8.1. We can derive r(1,4) by equating the payoff from a spot four-year loan with the payoff from a spot one-year loan plus a forward loan taken out at the end of year 1 and paid back at the end of year 4:

$$[1 + r(0,4)]^4 = [1 + r(0,1)][1 + r(1,4)]^3.$$

Note that $1 + r(1,4)$ is raised to the third power because it is a three-year loan. The implied forward rate is

$$r(1,4) = \left[\frac{\left[1+r(0,4)\right]^4}{1+r(0,1)}\right]^{1/3} - 1.$$

Because the rate r(1,4) is a three-year rate, the third root of the term in brackets is taken. This converts the three-year rate to an annual rate, which is the conventional method of quoting interest rates. The answer is r(1,4) = .1137. You should now be able to derive all the other forward rates. The answers are r(2,3) = .1103, r(3,4) = .1306, r(2,4) = .1204, and r(1,3) = .1053.

Now suppose the above relationships did not hold. For example, consider the two-year spot rate of .08 and the one-year spot rate of .06. Suppose a lender offered a forward rate, r(1,2), of .098 instead of the implied forward rate of .1004. Borrowers would besiege the lender for one-year spot loans at 6 percent and one-year forward loans at 9.8 percent. These borrowers would then become lenders themselves by using the proceeds of their loans to make two-year spot loans at 8 percent. At the end of two years, they would owe (1.06)(1.098) = 1.1639 for every dollar borrowed but would receive $(1.08)^2 = 1.1664$ for every dollar lent. Because the transaction would be riskless, this type of arbitrage would be attractive and would increase the demand for one-year spot loans and one-year forward loans and the supply of two-year spot loans. This would force a realignment of rates until the forward and spot rates offered no further arbitrage opportunities.

Theories of the Term Structure

If we plotted the relationship between interest rate and maturity for a set of bonds of a given level of risk, we might get any of the three general types of curves shown in Figure 8.2. Actual term structures are difficult to construct and seldom produce the smooth curves shown in the figure. Although some term structures are humped, in general the curves tend to be upward sloping, downward sloping, or approximately flat. Why the term structure takes on the shape it does has been a subject of much conjecture for most of this century. Economists have posited three possible explanations: expectations, liquidity preference, and market segmentation.

THE EXPECTATIONS THEORY   The *expectations theory* assumes there are no transaction costs and either there is no uncertainty or investors are risk neutral, that is, unconcerned about risk. Under these conditions, forward rates will be the market's expectations of future spot rates.

Let the borrower take out a one-year loan. One year later, the borrower takes out another one-year loan. Under the expectations theory, borrowers and lenders would be indifferent between this arrangement and a one-year loan plus a one-year forward loan. This means the implied forward rate represents the investor's expectation of the future spot rate. Thus, in the example in which $r(1,2) = .1004$, both borrower and lender believe that in one year the spot rate on one-year loans will be 10.04 percent. Because of their risk neutrality, they are willing to engage in the transaction without considering that the actual rate one year from now may turn out to be something other than 10.04 percent.

Recall that the formula for $r(1,2)$ is.

$$r(1,2) = \frac{[1 + r(0,2)]^2}{[1 + r(0,1)]} - 1.$$

An upward-sloping term structure would be one in which the two-year rate, $r(0,2)$, was greater than the one-year rate, $r(0,1)$. The above formula implies that if $r(0,2) > r(0,1)$, then $r(1,2) > r(0,1)$. Likewise, $r(0,2) < r(0,1)$ as $r(1,2) < r(0,1)$. In other words, an upward-sloping term structure implies that the one-year forward rate on one-year loans exceeds the spot rate on one-year loans. Since the one-year forward rate on one-year loans is the market's expectation of the future spot rate on one-year loans, the market is forecasting that spot rates on one-year loans will increase. Similarly, a downward-sloping term structure suggests a market forecast of declining spot rates on one-year loans. A flat term structure is a forecast of no change in spot rates.

The expectations theory assumes that forward rates are the market's expectations of futures spot rates and thus implies that the shape of the term structure indicates the expected direction of future interest rates.

THE LIQUIDITY PREFERENCE THEORY   The *liquidity preference theory* states that lenders prefer to maintain liquidity and thus have a preference for short-term loans. To justify long-term loans, lenders must expect a higher return in the form of a liquidity premium. Thus, long-term rates should naturally be above short-

FIGURE 8.2
Term Structures

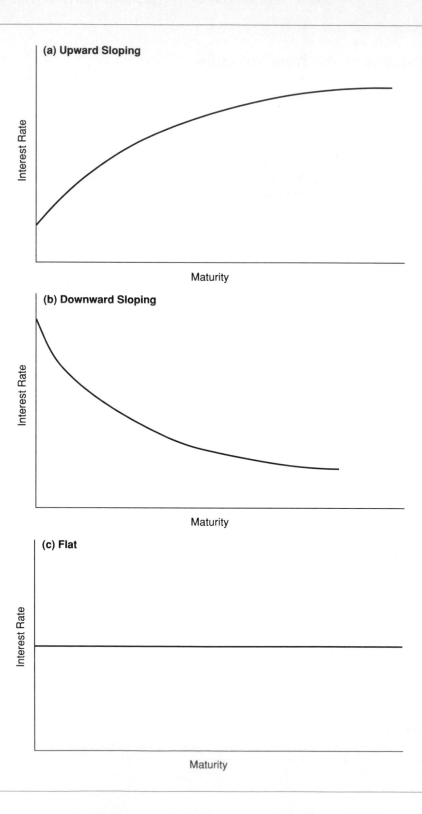

term rates. This would explain an upward-sloping term structure. If this theory is correct, the forward rate will systematically overestimate the expected future spot rate.

For example, assume the expectations theory holds and investors believe there will be no change in interest rates. Let the one-year rate be 6 percent. This means the two-year rate will be 6 percent and the implied forward rate will be 6 percent. Now let us propose that investors suddenly recognize that making two-year loans means giving up some liquidity. Lenders decide they do not particularly want to make two-year loans, so they start charging 7 percent for them. Now the forward rate will be $(1.07)^2/(1.06) - 1 = .0801$. Although the implied forward rate is 8.01 percent, investors still expect one-year rates in one year to be 6 percent. Because it contains the liquidity premium, the forward rate will consistently overestimate the future spot rate. Thus, forward rates are *biased* estimates of future spot rates.

THE MARKET SEGMENTATION THEORY The *market segmentation theory*, sometimes called the *preferred habitat theory*, argues that long- and short-term markets are separate. Long-term borrowers and lenders transact only in long-term markets, while short-term borrowers and lenders deal only in short-term markets. Because of this, the arbitrage transactions necessary for forcing a mathematical relationship between long- and short-term rates are not executed. Instead, supply and demand conditions in the respective markets define the term structure. An upward-sloping term structure is caused by tighter monetary conditions in long-term markets than in short-term markets.

To see the market segmentation theory at work, consider a market in which the expectations theory holds. Now suppose a new, totalitarian government passes a law that defines three distinct types of lenders. One lender can make only one-year loans, one only ten-year loans, and one only nine-year forward loans that will start in one year. As one of the few freedoms left, each lender can charge whatever rate it wants. The first lender offers the one-year loans at 6 percent, the second offers the ten-year loans at 10 percent, and the third offers the nine-year forward loans at 10.25 percent. A simple calculation reveals that a 6 percent one-year rate and a 10 percent ten-year rate produce an implied forward rate of not 10.25 percent but 10.45 percent. Obviously, an arbitrage transaction is possible, but wait—we said there were only three types of lenders and each lender could make only one type of loan. To execute the arbitrage, someone would have to make one of the other types of loans. Depending on the government's law enforcement and judicial policies, this could land the arbitraging lender in jail or worse! Thus, the arbitrage would not be made, and short- and long-term rates would bear no necessary relationship to each other as they would if the expectations (or liquidity preference) theory held.

WHICH THEORY IS CORRECT? It probably is safe to say that each theory has some merit. The expectations theory has been extensively tested, and while forward rates are not especially valid predictors of future spot rates, they are as good as any other predictions. The other two theories are much more difficult to test,

The liquidity preference theory assumes that long-term rates must exceed short-term rates to induce lenders to give up their liquidity and make long-term loans. Thus, it implies that forward rates will be biased expectations of future spot rates.

The market segmentation theory assumes that short-term and long-term markets are completely separate and that supply and demand conditions in the two markets determine their respective rates.

and the evidence has been mixed. While it is difficult to argue with the concept of a liquidity premium, it is also hard to measure it. For our purposes, it probably is safe to assume the expectations theory is correct. It is important to note, however, that the expectations theory need not be correct for us to use the forward rate concept. The expectations theory imbues the forward rate only with the special characteristic of being the market's forecast of the future spot rate. That certainly helps explain the term structure, but we do not require it to apply the concept of a forward rate.

The Pricing of Bonds

Consider an investor holding a portfolio of four pure-discount bonds. One bond matures at the end of one year; the others mature at the end of two, three, and four years, respectively. The first three bonds have face values of $80 and the fourth a face value of $1,080. Let the term structure be defined as in the previous example: $r(0,1) = .06, r(0,2) = .08, r(0,3) = .09$, and $r(0,4) = .10$. The prices of the four bonds are

$$
\begin{aligned}
&\text{Bond 1:} &80(1.06)^{-1} &= &75.47 \\
&\text{Bond 2:} &80(1.08)^{-2} &= &68.59 \\
&\text{Bond 3:} &80(1.09)^{-3} &= &61.77 \\
&\text{Bond 4:} &1,080(1.10)^{-4} &= &737.65.
\end{aligned}
$$

The total value of the investor's portfolio of bonds is $75.47 + $68.59 + $61.77 + $737.65 = $943.48.

Now consider a second investor who holds a four-year, $1,000-face-value bond paying coupons of 8 percent annually.[3] The two investors will receive identical cash flows; thus, their portfolios' values must be the same. This means the four-year bond must be worth $943.48. This value can, of course, be found as the present value of each coupon and the final principal payment, with each cash flow discounted by the respective spot rate given by the term structure:

$$
\begin{aligned}
B &= \sum_{t=1}^{T} CI_t \left[1 + r(0,t)\right]^{-t} + FV \left[1 + r(0,T)\right]^{-T} \\
&= 80(1.06)^{-1} + 80(1.08)^{-2} + 80(1.09)^{-3} + 80(1.10)^{-4} + 1,000(1.10)^{-4} \\
&= 943.48,
\end{aligned}
$$

where

CI_t = coupon interest at time t
FV = principal repayment at time T
T = time to maturity

---

[3]Most bonds pay interest semiannually, but we shall use annual interest at this point. Later, and in the chapters in which we begin working with actual bonds, we shall use semiannual interest.

In the real world, the spot rates given by the term structure are not easy to obtain. Spot rates for pure discount bonds are represented by Treasury bill rates, but these exist only for maturities of up to one year. Longer-term pure-discount bonds, called *zero coupon bonds*, do exist, but they are subject to complex tax rules that affect the interpretation of the rates. Instead, the yield is the concept used to price most bonds.

THE BOND YIELD   The *yield to maturity*, or simply *yield*, is the single discount rate that when applied to the bond's coupons and face value gives a present value equal to the actual market price. The formula for the price is

$$B = \sum_{t=1}^{T} CP_t \left(1 + y\right)^{-t},$$

where y is the yield and CP_t is the cash payment, the coupon or principal, at time t. Assuming the coupons are fixed, we can express them as a series of equivalent values, CI, followed by the principal repayment of FV. Then the formula can be expressed as

$$B = CI\left[\sum_{t=1}^{T} \left(1 + y\right)^{-t}\right] + FV\left(1 + y\right)^{-T}.$$

The term in brackets is the compound factor for an annuity and has a known formula. Using that formula, the price of the bond can be expressed as

$$B = CI\left[\frac{1 - \left(1 + y\right)^{-T}}{y}\right] + FV\left(1 + y\right)^{-T}.$$

Normally we would know the price and would have to solve for the yield. This is a tedious task best left to computers and financial calculators. In this problem, the yield that equates the present value of a four-year, 8 percent coupon bond to a price of $943.48 is approximately 9.77 percent. The reader can verify this answer by plugging .0977 into the above formula for B where CI = 80, FV = 1,000, T = 4, and B = 943.48.

TREASURY BOND PRICE QUOTATIONS   To apply the principles of bond pricing to actual bonds, we must first examine how bond prices are quoted. Consider the set of U.S. Treasury bond and note price quotes taken from *The Wall Street Journal* shown in Figure 8.3.

Note the first bond listed. In the first column is the annual coupon rate of 6 3/4 percent, paid in semiannual installments of $33.75 for a $1,000-par-value bond.[4] The next two columns give the maturity year and month, March 1991. Most government bonds mature on the fifteenth of the month. The interest payment days are the maturity day and the day exactly six months prior (or hence). Some

---

[4]In the language of financial markets, the notes are said to be the 6 3/4s of 91.

FIGURE 8.3

Treasury Bond Quotations in *The Wall Street Journal*, Trading Day of March 22, 1991

TREASURY BONDS, NOTES & BILLS

Friday, March 22, 1991

Representative Over-the-Counter quotations based on transactions of $1 million or more.

Treasury bond, note and bill quotes are as of mid-afternoon. Colons in bid-and-asked quotes represent 32nds; 101:01 means 101 1/32. Net changes in 32nds. n-Treasury note. Treasury bill quotes in hundredths, quoted on terms of a rate of discount. Days to maturity calculated from settlement date. All yields are to maturity and based on the asked quote. For bonds callable prior to maturity, yields are computed to the earliest call date for issues quoted above par and to the maturity date for issues below par. *-When issued.

Source: Federal Reserve Bank of New York.

U.S. Treasury strips as of 3 p.m. Eastern time, also based on transactions of $1 million or more. Colons in bid-and-asked quotes represent 32nds; 101:01 means 101 1/32. Net changes in 32nds. Yields calculated on the bid quotation. cl-stripped coupon interest. bp-Treasury bond, stripped principal. np-Treasury note, stripped principal.

Source: Bear, Stearns & Co. via Street Software Technology Inc.

GOVT. BONDS & NOTES

Rate	Maturity Mo/Yr	Bid	Asked	Chg.	Ask Yld.
6 3/4	Mar 91n	99:31	100:01	− 1	4.33
9 3/4	Mar 91n	100:01	100:03	....	2.79
12 3/8	Apr 91n	100:11	100:13	− 1	4.70
9 1/4	Apr 91n	100:09	100:11	− 1	5.47
8 1/8	May 91n	100:08	100:10	....	5.68
14 1/2	May 91n	101:05	101:09	− 1	4.90
8 3/4	May 91n	100:14	100:16	....	5.80
7 7/8	Jun 91n	100:13	100:15	....	5.97
8 1/4	Jun 91n	100:16	100:18	− 1	5.98
13 3/4	Jul 91n	102:08	102:10	− 2	5.91
7 3/4	Jul 91n	100:15	100:17	− 2	6.13
7 1/2	Aug 91n	100:15	100:17	....	6.06
8 3/4	Aug 91n	100:30	101:00	− 1	6.08
14 7/8	Aug 91n	103:13	103:17	....	5.59
8 1/4	Aug 91n	100:24	100:26	− 1	6.27
8 3/8	Sep 91n	101:01	101:03	− 1	6.18
9 1/8	Sep 91n	101:14	101:16	....	6.12
12 1/4	Oct 91n	103:06	103:08	− 1	6.21
7 5/8	Oct 91n	100:24	100:26	....	6.22
6 1/2	Nov 91n	100:02	100:04	+ 1	6.30
8 1/2	Nov 91n	101:09	101:11	− 1	6.32
14 1/4	Nov 91n	104:29	105:01	....	6.11
7 3/4	Nov 91n	100:27	100:29	....	6.37
7 5/8	Dec 91n	100:28	100:30	....	6.35
8 1/4	Dec 91n	101:11	101:13	....	6.34
11 5/8	Jan 92n	104:01	104:03	− 1	6.35
8 1/8	Jan 92n	101:11	101:13	....	6.40
6 5/8	Feb 92n	100:00	100:02	− 1	6.55
9 1/8	Feb 92n	102:04	102:06	− 1	6.56
14 5/8	Feb 92n	107:15	107:19	....	5.78
8 1/2	Feb 92n	101:22	101:24	....	6.53
7 7/8	Mar 92n	101:08	101:10	+ 1	6.52
8 1/2	Mar 92n	101:27	101:29	+ 1	6.53
11 3/4	Apr 92n	105:04	105:06	+ 1	6.58
8 7/8	Apr 92n	102:09	102:11	....	6.63
6 5/8	May 92n	99:30	100:00	+ 1	6.63
9	May 92n	102:13	102:15	....	6.71
13 3/4	May 92n	107:17	107:19	− 1	6.72
8 1/2	May 92n	101:28	101:30	....	6.77
8 1/4	Jun 92n	101:23	101:25	....	6.76
8 3/8	Jun 92n	101:27	101:29	....	6.78
10 3/8	Jul 92n	104:10	104:12	....	6.82
8	Jul 92n	101:13	101:15	....	6.84
4 1/4	Aug 87-92	96:07	97:07	+32	6.37
7 1/4	Aug 92	100:18	100:22	....	6.72
7 7/8	Aug 92n	101:05	101:07	....	6.94
8 1/4	Aug 92n	101:22	101:24	+ 1	6.91
8 1/8	Aug 92n	101:19	101:21	....	6.89
8 1/8	Sep 92n	101:17	101:19	− 2	7.00
8 3/4	Sep 92n	102:18	102:20	+ 2	6.89
9 3/4	Oct 92n	103:30	104:00	− 1	6.99
7 3/4	Oct 92n	101:00	101:02	....	7.04

Rate	Maturity Mo/Yr	Bid	Asked	Chg.	Ask Yld.
7 1/4	Nov 96n	96:24	96:28	....	7.95
8	Jan 97n	100:02	100:06	+ 1	7.96
8 1/2	Apr 97n	102:10	102:14	+ 1	7.98
8 1/2	May 97n	102:08	102:12	+ 1	8.00
8 1/2	Jul 97n	102:08	102:10	+ 2	8.03
8 5/8	Aug 97n	102:27	102:31	+ 1	8.02
8 3/4	Oct 97n	103:15	103:17	+ 2	8.05
8 7/8	Nov 97n	104:02	104:06	....	8.05
7 7/8	Jan 98n	99:08	99:10	+ 1	8.01
8 1/8	Feb 98n	100:12	100:16	+ 3	8.03
7	May 93-98	94:13	94:21	+ 2	8.00
9	May 98n	104:27	104:31	+ 3	8.07
9 1/4	Aug 98n	106:05	106:09	+ 2	8.10
3 1/2	Nov 98	95:10	96:10	....	4.07
8 7/8	Nov 98n	104:04	104:08	+ 3	8.12
8 7/8	Feb 99n	104:04	104:08	+ 3	8.13
8 1/2	May 94-99	101:27	102:03	....	7.74
9 1/8	May 99n	105:17	105:21	+ 3	8.16
8	Aug 99n	99:02	99:06	+ 5	8.14
7 7/8	Nov 99n	98:06	98:10	+ 5	8.15
7 7/8	Feb 95-00	98:12	98:16	+ 6	8.12
8 1/2	Feb 00n	101:30	102:02	+ 5	8.17
8 7/8	May 00n	104:09	104:13	+ 5	8.18
8 3/8	Aug 95-00	101:02	101:06	+ 1	8.05
8 3/4	Aug 00n	103:17	103:19	+ 5	8.19
8 1/2	Nov 00n	101:31	102:01	+ 4	8.19
7 3/4	Feb 01n	97:14	97:16	+ 5	8.12
11 3/4	Feb 01	123:23	123:31	+ 5	8.17
13 1/8	May 01	133:16	133:24	+ 6	8.17
8	Aug 96-01	99:06	99:14	+ 7	8.08
13 3/8	Aug 01	135:22	135:30	+ 6	8.18
15 3/4	Nov 01	152:18	152:26	+ 9	8.21
14 1/4	Feb 02	142:12	142:20	+ 6	8.25
11 5/8	Nov 02	124:17	124:25	+ 5	8.27
10 3/4	Feb 03	118:03	118:11	+ 6	8.29
10 3/4	May 03	118:05	118:13	+ 6	8.31
11 1/8	Aug 03	121:02	121:10	+ 6	8.33
11 7/8	Nov 03	127:01	127:09	+ 7	8.34
12 3/8	May 04	131:14	131:22	+ 7	8.36
13 3/4	Aug 04	142:24	143:00	+ 8	8.35
11 5/8	Nov 04	125:24	125:28	+ 7	8.40
8 1/4	May 00-05	99:22	99:26	+ 3	8.27
12	May 05	129:07	129:11	+ 6	8.41
10 3/4	Aug 05	119:03	119:07	+ 7	8.42
9 3/8	Feb 06	108:22	108:26	+ 6	8.33
7 5/8	Feb 02-07	94:04	94:08	+ 4	8.28
7 7/8	Nov 02-07	96:05	96:09	+ 5	8.29
8 3/8	Aug 03-08	100:02	100:06	+ 5	8.35
8 3/4	Nov 03-08	102:15	102:19	+ 3	8.41
9 1/8	May 04-09	105:08	105:12	+ 1	8.44
10 3/8	Nov 04-09	114:23	114:27	+ 5	8.51
11 3/4	Feb 05-10	126:02	126:06	+ 6	8.50
10	May 05-10	112:13	112:17	+ 6	8.46

Mat.	Type	Bid	Asked	Chg.	Bid Yld.
Nov 99	ci	48:27	48:31	....	8.47
Nov 99	np	49:18	49:22	+ 1	8.29
Feb 00	ci	47:26	47:30	+ 2	8.47
Feb 00	np	48:18	48:22	+ 1	8.29
May 00	ci	46:27	46:31	+ 2	8.47
May 00	np	47:18	47:22	+ 1	8.30
Aug 00	ci	45:27	45:31	+ 3	8.48
Aug 00	np	46:19	46:23	+ 2	8.30
Nov 00	ci	44:29	45:01	+ 2	8.48
Nov 00	np	45:23	45:27	+ 2	8.29
Feb 01	ci	43:27	43:31	+ 2	8.51
Feb 01	np	44:17	44:21	+ 2	8.35
May 01	ci	42:31	43:03	+ 3	8.51
Aug 01	ci	42:02	42:06	+ 3	8.51
Nov 01	ci	41:07	41:11	+ 3	8.51
Feb 02	ci	40:04	40:08	+ 1	8.56
May 02	ci	39:09	39:13	+ 2	8.57
Aug 02	ci	38:13	38:17	+ 1	8.58
Nov 02	ci	37:21	37:25	+ 1	8.57
Feb 03	ci	36:21	36:25	+ 1	8.62
May 03	ci	35:29	36:01	+ 1	8.62
Aug 03	ci	35:03	35:07	+ 1	8.63
Nov 03	ci	34:12	34:16	+ 1	8.63
Feb 04	ci	33:17	33:21	+ 2	8.66
May 04	ci	32:27	32:31	+ 2	8.66
Aug 04	ci	32:04	32:08	+ 1	8.66
Nov 04	ci	31:15	31:19	+ 1	8.66
Nov 04	bp	31:16	31:20	+ 1	8.65
Feb 05	ci	30:24	30:28	+ 1	8.67
May 05	ci	30:04	30:08	+ 1	8.67
May 05	bp	30:08	30:12	+ 2	8.64
Aug 05	ci	29:15	29:19	+ 1	8.67
Aug 05	bp	29:21	29:24	+ 2	8.63
Nov 05	ci	28:27	28:30	+ 2	8.68
Feb 06	ci	28:07	28:11	+ 1	8.68
Feb 06	bp	28:22	28:26	+ 1	8.56
May 06	ci	27:20	27:24	+ 1	8.68
Aug 06	ci	27:01	27:05	+ 1	8.68
Nov 06	ci	26:15	26:19	+ 1	8.68
Feb 07	ci	25:29	26:01	+ 1	8.68
May 07	ci	25:12	25:16	+ 1	8.68
Aug 07	ci	24:27	24:31	+ 1	8.68
Nov 07	ci	24:10	24:14	+ 1	8.68
Feb 08	ci	23:26	23:29	+ 2	8.68
May 08	ci	23:10	23:14	+ 1	8.68
Aug 08	ci	22:26	22:30	+ 1	8.68
Nov 08	ci	22:11	22:15	....	8.68
Feb 09	ci	21:28	21:31	+ 3	8.68
May 09	ci	21:13	21:17	+ 2	8.68
Aug 09	ci	20:31	21:02	+ 3	8.68
Nov 09	ci	20:17	20:20	+ 3	8.68
Nov 09	bp	20:02	20:05	+ 2	8.81
Feb 10	ci	20:03	20:06	+ 3	8.68
May 10	ci	19:21	19:25	+ 2	8.68
Aug 10	ci	19:08	19:11	+ 2	8.68
Nov 10	ci	18:27	18:31	+ 2	8.68
Feb 11	ci	18:15	18:19	+ 2	8.67
May 11	ci	18:03	18:07	+ 2	8.67
Aug 11	ci	17:23	17:26	+ 2	8.67
Nov 11	ci	17:11	17:14	+ 2	8.67
Feb 12	ci	17:00	17:04	+ 3	8.66
May 12	ci	16:21	16:24	+ 3	8.66
Aug 12	ci	16:10	16:13	+ 3	8.66
Nov 12	ci	15:31	16:02	+ 3	8.66
Feb 13	ci	15:21	15:24	+ 3	8.65
May 13	ci	15:11	15:14	+ 2	8.65
Aug 13	ci	15:00	15:04	+ 2	8.65
Nov 13	ci	14:23	14:26	+ 3	8.65
Feb 14	ci	14:15	14:18	+ 2	8.63
May 14	ci	14:05	14:08	+ 2	8.63

Source: The Wall Street Journal, *March 25, 1991.*

bonds, including this one, have an *n* beside the year, which indicates a Treasury note.[5] Some bonds have two maturity dates indicating that the bond is callable beginning on the first date and matures on the second. The next two columns give the bid and ask price in units of par value of 100 and thirty-seconds. Here the bid price is 99 31/32 and the ask price is 100 1/32. The next column is the bid change in thirty-seconds. The final column is the yield.

In the first column is a Treasury note with a coupon rate of 12 1/4 percent and maturing in October 1991. Its actual dollar coupons are $(.1225/2)(1,000) = 61.25$, payable on October 15 and April 15. Its ask price is 103 8/32, or $1,032.50, for a $1,000-par-value bond. The actual price paid is the quoted ask price plus the accrued interest.

ACCRUED INTEREST   In real-world applications, the pricing of fixed-income securities is complicated slightly by the fact that we may wish to measure the price at a time that falls between coupon payment dates. In that case, we must determine how much interest has accumulated since the last coupon payment date. This figure is called the *accrued interest*.

The reason behind the accrued-interest calculation is that the bond buyer will receive the entire next coupon payment despite having held the bond for only a fraction of the period since the last payment date. Even though interest does not accrue linearly, it is assumed that it does. We will describe the procedure for the 12 1/4 percent Treasury notes of October 1991 with information as of March 22.

First we count the number of days between the last coupon payment and the next; that is, 16 in October, 30 in November, 31 in December, 31 in January, 28 in February, 31 in March, and 15 in April, for a total of 182 days. Then we count the number of days since the last coupon payment date, which comes to $16 + 30 + 31 + 31 + 28 + 22 = 158$. Then we prorate the next interest payment, which gives us $61.25(158/182) = 53.173$. Finally, we add this figure to the ask price for a total of $1,032.50 + 53.173 = 1,085.673$. This is the price that one would have paid to buy the bond.

In this case, the person who sold the bond held it for 158 days since the last coupon payment date and thus is entitled to a fraction of the next interest payment.[6] Now suppose the bond buyer goes on to sell the bond before the next coupon payment date. Then the buyer becomes the seller and is entitled to receive accrued interest from the new buyer.

The final column in Figure 8.3 is a portion of a listing of a group of bonds called *stripped treasuries*. These are actually zero coupon Treasury bonds. This is a fairly recent phenomenon, in which firms that have bought coupon Treasury securities sell claims on the underlying coupons and principal. The notation *np* or *bp*

---

[5]Treasury notes have initial maturities of from two to ten years; Treasury bonds have initial maturities of ten years or more.

[6]Actually, the person who sold the bond did not necessarily hold it for the full 158 days since the last coupon payment. However, that person did pay the accrued interest up to the point of the bond's purchase.

means that it is either Treasury note or bond principal; ci indicates that the bond is a claim on coupon interest. Recall that earlier we saw how a coupon bond can be shown to consist of an equivalent combination of zero coupon bonds. Firms that strip these Treasury bonds apply that result to create these long-term zero coupon bonds.

The Relationship between Bond Prices and Yields

There are several important mathematical relationships between bond prices and yields. The discussion in this book is limited to those that are useful for understanding futures markets. The other important bond pricing principles are presented in most investments texts, some of which are listed in the references.

First, let us introduce the concept of a basis point. A *basis point* is one one-hundredth of a percent. It is used to measure a yield or yield change. For example, a yield that increases from 9 to 9.5 percent is a change of 50 basis points.

BOND PRICE AND YIELD CHANGES   The first important principle is the inverse relationship between bond prices and yields.

Consider a ten-year bond with an 11.75 percent coupon and annual interest payments. Its price at a yield of 11.75 percent is

$$B = 117.50 \left[\frac{1 - (1.1175)^{-10}}{.1175} \right] + 1,000(1.1175)^{-10} = 1,000.$$

Bond prices and yields move inversely.

When the coupon equals the yield, the price equals the par value. Such a bond is said to be *selling at par*.

Now suppose the yield increases 25 basis points to 12 percent. Then the price will decrease to

$$B = 117.50 \left[\frac{1 - (1.12)^{-10}}{.12} \right] + 1,000(1.12)^{-10} = 985.87.$$

When the yield exceeds the coupon, the price will be less than par. That bond is said to be *selling at a discount*.

Now let the yield be 11 percent. Then the price will increase to

$$B = 117.50 \left[\frac{1 - (1.11)^{-10}}{.11} \right] + 1,000(1.11)^{-10} = 1,044.17.$$

When the coupon exceeds the yield, the price will be greater than par. Such a bond is said to be *selling at a premium*.

Figure 8.4 illustrates this relationship for this example.

FIGURE 8.4
Bond Prices and Yields

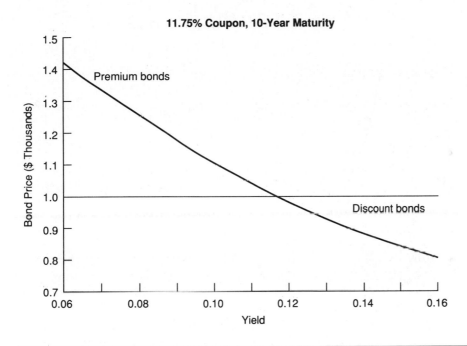

11.75% Coupon, 10-Year Maturity

BOND PRICE VOLATILITY AND MATURITY   The second important principle is that for a given change in yields, the bond price changes by a percentage that varies inversely with the bond's maturity.

Consider a bond with a coupon of 10 percent and an original yield of 10 percent. Both a 10- and a 20-year bond will have a price of $1,000. Suppose the yield increases by 100 basis points to 11 percent. The price of the 10-year bond will be

$$B = 100 \left[\frac{1 - (1.11)^{-10}}{.11} \right] + 1,000(1.11)^{-10} = 941.11,$$

a decrease of about 5.9 percent. The price of the 20-year bond will be

$$B = 100 \left[\frac{1 - (1.11)^{-20}}{.11} \right] + 1,000(1.11)^{-20} = 920.37,$$

a decrease of almost 8 percent. Had the yield decreased, the 20-year bond would have experienced the greater percentage increase.

FIGURE 8.5

Maturity and Bond Price Volatility

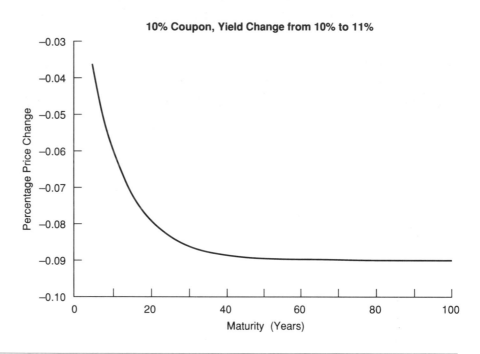

Figure 8.5 illustrates the relationship between maturity and percentage price change for a broad range of maturities for bonds with a coupon of 10 percent and a yield change of from 10 to 11 percent. As you can see, longer-maturity bonds experience greater percentage decreases in their prices. However, this relationship flattens out at a maturity of around 40 years.

Holding everything else constant, the longer the maturity, the greater the percentage change in the bond price for a given basis point change in the yield.

BOND PRICE VOLATILITY AND COUPON   The third important principle deals with the relationship between the bond price volatilty and the coupon. Consider two bonds alike in all respects except coupon. We know that if the yield decreases, both bonds will have price increases, but which one will experience the greater percentage increase? It will be the one with the lower coupon.

Consider two bonds, each with a maturity of five years. Let the yield be 11 percent. One bond has a coupon of 11 percent and the other a coupon of 10 percent. The 11 percent coupon bond will have a price of $1,000 (coupon = yield). The 10 percent bond will have a price of

$$B = 100\left[\frac{1-(1.11)^{-5}}{.11}\right]+1,000(1.11)^{-5} = 963.04.$$

FIGURE 8.6
Coupon and Bond Price Volatility

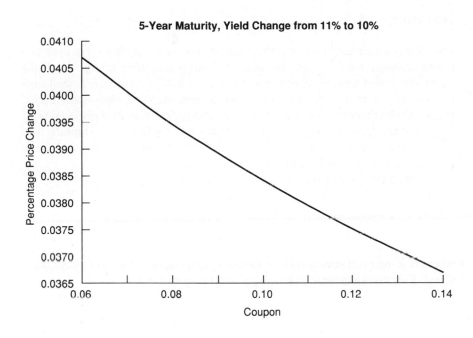

If the yield moves down 100 basis points to 10 percent, the bond with the 11 percent coupon will have a price of

$$B = 100 \left[\frac{1-(1.10)^{-5}}{.10} \right] + 1,000(1.10)^{-5} = 1,037.91.$$

We know that the bond with the 10 percent coupon will now be priced at $1,000. The percentage change of the 11 percent coupon bond is 3.79 percent (from $1,000 to $1,037.91); the percentage change of the 10 percent coupon bond is 3.84 percent. Had the yield increased, the lower-coupon bond again would have had the greater percentage price decrease.

Holding everything else constant, the greater the coupon, the lower the percentage change in the bond price for a given basis point change in the yield.

Figure 8.6 illustrates the percentage price change for five-year bonds of various coupons when the yield goes from 11 to 10 percent.

Putting our last two results together, we can see that the most volatile bonds will be those with longer maturities and lower coupons. If a portfolio manager is forecasting a decrease in interest rates, the portfolio should emphasize longer maturities and lower coupons. If an interest rate increase is expected, the portfolio should shift toward shorter maturities and higher coupons. This poses a problem when comparing, for example, a long-maturity, high-coupon bond with a short-maturity, low-coupon bond. Which is more volatile? For that, we turn to a one-dimensional measure of bond price volatility—duration.

Duration

Duration is a measure of the size and timing of a bond's cash flows. For example, a long-maturity bond requires its holder to wait a long time to receive all the payments. If that bond also has a low coupon, the holder will receive small cash flows over a long time period. In contrast, a short-maturity, high-coupon bond gives its holder large cash flows over a short time period. Clearly the second bond is less volatile and pays its return more promptly than the first bond. Duration thus captures the magnitude and timing of the cash flows and indicates which bond pays its return more quickly and which is more volatile.

Duration is given by the formula

$$DUR = \frac{\sum\limits_{t=1}^{T} t CP_t (1+y)^{-t}}{B},$$

where B is the bond price and CP_t is the cash payment, the coupon or principal, at time t. To better understand this formula, let us rewrite it as

$$DUR = \sum\limits_{t=1}^{T} t \left[\frac{CP_t (1+y)^{-t}}{B} \right].$$

Note that the value of t is weighted (multiplied) by the term in brackets, which is the present value of the cash flow received at time t divided by the total present value (price) of the bond. Thus, the values of t are multiplied by a set of weights. The sum of the weights is 1. Therefore, the formula for duration takes a weighted average of the numbers $t = 1, 2, \ldots, T$.

Consider a four-year bond with a coupon of 8 percent and a yield of 10 percent. The price would be 936.60. The duration would be

$$DUR = \frac{(1)(80)(1.10)^{-1} + (2)(80)(1.10)^{-2} + (3)(80)(1.10)^{-3} + (4)(1,080)(1.10)^{-4}}{936.60}$$

$$= 3.56.$$

For this bond, duration is a weighted average of the numbers 1, 2, 3, and 4. Note how the average tilts toward 4 because of the large principal repayment.

If the bond's life has many years remaining, adding up all the terms could be tedious. Fortunately, the duration formula has been simplified considerably. Caks, Lane, Greenleaf, and Joules (1985) showed that the formula reduces to

$$DUR = \frac{CI(1+y)\left[(1+y)^{T}-1\right] + Ty(FVy - CI)}{CIy\left[(1+y)^{T}-1\right] + FVy^2}.$$

In our example,

$$DUR = \frac{80(1.10)\left[(1.10)^4 - 1\right] + 4(.10)\left[1,000(.10) - 80\right]}{80(.10)\left[(1.10)^4 - 1\right] + 1,000(.10)^2} = 3.56.$$

The article also presents alternative versions of the formula for cases in which the bond is at par or the price and duration are calculated between coupon payment dates.

Table 8.1 presents some durations for a representative range of coupons and maturities at a yield of 10 percent. Note how for a given level of maturity, duration decreases as the coupon increases. For a given coupon, duration generally increases as maturity increases; however, there are some exceptions to that rule for low coupons. For discount coupon bonds, duration increases with maturity to a point and then starts to decrease. Given that most bonds have original maturities of no more than 30 years, we can say that duration normally increases with maturity. Note also that as maturity lengthens, duration increases, but at a decreasing rate.[7] For that reason, durations of more than 13 years would be somewhat rare.

Because duration is a measure of coupon and maturity, it should also be a measure of bond price volatility. In fact, duration is related to bond price volatility by the following approximation:[8]

$$\frac{\Delta B}{B} \cong -DUR\left(\frac{\Delta y}{1+y}\right),$$

where $\Delta B/B$ is the percentage price change for a yield change of Δy. For example, the four-year, 8 percent coupon bond with a 10 percent yield has a duration of 3.56. That means that if the yield increases by 100 basis points to 11 percent, the approximate percentage price change will be

$$\frac{\Delta B}{B} \cong -3.56\left(\frac{.01}{1.10}\right) = -.0324.$$

---

[7]Although not shown here, there is also a yield effect: The higher the yield, the lower the duration.

[8]The formula is only an approximation because it is based on derivatives, which hold only for very small yield changes. The exact relationship is

$$\frac{dB}{B} = -DUR\left(\frac{dy}{1+y}\right),$$

where dB/dy is the derivative of price with respect to yield. Also, if the bond pays coupons semiannually, dy (or Δy) should be divided by $1 + (y/2)$ instead of $1 + y$.

TABLE 8.1

Bond Durations for Various Coupons and Maturities (10 Percent Yield)

Maturity (Years)	Coupon (%)								
	0	2	4	6	8	10	12	14	16
5	5	4.76	4.57	4.41	4.28	4.17	4.07	3.99	3.92
10	10	8.73	7.95	7.42	7.04	6.76	6.54	6.36	6.21
15	15	11.61	10.12	9.28	8.74	8.37	8.09	7.88	7.71
20	20	13.33	11.30	10.32	9.75	9.36	9.09	8.89	8.74
25	25	14.03	11.81	11.86	10.32	9.98	9.75	9.58	9.45
30	30	14.03	11.92	11.09	10.65	10.37	10.18	10.04	9.94
35	35	13.64	11.84	11.17	10.82	10.61	10.46	10.36	10.28
40	40	13.13	11.70	11.18	10.92	10.76	10.65	10.57	10.51
50	50	12.19	11.40	11.40	10.99	10.91	10.85	10.81	10.78
100	100	11.02	11.01	11.00	11.00	11.00	11.00	11.00	11.00

The actual bond price at a yield of 11 percent is 906.93, a percentage price decrease of 3.17 percent.[9]

Thus, given two bonds, each assumed to have an equal chance of a given yield change, the bond with the longer duration is more volatile. Figure 8.7 illustrates the percentage price change for two bonds, one with a 6 percent coupon and one with an 8 percent coupon. For both bonds, the initial yield is 10 percent and the yield changes to 9 percent. A given curve represents a bond with a particular coupon and different maturities and, thus, different durations. The percentage price change increases with maturity and duration, although the rate of increase is not constant. At a maturity of around 28 years, the percentage price change increases only slightly with further increases in maturity and duration. Note that for the entire range of maturities, the lower-coupon, longer-duration bond is more volatile.

In addition to being a measure of bond price volatility, duration is an important portfolio management concept. Bonds whose holding period equals the duration are protected against losses resulting from interest rate changes. This strategy, called *immunization*, has been very popular, particularly during periods of high and volatile interest rates. For more on immunization strategies, the reader is referred to Bierwag (1987).

[9]The slight difference between the predicted percentage price change and the actual percentage price change can be quite large if the yield change is much larger. In that case, a more accurate prediction can be obtained by adding an additional term called *convexity*. For a discussion of convexity, see Chicago Board of Trade (1990). This paper may be ordered from the Literature Services Department of the CBOT. For formulas for convexity, see Brooks and Livingston (1989).

FIGURE 8.7
Duration and Bond Price Volatility

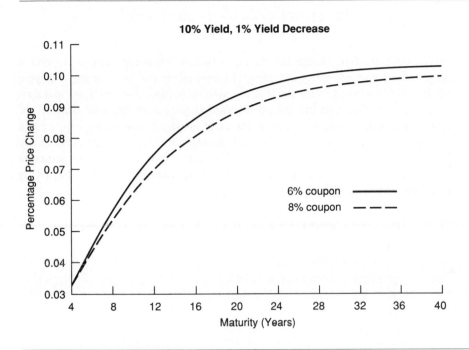

The Term Structure and the Yield Curve

The term structure is the relationship between the rates on pure-discount bonds and their maturities. The yield curve is the relationship between yields on coupon bonds and their maturities. The two curves are similar, but there are some differences. For example, let the term structure be defined as follows:

$$r(0,1) = .16$$
$$r(0,2) = .14$$
$$r(0,3) = .12$$
$$r(0,4) = .10.$$

A four-year bond with an 8 percent coupon would be priced as

$$B = 80(1.16)^{-1} + 80(1.14)^{-2} + 80(1.12)^{-3} + 1,080(1.10)^{-4}$$
$$= 925.12.$$

The yield would be the value of y that solves the equation

$$925.12 = 80\left[\frac{1-(1+y)^{-4}}{y}\right]+1,000(1+y)^{-4},$$

and y would be .1038. Notice that the term structure is quoting a rate of 10 percent on four-year investments, while the yield implied by the price of the four-year bond is 10.38 percent. Note too that the yield is greater than the four-year spot rate. This will always be true for a downward-sloping term structure. Thus, if the term structure is downward sloping, the yield on any T-year bond will be more than the T-year spot rate. For an upward-sloping term structure, the yield on any T-year bond will be less than the T-year spot rate. Only for a flat term structure will the yield on a T-year bond equal the T-year spot rate. These relationships are illustrated in Figure 8.8.

Estimating the Yield Curve

As noted earlier, the term structure is not easily observable. There are, however, several sophisticated mathematical techniques for estimating it. For the most part, the yield curve derived from U.S. Treasury securities usually serves as a proxy for the term structure. An example of such a yield curve is shown in Figure 8.9.

This yield curve is upward sloping; thus, we know that the true term structure lies above it and that the yield will underestimate the anticipated return on a bond. Also, note that the yield curve observed in reality is not smooth, as the theory implies. This is partly due to the fact that all of the bonds used should have the same coupon but do not because it is difficult to locate bonds with the same coupon over a broad range of maturities.

So far we have said a lot about spot and forward rates. Our objective, of course, is to establish a foundation for understanding futures prices. At this point, we can cheat a little and treat forward prices as though they were the same as futures prices. As we shall see in Chapter 9, they are not exactly equal either in theory or in reality, but the differences are quite small. Since we are discussing yield curves, this will be a good place to look at the yield curve implied by the Treasury bill futures market.

THE FUTURES YIELD CURVE   The Treasury bill futures contract at the International Monetary Market of the Chicago Mercantile Exchange calls for delivery of a 91-day Treasury bill. The contract expirations are March, June, September, and December, with maturities extending out about two years. Consider the prices on July 2 of a particular year.

The September contract is quoted at a price of 92.52, which is interpreted as a discount of $100 - 92.52 = 7.48$. Using the convention of the Treasury bill spot market as explained in Chapter 3, the price per $100 of par value is

$$100 - 7.48\,(91/360) = 98.1092.$$

FIGURE 8.8
Term Structure and Yield Curve

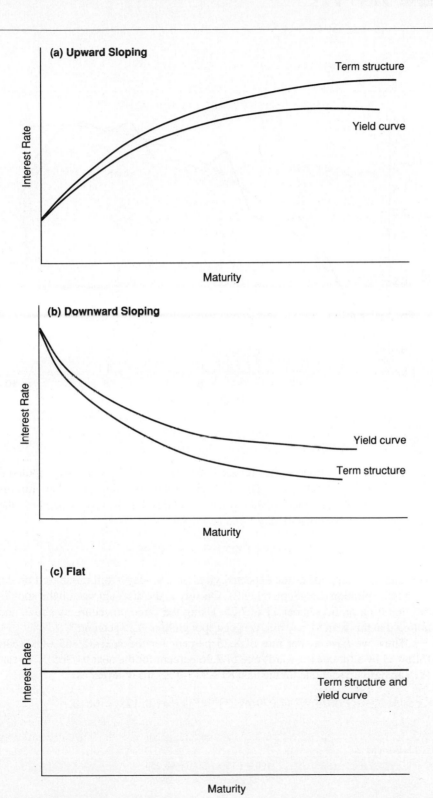

FIGURE 8.9

Treasury Yield Curve

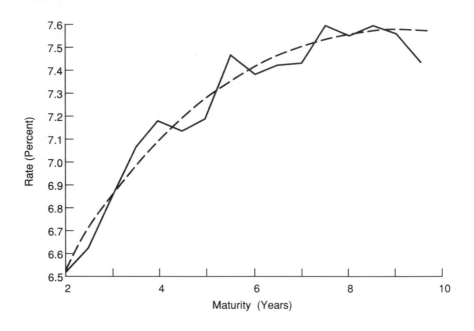

Although the actual futures price is based on a 90-day T-bill, we have computed it here as a 91-day T-bill price. That is because we are using the T-bill futures market to derive an implied forward price for 91-day T-bills. From Chapter 3, the yield on the purchase of a 91-day T-bill at 98.1092 is

$$(100/98.1092)^{365/91} - 1 = .0796.$$

This can be interpreted as the expected yield on a 91-day T-bill purchased on the contract expiration date, September 21. On July 2, the discount rate on the spot T-bill maturing on September 21 is 7.75. Using the same procedure as above and noting that this is an 81-day bill, we get a spot yield of 8.25 percent.[10]

Thus, we have a spot rate of 8.25 percent for the next 81/365 of a year, followed by a futures (forward) rate of 7.96 percent for the next 91/365 of a year. We can derive a spot rate for the next $81 + 91 = 172/365$ of a year as

$$[(1.0825)^{81/365}(1.0796)^{91/365}]^{365/172} - 1 = r(0, 172) = .0810.$$

---

[10]This is found as

$$100 - 7.75(81/360) = 98.2563$$
$$(100/98.2563)^{365/81} - 1 = .0825.$$

This rate is interpreted as the annualized spot rate for the next 172 days.

There are also futures contracts expiring in later months, although the liquidity of some of them is fairly low, which leaves their prices somewhat inaccurate. However, let us use one more futures contract to extend the yield curve a bit further. The December contract has a discount rate of 7.37. The bill matures March 22, which is 91 days after the December expiration of the bill underlying the September contract. Thus, we can extend the yield curve out to $172 + 91 = 263$ days.

The futures price for a discount of 7.37 is

$$100 - 7.37(91/360) = 98.1370.$$

This implies a yield of

$$(100/98.1370)^{365/91} - 1 = .0783.$$

Since we already know that the rate for the 172 days from July 2 to December 21 is .081, we link it with the 7.83 percent rate that applies to the period from December 21 to March 22.

$$[(1.081)^{172/365}(1.0783)^{91/365}]^{365/263} - 1 = r(0, 263) = .0801.$$

Thus, our term structure is 7.96 percent for 81 days, 8.1 percent for 172 days, and 8.01 percent for 263 days. As we shall see in a later chapter, a difference between the term structure implied by the futures market and the term structure implied by the spot market can imply either that arbitrage opportunities exist or that forward and futures prices should not be equal.

In this chapter, we examined a number of principles of pricing fixed-income securities. Because of their widespread use in the design of futures contracts, we have focused on U.S. Treasury securities. Corporate and municipal bonds play a lesser role in the futures markets, and an understanding of those bonds requires attention to factors such as default risk and taxes. Also, we have ignored a number of other factors that might be associated with a bond, such as the ability of the bondholder to convert the bond to stock and the ability of the issuing firm or government to call the bond and retire it early. These issues are important but are beyond the scope of this book.

This completes our discussion of the pricing of fixed-income securities. We will use these principles frequently in later chapters. For now, we turn to the pricing of equity securities.

EQUITIES

We said a great deal about equity securities in Part One. We have not, however, dealt with the pricing of equities. That is because option pricing theory takes the price of the stock as given. This allowed us to price the option without regard for how the stock is priced or even whether it is priced correctly. To some extent, that is also true of futures. However, we shall need to understand some of the methods of equity pricing to fully appreciate the utility of stock index futures and, in particular, to apply hedging techniques.

An Equity Pricing Equation

When we discussed the pricing of bonds, we noted that the bond price is the present value of the interest and principal payments over the bond's life. In general, the price of any asset is the present value of the cash flows that will go to the asset's owner. In the case of equities, those cash flows are dividends and capital gains. Specifically, the price of a stock is given as

$$S = \sum_{t=1}^{T(1)} D_t (1+k)^{-t} + S_{T(1)} (1+k)^{-T(1)},$$

where

S = stock price
D_t = expected dividend paid at time t
k = required rate of return or discount rate
$T(1)$ = time at which the owner sells the stock
$S_{T(1)}$ = price at time of sale of the stock

For example, suppose you buy a stock that is expected to pay a dividend of $4 in one year and $4.25 one year later. You expect to sell the stock at $54 at the end of two years. You believe a return of 16 percent is reasonable. A fair price is

$$S = 4(1.16)^{-1} + 4.25(1.16)^{-2} + 54(1.16)^{-2} = 46.74.$$

You would be willing to buy the stock for up to $46.74. If it sold for more than $46.74, you would consider it overpriced and might wish to sell it short.

In this example, we assume you sell the stock in two years for $54. How would that price be determined? Obviously the person who purchases the stock from you will price it as the present value of the remaining dividends and the price at which it subsequently will be sold; that is,

$$S_{T(1)} = \sum_{t=T(1)+1}^{T(2)} D_t (1+k)^{-[t-T(1)]} + S_{T(2)} (1+k)^{-[T(2)-T(1)]},$$

where time $T(2)$ is the time at which the stock is sold and $S_{T(2)}$ is the selling price. We could go on to define $S_{T(2)}$ in the same manner. By successively substituting these formulas, we would find that the price of the stock is

$$S = \sum_{t=1}^{\infty} D_t (1+k)^{-t}.$$

This formula simply means that the stock price is the present value of all future dividends. We need not be concerned with any interim stock prices. As a practical matter, however, we cannot possibly estimate the stream of all dividends until infinity. At this point, we usually appeal to some assumptions about growth.

THE EFFECT OF GROWTH   In many cases, dividends grow at a fairly constant rate for a period of time. In the most extreme case, dividends grow at a constant rate forever. This assumption is convenient because it simplifies the model into a form we can easily apply.

Suppose we define a growth rate, g, such that all future dividends are related to the first dividend by the formula

$$D_t = D_1(1 + g)^{t-1}.$$

For example, suppose the dividend in one year is $2. If it is expected to grow at a 4 percent rate, the dividend in five years will be

$$D_5 = 2(1.04)^4 = 2.34.$$

Stated in this manner, we can determine any future dividend by knowing only the first dividend, the growth rate, and the length of time until that dividend is paid. This type of specification results in the following formula for the stock price:

$$S = \frac{D_1}{k - g}.$$

This model is sometimes known as the *constant growth discounted cash flow model* or the *Gordon growth model*, named for Myron Gordon, an economist who studied it extensively many years ago.

Suppose the dividend in one year is expected to be $3.50, the required rate is 15 percent, and the growth rate is 9 percent. Then the stock price is

$$S = \frac{3.50}{.15 - .09} = 58.33.$$

The constant growth formulation allows us to avoid having to forecast any future dividends beyond the first year; however, it does so at the expense of reality. No firm can maintain a truly constant growth rate forever. For that reason, there are variations of the model that allow dividends to grow at different rates over various time periods. Nonetheless, the simplicity of the basic model is a worthwhile feature, and it illustrates most of the concepts we need here. For example, we can rearrange the equation to give the required rate,

$$k = \frac{D_1}{S} + g,$$

and we see that the required rate equals the dividend yield, D_1/S, plus the growth rate, g, and is inversely related to the price.

Where does the required rate come from? In Chapter 1, we alluded to the idea that investors require returns consisting of a risk-free rate plus a risk premium, the latter being the additional return expected for bearing risk. In the next section, we shall look at where these risk premia come from. For this we will appeal to a branch of investment analysis called *portfolio theory*.

Portfolio Theory

Portfolio theory is the study of the relationship between the expected return and the risk of securities and portfolios. Starting with the assumption that investors like return and dislike risk, it proceeds to derive several important properties about the way in which people invest their money. One of the most important results is that investors should diversify their portfolios.

Diversification simply means not putting all your eggs in one basket. If an investor holds a broadly diversified portfolio, the performance of the overall portfolio will be relatively insensitive to the ups and downs of the individual securities. While some securities will go up, others will go down. To at least some extent, these ups and downs will be offsetting.

Unsystematic risk is the risk associated with the uncertainty of individual securities. Holding the optimal number of securities in a portfolio provides the diversification capable of eliminating unsystematic risk. For obvious reasons, unsystematic risk is also called *diversifiable risk*. What remains is *systematic* or *nondiversifiable risk*.

Systematic risk is the risk associated with broad market movements resulting from uncertainty about the economy as a whole. In contrast, the uncertainty associated with an individual firm is unsystematic risk. An example of unsystematic risk would be the recall of a potentially dangerous product. Because this risk would not be associated with firms in general, it would not be systematic.[11] However, a major change in Federal Reserve monetary policy would have an impact on the entire economy and thus would be a source of systematic risk.

Earlier we noted that holding enough securities in a portfolio will eliminate unsystematic risk. Portfolio theory has provided mathematical algorithms for determining how to do this. It turns out, however, that we need not hold very many securities or combine them in any prescribed manner to see the effects of diversification. Figure 8.10 depicts the relationship between a portfolio's standard deviation and the number of securities in the portfolio. Studies have revealed that it takes surprisingly few securities to reach a point where portfolio standard deviation

---

[11]If consumers fear similar defects in competing products, some of the effects might carry over to other firms in the industry. This would be a type of industry effect, a risk associated with firms in an industry but not with the economy as a whole.

FIGURE 8.10
Portfolio Size and Diversification

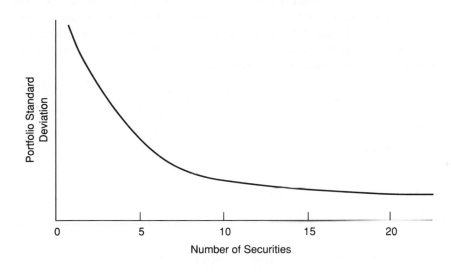

will decline very little with the addition of more securities.[12] The graph shows that somewhere between 10 and 20 securities are all one needs to achieve diversification.

The reduction in standard deviation as we add more securities reflects the diversification effect. The minimum level of risk remaining is the systematic risk, which cannot be eliminated by further diversification. Although investors can modify their portfolios' risk levels by investing a portion of their funds in low-risk or risk-free assets such as Treasury bills, the systematic risk associated with their security holdings will remain. Before the introduction of stock index futures, systematic risk could not be eliminated. In later chapters, we shall see how these contracts can be used to modify or eliminate systematic risk.

To understand how to measure systematic risk, we need a model that will explain how risk is reflected in the market prices of securities. Asset pricing theory, an outgrowth of portfolio theory, will give us some of these answers.

[12]John Evans and Stephen H. Archer, "Diversification and the Reduction of Dispersion: An Empirical Analysis," *The Journal of Finance* 23 (December 1968): 761–767; and Wayne Wagner and Sheila Lau, "The Effect of Diversification on Risk," *Financial Analysts Journal* 27 (November–December 1971): 48–53.

Asset Pricing Theory

Previously we assumed investors like return and dislike risk. As a result, they will diversify their holdings. If we add the assumption that everyone has equal access to information and reaches the same assessments of securities' expected returns, variances, and the correlations among securities, we obtain the *Capital Asset Pricing Model (CAPM)*.[13] The model is written as follows:

$$E(r_S) = r + [E(r_M) - r]\beta,$$

where

$E(r_S)$ = expected return on the asset
r = risk-free rate
$E(r_M)$ = expected return on the market
β = beta, or systematic risk

If the market is efficient, the expected rate equals the required rate.

The security's *beta* is its measure of risk and is defined as

$$\beta = \frac{\sigma_{SM}}{\sigma_M^2}.$$

The numerator is the covariance between the returns on the security and the market. It measures the extent to which the security and the market move together. The relationship between security and market, as reflected in the covariance, captures the systematic risk. The denominator is the variance of the return on the market.

Note that the security's variance, which reflects both its systematic and unsystematic risk, is not a factor in the equation. The market defines risk as systematic risk. Because unsystematic risk can be eliminated by diversification, investors cannot expect to earn a return by assuming it. In the absence of systematic risk, $\beta = 0$ and $E(r_S) = r$, meaning that the expected return is the risk-free rate. The amount $[E(r_M) - r]\beta$ is called the *risk premium*, because it is the additional return investors expect as a result of the stock's risk.

The market portfolio has a special role in the model: Its beta is 1. All individual stocks' betas can be regarded as measures of the securities' risk relative to the market beta. Securities with betas greater than 1 are considered to be of above-average risk and securities with betas less than 1 of below-average risk. The market portfolio, therefore, defines the average level of risk.

[13]Three articles originally developed the model: William F. Sharpe, "Capital Asset Prices: A Theory of Market Equilibrium under Conditions of Risk," *The Journal of Finance* 19 (September 1964): 425–442; John Lintner, "The Valuation of Risk Assets and the Selection of Risky Investments in Stock Portfolios and Capital Budgets," *Review of Economics and Statistics* 47 (February 1965): 13–37; and Jan Mossin, "Equilibrium in a Capital Asset Market," *Econometrica* 34 (October 1966): 768–783.

FIGURE 8.11
The Capital Asset Pricing Model

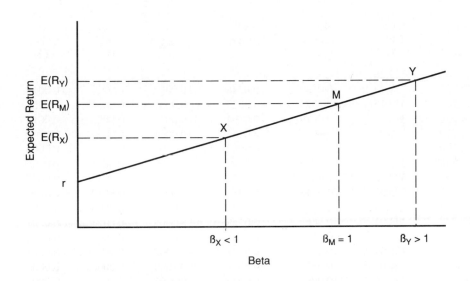

The CAPM is illustrated in Figure 8.11. Two stocks, X and Y, are shown. The beta of X is less than the market beta of 1; thus, its expected return is less than the expected return on the market. The beta of Y is greater than the market beta; hence, its expected return is greater than the expected return on the market.

Primarily because of its simplicity, the CAPM has been a very popular model. In recent years, however, it has been criticized for its dependence on the market portfolio of all risky assets. The next major revolution in asset pricing theory seems to be the Arbitrage Pricing Theory, or APT.[14] The APT allows security returns to be generated by a larger number of factors than simply the market portfolio. In fact, the market portfolio need not even be a determinant of security returns. Although most experts agree that general market movements will always play a role in the pricing of securities, the APT goes beyond that assumption to allow various other factors to determine security prices.

Although the CAPM has lost some of its luster in recent years, the concept of systematic risk remains on firm ground, even in the APT framework. We next turn to the problem of measuring systematic risk.

[14]For an excellent treatment of Arbitrage Pricing Theory, see Richard Roll and Stephen A. Ross, "The Arbitrage Pricing Theory Approach to Strategic Portfolio Planning," *Financial Analysts Journal* 40 (May–June 1984): 14–26.

TABLE 8.2

Data Set for Estimation of Beta

Obs. (1)	Mo. (2)	Day (3)	Disney Price (4)	S&P 500 (5)	Disney Return (6)	S&P Return (7)	(6) x (7) (8)	(6)² (9)	(7)² (10)
	1	5	116.000	352.20					
1	1	12	109.750	339.93	−0.0539	−0.0348	0.0019	0.0029	0.0012
2	1	19	109.500	339.15	−0.0023	−0.0023	0.0000	0.0000	0.0000
3	1	26	104.250	325.80	−0.0479	−0.0394	0.0019	0.0023	0.0015
4	2	2	104.750	330.92	0.0048	0.0157	0.0001	0.0000	0.0002
5	2	9	108.500	333.62	0.0358	0.0082	0.0003	0.0013	0.0001
6	2	16	109.750	332.72	0.0115	−0.0027	0.0000	0.0001	0.0000
7	2	23	104.750	324.15	−0.0456	−0.0258	0.0012	0.0021	0.0007
8	3	2	109.125	335.54	0.0418	0.0351	0.0015	0.0017	0.0012
9	3	9	110.875	337.93	0.0160	0.0071	0.0001	0.0003	0.0001
10	3	16	116.000	341.91	0.0462	0.0118	0.0005	0.0021	0.0001
11	3	23	114.250	337.22	−0.0151	−0.0137	0.0002	0.0002	0.0002
12	3	30	111.125	339.94	−0.0274	0.0081	−0.0002	0.0007	0.0001
13	4	6	113.875	340.08	0.0247	0.0004	0.0000	0.0006	0.0000
14	4	12	114.625	344.34	0.0066	0.0125	0.0001	0.0000	0.0002
15	4	20	111.750	335.12	−0.0251	−0.0268	0.0007	0.0006	0.0007
16	4	27	109.625	329.11	−0.0190	−0.0179	0.0003	0.0004	0.0003
17	5	4	112.750	338.39	0.0285	0.0282	0.0008	0.0008	0.0008
18	5	11	112.125	352.00	−0.0055	0.0402	−0.0002	0.0000	0.0016
19	5	18	115.000	354.64	0.0256	0.0075	0.0002	0.0007	0.0001
20	5	25	117.625	354.58	0.0228	−0.0002	0.0000	0.0005	0.0000
21	6	1	128.500	363.16	0.0925	0.0242	0.0022	0.0085	0.0006
22	6	8	123.375	358.71	−0.0399	−0.0123	0.0005	0.0016	0.0002
23	6	15	131.755	362.91	0.0679	0.0117	0.0008	0.0046	0.0001
24	6	22	127.750	355.43	−0.0304	−0.0206	0.0006	0.0009	0.0004
25	6	29	128.250	358.01	0.0039	0.0073	0.0000	0.0000	0.0001
					0.11672	0.02159	0.01344	0.03318	0.01044

Measuring Systematic Risk

Since beta is a measure of systematic risk, we can attempt to measure it by estimating the covariance between a security's return and the market's return and the variance of the market's return. Table 8.2 presents some data for estimating the beta of Disney stock. We used the S&P 500 return as a proxy for the market. The data are weekly prices from the period of January 5 through June 29 of a particular year.

Recall that we performed similar calculations to obtain a historical estimate of the standard deviation for the Black-Scholes model in Chapter 4. That example used logarithmic (continuously compounded) returns. This example uses only simple returns, primarily because the results will differ only slightly. The simple returns are given in columns 6 and 7 of Table 8.2.

Column 8 gives the cross-product, which is the return on the stock multiplied by the return on the market. Columns 9 and 10 give the squared returns on the stock and the market. The summations of Columns 6 through 10 are used in the calculations for beta.

Covariance is estimated as follows:

$$\sigma_{SM} = \frac{\sum\limits_{t=1}^{J} r_{St} r_{Mt} - \left(\sum\limits_{t=1}^{J} r_{St} \sum\limits_{t=1}^{J} r_{Mt}\right) / J}{J - 1},$$

where r_{St} and r_{Mt} are the returns at time t for the stock and market, respectively, and J is the number of returns. The variance of the market is estimated by the formula

$$\sigma_{M}^{2} = \frac{\sum\limits_{t=1}^{J} r_{Mt}^{2} - \left(\sum\limits_{t=1}^{J} r_{Mt}\right)^{2} / J}{J - 1},$$

The beta estimate is the ratio of the covariance over the variance. Note that the J − 1 in both denominators cancels. Referring to Table 8.2, we obtain the summed terms and compute the beta as follows:

$$\beta = \frac{0.01344 - (0.11672)(0.02159) / 25}{0.01044 - (0.02159)^{2} / 25} = 1.28.$$

In this example, Disney's beta is 1.28. Since it is greater than 1, it is considered more volatile than the market.

This procedure is a simple linear regression of the stock's return on the market return. The computed beta is an estimate obtained by an optimal statistical technique. Nonetheless, the estimate may vary from one time period to the next. Betas are known to be highly unstable, and it is best to use the most current data available. From this point on, we shall take our regression estimates of betas as being accurate. Still, we should keep in mind that these estimates can be suspect at times, a point that will become apparent in some of the strategies illustrated in later chapters.

We have now seen that beta is an appropriate measure of risk for a security. It is also a good measure of risk for a portfolio. The beta of a portfolio is simply a weighted average of the betas of the component stocks. The weight of a given security's beta is the market value of the stock held in the portfolio divided by the portfolio's total market value. In Chapter 10, we shall see in more detail how to compute and apply the concept of a portfolio beta.

Equity Market Indices

There are over 1,500 stocks on the New York Stock Exchange, and several thousand more trade on various other exchanges and over the counter. To assess the overall performance of the equity market, indices often are constructed. One of the most widely cited indices is the Dow Jones Industrial Average (DJIA). The DJIA is an average of the prices of 30 large industrial stocks. It originally was constructed by adding up the prices of the stocks and dividing by the number of stocks. However, when there are stock splits or stock dividends, the average will be distorted if adjustments are not made. Thus, the divisor is changed to leave the average unaltered by the split or dividend.

While the DJIA is the most widely cited average, it suffers from two major deficiencies. First, it consists of only 30 stocks, and thus may not be representative of the market as a whole. Second, its performance tends to be influenced more strongly by higher-priced stocks. Dow Jones and Company has prohibited the trading of futures and options on its stock. As a result, the Chicago Board of Trade and the American Stock Exchange created the *Major Market Index (MMI)*, which consists of 20 industrial stocks, 15 of which are in the DJIA. The MMI is constructed like the DJIA. The CBOT trades futures on the MMI, and the AMEX trades options on it. Let us see how the MMI is constructed.

THE MAJOR MARKET INDEX   Suppose we wish to construct an index with three stocks, A, B, and C. The prices and number of shares of each stock on day 1 and day 2 are as follows:

Stock	Day 1 Price	Day 1 Number of Shares	Day 2 Price	Day 2 Number of Shares
A	19	5,700	18	5,700
B	36	4,100	17.5	8,200
C	71	2,300	73	2,300

On day 1, the MMI would be a simple average of the three stock prices:

$$\text{MMI}_1 = \frac{19 + 36 + 71}{3} = 42.$$

On day 2, we see that stock B has had a 2-for-1 stock split, meaning that for each share owned on day 1, the investor receives one additional share on day 2. Thus, there will be twice as many shares oustanding. This does nothing for the wealth of the shareholders, so the price should fall to one-half of its day 1 value. However, we see that the price fell to slightly less than one-half of its day 1 value, probably due to some negative information about the company. The MMI, however, must be adjusted so that it does not fall as a result of the stock split alone. This is accomplished by taking the day 1 prices for the nonsplit stocks and adding them to the day 1 price of the split stock after adjusting for the split; that is, 19 + 18 + 71 = 108. This total is divided by the day 1 value of the MMI to get the new divisor:

$$\text{New divisor} = \frac{19 + 18 + 71}{42} = 2.5714.$$

This divisor is then used with the actual day 2 prices to obtain the day 2 MMI:

$$\text{MMI}_2 = \frac{18 + 17.5 + 73}{2.5714} = 42.19.$$

Thus, our MMI increased by 0.19.

Although options and futures trade on the MMI, this average, like the DJIA, suffers from the same criticisms of having a small number of companies and being influenced more strongly by high-priced stocks. One market average that does not suffer from these criticisms is the Standard and Poor's 500 (S&P 500).

THE S&P 500 The *S&P 500* is a market-value-weighted average index of 500 stocks listed on the New York and American Stock Exchanges. It is influenced more strongly by stocks of firms that have the largest market value of their equity, not just the highest prices. Let us illustrate the computation of the S&P 500 index with our sample of three stocks. We shall call this the S&P 3.

On day 1, we compute the market value of the three stocks:

$$19(5,700) + 36(4,100) + 71(2,300) = 419,200.$$

On the first day, the index is given an arbitrary starting value; we shall use 10. Thus, the S&P 3 on day 1 is at 10. On day 2, we take the market value of the stocks on day 2, divide by the market value of the stocks on day 1, and multiply the result by the base value of 10. Thus, the S&P 3 on day 2 is

$$\text{S\&P3}_2 = 10\left[\frac{18(5,700) + 17.5(8,200) + 73(2,300)}{419,200}\right] = 9.88.$$

Note that we need not make any adjustments as a result of the stock split. Since both the shares and the price adjust, the index is not biased by the split. However, note also that the S&P 3 fell from 10 to 9.88, yet our MMI rose from 42 to 42.19. This illustrates the weakness of price-weighted indices. The increase in the MMI was a result of the $2 increase in the price of the highest-priced stock, C. Yet the S&P 3 accurately reflected the fact that the market value of the shareholders' equity in all three firms combined did indeed fall.

In the real world, the S&P index consists of 500 stocks and has a base value of 10 established over the 1941–1943 period. Each day the S&P 500 is constructed by determining the market value of the 500 stocks divided by the market value of the same stocks averaged over the 1941–1943 period and multiplied by the base value.

A number of other indices are constructed in the same manner. In fact, we already have said a lot about index options on the S&P 100. In addition, there are options and futures on the New York Stock Exchange index, which is constructed in the same basic way as the S&P 500 but includes all NYSE stocks. We already mentioned S&P 500 options, which trade on the CBOE. However, the volume of these options is rather small compared to the volume of futures contracts traded on the S&P 500 at the CME. In the next several chapters, we shall illustrate a number of principles and strategies using the S&P 500 stock index futures contract.

In the final section of this chapter, we shall take a break from stocks and bonds and simply discuss a generic commodity. By this we mean any kind of asset that one could hold. Our goal is to develop a simple framework for determining the commodity's spot price.

THE FORMATION OF SPOT PRICES

In the first part of this chapter, we examined some basic concepts for pricing bonds and stocks. These principles will serve us well, and we will retain them throughout. In this section, we shall look at a simple model for determining spot prices. For convenience, we will assume the asset is a commodity such as corn or wheat (it could just as easily be a stock or a bond). In some cases, it will be important to point out the differences among the various types of commodities. We start our discussion of the model in a world of certainty.

The Spot Pricing Model under Certainty

Consider a commodity that is consumed at a constant, known rate. There is an initial supply that steadily decreases until replenished. This would be the case for an agricultural commodity that has a constant demand and a supply that increases at a harvest date. At that point, the crop is immediately harvested and its size is known. These assumptions mean that we are operating in a world of certainty. Figure 8.12 illustrates the model.

In panel a, the supply of the good is shown on the vertical axis and time on the horizontal axis. Supply follows a saw-toothed pattern, falling at a steady rate from a high of Q_2 immediately after the harvest to a low of Q_1 immediately before the next harvest. The times T_1, T_2, T_3, and T_4 are the harvest dates.

Panel b shows the evolution of the commodity price. When the supply is highest (at Q_2), the price is lowest (S_1). Then the price steadily increases as the supply decreases. Immediately before the next harvest, when the supply is lowest (Q_1), the price is highest (S_2).

FIGURE 8.12
A Simple Spot Pricing Model

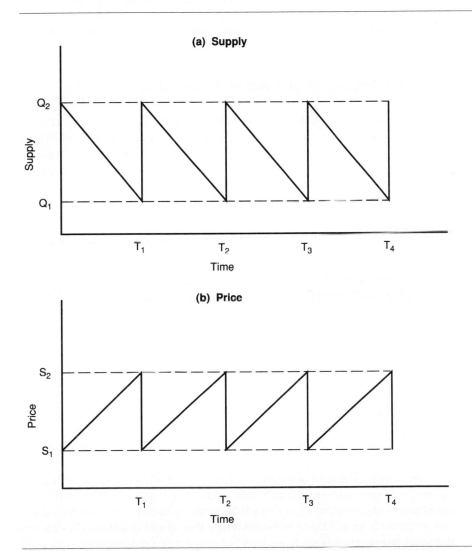

(a) Supply

(b) Price

Now imagine a person who purchases the commodity at the lowest price, S_1, at T_1 and stores it until time T_2 an instant before the harvest. Then the person sells the commodity at price S_2. During the time the commodity is stored, costs are incurred, which include the interest forgone on funds tied up. Storage will be profitable as long as the profit from the sale of the commodity exceeds the cost. However, if that is true, there will be an incentive to buy the good and store it. This will place upward pressure on the good's spot price and the price of storage. The additional storage will also tend to increase the future supply of the good,

Under certainty, today's spot price equals the future spot price minus the cost of storage and the interest forgone.

leading to a lower future spot price. If buying the good and storing it is unprofit-
able, this fact will discourage storage and encourage immediate consumption.
This will drive down the spot price and the price of storage. It follows that today's
spot price must equal the future spot price minus the cost of storage and the
interest forgone.

The Spot Pricing Model under Uncertainty

Now let us remove the certainty assumption and suppose that future demand and
supply are uncertain. For the present, however, let us assume individuals are
indifferent to risk; that is, they are said to be *risk neutral*. We encountered this
concept in Part One, where we noted that options can be priced as though investors do not consider risk. As unrealistic as this assumption seems, it is useful in
keeping the models simple without loss of practicality.

UNCERTAINTY AND RISK NEUTRALITY   If there is uncertainty, the future spot
price is unknown. Therefore, let us define investors' expectation of the spot price
at a future time T as $E(S_T)$. The current spot price is S. Then we should expect to
be able to buy the good at S, store and incur costs of s, forgo interest of i on the
funds tied up, and sell the good at a price of $E(S_T)$. The market will price the good
and the storage service such that there will be an incentive to store some of the
good; that is,

$$S + s + i = E(S_T),$$

> *Under uncertainty and risk
> neutrality, the spot price equals
> the expected future spot price
> minus the cost of storage and
> the interest forgone.*

or

$$S = E(S_T) - s - i.$$

Inefficient storers—those whose costs are higher than s—will be driven out of
business.

The inappropriateness of the risk neutrality assumption is seen by noting that
because the future spot price is uncertain, no rational person would be willing to
undertake storage without expecting a risk premium. Recall from Chapter 1 that a
risk premium is an additional expected return that an individual requires for undertaking risk. Up to this point, we have not introduced a risk premium. Let us do
so now.

UNCERTAINTY AND RISK AVERSION   Suppose individuals are not indifferent
to risk. To induce someone to buy the good, store it, and sell it at an uncertain
future price will require a risk premium. We denote this risk premium as $E(\phi)$. The
relationship among the variables is

$$S + s + i + E(\phi) = E(S_T),$$

or

$$S = E(S_T) - s - i - E(\phi).$$

Thus, to offer a risk premium, the expected spot price must exceed the current spot price by a greater amount. Individuals who are unable to keep storage costs at or below s and whose risk aversion is so high as to make $E(\phi)$ an unacceptable risk premium will not engage in storage.

Recall from our earlier discussion that the Capital Asset Pricing Model also gives a risk premium, which we identified as $[E(r_M) - r]\beta$. This equation is entirely consistent with the above risk premium expression. When we used the CAPM, we expressed things in terms of percentages; in this section, we express things in terms of dollars. Suppose we rewrite the preceding equation as follows:

$$E(S_T) - S = s + i + E(\phi).$$

Now we divide everything by S. We can then write $[E(S_T) - S]/S$ as $E(r_s)$:

$$\frac{E(S_T) - S}{S} = E(r_s) = \left(\frac{s+i}{S}\right) + \left(\frac{E(\phi)}{S}\right).$$

> *Under uncertainty and risk aversion, the spot price equals the expected future spot price minus the cost of storage, the interest forgone, and the risk premium.*

The first expression on the right, $(s + i)/S$, is the percentage opportunity cost of storing or investing in the asset. The interest forgone as a percentage of the price, i/S, is equivalent to the risk-free rate. The overall percentage opportunity cost differs only from the risk-free rate in that here we have included a storage cost, s. In the CAPM, we traditionally omit the storage cost because we tend to apply the CAPM to securities, which have no storage costs. If we applied the CAPM to commodities that are costly to store, we would have to include a storage cost with the risk-free rate. Thus, the expected return on such an asset would be the risk-free rate plus the storage cost expressed as a percentage of the asset's price.

The second term on the right is the expected risk premium expressed as a percentage of the spot price, $E(\phi)/S$. This is equivalent to the term $[E(r_M) - r]\beta$ in the CAPM. The CAPM simply provides a more explicit statement of the source of the risk premium, which is the systematic risk. Thus, we see that the equation developed in this section is a more general statement of the risk-return relationship. It is true regardless of whether or not the CAPM is valid.

A Further Word on Storage

The physical process of storage incurs costs that we have defined as s. For some goods, such as agricultural commodities, these costs can be substantial. They include the direct costs of the storage facility, plus insurance and a factor that reflects spoilage and obsolescence. For other goods, such as stocks and bonds, the direct costs of storage are insignificant. In addition, some securities even offer a return from storage in the form of dividends or coupon interest.

Let us now define the important concept of the *cost of carry* as the cost of storage, s, plus the interest forgone, i. The cost of carry is positive if storage creates a net cash outflow and negative if dividends or coupon interest are large enough to offset the cost of storage and the interest forgone. Sometimes, however, this concept is referred to as simply the *carry*. The carry is the coupon interest or dividends earned minus the cost of storage and the interest forgone. Thus, assets that offer dividends or coupon interest in excess of the costs of storing and the forgone interest are said to have a positive carry. In this text, we shall prefer to use the concept of the *cost of carry*.

While the cost of carry is an important concept in spot market pricing, it is even more vital in defining the relationship among the spot price, expected future spot price, and futures price. We shall have much more to say about the cost of carry in Chapter 9. Now let us consider two extreme cases: goods that are nonstorable and goods that are indefinitely storable.

There really are no truly nonstorable goods, but something highly perishable, like fresh fish, would approximate it. For such a good, there would not necessarily be a relationship between today's spot price and the expected future spot price. Supply and demand conditions today and in the future would be independent. The risk of uncertain future supplies could not be reduced by storing some of the good currently owned. Large price fluctuations likely would occur. The cost of carry would be a meaningless concept.

At the other extreme, a commodity might be indefinitely storable. Some financial assets, metals, and natural resources such as oil are examples. Their spot prices would be set in accordance with current supply and demand conditions, the cost of carry, investors' expected risk premia, and expected future supply and demand conditions.

For many agricultural commodities, limited storability is the rule. Grains have a fairly long storage life, while frozen concentrated orange juice has a more limited one. In the financial markets Treasury bills, which mature in less than a year, have a short storage life. Treasury bonds, with their longer maturities, have a much longer storage life.

For any storable commodity, the spot price is related to the expected future spot price by the cost of carry and the expected risk premium. This important relationship will carry through to Chapter 9, where we introduce futures markets into the model.

SUMMARY

To understand how futures prices are determined, we must first look at how spot prices are calculated. In this chapter, we examined basic principles of the spot pricing of stocks, bonds, and commodities. We saw how a bond is priced as the present value of the future coupon and principal payments. We considered the role of the discount rate by examining the term structure of interest rates and the behavior of bond prices in response to yield changes. We also looked at the concept of duration and how the yield curve and the term structure are related.

Next, we turned to equities and observed how they too are priced as the present value of future cash flows. We briefly examined the principles of portfolio theory and developed the concepts of diversification and the Capital Asset Pricing Model. We illustrated a simple regression technique for estimating systematic risk.

Finally, we looked at a simple model of the pricing of a commodity in the spot market. We developed the concept first under a world of certainty, then under a world of uncertainty and risk neutrality, and finally in a world of uncertainty with risk-averse investors. We found that spot prices are formed by taking into account the cost of storage, the interest forgone on the money tied up, the expected risk premium, and the expected future spot price. This model can apply to any commodity that is storable for at least a limited time period. This would include most agricultural commodities as well as financial instruments.

In Chapter 9, we shall introduce futures contracts into the model. We shall see how futures prices, spot prices, the cost of carry, risk premia, and expected future spot prices are related. In addition, we shall see how futures prices are related to other futures prices and to the prices of forward contracts.

Questions and Problems

1. Explain and distinguish between the concepts of spot and forward rates.

2. To which of the three theories of the term structure do each of the following statements refer? Explain your answers.

    a. Long-term rates are higher than short-term rates because the U.S. Treasury currently is shifting the average maturity of its debt by borrowing more heavily with Treasury bonds than with Treasury bills.

    b. The current structure of interest rates is the market's way of saying that interest rates are expected to increase in the future.

    c. The term structure is upward sloping because lenders are reluctant to make long-term loans.

3. Use the following term structure to derive the requested forward rates:

$$r(0,1) = .08$$
$$r(0,2) = .085$$
$$r(0,3) = .09.$$

    a. $r(1,2)$

    b. $r(1,3)$

    c. $r(2,3)$

4. Find the price of a 9 percent coupon bond with annual coupons, a three-year maturity, $1,000 face value, and a yield of 8.94 percent.

5. Verify that if the price of the bond in problem 4 is $898, the yield is 13.35 percent.

6. On July 2, 1990, a Treasury bond maturing on August 15, 1992, had a coupon of 7 1/4 percent, payable semiannually, a yield of 8.22 percent, and an ask price of 98 5/32. Find the actual price you would pay for the bond.

7. Find the price and duration of a bond with a coupon of 12 percent, payable annually, a yield of 14 percent, a face value of $1,000, and a maturity of five years. Use both formulas to calculate duration.

8. Consider two bonds with 10 percent coupons, paid annually, and 10 percent yields. One bond has a maturity of 8 years and the other a maturity of 12 years. Show that the 12-year bond is more volatile for a given yield change.

9. Consider two bonds each with an eight-year maturity and a 10 percent yield. One bond has an 8 percent coupon and the other a 10 percent coupon. Show that the 8 percent coupon bond is more volatile for a given yield change. Both bonds pay coupons annually.

10. On March 15, the spot discount rate on 91-day T-bills is 8.48. This rate is based on a 360-day year. The following rates are discount rates on that day for the 90-day T-bill futures contracts expiring on the dates indicated. Derive the futures yield curve.

Contract	Rate	Expiration
June	9.22	June 20
September	9.74	September 19
December	10.06	December 19

11. Consider a stock that is expected to pay a dividend in one year of $4. The dividend is expected to grow at a 10 percent rate each year forever. If investors require a return of 18 percent, what is an appropriate price for the stock?

12. If the stock price in problem 11 is $65, what is the expected rate of return it offers? What action is suggested?

13. Carefully explain the distinction between systematic and unsystematic risk. Then identify whether each of the following is a source of systematic or unsystematic risk:

   a. A strike by employees of a firm whose stock you own

   b. A change in the Federal Reserve discount rate

   c. A major recall of a product owned by a firm whose stock you do not own (however, you do own a competitor's stock)

14. Write out the equation for the Capital Asset Pricing Model. Explain what each term means. Then discuss why investors earn returns only for assuming systematic risk.

15. The following prices for MMM stock and the S&P 500 index are given at weekly intervals at the dates indicated. Estimate the beta for MMM.

Date	MMM	S&P 500
3/7	81.25	336.95
3/14	81.625	336.87
3/21	84.250	339.74
3/28	83.625	342.00
4/4	81.500	341.09
4/11	82.250	341.92
4/18	82.500	340.72
4/25	79.750	332.03
5/2	79.000	334.48
5/9	81.875	342.86
5/16	83.625	354.00
5/23	82.750	359.29
5/30	82.625	360.86

16. Suppose you are interested in constructing market indices using three component stocks. The index is begun on day 1 and computed every day thereafter. The data for day 1 and day 2 are as follows:

Stock	Day 1		Day 2	
	Number of Shares	Price	Number of Shares	Price
X	100	$21.50	100	$22.00
Y	225	11.00	225	12.75
Z	80	32.00	240	11.00

a. Construct an index like the Major Market Index, and determine its value on day 1 and day 2.

b. Construct an index like the S&P 500, and determine its value on day 2 assuming a base value of 100 on day 1.

17. Consider a stock priced at $80. An investor plans to buy the stock and hold it for one year. During that time, the investor will forgo $4 of interest on the money invested. There are no storage costs involved in holding the stock.

Determine the expected future stock price under the conditions described in parts a, b, and c. Then answer part d.

a.   The investor lives in a world of certainty.

b.   The investor lives in a world of uncertainty but is considered risk neutral.

c.   The investor lives in a world of certainty but is considered risk averse. The expected risk premium for holding this stock for one year is deemed to be $12.

d.   Now suppose the investor determines that the expected return on the market is .22. If the CAPM describes expected returns, determine the beta of the stock.

18. Explain how storage costs enter into the determination of the current spot price and expected return. How is your answer affected if the asset is perishable?

19. (Concept Problem) In the text and in problem 17, we determined the expected future spot price based on the current spot price plus other parameters. Why, in reality, is this perhaps like putting the chicken before the egg?

References

Bierwag, Gerald O. *Duration Analysis*. Cambridge, Mass.: Ballinger, 1987.

Bodie, Zvi, Alex Kane, and Alan J. Marcus. *Investments*, Chapters 8–9, 14–16. Homewood, Ill.: Irwin, 1989.

Brooks, Robert, and Miles Livingston. "A Closed-Form Equation for Bond Convexity." *Financial Analysts Journal* 45 (November–December 1989): 78–79.

Caks, John, William R. Lane, Robert W. Greenleaf, and Reginald G. Joules. "A Simple Formula for Duration." *The Journal of Financial Research* 8 (Fall 1985): 245–249.

Chicago Board of Trade. "Understanding Duration and Convexity." Chicago: Chicago Board of Trade, 1989.

Evans, John, and Stephen H. Archer. "Diversification and the Reduction of Dispersion: An Empirical Analysis." *The Journal of Finance* 23 (December 1968): 761–767.

Fabozzi, Frank, and Irving M. Pollack, eds. *The Handbook of Fixed Income Securities*, 2d ed., Chapters 1, 4, 5, 30, 31, 32, 53. Homewood, Ill.: Dow Jones–Irwin, 1987.

Figlewski, Stephen. *Hedging with Financial Futures for Institutional Investors*, Chapter 1. Cambridge, Mass.: Ballinger, 1986.

Garbade, Kenneth D. *Securities Markets*, Chapters 12, 14. New York: McGraw-Hill, 1984.

Homer, Sydney, and Martin L. Leibowitz, Jr. *Inside the Yield Book*, Chapters 1–5, 8–13. New York: Prentice-Hall and the New York Institute of Finance, 1971.

Kolb, Robert W. *Interest Rate Futures: A Comprehensive Introduction*, Chapter 2. Richmond, Va.: R. F. Dame, 1982.

Lintner, John. "The Valuation of Risk Assets and the Selection of Risky Investments in Stock Portfolios and Capital Budgets." *Review of Economics and Statistics* 47 (February 1965): 13–37.

Livingston, Miles. *Money and Capital Markets: Financial Instruments and Their Uses*, Chapters 8, 9. Englewood Cliffs, N.J.: Prentice-Hall, 1990.

Mossin, Jan. "Equilibrium in a Capital Asset Market." *Econometrica* 34 (October 1966): 768–783.

Roll, Richard, and Stephen A. Ross. "The Arbitrage Pricing Theory Approach to Strategic Portfolio Planning." *Financial Analysts Journal* 40 (May–June 1984): 14–26.

Rothstein, Nancy H., ed. *The Handbook of Financial Futures*, Chapter 15. New York: McGraw-Hill, 1984.

Schwarz, Edward W., Joanne M. Hill, and Thomas Schneeweis. *Financial Futures: Fundamentals, Strategies, and Applications*, Chapter 5. Homewood, Ill.: Irwin, 1986.

Sharpe, William F., and Gordon J. Alexander. *Investments*, 4th ed., Chapters 12–16. Englewood Cliffs, N.J.: Prentice-Hall, 1990.

Sharpe, William F. "Capital Asset Prices: A Theory of Market Equilibrium under Conditions of Risk." *The Journal of Finance* 19 (September 1964): 425–442.

Van Horne, James C. *Capital Market Rates and Flows*, 3rd. ed., Chapters 5, 6. Englewood Cliffs, N.J.: Prentice-Hall, 1990.

Wagner, Wayne, and Sheila Lau. "The Effect of Diversification on Risk." *Financial Analysts Journal* 27 (November–December 1971): 48–53.

PRINCIPLES OF FUTURES PRICING II: FUTURES MARKET PRICING

> *The price of an article is charged according to difference in location, time or risk to which one is exposed in carrying it from one place to another or in causing it to be carried. Neither purchase nor sale according to this principle is unjust.*
>
> ST. THOMAS AQUINAS, c. 1264

In Chapter 8, we examined some basic principles of the pricing of the underlying spot market instruments. We saw how the term structure of interest rates determines bond prices and how dividends and discount rates affect the pricing of equities. The Capital Asset Pricing Model and the beta are fundamental determinants of the relationship between return and risk. Expectations of the future price, the opportunity cost of money, and the risk premium combine to produce the current price.

We can now move directly into the pricing of futures contracts. The very nature of the word *futures* suggests that futures prices concern expectations of prices in the future. In this chapter, we shall see how futures prices, spot prices, expectations, and the cost of carry are interrelated. As with options, our objective is to link the price of the futures contract to the price of the underlying instrument and to identify factors that influence the relationship between these prices.

In the early part of this chapter, we shall treat forward and futures contracts as though they were entirely separate instruments. Recall that a forward contract is an agreement between two parties to exchange an asset for a fixed price at a future date. No money changes hands, and the agreement is binding; it cannot be reversed

327

by selling the asset back in a market. A futures contract is also an agreement between two parties to exchange an asset for a fixed price at a future date. However, the agreement is made on a futures exchange and is regulated by that exchange. The contract requires that the parties make margin deposits, and their accounts are marked to market every day. The contracts are standardized and can be bought and sold during regular trading hours. These differences between forward and futures contracts, particularly the marking to market, create some differences in their prices and values. As we shall see later, these differences may prove quite minor; for now, we shall proceed as though the forward and futures contracts were entirely different instruments.

SOME PROPERTIES OF FORWARD AND FUTURES PRICES

The Concept of Price versus Value

In Chapter 1, we discussed how an efficient market means that the price of an asset equals its true economic value. The holder of an asset has money tied up in the asset. If the holder is willing to retain the asset, the asset must have a value at least equal to its price. If the asset's value were less than its price, the owner would sell it. The value is the present value of the future cash flows, with the discount rate reflecting the opportunity cost of money and a premium for the risk assumed.

While this line of reasoning is sound in securities markets, it can get one into trouble in futures markets. A futures contract is not an asset. You can buy a futures contract, but do you actually pay for it? Indeed there is a small margin deposit, but is this really the price? You can buy 100 shares of a $20 stock by placing $1,000 in a margin account and borrowing $1,000 from a broker. Does that make the stock worth $10 per share? Certainly not. The stock is worth $20 per share: You have $10 per share invested and $10 per share borrowed.

The margin requirement on a futures contract is not really a margin in the same sense as the margin on a stock. You might deposit 3 to 5 percent of the price of the futures contract in a margin account, but you do not borrow the remainder. The margin is only a type of security deposit. Thus, the buyer of a futures contract does not actually "pay" for it, and, of course, the seller really receives no money for it. As long as the price does not change, neither party can execute an offsetting trade that would generate a profit.

When dealing with futures contracts, we must be careful to distinguish between *price* and *value*. The futures price is an observable number. The value is less obvious. However, the contract's initial value is zero. This is because neither party pays anything and neither party receives anything of monetary value. That does not imply, however, that neither party will pay or receive money at a later date.

The value of a futures contract when written is zero.

We stated this point in reference to futures contracts. It is equally applicable to forward contracts. The values of futures and forward contracts during their lives, however, are not necessarily equal either to each other or to zero.

The value of a forward contract when written is zero.

The Value of a Forward Contract

AT EXPIRATION At expiration, the value of a forward contract is easily found. Ignoring delivery costs and multiple deliverable grades, the forward price, F_T, must equal the spot price, S_T. The value of a forward contract at expiration, V_T, is the profit on the forward contract, $F_T - F = S_T - F$.

PRIOR TO EXPIRATION To understand how a forward contract can have value during its life prior to expiration, let us introduce the following notation for forward contracts expiring at time T:

F = price of a forward contract written today

F_t = price at time t of a forward contract written at time t $(t < T)$

V_t = value at time t of a forward contract written today

V_T = value at time T (expiration) of a forward contract written today. This equals $S_T - F$, or $F_T - F$, since $F_T = S_T$.

Note that we have two distinct forward contracts—one written today with a price of F and one written at time t with a price of F_t. Both contracts expire at T. To keep these separate, let us call them the first and second forward contracts, respectively.

The value of the first forward contract when written is zero. The value of the second forward contract when written is also zero. We wish to know the value of the first forward contract at a point, t, during its life. This contract is not liquid, so it cannot be sold to someone else; however, it does have value. The first forward contract is an agreement to buy the commodity at time T at price F. Suppose we buy one of these. Then, at time t, we find that new forward contracts are being sold at a price of F_t. We then sell the second forward contract. At expiration, the profit is $S_T - F$ from the first contract and $-(S_T - F_t)$ from the second contract, for a total of $F_t - F$. This means the overall transaction guarantees that we can buy the commodity at expiration at price F and sell it at F_t, so we have a guaranteed payoff of $F_t - F$ waiting at expiration. Thus, the value of our position should equal the present value of $F_t - F$. The value of the position is the value of the first forward contract minus (because we are short) the value of the second forward contract, or

Value of position = V_t – value of second contract when written.

But because the second forward contract has just been written, it has a value of zero. Thus, the value of the position is simply the value of the first forward contract, V_t. Therefore,

$$V_t = (F_t - F)(1 + r)^{-(T-t)},$$

where r is the risk-free rate. Note that this is simply the present value of the difference in forward prices. This value can be positive or negative. While there may not be a liquid market for a forward contract, we see that it is possible to sell a

The value of a forward contract at expiration is the forward price at expiration minus the original forward price. This also equals the spot price at expiration minus the original forward price.

The value of a forward contract prior to expiration is the difference in the new forward price and the original forward price discounted at the risk-free rate over the remaining time to expiration.

new contract that offsets the original one and has essentially the same effect as selling the first contract.

A NUMERICAL EXAMPLE   Suppose you buy a forward contract today at a price of $100. The contract expires in 45 days. The risk-free rate is 10 percent. The forward contract is an agreement to buy the commodity at a price of $100 in 45 days. Now, 20 days later, new forward contracts expiring at the same time—in 25 days—are being written at a price of $104. The value of your forward contract is

$$(104 - 100)(1.10)^{-25/365} = 3.974.$$

Why is your contract worth $3.974? You cannot liquidate the contract, but you can sell a new forward contract at the new price of $104. When both contracts expire in 25 days, you will buy the commodity at $100 using your first contract and sell it at $104 using your second contract. Your total payoff will be $4. At 25 days before expiration, you know you will receive $4 at expiration. The present value of $4 at the risk-free rate is $3.974. To the seller, the first forward contract has a value at t of –$3.974.

The Value of a Futures Contract

We already noted that the value of a futures contract when originally written is zero. The value of a futures contract during its life is influenced by marking to market. Because futures contracts are marked to market daily, we shall arbitrarily let the time period from today to time t be one day and the time period from time t to time T be one day. Thus, the contract is marked to market at time t and expires at time T.

Now suppose you purchase a futures contract today, when the futures price is f. The next day, the price increases to f_t. At that point, the contract has a value of f_t – f. Why? You can liquidate the contract by selling it in the market and earn a profit of f_t – f. However, once the account is marked to market, the contract's value goes back to zero. When the price changes again, the contract has value. Note that a futures contract, like a forward contract, can have a negative value. If the price decreases, the contract has a negative value. When it is marked to market, the value goes back to zero.

A NUMERICAL EXAMPLE   Suppose that on December 9 you buy the March T-bond futures contract at the closing price of 82 17/32, which also turns out to be the settlement price. Since the contract is for $100,000 of par-value bonds, the contract price is $82,531.25. The value at the time the contract is purchased is zero.

The next day the opening price is 83, or $83,000. The value of the contract is now $83,000 – $82,531.25 = $468.75. You could sell the contract and net a profit of $468.75. Later in the day the price fluctuates, reaching a high of 83 16/32. At that point, the contract value is $83,500 – $82,531.25 = $968.75. At the end of the day, the settlement price is 83 10/32. The account is marked to market, and the profit is \$83,312.50 − \$82,531.25 = \$781.25, which is credited to your margin account. The value of the contract is now zero. The next day, the contract price fluctuates and the contract takes on a positive or negative value based on the difference between the current price and the previous day's settlement price of 83 10/32.

Forward versus Futures Prices

At expiration, forward and futures prices equal the spot price. Are they equal at any other time? Do forward and futures contracts accomplish the same result? In this section we shall see. We shall examine two cases: (1) one day prior to expiration (time t) and (2) two days prior to expiration.

ONE DAY PRIOR TO EXPIRATION   Consider the following strategy: Buy a forward contract at price F_t, and sell a futures contract of the same size at price f_t. Both contracts expire in one day. This transaction costs no money. What will happen at expiration?

Using the forward contract, you buy the commodity at a price of F_t. You then deliver the commodity in fulfillment of your futures contract, receiving f_t for it. Your margin account is liquidated and contains the amount $-(f_T - f_t)$. Your total profit thus is $- F_t + f_T - (f_T - f_t) = f_t - F_t$. This means that you effectively bought the commodity at price F_t and sold it at f_t. Your profit of $f_t - F_t$ is known at time t, one day prior to expiration.

Remember that since it costs no money to trade the forward and futures contracts, the profit at expiration must be zero. The only way for this to occur is for the forward price to equal the futures price.

What happens if the futures price exceeds the forward price? The profit at expiration will be positive. Because this profit is certain and requires no initial outlay, arbitrageurs will enter the market and buy forward contracts and sell futures contracts. This will drive the forward price up and the futures price down until they are equal.

If the forward price exceeds the futures price, a portfolio consisting of a long futures contract and a short forward contract will produce a sure profit at expiration of $F_t - f_t$, which is positive. Then arbitrageurs will buy futures contracts and sell forward contracts, which will drive forward prices down and futures prices up until they are equal.

Now let us back up one more day.

Forward and futures prices are equal one day prior to expiration.

TWO DAYS PRIOR TO EXPIRATION   Now we are forced to make an important assumption: The interest rate on both days is r; that is, r does not change.[1] The futures price is f, and the forward price is F.

Consider the following transaction: Buy one forward contract, and sell $(1 + r)^{-(T-t)}$ futures contracts. The time interval is one day, so $-(T-t)$ will be $-1/365$.

---

[1]Technically, the interest rate can change as long as we know what it will change to.

Now move forward one day to time t. The futures price is f_t, and the futures account is marked to market. Remember that we are short $(1 + r)^{-1/365}$ futures contracts, so the profit is $-(1 + r)^{-1/365}(f_t - f)$. This amount could be either positive or negative. If it is positive, we invest it in risk-free bonds. If it is negative, we borrow money at the risk-free rate and use it to replenish the margin account. Now we close the futures position and sell one new futures contract.

One day later, when the contracts expire, we buy the commodity at the forward contract price of F. We deliver it in fulfillment of the new futures contract and effectively receive a price of f_t. We also have the profit from the first futures contract of $-(1 + r)^{-1/365}(f_t - f)$ carried over for one day with an interest factor of $(1 + r)^{1/365}$. This equals $-(1 + r)^{-1/365}(f_t - f)(1 + r)^{1/365} = -(f_t - f)$. Thus, the total amount of cash we shall have is $(f_t - F) - (f_t - f) = f - F$.

This is the difference in the original forward and futures prices. Because this amount is certain and the transactions require no initial outlay, it must generate a zero profit. Thus, the futures price, f, must equal the forward price, F. It should be apparent that this argument can be extended farther back in time.

If the futures price exceeds the forward price, the transaction will generate a positive profit at expiration. Because no initial outlay is required, arbitrageurs will sell futures contracts and buy forward contracts and earn a profit of $f - F$. This will put upward pressure on forward prices and downward pressure on futures prices until they are driven together.

If the forward price exceeds the futures price, the transaction should be reversed: Arbitrageurs will sell forward contracts and buy futures contracts and will earn a profit of $F - f$ until the prices are driven together.

If the interest rate does not change, the forward price will equal the futures price at any time prior to expiration.

A NUMERICAL EXAMPLE   Consider a September S&P 500 futures contract. On September 18, two days prior to expiration, the contract was priced at 332.15. There are no forward markets for the S&P 500, but assume one can buy a forward contract at 330. Thus, the futures price exceeds the forward price by 2.15. The interest rate is 8 percent and will not change for two days. An arbitrageur would observe that the futures price is too high and/or the forward price too low. Suppose the arbitrageur has sufficient capital to undertake a transaction of 10,000 forward contracts. Thus, the arbitrageur will attempt to capture a risk-free profit of $10,000(\$2.15) = \$21,500$ by selling futures contracts and buying forward contracts. The number of futures contracts is $10,000 \times (1.08)^{-1/365} = 9,998$, and the number of forward contracts is 10,000.

The next day, the futures price is 333.25. The arbitrageur has incurred a loss on the futures contracts of $9,998(333.25 - 332.15) = 10,998$. The loss must be made up, so the arbitrageur borrows \$10,998 for one day at 8 percent. The futures contracts are closed out, and a new position of 10,000 short futures is opened.

At expiration, the loan is due and the arbitrageur owes $10,998(1.08)^{1/365} = 11,000$. Let the S&P spot index be 334 on the expiration day. To keep things simple we will assume the S&P forward contract is cash settled, so the arbitrageur settles the forward contract by receiving a payment equal to the spot price at expiration minus the original forward price times the number of contracts, or $10,000(334 - 330) = 40,000$. The futures is settled in cash, so the arbitrageur makes a payment of $10,000(334 - 333.25) = 7,500$. Thus, the net cash flow to the arbitrageur on the expiration day is $-11,000 + 40,000 - 7,500 = 21,500$. This is the original amount the arbitrageur set out to capture with this riskless hedge. The combined effects of numerous arbitrageurs buying forward contracts and selling futures contracts will drive the forward and futures prices together.

WHY FORWARD AND FUTURES PRICES MAY NOT BE EQUAL   Once again we see that forward and futures prices should be equal. Our key assumption is that the interest rate was constant. Note that we sold $(1 + r)^{-1/365}$ futures contracts for every forward contract. If $f_t > f$, we covered the loss by borrowing additional funds. The amount of interest paid on the loan was completely offset by the fact that we had only $(1 + r)^{-1/365}$ contracts for every forward contract. We borrowed $(1 + r)^{-1/365}$ $(f_t - f)$ times the number of forward contracts and the next day paid back $(1 + r)^{-1/365}$ $(f_t - f)(1 + r)^{1/365} = (f_t - f)$ times the number of forward contracts. If $f_t < f$, the interest earned on the reinvested profit was offset by having only $(1 + r)^{-1/365}$ futures contracts for every forward contract.

When short-term interest rates are known in advance, forward prices will equal futures prices. When short-term interest rates are uncertain, arbitrageurs will not know how many futures contracts to trade to ensure a risk-free profit. Then futures and forward prices may differ. With a little intuition, we can see which would be greater.

Suppose the futures price increases over the contract's life. Then holders of long futures contracts will receive positive cash flows from marking to market. If during the same time interest rates increase, the daily reinvestment of the profits will earn more interest. If futures prices decrease, the holder of a long position will incur losses. If those losses occur during a period of falling interest rates, they can be covered by borrowing at increasingly lower rates. Thus, if interest rates and futures prices are positively correlated, futures contracts will offer an advantage over forward contracts and will be priced higher.

If futures prices and interest rates move in opposite directions, profits from rising futures prices will be reinvested in a falling interest rate environment. Losses from falling futures prices will be covered by borrowing in a rising interest rate environment. This will create a preference for forward contracts and will cause forward prices to exceed futures prices.

Futures prices will exceed forward prices when futures prices and interest rates are positively correlated. Forward prices will exceed futures prices when futures prices and interest rates are negatively correlated.

A COMPARISON OF FORWARD AND FUTURES PRICES   Are forward and futures prices equal? Let us examine some forward and futures prices of Treasury bills.

On January 6, the spot price of a Treasury bill expiring on March 20 is quoted at a discount of 7.01. From Chapter 3, we know the price is calculated as

$$100 - 7.01(73/360) = 98.5785,$$

which reflects the fact that 73 days remain until expiration. The annualized yield is

$$(100/98.5785)^{365/73} - 1 = .0742.$$

The T-bill maturing on June 19, 164 days from now, has a discount of 7.09. Its price is

$$100 - 7.09(164/360) = 96.7701,$$

which implies a yield of

$$(100/96.7701)^{365/164} - 1 = .0758.$$

We can now derive a forward rate for the period of March 20 to June 19, which is 91 days. The forward rate is derived as

$$(1.0758)^{164/365} = (1.0742)^{73/365}[1 + r(73,164)]^{91/365}.$$

This statement says that the return for a 164-day investment equals the returns from a 73-day investment followed by a 91-day investment at the rate $r(73,164)$. Solving this equation for $r(73,164)$ gives 7.71 percent, the implied forward rate. The forward price is the value of F in the equation

$$(100/F)^{365/91} - 1 = .0771.$$

Solving for F gives 98.1653. The forward price of a 91-day bill of 98.1653 gives an implied forward rate of 7.71 percent.

On the same day, the price of the March futures contract is 98.2659. In this instance, the futures price was higher than the forward price. Figure 9.1 shows the forward and futures prices over the next ten weeks. With the exception of one week, the futures price is above the forward price.

It is interesting that this result contrasts with our earlier statement. Since Treasury bill spot, forward, and futures prices should be inversely correlated with interest rates, we should observe futures prices that are lower than forward prices. Obviously, there must be some other factors not explained by the model. For example, some people argue that futures contracts have a lower risk of default than forward contracts, a result of the role of the clearinghouse and of marking to market.[2] Others have noted that the market for forward contracts is less liquid than that for futures contracts. These factors would create a greater demand for futures contracts. Still others would say that the difference between futures and forward prices is not economically significant. In fact, that is the general conclusion in studies conducted by Rendleman and Carabini (1979) and Elton, Gruber, and Rentzler (1984). Although some unexplained differentials do exist, they are not consistent, and we will benefit greatly from assuming that forward and futures prices are essentially equal.

We have now established some important principles of futures pricing. In the next section, we develop a futures pricing model.

---

[2]See Kane (1980).

FIGURE 9.1
Forward and Futures Prices: March and June Treasury Bills

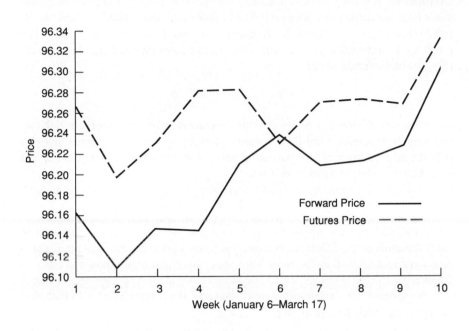

THE FORMATION OF FUTURES PRICES

In this section, we shall look more closely at how futures prices are influenced by the cost of carry, dividends or other cash flows, and the risk premium on the underlying instrument. As we already have seen, forward and futures prices may not be equal. However, in this section we shall disregard the marking to market effect and thus treat futures contracts as though they were forward contracts. In addition, we will assume spot and futures prices are equal at expiration and the margin requirement is zero. Finally, we shall recall from Chapter 8 the relationship between today's spot price and the expected future spot price,

$$S = E(S_T) - \theta - E(\phi),$$

where θ is the cost of carry and equals the storage cost (s) plus the opportunity cost of money (i) and $E(\phi)$ is the expected risk premium, the reward for assuming risk. First let us look at the role the cost of carry plays.

The Cost of Carry

Consider the following transaction: Buy the spot commodity at a price of S, and sell a futures contract at a price of f. At expiration, the spot price is S_T and the futures price is f_T, which equals S_T. At expiration, you deliver the commodity. The profit on the transaction is f – S minus the storage costs incurred and the opportunity cost of the funds tied up:

$$\Pi = f - S - s - i = f - S - \theta.$$

Since the expression f – S involves no unknown terms, the profit is riskless, meaning the transaction should not generate a risk premium. The amount invested is S, the original price of the spot commodity.[3] The profit from the transaction is f – S – θ, which should equal zero. Thus,

$$f = S + \theta.$$

In equilibrium, the futures price equals the spot price plus the cost of carry.

Thus, the futures price equals the spot price plus the cost of carry. The cost of carry therefore is the difference between the futures price and the spot price and is sometimes referred to as the basis.[4] We shall say much more about the basis in Chapter 10.

What makes this relationship hold? Assume the futures price is higher than the spot price plus the cost of carry:

$$f > S + \theta.$$

Arbitrageurs will then buy the spot commodity and sell the futures contract. This will generate a positive profit equal to f – S – θ. Many arbitrageurs will execute the same transaction, which will put downward pressure on the futures price. When f = S + θ, the opportunity to earn this profit will be gone.

Now suppose the futures price is less than the spot price plus the cost of carry; that is,

$$f < S + \theta.$$

First, let us assume the commodity is a financial instrument. Then arbitrageurs will sell short the commodity and buy the futures. When the instrument is sold short, the short seller will not incur the storage costs. Instead of incurring the opportunity cost of funds tied up in the commodity, the short seller can earn interest on the funds received from the short sale.

Thus, the cost of carry is not paid but received. The profit thus is S + θ – f, which is positive. The combined actions of arbitrageurs will put downward pressure on

---

[3]Remember that futures contracts do not require an initial outlay.

[4]The basis usually is defined as the spot price minus the futures price, and we shall use this definition in Chapter 10.

the spot price and upward pressure on the futures price until the profit is eradicated. At that point, $f = S + \theta$.

Short selling actually is not necessary for inducing the arbitrage activity. Consider an investor who holds the commodity unhedged. That person could sell the commodity and buy a futures contract. While the commodity is not owned, the arbitrageur avoids the storage costs and earns interest on the funds received from its sale. At expiration, the arbitrageur takes delivery and again owns the commodity unhedged. The profit from the transaction is $S + \theta - f$, which is positive. Thus, the transaction temporarily removes the commodity from the investor's assets, earns a risk-free profit, and then replaces the commodity into the investor's assets. Because many arbitrageurs will do this, it will force the spot price down and the futures price up until no further opportunities exist.

There has been some confusion even among experts over whether futures prices reflect expectations about future spot prices. Some have said that futures prices provide expectations abut future spot prices, while others have argued that futures prices reflect only the cost of carry. Still others have said that part of the time futures reveal expectations and part of the time they reveal the cost of carry. We shall more fully address the issue of whether futures prices reveal expectations in a later section; here we should note that both positions are correct. Because the futures price equals the spot price plus the cost of carry, the futures price definitely reflects the cost of carry. The spot price, however, reflects expectations. This is a fundamental tenet of spot pricing that we examined in Chapter 8. Because the futures price will include the spot price, it too reflects expectations; however, it does so indirectly through the spot price.

For storable commodities, as well as for securities that do not pay interest or dividends, the cost of carry normally is positive. This would cause the futures price to lie above the current spot price. A market of this type is referred to as a *contango*.

Table 9.1 presents some spot and futures prices from a contango market. The example is for cotton traded on the New York Cotton Exchange. The cost of carry implied for the October contract is $41.60 - 36.75 = 4.85$. Remember that this figure includes the interest forgone on the investment of 36.75¢ for a pound of cotton and the actual physical costs of storing the cotton from late September until the contract's expiration in October.

It would be convenient if fact always conformed to theory. If that were the case, we would never observe the spot price in excess of the futures price. In reality, spot prices sometimes exceed futures prices. A possible explanation is the *convenience yield*.

The Convenience Yield

We are seeking an explanation for the case in which the futures price is less than the spot price. If $f = S + \theta$ and $f < S$, then $\theta < 0$. What type of market condition might produce a negative cost of carry?

Suppose the commodity is in short supply; current consumption is unusually high relative to supplies of the good. This is producing an abnormally high spot

TABLE 9.1

A Contango Market: Cotton, September 26 (NYCE)

Expiration	Settlement Price (Cents per Pound)
Spot	36.75
October	41.60
December	42.05
March	42.77
May	43.50
July	43.80
October	45.20
December	45.85

price. The current tight market conditions discourage individuals from storing the commodity. If the situation is severe enough, the current spot price could be above the expected future spot price. If the spot price is sufficiently high, the futures price may lie below it. The relationship between the futures price and the spot price is then given as

$$f = S + \theta - \chi,$$

where χ is simply a positive value that accounts for the difference between f and S + θ. If χ is sufficiently large, the futures price will lie below the spot price. This need not be the case, however, since χ can be small.

The value χ often is referred to as the *convenience yield*. It is the premium earned by those who hold inventories of a commodity that is in short supply. By holding inventories of a good in short supply, one earns an additional return, the convenience yield. Note that we are not saying that the commodity is stored for future sale or consumption. Indeed, when the spot price is sufficiently high, the return from storage is negative. There is no incentive to store the good. In fact, there is an incentive to borrow as much of the good as possible and sell short.

When the commodity has a convenience yield, the futures price will be less than the spot price plus the cost of carry. In that case, the futures is said to be at *less than full carry*.

A market in which the futures price lies below the current spot price is referred to as *backwardation* or sometimes an inverted market. An example of a backwardation market is presented in Table 9.2. Notice that the March Treasury bill futures price (as well as the remaining futures prices) lies below the spot price. When we were studying the term structure, we might have explained this by appealing to the expectations theory. Under this explanation, the market is forecasting lower future spot prices. This conclusion is entirely consistent with what we have learned in this section. The futures prices imply that either demand for Treasury bills is expected to decrease or the supply to increase in the future. Backwardation

TABLE 9.2

A Backwardation Market: Treasury Bills, February 28 (IMM)

Expiration	Price
Spot	91.50
March	91.42
June	90.80
September	90.30
December	89.94
March	89.67
June	89.47
September	89.30
December	89.14

in the financial futures markets is the market's way of stating that future interest rates are expected to be higher. In addition, there may be a liquidity premium that keeps long-term rates higher. This, of course, is what we see with an upward-sloping yield curve. Backwardation in commodities markets is nearly always due to expectations of a good harvest and/or decreased demand.

It is not uncommon to see characteristics of both backwardation and contango in the same commodity at the same time. Table 9.3 illustrates this case with soybeans. The spot price is lower than the November futures price, and each succeeding futures price through the July expiration is a little higher. The August futures price is lower than the July futures price, and the September futures price is lower than the August futures price. Then the November price is higher. Up through July, the futures price is dominated by the cost of carry. Starting with the August contract, the market reflects the fact that the August harvest will drive down the spot price. This will continue through September. Once the harvest date has passed, the cost of carry will again be the primary determinant of the futures price.

The cost of carry model has been tested extensively, particularly in the Treasury bill futures markets. Vignola and Dale (1980), Rendleman and Carabini (1979), and Elton, Gruber, and Rentzler (1984) discovered a surprising number of cases in which arbitrage profits were possible. However, it would be difficult for most investors to exploit these situations. Thus, for the most part the model is reasonably accurate in pricing T-bill futures. Similar conclusions for Treasury bond futures can be drawn from Resnick (1984) and Resnick and Hennigar (1983).

With these concepts in mind, we now turn to an important and highly controversial issue in futures markets: Do futures prices contain a risk premium?

TABLE 9.3

Backwardation and Contango: Soybeans, September 26 (CBOT)

Expiration	Price (Cents per Bushel)
Spot	473
November	481 3/4
January	489 3/4
March	498 1/4
May	505 1/4
July	508 1/4
August	507 3/4
September	503
November	505 1/2

Futures Prices and Risk Premia

We already discussed the concept of a risk premium in spot prices. No one would hold the spot commodity unless a risk premium were expected. Although investors do not always earn a risk premium, they must do so on average. Is there a risk premium in futures prices? Are speculators in futures contracts rewarded, on average, with a risk premium? There are two schools of thought on the subject.

THE NO-RISK-PREMIUM HYPOTHESIS   Consider a simple futures market in which there are only speculators. The underlying commodity is the total number of points scored by all National Football League teams in a given week. Each contract trades every day for a week. On Tuesday morning, the contracts are cash settled. During the week, individuals can buy or sell contracts at whatever price they agree on.

For example, suppose two individuals make a contract at a price of 380. If the total number of points is above 380 at expiration, the trader holding the short position pays the holder of the long position a sum equal to the total number of points minus 380. Because no one can "hold" the commodity, there is no hedging or arbitrage.

Now suppose that after a period of several weeks, it is obvious that the longs are consistently beating the shorts. The shorts conclude that it is a very good year for the offense. Determined to improve their lot, those individuals who have been going short begin to go long. Of course, those who have been going long have no desire to go short. Now everyone wants to go long, and no one will go short. This drives up the futures price to a level at which someone finds it so high that it looks good to go short. Now suppose the price has been driven up so high that the opposite occurs: The shorts begin to consistently beat the longs. This causes the longs to turn around and go short. Ultimately an equilibrium must be reached in which neither the longs nor the shorts consistently beat the other side. In such a market, there is no risk premium. Neither side wins at the expense of the other.

In futures markets, this argument has been advanced by Telser (1958) and Gray (1961). They contend that on average the futures price today equals the expected price of the futures contract at expiration; that is, $f = E(f_T)$. Because the expected futures price at expiration equals the expected spot price at expiration, $E(f_T) = E(S_T)$, we obtain the following result:

$$f = E(S_T).$$

This is an extremely important and powerful statement. It says that *the futures price is the market's expectation of the future spot price*. If one wishes to obtain a forecast of the future spot price, one need only observe the futures price. In the language of economists, *futures prices are unbiased expectations of future spot prices*.

As an example, on September 26 of a particular year the spot price of silver was $5.58 per troy ounce. The December futures price was $5.64 per troy ounce. If futures prices contain no risk premium, the market is forecasting that the spot price of silver in December will be $5.64. Futures traders who buy the contract at $5.64 expect to sell it at $5.64.

Figure 9.2 illustrates a situation that is reasonably consistent with this view. The May wheat futures contract is shown along with the spot price for a period of 20 weeks prior to expiration. Both prices fluctuate, and the spot price exhibits a small risk premium as evidenced by the slight upward trend. The futures price, however, follows no apparent trend.

We must caution, of course, that this is just an isolated case. The question of whether futures prices contain a risk premium must be answered by empirical studies. First, however, let us turn to the arguments supporting the view that futures prices do contain a risk premium.

THE RISK PREMIUM HYPOTHESIS   If a risk premium were observed, we would see that

$$E(f_T) > f.$$

The futures price would be expected to increase. Buyers of futures contracts at price f would expect to sell them at $E(f_t)$. Since we assume that futures and spot prices converge at expiration, $E(f_T) = E(S_T)$,

$$E(f_T) = E(S_T) > f.$$

From this we conclude that the futures price is a low estimate of the expected future spot price.

Consider a contango market in which the cost of carry is positive. Holders of the commodity expect to earn a risk premium, $E(\phi)$, given by the following formula from Chapter 8:

$$E(S_T) = S + \theta + E(\phi),$$

FIGURE 9.2

No Risk Premium: May Wheat

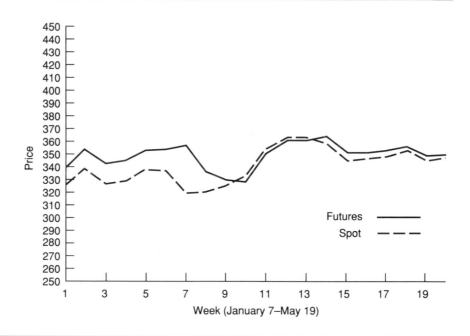

where θ is the cost of carry and $E(\phi)$ is the risk premium. Because $f = S + \theta$, then $S = f - \theta$. Substituting for S in the formula for $E(S_T)$, we get

$$E(S_T) = f - \theta + \theta + E(\phi),$$

or simply

$$E(S_T) = f + E(\phi) = E(f_T).$$

The expected futures price at expiration is higher than the current futures price by the amount of the risk premium. This means that buyers of futures contracts expect to earn a risk premium. However, they do not earn a risk premium because the futures contract is risky. They earn the risk premium that existed in the spot market; it was merely transferred to the futures market.

Now consider the silver example in the previous section. The spot price is $5.58, and the December futures price is $5.64. The interest lost on $5.58 for two months is about $.05. Let us assume that the cost of storing silver for two months is $.01. Let us also suppose that buyers of silver expect to earn a $.02 risk premium. Thus, the variables are

$$S = 5.58$$
$$f = 5.64$$

$$\theta = .05 + .01 = .06$$
$$E(\phi) = .02.$$

The expected spot price of silver in December is

$$E(S_T) = S + \theta + E(\phi) = 5.58 + .06 + .02 = 5.66.$$

Because the expected spot price of silver in December equals the expected futures price in December, $E(f_T) = 5.66$. This can also be found as

$$E(f_T) = f + E(\phi) = 5.64 + .02 = 5.66.$$

Futures traders who buy the contract at 5.64 expect to sell it at 5.66 and earn a risk premium of .02. The futures price of 5.64 is an understatement of the expected spot price in December by the amount of the risk premium.

The process is illustrated as follows:

Spot:		Store and	Expected	Expected
	Buy silver	incur costs	risk premium	selling price
	$5.58	+ $0.06	+ $0.02	= $5.66
Futures:	Buy silver		Expected	Expected
	futures		risk premium	selling price
	$5.64		+ $0.02	= $5.66

The idea that futures prices contain a risk premium was proposed by two famous economists, Keynes (1930) and Hicks (1939). They argued that futures and spot markets are dominated by individuals who hold long positions in the underlying commodities. These individuals desire the protection afforded by selling futures contracts. That means they need traders who are willing to take long positions in futures. To induce speculators to take long positions in futures, the futures price must be below the expected price of the contract at expiration, which is the expected future spot price. Therefore, Keynes and Hicks argued, *futures prices are biased expectations of future spot prices*, with the bias attributable to the risk premium. The risk premium in futures prices exists only because it is transferred from the spot market.

An example of such a case is shown in Figure 9.3, which illustrates a September S&P 500 futures contract. Both the spot and futures prices exhibit an upward trend. Again, however, we must caution that this is only an isolated case.

How can we explain the existence of a risk premium when we argued earlier that neither longs nor shorts would consistently win at the expense of the other side? The major difference in the two examples is the nature of the spot market. In the first example, in which the futures contract was on the point total of NFL teams, there was no opportunity to take a "position" in the spot market. In fact, there was no spot market; futures traders were simply competing with one another. When we allow for a spot market, we introduce individuals who hold speculative long positions in commodities. If the positions are unhedged, these individuals

FIGURE 9.3
Risk Premium: September S&P 500

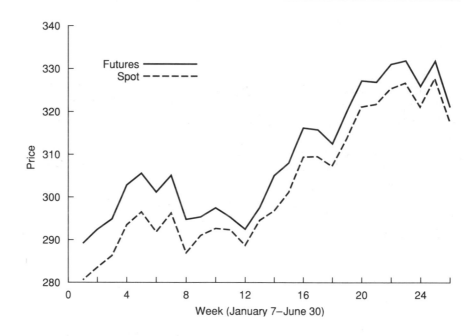

expect to earn a risk premium. If they are unwilling to accept the risk, they sell futures contracts. They are, in effect, purchasing insurance from the futures traders, and in so doing they transfer the risk and the risk premium to the futures markets.

What about situations in which the hedgers buy futures? This would occur if hedgers were predominantly short the commodity. This would drive up futures prices, and futures prices would, on average, exhibit a downward trend as contracts approached expiration. Futures prices would overestimate future spot prices. Speculators who sold futures would earn a risk premium.

A market in which the futures price is below the expected future spot price is called *normal backwardation*, and one in which the futures price is above the expected future spot price is called *normal contango*. The choice of names for these markets is a bit confusing, and they must be distinguished from simply contango and backwardation:

$$\text{Contango: } S < f$$
$$\text{Backwardation: } f < S$$
$$\text{Normal contango: } E(S_T) < f$$
$$\text{Normal backwardation: } f < E(S_T)$$

Because the spot price can lie below the futures price, which in turn can lie below the expected future spot price, we can have contango and normal backwardation simultaneously; indeed, this is the more typical occurrence. We can also have backwardation and normal contango simultaneously, although this is less likely.

Which view on the existence of a risk premium is correct? Since there is almost certainly a risk premium in spot prices, the existence of hedgers who hold spot positions means that the risk premium is transferred to futures traders. Thus, there would seem to be a risk premium in futures prices. However, if there are not enough spot positions being hedged or if most hedging is being done by investors who are short in the spot market, there may be no observable risk premium in futures prices. Early studies by Telser (1958) and Gray (1961) in cotton, wheat, and corn futures markets found no support for the existence of a risk premium. Dusak (1973) corroborated these findings in a study of wheat, corn, and soybean markets. However, Chang (1985) tested the same wheat, corn, and soybean markets and found significant risk premia. Breeden (1980) and Carter, Rausser, and Schmitz (1983) also found substantial risk premia. Such conflicting findings have been common in research and suggest that the issue is still unresolved.

The Effect of Intermediate Cash Flows

Until now we have avoided any consideration of how intermediate cash flows, such as interest and dividends, affect the futures price. We did note in Chapter 8 that these cash payments would have an effect on the cost of carry, possibly making it negative. Now we shall look more closely at how they affect futures prices.

The contracts in which these factors apply are stock and bond futures. We shall concentrate on stock index futures, although the general principles are the same in both cases.

For simplicity, assume there is only one stock in the index, which pays a sure dividend of D_T on the expiration date. Now suppose an investor buys the stock at a spot price of S and sells a futures contract at a price of f.

At expiration, the stock is sold at S_T, the dividend D_T is collected, and the futures contract generates a cash flow of $-(f_T - f)$, which equals $-(S_T - f)$. Thus, the total cash flow at expiration is $D_T + f$. This amount is known in advance; therefore, the current value of the portfolio must equal the present value of $D_T + f$. The current portfolio value is simply the amount paid for the stock, S. Putting these results together gives

$$S = (f + D_T)(1 + r)^{-T}$$

or

$$f = S(1 + r)^T - D_T.$$

Here we see that the futures price is the spot price compounded at the risk-free rate minus the dividend.

To take our model one step closer to reality, let us assume the stock pays several dividends. In fact, our stock could actually be a portfolio of stocks that is identical to an index such as the S&P 500. Suppose N dividends will be paid during the life of the futures. Each dividend is denoted as D_t and is paid t years from today. Now suppose we buy the stock and sell the futures. During the life of the futures, we collect each dividend and reinvest it in risk-free bonds earning the rate r. Thus, dividend D_t will grow to a value of $D_t(1 + r)^{(T-t)}$ at expiration. At expiration the stock is sold for S_T, and the futures is settled and generates a cash flow of $-(f_T - f)$, which equals $-(S_T - f)$. Thus, the total cash flow at expiration is

$$S_T - (S_T - f) + \sum_{t=1}^{N} D_t (1+r)^{(T-t)}$$

or

$$f + \sum_{t=1}^{N} D_t (1+r)^{(T-t)}.$$

This amount is also known in advance, so its present value, discounted at the risk-free rate, must equal the current value of the portfolio, which is the value of the stock, S. Setting these terms equal and solving for f gives

$$f = S(1+r)^T - \sum_{t=1}^{N} D_t (1+r)^{(T-t)}.$$

Thus, the futures price is the spot compounded at the risk-free rate minus the compound future value of the dividends. In the first pricing equation we developed, the lone dividend did not need to be compounded because we assumed it was paid at the expiration.

It might appear that our futures pricing model is inconsistent with the cost of carry equation we previously developed, in which $f = S + \theta$. We can show, however, that the formulas are identical and that the cost of carry will reflect the interest minus any offsetting dividends. Suppose we add and substract S on the right-hand side of the above equation:

$$f = S + S(1+r)^T - S - \sum_{t=1}^{N} D_t (1+r)^{(T-t)}.$$

Then rearranging terms gives

$$f = S + \left\{ \left(S\left[(1+r)^T - 1\right] \right) - \sum_{t=1}^{N} D_t (1+r)^{(T-t)} \right\}.$$

The term in braces is θ, the cost of carry. Within the braces, the first term, $(S[(1 + r)^T - 1])$, is the interest forgone on an investment of S dollars for a period of T years. The second term represents the compound future value of the dividends earned. Thus, the entire term added to S is the cost of carry.

A stock index is a weighted combination of securities, most of which pay dividends. In reality, the dividend flow is more or less continuous, although not of a constant amount. However, as we did with options, we can fairly safely assume a continuous flow of dividends at a constant yield, δ. If r is interpreted as the continuously compounded risk-free rate and S as the spot price of the index, the model is written as

$$f = Se^{(r-\delta)T}.$$

This format makes an interpretation somewhat easier. Suppose an investor is considering speculating on the stock market. There are two ways to do this: buy the stock index portfolio or buy the futures contract. If the portfolio is purchased, the investor receives dividends at a rate of δ. If the futures contract is purchased, the investor receives no dividends. The dividend yield enters the model as the factor $e^{-\delta T}$, which is less than 1. Thus, the effect of the dividend is to make the futures price lower than it would be without it. Note that the futures price will exceed (be less than) the spot price if the risk-free rate is higher (lower) than the dividend yield.

The futures pricing equation for the case of continuous dividends is also consistent with our simple cost of carry equation, $f = S + \theta$. To see this, we add and substract S to the right-hand side, giving

$$f = Se^{(r-\delta)T} + S - S,$$

which we can then express as

$$f = S + \{S[e^{(r-\delta)T} - 1]\}.$$

The term in braces on the right-hand side is the cost of carry, θ. The exponential function determines the compound future value of S growing at the rate of $r - \delta$. Subtracting the 1 removes the original value of S, leaving the interest minus dividends that accumulate over the life of the futures.

Consider the following problem. The stock is at 50, the risk-free rate is 8 percent, the dividend yield is 6 percent, and the time to expiration is 60 days, so T is $60/365 = .164$. Then the futures price is

$$f = 50e^{(.08-.06)(.164)} = 50.16.$$

If the risk-free rate were 5 percent, the futures price would be

$$f = 50e^{(.05-.06)(.164)} = 49.92.$$

This version of the futures pricing model is used extensively by traders and institutions to evaluate stock index and bond futures contracts. If the futures price does not conform to the model, an opportunity to earn a riskless profit in excess of the risk-free rate is possible. Empirical research by Cornell and French (1983), Cornell (1985), and Modest and Sundaresan (1983) tends to support the pricing model, but we shall defer further discussion and illustration of this issue until Chapter 11. For now, let us look at how futures contracts of different expirations are related.

Prices of Futures Contracts of Different Expirations

Earlier we presented the important relationship

$$f = S + \theta,$$

which, with no dividend or interest payments or a shortage of the good, means that the futures price is above the spot price. Now consider two futures contracts on the same commodity but with different expirations. Let those two expirations be $T(1)$ and $T(2)$, where $T(2) > T(1)$. We shall use the notation 1 and 2 to denote the respective time points. Thus,

$$f_1, f_2 = \text{futures prices}$$
$$\theta_1, \theta_2 = \text{cost of carry on each contract, respectively.}$$

Because it costs more to carry a commodity longer, the cost of carry for the contract expiring at $T(2)$ is greater than that for the contract expiring at $T(1)$. The futures–spot price relationships for the two contracts are

$$f_1 = S + \theta_1$$
$$f_2 = S + \theta_2.$$

Solving each of these for the spot price, S, gives

$$S = f_1 - \theta_1$$
$$S = f_2 - \theta_2.$$

We then can set these equal to each other and solve for $f_2 - f_1$:

$$f_2 - f_1 = \theta_2 - \theta_1.$$

This equation defines the spread between futures prices. The spread between the nearby and deferred contracts is the difference in their respective costs of carry. The term $\theta_2 - \theta_1$ is the cost of carry for the time interval between $T(1)$ and $T(2)$. The term $-(\theta_2 - \theta_1) = \theta_1 - \theta_2$ is sometimes referred to as the *spread basis*. It defines the relationship among prices of contracts with different expirations.

As an example, consider the following soybean oil contract. On September 26 of a particular year, the December contract was priced at 14.64 cents per pound and the January contract at 14.75 cents per pound. The difference of 11 cents per pound is the cost of carry of soybean oil from December to January.

It is important to examine the behavior of the spread through time. Figures 9.4 and 9.5 illustrate these relationships for June and September Eurodollar con-

FIGURE 9.4

Eurodollar Spread Basis: June–September Contract

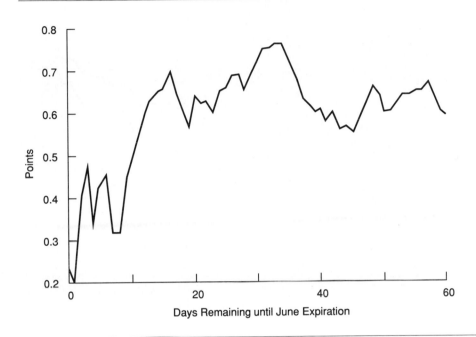

tracts. Figure 9.4 is the spread basis—the June futures price minus the September futures price—starting at about 60 days prior to the June expiration. The graph reads from right to left. Figure 9.5 presents the June and September futures prices and the spot price. Note that the September contract price is less than the June contract price. As the two contracts approach the June expiration, the spread basis narrows. This reflects the fact that the cost of carry of the June contract is approaching zero. The June contract is beginning to behave like the spot Eurodollar. The cost of carry of the September contract also declines, but less rapidly than that of the June contract. The spread basis obviously does not change in a perfectly predictable manner, which is one reason spread trading is so popular among futures traders. As we shall see in Chapter 11, there are strategies to take advantage of changes in the spread basis.

SUMMARY

This chapter introduced several approaches to understanding the pricing of futures contracts. It developed the concept of cost of carry and examined the relationship between futures and spot prices. It also addressed the joint issues of whether futures prices are unbiased estimators of future spot prices and whether futures

FIGURE 9.5

Spot, Nearby, and Deferred Prices: June–September Eurodollar Contracts

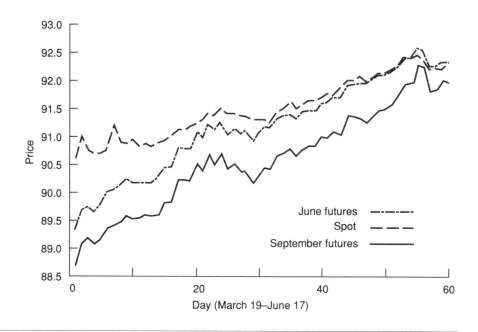

prices offer risk premia to speculators. The chapter examined the relationship be-tween forward and futures prices. We saw that if future interest rates are uncertain, forward prices need not equal futures prices.

As we move into Chapter 10, we should keep a few points in mind. We can reasonably accept the fact that futures prices and spot prices are described by the cost of carry relationship. We do not know whether futures prices are unbiased, but it seems logical to believe that holders of spot positions expect to earn a risk premium. When they hedge, they transfer the risk to futures traders. Therefore, it is reasonable to expect futures traders to demand a risk premium. Finally, although we have good reason to believe that forward prices are not precisely equal to futures prices, we see little reason to give much weight to the effect of marking to market on the performance of trading strategies. Accordingly, we shall ignore its effects in Chapter 10, which covers hedging strategies, and Chapter 11, which presents advanced futures strategies.

Questions and Problems

1.   Assume there is a forward market for a commodity. The forward price of the commodity is $45. The contract expires in one year. The risk-free rate is 10 percent. Now, six months later, new forward contracts are being written at a

price of $54. What is the original forward contract worth at this time? Explain why this is the correct value of the forward contract in six months by showing how the contract holder can capture that value even though the original contract cannot be sold.

2. Why is the value of a futures contract at the time it is purchased equal to zero? Contrast this with the value of the corresponding spot commodity.

3. On November 18, the S&P 500 futures settlement price was 199.30. You buy one contract at around the close of the market at the settlement price. The next day, the contract opens at 199.70 and the settlement price at the close of the day is 199.10. Determine the value of the futures contract at the opening, an instant before the close, and after the close. Remember that the S&P futures contract has a $500 multiplier.

4. The March Major Market Index futures expires on March 15. On March 13, the contract is selling at 253.625. Assume that there is a forward contract that also expires on March 15. The current forward price is 253. The risk-free rate is 5 percent per year, and you can assume that this rate will remain in effect for the next two days. Answer the following questions:

    a. Identify the existence of an arbitrage opportunity. What transactions should be executed on March 13?

    b. On March 14 the futures price is 253.35, and on March 15 the futures expires at 250.125. Show that the arbitrage works.

    c. Given your answer in part b, what effect will this have on market prices?

5. Name and explain the four conditions under which forward and futures prices would be equal.

6. On June 28, the price of the September Treasury bill futures is 92.95. The spot price of 91-day Treasury bills is quoted at a discount of 7.06, while the spot price of 182-day Treasury bills is 7.24. Estimate the forward rate on 91-day Treasury bills, and compare it to the rate implied by the futures market.

7. Construct an arbitrage example involving a commodity that can be sold short, and use it to explain the cost of carry model for pricing futures.

8. Comment on the following statement made by a futures trader: "Futures prices are determined by either expectations or the cost of carry."

9. If futures prices are less than spot prices, the explanation usually given is the convenience yield. Explain what the convenience yield is. Then identify certain assets on which convenience yields are more likely to exist and other assets on which they are not likely to be found.

10. Suppose there is an asset on which you know there is no convenience yield, yet the futures price is below the spot price. Can you think of an explanation for this?

11. What is a contango market? How do we interpret the cost of carry in a contango market? What is a backwardation market? How do we explain the cost of carry in a backwardation market?

12. On September 26, the spot price of wheat was $2.5225 per bushel and the price of a December wheat futures was $2.64 per bushel. How do you interpret the futures price if there is no risk premium in the futures market?

13. Reconsider the wheat example in problem 12. The interest forgone on money tied up in a bushel until expiration is .03, and the cost of storing the wheat is .0875 per bushel. The risk premium is .035 per bushel.

   a. What is the expected price of wheat on the spot market in December?

   b. Show how the futures price is related to the spot price.

   c. Show how the expected spot price at expiration (your answer in part a) is related to the futures price today.

   d. Show how the expected futures price at expiration is related to the futures price today.

   e. Explain who earns the risk premium and why.

14. On July 10, the September S&P 500 stock index futures was priced at 360.50. The contract expires on September 21. The S&P 500 index was at 356.49. The risk-free rate is 7.96 percent, and the dividend yield on the index is 3.75 percent. Is the futures overpriced or underpriced?

15. How do you interpret the difference between the January frozen concentrated orange juice futures price of $1.077 per pound and the March futures price of $1.0785? The prices are as of the previous September. Explain why these values differ.

16. Suppose there is a commodity in which the expected future spot price is $60. To induce investors to buy futures contracts, a risk premium of $4 is required. To store the commodity for the life of the futures contract would cost $5.50. Find the futures price.

17. On July 10, a farmer observes that the spot price of corn is $2.735 per bushel and the September futures price is $2.76. The farmer would like a prediction of the spot price in September but believes the market is dominated by hedgers holding long positions in corn. Eplain how the farmer would use this information in a forecast of the future price of corn.

18. Suppose the futures contract with the earliest expiration is priced higher than the one with the next earliest expiration. What explanation can you give for this condition?

19. The cost of carry futures pricing equation may appear slightly flawed to some people. To derive it, we equated a payoff at expiration with the initial outlay for the asset. Since these cash flows occur at different points in time, the time value of money seems to have been omitted. Explain why this interpretation is not correct.

20. (Concept Problem) Suppose there is a futures contract on a portfolio of stocks that currently are worth $100. The futures has a life of 90 days, and during that time the stocks will pay dividends of $0.75 in 30 days, $0.85 in 60 days, and $0.90 in 90 days. The simple interest rate is 12 percent.

a. Find the price of the futures contract assuming no arbitrage opportunities are present.

b. Find the value of θ, the cost of carry in dollars.

References

Breeden, Douglas. "Consumption Risk in Futures Markets." *The Journal of Finance* 35 (March 1980): 503–520.

Carter, A. Colin, Gorden C. Rausser, and Andrew Schmitz. "Efficient Asset Portfolios and the Theory of Normal Backwardation." *Journal of Political Economy* 91 (April 1983): 319–331.

Chang, Eric C. "Returns to Speculators and the Theory of Normal Backwardation." *The Journal of Finance* 40 (March 1985): 193–208.

Chicago Board of Trade. *Financial Instrument Markets: An Advanced Study of Cash-Futures Relationships.* Chicago: Board of Trade of the City of Chicago, 1986.

Cornell, Bradford. "Taxes and the Pricing of Stock Index Futures: Empirical Results." *The Journal of Futures Markets* 5 (1985): 89–101.

Cornell, Bradford, and Kenneth R. French. "Taxes and the Pricing of Stock Index Futures." *The Journal of Finance* 38 (June 1983): 675–693.

Duffie, Darrell. *Futures Markets*, Chapters 4, 5. Englewood Cliffs, N.J.: Prentice-Hall, 1989.

Dusak, Katherine. "Futures Trading and Investor Returns: An Investigation of Commodity Risk Premiums." *Journal of Political Economy* 81 (December 1973): 1387–1406.

Elton, Edwin, Martin J. Gruber, and Joel Rentzler. "Intra-Day Tests of the Efficiency of the Treasury Bill Futures Market." *Review of Economics and Statistics* 66 (February 1984): 129–137.

Figlewski, Stephen. *Hedging with Financial Futures for Institutional Investors*, Chapter 3. Cambridge, Mass.: Ballinger, 1986.

Garbade, Kenneth D. *Securities Markets*, Chapter 16. New York: McGraw-Hill, 1984.

Gray, Roger W. "The Search for a Risk Premium." *Journal of Political Economy* 64 (June 1961): 250–260.

Hicks, J. R. *Value and Capital*, 2d ed., Chapter 10. Oxford: Clarendon Press, 1939.

Houthakker, H. S. "Can Speculators Forecast Prices?" *Review of Economics and Statistics* 39 (1957): 143–151.

Hull, John. *Options, Futures, and Other Derivative Securities,* Chapters 1, 2. Englewood Cliffs, N.J.: Prentice-Hall, 1989.

Kane, Edward J. "Market Incompleteness and Divergences between Forward and Futures Interest Rates." *The Journal of Finance* 35 (May 1980): 221–234.

Keynes, John Maynard. *A Treatise on Money*. London: Macmillan, 1930.

Leuthold, Raymond M., Joan C. Junkus, and Jean E. Cordier. *The Theory and Practice of Futures Markets*, Chapters 3, 6, 7, 9, 11. Lexington, Mass.: Lexington Books, 1989.

Modest, David M., and Mahedevan Sundaresan. "The Relationship between Spot and Futures Prices in Stock Index Futures Markets: Some Preliminary Evidence." *The Journal of Futures Markets* 3 (1983): 15–41.

Rendleman, Richard J., and Christopher Carabini. "The Efficiency of the Treasury Bill Futures Market." *The Journal of Finance* 44 (September 1979): 895–914.

Resnick, Bruce G. "The Relationship between Futures Prices for U.S. Treasury Bonds." *Review of Research in Futures Markets* 3 (1984): 88–104.

Resnick, Bruce G., and Elizabeth Hennigar. "The Relationship between Futures and Cash Prices for U.S. Treasury Bonds." *Review of Research in Futures Markets* 2 (1983): 282–298.

Rothstein, Nancy H., ed. *The Handbook of Financial Futures*, Chapters 15–18. New York: McGraw-Hill, 1984.

Schwarz, Edward D., Joanne M. Hill, and Thomas Schneeweis. *Financial Futures: Fundamentals, Strategies, and Applications*, Chapters 6, 7. Homewood, Ill.: Irwin, 1986.

Siegel, Daniel R., and Diane F. Siegel. *Futures Markets*, Chapter 2. Hinsdale, Ill.: Dryden Press, 1990.

Telser, Lester G. "Futures Trading and the Storage of Cotton and Wheat." *Journal of Political Economy* 66 (June 1958): 233–255.

Vignola, Anthony, and Charles Dale. "The Efficiency of the Treasury Bill Futures Market: An Analysis of Alternative Specifications." *The Journal of Financial Research* 3 (1980): 169–188.

FUTURES HEDGING STRATEGIES

Nothing stings more sharply than the loss of money.

TITUS LIVIUS, c. AD 5

Hedging is a transaction designed to reduce or, in some cases, eliminate risk. The material on options presented numerous examples of hedges, the most obvious one being the covered call strategy. There a long position in stock was protected by holding a short position in calls. We saw that it is possible to do simply a covered call that will reduce risk or to hedge with the optimal number of options to eliminate risk. Similar principles apply to futures hedges.

Before illustrating the futures hedging strategies, we shall discuss some basic hedging concepts and techniques. Then we will examine some special features of various contracts. After mastering this basic material, we will present examples of each type of hedge. The examples come from actual market conditions. Although the hedges did not necessarily take place, the outcomes shown are those that would have occurred had the hedges been executed.

HEDGING CONCEPTS

Before we can understand why a certain hedge is placed or how it works, we must become acquainted with a few basic hedging concepts. We have mentioned some of these points before but have not specifically applied them to hedging strategies.

Short Hedge and Long Hedge

The terms *short hedge* and *long hedge* distinguish hedges that involve short and long positions in the futures contract, respectively. A hedger who holds the commodity and is concerned about a decrease in its price might consider hedging it with a short position in futures. If the spot price and futures price move together, the hedge will reduce some of the risk. For example, if the spot price decreases, the futures price also will decrease. Since the hedger is short the futures contract, the futures transaction produces a profit that at least partially offsets the loss on the spot position. This is called a *short hedge* because the hedger is short futures.

Another type of short hedge can be used in anticipation of the future sale of the commodity. An example of this occurs when a firm decides that it will need to borrow money at a later date. Borrowing money is equivalent to issuing or selling a bond or promissory note. If interest rates increase before the money is borrowed, the loan will be more expensive. To hedge this risk, the firm might short an interest rate futures contract. If rates increase, the futures transaction will generate a profit that will at least partially offset the higher interest rate on the loan. Because it is taken out in anticipation of a future transaction in the spot market, this type of hedge is known as an *anticipatory hedge*.

Another type of anticipatory hedge involves an individual who plans to purchase the commodity at a later date. Fearing an increase in the commodity's price, the investor might buy a futures contract. Then, if the price of the commodity increases, the futures price also will increase and produce a profit on the futures position. That profit will at least partially offset the higher cost of purchasing the commodity. This is referred to as a *long hedge*, because the hedger is long in the futures market.

Another type of long hedge might be placed when one is short the commodity. Although this hedge is less common, it would be appropriate for someone who has sold short a stock and is concerned that the market will go up. Rather than close out the short position, one might buy futures and earn a profit on the long position in futures that will at least partially offset the loss on the short position in the stock.

In each of these cases, the hedger held a position in the spot market that was subject to risk. The futures transaction served as a temporary substitute for a spot transaction. Thus, when one holds the spot commodity and is concerned about a price decrease but does not want to sell it, one can execute a short futures trade. Selling the futures contract would substitute for selling the commodity.

The Basis

The basis is one of the most important concepts in futures markets. The *basis* usually is defined as the spot price minus the futures price. However, some books and articles define it as the futures price minus the spot price. In this book, we shall use the former definition:

$$\text{Basis} = \text{Spot price} - \text{Futures price}.$$

HEDGING AND THE BASIS   The basis plays an important role in understanding the process of hedging. Here we will look at the concept of hedging and how the basis affects the performance of a hedge. Ultimately we shall need to understand the factors that influence the basis.

Let us define the following terms:

T = time to expiration
t = a time point prior to expiration
S = spot price today
f = futures price today
S_T = spot price at expiration
f_T = futures price at expiration
S_t = spot price at time t prior to expiration
f_t = futures price at time t prior to expiration
Π = profit from the strategy

For the time being, we shall ignore marking to market, any costs of storing the asset, and other transaction costs.

The concept of a hedge is not new. When we looked at options, we constructed several types of hedges, some of which were riskless. By taking a position in a stock and an opposite position in an option, gains (losses) on the stock are offset by losses (gains) on the option. We can do the same thing with futures: hold a long (short) position in the spot market and a short (long) position in the futures market. For a long position in the spot market, the profit from a hedge held to expiration is

$$\Pi = S_T - S \text{ (from the spot market)} - (f_T - f) \text{ (from the futures market).}$$

For a short position in the spot market and a long position in the futures market, the sign of each term in the above equation is reversed; that is,

$$\Pi = -S_T + S + (f_T - f).$$

In some cases, we might wish to close out the position at time t, that is, before expiration. Then the profit from the hedge that is long in the spot market is

$$\Pi = S_t - S - (f_t - f).$$

At expiration, a person buying a futures contract can expect to receive immediate delivery of the good. Thus, an expiring futures contract is the same as the purchase of the spot commodity; therefore, $S_T = f_T$. Thus, the profit if the hedge is held to expiration is simply $f - S$. That means that the hedge is equivalent to buying the asset at price S and immediately guaranteeing a sale price of f.

As an example, suppose you buy an asset for $100 and sell a futures contract on the asset at $103. At expiration, the spot and futures prices are both $97. You sell the asset for $97, taking a $3 loss, and close your futures contract at $97, making a $6 gain, for a net profit of $3. Alternatively, you could deliver the asset on your futures contract, receiving $97, and collect the $6 that has accumulated in your futures account, making the effective sale price of the asset $103. In either case, the transaction is equivalent to selling the asset for $103, the original futures price.

Since the basis is defined as the spot price minus the futures price, we can write it as a variable, b, where

$b = S - f$ (initial basis)
$b_t = S_t - f_t$ (basis at time t)
$b_T = S_T - f_T$ (basis at expiration)

Thus, for a position closed out at time t,

$$\Pi = S_t - f_t - (S - f),$$
$$= b_t - b.$$

The profit from the hedge is simply the change in the basis. The uncertainty regarding how the basis will change is called *basis risk*. A hedge substitutes the change in the basis for the change in the spot price. The basis change is far less variable than the spot price change; hence, the hedged position is less risky than the unhedged position. Because basis risk results from the uncertainty over the change in the basis, hedging is a speculative activity but produces a risk level much lower than that of an unhedged position.

If the spot price increases by more than the futures price, the basis will increase. This is said to be a *strengthening basis*, and it improves the performance of the short hedge. If the futures price increases by more than the spot price, the basis will decrease, reducing the performance on the hedge. In that case, the basis is said to be *weakening*.

For a long hedger, however, everything we just said is reversed. The profit is $-(S_t - S) + (f_t - f) = -b_t + b$. Now a weakening basis improves the performance and a strengthening basis reduces the performance.

Suppose a hedge is held all the way to expiration so that the spot position is closed at a price of S_T and the futures position is closed at a price of f_T. Assuming $S_T = f_T$, the basis goes to zero. In that case, the profit is simply $-b$ from a short hedge and $+b$ from a long hedge. This raises an interesting point: If the short hedger knows the basis will go to zero and the profit will be $-b$, why hedge at all? There are two possible reasons. First, the original basis could be negative; therefore, the hedge would lock in a small profit. Second, in some cases knowledge of a small loss is preferable to the risk of a potentially large loss.

Finally, we should remember that hedging incurs costs such as the transaction costs of the futures. In addition the asset itself will incur costs of storage. These will reduce the profit but their effects are generally known in advance and, thus, do not impose any additional risk.

A HEDGING EXAMPLE   Let us consider an example using gold. On September 26, the price of a gold futures expiring in December was $431.50 per troy ounce. The spot price of gold was $433.40. Suppose a gold dealer held 100 troy ounces of gold worth $100(433.40) = 43,340$. To protect against a decrease in the price of gold, the dealer might sell one futures contract on 100 troy ounces. In our notation,

$$S = 433.40$$
$$f = 431.50$$
$$b = 433.40 - 431.50 = 1.90.$$

If the hedge is held to expiration, the basis should converge to zero. However, it might not go precisely to zero, and we shall see why later. If it does, the profit should be -1 times the original basis times the number of ounces:

$$\Pi = -1(1.90)(100) = -190.$$

Suppose that at expiration the spot price of gold is $448.50. Then the dealer sells the gold in the spot market for a profit of $100(448.50 - 433.40) = 1,510$. The short futures contract is offset by purchasing it in the futures market for a profit of $-100(448.50 - 431.50) = -1,700$. The overall profit therefore is $-1,700 + 1,510 = -190$, as we predicted.

Now suppose we close the position prior to expiration. For example, on November 5 the spot price of gold was $405.65 and the December futures price was $408.50. In our notation, $S_t = 405.65$ and $f_t = 408.50$. If the gold is sold in the spot market, the profit is $100(405.65 - 433.40) = -2,775$. The futures contract is bought back at 408.50 for a profit of $-100(408.50 - 431.50) = 2,300$. The net loss is $-2,775 + 2,300 = -475$. As we said earlier, this should equal the change in the basis, $b_t - b$. The original basis was 1.90. The basis when the position is closed is $S_t - f_t$, or $405.65 - 408.50 = -2.85$. The profit therefore is,

$$-2.85 - (1.90) = -4.75,$$

which is the loss on the hedge per ounce of gold.

THE BEHAVIOR OF THE BASIS   Figure 10.1 shows the basis on a June Eurodollar contract for a period of 60 days prior to expiration. The graph reads from right to left. Notice how the basis starts off at about 1.0 and then gradually decreases as expiration nears. At around ten days before expiration, the basis actually becomes

FIGURE 10.1

The June Eurodollar Basis, March 19–June 17

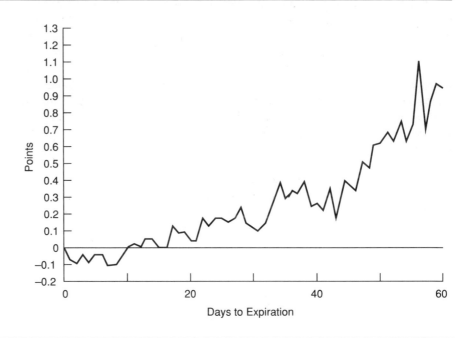

slightly negative. Because the Eurodollar contract is settled in cash, the basis on the expiration day automatically is zero.

In some cases, however, the basis does not converge exactly to zero. In the case of gold, for example, an investor who purchased gold on the spot market and immediately sold a futures contract that is about to expire would have to deliver the gold. There is a potentially significant delivery cost that would leave the futures price slightly above the spot price. For some commodities, there are several acceptable grades that can be delivered, so there are multiple spot prices. The short has control over the delivery and will choose to deliver the most economical grade. The futures price will tend to converge to the spot price of the commodity that is most likely to be delivered.

Some Risks of Hedging

Sometimes the commodity being hedged and the commodity underlying the futures contract differ. A typical example, which we shall illustrate later, is the hedging of a corporate bond with a Treasury bond futures contract. This is referred to as a *cross hedge* and is a type of basis risk much greater than that encountered by hedging government bonds with Treasury bond futures. Corporate and government bond prices tend to move together, but the relationship is weaker than that of two government bonds. In addition, bonds with higher ratings would be more highly correlated with government bonds. Thus, lower-quality corporate bonds would carry some additional basis risk, and hedges would tend to be less effective.

In some cases, the price of the commodity being hedged and that of the futures contract move in opposite directions. Then a hedge will produce either a profit or a loss on both the spot and the futures positions. If one chooses the correct futures contract, this is unlikely to occur. If it occurs frequently, the hedger should find a different contract.

Hedging also entails another form of risk called *quantity risk*. As an example, suppose a farmer wishes to lock in the price at which an as yet unharvested crop will be sold. The farmer might sell a futures contract and thereby establish the future selling price of the crop. Yet what the farmer does not know and cannot hedge is the uncertainty over the size of the crop. This is the farmer's quantity risk. The farmer's total revenue is the product of the crop's price and its size. In a highly competitive market, the farmer's crop is too small to influence the price, but there are systematic factors, such as weather, that could influence everyone's crop. Thus, the crop size could be small when prices are high and large when prices are low. This situation creates its own natural hedge. When the farmer hedges, the price volatility no longer offsets the uncertainty of the crop size. Thus, the hedge actually can *increase* the overall risk.

Quantity uncertainty is common in farming but is by no means restricted to it. Many corporations and financial institutions do not know the size of future hedge positions and thus must contend with quantity risk.

Contract Choice

The choice of futures contract actually consists of four decisions: (1) which futures commodity, (2) which expiration month, (3) whether to be long or short, and (4) the number of contracts. The number of contracts is called the *hedge ratio* and is so important that we defer it to the next main section.

WHICH FUTURES COMMODITY?   From the previous section, we can see that it is important to select a futures contract on a commodity that is highly correlated with the underlying commodity being hedged. For example, if one were hedging soybeans, the soybean futures contract would provide the best hedge; for Treasury bonds, the Treasury bond futures contract would provide the best hedge. In many cases the choice is obvious, but in some it is not.

For example, suppose one wishes to hedge the rate on bank CDs, short-term money market instruments issued by commercial banks. Bank CD contracts used to trade at the IMM, but not actively. Liquidity is important, because the hedger must be able to close the contract easily. If the futures contract lacks the necessary liquidity, the hedger should select a contract that has sufficient liquidity and is highly correlated with the spot commodity being hedged. Since both Treasury bills and Eurodollars are short-term money market instruments, their futures contracts, which are quite liquid, would seem appropriate for hedging bank CD rates.

Another factor one should consider is whether the contract is correctly priced. A short hedger will be selling futures contracts and therefore should look for contracts that are overpriced or, in the worst case, correctly priced. A long hedger should hedge by buying underpriced contracts or, in the worst case, correctly priced contracts.

Sometimes the best hedge can be obtained by using more than one futures commodity. For example, a hedge of a corporate bond position might be more effective if *both* Treasury and municipal bond futures are used.

WHICH EXPIRATION?   Once one has selected the futures commodity, one must decide on the expiration month. As we know, only certain expiration months trade at a given time. For example, in September the Treasury bond futures contract has expirations of December of the current year, March, June, September, and December of the following year, and March, June, and September of the year after that. If the Treasury bond futures contract is the appropriate hedging vehicle, the contract used must come from this group of expirations.

In most cases, there will be a time horizon over which the hedge remains in effect. To obtain the maximum reduction in basis risk, a hedger should hold the futures position until as close as possible to expiration. Thus, an appropriate contract expiration would be one that corresponded as closely as possible to the expiration date. However, hedgers are advised to avoid holding a futures position in the expiration month. This is because unusual price movements sometimes are observed in the expiration month, and this would pose an additional risk to hedgers. Thus, the hedger should choose an expiration month that is as close as possible to but after the month in which the hedge is terminated.

Table 10.1 lists possible hedge termination dates for a Treasury bond futures hedge and the appropriate contracts for use. Consider, however, that *the longer the time to expiration, the less liquid the contract*. Therefore, the selection of a contract according to this criterion may need to be overruled by the necessity of using a liquid contract. If this happens, one should use a contract with a shorter expiration. When the contract moves into its expiration month, the futures position is closed out and a new position is opened in the next expiration month. This process, called *rolling the hedge forward*, generates some additional risk but is still quite effective.[1]

LONG OR SHORT?   After selecting the futures commodity and expiration month, the hedger must decide whether to be long or short. This decision requires thinking through the problem and understanding the direction of the risk. One approach is to identify the worst that could happen. If you hold the commodity, the worst that could happen is that its price decreases. Now assume this is what happens, and ask yourself how this could produce a profit in the futures contract. To make a profit in futures with a falling price, you would require a short position. If you are planning to purchase the commodity, the worst that could happen would be an

---

[1]See McCabe and Franckle (1983) for empirical evidence on the effectiveness of this strategy.

TABLE 10.1

Contract Expirations for Planned Hedge Termination Dates (Treasury Bond Futures Hedge Initiated on September 30, 1990)

Hedge Termination Date	Appropriate Contract
10/1/90 – 11/30/90	Dec 90
12/1/90 – 2/28/91	Mar 91
3/1/91 – 5/31/91	Jun 91
6/1/91 – 8/31/91	Sep 91
9/1/91 – 11/30/91	Dec 91
12/1/91 – 2/29/92	Mar 92
3/1/92 – 5/31/92	Jun 92
6/1/92 – 8/31/92	Sep 92
9/1/92 – 11/30/92	Dec 92

Note: The appropriate contract is based on the rule that the expiration date should be as soon as possible after the hedge termination date subject to no contract being held in its expiration month. Liquidity considerations may make some more distant contracts inappropriate.

increase in its price. If the price increased, you could make a profit by being long in futures.

Another way to understand the problem is to determine what transaction to make in the spot market when the hedge is terminated. At that time, you must make the opposite transaction in futures. This should tell you which futures transaction to execute today. For example, if you hold the spot commodity and plan to sell it when the hedge is lifted, you will buy futures at that time. Thus, you need to sell futures today.

Margin Requirements and Marking to Market

Two other considerations in hedging are the margin requirement and the effect of marking to market. We discussed these factors earlier, but now we need to consider their implications for hedging.

Margin requirements, as we know, are very small and virtually insignificant in relation to the size of the position being hedged. Moreover, margin requirements for hedges are even smaller than speculative margins. In addition, margins can be posted with Treasury bills; thus, interest on the money can still be earned. Therefore, the initial amount of margin posted is really not a major factor in hedging.

What is important, however, is the effect of marking to market and the potential for margin calls. Remember that the profit on a futures transaction is supposed to offset the loss on the spot commodity. At least part of the time, there will be profits on the spot commodity and losses on the futures contract. On a given day when the futures contract generates a loss, the hedger must deposit additional margin money to cover that loss. Even if the spot position has generated a profit in excess of the loss on the futures contract, it may be impossible, or at least inconvenient, to withdraw the profit on the spot position to cover the loss on the futures.

This is one of the major obstacles to more widespread use of futures by banks and corporations. Because futures profits and losses are realized immediately and spot profits and losses do not occur until the hedge is terminated, many potential hedgers tend to weigh the losses on the futures position more heavily than the gains on the spot. They also tend to think of hedges on an ex post rather than ex ante basis. If the hedge produced a profit on the spot position and a loss on the futures position, it would be apparent *after the fact* that the hedge should not have been done. But this would not be known *before the fact*.

Thus, a hedger must be aware that hedging will produce both gains and losses on futures transactions and will require periodic margin calls. The alternative to not meeting a margin call is closing the futures position. It is tempting to do this after a streak of losses and margin calls. If the futures position is closed, however, the hedge will no longer be in effect and the individual or firm will be exposed to the risk in the spot market, which is greater than the risk of the hedge.

To meet margin calls, a hedger must set aside a pool of funds. The size of that pool can be gauged by simulating the historical behavior of similar hedges or with mathematical formulas.[2]

In Chapter 9, we examined the effect of marking to market on the futures price. We concluded that the impact is fairly small. If, however, the interest earned or paid on the variation margin is not insignificant, it is possible to take it into account when establishing the optimal number of contracts. We shall cover this topic in a later section.

Micro Hedging versus Macro Hedging

Another type of hedging decision is whether to hedge individual transactions or hedge all of the firm's assets and liabilities as a group. The former is called *micro hedging* and the latter *macro hedging*.

In micro hedging, a firm selectively hedges certain assets and liabilities from time to time. For example, a firm that buys wheat as a raw material may choose to hedge wheat but not hedge other raw materials. Similarly, it may choose to hedge wheat at some times and not at others.

Macro hedging, on the other hand, occurs when a firm hedges its entire risk exposure. Banks sometimes do this. A bank is a fairly homogeneous firm. It consists of interest-sensitive assets and liabilities.[3] If its assets are more interest sensitive than its liabilities, the bank will profit when interest rates decrease and lose when they increase. To eliminate its exposure to interest rate changes, the bank might sell futures contracts. Then, when rates increase, its assets will de-

---

[2]Kolb, Gay, and Hunter (1985) show how to determine the cash reserve necessary for supporting margin calls.

[3]Of course, not all bank assets and liabilities are interest sensitive, but most are.

crease in value more than its liabilities, but the loss will be somewhat offset by the profit from the short futures position.

Because it is more difficult for a firm to determine its overall exposure, most firms use macro hedging less often than micro hedging. If the firm always hedges its total position, there is little reason to be in business in the first place. A firm usually hedges because of temporary uncertainty about the future of a particular commodity or to lock in an existing price at which it can make a profit on another segment of its business. A policy of continuous hedging without regard for the commodity's outlook is like a football team that always runs three simple handoffs. The game is dull and predictable, and long-term success is seldom achieved.

These are several of the most important factors one must consider before initiating a hedge. As we noted earlier, another important consideration is the correct number of futures contracts, or the hedge ratio.

DETERMINATION OF THE HEDGE RATIO

The *hedge ratio* is the number of futures contracts one should use to hedge a particular exposure in the spot market. The hedge ratio should be the one in which the futures profit or loss matches the spot profit or loss. There is no exact method of determining the hedge ratio before performing the hedge. However, there are several ways to estimate it.

The most elementary method is to take a position in the futures market equivalent in size to the position in the spot market. For example, if you hold $10 million of the commodity and the futures price is $80,000, you should hold $10,000,000/$80,000 = 125 contracts. This approach is relatively naive, because it fails to consider that the futures and spot prices might not change in the same proportions. In some cases, however, particularly when the commodity being hedged is the same as the commodity underlying the futures contract, such a hedge ratio will be appropriate.

Nevertheless, in most other cases the futures and spot prices will change by different percentages. Suppose we write the profit from a hedge as follows:

$$\Pi = \Delta S + \Delta f N_f,$$

where the symbol Δ means *change in*. Thus, the profit is the change in the spot price (ΔS) plus the change in the futures price (Δf) multiplied by the number of futures contracts (N_f). A positive N_f means a long position and a negative N_f means a short position. For the futures profit or loss to completely offset the spot loss or profit, we set $\Pi = 0$ and find the value of N_f as

$$N_f = -\frac{\Delta S}{\Delta f}.$$

Because we assume futures and spot prices will move in the same direction, ΔS and Δf have the same sign; thus, N_f is negative. This example therefore is a short hedge, but the concept is equally applicable to a long hedge, where $\Pi = -\Delta S + \Delta f N_f$ and N_f would be positive.

Now we need to know the ratio $\Delta S/\Delta f$. There are several approaches to estimating this value.

Minimum Variance Hedge Ratio

The objective of a hedge—indeed, of any investment decision—is to maximize the investor's expected utility. In this book, however, we do not develop the principles of expected utility maximization. Therefore, we shall take a much simpler approach to the hedging problem and focus on risk minimization. The model used here comes from the work of Johnson (1960) and Stein (1961).

The profit from the short hedge is[4]

$$\Pi = \Delta S + \Delta f N_f.$$

The variance of the profit is

$$\sigma_\Pi^2 = \sigma_{\Delta S}^2 + \sigma_{\Delta f}^2 N_f^2 + 2\sigma_{\Delta S \Delta f} N_f,$$

where

σ_Π^2 = variance of hedged profit

$\sigma_{\Delta S}^2$ = variance of change in the spot price

$\sigma_{\Delta f}^2$ = variance of change in the futures price

$\sigma_{\Delta S \Delta f}$ = covariance of change in the spot price and change in the futures price[5]

The objective is to find the value of N_f that gives the minimum value of σ_Π^2. (Appendix 10A presents the procedure.) The formula for N_f is

$$N_f = -\frac{\sigma_{\Delta S \Delta f}}{\sigma_{\Delta f}^2}.$$

This formula gives the number of futures contracts that will produce the lowest possible variance. The negative sign means that the hedger should sell futures. If the problem were formulated as a long hedge, the sign would be positive.

---

[4]The problem as formulated here is in terms of the profit. An alternative, and in some ways preferable, formulation is in terms of the rate of return on the hedger's wealth. We shall use the profit formulation here because it is more frequently seen in the literature.

[5]Covariance, as we saw in Chapter 8, is a measure of the degree of association between two variables.

You may recognize that the formula for N_f is very similar to that for β from a regression, which we covered in Chapter 8. In fact, we can estimate N_f by running a regression with ΔS as the dependent variable and Δf as the independent variable. Of course, this can give us the correct value of N_f only for a historical set of data. We cannot know the actual value of N_f over an upcoming period. Extrapolating the future from the past is risky, but at least it is a starting point.

The effectiveness of the minimum variance hedge can be determined by examining the percentage of the risk reduced. Suppose we define hedging effectiveness as

$$e^* = \frac{\text{Risk of unhedged position} - \text{Risk of hedged position}}{\text{Risk of unhedged position}}.$$

This can be written as

$$e^* = \frac{\sigma_{\Delta S}^2 - \sigma_\Pi^2}{\sigma_{\Delta S}^2}.$$

Thus, e^* gives the percentage of the unhedged risk that the hedge eliminates. By substituting the formulas for σ_Π^2 and N_f in the formula for e^* and rearranging terms, we get

$$e^* = \frac{N_f^2 \sigma_{\Delta f}^2}{\sigma_{\Delta S}^2}.$$

This happens to be the formula for the coefficient of determination from the regression. This is the square of the correlation coefficient. It indicates the percentage of the variance in the dependent variable, ΔS, that is explained by the independent variable, Δf.

Price Sensitivity Hedge Ratio

The price sensitivity hedge ratio comes from the work of Kolb and Chiang (1981). The objective here is to determine the value of N_f that will result in no change in the portfolio's value. Because the strategy is designed to be used with interest rate futures, we will illustrate it with reference to a bond and a bond futures contract.

Suppose changes in interest rates on all bonds are caused by a change in a single interest rate, r, which can be viewed as a risk-free government bond rate. Thus, when r changes, all other bond yields change. Let S be the price of the bond held in the spot market and y_s be its yield. We will assume the bond futures contract is based on a single government bond.[6] The futures contract has a price of f, and that price implies a yield of y_f, as discussed in Chapter 7.

---

[6]The actual futures contract is based on several eligible bonds. Later we shall examine how this affects hedging strategies.

The profit from a hedge is the change in value of the hedger's position as a result of a change in the rate, r. If we are hedged, this change in value is zero. (Details of the solution are presented in Appendix 10A). The formula for N_f is

$$N_f = -\frac{\Delta S / \Delta y_s}{\Delta f / \Delta y_f}.$$

This expression can be considerably simplified. Recall that in Chapter 8 we discussed the concept of duration, a measure of the sensitivity of a bond's price to interest rates. Duration can be written as

$$DUR_s \cong -\frac{(\Delta S / S)(1 + y_s)}{\Delta y_s}.$$

The duration of a futures contract can be expressed in a similar manner. However, we must be careful to define it as the duration of the bond underlying the futures contract on the date of the contract's expiration. For example, suppose we are planning to hedge with a futures contract that expires in six months. The bond underlying the futures contract has a maturity of exactly 20 years. The duration of the futures contract is the duration of the underlying bond when the futures contract expires. At that time, the bond will have a maturity of 19 1/2 years. Thus, we would calculate the duration using the bond's coupon, the current futures price, the implicit yield, y_f, and 19 1/2 years to maturity. We can write the duration of the futures contract as

$$DUR_f \cong -\frac{(\Delta f / f)(1 + y_f)}{\Delta y_f}.$$

Letting $\Delta y_f = \Delta y_s$ and substituting in the expression for N_f gives

$$N_f = -\frac{DUR_s S(1 + y_f)}{DUR_f f(1 + y_s)}.$$

There is yet another version of the price sensitivity hedge ratio that is often used in practice. It is given as

$$N_f = -(\text{Yield beta})\frac{PVBP_s}{PVBP_f},$$

where $PVBP_s$ is the present value of a basis point change for the spot and is specifically defined as $\Delta S / \Delta y_s$, which we know is $-DUR_s S/(1 + y_s)$. $PVBP_f$ is the present value of a basis point change for the futures and is defined as $\Delta f / \Delta y_f$, which is $-DUR_f f/(1 + y_f)$. These variables are, in effect, the change in the price of the spot or futures for a change in the yield of Δy_s or Δy_f.

The *yield beta* is the regression coefficient from a regression of the spot yield on the futures yield. In the price sensitivity formula, we assumed the spot yield changes one for one with the futures yield (see Appendix 10A). This makes the yield beta 1. Thus, if the yield beta is 1, the preceding equation becomes

$$N_f = -\frac{DUR_s S / (1 + y_s)}{DUR_f f / (1 + y_f)},$$

which is equivalent to the price sensitivity formula. However, if the hedger does not believe the spot and futures prices will change in a one-to-one ratio, the yield beta actually should be estimated. In the examples used in this chapter, we shall assume the yield beta is 1.

The price sensitivity formula takes into account the volatility of the spot and futures prices. Thus, it incorporates information from current prices rather than regressing past spot prices on past futures prices. There are merits to both approaches, and in practice one approach sometimes may be easier to implement than the other. We shall illustrate both methods in some hedging examples later in the chapter.

Stock Index Futures Hedge

Because the price sensitivity hedge is not applicable to stock index futures, the minimum variance hedge usually is employed. Suppose we define ΔS as Sr_s, where r_s is the return on the stock, which is the percentage change in price. Then we define Δf as fr_f, where r_f is the percentage change in the price of the futures contract. Note that this is not the return on the futures contract. Because there is no initial outlay, there is no return on a futures contract. If we substitute Sr_s and fr_f for ΔS and Δf in the minimum variance formula for N_f, we get

$$N_f = -\frac{S\sigma_{sf}}{f\sigma_f^2},$$

where σ_{sf} is the covariance between r_s and r_f and σ_f^2 is the variance of r_f. If we run a regression of the percentage change in the spot price on the percentage change in the futures price, we obtain a regression coefficient we can call β_s. Is this the beta from the Capital Asset Pricing Model? Not exactly, but since the futures contract is based on a market index, the beta will be very close—probably close enough for our purposes. In that case,

$$N_f = -\beta_s \left(\frac{S}{f}\right)$$

is the minimum variance hedge ratio for a stock index futures contract where β_s is the beta of the stock portfolio.

This hedge ratio is widely used in practice even though it ignores a few problems. For one, it disregards dividends on the portfolio of stocks. Also, it assumes the futures contract behaves exactly like the market portfolio or the underlying stock index. In other words, it assumes that the beta of the futures is 1. This will not be precisely the case. Thus, there is some basis risk that can impair the hedge's effectiveness. For our purposes, however, we shall stay with the above formula so we can concentrate on the essential concepts underlying the stock index futures hedge.

Tailing a Hedge

In Chapter 9, we discussed the impact of marking to market on futures prices. We saw that the effect is likely to be small, so we can treat forward contracts as though they were futures contracts and permit the profit from the contract to be earned entirely at expiration. In reality, there are some cases where the interest earned on daily profits and losses from futures positions can be significant enough to require consideration in the design of hedging models. The effect of marking to market is to reduce the hedge ratio below the optimum. This is called *tailing the hedge*.

Suppose we set up a hedge consisting of a long position in the spot asset priced at S and a short position in the futures priced at f. We shall hold the position until the futures expires at T. During the interim at times $T(1)$ and $T(2)$, the futures will be marked to market. This implies that from today until $T(1)$ is one day, from $T(1)$ until $T(2)$ is one day, and from $T(2)$ to T is one day. We shall assume the interest rate applied to settlement gains and losses is the risk-free rate, r, and this rate is constant until expiration.

We set up the hedge by selling N futures today. At time $T(1)$, we shall have a futures profit of $-N(f_{T(1)} - f)$. We shall reinvest this (or, if a loss, borrow the money) at the rate r for two more days. At expiration, the profit will have grown to $-N(f_{T(1)} - f)(1 + r)^{T - T(1)}$. Then, at time $T(1)$, we shall close out that futures position and open a new short position of $N_{T(1)}$ contracts. At time $T(2)$, we shall have a futures profit of $-N_{T(1)}(f_{T(2)} - f_{T(1)})$. We shall reinvest this (or, if a loss, borrow the money) at the rate r for one more day. At expiration, the profit will have grown to $-N_{T(1)}(f_{T(2)} - f_{T(1)})(1 + r)^{T - T(2)}$. At time $T(2)$, we shall close that futures position and open up a new one by selling one futures contract. Thus, our new hedge ratio will be $N_{T(2)} = 1$.

At expiration, we shall deliver the spot asset and effectively receive $f_{T(2)}$, the futures price at the time we opened the contract. We shall also have accumulated $-N(f_{T(1)} - f)(1 + r)^{T - T(1)} - N_{T(1)}(f_{T(2)} - f_{T(1)})(1 + r)^{T - T(2)}$. With simple algebra, we can see that if N is set equal to $(1 + r)^{-(T - T(1))}$ and $N_{T(1)}$ is set equal to $(1 + r)^{-(T - T(2))}$, the total amount will be $f_{T(2)} - f_{T(1)} + f - f_{T(2)} + f_{T(1)}$, which equals f. Thus, the amount of money accumulated at expiration will be simply f, the price at which the futures position was originated. This will make the hedge do what it is supposed to do: lock in a price of f for the asset at expiration. Thus, in general the number of

TABLE 10.2

Tailing the Hedge

The time pattern

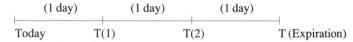

Today

Buy asset in spot market

Sell $N = (1 + r)^{-(T - T(1))}$ futures contracts

At T(1)

Profit on futures $= -(1 + r)^{-(T - T(1))}(f_{T(1)} - f)$ (where $(1 + r)^{-(T - T(1))}$ is the number of contracts and $f_{T(1)} - f$ is the price change.)

Reinvest or borrow this amount for the period $T - T(1)$ at the rate r. It will grow to $-(1 + r)^{-(T - T(1))}(f_{T(1)} - f)(1 + r)^{(T - T(1))} = f - f_{T(1)}$ at T.

Add this amount to your dollars at T.

Buy back the N futures and sell $N_{T(1)} = (1 + r)^{-(T - T(2))}$ futures.

At T(2)

Profit on futures $= -(1 + r)^{-(T - T(2))}(f_{T(2)} - f_{T(1)})$ (where $(1 + r)^{-(T - T(2))}$ is the number of contracts and $f_{T(2)} - f_{T(1)}$ is the price change.)

Reinvest or borrow this amount for the period $T - T(2)$ at the rate r. It will grow to $-(1 + r)^{-(T - T(2))}(f_{T(2)} - f_{T(1)})(1 + r)^{(T - T(2))} = f_{T(1)} - f_{T(2)}$ at T.

Add this to your dollars at T.

Buy back your futures and sell $N_{T(2)} = 1$ new futures.

At T

Deliver the spot asset and receive S_T.

Profit on futures $= -1(f_T - f_{T(2)}) = f_{T(2)} - S_T$ (where 1 is the number of contracts and $f_T - f_{T(2)}$ is the price change. Note $f_T = S_T$.) so we effectively receive $f_{T(2)}$.

Accumulation of reinvested (borrowed) profits (losses) from above $= f - f_{T(1)} + f_{T(1)} - f_{T(2)}$.

Total cash $= S_T + f_{T(2)} - S_T + f - f_{T(1)} + f_{T(1)} - f_{T(2)} = f$.

---

futures on a given day should be

$$N = N_f(1 + r)^{-(\text{Days until expiration} - 1)/365},$$

where N_f is the number of futures contracts without the tail. Table 10.2 outlines the above procedure.

Consider the following simple example. Let S be 100 and f be 105. The interest rate, r, is .10. Without tailing the hedge, the hedger would buy 1 unit of the spot at 100 and sell 1 unit of the futures at 105. With the tail, however, the hedger should sell $(1.10)^{-2/365}$ futures when there are two days to go and $T - T(2)$ is 2/365. This amounts to 0.9995 contracts. Thus, if the investor held 10,000 units of the spot, the hedge ratio would be 0.9995(10,000) futures, or 9,995 contracts. At time $T(1)$, the hedge ratio would be changed to $(1.10)^{-(1/365)}$ or 9.9997, or 9,997 contracts. At time $T(2)$, the hedge ratio would change to 1, or 10,000 contracts.

These adjustments to the hedge ratio may seem insignificant, but that is primarily because we let the hedge begin three days before expiration. Had we extended our example to, say, 100 days before expiration, and assuming marking to market daily, the hedge ratio would have been $(1.10)^{99/365}$ or 9,745 contracts. Each day this ratio would change by incrementing the exponent by 1/365 until the day before expiration, when it would become 365/365, or 1. In practice, many professional hedgers do not necessarily adjust the hedge ratio daily; they do so only periodically and achieve results quite close to those of a daily adjustment. To keep our hedge examples fairly basic, we shall not use this tailing procedure, but you should keep it in mind for situations you may encounter in the real world.

The instruments on which we shall focus in this chapter are short-term interest rate futures, intermediate- and long-term interest rate futures, and stock index futures. Before we begin looking at specific hedges, we must become familiar with the unique characteristics of these types of futures contracts. The short-term interest rate futures we shall examine are Treasury bill and Eurodollar futures. The intermediate- and long-term interest rate futures are Treasury note and Treasury bond futures. The stock index futures contract is the S&P 500.

CONTRACT CHARACTERISTICS

Treasury Bills and Eurodollars

Treasury bill and Eurodollar contracts trade on the International Monetary Market of the Chicago Mercantile Exchange. They are the most actively traded futures contracts on short-term money market instruments.

TREASURY BILLS   We introduced T-bills in Chapter 3 when we needed a return to use as the risk-free rate. T-bills are auctioned each week and normally mature in 91 days. T-bills are pure-discount instruments, and the discount is quoted on a 360-day basis.

Although generally 91-day bills are delivered, the futures contract allows delivery of a 90-, 91-, or 92-day bill. To augment the supply of deliverable bills, the futures contract expiration is timed to correspond to the date on which the U.S. Treasury's 365-day bill, which is auctioned every four weeks, has 90, 91, or 92 days remaining. However, the contract price is always quoted based on a 90-day bill. For example, suppose a T-bill futures contract is priced such that the discount is 8.25. The IMM quotes the bill price as $100 - 8.25 = 91.75$. This is called the *IMM Index*. Therefore, when you observe the futures price, it will be 91.75. However, that is not the actual price at which you trade the contract and thus is not the real futures price. The actual futures price per $100 is given by the formula

$$f = 100 - (100 - \text{IMM Index})(90/360).$$

For example, if the IMM Index is 91.75,

$$f = 100 - (100 - 91.75)(90/360) = 97.9375.$$

The standard size of a single contract is $1 million face value of T-bills; thus, the futures price is $979,375.

The purpose of assuming a 90-day bill in the formula is that it implies that a one-point move in the IMM Index converts to a $25 change in the futures price. For example, if the IMM Index goes up to 91.76, the futures price will be $979,400. Thus, followers of the contract can quickly assess the dollar impact of a change in the IMM Index. If the holder of the short position elects to make delivery of a 90- or 92-day bill, the formula is adjusted on the delivery day so that 90 or 92 is used instead of 90 in calculating the final price.

The contract expiration months are March, June, September, and December, going out about two years. The last trading day is the business day prior to the date of issue of T-bills in the third week of the month. Delivery can take place on the business day after the last trading day and any day thereafter during the expiration month.

EURODOLLARS   The Eurodollar contract has many of the characteristics of the T-bill contract. We briefly discussed Eurodollars in Chapter 7. Recall that these are dollar deposits in foreign banks or foreign branches of U.S. banks. The Eurodollar interest rate is called *LIBOR* for *London Interbank Offer Rate*. This is the interest rate offered on Eurodollar deposits by large London banks. Although there are no longer ceilings on U.S. interest rates, the Eurodollar rate still is normally higher than U.S. rates on CDs and T-bills due to the credit risk of the issuing bank, the absence of deposit insurance, and the remote possibility of the fall of the foreign government, nationalization of the banks, or other unforeseen political or economic problems.

Another difference between T-bills and Eurodollars is the manner in which their rates are interpreted. The T-bill is a discount instrument, and the Eurodollar is an add-on instrument. For example, although we noted that T-bills and Eurodollars would not have equivalent rates, suppose we assume the quoted rate is 10 percent for both 90-day T-bills and Eurodollars. Then we know that the T-bill price per $100 face value would be $(100 - 10)(90/360) = 97.5$ and that the yield would be $(100/97.5)^{365/90} - 1 = .1081$. Thus, the investor puts down $97.50 today and receives $100 in 90 days. For a Eurodollar deposit of $97.50, the interest would be figured as $97.50(.10)(90/365) = $2.40; thus, the investor would get back $97.50 + $2.40 = $99.90 at expiration. The return would be $(99.90/97.50)^{365/90} - 1 = .1036$. While these differences in rates are significant, T-bills may not yield more than Eurodollars in general, because the Eurodollar rate would simply be quoted higher.

The Eurodollar futures contract is based on a three-month Eurodollar (LIBOR) rate. The contract is for $1 million face value and is quoted by the IMM Index method—the same procedure used for T-bills. However, the Eurodollar contract is settled in cash. The settlement price on the last day of trading is the LIBOR rate as determined by the CME clearinghouse. Contract expirations are March, June, September, and December and extend out about two years. The last trading day is the second London business day before the third Wednesday of the month.

The Eurodollar contract is very actively traded and is much more liquid than the T-bill contract. It is considered an excellent contract for hedging or speculating on short-term interest rates.

Treasury Notes and Bonds

Treasury note and bond contracts, which are traded on the Chicago Board of Trade, are virtually identical except that there are three T-note contracts that are based on 0–2 year, 4–6 year, and 6 1/2–10 year maturities while the T-bond contract is based on Treasury bonds with maturities of at least 15 years that are not callable for at least 15 years. Thus, the T-note contracts are intermediate-term interest rate futures contracts and the T-bond contract is a long-term interest rate futures contract. The T-note contracts are traded quite actively, but the T-bond contract is the most active of all futures contracts. Other than the difference in maturity of the underlying instruments and the margin requirements, the contract terms are essentially identical. We shall, therefore, discuss only the T-bond contract.

The T-bond contract is based on the assumption that the underlying bond has an 8 percent coupon and, as mentioned, a maturity or call date of not less than 15 years. The 8 percent coupon requirement is not restrictive, however. The CBOT permits delivery of bonds with coupons other than 8 percent, with an appropriate adjustment made to the price received for the bonds. There can easily be 30 or more different bond issues eligible for delivery on a given contract.

Recall from Chapter 8 that T-bond prices are quoted in dollars and thirty-seconds of par value of $100. T-bond futures prices are quoted similarly. For example, a futures price of 93-14 is 93 14/32, or 93.4375. The face value of T-bonds underlying the contract is $100,000; therefore, a price of 93.4375 is actually $93,437.50. Expiration months are March, June, September, and December, extending out about two years. The last trading day is the business day prior to the last seven days of the expiration month. The first delivery day is the first business day of the month.

As with most other futures contracts, delivery seldom takes place, but the possibility of delivery is what keeps the contract price in line with conditions in the spot market. We described the delivery procedure in Chapter 7. There are several other delivery issues, which we shall address in the next chapter. For now, however, let us examine how the price the holder of the long position receives for the bond upon delivery is determined.

Suppose you are short the June 1990 contract. As the holder of the short position, you have the choice of which day during the delivery month to make delivery and which bond from among the eligible bonds you will deliver. Let us assume you have decided to deliver the 10 5/8s of August 15, 2015 on June 11.

Since the contract assumes delivery of a bond with an 8 percent coupon, the delivery of the 10 5/8s requires an adjustment to the price paid by the long to the short. The adjustment is based on the CBOT's conversion factor system. The *conversion factor*, *CF*, is defined for each eligible bond for a given contract. The CF is the price of a bond with a face value of $1, coupon and maturity equal to that of the deliverable bond, and yield of 8 percent. The *maturity* is defined as the maturity of the bond on the first day of the delivery month. If the bond is callable, the call date is substituted for the maturity date. The CF for the 10 5/8s of 2015 would be the price of a bond with a face value of $1, coupon of 10 5/8 percent, maturity equal to the time remaining from June 1, 1990, to August 15, 2015, the maturity date of the bond, and yield of 8 percent. That same bond delivered on the September 1990 contract would have a different CF because it would have a different maturity on September 1 than on June 1. A different bond delivered on the March 1990 contract would have a different conversion factor.

The conversion factor system is designed to place all bonds on an equivalent basis for delivery purposes. If the holder of the short position delivers a bond with a coupon greater than 8 percent, the CF will be greater than 1. The short will then receive more than the futures price in payment for the bond. If the coupon is less than 8 percent, the CF will be less than 1 and the short will receive less than the futures price in payment for the bond.

Tables of conversion factors are available, and there is a specific formula for determining the conversion factor, which is provided in Appendix 10B. In this problem, the CF for the 10 5/8s of 2015 delivered on the June 1990 contract would be 1.282. To determine the invoice price—the amount the long pays to the short for the bond—multiply the CF by the settlement price on the position day. Then the accrued interest from the last coupon payment date until the delivery date is added:

$$\text{Invoice price} = (\text{Settlement price on position day})(\text{Conversion factor}) + \text{Accrued interest}.$$

In this problem, the settlement price on June 7, the position day, was 94-02, or $94,062.50. The bond has coupon payment dates of February 15 and August 15. Thus, the last coupon payment date was February 15, 1990. The number of days from February 15 to June 11 is 116, and the number of days between coupon payment dates of February 15, 1990, and August 15, 1990, is 181. Thus, the accrued interest is

$$\$100,000(.10625/2)(116/181) = \$3,404.70.$$

The invoice price therefore is

$$\$94,062.50(1.282) + \$3,404.70 = \$123,992.83.$$

On the notice of intention day, the holder of the long position receives an invoice of $123,992.83 and must pay this amount and accept the bond on the delivery day.

Table 10.3 presents CFs and invoice prices for other bonds deliverable on the June 1990 contract. Note how the CFs vary directly with the level of the coupon.

TABLE 10.3

Some Conversion Factors and Invoice Prices for Deliverable Bonds (June 1990 T-Bond Futures Contract)

Contract price: 94.0625
Delivery date: June 11, 1990

Coupon	Maturity Date	CF	Accrued Interest	Invoice
11 1/4s	2/15/15	1.3468	$3,605	$130,228
10 5/8s	8/15/15	1.2820	3,405	123,993
7 1/2s	11/15/16	0.9453	550	89,467
8 3/4s	5/15/17	1.0820	642	102,418
9 1/8s	5/15/18	1.1245	669	106,442
8 7/8s	2/15/19	1.0977	2,844	106,096
8 1/2s	2/15/20	1.0563	2,724	102,082
8 3/4s	5/15/20	1.0844	642	102,643

Stock Index Futures

The stock index futures contract is based on an index of common stocks. The most widely traded contract is the S&P 500 futures at the Index and Option Market of the Chicago Mercantile Exchange. In Chapter 8, we saw how this index and others are computed. Recall that the S&P 500 originally was set at a base value of 10 in the period 1941 to 1943. The value of the index on March 28, 1991, was 375.22. Thus, the market value of the stocks increased by a factor of 375.22/10 = 37.5 over the approximately 49-year period.

The futures price is quoted in the same manner as the index. The futures contract, however, has an implicit multiplier of $500. Thus, if the futures price is 350, the actual price is 350($500) = $175,000. At the end of the expiration day, the settlement price is set at the price of the S&P 500 index and the contract is settled in cash. The contract expires in March, June, September, and December. Normally only the first two expiration months have much liquidity. The last trading day is the Thursday before the third Friday of the expiration month.

HEDGING STRATEGIES

So far we have examined some basic principles underlying the concept of hedging and the unique characteristics of some of the most popular financial futures contracts. The next step is to illustrate how these hedges are executed. We shall look at some real-world situations chosen from a variety of interest rate environments and illustrating several hedging principles. In all cases, however, we will see the outcomes of actual hedges that could have taken place.

The examples are divided into three groups: short-term interest rate hedges, intermediate- and long-term interest rate hedges, and stock hedges. We begin with short-term interest rate hedges.

Short-Term Interest Rate Hedges

HEDGING THE FUTURE PURCHASE OF A TREASURY BILL   Consider the following scenario. On February 15, a corporate treasurer learns that $1 million will be available on May 17. The funds will be needed for long-term investment later in the year, but meanwhile they should be invested in liquid, interest-earning securities. The treasurer decides to purchase 91-day Treasury bills at the weekly auction on May 17.

T-bills currently are offered at a discount of 8.20. The treasurer is concerned that rates will fall over the next three months, which would mean that the money would be invested at a lower rate. To hedge against falling interest rates, the treasurer decides to use T-bill futures.

Should this be a long or short hedge? Recall from our earlier discussion that the hedger should assume the worst outcome. In this case, that means falling interest rates. How can the hedger make a profit in futures from falling rates? If rates fall, T-bill futures prices, like T-bill spot prices, will rise. Therefore, the hedger should buy the futures.

Because the hedge is to be closed on May 17, the June futures contract should be chosen. Since each contract has a face value of $1 million and a price of close to $1 million, the hedger should purchase one contract.[7] Table 10.4 summarizes the hedge's performance.

If the funds were available, the firm could purchase the T-bills at a discount of 8.20. Recall that this is stated on a 360-day basis. The price per $100 face value therefore is 97.9272. The annualized yield, then, is

$$(100/97.9272)^{365/91} - 1 = .0876.$$

Thus, if the firm could buy the bills now, it would get a yield of 8.76 percent. The $1 million of bills would cost $979,272.

The hedger buys futures at the IMM Index of 91.32. This is a discount of 8.68 and a futures price per $100 of 97.83. Thus, the contract price is $978,300.

Over the next three months, the treasurer's worst fears are realized. Rates have declined and on May 17, the 91-day T-bill is purchased at a discount of 7.69. As Table 10.4 shows, the price of $1 million of T-bills is $980,561. This is a yield

---

[7]Recall that the optimal hedge ratio requires the duration of the spot and futures contracts and the ratio of the yields on the spot and futures instruments. Since we are hedging 91-day T-bills with 90-day T-bill futures, the durations are essentially the same: .25. The yield implied by the futures price of 97.83 is 9.31 percent and the yield on the spot T-bill is 8.76 percent. Using the price sensitivity formula gives a value of N_f of one contract. In other examples in this chapter, we shall illustrate how differences in these factors affect the hedge ratio.

TABLE 10.4

Anticipatory Hedge of a Future Purchase of a Treasury Bill

Scenario: On February 15, a corporate treasurer learns that $1 million will be available on May 17. The treasurer plans to purchase Treasury bills at the weekly auction.

February 15

Spot market: 91-day T-bills are selling at a discount of 8.20

    Price per $100: $100 - 8.20(91/360) = 97.9272$

    Proceeds per $1,000,000: $979,272

    Yield: $(100/97.9272)^{365/91} - 1 = .0876$

Futures market: June T-bill IMM Index is 91.32

    Price per $100: $100 - 8.68(90/360) = 97.83$

    Price per contract: $978,300

Buy one contract

May 17

Spot market: Buy T-bills at a discount of 7.69

    Price per $100: $100 - 7.69(91/360) = 98.0561$

    Proceeds per $1,000,000: $980,561

Futures market: Sell June T-bill futures at IMM Index of 92.54

    Price per $100: $100 - 7.46(90/360) = 98.135$

    Price per contract: $981,350

Sell one contract

Results

Yield on T-bills without hedge: $(100/98.0561)^{365/91} - 1 = .0819$

Profit on futures transaction: $981,350 - $978,300 = $3,050

Effective price of T-bills with hedge:

    $980,561   (price of T-bills)

    <u> - 3,050</u>   (futures profit)

    $977,511   (effective price)

Effective yield: $(1,000,000/977,511)^{365/91} - 1 = .0955$

---

of 8.19 percent. The June futures price on the IMM Index was 92.54, which is a price of $981,350. The futures is sold for a profit of $3,050.

    The profit on the futures contract can be viewed as implicitly lowering the cost of the T-bills purchased in the spot market; that is, the T-bills cost $980,561, but the profit of $3,050 on the futures contract offsets a portion of this, leaving a net cost of $977,511. If $1 million of bills is purchased at $977,511, the annualized yield, as shown in the table, is 9.55 percent, which is substantially above the 8.19 percent yield for the unhedged position.

    Note that we have described this hedge as though the treasurer were attempting to lock in the yield of 8.76 percent on February 15. In fact, however, a futures hedge attempts to lock in not the current spot rate but the current forward rate that spans the time period beginning at the date on which the hedge is terminated and ending when the deliverable instrument matures. Thus, in this problem it is the forward rate from May 17 to August 16, 91 days thereafter. The spot and forward rates will be equal when the term structure is flat. Because forward prices are essentially equal to futures prices, we know that this rate is approximately the return earned by buying a T-bill at the original futures price of 97.83 and holding it for 91 days until it matures. This rate would be $(100/97.83)^{365/91} - 1 = .0920$. Thus, we are actually attempting to lock in a yield of 9.20 percent. Because of a favorable move in the basis, the rate actually received was even better: 9.55 percent.

The hedge has worked because the spot and futures T-bill prices moved in the same direction. In this case, rates declined. Had rates risen, the T-bills would have been less expensive, thus offering a higher yield. The futures position would have produced a loss, however, and this would have offset some or all of the gain made in the spot market. In that case, the hedge would have been effective, but the hedger would have wished that the hedge had not been done. The price one pays for hedging is that it will occasionally produce losses on the futures position that will absorb gains made in the spot market.

The above hedge is just one of many types of long hedges one can execute with interest rate futures contracts on short-term instruments. Many types of firms and some individuals determine that they will be investing funds in money market instruments at a later date. As long as the decision to invest the funds is unlikely to be reversed, a hedge is appropriate. This does not mean, however, that one should always hedge. If the hedger believes rates are abnormally low and likely to rise, the hedge will lock in the low rate while money market rates might increase. Thus, the hedger should not blindly hedge in all interest rate environments. Although in an efficient market the hedger should be unable to effectively time the interest rate cycle, it would still be inappropriate for the hedger to ignore his or her own expectations. This will be true for all of the remaining cases.

HEDGING A FUTURE COMMERCIAL PAPER ISSUE Corporations continuously borrow funds in short-term markets. These funds supply working capital that firms use to finance inventory and accounts receivable and provide liquidity with which to meet interest payments on long-term loans. Large, creditworthy corporations frequently borrow by issuing commercial paper, a short-term promissory note.

Suppose that on April 6 a corporate treasurer determines that on July 20, the firm will need to issue $10 million of commercial paper with a maturity of 180 days. Commercial paper rates are quoted on a 360-day basis, and the paper is discounted. Thus, commercial paper is like Treasury bills, and the calculations for determining the purchase price and effective yield are the same. Table 10.5 shows the results of the hedge.

For simplicity, we shall assume a flat yield curve, so the forward rate is the rate that the hedger is attempting to lock in. If the paper were issued on April 6, the discount rate would be 10.17 percent. The $10 million would be discounted, and the firm would receive $9,491,500.[8] The annualized yield on the paper thus

---

[8]We assume the firm can get by with slightly less than $10 million in cash. Otherwise, it would need to issue more than $10 million of face value of commercial paper.

TABLE 10.5

Anticipatory Hedge of a Future Commercial Paper Issue

Scenario: On April 6, a corporate treasurer learns that on July 20 the firm will have to issue $10 million of commercial paper.

April 6
Spot market: Current rate on 180-day paper is 10.17
   Proceeds per $100: $100 - 10.17(180/360) = 94.915$
   Proceeds per $10,000,000: $9,491,500
   Yield: $(100/94.915)^{365/180} - 1 = .1116$
Futures market: September Eurodollar IMM Index is 88.23
   Price per $100: $100 - 11.77(90/360) = 97.0575$
   Price per contract: $970,575
   Implied yield: $(100/97.0575)^{365/90} - 1 = .1288$
Sell 20 contracts

July 20
Spot market: Issue paper at 11.34
   Proceeds per $100: $100 - 11.34(180/360) = 94.33$
   Proceeds per $10,000,000: $9,433,000
Futures market: September Eurodollar IMM Index is 87.47
   Price per $100: $100 - 12.53(90/360) = 96.8675$
   Price per contract: $968,675
Buy 20 contracts

Results
Cost of paper without hedge: $(100/94.33)^{365/180} - 1 = .1257$
Profit on futures transaction: $-20($968,675 - $970,575) = $38,000$
Effective proceeds with hedge:
   $9,433,000   (proceeds of issue)
       38,000   (futures profit)
   $9,471,000   (effective proceeds)
Effective cost of paper: $(10,000,000/9,471,000)^{365/180} - 1 = .1165$

would be 11.16 percent. This means the firm would be borrowing at a rate of 11.16 percent. The treasurer is concerned that interest rates will increase and that the loan therefore will be more costly. If rates do increase, the firm can earn a profit in the futures market by being short.

What is the appropriate futures commodity? T-bills or Eurodollars would be the prime candidates. The treasurer has heard that the Eurodollar contract is more liquid than the T-bill contract and responds more rapidly to changes in short-term interest rates. Moreover, Eurodollars represent rates on loans made by private borrowers, namely European banks, and T-bills reflect government borrowing rates. Since the firm is a private borrower, the Eurodollar contract seems more appropriate. Because the hedge will be terminated on July 20, the treasurer chooses the September contract.

Recall that the price sensitivity formula for the number of futures contracts, N_f, is

$$N_f = -\frac{DUR_s S(1+y_f)}{DUR_f f(1+y_s)}.$$

The spot instrument is 180-day commercial paper, and the futures commodity is 90-day Eurodollars. Because neither commercial paper nor Eurodollars pay coupons, their durations are simply their maturities. Thus, $DUR_s = 180/365$, $DUR_f = 90/365$, and $DUR_s/DUR_f = 2$.

The value of S is the current proceeds from the commercial paper, $9,491,500. The value of f is the price of one futures contract, which, based on an IMM Index of 88.23, is $970,575. The term y_s is the yield on the commercial paper if issued now; this is 11.16 percent. The term y_f is the yield on 90-day Eurodollars that is implied by the current futures price. Thus, we simply find the annualized yield on a 90 day Eurodollar selling for 97.0575 per $100 face value. As Table 10.5 shows, this is 12.88 percent.

Plugging these numbers into the formula for N_f gives

$$N_f = -2\left(\frac{9,491,500}{970,575}\right)\left(\frac{1.1288}{1.1116}\right) = -19.86.$$

Because fractional contracts cannot be held, the hedger should sell 20 contracts.

On May 17, the firm issues the commercial paper at a discount of 11.34 percent. This nets proceeds of $9,433,000. In the last section of Table 10.5, we see that the cost of the paper is 12.57 percent. The September futures contract is selling for an IMM Index price of 87.47. This converts to a price per contract of $968,675. Thus, the 20 futures contracts generate a profit of −20($968,675 − $970,575), or $38,000.

The profit on the futures contract effectively raises the proceeds from issuing the paper to $9,471,000. Thus, the firm is issuing $10 million of paper and essentially receiving $9,471,000 for it. As the last line of Table 10.5 shows, this results in a cost of 11.65 percent. Thus, the hedge has reduced the firm's cost of borrowing from 12.57 to 11.65 percent. It is obvious that had we not taken into account the different volatilities of the spot and futures prices, we would have used only ten contracts and the hedge would have been far less effective.

The hedge worked because Eurodollar and commercial paper rates moved in the same direction—in this case, upward. Had rates moved downward, there would have been a loss on the futures transaction and the loan would have been less expensive without the hedge. However, the firm would not have known that rates would have decreased; thus, it bought the protection of the hedge at the risk of a decrease in interest rates.

What we have just seen is a short hedge. The example is applicable to a wide variety of similar situations. For example, the firm could take out a bank loan rather than issue commercial paper. A bank could plan to borrow funds by issuing CDs. Any type of firm that anticipated borrowing money at a future time would be able to reduce the uncertainty of the rate at which it would borrow by selling futures contracts.

HEDGING A FLOATING RATE LOAN   In addition to interest rate futures, there are other ways to hedge the risk of changing interest rates. For example, a bank might require that the interest rate on a loan float with market interest rates. If interest rates increase, the rate the bank charges on the loan will go up and at least partially cover the additional cost to the bank of borrowing the money. Thus, the bank will pass on the interest rate risk to its loan customers.

This will place the burden of hedging on the borrower. If the loan rate is tied to a floating market rate, the borrower must get into a position to profit when interest rates increase. It can do this by selling interest rate futures contracts.

Consider the following situation. On February 3, a firm decides to take out a three-month, $10 million loan from a bank. The rate on the loan will be set on the first Friday of the month and will equal that day's LIBOR rate plus 100 basis points. For simplicity, we shall assume the monthly rate will be one-twelfth of the annual rate. Here, as in reality, the exact number of days in the interest payment period are counted. The firm can repay any part or all of the loan at any time.

February 3   Since the current annual LIBOR rate is 9.68 percent, the first month's annual rate will be 10.68 percent. We shall assume a flat term structure, so the borrower will attempt to lock in this rate for the next three months. If the borrower does so, the effective annualized borrowing rate on the loan will be

$$[1 + (.1068/12)]^{12} - 1 = .1122.$$

Since the loan rate is tied to the LIBOR rate, the Eurodollar futures contract is the appropriate hedging vehicle. Determining the number of contracts, however, is not a straightforward process. The new rates will be set on March 2 and April 6. If interest rates increase, the loan rate will go up and the hedger will need to be short futures contracts. This problem can be thought of as two anticipatory hedges, one of the new rate in effect on March 2 and one of the new rate in effect on April 6.

Let us use the price sensitivity formula to compute the hedge ratio. The spot position, S, is $10 million, and the yield, y_S, is 11.22 percent. Because the March contract expires before the hedge is terminated, the June contract should be used. The June IMM Index is 90.75, which gives a price of $976,875 per contract. The yield implied on a 90-day Eurodollar deposit of $976,875 is $(\$1,000,000/\$976,875)^{365/90} - 1 = .0995$. Thus, f = $976,875 and y_f = 9.95 percent.

Now we need the durations, DUR_S and DUR_f. The spot duration is its maturity of one month. The futures duration is the maturity of the underlying Eurodollar deposit at expiration, which is three months. Thus, $DUR_S = 1/12$ and $DUR_f = 1/4$. The value of N_f is

$$N_f = -\frac{(1/12)(\$10,000,000)(1.0995)}{(1/4)(\$976,875)(1.1122)} = -3.37.$$

Rounding off gives three contracts. However, remember that the firm is hedging two interest rate adjustments, one on March 2 and one on April 6. Thus, the firm should use six contracts, with three to be closed out on March 2 and three to be closed out on April 6. Therefore, let the firm sell six contracts.

March 2   With the first month's rate set at 10.68 percent, the accumulated principal and interest on the loan are

$$\$10,000,000[1 + (.1068/12)] = \$10,089,000.$$

The LIBOR rate on that day is 10.09 percent, so the next month's rate will be 11.09 percent. The June IMM Index is at 90.47, giving a futures price of $976,175. The firm buys back three contracts and makes a profit of

$$-3(\$976,175 - \$976,875) = \$2,100.$$

The funds are applied toward the loan balance, reducing it to

$$\$10,089,000 - \$2,100 = \$10,086,900.$$

April 6   Based on a rate of 11.09 percent, the accumulated principal and interest are

$$\$10,086,900[1 + (.1109/12)] = \$10,180,211.$$

The new LIBOR rate is 10.79 percent, so next month's interest rate will be 11.79 percent. The June IMM Index is 89.99, which gives a futures price of $974,975. The firm buys back the remaining three contracts, producing a profit of

$$-3(\$974,975 - \$976,875) = \$5,700.$$

This is applied toward the loan balance, reducing it to

$$\$10,180,211 - \$5,700 = \$10,174,511.$$

There are now no futures positions outstanding.

May 4   At 11.79 percent, the principal and interest add up to

$$\$10,174,511[1 + (.1179/12)] = \$10,274,476.$$

This is the final amount to be repaid. The effective rate on the loan is, thus,

$$(\$10,274,476/\$10,000,000)^4 - 1 = .1140,$$

which is slightly higher than the 11.22 percent the firm was attempting to lock in. However, had the firm not hedged, the rate on the loan would have been

$$\{[1 + (.1068/12)][1 + (.1109/12)][1 + (.1179/12)]\}^4 - 1 = .1178$$

Thus, the hedge reduced the effective cost of the loan from 11.78 to 11.40 percent. Each time the LIBOR rate increased, the Eurodollar futures price decreased. The futures transactions produced a profit that was applied to the balance of the loan and reduced the effect of the higher interest rate over the next month. Had rates decreased, the futures contracts would have produced a loss that would have offset some of the benefits of the lower loan rate for the upcoming month.

Floating-rate loans are very common in our financial system. They are but one means of passing on the interest rate risk to the borrower. Some banks prefer to offer their customers fixed-rate loans, but the rates on the CDs they issue float with market interest rates. The bank can then hedge its floating-rate financing and offer its loan customers a fixed rate. Since banks are probably more knowledgeable about the benefits of hedging, this type of arrangement should be common. Unfortunately, it is not. As we shall see later, banks do not use interest rate futures as much as one would think given their central position in the financial system and the risk exposure they face.

The type of hedge described in this section is called a *strip hedge* or simply a *strip*. It can also be used as an arbitrage strategy whereby the investor effectively creates a synthetic 90-day (or longer) fixed rate security. The return on this security can be compared against the return from actual 90-day securities or from swaps, a topic to be covered in Chapter 14. A variation of the strip hedge is called a *rolling strip hedge*, in which the hedger attempts to extend the effective maturity further out than the availability of the futures contracts permits. In that case, the hedger simply rolls forward the expiring contracts into new contracts as they become available. When the liquidity of contracts with longer maturities raises concerns about using them, the hedger might wish to use a larger quantity of the shorter-term futures and gradually roll over into the longer-term futures as their expirations become shorter and they become more liquid. This transaction is referred to as a *stack hedge*. Of course, all the strategies involving rolling over into new contracts will entail some additional basis risk.

Intermediate- and Long-Term Interest Rate Futures Hedges

HEDGING A LONG POSITION IN A GOVERNMENT BOND   Portfolio managers constantly face decisions about when to buy and sell securities. In some cases, such decisions are automatic. Securities are sold at certain times to generate cash for meeting obligations such as pension payments. Consider the following example.

On February 25, a portfolio manager holds $1 million face value of government bonds with a coupon of 11 7/8 percent and maturing in about 19 years. The bond currently is priced at 101 per $100 par value, and the yield is 11.74 percent. The duration is 7.83 years. The bond must be sold on March 28.

The portfolio manager is concerned that interest rates will increase, resulting in a lower bond price and the possibility that the proceeds from the bond's sale will be inadequate for meeting the pension obligation. The manager knows that if interest rates increase, a short futures position will yield a profit that can offset at least part of any decrease in the bond's value. Since this is a government bond, the Treasury bond futures contract should be used.

Because the hedge will be closed on March 28, the June contract should be used. Currently it is selling for 70 16/32, or $70,500 per contract. The number of contracts should be determined by the formula for N_f.

To determine the duration and implied yield on the futures contract, the firm must identify which of the many eligible deliverable bonds the contract is tracking. By *tracking* we mean that the futures contract behaves as if this bond is the instrument to be delivered. The choice of bonds is a type of arbitrage decision that we cover in Chapter 11. For now, let us assume the contract is tracking the T-bond that has a coupon of 10 3/8 percent and matures in about 25 years.

We assume the futures contract expires on the first day of the delivery month, June 1. Using the futures price of 70.5 per $100, the deliverable bond would have a duration of 7.20 years. The yield would be 14.92 percent.

Plugging into the formula for N_f, we get

$$N_f = -\left(\frac{7.83}{7.20}\right)\left(\frac{1,010,000}{70,500}\right)\left(\frac{1.1492}{1.1174}\right)$$

$$= -16.02.$$

Thus, the manager sells 16 contracts. Table 10.6 shows the results of the hedge.

The amount the portfolio manager is trying to hedge is the current value of the bonds, $1,010,000.[9] On March 28, the bond price indeed was down to 95 22/32, so the manager sells the bonds for $956,875—a loss of $53,125. The June futures contract is at 66 23/32, a price of $66,718.75, for a profit of $3,781.25. Since the manager sold 16 contracts, the profit was $60,500, which produced an overall profit on the bond of $7,375.

Because the bond price was positively correlated with the futures price, the hedge was effective in covering the loss and actually produced a small gain. Had bond yields moved down, the futures price would have increased and, being short in futures, the hedge would have shown a loss on the futures transaction. This would have absorbed some or all of the gain made from the increased value of the bond.

---

[9]Technically, the accrued interest would be included here, but it is not subject to any uncertainty, so we leave it out of the hedging examples.

TABLE 10.6
Hedging a Long Position in a Government Bond

Scenario: On February 25, a portfolio manager holds $1 million face value of a government bond, the 11 7/8s maturing in about 19 years. The bond is currently priced at 101 and will be sold on March 28.

February 25
Spot market: Current price of bonds is 101
　Value of position: $1,010,000
Futures market: June T-bond futures are at 70 16/32
　Price per contract: $70,500
Sell 16 contracts

March 28
Spot market: Sell bonds at 95 22/32
　Price per bond: $956.875
　Value of portfolio: $956,875
Futures market: June T-bond futures are at 66 23/32
　Price per contract: $66,718.75
Buy 16 contracts

Results
Profit on portfolio: $956,875 − $1,010,000 = − $53,125
Profit on futures: − 16($66,718.75 − $70,500) = $60,500
Overall profit: − $53,125 + $60,500 = $7,375

This short hedge represents one of the most common hedging applications, and we shall see a slight variation of it later, when we examine stock index futures hedging. This hedge is applicable to many firms and institutions, such as banks, insurance companies, pension funds, and mutual funds.

ANTICIPATORY HEDGE OF A FUTURE PURCHASE OF A TREASURY NOTE Previously we saw how one could hedge the future purchase of a Treasury bill. In this example, we do the same with a Treasury note. We also take a slightly different approach to determining the hedge ratio.

Suppose that on March 29, a portfolio manager determines that approximately $1 million will be available on July 15. The manager decides to purchase the 11 5/8 Treasury notes maturing in about nine years. The current price of the notes is 97 28/32, or $978,750, for $1 million face value. If yields decline, the notes' price will increase and the manager may be unable to make the purchase. If this happens, a profit could have been made by purchasing futures contracts. Because the Treasury note futures contract is quite liquid, the manager decides to buy T-note futures.

Because the hedge is to be terminated on July 15, the September contract is appropriate. In this example, let us illustrate an alternative approach to estimating

TABLE 10.7

Anticipatory Hedge of a Future Purchase of a Treasury Note

Scenario: On March 29, a portfolio manager determines that approximately $1 million will be available for investment on July 15. The manager plans to purchase the 11 5/8s Treasury notes maturing in about nine years.

March 29
Spot market: Current price of notes is 97 28/32
  Price per note: $978.75
  Cost of notes: $978,750
Futures market: September T-note futures are at 78 21/32
  Price per contract: $78,656.25
Buy 11 contracts

July 15
Spot market: Buy T-notes at 107 19/32
  Price per note: $1,075.9375
  Cost of notes: $1,075,937.50
Futures market: September T-note futures are at 86 6/32
  Price per contract: $86,187.50
Sell 11 contracts

Results
Change in cost of T-notes: $1,075,937.50 – $978,750 = $97,187.50
Profit on futures transaction: 11($86,187.50 – $78,656.25) = $82,843.75
Net additional cost of T-notes: $97,187.50 – $82,843.75 = $14,343.75

the hedge ratio. Recall that N_f should equal $-\Delta S/\Delta f$. This can be estimated from the price sensitivity formula we applied in previous examples or from a historical regression of the change in the portfolio value on the change in the futures price. The portfolio manager ran that regression using daily spot and futures prices over the period of January 2 through March 28. The regression coefficient was 10.5, and the measure of hedging effectiveness was 59.5 percent. Thus, the optimal number of futures contracts should be 10.5. Therefore, the hedger buys 11 contracts. The results of the hedge are shown in Table 10.7.

On July 15, the T-note price is 107 19/32. The cost of the $1 million-face-value notes is $1,075,937.50, which is $97,187.50 higher. The futures price is 86 6/32, or $86,187.50 per contract. This produces a profit of $82,843.75, which offsets about 85 percent of the increased cost of the notes. The net effect is that the notes cost only about $14,000 more.

Had bond prices moved down, the hedger would have regretted doing the hedge. The notes would have cost less, but this would have been offset by a loss on the futures contract. Once again, this is the price of hedging—forgoing gains to limit losses.

HEDGING A CORPORATE BOND ISSUE   One interesting application of an interest rate futures hedge occurs when a firm decides to issue bonds at a future date. There is an interim period during which the firm prepares the necessary paperwork and works out an underwriting arrangement for distributing the bonds. During that period, interest rates could increase so that when the bonds ultimately are issued, they will command a higher yield. This will be more costly to the issuer.

Consider the following example. On February 24, a corporation decides to issue $5 million face value of bonds on May 24. As a standard of comparison, the firm currently has a bond issue outstanding with a coupon of 9 3/8 percent, a yield of 13.76 percent, and a maturity of about 21 years. Any new bonds issued will require a similar yield. If the bonds are issued now, the coupon will be set at 13.76 percent, so the bonds will go out at par.

If rates increase, the firm will have to discount the bonds or adjust the coupon upward to the new market yield. We shall assume that the coupon is fixed so that the price will decrease. In either case, the firm will incur a loss. The firm realizes that if rates increase, it can make a profit from a short transaction in futures. Thus, it decides to hedge the issue by selling futures contracts.

The corporate bond futures contract introduced at the Chicago Board of Trade in the fall of 1987 would have been the preferred hedging vehicle, but that contract did not succeed. Therefore, the hedger chooses the Treasury bond futures contract. Because the hedge will be closed on May 24, the June contract is chosen. The current price of the June contract is 68 11/32, or $68,343.75 per contract. The firm uses the price sensitivity formula to compute the hedge ratio.

To compute the value of N_f, the firm must identify which T-bond the futures contract is tracking. As noted earlier, we shall cover this in Chapter 11. For now, let us assume it is the 9 1/8s maturing in about 25 years. Applying the duration formula on the first day of the delivery month to the deliverable bond with a price of 68.34375 gives a duration of 7.83 years. The implied yield is 13.60 percent.

The firm plans to issue 20-year bonds with a coupon and yield of 13.76 percent on February 24. The duration of the bond is 7.22. Now we have all the variables and can plug into the formula for N_f:

$$N_f = -\left(\frac{7.22}{7.83}\right)\left(\frac{5,000,000}{68,343.75}\right)\left(\frac{1.1360}{1.1376}\right)$$

$$= -67.4.$$

The firm decides to use 67 contracts. Table 10.8 shows the results.

On May 24, the yield on comparable bonds is 15.25 percent. Thus, we assume the bonds will be issued at a yield of 15.25 percent. The bonds are discounted in the market and go out at a price of 90.74638 per $100 face value. Thus, the firm nets only $4,537,319, which is $462,681 less. The futures price is 60 25/32, or $60,781.25. The profit on the 67 futures contracts is $506,687.50. Thus, the futures profit absorbs the loss on the issuance of the bonds and leaves a net gain of $44,006.50.

TABLE 10.8
Hedging a Corporate Bond Issue

Scenario: On February 24, a corporation decides to issue $5 million of bonds on May 24. The firm currently has comparable bonds outstanding with a coupon of 9 3/8, a yield of 13.76 percent, and a maturity of about 21 years. If the bonds were issued now, it is believed that they would go out with a 13.76 percent coupon and be priced at par with a 20-year maturity.

February 24

Spot market: If issued now, bonds would offer a coupon of 13.76 percent and be priced at par

   Value of bonds: $5,000,000

Futures market: June T-bond futures are at 68 11/32

   Price per contract: $68,343.75

Sell 67 contracts

May 24

Spot market: The yield on comparable bonds is 15.25 percent. The bonds are issued at 13.76 percent coupon and price of 90.74638.

   Price per bond: $907.46

   Value of bonds: $4,537,319

Futures market: June T-bond futures are at 60 25/32

   Price per contract: $60,781.25

Buy 67 contracts

Results

Change in value of bonds: $4,537,319 – $5,000,000 = – $462,681

Profit on futures transaction: – 67($60,781.25 – $68,343.75) = $506,687.50

Net change in value of bonds: $44,006.50

Had interest rates declined, the firm would have obtained a higher price for the bonds; however, this would have been at least partially offset by a loss on the futures transaction. By executing the hedge, the firm was able to protect itself against an interest rate change while preparing the issue. In a similar vein, investment bankers might do this type of hedge. An investment banker purchases the bonds from the firm and then resells them to investors. Between the time the bonds are purchased and resold, the investment banker is exposed to the risk that bond yields will increase.[10] Therefore, a short hedge such as this would be appropriate. Many investment banking firms have been able to protect themselves against large losses by hedging with interest rate futures.

[10]Investment bankers do employ other means of minimizing their risk exposure. The use of a syndicate, in which a large number of investment bankers individually take a small portion of the issue, spreads out the risk. Many issues are taken on a "best efforts" basis. This allows the investment banker to return the securities to the issuing firm if market conditions make the sale of the securities impossible without substantial price concessions.

Stock Index Futures Hedges

Many of the hedging examples illustrated with T-note and T-bond futures are similar to stock index futures hedges. In both cases, a firm attempts to hedge a position in a long-term security, whether a stock or a bond. The first example we shall look at is the hedge of a stock portfolio.

STOCK PORTFOLIO HEDGE   A central tenet of modern investment theory is that diversification eliminates unsystematic risk, leaving only systematic risk. Until the creation of stock index futures, investors had to accept the fact that systematic risk could not be eliminated. Now investors can use stock index futures to hedge the systematic risk. But should they do that? If all systematic and unsystematic risk is eliminated, the portfolio can expect to earn only the risk-free return. Why not just buy T-bills? The answer is that investors occasionally wish to change or eliminate systematic risk for brief periods. During periods of unusual volatility in the market, they can use stock index futures to adjust or eliminate the systematic risk. This is much easier and less costly than adjusting the relative proportions invested in each stock. Later the portfolio manager can close out the futures position, and the portfolio systematic risk will be back at its original level. The next example concerns a portfolio manager who has accumulated a profit on a portfolio and wishes to protect that profit during the time remaining before the portfolio's liquidation.

On January 3, a portfolio manager is concerned about the market over the next quarter, which ends on March 30. The portfolio has accumulated an impressive return, and the manager wishes to protect that position against any declines in the stock market over the approximately three-month period.

If the stock market falls, a short position in stock index futures will produce a profit. The manager decides to sell S&P 500 stock index futures contracts. Because the hedge will be closed on March 30, the June contract is the appropriate choice. The number of contracts will depend on the portfolio's beta. Table 10.9 provides information about the component stocks as well as details of the hedge transaction.

The second column, the current price, times the third column, the number of shares owned, gives the fourth column, the market value of each stock. The total market value of the portfolio is $2,369,650. The weights shown in the fifth column are each stock's market value divided by the portfolio's total market value. For example, the market value of the Federal Mogul stock is $338,400, which is 14.3 percent of the total market value of $2,369,650.

The beta of each stock is shown in the last column. The portfolio beta is given by the formula

$$\beta_p = \sum_{j=1}^{K} w_j \beta_j ,$$

TABLE 10.9
Stock Portfolio Hedge

Scenario: On January 3, a portfolio manager is concerned about the market over the next quarter, which ends on March 30. The portfolio has accumulated an impressive profit, which the manager wishes to protect. The prices, number of shares, and betas are given below:

Stock	Price (1/3)	Number of Shares	Market Value	Weight	Beta
Federal Mogul	36	9,400	$338,400	.143	.80
Martin Marietta	36	8,000	288,000	.121	1.25
R. J. Reynolds	60.5	6,000	363,000	.153	.90
Telex	25.125	9,300	233,663	.099	1.60
Tandy	42.75	6,600	282,150	.119	1.40
Chase Manhattan	45.5	9,500	432,250	.182	.95
American Brands	59.375	3,700	219,687	.093	.70
Emery	25	8,500	212,500	.090	1.10
Total value			$2,369,650		

Portfolio Beta: $.80(.143) + 1.25(.121) + .90(.153) + 1.60(.099) + 1.40(.119) + .95(.182) + .70(.093) + 1.10(.09) = 1.065$

S&P 500 June futures price: 167.95

Price per contract: $167.95(\$500) = \$83,975$

$N_f = -(\$2,369,650/\$83,975)(1.065) = -30.05$

Sell 30 contracts

Results: The values of the stocks on March 30 are shown below:

Stock	Price (3/30)	Market Value
Federal Mogul	32.75	$307,850
Martin Marietta	33.375	267,000
R. J. Reynolds	56.875	341,250
Telex	22.25	206,926
Tandy	31.375	207,075
Chase Manhattan	48.625	461,938
American Brands	54.5	201,650
Emery	18.25	155,125
Total value		$2,148,812

S&P 500 futures price: 161.05

Price per contract: $161.05(\$500) = \$80,525$

Profit on portfolio: $\$2,148,812 - \$2,369,650 = -\$220,838$

Profit on futures: $-30(\$80,525 - \$83,975) = \$103,500$

Net profit on hedge: $-\$220,838 + \$103,500 = -\$117,338$

where

β_p = portfolio beta
K = number of stocks
w_j = weight of stock j
β_j = beta of stock j

Thus, the portfolio beta is a weighted average of the individual security betas. As Table 10.9 shows, the portfolio beta is 1.065.

In the formula for the hedge ratio for stock index futures, we had

$$N_f = -\beta_s \left(\frac{S}{f} \right).$$

The term β_s is the stock's beta. In the case of a portfolio, it is the portfolio's beta. The value of S is the market value of the stock, $2,369,650. The only other term is f, the futures price. The S&P contract is priced at 167.95. With a multiplier of $500, this gives a contract price of $83,975. Plugging into the formula for N_f gives

$$N_f = -\frac{\$2,369,650}{\$83,975}(1.065) = -30.05.$$

Thus, the manager should sell 30 contracts.

The lower half of Table 10.9 shows the price and market value of the stocks on March 30, the date on which they are sold. The market did decline, and the portfolio is now worth $2,148,812. This is a loss of $220,838. However, the futures price on March 30 was 161.05, so the price per contract was $80,525. The 30 contracts generated a futures profit of $103,500. This reduced the overall loss to $117,338.

The objective of the hedge was to eliminate systematic risk. Clearly systematic risk was reduced but not eliminated. The stock portfolio value declined about 9.3 percent, while the futures price decreased a little over 4 percent.

There are several possible explanations for this result. One is that the betas are only an estimate taken from a popular investment advisory service. Beta estimates over the recent past have not necessarily been stable. It is also possible that the portfolio was not fully diversified and some unsystematic risk contributed to the loss. Some of the stocks may have paid dividends during the hedge period. We did not account for these dividends in illustrating the hedge results. Dividends would have reduced the loss on the portfolio and made the hedge more effective.

Had the market moved up, the portfolio would have shown a profit, but this would have been at least partially offset by a loss on the futures transaction. In either outcome, however, the portfolio manager would have been reasonably successful in capturing at least some of the accumulated profit on the portfolio.

ANTICIPATORY HEDGE OF A TAKEOVER   The exciting world of mergers and takeovers offers an excellent opportunity to apply hedging concepts. The acquiring firm identifies a target firm and intends to make a bid for the latter's stock. Typically the acquiring firm plans to purchase enough stock to obtain control. Because of the large amount of stock usually involved and the speed with which takeover rumors travel, the acquiring firm frequently makes a series of smaller purchases until it has accumulated sufficient shares to obtain control. During the period in which the acquiring firm is slowly and quietly buying the stock, it is exposed to the risk that stock prices in general will increase. This means that either the shares will cost more or fewer shares can be purchased.

Consider the following situation. On November 17, a firm has identified Lotus Development Corporation as a potential acquisition.[11] Lotus stock currently is selling for $49.50. The acquiring firm plans to buy 100,000 shares, so it will cost $4,950,000. The purchase will be made on December 17. This could be viewed as one purchase in a series of purchases designed to ultimately acquire controlling interest in the target firm. The acquiring firm realizes that if stock prices as a whole increase, the shares will be more expensive. In fact, Lotus has a beta of 2, so the shares are expected to increase at twice the rate of the market as a whole. However, if the firm purchases stock index futures, any general increase in stock prices will lead to a profit in the futures market.

Because the hedge will be terminated on December 17, the acquiring firm chooses to buy March S&P 500 futures. The price of 244.05 and multiplier of $500 give a contract price of $122,025. Given the beta of 2, the number of contracts is

$$N_f = -2(\$4,950,000/\$122,025) = -81.13.$$

Since the firm is buying futures, we ignore the negative sign. Thus, the firm buys 81 contracts. Table 10.10 shows the results of the hedge.

On December 17, the Lotus stock price is $52.25. The shares thus cost an additional $275,000.[12] However, the futures price is 248.5, which converts to a contract price of $124,250. The profit on the futures transaction was $180,225. Thus, the net additional cost of the shares is $94,775.

The hedge was successful in reducing the additional cost of the shares by about two-thirds; however, the unsystematic risk cannot be hedged.[13] In takeover situations, the unsystematic risk is likely to be very high. For example, if word leaks out that someone is buying up the stock, the price will tend to rise substantially. This can occur even if the market as a whole is going down. Also, federal regulations require that certain takeover attempts be announced beforehand.

The takeover game is intense and exciting, with high risk and the potential for large profits. Stock index futures can play an important role, but the extent to

---

[11]A specific firm was chosen for this example so that we could use actual market prices. At the time of this writing, Lotus was not known to be a takeover target.

[12]It is unlikely that all of the 100,000 shares could have been purchased at the same price. Therefore, we should treat $52.25 as the average price at which the shares were acquired.

[13]However, if there were options on the target firm's stock, the acquiring firm could use these to hedge the unsystematic risk.

TABLE 10.10

Anticipatory Hedge of a Takeover

Scenario: On November 17, a firm has identified Lotus Development Corporation as a potential acquisition. The acquisition will be made by purchasing lots of about 100,000 shares until sufficient control is obtained. The first purchase of 100,000 shares will take place on December 17.

November 17

Spot market: Lotus stock currently is priced at 49.5.
   Total cost of 100,000 shares: $4,950,000
   Lotus's beta: 2
Futures market: March S&P 500 futures are priced at 244.05
   Price per contract: (244.05)($500) = $122,025
Buy 81 contracts

December 17

Spot market: Buy 100,000 shares of Lotus at 52.25
   Total cost of 100,000 shares: $5,225,000
Futures market: March S&P 500 futures are priced at 248.5
   Price per contract: (248.5)($500) = $124,250
Sell 81 contracts

Results

Additional cost of 100,000 shares: $5,225,000 – $4,950,000 = $275,000
Profit on futures transaction: 81($124,250 – $122,025) = $180,225
Net additional cost: $275,000 – $180,225 = $94,775

which futures are used to hedge this kind of risk is not known, because much of this kind of activity is done with a minimum of publicity.

The takeover example is but one type of situation wherein a firm can use a long hedge with stock index futures. Any time someone is considering buying a stock, there is the risk that the stock price will increase before the purchase is made. Stock index futures cannot hedge the risk that factors specific to the company will drive up the stock price, but they can be used to protect against increases in the market as a whole.

Is hedging really effective in reducing risk? There probably has been no topic in the area of futures more extensively examined than hedging. There have been numerous studies of the effectiveness of hedging employing the various types of hedge ratios and using the coefficient of determination from the regression of spot price changes on futures price changes. Studies by Ederington (1979), McCabe and Solberg (1989), and Senchak and Easterwood (1983) showed the effectiveness of T-bill hedges in reducing the risk of short-term interest rates. Hill and Schneeweis (1982), Gay, Kolb, and Chiang (1983), and Chance, Marr, and Thompson (1986) found evidence of the effectiveness of T-bond futures hedges. Figlewski

(1984) and Graham and Jennings (1987) showed the effectiveness of stock index futures hedges.

Ironically, knowledge of the benefits of hedging has taken a long time to reach those who would gain from it. In fact, the U.S. savings and loan crisis, though partly a result of fraud, is at least partially due to the failure of thrifts to hedge. Block and Gallagher (1986) and Veit and Reiff (1983) reported that corporations and banks hedge very little. It has been awhile, however, since those studies were conducted, and it remains to be determined whether hedging has become more or less widely used. There is no question that today many large firms and financial institutions are actively involved in hedging, but many smaller ones are still somewhat hesitant.

Thus, it appears that those who stand to benefit the most from hedging do not use it. There are probably two reasons for this. One is that they are unaware of what futures can do and believe it is very time consuming to learn. The other is that they have a negative image of futures markets. As we discussed at some length in Chapter 1, this is inaccurate and unfortunate. As you no doubt have found, learning about futures does take some effort, but the greater flexibility afforded in managing a firm's risk would seem to far exceed the cost. In this case, the expression "A little learning is a dangerous thing" should be restated as "Lack of a little learning is even more dangerous."[14]

This concludes our presentation of various types of hedging applications. As we noted in many of the examples, there are numerous similar situations in which the same type of hedge would be appropriate. One purpose of this book is to bring you up to a level at which you will understand how options and futures strategies are used and when to use them. If you recognize the principles illustrated in each hedge, you should be able to see where hedging can be used in other, similar situations.

SUMMARY

This chapter looked at hedging with interest rate and stock index futures. It began by examining some basic concepts necessary for understanding and formulating hedge strategies. It explored the concepts of long and short hedging and basis risk and identified rules that help determine which contract to select, including the choice of commodity, expiration month, and whether to be long or short.

The chapter examined techniques for determining the optimal number of futures contracts for providing the volatility needed to offset the spot market risk. Then it looked at some special contract characteristics such as pricing conventions and conversion factors.

The hedge examples were grouped by type of contract—short-term interest rate futures hedges, intermediate- and long-term interest rate futures hedges, and

---

[14]The original expression is attributed to Alexander Pope, *An Essay on Criticism* (1771).

stock index futures hedges. While these examples span a broad range of applications, there are numerous similar situations in which virtually the same type of hedge would apply. The emphasis was on understanding the concept of hedging by observing it in practical examples.

While hedging seems to be effective in reducing risk, those who would benefit the most from it do not seem to take advantage of it.

Chapter 11 continues our look at futures strategies by examining arbitrage, speculative, and spread strategies. These strategies are somewhat more complex and require more frequent reference to concepts developed in previous chapters. The reader may wish to review Chapters 8 and 9 before reading Chapter 11.

Questions and Problems

1. Explain the difference between a short hedge and a long hedge. Give an example of each.

2. What is the basis? How is the basis expected to change over the life of a futures contract?

3. Explain why a strengthening basis benefits a short hedge and hurts a long hedge.

4. Suppose you are a dealer in sugar. It is September 26, and you hold 112,000 pounds of sugar worth $0.0479 per pound. The price of a futures contract expiring in January is $0.0550 per pound. Each contract is for 112,000 pounds. Determine the original basis. Then calculate the profit from a hedge if it is held to expiration and the basis converges to zero. Show how the profit is explained by movements in the basis alone.

5. Rework problem 4, but assume the hedge is closed on December 10, when the spot price is $0.0574 and the January futures price is $0.0590.

6. What factors must one consider in deciding on the appropriate futures commodity for a hedge?

7. For each of the following hedge termination dates, identify the appropriate contract expiration. Assume the available expiration months are March, June, September, and December.

   a. August 10

   b. December 15

   c. February 20

   d. June 14

8. What is the difference between micro and macro hedging? What type of hedging do most firms do? Why?

9. What is the minimum variance hedge ratio and the measure of hedging effectiveness? What do these two parameters tell us?

10. What is the price sensitivity hedge ratio? How are the price sensitivity and minimum variance hedge ratios alike? How do they differ?

11. Suppose you are an oil dealer and hold a position of 1 million barrels of crude oil. You hedge by trading futures each of which is on 10,000 barrels. However, you consider the effects of marking to market to be sufficient to justify tailing the hedge. The hedge will be on for 60 days. The interest rate is 8.5 percent. You plan to hold the hedge all the way to the expiration date. Determine the number of contracts you should sell at the beginning of the hedge. Then determine the number of contracts you should be holding when the hedge has 20 days to go. Assume each futures contract covers one barrel.

12. Following are prices for IMM T-bill and Eurodollar futures contracts. The quotes are based on the IMM Index. Determine the actual contract price.

    a.   T-bills: 89.72

    b.   Eurodollars: 87.24

13. For each of the following bonds, determine whether the bond is eligible for delivery on the March 1991 T-bond futures contract. (Assume all bonds mature on the fifteenth.)

    a.   10 3/4s of August 2005

    b.   11 1/4s of February 2015

    c.   11 5/8s of November 2004

    d   13 7/8s of May 2011, callable in May 2006

    e.   10s of May 2010, callable in May 2005

14. On March 13, you are short the March T-bond futures contract. You plan to deliver a Treasury bond that has a coupon of 11 1/4 percent payable semiannually on May 15 and November 15 and a conversion factor of 1.3661. The delivery date is Friday, March 15. The settlement price on March 13 is 69 6/32. Determine the invoice price, and describe the three-day sequence leading to delivery. (Refer back to Chapter 7 for the delivery procedure.)

15. On October 26, a bank is considering making a $20 million, three-month, fixed-rate loan to a corporation. The loan will be taken out immediately and repaid on January 25. The bank knows it will have to finance the loan by issuing one-month CDs that will pay interest at the LIBOR rate. The CDs will mature on the last Friday of the month and will be repaid by issuing a new CD at the new rate.

    The current LIBOR rate is 10.16 percent. The bank must keep its cost of financing as low as possible and will lose money on the loan if that cost exceeds 11 percent. December Eurodollar futures currently are at 89.33. March Eurodollar futures are at 88.89. Both figures are IMM Index values. The dates on which the CDs will be rolled over are November 30 and December 28.

    a.   What should the firm do on October 26?

    b.   On November 30, the December Eurodollar futures is at 90.54. The March contract is at 89.93. The LIBOR rate is 9.10 percent. Describe what happens on this day.

    c.   On December 28, the March contract is at 90.56. The LIBOR rate is 8.63 percent. Describe what happens on this day.

    d.   On January 25, the fixed-rate loan is repaid. The March contract is at 91.28. Determine the overall outcome of the hedge. Be sure to determine whether the firm met its objective of keeping the rate below 11 percent.

16. On July 6, a firm learns that it will have approximately $10 million available for short-term investment on November 30. It believes that the best use of the funds is to make a Eurodollar deposit. The current rate on 90-day Eurodollar deposits is 12.25 percent. The firm is concerned that Eurodollar rates will decrease over the next few months. The December Eurodollar IMM Index is 86.30.

    a.   Describe the transaction the firm should execute to hedge the risk of a decrease in Eurodollar rates. What is the yield on Eurodollar deposits on July 6?

    b.   On November 30, the December Eurodollar IMM Index is at 90.54. The three-month Eurodollar deposit rate is 9.10 pecent. Determine the outcome of the hedge. Calculate the effective yield on the Eurodollar deposit.

17. On February 15, a firm learns that it will need to borrow $10 million on August 15 for 90 days. The loan will be at a fixed rate equal to the prime rate, which currently is 11 percent. The loan will be discounted and the rate stated on a 360-day basis. The company is concerned about rising interest rates and is considering hedging that risk. However, it is uncertain whether the T-bill or Eurodollar contract is a better hedge. The prime rate is administered by the bank and is not necessarily highly correlated with market rates. Lacking any specific knowledge of how to handle this problem, the firm decides to assume the prime rate changes one point for every one-point change in T-bill and Eurodollar rates. The firm elects to use T-bill futures for the hedge but, for future reference, to track the performance of a Eurodollar hedge.

        The September T-bill IMM Index is 90.25, and the September Eurodollar IMM Index is 89.06. For each of the following questions, work out the results for both a T-bill and a Eurodollar hedge.

    a.   Determine the transaction the firm would make on February 15 to set up the hedge. Use the price sensitivity hedge ratio. Identify the effective rate if the loan were taken out today.

    b.   On August 15, the prime rate is at 13 percent. The September T-bill IMM Index is at 89.84, and the Eurodollar IMM Index is at 88.14. Determine the outcome of the hedge. What is the effective cost of borrowing?

18. On January 31, a firm learns that it will have $5 million available on May 31. It will use the funds to purchase the APCO 9 1/2 percent bonds maturing in about 21 years. Interest is paid semiannually on March 1 and September 1. The bonds are rated A2 by Moody's and are selling for 78 7/8 per 100 and yielding 12.32 percent. The duration is 7.81.

The firm is considering hedging the anticipated purchase with September T-bond futures. The futures price is 71 8/32. The firm believes the futures contract is tracking the Treasury bond with a coupon of 12 3/4 percent and maturing in about 25 years. It has determined that the implied yield on the futures contract is 11.40 percent and the duration of the contract is 8.32.

The firm believes the APCO bond yield will change one point for every one-point change in the yield on the bond underlying the futures contract.

a.   Determine the transaction the firm should conduct on January 31 to set up the hedge.

b.   On May 31, the APCO bonds were priced at 82 3/4. The September futures price was 76 14/32. Determine the outcome of the hedge.

19. On July 1, a portfolio manager holds $1 million face value of Treasury bonds, the 11 1/4s maturing in about 29 years. The price is 107 14/32. The bond will need to be sold on August 30. The manager is concerned about rising interest rates and believes a hedge would be appropriate. The September T-bond futures price is 77 15/32.

The manager decides to compute the minimum variance hedge ratio by regressing the daily change in the portfolio value on the change in the September futures price. The regression produces the following results:

$$b = 13$$
$$\text{Coefficient of determination} = .95$$

a.   What transaction should the firm make on July 1?

b.   On August 30, the bond was selling for 101 12/32 and the futures price was 77 5/32. Determine the outcome of the hedge.

20. You are the manager of a stock portfolio. On October 1, your holdings consist of the eight stocks listed in the following table, which you intend to sell on December 31. You are concerned about a market decline over the next three months. The number of shares, their prices, and the betas are shown, as well as the prices on December 31.

Stock	Number of Shares	Beta	10/1 Price	12/31 Price
R. R. Donnelley	10,000	1.00	19 5/8	27 3/8
B. F. Goodrich	6,200	1.05	31 3/8	32 7/8
Raytheon	15,800	1.15	49 3/8	53 5/8
Maytag	8,900	.90	55 3/8	77 7/8
Kroger	11,000	.85	42 1/8	47 7/8
Comdisco	14,500	1.45	19 3/8	28 5/8
Cessna	9,900	1.20	29 3/4	30 1/8
Foxboro	4,500	.95	24 3/4	26

On October 1, you decide to execute a hedge using S&P 500 futures. The March contract price is 188.10. On December 31, the March contract price is 212.45. Determine the outcome of the hedge.

21. On April 1, a securities analyst recommended General Cinema stock as a good purchase in the early summer. The portfolio manager plans to buy 20,000 shares of the stock on June 1 but is concerned that the market as a whole will be bullish over the next three months. General Cinema's stock currently is at 32 7/8, and the beta is 1.10.

    Construct a hedge that will protect against movements in the stock market as a whole. Use the September S&P 500 futures, which is priced at 187.65 on April 1. Evaluate the outcome of the hedge if on June 28 the futures price is 193.65 and General Cinema's stock price is 38 5/8.

22. (Concept Problem) As we discussed in the chapter, futures can be used to eliminate systematic risk in a stock portfolio, leaving it essentially a risk-free portfolio. However, a portfolio manager can achieve the same result by selling the stocks and replacing them with T-bills. Consider the following stock portfolio.

Stock	Number of Shares	Price	Beta
Northrup	14,870	18.125	1.10
H. J. Heinz	8,755	36.125	1.05
Washington Post	1,245	264	1.05
Disney	8,750	134.5	1.25
Wang Labs	33,995	4.25	1.20
Wisconsin Energy	12,480	29	0.65
General Motors	14,750	48.75	0.95
Union Pacific	12,900	71.5	1.20
Royal Dutch Shell	7,500	78.75	0.75
Illinois Power	3,550	15.5	0.60

Suppose the portfolio manager wishes to convert this portfolio to a riskless portfolio for a period of one month. The price of an S&P 500 futures (with a $500 multiplier) is 369.45. To sell each share would cost $20 per order plus $0.03 per share. Each company's shares would constitute a separate order. The futures contract would entail a cost of $27.50 per contract, round-trip. T-bill purchases cost $25 per trade for any number of T-bills. Determine the most cost-effective way to accomplish the manager's goal of converting the portfolio to a risk-free position for one month and then converting it back.

23. (Concept Problem) On January 2, a bank learns it will have about $10 million to invest in T-bills on November 28. The current T-bill discount rate is 7.11 percent. The bank believes T-bill rates will fall over the next nine months. It would like to hedge in the T-bill futures market but believes that only the nearby contract is sufficiently liquid to justify a hedge. Thus, it will use the March contract until February 28, the June contract from February 28 to May 30, the September contract from May 30 to August 29, and the December contract from August 29 to November 28. When it rolls out of one contract and into the next, it will take its futures gain (loss) and reinvest (borrow) at the market rates for the time remaining until November 28. These rates are, of course, unknown when the hedge is begun. The reinvestment (borrowing) rates turned out to be 8 percent from February 28 to November 28, 6.875 percent from May 30 to November 28, and 5.6875 percent from August 29 to November 28. Whatever amount is invested on the given date earns the rate indicated for the time remaining until November 28 (however, these are annual rates, so adjust accordingly). The prices of the T-bill futures on the appropriate dates were as follows:

March contract: January 2 (93.18), February 28 (93.10)
June contract: February 28 (93.39), May 30 (93.71)
September contract: May 30 (93.77), August 29 (94.94)
December contract: August 29 (95.06), November 28 (94.71)

On November 28, the discount spot rate on 91-day T-bills was 5.41 percent. Determine the rate the bank would earn on the purchase of the spot T-bills on November 28 both with and without the hedge. Remember to account for the reinvestment of futures profits and losses as the hedge is rolled forward on the given dates.

References

Block, Stanley B., and Timothy J. Gallagher. "The Use of Interest Rate Futures and Options by Corporate Financial Managers." *Financial Management* 15 (Autumn 1986): 73–78.

Chance, Don M., M. Wayne Marr, and G. Rodney Thompson. "Hedging Shelf Registrations." *The Journal of Futures Markets* 6 (Spring 1986): 11–27.

Chicago Board of Trade. *A Guide to Financial Futures at the Chicago Board of Trade*. Chicago: Board of Trade of the City of Chicago, 1983.

Chicago Board of Trade. *Hedging Workbook*. Chicago: Board of Trade of the City of Chicago, 1984.

Chicago Board of Trade. *Introduction to Hedging*. Chicago: Board of Trade of the City of Chicago, 1984.

Chicago Board of Trade. *Commodity Trading Manual*, Chapter 8. Chicago: Board of Trade of the City of Chicago, 1989.

Chicago Board of Trade. *Interest Rate Futures for Institutional Investors*. Chicago: Board of Trade of the City of Chicago, 1989.

Duffie, Darwell. *Futures Markets*, Chapter 7. Englewood Cliffs, N.J.: Prentice-Hall, 1989.

Ederington, Louis H. "The Hedging Performance of the New Futures Market." *The Journal of Finance* 34 (March 1979): 157–170.

Figlewski, Stephen. *Hedging with Financial Futures for Institutional Investors*, Chapters 2, 4, 6. Cambridge, Mass.: Ballinger, 1986.

Figlewski, Stephen. "Hedging Performance and Basis Risk in Stock Index Futures." *The Journal of Finance* 39 (July 1984): 657–669.

Franckle, Charles T. "The Hedging Performance of the New Futures Market: Comment." *The Journal of Finance* 35 (December 1980): 1273–1279.

Gay, Gerald D., Robert W. Kolb, and Raymond Chiang. "Interest Rate Hedging: An Empirical Test of Alternative Strategies." *The Journal of Financial Research* 6 (Fall 1983): 187–197.

Graham, David, and Robert Jennings. "Systematic Risk, Dividend Yield, and the Hedging Performance of Stock Index Futures." *The Journal of Futures Markets* 7 (February 1987): 1–13.

Hill, Joanne, and Thomas Schneeweis. "Risk Reduction Potential of Financial Futures for Corporate Bond Positions." In *Interest Rate Futures: Concepts and Issues*, edited by R. W. Kolb and G. D. Gay. Richmond, Va.: R. F. Dame, 1982.

Hull, John. *Options, Futures, and Other Derivative Securities*, Chapters 2, 6, 8. Englewood Cliffs, N.J.: Prentice-Hall, 1989.

Johnson, L. L. "The Theory of Hedging and Speculation in Commodity Futures Markets." *Review of Economic Studies* 27 (October 1960): 139–151.

Kawaller, Ira G. "Hedging with Futures Contracts: Going the Extra Mile." *Journal of Cash Management* 6 (July–August 1986): 34–36.

Kolb, Robert W., and Raymond Chiang. "Improving Hedging Performance Using Interest Rate Futures." *Financial Management* 10 (Autumn 1981): 72–79.

Kolb, Robert W., Gerald D. Gay, and William C. Hunter. "Liquidity Requirements for Financial Futures Hedges." *Financial Analysts Journal* 41 (May–June 1985): 60–68.

Kolb, Robert W., and Gerald D. Gay, eds. *Interest Rate Futures: Concepts and Issues*. Richmond, Va.: R. F. Dame, 1982.

Leuthold, Raymond M., Joan C. Junkus, and Jean E. Cordier. *The Theory and Practice of Futures Markets*, Chapters 8, 10, 11. Lexington, Mass.: Lexington Books, 1989.

McCabe, George M., and Charles T. Franckle. "The Effectiveness of Rolling the Hedge Forward in the Treasury Bill Futures Market." *Financial Management* 12 (Summer 1983): 21–29.

McCabe, George M., and Donald P. Solberg. "Hedging in the Treasury Bill Futures Market When the Hedged Instrument and the Delivered Instrument Are Not Matched." *The Journal of Futures Markets* 9 (December 1989): 529–537.

Powers, Mark J. *Inside the Financial Futures Markets*, 2d ed. New York: Wiley, 1984.

Quinn, Lawrence R. "Thrift Industry Hasn't Learned How to Handle Its Risks by Hedging." *Futures* 18 (April 1989): 54–57.

Rothstein, Nancy H., ed. *The Handbook of Financial Futures*, Chapters 10-12. New York: McGraw-Hill, 1984.

Schwarz, Edward W., Joanne M. Hill, and Thomas Schneeweis. *Financial Futures: Fundamentals, Strategies, and Applications*, Chapters 7–13. Homewood, Ill.: Irwin, 1986.

Senchak, Andrew J., and John C. Easterwood. "Cross Hedging CD's with Treasury Bill Futures." *The Journal of Futures Markets* 3 (1983): 429–438.

Siegel, Daniel R., and Diane F. Siegel. *Futures Markets*, Chapters 4, 5, 6, 8. Hinsdale, Ill.: Dryden Press, 1990.

Stein, Jerome L. "The Simultaneous Determination of Spot and Futures Prices." *American Economic Review* 51 (December 1961): 1012–1025.

Teweles, Richard J., and Frank J. Jones. *The Futures Game*. New York: McGraw-Hill, 1987.

Veit, W. Theodore, and Wallace W. Reiff. "Commercial Banks and Interest Rate Futures: A Hedging Survey." *The Journal of Futures Markets* 3 (1983): 283–293.

appendix 10A

Derivation of the Hedge Ratio[*]

MINIMUM VARIANCE HEDGE RATIO

The variance of the profit from the hedge is

$$\sigma_{\Pi}^2 = \sigma_{\Delta S}^2 + \sigma_{\Delta f}^2 N_f^2 + 2\sigma_{\Delta S \Delta f} N_f.$$

The value of N_f that minimizes σ_{Π}^2 is found by differentiating σ_{Π}^2 with respect to N_f:

$$\frac{\partial \sigma_{\Pi}^2}{\partial N_f} = 2\sigma_{\Delta f}^2 N_f + 2\sigma_{\Delta S \Delta f}.$$

Setting this equal to zero and solving for N_f gives

$$N_f = -\frac{\sigma_{\Delta S \Delta f}}{\sigma_{\Delta f}^2}.$$

A check of the second derivative verifies that this is a minimum.

PRICE SENSITIVITY HEDGE RATIO

The value of the position can be specified as

$$V = S + V^f N_f,$$

where V^f is the value of the futures contract. Now we wish to find the effect of a

[*]This appendix requires the use of calculus.

change in r on V. Since $\partial V^f/\partial r = \partial f/\partial r$,

$$\frac{\partial V}{\partial r} = \frac{\partial S}{\partial r} + \frac{\partial f}{\partial r} N_f.$$

The optimal value of N_f is the one that makes this derivative equal to zero. We do not know the derivatives, $\partial S/\partial r$ and $\partial f/\partial r$, but we can use the chain rule to express the equation as

$$\frac{\partial V}{\partial r} = \frac{\partial S}{\partial y_s} \frac{\partial y_s}{\partial r} + \frac{\partial f}{\partial y_f} \frac{\partial y_f}{\partial r} N_f = 0.$$

This procedure introduces the yield changes, ∂y_s and ∂y_f, into the problem. Usually it is assumed that $\partial y_s/\partial r = \partial y_f/\partial r$. Substituting and solving for N_f give

$$N_f = -\frac{(\partial S / \partial y_s)}{(\partial f / \partial y_f)}.$$

This is approximated as

$$N_f = -\frac{(\Delta S / \Delta y_s)}{(\Delta f / \Delta y_f)}.$$

---

appendix 10B

Determining the CBOT Conversion Factor

Step 1   Determine the maturity of the bond in years, months, and days as of the first day of the expiration month. If the bond is callable, use the first call date instead of the maturity date. Let YRS be the number of years and MOS the number of months. Ignore the number of days. Let c be the coupon rate on the bond.

Step 2   Round the number of months down to 0, 3, 6, or 9. Call this MOS*.

Step 3   If MOS* = 0,

$$CF_0 = \frac{c}{2}\left[\frac{1-(1.04)^{-2*YRS}}{.04}\right] + (1.04)^{-2*YRS}.$$

If MOS* = 3,

$$CF_3 = \left(CF_0 + c/2\right)\left(1.04\right)^{-.5} - c/4.$$

If MOS* = 6,

$$CF_6 = \frac{c}{2}\left[\frac{1-\left(1.04\right)^{-(2*YRS+1)}}{.04}\right] + \left(1.04\right)^{-(2*YRS+1)},$$

If MOS* = 9,

$$CF_9 = \left(CF_6 + c/2\right)\left(1.04\right)^{-.5} - c/4.$$

Example: Determine the CF for delivery of the 9 1/8s of May 15, 2018, on the June 1990 T-bond futures contract.

On June 1, 1990 the bond's remaining life is 27 years, 11 months, and 14 days. Thus, YRS = 27 and MOS = 11. Rounding down gives MOS* = 9. First, we must find CF_6:

$$CF_6 = \frac{.09125}{2}\left[\frac{1-\left(1.04\right)^{-(2(27)+1)}}{.04}\right] + \left(1.04\right)^{-(2(27)+1)}$$

$$= 1.1244.$$

Then we find CF_9 as

$$CF_9 = \left(1.1237 + .09125/2\right)\left(1.04\right)^{-.5} - .09125/4 = 1.1245,$$

which is shown in Table 10.3 in the chapter.

chapter 11

ADVANCED FUTURES STRATEGIES

This chapter looks at some advanced futures trading strategies. Some of these strategies are spreads and some are arbitrage strategies. Let us start out by defining these terms.

A *spread strategy* is a long or short position in one futures contract and an opposite position in another. The concept of a spread certainly should not be new to you. We already covered time spreads in options, and we discussed futures spreads briefly in Chapter 9. A spread is a relatively low-risk strategy with several objectives. However, to regard a spread as a nonspeculative strategy is misleading. A spread involves an element of speculation, but the risk is much lower than that in an outright long or short position.

We discussed arbitrage frequently in previous chapters. Arbitrage is the mechanism that links futures prices to spot prices. Without arbitrage, the markets would be far less efficient. However, futures and spot prices do not always conform to their theoretical relationships. When this happens, arbitrageurs step in and execute profitable transactions that quickly drive prices back to their theoretical levels. This chapter illustrates some of the arbitrage transactions important to the proper functioning and efficiency of the futures markets.

407

Our approach here is to examine three groups of contracts: short-term interest rate futures contracts, intermediate- and long-term interest rate futures contracts, and stock index futures. Within each group of contracts, we shall examine several popular trading strategies.

SHORT-TERM INTEREST RATE FUTURES STRATEGIES

In the category of short-term interest rate futures, we shall look at Treasury bill and Eurodollar futures strategies. The reader may first wish to review the contract specifications and hedging examples in Chapter 10.

Treasury Bill Cash and Carry/Implied Repo

In Chapter 9, we saw that the futures price is determined by the spot price and the cost of carry. The basic arbitrage transaction that determines this relationship often is referred to as a *cash and carry*. The investor purchases the security in the spot market and sells a futures contract. If the futures contract is held to expiration, the security's sale price is guaranteed.[1] Since the transaction is riskless, it should offer a return sufficient to cover the cost of carry. Because there is no risk, the investor will not earn a risk premium.

Another way to approach this problem is to focus on the rate at which the security's purchase can be financed. Often the financing is obtained by means of a repurchase agreement. A *repurchase agreement*, or *repo*, is an arrangement with a financial institution in which the owner of a security sells that security to the financial institution with the agreement to buy it back, usually a day later. This transaction is referred to as an *overnight repo*. The repo thus is a form of a secured loan. The investor obtains the use of the funds to buy the security by pledging it as collateral. The interest charged on a repo is usually quoted and calculated as if there were 360 days in a year, but here we shall use the assumption of a full 365-day year.

Repurchase agreements are frequently used in transactions involving government securities. Overnight repos are more common, but longer-term arrangements, called *term repos*, of up to two weeks are sometimes employed. In cash-and-carry transactions, the security is considered as being financed by using a repo. If the return from the transaction is greater than the repo rate, the arbitrage will be profitable.

From Chapter 9, the futures–spot price relationship is

$$f = S + \theta.$$

---

[1]Recall that this is true because the spot price at expiration equals the futures price at expiration. The profit on the spot transaction is $S_T - S$, and the profit on the futures transaction is $-(f_T - f)$. The total profit is $f - S$. Thus, f is the effective sale price of the underlying commodity.

Since we are focusing on securities here, there is no significant storage cost; thus, the cost of carry, θ, is strictly the interest, i. Now let us define the implicit interest cost as

$$\theta = f - S.$$

Thus, θ is the implied cost of financing expressed in dollars. Suppose we express it as a percentage of the spot price, θ/S, and define this as R. Then R is the implied repo rate. If the cost of financing the position—the actual repo rate—is less than the implied repo rate, the arbitrage will be profitable.

Readers familiar with the concept of internal rate of return will find that it is analogous to the implied repo rate. If the arbitrage brings no profit, the cost of financing is the implied repo rate. In a capital budgeting problem, a zero net present value defines the internal rate of return. If the opportunity cost is less than the IRR, the project is favorable and produces a positive NPV. Likewise, an arbitrage is profitable if it can be financed at a rate lower than the implied repo rate.

For example, suppose there is a security that matures at time T and an otherwise identical security that matures at an earlier time, t. There is also a futures contract that matures at time t. You buy the security at a price of S, finance it at the rate R (an annualized rate), and sell a futures contract. At time t, the futures expires and you deliver the security. You have effectively sold the security at t for a price of f. The profit from the transaction is

$$\Pi = f - S(1 + R)^t.$$

The term $S(1 + R)^t$ reflects what you paid for the security, factored up by the cost of financing over period t. Thus, the implied repo rate is the cost of financing that produces no arbitrage profit; therefore,

$$R = \left(\frac{f}{S}\right)^{(1/t)} - 1.$$

There is yet another approach to understanding the basic cash-and-carry arbitrage. Suppose we buy the security that matures at time T and simultaneously sell the futures contract that expires at time t $(t < T)$. When the futures contract expires we deliver the security, which has a remaining maturity of $T - t$. The net effect is that we have taken a security that matures at T and shortened its maturity to t. Thus, we have created a synthetic t-period instrument. If the return from the synthetic t-period instrument is greater than the return from an actual security maturing at t, prices are out of line and an arbitrage profit is possible.

An example of this strategy is to buy a six-month T-bill and sell a futures contract expiring in three months. This transaction creates a synthetic three-month T-bill, with a return that should equal the return on an actual three-month T-bill. If it does not, investors will be attracted to the strategy and their transactions will drive up the price of the six-month T-bill and drive down the futures price (or vice versa) until the synthetic T-bill and the actual T-bill have the same returns.

> *The implied repo rate is the return implied by the cost of carry relationship between spot and futures prices.*

TABLE 11.1

Treasury Bill Cash and Carry/Implied Repo

Scenario: On September 26 of a particular year, the T-bill maturing on December 18 has a discount rate of 5.19. The T-bill maturing on March 19 has a discount rate of 5.35. The December T-bill futures is priced at the IMM Index of 94.80. An arbitrage opportunity is available.

September 26

Spot market: Buy the March 19 T-bill at a discount of 5.35
  Price per 100: 97.4142 (based on 174 days)

Futures market: Sell the December T-bill futures at IMM Index of 94.80
  Price per 100: 98.70

Sell one contract

December 18

Spot market: Deliver the March 19 T-bill and receive an effective price of 98.70

Effective return: The bill was bought for 97.4142 and sold for 98.70. The holding period was 83 days (9/26-12/18). The return (implied repo rate) is

$$\left(\frac{98.70}{97.4142} \right)^{(365/83)} - 1 = .0594$$

This can be compared to the return from buying an actual 83-day T-bill. Its price is $100 - 5.19(83/360) = 98.8034$ and its return is

$$\left(\frac{100}{98.8034} \right)^{(365/83)} - 1 = .0544$$

which is 50 basis points lower.

AN EXAMPLE   Table 11.1 illustrates the cash-and-carry transaction with Treasury bills. On September 26 of a particular year, the T-bill maturing on December 18 has a discount rate of 5.19 while the T-bill maturing on March 19 has a discount rate of 5.35. The futures contract expiring in December is priced by the IMM Index at 94.80.

Let us see why an arbitrage opportunity exists. The T-bill maturing on December 18 has a maturity of 83 days. Its price is found (using the same method as before) as

$$100 - 5.19(83/360) = 98.8034.$$

The return on the bill is

$$\left(\frac{100}{98.8034} \right)^{(365/83)} - 1 = .0544.$$

Using the same technique for the bill maturing on March 19, 174 days from now, gives a price of 97.4142. The same technique gives us the futures price of 98.70.[2] If we buy the bill at 97.4142 and sell a futures contract at 98.70, we can deliver the bill on December 18 and receive a price of 98.70. Thus, we will have earned a return of

$$\left(\frac{98.70}{97.4142} \right)^{(365/83)} - 1 = .0594.$$

Note that this is the same formula we illustrated earlier for the implied repo rate, R = $(f/S)^{(1/t)} - 1$. In fact, 5.94 percent is the implied repo rate. If the T-bill can be financed at less than the implied repo rate of 5.94 percent, an arbitrage profit is possible.

It is interesting to compare the return on the cash-and-carry transaction with the return on the actual bill maturing on December 18. The cash-and-carry transaction guarantees a return of 5.94 percent, less any financing costs. An actual T-bill maturing on December 18 was shown as offering a return of 5.44 percent. Thus, the synthetic T-bill offers a return 50 basis points higher than that of the actual T-bill. Investors wanting to hold T-bills maturing on December 18 will find it more profitable to create the synthetic T-bill.

There are, however, some limitations to the effectiveness of this strategy. These prices were closing prices from *The Wall Street Journal*. As we acknowledged when studying options, the prices may not necessarily be synchronized. A professional arbitrageur would, of course, have access to current synchronized prices, but even in that case the prices might change before the transaction is completed.

Another limitation to the cash-and-carry arbitrage is that the repo rate is not fixed for the full time period. As noted earlier, some term repos for up to two weeks are available, but most repo financing is overnight. In either case, the financing rate on the T-bill is unknown when the arbitrage is executed. Each time a repo matures, new financing must be arranged, and the rate may well be much higher than originally expected. A number of other limitations come into play when determining the implied repo rate from other futures instruments. In fact, Kawaller (1987) has argued that there may not be a true risk-free arbitrage strategy, even though billions of dollars are committed to these types of transactions.

Eurodollar Arbitrage

Suppose it is September 16 and a London bank needs to issue $10 million of 180-day Eurodollar CDs. The current discount rate on the CDs is 8.75. One way to

---

[2]In Chapter 10, we saw how the IMM Index value, here 94.80, is converted to the futures price as follows:

$$100 - 5.20(90/360) = 98.70,$$

where 5.20 = 100 − 94.80.

construct a synthetic 180-day CD is to issue a 90-day CD at the current rate of 8.25 and simultaneously sell a Eurodollar futures contract expiring in three months. The current IMM Index on the futures contract is 91.37.

Selling a 90-day CD and a futures contract expiring in three months is equivalent to selling a 180-day CD. When the 90-day CD matures, the bank issues a new 90-day CD. The rate at which it will issue the new CD is effectively locked in by the futures contract. Why? Recall the hedge examples. When a firm anticipates borrowing money at a future date, it will sell a futures contract. This hedges the rate at which it ultimately would borrow the funds. If the Eurodollar contract allowed delivery, the bank could simply issue a Eurodollar CD and deliver it. But the Eurodollar contract is a cash settlement contract. Thus, the firm will have to issue a CD and use the profit or loss on the futures contract to offset any difference between the rate at which it issues the CD and the rate at which it expected to issue it. Table 11.2 shows the results of this transaction.

If the bank issues a 180-day Eurodollar CD, it will receive $10 million and in six months will pay back

$$\$10,000,000[1 + .0875(180/360)] = \$10,437,500.$$

The annualized cost of borrowing therefore is

$$(\$10,437,500/\$10,000,000)^{(365/180)} - 1 = .0907.$$

Now suppose the bank issues a 90-day Eurodollar CD at a rate of 8.25 and simultaneously sells a Eurodollar futures contract at the IMM Index of 91.37. Using the same method as for T-bill futures, we compute the futures price as $978,425. Because the spot position is about ten times the price of one futures contract, the bank sells ten contracts. At maturity, the bank will need $10,000,000[1 + .0825(90/360)] = $10,206,250.

On December 16, the rate on new 90-day Eurodollar CDs is 7.96 percent. The original 90-day CD is due; thus, the bank needs $10,206,250. The futures contract expires and converges to the spot rate of 7.96 percent (IMM Index of 92.04). This is equivalent to a futures price of $980,100. The loss for ten contracts is $16,750. To cover the loss and to pay off the maturing CD, the bank needs $10,206,250 + $16,750 = $10,223,000. The bank can issue a new CD for $10,223,000 at a rate of 7.96 percent. When the new CD matures on March 16, the bank will owe

$$\$10,223,000[1 + .0796(90/360)] = \$10,426,438.$$

The net result is that on September 16, the bank received $10,000,000 and on March 16 paid back $10,426,438. The cost of funds for the 180 days therefore is

$$(\$10,426,438/\$10,000,000)^{(365/180)} - 1 = .0884.$$

This is 23 basis points less than the original 180-day Eurodollar rate. Thus, the bank created a synthetic 180-day CD that was less expensive than the actual 180-day CD.

TABLE 11.2
Eurodollar Arbitrage

Scenario: On September 16 of a particular year, a London bank needs to issue $10 million of 180-day Eurodollar CDs. The current rate on such CDs is 8.75. The bank is considering the alternative of issuing a 90-day CD at a rate of 8.25 and selling a Eurodollar futures contract.

If the 180-day CD is issued, the bank will have to pay back

$$\$10,000,000[1 + .0875(180/360)] = \$10,437,500.$$

The rate thus would be

$$(\$10,437,500/\$10,000,000)^{(365/180)} - 1 = .0907.$$

The rates available in the spot and futures markets are such that the bank can obtain a better rate with the following transaction.

September 16
Spot market: Issue 90-day CD at 8.25

Futures market: December futures IMM Index is at 91.37
   Price per 100: 97.8425
   Contract price: $978,425
Sell 10 contracts

December 16
Futures market: December futures IMM Index is at 92.04
   Price per 100: 98.01
   Contract price: $980,100
Buy 10 contracts
   Profit: – $16,750
Spot market: New 90-day CDs are at 7.96
   Issue $10,223,000 face value of CDs
   Use $16,750 to cover loss on futures and $10,206,250 to pay off maturing CD

Results
On September 16, the bank received $10,000,000 and on March 16 paid back $10,426,438. The cost of funds for the 180 days is

$$(\$10,426,438/\$10,000,000)^{(365/180)} - 1 = .0884.$$

This is 23 basis points less than the cost of a 180-day Eurodollar CD.

It might appear that the result was contingent on the rate on the CD issued on December 16—a rate that was not known back in September. In fact, the result of this transaction was known when it was executed. The 90-day CD was issued at a rate of .0825(90/360) = .020625 for the 90 days. The Eurodollar futures was sold at a rate of .0863(90/360) = .021575. Thus, if the bank issued a 90-day CD at .020625 and followed that with a 90-day CD at .021575, the overall rate for 180 days would be

$$(1.020625)(1.021575) - 1 = .042645.$$

Annualizing this rate gives

$$(1.042645)^{(365/180)} - 1 = .0884,$$

which is the rate obtained by the bank.

INTERMEDIATE- AND LONG-TERM INTEREST RATE FUTURES STRATEGIES

Intermediate- and long-term interest rate futures include Treasury note and Treasury bond futures. As we noted in earlier chapters, these instruments are virtually identical. Here we shall concentrate on the Treasury bond contract.

Determining the Best Bond to Deliver

As previously explained, the specifications on the Treasury bond contract allow delivery of many different bonds, subject to the 15-year requirement stated above. At any given time prior to expiration, it is impossible to determine which bond will be delivered. It is, however, possible to identify the bond that is most likely to be delivered. That bond is referred to as the *cheapest to deliver* or sometimes the *best bond to deliver*.

Suppose it is September 26 of a given year and you are interested in determining the bond that is most likely to be delivered on the upcoming December contract. The procedure involves a series of calculations that we shall illustrate for one particular bond—the 12 1/2s that mature on August 15 in about 23 years.

If the holder of a long position in this bond also holds a short position in the T-bond futures contract, that trader can elect to maintain the position until expiration and deliver this particular bond. Even if another bond would be cheaper to deliver, the trader always has the option to deliver the bond already held, provided, of course, that that bond is still eligible for delivery. The cost of delivering the particular bond is the net profit or loss from buying the bond, selling a futures, holding the position until expiration, and then delivering the bond. Thus, the trader incurs the cost of carry on the bond held. Remember that this cost is somewhat offset by the coupons received on the bond.

For evaluating at time t, the best bond to deliver at time T, the general expression for the cost of delivering a bond is

$$f(CF) + AI_T - [(B + AI_t)(1 + r)^{(T-t)} - FV \text{ of coupons at T}],$$

where AI_T is the accrued interest on the bond at T, the delivery date; AI_t is the accrued interest on the bond at t, today; and r is the risk-free rate that represents the interest lost on funds invested in the bond. The term inside the brackets is the spot price of the bond (quoted price plus accrued interest) factored up by the cost of carry and reduced by the compound future value of any coupons received while the position is held. These coupons, of course, help offset the cost of carry, and by subtracting them we are simply reflecting the net cost of carry. The first two terms are the amount the trader would receive from delivering the bond. This is the invoice price, which we covered in Chapter 10.

For our bond, the futures price is 95.65625 and the conversion factor is 1.4662. The accrued interest on September 26 is 1.43, and the accrued interest on December 1, the day we shall assume delivery, is 3.63. The price quoted for the bond is 141.5. The risk-free rate is .053. There are 66 days between September 26 and December 1. The invoice price for the futures is

$$95.65625(1.4662) + 3.63 = 143.88.$$

Since the coupons are paid on August 15 and February 15, no coupons are paid during the time the bond is held. Thus, the spot price of the bond factored up by the cost of carry is

$$(141.5 + 1.43)(1.053)^{(66/365)} = 144.27.$$

Hence, the bond would cost .39 more than it would return.

This conclusion by itself does not enable us to make a decision. We can only compare this figure for one bond to that for another. Let us consider a second bond, the 9 7/8s maturing in about 29 years. Its conversion factor is 1.2096, and its price is 119.50. In this case, however, the bond will make coupon payments on May 15 and November 15, so there will be a coupon payment while the bond is held. The accrued interest is .44 on December 1 and 3.60 on September 26. The coupon of 4.9375 received on November 15 is reinvested at 5.3 percent for 16 days and grows to a value of

$$4.9375(1.053)^{(16/365)} = 4.9487.$$

Thus, the cost of the bond factored up by the cost of carry is

$$(119.50 + 3.60)(1.053)^{(66/365)} - 4.9487 = 119.3062.$$

The invoice price is

$$95.65625(1.2096) + .44 = 116.1458.$$

Thus, the difference between the amount received and the amount paid is 116.1458 − 119.3062 = −3.16.

Therefore, it is clear that the 12 1/2 percent bond is better to deliver than the 9 7/8 percent bond. Of course, this calculation should be done for all bonds that are

The best bond to deliver is the bond for which the difference between the revenue received from delivery of the bond and the cost incurred to buy and hold the bond is maximized.

eligible for delivery. The bond for which the difference between the amount received and the amount paid is the maximum is the best bond to deliver.

The best bond to deliver is important for several reasons. Any futures contract must reflect the behavior of the spot price. In the case of Treasury bond (and note) futures, the so-called "spot price" is not easy to determine. The best bond to deliver is the bond that represents the spot instrument on which the futures contract is tracking. The futures price tracks the spot price of the best bond to deliver. Therefore, the cost of carry model examined in Chapter 9 would apply only to the best bond to deliver. Also, the optimal hedge ratio would require knowledge of the best bond to deliver.

Delivery Options

The characteristics of the Treasury bond futures contract create some interesting opportunities for alert investors. Specifically, the contract contains several imbedded options. While these options are not formally traded in the same way stock options are, they have many of the characteristics of the options we studied in earlier chapters. We shall examine some of these options here.

THE WILD CARD OPTION   The *wild card option* results from a difference in the closing times of the spot and futures markets. The Treasury bond futures contract stops trading at 3:00 p.m. Eastern time. However, the spot market for Treasury bonds operates until 5:00 p.m. Eastern time. During the delivery month, the holder of a short position knows the settlement price for that day at 3:00 p.m. Multiplying the settlement price by the conversion factor gives the invoice price the holder would receive if a given bond were delivered. This figure is locked in until the next day's trading starts.

During the two-hour period after the futures market closes, the spot market continues to trade. If the spot price declines during those two hours, the holder of a short futures position may find it attractive to buy a bond and deliver it. Because the futures market is closed and the invoice price is fixed, the futures market is unable to react to the new information that drove the spot price down. Moreover, the short has until 9:00 p.m. to make the decision to deliver.

Let us use the following symbols:

f_3 = futures price at 3:00 p.m.
S_3 = spot price at 3:00 p.m.
CF = conversion factor of bond under consideration

You hold a short position in the futures contract that is expiring during the current month. Assume you own $1/CF$ bonds. Why? If you do not own at least some bonds, your position will be quite risky. Also, the bond under consideration should be the best bond to deliver. That way your risk is quite low. Unexpected changes in the futures price will be approximately matched by changes in the value of the $1/CF$ bonds.

If you make delivery that day, you will be required to deliver one bond per contract. You own only 1/CF bonds, so you will have to buy $1 - 1/\text{CF}$ additional bonds. If the bonds' spot price declines sufficiently between 3:00 and 5:00, you may be able to buy the additional bonds at a price low enough to make a profit. These additional bonds are referred to as the *tail*.

Now suppose that at 5:00 p.m. the bond price is S_5. If you buy the additional $1 - 1/\text{CF}$ bonds at the price of S_5 and deliver them, your profit will be

$$\Pi = f_3(\text{CF}) - \left[\left(\frac{1}{\text{CF}}\right)S_5 + \left(1 - \frac{1}{\text{CF}}\right)S_5\right] = f_3(\text{CF}) - S_5.$$

The first term, $f_3(\text{CF})$, is the invoice price. This is simply the 3:00 p.m. settlement price on the futures contract times the conversion factor on the bond. The invoice price is the amount you receive upon delivery. The terms in brackets denote values of the bonds you are delivering. The first term, $(1/\text{CF})S_5$, is the 5:00 p.m. value of the 1/CF bonds. The second term is the cost of the $1 - 1/\text{CF}$ bonds bought at the 5:00 p.m. price. As indicated above, the expression simplifies to $f_3(\text{CF}) - S_5$. Note that the 3:00 p.m. bond price does not enter into the decision to deliver because the delivery decision is made at 5:00 p.m. By that time, the 1/CF bonds are worth $(1/\text{CF})S_5$ and can be sold for that amount.

If the transaction is profitable, $\Pi > 0$. This requires that

$$S_5 < f_3(\text{CF}).$$

A trader can observe the spot price at 5:00. If the price is sufficiently low, the trader should buy the remaining $1 - 1/\text{CF}$ bonds and make delivery. The wild card option thus will be profitable if the spot price at 5:00 p.m. falls below the invoice price established at 3:00 p.m.

As an example, suppose that on March 2 the March futures contract has a settlement price at 3:00 p.m. of 101.8125. The best bond to deliver was the 12 1/2s maturing in about 22 years, which have a conversion factor of 1.464. We do not have the 3:00 p.m. spot price, but let us assume it is 149.65. Suppose we are short 100 contracts, which obligates us to deliver bonds with a face value of 100($100,000) = $10,000,000. Assume each bond has a face value of $1,000. Thus, we will have to deliver 10,000 bonds. To begin this strategy, we must have a position in the spot T-bonds; otherwise, our risk will be quite high. We weight that position by the conversion factor; that is, we hold bonds with a face value of $10,000,000(1/1.464) = $6,830,601, in other words, about 6,831 bonds. To make delivery, we will need to buy 3,169 bonds. For us to make a profit, the 5:00 p.m. price must decline to

$$S_5 < 101.8125(1.464) = 149.05$$

or less. Thus, if the spot price declined by at least .60 by 5:00 p.m., it would pay to buy the remaining 3,169 bonds and make delivery.

The wild card option is the opportunity the holder of the short futures contract has to lock in the invoice price at 3:00 p.m. and make delivery if the spot price falls below the established invoice price between 3:00 and 5:00 p.m. The option exists only during the delivery month and only on Treasury bond and note contracts at the Chicago Board of Trade.

The alternative to making delivery is to hold the position until the next day. If we work from the assumption that there will be no overnight news, we can project that tomorrow's opening futures price will equal the 5:00 p.m. spot price divided by the conversion factor. This is because the 5:00 p.m. futures price times the conversion factor should approximately equal the spot price. Thus, if we wait until the next day, our profit from marking to market will be $f_3 - S_5/CF$. Thus, we should mark to market rather than deliver if $f_3 - S_5/CF > 0$, but this is simply the rule we established for delivering; that is, we deliver if $S_5 < f_3(CF)$. Otherwise, we should hold our position and mark to market.

THE QUALITY OPTION   The holder of the short position has the right to deliver any of a number of acceptable bonds. Sometimes the holder of the short position will be holding a bond that is not the best to deliver. A profit is sometimes possible by switching to another bond. This is called the *quality option*, because the deliverable bonds are considered to be of different quality for delivery; it is also sometimes called the *switching option*.

Suppose it is September 5 and you are the holder of a short position in 112 September T-bond futures contracts selling at 89 1/4 or $89,250. You also hold 10,000 individual bonds with a coupon of 9 3/8 percent and a maturity of about 15 1/2 years. Each bond has a face value of $1,000. The ask price of each bond is 103 1/32. You are considering giving notice to make delivery in two days. The accrued interest on the bond on delivery day will be $0.59 per $100. The bonds have a conversion factor of 1.1197. This is how the ratio of 112 futures with an underlying face value of $11,200,000 to 10,000 bonds with an underlying face value of $10,000,000 was chosen. Unexpected changes in the value of the futures will be approximately matched by unexpected changes in the value of the bonds. If you make delivery, the invoice price per $100 will be

$$1.1197(89.25) + 0.59 = 100.52,$$

or $10,052,000 in total. Of course, you would buy back 12 futures.

If the bonds were sold, the price per $100 face value would be the ask price of 103.03125 plus the accrued interest of 0.59, or 103.62125. The overall total thus would be $10,362,125. Therefore, you are holding bonds that could be sold for about $300,000 more than you would receive if you made delivery. Because many bonds are deliverable, at this point you should be especially alert to the possibility that some other bond might be more attractive to deliver. You can often profitably discharge your obligation on the futures contracts by selling the bond you hold, buying a new bond at a favorable price and making delivery.

We consider the alternative of switching to another bond, the 10 5/8s that mature in about 28 years, have a conversion factor of 1.2902, and a price of 115 per $100 face value. The accrued interest is 3.32. Because you are short $11,200,000 face value of futures, you buy $11,200,000 face value of these bonds. This will cost you 118.32 per $100, or $13,251,840 in total. Now you deliver these bonds. The invoice price is $1.2902(89.25) + 3.32 = 118.47$ per $100 face value, or $13,268,679 in total.

The net result is that you have done the following:

Forgone the delivery of the 9 3/8s	– $10,052,000
Sold the 9 3/8s	+ $10,362,125
Bought the 10 5/8s	– $13,251,840
Delivered the 10 5/8s	+ $13,268,679
Total	+ $326,964

Thus, the switch has netted you over $300,000.

This evaluation should be made for all eligible bonds. The best bond to deliver, which has the largest gain from switching, should be acquired. The quality option also exists on other futures contracts that permit delivery of one of several underlying assets.

THE END-OF-THE-MONTH OPTION   The last day for trading a T-bond futures contract is the eighth to last business day of the delivery month. Delivery can take place during the remaining business days. The invoice price during those final delivery days is based on the settlement price on the last trading day. Thus, during the last seven delivery days, the holder of the short position has full knowledge of the price that would be received for delivery of the bonds. This gives the holder of the short position the opportunity to watch the spot market for a fall in bond prices. The trader can continue to wait for spot prices to fall until the second to last business day, because delivery must occur by the last business day.

The *end-of-the-month option*, thus, is similar to the wild card option. There is a period during which spot prices can change while the delivery price is fixed. It is also related to the quality option, for the holder of the short position can also switch to another bond.

There are many other ways to evaluate these options. For example, the right to switch bonds can be evaluated well in advance of the delivery month. We shall not cover all of these procedures here, but a full understanding of them is necessary for actual trading of Treasury bond futures.

These options are, like any other type of option, valuable to their owners, which in these cases are holders of short positions. They are effectively "written" by holders of long positions, because those investors are granting the right to choose the bond for delivery and the date of delivery to the holders of the short positions. It should not surprise you that these options must be "priced." This is done by having the futures price be lower than it would be if there were no delivery options. The lower futures price means that the buyer can buy the contract for less, but in so doing grants the seller the right to exercise these options.

The quality option is the opportunity the holder of the short futures contract has to lock in the invoice price and switch to another bond if it becomes more favorably priced. The option exists on any futures contract that permits delivery of one of several underlying assets, with the decision made by the holder of the short position.

The valuation of these options has been extensively examined. However, it is difficult to break down the total value of all the options into their individual components. Hemler (1990) and Hegde (1988) estimated the quality option to be worth less than 1 percent of the price of the futures. Kane and Marcus (1986) estimated that the wild card option is worth less than .002 of par. However, there is considerable disagreement among researchers, and the issues are still under investigation.

Implied Repo/Cost of Carry

Earlier in this chapter, we examined the concept of the implied repo rate in the context of the cost of carry model for Treasury bill futures. Although slightly more complex, the concept is equally applicable to Treasury bond futures.

First, we must identify the best bond to deliver. If we buy that bond, we pay the spot price plus the accrued interest. The sale of a repo finances the bond's purchase. This means that we borrow the funds by selling the bond and agreeing to buy it back at a specified later date. We simultaneously sell a futures contract expiring at T. We hold the position until expiration, deliver the bond, and effectively receive f(CF), the futures price times the conversion factor, plus accrued interest for it. In an efficient market, there should be no arbitrage profit. Therefore, the amount we receive for the bond must equal the amount we paid for it plus the cost of carry:

$$f(CF) + AI_T = (S + AI)(1 + R)^T,$$

where AI_T is the accrued interest on the bond at expiration, AI is the accrued interest when the bond originally is bought, and R is the implied repo rate. The left-hand side of the formula is the amount we receive upon delivery. The right-hand side is the amount paid for the bond, S + AI, factored up by the cost of financing over the holding period, T. Solving for R,

$$R = \left[\frac{f(CF) + AI_T}{S + AI} \right]^{(1/T)} - 1.$$

If the bond can be financed in the repo market at a rate of less than R, profitable arbitrage is possible.

AN EXAMPLE   On September 26 of a particular year, the best bond to deliver on the December contract is the 12 1/2s maturing in about 23 years. The spot price is 141 16/32, the accrued interest is 1.43, the conversion factor is 1.4662, and the futures price is 95.65625. The accrued interest on December 1 is 3.669. From September 26 to December 1 is 66 days, so T = 66/365 = .1808.

The implied repo rate is

$$R = \left[\frac{95.65625(1.4662)+3.669}{141.5+1.43}\right]^{(1/.1808)} -1 = .0389.$$

If the bond can be financed in the repo market for less than 3.89 percent, the arbitrage will be profitable. With the government borrowing at 5 to 6 percent on T-bills, it would not be possible to borrow at a rate that low. Thus, no arbitrage opportunity exists.

If a coupon is paid during the life of this cash and carry arbitrage, we must make a minor adjustment: The amount AI_T must reflect the accrual of any coupons and any interest earned from reinvesting the coupons. For example, suppose a position was held for 50 days. After 32 days, the bond payed a coupon of $4.50 per $100 of face value. In that case, the coupon was received on day 32 and reinvested for 18 days. We must assume a reinvestment rate, so let us use 5.3 percent. There are 181 days between the bond's coupon payment dates. The forthcoming coupon accrues for 18 days, so the total for AI_T is

$$4.50(1.053)^{(18/365)} + 4.50(18/181) = 4.96.$$

A Treasury Bond Spread

Treasury bond futures traders frequently use spreads. Suppose a trader takes a long position in a futures contract. If this is the only transaction, the risk is quite high. One way to modify the risk is to sell short a Treasury bond, but short selling requires that the trader execute a transaction in the spot market. In addition, there are large margin requirements on short sales. An alternative that is easy to execute is to simply sell another Treasury bond futures contract. That transaction could be executed within the same trading pit. In addition, the margin requirement on a spread is much lower than the margin requirement on either a long or a short position.

AN EXAMPLE   It is July 6, and interest rates have steadily risen over the last six months. The yield on long-term government bonds is 13.54 percent. Your analysis of the economy indicates that rates are likely to continue upward, but your belief is buffered somewhat by the fact that the economy remains healthy and the Fed shows no inclination to tighten the money supply. You want to take a speculative short position in interest rate futures but are concerned that rates will not move upward by the end of August. Thus, you sell a September Treasury bond futures contract and, for protection, buy a December contract.

The September contract price is 60.6875, and the December contract price is 60.0625. Thus, the spread basis is 60.6875, the nearby futures price, minus 60.0625, the deferred futures price, or .625. Table 11.3 shows the results of the transaction.

When the spread is closed out on August 31, the September contract is priced at 65.84375 and the December contract at 65.15625, so the spread is 65.84375

TABLE 11.3

A Treasury Bond Futures Spread

Scenario: It is July 6. Interest rates have steadily risen over the last six months. The current yield on long-term government bonds is 13.54 percent. You anticipate that rates will continue upward; however, the economy remains healthy and there are no indications that the Fed will tighten the money supply, which would drive rates upward. Thus, while you are bearish, you are encouraged by other economic factors. You want to take a speculative short position in T-bond futures but are concerned that rates will fall. You believe that if rates have not changed by late August, they will not change at all. Thus, you short the September contract and buy the December contract.

July 6
Sell one September T-bond contract at 60-22.
    Price per contract: $60,687.50
Buy one December T-bond contract at 60-02
    Price per contract: $60,062.50

August 31
Buy one September T-bond contract at 65-27.
    Price per contract: $65,843.75
Sell one December contract at 65-05
    Price per contract: $65,156.25

Results
Profit on September contract: $60,687.50 – $65,843,75 = – $5,156.25
Profit on December contract: $65,156.25 – $60,062.50 = $5,093.75
Net profit: – $5,156.25 + $5,093.75 = – $62.50

– 65.15625 = .6875. Interest rates obviously did not move in the expected direction—in fact, they declined. As the table indicates, the September contract produced a loss of $5,156.25. By having a long position in the profitable December contract, the overall loss was reduced to only $62.50. Note that the overall profit can be shown as the change in the basis, .625 – .6875 = – .0625, which is – $62.50 on a $100,000 contract.

Treasury Bond Spread/Implied Repo Rate

The concept of an implied repo rate also applies to Treasury bond spreads. The implied repo rate can be used to help determine if the spread is correctly priced.

Suppose there is a futures contract expiring at time t and another expiring at time T with t coming before T. Suppose we sell the longer-term contract and buy the shorter-term contract. At time t, the shorter-term contract expires. We take delivery of the bond, financing it at the repo rate, R, and hold it until time T, when the longer-term contract expires. Because we are short that contract, we simply deliver the bond. Assume we can identify today the best bond to be delivered on the shorter-term contract.

Consider the following notation:

CF^t = conversion factor for bond delivered at t
CF^T = conversion factor for same bond delivered at T
f^t = today's futures price for contract expiring at t
f^T = today's futures price for contract expiring at T
AI_t = accrued interest on bond as of time t
AI_T = accrued interest on bond as of time T

At time t, we take delivery of the bond and pay the invoice price,

$$f^t(CF^t) + AI_t.$$

To finance the acceptance and holding of this bond, we borrow this sum at the rate R. Then, at time T, we deliver the bond and receive the invoice price,

$$f^T(CF^T) + AI_T.$$

Since this transaction is riskless, the profit from it should be zero. Therefore,

$$[f^t(CF^t) + AI_t](1 + R)^{T-t} = f^T(CF^T) + AI_T.$$

The bracketed term on the left-hand side is the amount we paid for the bond at t. Since we borrowed this amount, we must factor it up by the interest rate compounded over the period T − t. The right-hand side is the amount received from delivering the bond at T. We can now solve for R, the implied repo rate:

$$R = \left[\frac{f^T(CF^T) + AI_T}{f^t(CF^t) + AI_t} \right]^{1/(T-t)} - 1.$$

The numerator is the amount received for the bond, and the denominator is the amount paid for it. Dividing these two numbers gives the rate of return over the period T − t. Raising this term to the power $1/(T - t)$ annualizes the rate. The implied repo thus is the return we could earn over the period T − t. If the bond can be financed at less than this rate, the transaction will be profitable.

AN EXAMPLE   Assume that on September 26, the best bond to deliver was the 12 1/2s maturing on August 15 in about 29 years. Let us examine the December-March Treasury bond futures spread. The December contract is priced at 95.65625, and the conversion factor is 1.4662. The March futures price is 94.6875. The conversion factor for the 12 1/2s of 2009 delivered on the March contract is 1.464. The accrued interest on the bond on December 1, the assumed delivery date, is

3.67, and the accrued interest on March 1 is approximately 6.74. This reflects the payment of the coupon on February 15.[3]

Since the time from December 1 to March 1 is 90 days, the implied repo rate is

$$R = \left[\frac{94.6875(1.464) + 6.74}{95.65625(1.4662) + 3.67} \right]^{365/90} - 1 = .0412.$$

The implied repo rate thus is 4.12 percent. Note that this is a forward rate, because it reflects the repo rate over the period from December 1 to March 1. If the bond can be financed at a rate of less than 4.12 percent from December 1 to March 1, the transaction will be profitable.

One way traders determine if the implied repo rate on the spread is attractive is to evaluate what is called a *turtle trade*. The implied repo rate of 4.12 percent is an implied forward rate. It can be compared to the implied rate in the T-bill futures market. If the T-bill futures rate is lower, the trader sells the T-bill futures and buys the T-bond spread. This creates a risk-free position and earns the difference between the implied repo rate on the T-bond spread and the implied rate on the T-bill futures. If the implied rate on the T-bill futures is higher, the investor reverses the T-bond spread and buys the T-bill futures.

In this problem, the T-bill futures price was the IMM Index of 94.80, which implies a discount of 5.20. This produces a futures price $100 - 5.20(90/360) = 98.70$, which implies a rate of $(100/98.70)^{(365/90)} - 1 = .0545$. Thus, if the investor reversed the T-bond spread—sold the December contract and bought the March contract—the transaction would be equivalent to borrowing forward at a rate of 4.12 percent. By buying the T-bill futures, the investor would be lending forward at a rate of 5.45 percent. Thus, the turtle trade would lock in a return of 1.33 percent.

Unfortunately, there are a number of impediments to executing a turtle trade, and the return is not truly risk free. In discussing some of the difficulties in the turtle trade, Rentzler (1986) found that despite the problems, a number of profitable arbitrage opportunities existed.

Intermarket Spreads

We have discussed two forms of intramarket spreads. There are also a number of intermarket spreads. These are transactions in which the two futures contracts are on different underlying instruments. For example, many traders execute what is called the NOB (notes over bonds) spread. This spread involves a long (short) position in T-note futures and a short (long) position in T-bond futures. This trade

---

[3]This was found by assuming a 5 percent reinvestment rate on the coupon paid on February 15. It earns 14 days of interest until March 1. The next coupon accrues 14 days until March 1. Thus,

$$AI_T = 6.25(1.053)^{14/365} + 6.25(14/181) = 6.74.$$

would be used to capitalize on shifts in the yield curve. For example, if a trader believes that rates on the 7-to-10-year range of the yield curve will fall and rates on the 15-plus-year range will either rise or fall by less, a long position in the NOB spread might be warranted. If the investor's expectations prove correct, a profit could be made as T-note futures will rise and T-bond futures will either fall or rise by a smaller amount. Of course, if yields on the long-term end of the market fall, the trader could end up losing money because long-term bond prices will be expected to rise by a greater amount for a given yield change. Thus, the trader might prefer to take a weighted position in which the ratio of T-note to T-bond futures is something other than one to one. Thus, the NOB spread is designed to capitalize on changes in the relationship between Treasury note and Treasury bond futures prices.

Another intermarket spread is the MOB (municipals over bonds) spread. This spread involves a long (short) position in the municipal bond futures contract and a short (long) position in the T-bond futures contract. There is no specific arbitrage relationship that defines the MOB spread, simply because T-bonds and municipals are not perfect substitutes; however, a perceived historical relationship has prevailed. Traders often watch that relationship for signs of abnormal behavior that might signal profit opportunities. Arak et al. (1987) analyzed this historical relationship and provided some rules for identifying profitable opportunities.

This completes our discussion of Treasury note and bond futures transactions. We now turn to stock index futures.

STOCK INDEX FUTURES STRATEGIES

Stock index futures contracts offer several interesting applications. We shall look at two: cash-and-carry arbitrage and speculating on unsystematic risk.

Cash-and-Carry Arbitrage

We discussed cash-and-carry arbitrage with Treasury bill and bond futures. The concept is equally applicable to stock index futures. In fact, this type of transaction is one of the most widely used in the futures markets. It is called index arbitrage.

Recall that the model for the stock index futures price is

$$f = Se^{(r-\delta)T},$$

where r is the risk-free rate and δ is the dividend yield. On October 27 of a particular year, the December S&P 500 futures price was 337.20 and the S&P index was at 335.06. The dividend yield was 3.13 percent. The contract expires on December 14, so the time to expiration is .1315 based on 48 days between October 27 and December 14. The continuously compounded Treasury bill yield was 7.74

percent. The model gives the futures price as

$$f = 335.06e^{(.0774 - .0313)(.1315)} = 337.10.$$

The actual futures price was 337.20. Thus, the futures was very slightly overpriced. We would sell the futures and buy the stocks in the S&P 500 in the same proportions as in the index. At expiration, the futures price would equal the spot price of the S&P 500 index. We then would sell the stocks. The transaction is theoretically riskless and would earn a return in excess of the risk-free rate.

What actually happened is that on December 14, the S&P 500 index closed at 350.30. The profit on the futures contract was $-350.30 + 337.20 = -13.10$. We sold the stocks for 350.30, but, combined with the loss on the futures of 13.10, effectively sold the stocks for $350.30 - 13.10 = 337.20$. We bought the stocks for 335.06. While we held them, we lost interest on the money at a rate of 7.74 percent, but this was partially offset by the dividend paid at a rate of 3.13 percent. Thus, we effectively bought the stocks for

$$335.06e^{(.0774 - .0313)(.1315)} = 337.10.$$

Note that this is simply the price of the futures contract given by the model. After accounting for the opportunity cost of the interest and the receipt of the dividends, we invested 337.10 and received 337.20 for a net profit at expiration of .10, which is the difference between the model price of the futures contract and its market price.

SOME PRACTICAL CONSIDERATIONS   There are several problems in implementing the stock index futures cash-and-carry arbitrage. We referred to the arbitrageur as buying the stock index at 335.06. In reality, the arbitrageur would have to purchase all 500 stocks in the appropriate proportions as the index and immediately execute all of the trades. The New York Stock Exchange has established a computerized order processing system, called the *Designated Order Turnaround*, or *DOT*, that expedites trades. Nonetheless, it is still difficult to get all the trades in before the price of any single stock changes. Thus, most arbitrageurs do not duplicate the index but use a smaller subset of the stocks. Of course, this introduces some risk into what is supposed to be a riskless transaction.

Let us assume, however, that the trades can be executed simultaneously. Let the index be 335.06. Now assume an arbitrageur has $2 million to use. Then the arbitrageur will buy the appropriately weighted 500 stocks with that amount. Since the S&P 500 is actually priced at 335.06($500) = $167,530, the arbitrageur will need to buy $2,000,000/$167,530 = 11.94 futures contracts. Because one cannot buy fractional contracts, the transaction will not be weighted precisely.

In addition, there are transaction costs, estimated by Stoll and Whaley (1987) at about .006125 of the market value of the stocks. Would this consume the profit in this example? If the index is 335.06 and the net profit is .10, the profit is .0003 of the index and clearly would be absorbed by the transaction costs.

In addition, there are problems involved in simultaneously selling all of the stocks in the index at expiration. These transactions must be executed such that the portfolio will be liquidated at the closing values of each stock. This is very difficult to do and frequently causes unusual stock price movements at expiration.

Nonetheless, many large financial institutions execute this arbitrage transaction. Every day billions of dollars trade on the basis of this futures pricing model. This kind of activity often is referred to as *program trading*.[4] The stock index futures pricing model is programmed into a computer, which continuously monitors the futures price and the individual stock prices. When the computer identifies a deviation from the model, it sends a signal to the user. Many large institutions have established procedures for immediately executing the many simultaneous transactions, usually sending the orders through the DOT system. We shall say more about program trading and its implications in Chapter 14.

Are stock index futures contracts correctly priced? Is it truly possible to profit from index arbitrage? This question has been studied at great length. In the early days of stock index futures trading, there was considerable evidence that stock index futures prices were too low (Figlewski, 1984). In time, prices began to conform more closely to the model, as shown by Cornell (1985). However, deviations from the model remain, and some can be exploited by traders with sufficiently low transaction costs. MacKinlay and Ramaswamy (1988) revealed that (1) mispricing is more common the longer the remaining time to expiration and (2) when a contract becomes overpriced or underpriced, it tends to stay overpriced or underpriced rather than reversing from overpriced to underpriced or vice versa. It is still not obvious that any such profits from index arbitrage are truly earned, however, because the transactions remain quite risky and may simply be earning a risk premium for the risk taken.

One consequence of program trading is that large stock price movements often occur quickly and without an apparent flow of new information. For example, when the index or futures price becomes out of line with the cost of carry model, many investors recognize this event simultaneously and react by buying and selling large quantities of stock and futures. Such actions have attracted considerable attention from the media. Critics have charged that program trading has led to increased volatility in the spot markets. Regulators and legislators have called for restrictions on such trading in the form of circuit breakers and reduced access to the DOT system for rapidly executing orders. Others have argued for imposing higher margins on futures trading. We shall defer a discussion of these issues until Chapter 14, where we look at a number of contemporary controversial issues.

---

[4]This type of program trading is index arbitrage. There are other forms of program trading, such as portfolio insurance, which is covered in Chapter 14. See Hill and Jones (1988) for a discussion of the different forms of program trading.

Speculating on Unsystematic Risk

In Chapter 8, we saw how stock returns contain both systematic and unsystematic risk. We already have seen that the systematic risk of a diversified portfolio can be hedged by using stock index futures. Because the portfolio is diversified, there is no unsystematic risk and therefore the portfolio is riskless. With some undiversified portfolios, an investor might wish to hedge the systematic risk and retain the unsystematic risk.

In an efficient market, investors cannot expect to earn returns by assuming unsystematic risk. However, professional financial analysts do not believe this is true. Thousands of analysts devote all of their time to identifying over- and underpriced stocks. An analyst who thinks a stock is underpriced normally recommends it for purchase. If the stock is purchased and the market goes down, the stock's overall performance may be hurt. For example, a drug firm may announce an important new drug that can help cure diabetes. If that announcement occurs during a strong bear market, the stock may be pulled down by the market effect. The extent of the stock's movement with the market is measured by its beta.

We will use the following notation:

S = stock price
M = value of market portfolio of all risky assets
$r_S = \Delta S/S$ = return on stock
$r_M = \Delta M/M$ = return on market
β = beta of the stock

The stock's return consists of its systematic return, βr_M, and its unsystematic return, which we shall call μ_S. Thus,

$$r_S = \beta r_M + \mu_S.$$

If we multiply both sides of the equation by S, we have

$$Sr_S = S\beta r_M + S\mu_S,$$

which is equivalent to

$$\Delta S = S\beta(\Delta M/M) + S\mu_S.$$

This is the return on the stock expressed in dollars. The objective of the transaction is to capture a profit equal to the unsystematic return, $S\mu_S$.

The profit from a transaction consisting of the stock and N_f futures contracts is

$$\Pi = \Delta S + N_f \Delta f.$$

Recall from Chapter 10 that the formula for N_f in an ordinary stock index futures hedge is $-\beta(S/f)$. Let us substitute this for N_f:

$$\Pi = \Delta S - \beta(S/f)\Delta f.$$

Now we need to substitute $S\beta(\Delta M/M) + S\mu_s$ for ΔS and assume the futures price change will match the index price change. In that case, $\Delta M/M = \Delta f/f$. Making these substitutions gives

$$\Pi = S\mu_s.$$

Thus, if we use N_f futures contracts where N_f is the ordinary hedge ratio for stock index futures, we will eliminate systematic risk and the profit will be the unsystematic risk.

AN EXAMPLE   Table 11.4 illustrates an application of this method. On July 1, you have identified Helene Curtis stock as likely to have share price appreciation of about 10 percent by the end of September. The 10 percent return is unsystematic and associated only with the company's performance and not with the market as a whole. The stock currently is at 17 3/8 and has a beta of 1.10. The market as a whole is expected to decline about 8 percent during that time. Because the stock has a beta of 1.10, the systematic return is expected to be

$$(-.08)(1.10) = -.088,$$

while the unsystematic return is 10 percent. This leaves the overall return at $-.088 + .10 = .012$.

If you own 50,000 shares, the value of the stock is $50,000(\$17.375) = \$868,750$. The December futures contract is priced at 197.60. With the multiplier of $500, the actual price is $197.60(\$500) = \$98,800$. The appropriate number of futures contracts is

$$N_f = 1.10(\$868,750/\$98,800) = 9.67.$$

You would then sell 10 contracts.

On September 30, the stock price is at $17.75. Thus, the stock is worth $887,500, a profit of $18,750. However, the futures price is 182.80, or $91,400, per contract for a profit on ten contracts of $74,000. The overall profit therefore is $92,750.

The market as a whole, as measured by the futures contract, declined from 197.60 to 182.80, a drop of 7.49 percent. The stock increased from 17.375 to 17.75, an increase of only 2.16 percent. With a beta of 1.10, it is apparent that the market factor indeed had an effect on the stock. By hedging away the market effect, the overall return was

$$\$92,750/\$868,750 = .1068,$$

which was close to—in fact, higher than—the return originally expected.

TABLE 11.4
Speculating on Unsystematic Risk

Scenario: On July 1, you are following the stock of Helene Curtis, which has a price of 17 3/8 and a beta of 1.10. Barring any change in the general level of stock prices, you expect the stock to appreciate by about 10 percent by the end of September. However, your analysis of the market as a whole calls for about an 8 percent decline in stock prices in general over the same time period. Since the stock has a beta of 1.10, this will bring the stock down by 1.10(.08) = .088, or 8.8 percent, which will almost completely offset the expected 10 percent unsystematic increase in the stock price. You decide to hedge the market effect by selling stock index futures.

July 1
Spot market: Own 50,000 shares of Helene Curtis stock at 17.375
    Value of stock: $868,750
Futures market: December S&P 500 futures is at 197.60
    Price per contract: 197.60(500) = $98,800
Sell 10 contracts

September 30
Spot market: Helene Curtis stock is at 17.75
    Value of stock: $887,500
Futures market: December S&P 500 futures is at 182.80
    Price per contract: 182.80(500) = $91,400
Buy 10 contracts

Results
Profit on stock: $887,500 − $868,750 = $18,750
Profit on futures: − 10($91,400 − $98,800) = $74,000
Total profit: $18,750 + $74,000 = $92,750
Rate of return: $92,750/$868,750 = .1068

This transaction should not be considered riskless. As the title of this section indicates, it involves speculating on unsystematic risk. Suppose your analysis is incorrect and the company announces some bad news during a bull market. Selling the futures contract would eliminate the effect of the bull market while retaining the effect of the bad news announcement. Moreover, this type of trade depends not only on the correctness of the analysis but on the beta's stability.

SUMMARY

This chapter examined the application of some advanced futures trading strategies. It looked at how T-bill, Eurodollar, Treasury bond, and stock index futures can be used in arbitrage transactions. It also examined some spread strategies and the important concept of the implied repo rate. It examined speculative strategies and techniques for using stock index futures in exploiting information about unsystematic risk.

This completes the chapters devoted exclusively to futures. So far we have kept futures and options separate. That will change in the next three chapters. In Chapter 12 we shall examine options on futures, which require an understanding of both options and futures. In Chapter 13, we shall cover foreign currency instruments, which include both options and futures. In Chapter 14, we shall look at a number of products that have characteristics of both futures and options. In addition, we shall consider some advanced applications of futures and options.

Questions and Problems

1. Explain how the repurchase agreement plays a role in the pricing of futures contracts. What is the implied repo rate?

2. On November 1, the T-bill futures contract expiring on December 19 was priced at 93 (IMM Index). The T-bill maturing at that time was priced at a discount of 7.10 and the T-bill maturing on March 20 at a discount of 7.17. Determine the implied repo rate.

3. On November 1, the March T-bill futures price was 92.85. The T-bill maturing at around the futures expiration was selling at a discount of 7.17. You are interested in using the spot T-bill and the March futures contract to construct a synthetic T-bill maturing on June 20. The March contract expires on March 21.

    a. Determine the return on this T-bill.

    b. There is no actual T-bill maturing on June 20, but based on the discounts on bills maturing around that time, such a bill probably would have a discount of 7.31. Compare your result in part a with the return on the hypothetical T-bill maturing on June 20.

4. Why is it difficult to identify the spot instrument that the Treasury bond futures contract is following? How do futures traders determine the bond that the contract is most likely following?

5. On September 26 of a particular year, the March Treasury bond futures contract settlement price was 94-22. Compare the following two bonds and determine which is the better bond to deliver. Assume delivery will be made on March 1. Use 5.3 percent as the repo rate.

    a. Bond A: A 12 3/4 bond callable in about 19 years and maturing in about 24 years with a price of 148 9/32 and a CF of 1.4433. Coupons are paid on November 15 and May 15.

    b. Bond B: A 13 7/8 bond callable in about 20 years and maturing in about 25 years with a price of 159 27/32 and a CF of 1.5689. Coupons are paid on November 15 and May 15.

6. It is August 20, and you are trying to determine which of two bonds is the better bond to deliver on the December Treasury bond futures contract. The

futures price is 89 12/32. Assume delivery will be made on December 14, and use 7.9 percent as the repo rate. Find the better bond to deliver.

   a.   Bond X: A 9 percent non-callable bond maturing in about 28 years with a price of 100 14/32 and a CF of 1.1106. Coupons are paid on November 15 and May 15.

   b.   Bond Z: An 11 1/4 percent non-callable bond maturing in about 25 years with a price of 121 14/32 and a CF of 1.3444. Coupons are paid February 15 and August 15.

7.   Assume that on March 16, the best bond to deliver on the June T-bond futures contract is the 14s callable in about 19 years and maturing in about 24 years. Coupons are paid on November 15 and May 15. The price of the bond is 161 23/32, and the CF is 1.584. The June futures price is 100 17/32. Assume a 5.5 percent reinvestment rate. Determine the implied repo rate on the contract. Interpret your result.

8.   During the first six months of the year, yields on long-term government debt have fallen about 100 basis points. You believe the decline in rates is over, and you are interested in speculating on a rise in rates. You are, however, unwilling to assume much risk, so you decide to do a spread. Use the following information to construct a T-bond futures spread on July 15, and determine the profit when the position is closed on November 15.

July 15
December futures price: 76 9/32
March futures price: 75 9/32

November 15
December futures price: 79 13/32
March futures price: 78 9/32

---

9.   Explain how the implied repo rate on a spread transaction differs from that on a nearby futures contract.

10.   Explain what a turtle trade is, and give an example.

11.   On March 16, the June T-bond futures contract was priced at 100 17/32 and the September contract was at 99 17/32. Determine the implied repo rates on the spread. Assume the best bond to deliver on both contracts is the 11 1/4 maturing in 28 years and currently priced at 140 21/32. The CF for delivery in June was 1.3593, and the CF for delivery in September was 1.3581. Delivery is on the first of the month, and coupons are on 2/15 and 8/15. Use 5.3 percent as the reinvestment rate on the coupon.

12. On July 5, the September S&P 500 futures contract was at 194.85. The index was at 192.54, the risk-free rate was 6.83 percent, the dividend yield was 4.08 percent, and the contract expired on September 20. Determine if an arbitrage opportunity was available, and explain what transactions were executed.

13. Rework problem 12 assuming that the S&P 500 index was at 188.14 at expiration. Determine the profit from the arbitrage trade, and express it in terms of the profit from the spot and futures sides of the transaction. How does your answer relate to that in problem 12?

14. On August 20 the September S&P 500 futures, which expires on September 20, was priced at 329.70. The S&P 500 index was at 328.51. The dividend yield was 3.7 percent. Discuss the concept of the implied repo rate on an index arbitrage trade. Determine the implied repo rate on this trade, and explain how you would evaluate it.

15. Identify and explain some factors that make the execution of stock index futures arbitrage difficult in practice.

16. What is program trading? Why is it so controversial?

17. On November 1, an analyst who has been studying a firm called Computer Sciences believes the company will make a major new announcement before the end of the year. Computer Sciences currently is priced at 27 5/8 and has a beta of .95. The analyst believes the stock can advance about 10 percent if the market does not move. However, the analyst thinks the market might decline by as much as 5 percent, leaving the stock with a return of $.10 + (-.05)(.95) = .0525$. To capture the full 10 percent unsystematic return, the analyst recommends the sale of S&P 500 futures. The March contract currently is priced at 193. Assume the investor owns 100,000 shares of the stock. Set up a transaction by determining the appropriate number of futures contracts. Then determine the effective return on the stock if, on December 31, the stock is sold at 28 7/8 and the futures contract is at 212.45. Explain your results.

18. Consider the quality option problem discussed in the chapter. Recall that it is September 5 and you are short T-bond futures with a price of 89 1/4. You are considering making delivery on September 7. You own $10 million face value of the 13 7/8s, which have a maturity of about 16 years and a conversion factor of 1.5167. You hold an appropriately weighted short position in the futures contract. The accrued interest on the bond is 4.34, and the ask price is 138 19/32. Evaluate the possibility of switching to the 7 1/2s, which have a maturity of about 26 years and a conversion factor of .9456. The price of the bonds is 82 18/32, and the accrued interest is 2.34.

19. Explain the concept of the wild card option. Does the option have value like an ordinary option? Who "pays" for the option?

20. On March 16, the March T-bond futures settlement price was 101 21/32. Assume the 12 1/2 bond maturing in about 22 years is the best bond to deliver. The CF is 1.4639. Assume that the price at 3:00 p.m. was 150 15/32. Determine the price at 5:00 p.m. that would be necessary to justify delivery.

21. (Concept Problem) Recall from the chapters on options that we learned about bull and bear spreads. Intramarket futures spreads also are considered bull and bear spreads. Describe what you think might be a bull spread with T-bond futures. Of course, be sure to explain your reasoning.

22. (Concept Problem) Referring to problem 12, suppose transaction costs amounted to .5 percent of the value of the spot index. Explain how these costs would affect the profitability and the incidence of index arbitrage. Then calculate the range of possible futures prices within which no arbitrage would take place.

References

Arak, Marcelle, Philip Fischer, Laurie Goodman, and Raj Daryanani. "The Municipal-Treasury Futures Spread." *The Journal of Futures Markets* 7 (1987): 355–371.

Arak, Marcelle, Laurie Goodman, and Susan Ross. "The Cheapest to Deliver Bond on the Treasury Bond Futures Contract." *Advances in Futures and Options Research* 1, part B (1986): 49–74.

Chicago Board of Trade. *Commodity Trading Manual*, Chapters 10, 11. Chicago: Board of Trade of the City of Chicago, 1985.

Cornell, Bradford. "Taxes and the Pricing of Stock Index Futures: Empirical Results." *Journal of Futures Markets* 5 (1985): 89–101.

Duffie, Darrell. *Futures Markets*, Chapter 5. Englewood Cliffs, N.J.: Prentice-Hall, 1989.

Figlewski, Stephen. "Explaining the Early Discounts on Stock Index Futures: The Case for Disequilibrium." *Financial Analysts Journal* 40 (1984): 43–47, 67.

Figlewski, Stephen. *Hedging with Financial Futures for Institutional Investors*, Chapters 3, 4, 6. Cambridge, Mass.: Ballinger, 1986.

Gay, Gerald D., and Steven Manaster. "Implicit Delivery Options and Optimal Delivery Strategies for Financial Futures Contracts." *Journal of Financial Economics* 16 (1986): 41–72.

Gay, Gerald D., and Steven Manaster. "The Quality Option Implicit in Futures Contracts." *Journal of Financial Economics* 13 (1984): 353–370.

Hegde, Shantaram P. "An Empirical Analysis of Implicit Delivery Options in the Treasury Bond Futures Contract." *Journal of Banking and Finance* 12 (1988): 469–482.

Hegde, Shantaram P. "Coupon and Maturity Characteristics of the Cheapest-to-Deliver Bond in the Treasury Bond Futures Contract." *Financial Analysts Journal* 43 (March–April 1987): 70–76.

Hemler, Michael A. "The Quality Delivery Option in Treasury Bond Futures Contracts." *The Journal of Finance* 45 (December 1990): 1565–1586.

Hill, Joanne M., and Frank J. Jones. "Equity Trading, Program Trading, Portfolio Insurance, Computer Trading and All That." *Financial Analysts Journal* 44 (July–August 1988): 29–38.

Hull, John. *Options, Futures, and Other Derivative Securities*, Chapter 2. Englewood Cliffs, N.J.: Prentice-Hall, 1989.

Kane, Alex, and Alan J. Marcus. "Valuation and Optimal Exercise of the Wild Card Option in the Treasury Bond Futures Market." *The Journal of Finance* 41 (March 1986): 195–207.

Kawaller, Ira G. "A Note: Debunking the Myth of the Risk-Free Return." *The Journal of Futures Markets* 7 (1987): 327–331.

MacKinlay, A. Craig, and Krishna Ramaswamy. "Index-Futures Arbitrage and the Behavior of Stock Index Futures Prices." *Review of Financial Studies* 1 (1988): 137–158.

Modest, David M., and Mahadevan Sundaresan. "The Relationship between Spot and Futures Prices in Stock Index Futures Markets: Some Preliminary Evidence." *The Journal of Futures Markets* 3 (1983): 15–41.

Powers, Mark J. *Inside the Financial Futures Markets*, 2d ed., Chapters 11, 12, 15, 18. New York: Wiley, 1984.

Rentzler, Joel C. "Trading Treasury Bond Spreads against Treasury Bill Futures—a Model and Empirical Test of the Turtle Trade." *The Journal of Futures Markets* 6 (1986): 41–61.

Rothstein, Nancy H. *The Handbook of Financial Futures*, Chapters 12, 15, 17. New York: McGraw-Hill, 1984.

Schwarz, Edward W., Joanne M. Hill, and Thomas Schneeweis. *Financial Futures: Fundamentals, Strategies, and Applications*, Chapters 10, 11, 14, 15. Homewood, Ill.: Irwin, 1986.

Siegel, Daniel R., and Diane F. Siegel. *Futures Markets*, Chapters 4, 5, 6. Hinsdale, Ill.: Dryden Press, 1989.

Stoll, Hans, and Robert E. Whaley. "Program Trading and Expiration-Day Effects." *Financial Analysts Journal* 43 (July–August 1987): 44–54.

Teweles, Richard J., and Frank J. Jones. *The Futures Game: Who Wins? Who Loses? Why?*, Chapter 8. New York: McGraw-Hill, 1987.

part three
ADVANCED TOPICS

OPTIONS ON FUTURES

> *Nought may endure but Mutability.*
>
> PERCY BYSSHE SHELLEY, *Mutability*

One of the distinguishing features of U.S. financial markets is their ability to change. In this chapter, we shall examine one of the most successful new products in the financial markets: *options on futures*. These instruments combine many of the most attractive features of both options and futures. As a result, they give us an opportunity to extend the principles we learned in our study of options and futures in the preceding chapters.

Options on futures are not really new instruments. They existed many years ago. However, as a result of several scandals, they were banned in 1936. They were reauthorized in 1982, when the CFTC began a pilot program allowing each exchange to offer one option on futures contract. The program was so successful that in January 1987, options on futures were authorized permanently.

Options on futures are sometimes called *commodity options*, but that term is somewhat misleading. These are not options on commodities but options on futures contracts. There are, however, a number of options on futures contracts in which the futures is an agricultural commodity futures. However, the most successful options on futures have been the options on financial futures.

Options on futures are also referred to as *futures options*. In this book, however, we shall use the term *options on futures*.

CHARACTERISTICS OF OPTIONS ON FUTURES

An *option on a futures* is a contract that grants the holder the right, but not the obligation, to buy or sell a futures contract at a fixed price—the exercise price—up to a specified expiration date. An option to buy a futures is referred to as a *call*, and an option to sell a futures is called a *put*. Although an option on a futures is very similar to an option on a spot (in fact, in some cases they are identical), there are a number of important differences that will become apparent as we examine how they are priced.

An option on a futures contract differs from an option on the spot instrument in that upon exercise, the option holder establishes a position in the futures contract. For example, on March 28, 1991, an option on a Treasury bond futures contract was trading at the Chicago Board of Trade with an exercise price of 96. The underlying futures is the June Treasury bond futures, which trades up to the business day prior to the last seven days of the month. The Treasury bond option expires on the first Friday that is at least five business days before the first notice day of the futures. That effectively makes the option expire in the month before the futures. Thus, even though this option would be referred to as the June 96 call, it actually expires in late May. This particular feature of futures options is somewhat of an exception, however, as most options on futures expire on the same day as the futures expiration. The Treasury bond option on futures is an American option, meaning that it can be exercised on any day prior to and including the expiration day.

The option permits the purchase of the June T-bond futures at a price of 96. The option price on that day was 1 2/64, or 1.03125. The option is on one underlying futures, which, as we already learned, has a face value of $100,000. Thus, the option price per contract is $1,031.25. As with options on a spot instrument, the buyer of the option is bullish, in this case on the price of the underlying instrument, the futures.

Suppose that at expiration the futures price was at 97. Then the call holder exercises the option. This establishes for the call holder a long position in the T-bond futures contract at a price of 96. Remember that these prices are in terms of a par value of $100,000 of Treasury bonds. The futures is immediately marked to market, and the buyer thus receives a cash credit of $1,000 based on the difference between the current price, 97—actually $97,000—and the price at which the contract was established, 96—actually $96,000. The investor must either deposit sufficient funds to meet the futures' initial margin requirement or liquidate the futures. Upon exercise, a short position in the futures at a price of 96, or $96,000, is established for the writer. The writer's account is marked to market and must be supplied with sufficient margin or liquidated. If at expiration the stock price is less than the exercise price, the call simply expires unexercised and the writer retains the premium paid by the buyer.

FIGURE 12.1
Options on Futures Volume, 1983–1989

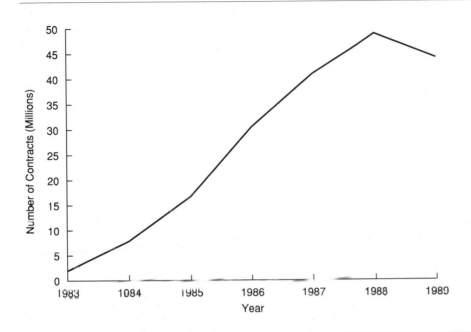

The June 96 put traded at a price of 1 35/64, or $1,546.875. Upon exercise, a short position in the futures at a price of 96, or $96,000, is established for the put holder. The position is marked to market, and sufficient margin funds must be deposited or the futures bought back. A long position in the futures at a price of 96, or $96,000, is established for the put writer. The position is marked to market, and sufficient margin funds must be deposited or the futures sold.

Buyers of these options are required to pay the full premium. Writers post margin for their short options in a manner similar to writers of options on spot instruments. In addition, the writers' accounts are marked to market.

Options on futures have been quite popular with investors. Figure 12.1 shows the annual volume from 1983 to 1989. Growth had been quite steady through 1988. Then a decline occurred in 1989. This partially reflected a decrease in public trading of these options since the market crash of 1987.

Figure 12.2 illustrates the composition of the market for options on futures in terms of the type of underlying instrument. As the pie chart indicates, financials comprise the largest single group, accounting for about 41 percent of volume. This is down, however, from the 72 percent financials accounted for in 1986. Currencies are the second largest group, accounting for around 20 percent. Agriculturals now comprise about 18 percent, up from 8 percent in 1986. Options on energy futures, which did not even exist in 1986, now account for almost 15 percent of the total. As we noted in Chapter 7, energy futures are one of the fastest

FIGURE 12.2

Options on Futures Volume by Type of Underlying Instrument, 1989

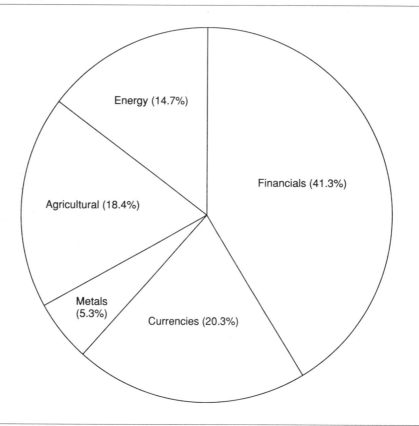

growing categories of futures, and this phenomenon is reflected in their options as well.

Table 12.1 presents the 1990 volume by exchange. Each of the U.S. futures exchanges has options on futures trading. The Chicago Board of Trade, which is first in futures volume, is also first in the volume of options on futures. The Chicago Mercantile Exchange is second and the New York Mercantile Exchange, with its highly successful energy futures and options, is third.

Figure 12.3 shows *The Wall Street Journal* quotations for some of the options on futures contracts. The tables are virtually the same as those for options on the spot. Beside the contract name and the exchange abbreviation is the contract size and units of quotation. Below the actual price quotations are volume and open interest figures.

Figure 12.4 contains some sample quotations for soybean options on futures from *Barron's*. They are arranged somewhat like the stock option quotes, but instead of intermingling the calls and puts, they are listed separately. *Barron's*

TABLE 12.1
1990 Options on Futures Trading Volume by Exchange

Exchange	1,000 Contracts
Chicago Board of Trade	33,461
Chicago Mercantile Exchange	18,156
New York Mercantile Exchange	6,101
Coffee, Sugar and Cocoa Exchange	3,021
Commodity Exchange	2,787
New York Cotton Exchange	448
Kansas City Board of Trade	66
MidAmerica Commodity Exchange	29
New York Futures Exchange	29
Minneapolis Grain Exchange	5
	64,103

Source: Consensus, *January 18, 1991.*

also shows the volume and open interest, the week's high, low, and settlement prices, the net change in the settlement price, and the settlement price of the futures.

Table 12.2 lists all options on futures contracts trading and regularly quoted in *The Wall Street Journal* as of March 28, 1991. Table 12.3 presents the ten most active options on futures contracts in 1990. The Treasury bond option on futures is the most active, followed by the Chicago Mercantile Exchange's Eurodollar option on futures contract. The list of most active options on futures contracts, in fact, is quite similar to that of most active futures contracts. This is not surprising, since trading in both the options and the futures occurs side by side. As you might expect, arbitrage between the option and the underlying futures is the basis for pricing these instruments.

PRICING OPTIONS ON FUTURES CONTRACTS

In this section, we shall look at some principles of pricing options on futures. We shall continue to employ the same notation previously used. We will make the assumptions that the options and the futures contract expire simultaneously and the futures price equals the forward price.

The Intrinsic Value of an American Option on Futures

The minimum value of an American call on a futures is its intrinsic value. We can formally state this as

$$C_a(f,T,E) \geq \text{Max}(0, f - E),$$

FIGURE 12.3

Options on Futures Quotations in *The Wall Street Journal*, Trading Day of March 22, 1991

T-BONDS (CBT) $100,000; points and 64ths of 100%

Strike	Calls–Last			Puts–Last		
Price	May-c	Jun-c	Sep-c	Apr-p	Jun-p	Sep-p
90	....	4-39	4-37	0-04	0-14	0-58
92	2-40	2-59	3-15	0-13	0-33	1-31

Strike	Calls–Last			Puts–Last		
Price	May-c	Jun-c	Sep-c	Apr-p	Jun-p	Sep-p
94	1-06	1-38	2-07	0-41	1-07	2-19
96	0-19	0-43	1-16	1-55	2-12	3-24
98	0-05	0-17	0-46	....	3-50	4-51
100	0-02	0-06	0-26	....	5-39	6-28

Est. vol. 50,000, Thur vol. 32,265 calls, 41,208 puts
Open Interest Thur 263,789 calls, 230,051 puts

T-NOTES (CBT) $100,000; points and 64ths of 100%

Strike	Calls–Last			Puts–Last		
Price	May-c	Jun-c	Sep-c	Apr-p	Jun-p	Sep-p
96	....	2-21	....	0-07	0-21	0-59
97	1-16	1-36	....	0-16	0-37	....
98	0-38	0-60	1-18	0-37	0-60	1-50
99	0-14	0-32	....	....	1-32	....
100	0-04	0-17	....	....	2-15	....
101	0-03	0-09	0-38	....	3-06	....

Est. vol. 1,000, Thur vol. 1,130 calls, 1,394 puts
Open Interest Thur 12,289 calls, 11,147 puts

MUNICIPAL BOND INDEX (CBT) $100,000; pts. & 64ths of 100%

Strike	Calls–Settle			Puts–Settle		
Price	Jun-c	Sep-c	Dec-c	Jun-p	Sep-p	Dec-p
88	....	....	....	0-26	....	....
89	1-56	1-62	....	0-39	1-14	....
90	1-16	1-28	....	0-63	1-41	....
91	....	1-02	....	....	2-13	....
92	0-32	0-47	....	2-12	2-56	....
93	0-19	0-33	....	2-62	3-40	....

Est. vol. 0, Thur vol. 0 calls, 0 puts
Open Interest Thur 13,011 calls, 13,118 puts

EURODOLLAR (IMM) $ million; pts. of 100%

Strike	Calls–Settle			Puts–Settle		
Price	Jun-c	Sep-c	Dec-c	Jun-p	Sep-p	Dec-p
9275	0.64	0.49	0.28	0.03	0.18	0.47
9300	0.43	0.33	0.20	0.06	0.27	0.63
9325	0.25	0.21	0.13	0.13	0.39	0.81
9350	0.13	0.13	0.08	0.26	0.56	0.99
9375	0.06	0.08	0.05	0.44	....	....
9400	0.03	0.04	0.03	0.65	....	....

Est. vol. 13,268, Thur vol. 20,802 calls, 6,875 puts
Open Interest Thur 143,497 calls, 165,609 puts

EURODOLLAR (LIFFE) $1 million; pts. of 100%

Strike	Calls–Settle			Puts–Settle		
Price	Mar-c	Jun-c	Sep-c	Mar-p	Jun-p	Sep-p
9275	0.65	0.47	0.29	0.04	0.18	0.50
9300	0.43	0.32	0.20	0.07	0.28	0.66
9325	0.25	0.20	0.12	0.14	0.41	0.83
9350	0.12	0.11	0.07	0.26	0.57	1.03
9375	0.06	0.07	0.04	0.45	0.78	1.25
9400	0.03	0.04	0.02	0.67	1.00	1.48

Est. Vol. Fri, 100 Calls, 10 Puts.
Open Interest Thur 1,618, Calls, 1,466 Puts.

CORN (CBT) 5,000 bu.; cents per bu.

Strike	Calls–Settle			Puts–Settle		
Price	May-c	Jly-c	Sep-c	May-p	Jly-p	Sep-p
230	23½	30	31½	¼	1	4
240	14¼	22½	24½	¾	2¾	7½
250	5¾	16¼	20	2¼	5¾	11¾
260	1¾	10⅞	15¾	8¼	10½	16¾
270	⅜	7	12	17¼	17	23
280	¼	4⅝	9	....	25	37

Est. vol. 5,500, Thur vol. 3,130 calls, 3,398 puts
Open Interest Thur 83,432 calls, 58,572 puts

SOYBEANS (CBT) 5,000 bu.; cents per bu.

Strike	Calls–Settle			Puts–Settle		
Price	May-c	Jly-c	Aug-c	May-p	Jly-p	Aug-p
525	....	65	....	¼	1½	3¼
550	26½	43½	....	1	5	7¾
575	8⅝	26½	35	8	13	16½
600	2⅜	15¾	24½	26¼	27½	30½
625	⅝	9½	16¾	50	45½	47¼
650	¼	6	12	74⅝	67	66¾

Est. vol. 5,500, Thur vol. 8,524 calls, 5,435 puts
Open Interest Thur 86,267 calls, 29,930 puts

SOYBEAN MEAL (CBT) 100 tons; $ per ton

Strike	Calls–Settle			Puts–Settle		
Price	May-c	Jly-c	Aug-c	May-p	Jly-p	Aug-p
155	....	....	....	....	....	....
160	6.50	....	....	1.00	2.10	3.00
165	3.50	8.40	....	2.50	3.50	4.80
170	1.50	6.00	....	5.50	6.40	7.10
175	.90	4.25	....	9.50	9.50	....
180	.55	3.10	5.25	14.20	13.20	13.25

Est. vol. 100, Thur vol. 169 calls, 22 puts
Open Interest Thur 4,138 calls, 2,962 puts

SOYBEAN OIL (CBT) 60,000 lbs.; cents per lb.

Strike	Calls–Settle			Puts–Settle		
Price	May-c	Jly-c	Aug-c	May-p	Jly-p	Aug-p
20	....	....	....	.020	.130	.160
21	.650	1.400	....	.070	.250	.300
22	.400	.800	....	.450	.600	.800
23	.150	.550	.680	1.300	....	....
24	.050	.300	....	....	....	....
25	.020	.200	....	....	....	....

Est. vol. 400, Thur vol. 194 calls, 462 puts
Open Interest Thur 4,585 calls, 3,268 puts

WHEAT (CBT) 5,000 bu.; cents per bu.

Strike	Calls–Settle			Puts–Settle		
Price	May-c	Jly-c	Sep-c	May-p	Jly-p	Sep-p
260	23	32¾	....	¾	1⅜	....
270	14¾	24½	33¾	2¼	3¼	4¾
280	8¼	17¾	27	5½	6¼	7½
290	4¼	12¾	21	11¼	10⅝	11¼
300	2	9	16¼	....	16½	16
310	1⅛	6¼	12	....	23¼	18½

Est. vol. 3,500, Thur vol. 1,207 calls, 779 puts
Open Interest Thur 20,607 calls, 18,228 puts

Source: The Wall Street Journal, *March 25, 1991.*

where Max(0, f – E) is the intrinsic value. It is easy to see that this statement must hold for options on futures in the same way as for options on the spot. If the call price is less than the intrinsic value, the call can be bought and exercised. This establishes a long position in a futures contract at the price of E. The futures is immediately sold at the price of f, and a risk-free profit is made.

Consider the December 230 S&P 500 option on futures on September 26 of a particular year. The futures price is 231.95. The intrinsic value is Max(0, 231.95

FIGURE 12.4
Options on Futures Quotations in *Barron's*, Week Ending March 22, 1991

FUTURES OPTIONS

Chicago Board of Trade

Soybeans

CALLS

Month	Strike	Vol	Open Int	Week's High	Low	Sett	PtChg	Future Sett
May 91	475	0	0	—	—	100.4	+ 1.6	575.4
May 91	500	19	0	80.0	74.3	75.4	+ 1.6	575.4
May 91	550	105	524	31.0	25.0	26.4	+ .4	575.4
May 91	575	2279	2793	12.7	8.0	8.5	− 1.5	575.4
May 91	600	4851	6234	4.2	2.2	2.3	− .7	575.4
May 91	625	2907	4553	1.4	.5	.5	− .3	575.4
May 91	650	854	3483	.4	.2	.2	unch	575.4
May 91	675	172	1992	.1	.1	.1	unch	575.4
May 91	700	20	1321	.1	.1	.1	unch	575.4
May 91	725	0	184	—	—	.1	unch	575.4
May 91	750	0	308	—	—	.1	unch	575.4
May 91	775	0	378	—	—	.1	unch	575.4
May 91	800	0	111	—	—	.1	unch	575.4
May 91	825	0	70	—	—	.1	unch	575.4

PUTS

Month	Strike	Vol	Open Int	Week's High	Low	Sett	PtChg	Future Sett
May 91	500	0	85	----	----	.1	unch	575.4
May 91	525	71	129	.4	.1	.2	− .1	575.4
May 91	550	1727	2117	2.4	.7	1.0	− 1.0	575.4
May 91	575	4231	4843	12.4	6.4	8.0	− 3.2	575.4
May 91	600	2238	3413	29.4	23.0	26.2	− 2.6	575.4
May 91	625	15	844	51.0	45.4	50.0	− 2.0	575.4
May 91	650	0	483	----	----	74.5	− 1.5	575.4
May 91	675	0	46	----	----	99.4	− 1.6	575.4
May 91	700	0	1	----	----	124.4	− 1.6	575.4
May 91	825	0	0	----	----	249.4	− 1.6	575.4
Jul 91	500	395	735	.4	.3	.3	− .2	588.4
Jul 91	525	676	1162	2.0	1.3	1.4	− .4	588.4
Jul 91	550	789	2102	6.4	4.2	5.0	− 1.0	588.4
Jul 91	575	1547	1807	16.0	11.4	13.0	− 2.0	588.4
Jul 91	600	557	2356	30.0	25.0	27.4	− 2.0	588.4
Jul 91	625	76	931	48.4	43.4	45.4	− 2.0	588.4
Jul 91	650	191	1497	70.0	64.0	67.0	− 2.0	588.4
Jul 91	675	150	1171	93.0	87.4	89.4	− 2.0	588.4
Jul 91	750	0	0	----	----	161.6	− 1.2	588.4
Jul 91	825	0	0	----	----	236.4	− 1.0	588.4
Jul 91	850	0	0	----	----	261.4	− 1.0	588.4

Source: Barron's, *March 25, 1991.*

$- 230) = 1.95$. The call is actually worth 9.35. The difference of $9.35 - 1.95 = 7.40$ is the time value. Like the time value on an option on the spot, the time value here decreases as expiration approaches. At expiration, the call must sell for its intrinsic value.

The intrinsic value of an American put option on futures establishes its minimum value. This is stated as

$$P_a(f,T,E) \geq \text{Max}(0, E - f),$$

where $\text{Max}(0, E - f)$ is the intrinsic value. Again, if this is not true, the arbitrageur can purchase the futures contract and the put, immediately exercise the put, and earn a risk-free profit.

The December 240 S&P 500 put option on futures was priced at 13.10 on September 26. The futures price was 231.95. The minimum value is

$$P_a(f,T,E) = \text{Max}(0, 240 - 231.95) = 8.05.$$

The difference between the put price, 13.10, and the intrinsic value, 8.05, is the time value, 5.05. The time value, of course, erodes as expiration approaches. At expiration, the put is worth the intrinsic value.

TABLE 12.2

Listed Options on Futures Contracts on U.S. Futures Exchanges Covered in *The Wall Street Journal* (as of March 28, 1991)

Contract	Exchange	Contract Size
Interest Rates		
Treasury bonds	CBOT	$100,000
6 1/2–10-year Treasury notes	CBOT	$100,000
Municipal bond index	CBOT	$100,000
5-year Treasury notes	CBOT	$100,000
Mortgage-backed securities	CBOT	$100,000
Eurodollars	IMM	$1,000,000
Treasury bills	IMM	$1,000,000
Stock Indices		
S&P 500 index	IOM	$500 x premium
NYSE Composite Index	NYFE	$500 x premium
Nikkei 225 Index	IOM	$5 x premium
Commodity Futures		
Corn	CBOT	5,000 bu.
Soybeans	CBOT	5,000 bu.
Soybean meal	CBOT	100 tons
Soybean oil	CBOT	60,000 lbs.
Wheat	CBOT	5,000 bu.
Wheat	KCBT	5,000 bu.
Cotton	CTN	50,000 lbs.
Orange juice	CTN	15,000 lbs.
Coffee	CSCE	37,500 lbs.
Sugar—world	CSCE	112,000 lbs.
Cocoa	CSCE	10 metric tons
Crude oil	MYMEX	1,000 bbls.
Heating oil no. 2	NYMEX	42,000 gals.
Gasoline—unleaded	NYMEX	42,000 gals.
Feeder cattle	CME	44,000 lbs.
Live cattle	CME	40,000 lbs.
Live hogs	CME	30,000 lbs.
Pork bellies	CME	40,000 lbs.
Copper	COMEX	25,000 lbs.
Gold	COMEX	100 troy ozs.
Silver	COMEX	5,000 troy ozs.
Silver	CBOT	1,000 troy ozs.
Lumber	CME	150,000 bd. ft.
Soybeans	MCE	1,000 bu.
Wheat	MPLS	5,000 bu.
Oats	CBOT	1,000 bu.
Foreign Currencies		
Japanese yen	IMM	12,500,000 yen
German mark	IMM	125,000 marks
Canadian dollar	IMM	100,000 Canadian dollars
British pound	IMM	62,500 pounds
Swiss franc	IMM	125,000 francs
Australian dollar	IMM	$100,000 Australian dollars
U.S. Dollar Index	FINEX	$500 x Index

TABLE 12.3
Most Active Options on Futures Contracts, 1990

Contract (Exchange)	1,000 Contracts
Treasury bonds (CBOT)	27,315
Eurodollars (IMM)	6,859
Crude oil (NYMEX)	5,255
Deutsche mark (IMM)	3,430
Japanese yen (IMM)	3,116
Sugar (CSCE)	2,393
Corn (CBOT)	2,116
Soybeans (CBOT)	2,089
Gold (COMEX)	1,932
S&P 500 (IOM)	1,638

Source: Consensus, *January 18, 1991.*

The Lower Bound of a European Option on Futures

The intrinsic values apply only to American options on futures. This is because early exercise is necessary to execute the arbitrage. As you should recall from our study of options on stocks, we can establish a lower bound for a European option.

Let us first look at the call option on futures. We construct two portfolios, A and B. Portfolio A consists of a single long position in a European call. Portfolio B consists of a long position in the futures contract and a long position in risk-free bonds with a face value of $f - E$. Note that if E is greater than f, this is actually a short position in bonds and thus constitutes a loan in which we pay back $f - E$ at expiration. We do not really care whether we are borrowing or lending. As long as we keep the signs correct, we will obtain the desired result in either case. Table 12.4 presents the outcomes of these portfolios.

If $f_T \leq E$, the call expires worthless. The futures contract is worth $f_T - f$, and the bonds are worth $f - E$; thus, portfolio B is worth $f_T - E$. If $f_T > E$, the call is worth $f_T - E$, the intrinsic value, and portfolio B is still worth $f_T - E$. As you can see, portfolio A does at least as well as portfolio B in all cases. Therefore, its current value should be at least as high as portfolio B's. We can state this as

$$C_e(f,T,E) \geq (f - E)(1 + r)^{-T}.$$

Because an option cannot have negative value,

$$C_e(f,T,E) \geq \text{Max}[0, (f - E)(1 + r)^{-T}].$$

Note that we used an important result from Chapter 9: The value of a futures contract when initially established is zero. Thus, portfolio B's value is simply the value of the risk-free bonds.

TABLE 12.4

The Lower Bound of a European Call Option on Futures: Payoffs at Expiration of Portfolios A and B

| Portfolio | Current Value | Payoffs from Portfolio Given Futures Price at Expiration | |
		$f_T \leq E$	$f_T > E$
A	$C_e(f,T,E)$	0	$f_T - E$
B	0	$f_T - f$	$f_T - f$
	$+ (f - E)(1 + r)^{-T}$	$+ (f - E)$	$+ (f - E)$
		$= f_T - E$	$= f_T - E$

This result establishes the lower bound for a European call on the futures. Remember that a European call on the spot has a lower bound of

$$C_e(S,T,E) \geq S - E(1 + r)^{-T}.$$

As we saw in Chapter 9, in the absence of dividends on the spot instrument, the futures price is

$$f = S(1 + r)^T.$$

Making this substitution for f, we see that these two lower bounds are equivalent. In fact, if the option and futures expire simultaneously, a European call on a futures is equivalent to a European call on the spot. This is because a European call can be exercised only at expiration, at which time the futures and spot prices are equivalent.

As an example of the lower bound, let us look at the December 230 S&P 500 call option on futures on September 26. The option expires on December 19; thus, there are 84 days remaining and T = 84/365 = .2301. The risk-free rate is 5.46 percent. The lower bound is

$$C_e(f,T,E) \geq Max[0, (231.95 - 230)(1.0546)^{-.2301}] = 1.926.$$

The actual call price is 9.35.

Note, however, that the lower bound established here is slightly less than the intrinsic value of 1.95. This should seem unusual. For ordinary equity options, the lower bound of $Max[0, S - E(1 + r)^{-T}]$ exceeds the intrinsic value of $Max(0, S - E)$. For options on futures, however, this is not necessarily so. As we shall see in a later section, this explains why some American call (and put) options on futures are exercised early.

Now let us look at the lower bound for a European put option on a futures. Again we shall establish two portfolios, A and B. Portfolio A consists of a long position in the put. Portfolio B consists of a short position in the futures contract

TABLE 12.5

The Lower Bound of a European Put Option on Futures: Payoffs at Expiration of Portfolios A and B

Portfolio	Current Value	Payoffs from Portfolio Given Futures Price at Expiration	
		$f_T < E$	$f_T \geq E$
A	$P_e(f,T,E)$	$E - f_T$	0
B	0	$-(f_T - f)$	$-(f_T - f)$
	$+ (E - f)(1 + r)^{-T}$	$+ E - f$	$+ E - f$
		$= E - f_T$	$= E - f_T$

and a long position in risk-free bonds with a face value of E – f. Again, if f is greater than E, this is actually a short position in bonds, or taking out a loan. Table 12.5 illustrates the outcomes.

By now you should be able to explain each outcome. If $f_T < E$, the put is exercised, so portfolio A is worth $E - f_T$. If $f_T > E$, the put expires worthless. In both cases, the futures contract in portfolio B is worth $-(f_T - f)$ and the bonds are worth E – f, for a total of $E - f_T$. Portfolio A does at least as well as portfolio B in both outcomes. Therefore, the current value of A should be at least as great as the current value of B,

$$P_e(f,T,E) \geq (E - f)(1 + r)^{-T}.$$

Because the option cannot have a negative value,

$$P_e(f,T,E) \geq Max[0, (E - f)(1 + r)^{-T}].$$

As we saw with calls, we can substitute S for $f(1 + r)^{-T}$ and see that the lower bound for a put option on a futures is the same as that for a put option on the spot. As is true for calls, European put options on futures in which the put and the futures expire simultaneously are equivalent to options on the spot.

As an example, let us look at the December 240 S&P 500 put option on futures on September 26 of a particular year. The futures price is 231.95, the time to expiration is .2301, and the risk-free rate is 5.46 percent. The lower bound is

$$P_e(S,T,E) \geq Max[0, (240 - 231.95)(1.0546)^{-.2301}] = 7.95.$$

The actual price of the put is 13.10. As we saw for equity puts, the European lower bound will be less than the American intrinsic value. Thus, the actual minimum price of this American put is its intrinsic value of $240 - 231.95 = 8.05$.

TABLE 12.6
Put-Call Parity of Options on Futures

Payoff from	Current Value	Payoffs from Portfolio Given Futures Price at Expiration	
		$f_T < E$	$f_T \geq E$
Long futures	0	$f_T - f$	$f_T - f$
Long put	$P_e(f,T,E)$	$E - f_T$	0
Short call	$-C_e(f,T,E)$	0	$-(f_T - E)$
Bonds	$+ (f - E)(1 + r)^{-T}$	$f - E$	$f - E$
		0	0

Put-Call Parity

We have looked at put-call parity for options on equities. We can also establish a put-call parity rule for options on futures.

First, let us construct a portfolio consisting of a long position in a European put option on futures, a short position in a European call option on futures, a long position in the futures contract, and a long position in bonds with a face value of f − E. Again, if E is greater than f, we issue rather than buy bonds. The results are presented in Table 12.6.

The portfolio has a zero cash flow at expiration. Thus, the initial portfolio value must be zero. This means that

$$P_e(f,T,E) - C_e(f,T,E) + (f - E)(1 + r)^{-T} = 0.$$

We usually write this as

$$P_e(f,T,E) = C_e(f,T,E) - (f - E)(1 + r)^{-T}$$

or

$$C_e(f,T,E) = P_e(f,T,E) + (f - E)(1 + r)^{-T}.$$

Note the similarity between put-call parity for options on futures and put-call parity for options on the spot:

$$P_e(S,T,E) = C_e(S,T,E) - S + E(1 + r)^{-T}.$$

Because the futures price is $S(1 + r)^T$, these two versions of put-call parity are equivalent. As we stated earlier, in many ways the options themselves are equivalent.

Let us look at the December 230 puts and calls on the S&P 500 futures on September 26 of a particular year. As we saw in Chapter 3, we can calculate the put price and compare it to the actual market price or calculate the call price and compare it to the actual market price. Here we shall calculate the call price. The put price is \$7.45. The other input values given earlier are f = 231.95, r = .0546, and T = .2301. The call price is

$$C_e(f,T,E) = 7.45 + (231.95 - 230)(1.0546)^{-.2301} = 9.38.$$

The actual call price was 9.35. This is very close, but we should expect a difference because these are American options and the formula is for European options. The formula price should be less than the market price, but in this case it is not. However, the effect of transaction costs might explain the difference. Jordan and Seale (1986) and Blomeyer and Boyd (1988) examined the prices of Treasury bond options on futures to determine if they conform to put-call parity and the boundary rules we have established. Their results showed that violations of these conditions rarely occur and, when they do occur, are difficult and costly to exploit.

Early Exercise of Call and Put Options on Futures

Recall that in the absence of dividends on a stock, a call option on the stock would not be exercised early; however, a put option might be. With an option on a futures contract, either a call or a put might be exercised early. Let us look at the call.

Consider a deep-in-the-money American call. If the call is on the spot instrument, it may have some time value remaining. If it is sufficiently deep-in-the-money, it will have little time value. However, that does not mean it should be exercised early. Disregarding transaction costs, early exercise would be equivalent to selling the call. If the call is on the futures, however, early exercise may be the better choice. The logic behind this is that a deep-in-the-money call behaves almost identically to the underlying instrument. If the call is on the spot instrument, it will move one for one with the spot price. If the call is on the futures, it will move one for one with the futures price. Thus, the call on the futures will act almost exactly like a long position in a futures contract. However, the investor has money tied up in the call but because the margin can be met by depositing interest-earning T-bills, there is no money tied up in the futures. By exercising the call and replacing it with a long position in the futures, the investor obtains the same opportunity to profit but frees up the funds tied up in the call. If the call were on the spot instrument, we could not make the same argument. The call may behave in virtually the same manner as the spot instrument, but the latter also requires the commitment of funds.

From an algebraic standpoint, the early-exercise problem is seen by noting that the minimum value of an in-the-money European call, $(f - E)(1 + r)^{-T}$, is less than the value of the call if it could be exercised, $f - E$. The European call cannot be exercised, but if it were an American call, it could be.

These points are illustrated in panel a of Figure 12.5. The European call option on futures approaches its lower bound of $(f - E)(1 + r)^{-T}$. The American call option on futures approaches its minimum value, its intrinsic value of $f - E$, which

FIGURE 12.5

American and European Calls and Puts on Futures

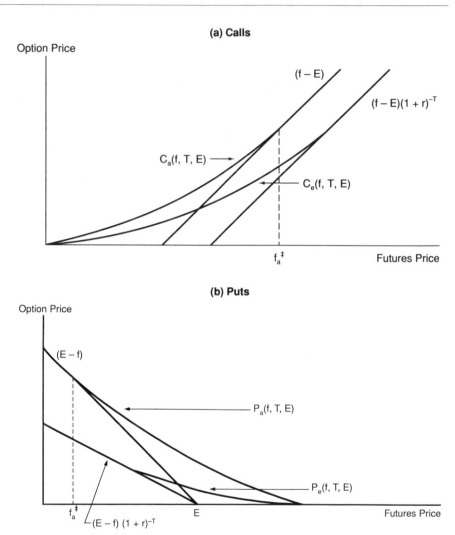

(a) Calls

Option Price

$(f - E)$

$(f - E)(1 + r)^{-T}$

$C_a(f, T, E)$

$C_e(f, T, E)$

$f_a^{\ddagger}$

Futures Price

(b) Puts

Option Price

$(E - f)$

$P_a(f, T, E)$

$P_e(f, T, E)$

$f_a^{\ddagger}$

$(E - f)(1 + r)^{-T}$

E

Futures Price

is greater than the European lower bound. Thus, there is a futures price, $f_a^{\ddagger}$, at which the American call will equal its intrinsic value. Above that price, the American call will be exercised early. Recall that for calls on spot instruments, the European lower bound was higher than the intrinsic value. Thus, there was no early exercise premium—provided, of course, that the underlying asset paid no dividends.

For put options on futures, the intuitive and algebraic arguments work similarly. Deep-in-the-money American puts on futures tend to be exercised early.

Panel b of Figure 12.5 illustrates the case for puts. The price of European put options on futures approaches its lower bound of $(E - f)(1 + r)^{-T}$, while the price of the American put option on futures approaches its intrinsic value of $E - f$. The American intrinsic value is greater than the European lower bound; thus, there is a price, $f_a^{\ddagger}$, at which the American put option on futures would equal its intrinsic value. Below this price, the American put would be exercised early.

Although these instruments are options on futures, it is conceivable that one would be interested in an option on a forward contract. Interestingly, these options would not be exercised early. This is because when exercised, a forward contract is established at the price of E. However, a forward contract is not marked to market, so the holder of a call does not receive an immediate cash flow of $F - E$. Instead, that person receives only a position with a value, as we learned in Chapter 9, of $(F - E)(1 + r)^{-T}$. This amount, however, is the lower bound of a European call on a forward contract. Early exercise cannot capture a gain over the European call value; thus, it offers no advantage. Similar arguments hold for early exercise of a European put on a forward contract.

The Black Option on Futures Pricing Model

Fischer Black (1976) developed a variation of his own Black-Scholes model for pricing European options on futures. Using the assumption that the option and the futures expire simultaneously, the option price is as follows:

$$C = e^{-rT}\left[fN(d_1) - EN(d_2)\right],$$

where

$$d_1 = \frac{\ln(f/E) + (\sigma^2/2)T}{\sigma\sqrt{T}}$$

$$d_2 = d_1 - \sigma\sqrt{T}$$

Note that the expression for d_1 does not contain the risk-free rate, r, as it does in the Black-Scholes model. That is because the risk-free rate captures the opportunity cost of funds tied up in the stock. If the option is on a futures contract, no funds are invested in the futures and therefore there is no opportunity cost. However, the price of the call on the futures will be the same as the price of the call on the spot. This is because when the call on the futures expires, it is exercisable into a futures position, which is immediately expiring. Thus, the call on the futures, when exercised, establishes a long position in the spot asset.

To prove that the Black option on futures pricing model gives the same price as the Black-Scholes model for an option on the spot, notice that in the Black model $N(d_1)$ is multiplied by fe^{-rT}, while in the Black-Scholes model it is multiplied by S. However, we learned in Chapter 9 that $f = Se^{(r-\delta)T}$ so that with no dividends on the underlying asset, the futures price will equal Se^{rT}. Thus, if we substitute Se^{rT} for f in the Black model, the formula will be the same as the Black-Scholes formula.[1]

We know that in the presence of dividends, the futures price is given by the formula $f = Se^{(r-\delta)T}$. Thus, $S = fe^{-(r-\delta)T}$. If we substitute this expression for S into the Black-Scholes model, we obtain the Black option on futures pricing model if the underlying spot asset—in this case, a stock—pays dividends. However, the dividends do not show up in the Black model, so we need not distinguish the Black model with and without dividends. Dividends do affect the call price, but only indirectly, as the futures price captures all the effects of the dividends.

Another useful comparison of the Black and Black-Scholes models is to consider how the Black-Scholes model might be used as a substitute for the Black model. Suppose we have available only a computer program for the Black-Scholes model, but we want to price an option on a futures contract. We can do this easily by using the version of the Black-Scholes model in Chapter 4, which had a continuous dividend yield, and inserting the risk-free rate for the dividend yield and the futures price for the spot price. The risk-free rate minus the dividend yield is the cost of carry, so it will equal zero. The Black-Scholes formula will then be pricing an option on an instrument that has a price of f and a cost of carry of zero. This is precisely what the Black model prices: an option on an instrument—in this case, a futures contract—with a price of f and a cost of carry of zero. Remember that the futures price reflects the cost of carry on the underlying spot asset, but the futures itself does not have a cost of carry because there are no funds tied up and no storage costs.

Let us now use the Black model to price the December 230 call option on the S&P 500 futures. Recall that the futures price is 231.95, the exercise price is 230, the time to expiration is .2301, and the risk-free rate is $\ln(1.0546) = .0532$. We now need only the standard deviation of the continuously compounded percentage change in the futures price. For illustrative purposes, we shall use .165 as the standard deviation.

---

[1]This may not be obvious in the formula for d_1. However, if we substitute Se^{rT} for f in the above formula for d_1, we obtain

$$d_1 = \frac{\ln\left(Se^{rT}/E\right)+\left(\sigma^2/2\right)T}{\sigma\sqrt{T}}.$$

The expression $\ln(Se^{rT}/E)$ is equivalent to $\ln S + \ln e^{rT} - \ln E$. Now $\ln e^{rT} = rT$, so d_1 becomes

$$d_1 = \frac{\ln\left(S/E\right)+\left(r+\sigma^2/2\right)T}{\sigma\sqrt{T}}.$$

which is d_1 from the Black-Scholes formula.

The values of d_1 and d_2 are

$$d_1 = \frac{\ln(231.95/230) + \left[(.165)^2/2\right].2301}{.165\sqrt{.2301}} = .1462$$

$$d_2 = .1462 - .165\sqrt{.2301} = .0671.$$

Using the normal probability table, Table 4.2 on page 122, gives

$$N(.15) = .5596$$
$$N(.07) = .5279.$$

Plugging into the formula for C gives

$$C = e^{-(.0532)(.2301)}[231.95(.5596) - 230(.5279)] = 8.28.$$

The actual value of the call is 9.35. Thus, the call would appear to be overpriced. As we showed in Chapter 4, an arbitrageur could create a risk-free portfolio by buying the underlying instrument, the futures contract, and selling the call. The hedge ratio would be $e^{-rT}N(d_1)$ futures contracts for each call. However, remember that the model gives the European option price, so we expect it to be less than the actual American option price.

The effect of the underlying variables on the call option price, called the comparative statics, is presented in Appendix 12B.

We can easily develop a pricing model for European put options on futures from the Black model and put-call parity. Using the continuously compounded version, put-call parity is expressed as $C - P = (f - E)e^{-rT}$. Rearranging this expression to isolate the put price gives

$$P = C - (f - E)e^{-rT}.$$

Now we can substitute the Black European call option on futures pricing model for C in put-call parity and rearrange the terms to obtain the Black European put option on futures pricing model,

$$P = Ee^{-rT}[1 - N(d_2)] - fe^{-rT}[1 - N(d_1)].$$

Some end-of-the-chapter problems will allow us to use this model and examine it further.

Earlier we noted that even in the absence of dividends, American calls on futures might be exercised early. Like options on the spot, American puts on futures might be exercised early. The Black model does not price American options, and we cannot appeal to the absence of dividends, as we could for some stocks, to allow us to use the European model to price an American option. Unfortunately, American option on futures pricing models are too complex to cover in this book. However, recall from Chapter 4 that the Barone-Adesi/Whaley pricing model provides an approximation of an American option price. Appendix 12C applies that model to futures.

In addition to the problem of using a European option pricing model to price American options, the Black model has difficulty pricing the most actively traded options on futures, Treasury bond options on futures. That problem is related to the interest rate component. The Black model, like the Black-Scholes model, makes the assumption of a constant interest rate. This generally is considered an acceptable assumption for pricing options on commodities and sometimes even stock indices. It is far less palatable for pricing options on bonds. There is a fundamental inconsistency in assuming a constant interest rate while attempting to price an option on a futures that is on an underlying Treasury bond, whose price changes because of changing interest rates. Merville and Overdahl (1986) confirm that the model has some difficulties pricing Treasury bond options on futures, although it is hard to tell whether those problems are unique to the contract it is pricing or associated with the model in general.

The Black model has been extensively tested in applications to other options on futures. Wolf and Pohlman (1987) examined gold and silver; Followill (1987) studied gold; and Jordan et al. (1987) tested soybeans. All of the results showed that the model performs reasonably well. It is widely used to price options on non–interest rate instruments.

Where does this leave us with regard to pricing options on Treasury bond futures and other interest rate instruments? A widely accepted, theoretically consistent, and easily understood model for pricing options on interest rate instruments has become the Holy Grail for option pricing theorists. Let us hope the financial researchers are more successful than their archaeological counterparts.

TRADING STRATEGIES FOR OPTIONS ON FUTURES

Virtually any strategy that can be done with options on the spot can be done with options on futures. Chapters 5 and 6 discussed many of the popular option strategies. There is little need for much repetition here, as most of those results transfer directly to options on futures. However, it will be helpful to briefly examine three basic option on futures strategies: buying a call, buying a put, and writing a covered call.

Buy a Call Option on Futures

The profit from a call option on futures that is held to expiration is given by the equation

$$\Pi = \text{Max}(0, f_T - E) - C.$$

FIGURE 12.6
Buy Call Option on Futures

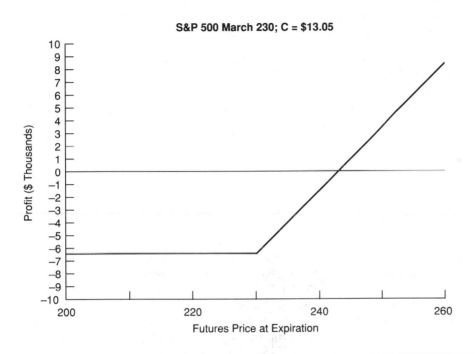

S&P 500 March 230; C = $13.05

The two outcomes are

$$\Pi = -C \qquad \text{if } f_T \le E$$
$$\Pi = f_T - E - C \quad \text{if } f_T > E.$$

The breakeven futures price at expiration is $E + C$. The outcome of this strategy is the same as it is for an option on the spot, provided, of course, that the futures and the option expire simultaneously.

As an example, let us buy the March 230 S&P 500 call option on futures. The price of the call is 13.05. Because the contract has a multiplier of 500, the actual premium is $500(\$13.05) = \$6,525$. The graph showing the profit for various values of the futures (and spot) price at expiration is presented in Figure 12.6.

Suppose the futures price ends up at 245. Then the call is exercised, which means the futures is purchased at the exercise price of 230 and immediately sold at 245. Subtracting the cost of the call of 13.05 gives a profit of $245 - 230 - 13.05 = 1.95$. The overall profit is $500(\$1.95) = \$975$. If the futures price ends up below 230, the option expires worthless and the option holder loses the premium, $6,525. The breakeven futures price is $230 + 13.05 = 243.05$.

We shall not illustrate the comparison of different exercise prices and different holding periods. The issues are the same as they are for options on the spot. The lower-exercise-price call is more expensive, but it offers greater profit potential. The shorter holding period produces a higher profit for a given futures price but allows less time for the futures price to move.

Buy a Put Option on a Futures

The profit for a put option on a futures contract held to expiration is given by the equation

$$\Pi = \text{Max}(0, E - f_T) - P.$$

The two possible outcomes are

$$\Pi = E - f_T - P \quad \text{if } f_T < E$$
$$\Pi = -P \qquad\quad \text{if } f_T \geq E.$$

The breakeven futures price at expiration is $E - P$. The profit is the same as that for a put option on the spot, provided that the two puts expire simultaneously.

As an example, consider the S&P 500 March 240 put option on futures. The cost of the put is $15.30. Because the multiplier is 500, the total premium is $7,650. Figure 12.7 illustrates the profit for various futures prices at expiration.

Suppose the futures price at expiration is 220. Then the investor buys the futures at 220 and exercises the put, selling the futures at 240. The profit is 240 − 220 − 15.30 (the cost of the put) = 4.70 times the multiplier (500), or $4.70(500) = $2,350. If the futures price at expiration is above 240, the put expires worthless and the investor loses the put premium of $7,650. The breakeven futures price is 240 − 15.30 = 224.70.

The investor should also consider the effect of different exercise prices and different holding periods. These issues are the same as for options on the spot.

Write A Covered Call Option on Futures

Recall from Chapter 5 that a covered call is a strategy in which the investor purchases the underlying instrument and writes a call. When the underlying instrument is a stock, the covered call protects the investor against a substantial decrease in the stock price. If that happens, the call will expire worthless and the investor will retain the premium. If the stock price rises above the exercise price at expiration, the call will be exercised and the investor will have effectively sold the stock for the exercise price.

The covered call option on futures is similar. A long position in a futures contract can be protected by selling a call option. If the futures price falls and the call ends up out-of-the-money, the investor retains the premium, which cushions

FIGURE 12.7
Buy Put Option on Futures

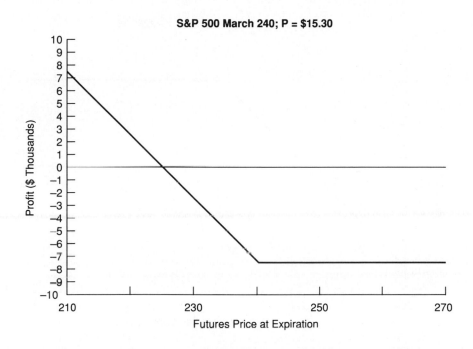

S&P 500 March 240; P = $15.30

the loss on the futures. If the futures price rises and the call is exercised, the investor effectively sells the futures contract at the exercise price.

The profit from a single long futures contract is

$$\Pi = f_T - f.$$

The profit from a short call option on the futures is

$$\Pi = -\operatorname{Max}(0, f_T - E) + C.$$

Combining these into the covered call strategy gives a profit of

$$\Pi = f_T - f - \operatorname{Max}(0, f_T - E) + C.$$

The profit at expiration for the two cases is

$$\Pi = f_T - f - f_T + E + C = E - f + C \quad \text{if } f_T > E$$
$$\Pi = f_T - f + C \qquad\qquad\qquad\qquad \text{if } f_T \le E.$$

The breakeven futures price at expiration is $f - C$.

FIGURE 12.8

Covered Call Option on Futures

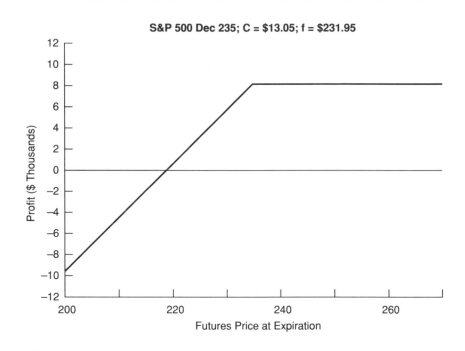

Figure 12.8 illustrates the possible outcomes for the covered call using the S&P 500 December 235 call. The call price is 13.05, and the futures price is 231.95. Suppose the futures price at expiration is 240. Then the call is exercised. The covered call writer is assigned a short futures contract at 235, which offsets the long futures position established at 231.95. This leaves a profit of 235 − 231.95 + 13.05 = 16.10. Multiplying this by 500 gives the overall profit of 500($16.10) = $8,050. If the futures price ends up at 210, the futures contract produces a loss of 231.95 − 210 = 21.95. This is partially offset by the call premium of 13.05, leaving a net loss of 8.90. Multiplying by 500 gives a loss of 500($8.90) = $4,450. The breakeven futures price is 231.95 − 13.05 = 218.90.

Almost any strategy than can be executed with options on the spot can also be executed with option on futures. Some examples of these are risk-free hedges using the option's delta, spreads, and portfolio insurance and dynamic hedges, two topics to be covered in Chapter 14. Some end-of-chapter problems ask you to apply options on futures to strategies that are not covered in this chapter but are covered under options on the spot.

OPTIONS ON FUTURES VERSUS OPTIONS ON THE SPOT

So far, we have seen that options on futures are equivalent to options on the spot when the options are European and the futures and options expire simultaneously. In this section, we shall introduce some real-world factors that make options on futures unique.

Consider an American call option on the spot and one on the futures. Assume the spot instrument does not pay a dividend. As we already know, the call on the spot will not be exercised early. The call on the futures may be exercised early if it is sufficiently in-the-money. We know that the futures price is given by the formula

$$f = S(1 + r)^T.$$

From the formula, it is apparent that prior to expiration the futures price is always higher than the spot price. Thus, an option on the futures is an option on a higher-priced instrument than is an option on the spot. Accordingly, its price should be higher. This is true, however, only because of the early exercise possibility. If the option could not or would not be exercised early, it would be equivalent to an option on the spot.

A similar line of reasoning holds for puts. A put option on a futures is an option to sell a higher-priced instrument—the futures. Because of the possibility of early exercise, the put will be priced lower than the put on the spot instrument itself.

If we add dividends to the picture, things can get very complicated. Dividends lower the spread between the futures and spot prices and, if high enough, can make the futures price be less than the spot price, thus complicating the relationship further.

If the option on the futures expires before the option on the spot, it should be obvious that even European options on the spot and those on the futures are not equivalent. However, even if they expire simultaneously and are European, there are other reasons why these instruments have their own unique properties.

The option on the futures may be more attractive because the underlying futures contract is more liquid, or easier to transact in, than the underlying spot instrument. As an example, options on Treasury bond futures at the Chicago Board of Trade are far more popular than options on Treasury bonds at the Chicago Board Options Exchange. One reason is that the T-bond futures market is much more liquid than the T-bond spot market. Because exercise may require establishing a position in the underlying instrument, the underlying instrument's liquidity is important to the option trader. Even if the option is not exercised, pricing the option off of the more liquid futures market is better than pricing it off of the bond market. Of course, the futures market still must price the futures contract off of the bond market.

Suppose an investor wishes to construct a hedge, covered call, or protective put using the S&P 500. The option on the spot would require the investor to simultaneously purchase the S&P 500 stocks in the appropriate proportions. The same strategy with the option on the futures would require only a position in the futures and the option. Obviously it would be easier to transact in the futures market than in the spot market.

Exercise of an option on the spot requires delivery of the underlying instrument. Although the possibility is somewhat remote, there is at least some likelihood that there would be a shortage of the deliverable instrument. This is more likely to occur with agricultural commodities, but it could happen with a Treasury bond or note. If using the option on the futures, one need not be concerned about obtaining the underlying commodity. Futures contracts can be created in virtually unlimited quantities. However, if a European option and the futures expire simultaneously, the option holder or writer must immediately execute an opposite transaction in the futures market to avoid having to make or take delivery on the futures contract, unless the futures is cash settled.

Finally, we come to what may well be the key attraction of options on futures. Options on spot instruments have traded on the CBOE and several stock exchanges for many years. Individuals who held memberships in the futures exchanges could not easily trade options on the other exchanges. If they wished to trade options, they had to place orders through brokers, who would execute the trades on the CBOE and the stock exchanges. When options on futures were introduced, they gave futures traders the opportunity to trade both futures and options. For most contracts, the trading pits for the options and the underlying futures are adjacent. This greatly facilitated simultaneous trading of the option and the underlying futures. Because options on stocks do not trade side by side with the underlying stocks, futures traders have an advantage over members of the stock and option exchanges. Thus, much of the success of options on futures has come from local traders. That is not meant to imply, however, that the public has not traded these instruments. As noted earlier in this section, options on futures have many attractive features not offered by options on the spot, but neither instrument has a clear advantage over the other. Each is unique and fills the needs of a given clientele of investors and traders.

SUMMARY

This chapter examined options on futures. These contracts are very similar to options on the spot instrument. Most of the basic rules for pricing these two types of options are similar. In particular, if the futures price equals the spot price compounded at the risk-free rate and the options expire simultaneously, a European option on the spot and a European option on the futures are equivalent. The lower bounds, put-call parity, and the Black option on futures pricing model are equivalent to their counterparts in equity options. The performance of trading strategies is also identical.

The chapter discussed several important differences between these two types of options. Prices of American options on the spot differ from those of American options on futures. In addition, options on futures may have more liquidity in the underlying instruments, the futures. Moreover, the options and the underlying futures trade side by side, which offers advantages to floor traders who must execute arbitrage transactions quickly.

In the next chapter, we shall examine some more instruments that are widely traded but differ slightly from traditional options and futures: options and futures on foreign currencies.

Questions and Problems

1. Use the following data from December 9 of a particular year for the March 210 S&P 500 call option on futures contract to answer parts a through g:
    -   Futures prices: 207.65
    -   Expiration: March 21
    -   Risk-free rate: 7.63 percent (simple)
    -   Call price: 4.10
    -   Put price: 6.40

    a. Determine the intrinsic value of the call.
    b. Determine the time value of the call.
    c. Determine the lower bound of the call.
    d. Determine the intrinsic value of the put.
    e. Determine the time value of the put.
    f. Determine the lower bound of the put.
    g. Determine whether put-call parity holds.

2. The put-call parity rule is that $C - P = (f - E)(1 + r)^{-T}$. Consider the following data: $f = 102$, $E = 100$, $r = .1$, $T = .25$, $C = 4$, and $P = 1.75$. A few calculations will show that the prices do not conform to the rule. Suggest an arbitrage strategy and show how it can be used to capture a risk-free profit. Assume no transaction costs. Be sure your answer shows the payoffs at expiration and proves these payoffs are riskless.

3. Explain why American call options on futures could be exercised early when call options on the spot are not. Assume no dividends.

4. Assume a standard deviation of .22, and use the Black model to determine if the call option in problem 1 is correctly priced. If not, suggest a riskless hedge strategy.

5. Describe two problems in using the Black option on futures pricing model for pricing options on Eurodollar futures.

6. Using the information in problem 4, calculate the price of the put described in problem 1 using the Black model for pricing puts.

7. Explain why the futures option pricing model is simply a pricing model for options on instruments with a zero cost of carry.

8. In Chapter 4, we examined the sensitivity of a call's price to different risk-free rates and volatilities. Compute the Black option on futures price using the data for the call given in problems 1 and 4 for the following risk-free rates and standard deviations. (Hint: You may wish to use the Black spreadsheet on the software diskette to save time on these calculations.)

   a. Use risk-free rates of 1 through 10 percent in increments of 100 basis points. From Appendix 12B, we know that the call price should increase as we increase r. What do you notice about the results? Try to explain. (Hint: Remember that $f = Se^{rT}$.)

   b. Use standard deviations of .05 through .50 in increments of .05. Comment on what you find.

9. In the chapter, we showed how the Black call option on futures pricing model is equivalent to the Black-Scholes call option pricing model if the two options expire at the same time. You were given the formula for the Black put option on futures pricing model and used it in problem 6, and you learned the Black put option pricing model in Chapter 4. Show that these models give equivalent prices if the options expire simultaneously. Do not use numerical examples. Show that the formulas will be equivalent.

10. Find the implied volatility, to three decimal places, of the call in problem 4 if the call is worth 5.25. (Hint: You may wish to use the Black spreadsheet on the software diskette to perform these calculations.)

11. Evaluate the following statement: "Dividends are relevant to the pricing of European call options but not to the pricing of European call options on futures. Amazingly enough, this is true even though the two calls will have the same price."

Problems 12 through 17 use the S&P 500 options on futures prices on October 15 of a particular year. Determine the profit from the strategy for each of the following futures prices at expiration: 180, 185, 190, 195, and 200. Graph the results. Determine the breakeven futures price at expiration.

12. The December 185 call price is 4.40. Construct a simple long call position.

13. The December 190 put price is 5.50. Construct a simple long put position.

14. The December futures price is 186.65. Using the December call data from problem 12, construct a covered call position.

15. Using the information in problems 13 and 14, construct a protective put with the December 190 put.

16. Discuss why options on futures have advantages not offered by options on the spot.

17. (Concept Problem) Redo problem 12, but close the position on November 25. The calls expire December 20. Let $\sigma = .22$ and $r = .08$.

18. (Concept Problem) Use the following information to calculate the call option price using the Black model: $f = 30$, $E = 25$, $r = .08$, $\sigma = .35$, and $T = .125$. Determine the option's delta. Then recommend a risk-free hedge position,

and show why the position is risk free by evaluating its performance if the futures price decreases by $1. (Hint: This was done in Chapter 4 for call options on the spot. Follow the same procedure.)

References

Black, Fischer. "The Pricing of Commodity Contracts." *Journal of Financial Economics* 3 (January–February 1976): 167–179.

Blomeyer, Edward C., and James C. Boyd. "Empirical Tests of Boundary Conditions for Options on Treasury Bond Futures." *The Journal of Futures Markets* 4 (1988): 185–198.

Bookstaber, Richard M. *Option Pricing and Investment Strategies*, Chapters 2, 3. Chicago: Probus Publishing, 1987.

Chicago Board of Trade. *Commodity Trading Manual*, Chapter 12. Chicago: Board of Trade of the City of Chicago, 1989.

Chicago Board of Trade. "Opportunities in Options on U.S. Treasury Bond Futures." Chicago: Board of Trade of the City of Chicago.

Duffie, Darrell. *Futures Markets*, Chapter 8. Englewood Cliffs, N.J.: Prentice-Hall, 1989.

Followill, Richard A. "Relative Call Futures Option Pricing: An Examination of Market Efficiency." *The Review of Futures Markets* 6 (1987): 354–381.

Hull, John. *Options, Futures, and Other Derivative Securities*, Chapter 6. Englewood Cliffs, N.J.: Prentice-Hall, 1989.

Index and Option Market. *Options on Futures: A New Way to Participate in Futures*. Chicago: Chicago Mercantile Exchange, 1983.

Jordan, James V., and William E. Seale. "Transactions Data Tests of Minimum Prices and Put-Call Parity for Treasury Bond Futures Options." *Advances in Futures and Options Research* 1, part A (1986): 63–87.

Jordan, James V., William E. Seale, Nancy C. McCabe, and David E. Kenyon. "Transaction Data Tests of the Black Model for Soybean Futures Options." *The Journal of Futures Markets* 7 (1987): 535–554.

Labuszewski, John F. "Using Dynamic Covered Calls to Enhance Portfolio Yields." *Futures* 18 (August 1989): 42, 44.

Leuthold, Raymond M., Joan C. Junkus, and Jean E. Cordier. *The Theory and Practice of Futures Markets*, Chapter 13. Lexington, Mass.: Lexington Books, 1989.

McMillan, Lawrence G. *Options as a Strategic Investment*, 2d ed., Chapter 34. New York: New York Institute of Finance, 1986.

Merville, Larry J., and James A. Overdahl. "An Empirical Examination of the T-Bond Futures (Call) Options Markets under Conditions of Constant and Changing Variance Rates." *Advances in Futures and Options Research* 1, part A (1986): 89–118.

Powers, Mark J. *Inside the Financial Futures Market*, 2d ed., Chapters 25, 26. New York: Wiley, 1984.

Ritchken, Peter. Options: *Theory, Strategy, and Applications*, Chapters 11, 13. Glenview, Ill.: Scott, Foresman, 1987.

Schwarz, Edward W., Joanne M. Hill, and Thomas Schneeweis. *Financial Futures: Fundamentals, Strategies, and Applications*, Chapter 17. Homewood, Ill.: Irwin, 1986.

Shastri, Kuldeep, and Kishore Tandon. "Options on Futures Contracts: A Comparison of European and American Pricing Models." *The Journal of Futures Markets* 6 (Winter 1986): 593–618.

Siegel, Daniel R., and Diane F. Siegel. *Futures Markets*, Chapter 9. Hinsdale, Ill.: Dryden Press, 1990.

Teweles, Richard J., and Frank J. Jones. *The Futures Game: Who Wins? Who Loses? Why ?*, Chapter 9. New York: McGraw-Hill, 1987.

Whaley, Robert E. "Valuation of American Futures Options: Theory and Tests." *The Journal of Finance* 41 (March 1986): 127–150.

Wolf, Avner S., and Lawrence F. Pohlman. "Tests of the Black and Whaley Models for Gold and Silver Futures Options." *The Review of Futures Markets* 6 (1987): 328–347.

Selected Options on Futures Contract Specifications

This table includes only certain information for the ten most active options on futures contracts. Other information can be obtained from the source of the table.

Contract	Contract Size	Exercise Price Increments	Minimum Price Change	Last Trading Day
Treasury Bonds and 6 1/2-to-10 year Treasury notes (CBOT)	One $100,000 futures contract	2 points	1/64 = $15.625	Noon on Friday at least five business days before first notice day on futures
Crude oil (NYMEX)	One 1,000-barrel futures contract	$1 per barrel	1 cent = $10 per contract	Second Friday of month prior to futures expiration
Eurodollars (IOM)	One $1 million futures contract	.5 when IMM < 88, .25 when IMM > 88	.01 = $25	Second London bank business day before third Wednesday of month
Deutsche mark (IMM)	One 125,000 futures contract	1 cent	$0.0001/DM = $12.50	Same as Eurodollars
Japanese yen (IMM)	One 12.5 million futures contract	$0.0001	$0.000001/JY = $12.50	Same as Eurodollars
World sugar (CSCE)	One 50-long-tons futures contract	Varies by price of futures	$0.0001/lb. = $11.20	Second Friday of month before futures expiration
Corn (CBOT)	One 5,000-bushel futures contract	10 cents	1/8 cent/bu. = $6.25	Last Friday before first notice day of futures
Swiss francs (IMM)	One 125,000 futures contract	1 cent	$0.0001/SF = $12.50	Same as Eurodollars
Gold (COMEX)	One 100-troy-oz. futures contract	Varies by price of futures	10 cents/contract = $10	Second Friday of month before futures expiration
S&P 500 (CME)	One S&P 500 stock index futures contract	5 points	.05 points = $25	Same day as futures for March cycle and third Friday for other months

Source: Chicago Board of Trade, Commodity Trading Manual (Chicago: Board of Trade of the City of Chicago, 1989). This information is believed to be current as of February, 1991. Contract specifications can change, so investors should consult the exchanges for the latest information.

appendix 12B

Comparative Statics of the Black Option on Futures Pricing Model[*]

The formula for the Black model is

$$C = e^{-rT}\left[fN(d_1) - EN(d_2)\right],$$

where

$$d_1 = \frac{\ln(f/E) + (\sigma^2/2)T}{\sigma\sqrt{T}}$$

$$d_2 = d_1 - \sigma\sqrt{T}$$

As illustrated in Appendix 4B for the Black-Scholes model, the changes in the option price for infinitesimally small changes in the underlying variables are called the *comparative statics*. These effects are the derivatives of the call price with respect to the variables of interest:

$$\frac{\partial C}{\partial f} = e^{-rT}N(d_1) > 0. \quad \text{This is called the } delta.$$

$$\frac{\partial C}{\partial E} = -e^{-rT}N(d_2) < 0.$$

$$\frac{\partial C}{\partial r} = ETN(d_2)e^{-rT} > 0. \quad \text{This is called the } rho.$$

$$\frac{\partial C}{\partial T} = \left[\left(\frac{fe^{-rT}\sigma}{2\sqrt{T}}\right)\left(\frac{\partial N(d_1)}{\partial d_1}\right)\right] + re^{-rT}EN(d_2) > 0.$$

The value $-\partial C/\partial T$ is called the *theta*.

$$\frac{\partial C}{\partial \sigma} = fe^{-rT}\sqrt{T}\left(\frac{\partial N(d_1)}{\partial d_1}\right) > 0.$$

This is called the *vega, lambda,* or *kappa*.

[*]This appendix requires the use of calculus.

$$\frac{\partial}{\partial f}\left(\frac{\partial C}{\partial f}\right) = \frac{e^{-rT}\left(\dfrac{\partial N(d_1)}{\partial d_1}\right)}{f\sigma\sqrt{T}} > 0.$$

This is called the *gamma*.

The interpretation and use of these measures of the price sensitivity of options on futures is much the same as those for options on the spot as covered in Appendix 4B.

---

appendix 12C

An Approximate American Option on Futures Pricing Model

Appendix 4C presented a model for pricing American options on stocks that was developed by Barone-Adesi and Whaley (1987). The BAW model provides an approximate price for American calls and puts on stocks. It requires the same information as the Black-Scholes model, plus the dividend yield. That model can also be used to price options on futures. The only change is to let the dividend yield equal the risk-free rate and use the futures price for the stock price. We shall present and illustrate the BAW model here.

The formula provides a critical stock price, above which an American call should be exercised and below which an American put should be exercised. The formula for calls is

$$C_a = C_e + A_2\left(\frac{f}{f^*}\right)^{q_2} \qquad \text{when } f < f^*,$$

$$C_a = f - E \qquad\qquad\quad \text{when } f \geq f^*,$$

where

C_a = American call price

C_e = European call price given by the Black formula, in which f, E, r, T, and σ are the parameters and were defined in the chapter

$$A_2 = \left(\frac{f^*}{q_2}\right)\left[1 - e^{-rT}N(d_1^*)\right]$$

$$q_2 = \frac{\left[1 + \sqrt{1 + \dfrac{4M}{K}}\,\right]}{2}$$

$$K = 1 - e^{-rT}$$

$$M = \frac{2r}{\sigma^2}$$

In the formula, f* is the critical futures price, above which the call would be exercised and would be worth f − E. We must find f* implicitly by solving the following equation:

$$f* - E = C_e^* + \frac{\left[1 - e^{-rT}N(d_1^*)\right]f*}{q_2},$$

where C_e^* is the Black model value when f* is the stock price and $N(d_1^*)$ is the cumulative normal probability when d_1 is computed using f*.

Let us work the same problem we worked in Appendix 4C. There we had the following input values: S = 100, E = 100, r = .05, T = .25, σ = .3, and δ = .08. The futures price is $f = Se^{(r-\delta)T}$, so f = $100e^{(.05-.08)(.25)}$ = 99.25. Thus, we shall use 99.25 as the futures price. We shall not require the dividend yield from this point on. The computed input values are

$$M = \frac{2(.05)}{(.3)^2} = 1.1111$$

$$K = 1 - e^{-(.05)(.25)} = 0.0124$$

$$q_2 = \frac{\left[1 + \sqrt{1 + \left(\dfrac{4(1.1111)}{0.0124}\right)}\right]}{2}$$

$$= 9.9792.$$

Now we must solve for f*. This is a tedious procedure and should be done with a spreadsheet. The solution is f* = 137.50 − 100 = 37.50. Let us check this out.

-   *Left-hand side*: f* − E = 137.50 − 100 = 37.50.
-   *Right-hand side*: Using 137.50 in the Black formula gives a value of $d_1^* = 2.198$ and N(2.198) = .9860 (using a computer algorithm). The Black European value is $C_e^* = 37.14$. Thus, the right-hand side is

$$37.14 + \frac{\left[1 - e^{-.05(.25)}(.9860)\right](137.50)}{9.9792} = 37.50.$$

Then

$$A_2 = \left(\frac{137.50}{9.9792}\right)\left[1 - e^{-.05(.25)}(.9860)\right]$$

$$= .3610,$$

and, since $f < f^*$ (i.e., $99.25 < 137.50$), we use the formula

$$5.5192 + .3610\left(\frac{99.25}{137.50}\right)^{9.9792} = 5.533,$$

where 5.5192 was obtained by using the Black formula with $f = 99.25$. The early exercise premium is $5.533 - 5.519 = .014$.

The formula for puts is

$$P_a = P_e + A_1\left(\frac{f}{f^{**}}\right)^{q_1} \qquad \text{when } f > f^{**},$$

$$P_a = E - S \qquad \text{when } f \le f^{**},$$

where

P_a = American put price

P_e = European put price given by the Black formula

$$A_1 = \left(-\frac{f^{**}}{q_1}\right)\left[1 - e^{-rT}N(-d_1^{**})\right]$$

$$q_1 = \frac{\left[1 - \sqrt{1 + \dfrac{4M}{K}}\right]}{2}$$

K and M are defined as before.

Here, f^{**} is the critical stock price, below which the put would be exercised and would be worth $E - f^{**}$. We must find f^{**} implicitly by solving the following equation:

$$E - f^{**} = P_e^{**} - \frac{\left[1 - e^{-rT}N(-d_1^{**})\right]f^{**}}{q_1},$$

where P_e^{**} is the Black model put value using f^{**} as the stock price and $N(-d_1^{**})$ is the cumulative normal probability when d_1 is computed using f^{**} and then multiplied by -1.

Working the same problem we worked with calls,

$$q_1 = \frac{1 - \sqrt{1 + \left(\dfrac{4(1.1111)}{0.0124}\right)}}{2}$$

$$= -8.9792.$$

The value of f** is 72.70. To check this, we compute as follows:

- *Left-hand side*: $E - f^{**} = 100 - 72.70 = 29.30$.
- *Right-hand side*: Using 72.70 in the Black formula gives a value of d_1 of -2.198. Then $-d_1^{**} = 2.198$, so $N(2.198) = .9798$. The Black European value is $P_e^{**} = 27.03$. Thus, the right-hand side is

$$27.03 - \frac{\left[1 - e^{-.05(.25)}(.9798)\right](72.70)}{-8.9792} = 27.29,$$

which is close enough.

Then

$$A_1 = -\left(\frac{72.70}{-8.9792}\right)\left[1 - e^{-.05(.25)}(.9798)\right] = 0.2621,$$

and, since $f > f^{**}$ (i.e., $99.25 > 72.70$), we use the formula

$$P_a = 6.2599 + (0.2621)\left(\frac{99.25}{72.70}\right)^{-8.9792} = 6.2760,$$

where 6.2599 was obtained using the Black formula with $f = 99.25$. The early exercise premium is very low at .017.

The software diskette that accompanies this book contains a spreadsheet that performs all of the model's calculations. It is set up to compute prices for options on the spot. Recall that all you have to do is to input f where you would put S and put the risk-free rate where you would put the dividend yield.

FOREIGN CURRENCY OPTIONS AND FUTURES

> *Peace is the natural effect of trade. Two nations who traffic with each other become reciprocally dependent; for if one has an interest in buying, the other has an interest in selling; and thus, their union is founded on their mutual necessities.*
>
> C. S. MONTESQUIEU, 1748

This chapter introduces the world of international finance and the exciting markets for currency options and futures. In so doing, it breaks away from the approach used thus far, which has focused on concepts rather than on specific types of contracts. In the case of currency futures and options, however, a slightly different approach is necessary. Foreign currencies often are seen as exotic and confusing. While indeed some discipline is needed to organize one's thinking, analyzing foreign currencies actually differs very little from analyzing ordinary stocks and bonds.

CHARACTERISTICS OF FOREIGN CURRENCIES AND MARKETS

The Nature of Exchange Rates

Each country has a designated currency. In the United States, of course, it is dollars. In the United Kingdom it is the British pound, in Germany the deutsche mark (pronounced "doychmark"), in Switzerland the Swiss franc, in Japan the

Japanese yen, and in Canada the Canadian dollar. To settle transactions among individuals, corporations, and governments in different countries, there is a rate at which the currency of one country can be converted into the currency of another. That rate is called the *exchange rate*.

For example, suppose you wish to convert U.S. dollars into British pounds. The exchange rate is $1.40 per pound. We denote this as $1.40/£, where £ is the symbol for pounds. Each pound is convertible into $1.40. Conversely, each dollar can be converted into 1/$1.40, or .7143 pounds. We can express the exchange rate as the dollar cost of pounds, $1.40, or the pound cost of dollars, £.7143.

This line of thinking often causes some confusion. An easy way to understand the exchange rate is to always think in terms of a single currency—normally the dollar—and treat the foreign currency as if it were a commodity, which it is. Just as you can buy stocks, bonds, wheat, or gold, so can you buy a foreign currency. When you convert dollars into pounds, you are simply buying a commodity that happens to be pounds. When you convert back into dollars, you are selling the commodity (pounds). The difference in the dollar price at which you buy the pounds and the dollar price at which you sell them generates a profit or loss that results from changes in the exchange rate.

The illustrations in this chapter primarily use the dollar-pound relationship. However, before we begin examining the foreign currency instruments, let us look at the history of foreign currency markets.

A Brief History of Foreign Currency Markets

From the early nineteenth to the mid-twentieth century, gold was the standard to which most countries fixed their currencies. International transactions were settled in gold, and most currency rates were expressed as a fixed ratio to the price of gold. In 1944, a group of Allied nations met in Bretton Woods, New Hampshire, and established the International Monetary Fund. As part of the agreement, each nation fixed its currency in relation to the gold content of the dollar. Currency rates were allowed to fluctuate within a very narrow range, but foreign governments were obligated to execute the necessary buying and selling of their currencies and the dollar to keep the exchange rate relatively stable. For the most part, exchange rates were fixed.

The system worked well as long as there was confidence that the fixed exchange rate accurately reflected the value of a given currency. When it did not, there was significant buying and selling of that currency. For example, if investors thought, as they did in the late 1940s, that the British pound was overvalued, they would sell pounds. With the price of pounds fixed, no one wanted to hold pounds. The British government finally was forced to devalue the pound, which meant lowering its official exchange rate.

By the late 1960s, the United States was running a record balance-of-payments deficit. This meant the United States was paying out more dollars than it was taking in. As foreigners were accumulating large quantities of dollars that were quickly losing value in light of record U.S. inflation levels, the dollar came under pressure and finally was devalued by the U.S. government in 1971. At the same

FIGURE 13.1
European Currency Unit's Value against the Dollar, 1979–1989

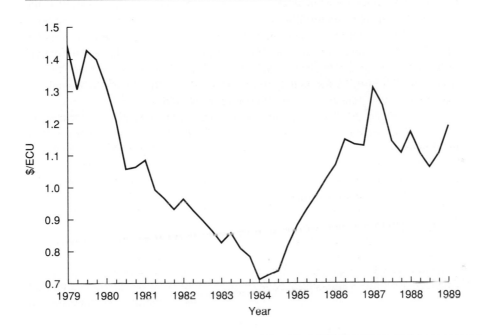

time, the dollar's convertibility to gold was suspended. The Bretton Woods system had failed.

An interim system developed in 1972, called the Smithsonian Agreement, allowed a wider range in which currencies could fluctuate, but it all too quickly proved inadequate. In 1973, the exchange rates of several countries began to fluctuate freely. Ultimately all exchange rates of free countries fluctuated with market conditions.

Figure 13.1 illustrates the fluctuations in the dollar since 1979. The series indicated is the *European Currency Unit*, or *ECU*, an index of the currencies of ten major European countries. The graph shows the dollar cost of a unit of the ECU. A rising value of ECU means the ECU is increasing relative to the dollar, which implies a weakening (depreciating) dollar. A falling ECU means the ECU is weakening or, conversely, the dollar is strengthening (appreciating).

As the graph indicates, the dollar appreciated during much of the early 1980s. This was due primarily to the very low U.S. interest and inflation rates, which led to improved confidence in the U.S. economy. Despite record U.S. fiscal and trade deficits, confidence in and demand for dollars by foreign investors was increasing. However, by 1985 record U.S. trade deficits and a weakening American economy led to the dollar's decline, which has generally continued, as Figure 13.1 shows.

What causes currency fluctuations? One major factor is a nation's balance of payments. As a country exports more than it imports, the demand for its currency increases. At some point, however, the currency becomes so expensive that the country's goods become prohibitively costly. This leads to a decrease in imports and a lower demand for the currency. A nation running a trade deficit finds the demand for its currency weakening. This lowers its currency's value and ultimately makes its currency, and hence its goods, cheap. This reverses the cycle and turns it into a trade surplus. Unfortunately, there are so many other factors involved that the system never quite works as the theory says it should.

For example, exchange rates are also influenced by economic conditions in a country, such as inflation and interest rates. If inflation is high, there is little confidence in the currency, and this weakens the demand for it. High interest rates attract foreigners to the currency; however, if interest rates are high because of high inflation, the effect may be offset. Government policies and political instability are still other factors that influence currency values.

Foreign Currency Spot and Forward Markets

The market for the exchange of foreign currency is large and sophisticated. Major financial institutions and central banks in the various countries are linked through computers and telecommunication systems. Transactions are executed quickly and efficiently.

The spot market is the market for immediate delivery of the foreign currency. This is done by book entry, which is made possible by the fact that the major banks in a given country have accounts with their counterparts in other countries. There is also a large forward market for foreign currency—in fact, the largest forward market of all commodities. Like the spot market, there is no central marketplace; it operates through telecommunication systems linking the major financial institutions. For example, if a corporation will need £1 million in 90 days, it can call a major money center bank, which will enter into a forward contract to deliver the pounds in that period. Recall that in a forward contract the price, which is the exchange rate, is agreed upon at the time the transaction is initiated. No money initially changes hands, but the bank may require a small margin deposit. Ninety days later, the corporation acquires the pounds at the forward price.

Figure 13.2 illustrates a sample of foreign currency spot rates from *The Wall Street Journal* for the trading day of March 22, 1991. For many of the major free countries, there are also 30-, 90-, and 180-day forward quotes. The rates are quoted in both U.S. dollars and foreign currency units per U.S. dollar.

Look at the British pound quotes. The spot rate for pounds is $1.7905, while the spot rate for dollars per pound is 1/$1.7905, or £.5585. The 30-day forward rate per pound is $1.7810 and per dollar is £.5615. Because the forward rates per pound decrease the longer the horizon, the pound is said to be selling at a *forward discount* and the dollar at a *forward premium*.

FIGURE 13.2

Foreign Currency Spot Quotations in *The Wall Street Journal,* Trading Day, March 22, 1991

EXCHANGE RATES

Friday, March 22, 1991

The New York foreign exchange selling rates below apply to trading among banks in amounts of $1 million and more, as quoted at 3 p.m. Eastern time by Bankers Trust Co.and other sources. Retail transactions provide fewer units of foreign currency per dollar.

Country	U.S. $ equiv. Fri.	Thurs.	Currency per U.S. $ Fri.	Thurs.
Argentina (Austral) ...	.0001075	.0001074	9300.08	9310.01
Australia (Dollar)	.7735	.7717	1.2928	1.2958
Austria (Schilling)	.08651	.08720	11.56	11.47
Bahrain (Dinar)	2.6525	2.6525	.3770	.3770
Belgium (Franc)				
Commercial rate	.02954	.02977	33.85	33.59
Brazil (Cruzeiro)	.00442	.00442	226.00	226.25
Britain (Pound)	1.7905	1.8000	.5585	.5556
30-Day Forward	1.7810	1.7908	.5615	.5584
90-Day Forward	1.7648	1.7749	.5666	.5634
180-Day Forward	1.7457	1.7570	.5728	.5692
Canada (Dollar)	.8638	.8651	1.1577	1.1560
30-Day Forward	.8614	.8624	1.1609	1.1596
90-Day Forward	.8567	.8580	1.1673	1.1655
180-Day Forward	.8508	.8520	1.1754	1.1737
Chile (Peso)	.003030	.003033	330.00	329.69
China (Renmimbi)	.191494	.191494	5.2221	5.2221
Colombia (Peso)	.001770	.001768	565.00	565.50
Denmark (Krone)	.1587	.1598	6.3025	6.2590
Ecuador (Sucre)				
Floating rate	.001024	.001024	976.51	976.51
Finland (Markka)	.25621	.25763	3.9030	3.8815
France (Franc)	.17886	.18006	5.5910	5.5536
30-Day Forward ..	.17843	.17963	5.6044	5.5670
90-Day Forward ..	.17765	.17884	5.6290	5.5916
180-Day Forward ..	.17655	.17773	5.6640	5.6266
Germany (Mark)	.6085	.6131	1.6435	1.6310
30-Day Forward	.6072	.6118	1.6470	1.6345
90-Day Forward	.6044	.6092	1.6546	1.6415
180-Day Forward	.6005	.6051	1.6652	1.6525
Greece (Drachma)	.005626	.005903	177.75	169.40
Hong Kong (Dollar) ...	.12849	.12847	7.7830	7.7840
India (Rupee)	.05236	.05236	19.10	19.10
Indonesia (Rupiah)	.0005222	.0005222	1915.01	1915.01
Ireland (Punt)	1.6215	1.6354	.6167	.6115
Israel (Shekel)	.4651	.4593	2.1500	2.1770
Italy (Lira)	.0008177	.0008234	1223.00	1214.51
Japan (Yen)	.007293	.007313	137.30	136.75
30-Day Forward	.007271	.007300	137.54	136.98
90-Day Forward	.007252	.007292	137.89	137.14
180-Day Forward	.007243	.007277	138.07	137.42
Jordan (Dinar)	1.4995	1.4995	.6669	.6669
Kuwait (Dinar)	z	z	z	z
Lebanon (Pound)	.001034	.001034	967.00	967.00
Malaysia (Ringgit)	.3644	.3644	2.7440	2.7445
Malta (Lira)	3.2154	3.2154	.3110	.3110
Mexico (Peso)				
Floating rate	.0003361	.0003361	2975.00	2975.00
Netherland (Guilder) .	.5400	.5442	1.8520	1.8375
New Zealand (Dollar) .	.5955	.5960	1.6793	1.6779
Norway (Krone)	.1562	.1571	6.4019	6.3650
Pakistan (Rupee)	.0451	.0451	22.19	22.19
Peru (New Sol)	1.8519	1.8567	.54	.54
Philippines (Peso)	.03676	.03676	27.20	27.20
Portugal (Escudo)	.007042	.007085	142.00	141.14
Saudi Arabia (Riyal) ..	.26667	.26667	3.7500	3.7500
Singapore (Dollar)	.5656	.5658	1.7680	1.7675
South Africa (Rand)				
Commercial rate	.3708	.3725	2.6968	2.6843
Financial rate	.3055	.3058	3.2730	3.2700
South Korea (Won)	.0013947	.0013947	717.00	717.00
Spain (Peseta)	.009799	.009872	102.05	101.30
Sweden (Krona)	.1670	.1678	5.9880	5.9585
Switzerland (Franc) ..	.7090	.7117	1.4105	1.4050
30-Day Forward	.7077	.7104	1.4131	1.4076
90-Day Forward	.7052	.7080	1.4180	1.4124
180-Day Forward	.7032	.7060	1.4221	1.4165
Taiwan (Dollar)	.036765	.037327	27.20	26.79
Thailand (Baht)	.03935	.03935	25.41	25.41
Turkey (Lira)	.0003030	.0002646	3300.00	3779.00
United Arab (Dirham) .	.2723	.2723	3.6725	3.6725
Uruguay (New Peso)				
Financial	.000570	.000570	1754.00	1754.00
Venezuela (Bolivar)				
Floating rate	.01887	.01884	53.00	53.09
SDR	1.36709	1.36930	.73148	.73030
ECU	1.24775	1.25698	....	....

Special Drawing Rights (SDR) are based on exchange rates for the U.S., German, British, French and Japanese currencies. Source: International Monetary Fund.

European Currency Unit (ECU) is based on a basket of community currencies. Source: European Community Commission.

z-Not quoted.

Source: The Wall Street Journal, *March 25, 1991.*

Foreign Currency Futures Markets

During the transition to freely floating exchange rates in 1972, the Chicago Mercantile Exchange established the International Monetary Market for the trading of futures contracts in foreign currencies. We already are familiar with the IMM's T-bill and Eurodollar contracts. However, the foreign currency contracts actually were the first financial futures contracts.

FIGURE 13.3
Foreign Currency Futures Volume (IMM, MACE, PBT), 1981–1989

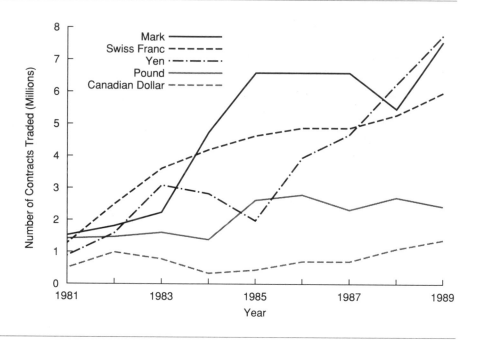

The foreign currency futures contracts call for delivery of a specified number of units of the foreign currency. Prices are always quoted in dollars per unit of that currency. Let us take the British pound contract as an example.

The pound contract calls for delivery of 62,500 pounds. The price is quoted in dollars per pound. For example, if the contract price is $1.786, the actual price is $1.786(62,500) = $111,625. The expiration months are January, March, April, June, July, September, October, December, and the current month. The contract expires on the second business day before the third Wednesday of the month. There are daily price limits at the opening but not for the rest of the day. Contract specifications for all of the IMM foreign currency contracts are provided in Appendix 13A.

Figure 13.3 presents the historical volume of trading in foreign currency contracts. As you can see, the growth has been quite phenomenal. The deutsche mark and yen have experienced rapid growth in recent years, while the Swiss franc has shown consistent growth, although at a lower rate. In contrast, the Canadian dollar and British pound have shown little growth. It is no coincidence that the growth patterns are consistent with the strength of the countries' economies, particularly their balances of trade.

Figure 13.4 illustrates the foreign currency futures quotations in *The Wall Street Journal* and *Barron's*. In *The Wall Street Journal* quotes for the British pound, the

FIGURE 13.4

Foreign Currency Futures Quotations: *The Wall Street Journal,* Trading Day of March 22, 1991, and *Barron's,* Week Ending March 22, 1991

FUTURES

	Open	High	Low	Settle	Change	Lifetime High	Low	Open Interest
JAPANESE YEN (IMM)—12.5 million yen; $ per yen (.00)								
June	.7237	.7280	.7233	.7253	− .0032	.8010	.6645	34,279
Sept	.7225	.7260	.7225	.7241	− .0032	.7995	.7127	1,384
Dec	....	....		.7243	− .0034	.7770	.7180	617
Mr92		....	....	.7254	− .0034	.7540	.7261	1,353

Est vol 26,509; vol Thur 23,171; open int 37,633, − 169.

	Open	High	Low	Settle	Change	Lifetime High	Low	Open Interest
DEUTSCHEMARK (IMM)—125,000 marks; $ per mark								
June	.6040	.6066	.6015	.6047	− .0044	.6870	.5925	52,997
Sept	.5996	.6019	.5980	.6008	− .0045	.6810	.5885	1,507

Est vol 33,434; vol Thur 38,536; open int 54,587, +1,160.

	Open	High	Low	Settle	Change	Lifetime High	Low	Open Interest
CANADIAN DOLLAR (IMM)—100,000 dirs.; $ per Can $								
June	.8568	.8576	.8565	.8574	− .0013	.8630	.7995	17,321
Sept	.8508	.8512	.8508	.8517	− .0013	.8574	.7985	1,798
Dec	....	....		.8469	− .0013	.8520	.8175	293
Mr92	....	....		.8431	− .0007	.8440	.8253	375
June	....	....		.8390	− .0007	.8370	.8330	150

Est vol 1,826; vol Thur 2,626; open int 19,935, +226.

	Open	High	Low	Settle	Change	Lifetime High	Low	Open Interest
BRITISH POUND (IMM)—62,500 pds.; $ per pound								
June	1.7622	1.7710	1.7572	1.7650	− .0114	1.9610	1.7230	25,973
Sept	.7428	1.7428	1.7510	1.7390	− .0120	1.9360	1.7050	326

Est vol 12,317; vol Thur 12,425; open int 26,301, 500.

	Open	High	Low	Settle	Change	Lifetime High	Low	Open Interest
SWISS FRANC (IMM)—125,000 francs; $ per franc								
June	.7035	.7084	.7024	.7058	− .0020	.8084	.6895	35,022
Sept	.7010	.7050	.7000	.7036	− .0022	.8055	.6875	470

Est vol 19,469; vol Thur 25,535; open int 35,506, − 369.

	Open	High	Low	Settle	Change	Lifetime High	Low	Open Interest
AUSTRALIAN DOLLAR (IMM)—100,000 dirs.; $ per A.$								
June	.7652	.7655	.7636	.7641	+ .0008	.7785	.7551	1,338

Est vol 145; vol Thur 194; open int 1,341, +71.

	Open	High	Low	Settle	Change	Lifetime High	Low	Open Interest
U.S. DOLLAR INDEX (FINEX)—500 times USDX								
June	90.30	90.61	90.00	90.25	+ .54	91.80	81.45	5,527
Sept	91.15	91.15	90.90	91.00	+ .58	92.35	83.17	423

Est vol 2,939; vol Thur 3,190; open int 5,950, −3,777.
The Index: High 89.64; Low 89.08; Close 89.28 +.48

BRITISH POUND
$ per pound; 1 point equals $0.0001

1.9600	1.7230	Jun	1.7850	1.7230	1.7650 −320	25,973
1.9340	1.7190	Sep	1.7660	1.7190	1.7460 −310	326
1.7900	1.7900	Dec	.....	.....	1.7320 −290	2

Last spot 1.7895, off 330.
Fri. to Thurs. sales 94,456.
Total open interest 26,301.

CANADIAN DOLLAR
$ per dir; 1 point equals $0.0001

.8630	.7995	Jun	.8604	.8554	.8574 −5	17,321
.8574	.7985	Sep	.8544	.8504	.8517 −4	1,798
.8520	.8175	Dec	.8488	.8460	.8469 +2	293
.8445	.8268	Mar	.8445	.8445	.8431 +14	373
.8430	.8330	Jun	.....	.....	.8390 +15	150

Last spot .8640, off 13.
Fri. to Thurs. sales 20,950.
Total open interest 19,935.

FRENCH FRANC
$ per franc; 1 point equals $0.00001
No open contracts.

GERMAN MARK
$ per mark; 1 point equals $0.0001

.6870	.5925	Jun	.6150	.5925	.6047 −120	52,997
.6810	.5885	Sep	.6108	.5885	.6008 −127	1,507
.6770	.5920	Dec	.6030	.5920	.5981 −124	83

Last spot .6088, off 137.
Fri. to Thurs. sales 256,903.
Total open interest 54,587.

JAPANESE YEN
$ per yen; 1 point equals $0.000001

.008010	.006645	Jun	.007290	.007130	.007253 +20	34,279
.007870	.007127	Sep	.007275	.007127	.007241 +24	1,384
.007559	.007180	Dec	.007245	.007180	.007243 +24	617
.007261	.007261	Mar	.....	.....	.007254 +29	1,353

Last spot .007286, up 19.
Fri. to Thurs. sales 158,542.
Total open interest 37,633.

SWISS FRANC
$ per franc; 1 point equals $0.0001

.8084	.6895	Jun	.7135	.6895	.7058 −77	35,022
.8055	.6916	Sep	.7105	.6950	.7036 −71	470
.8090	.6880	Dec	.7062	.6880	.7029 −56	14

Last spot .7089, off 95.
Fri. to Thurs. sales 158,475.
Total open interest 35,506.

AUSTRAL. DOLLAR
$ per dir; 1 point equals $0.0001

.7785	.7551	Jun	.7655	.7582	.7641 +46	1,338
.7544	.7520	Sep	.7544	.7520	.7571 +46	3

Last spot .7733, up 50.
Fri. to Thurs. sales 1,589.
Total open interest 1,341.

Source: The Wall Street Journal, *March 25, 1991;* Barron's, *March 25, 1991.*

first line indicates that the contract is at the IMM, it covers 62,500 pounds, and the quote is in dollars per pound. The column headings of the first four columns show the open, high, low, and settlement prices. Thus, the June contract opened at $1.7622, reached a high of $1.7710, reached a low of $1.7572, and had a settlement price of $1.7650. The next column gives the change in the settlement price, which in this case was − .0114. The next two columns give the high and low over the contract's life, and the final column gives the open interest. The last line is a summary of the volume and open interest for all contracts.

On the first line below the contract name, *Barron's* provides the dollar effect of a one-point move in the futures price—in this case, $.0001. The first two columns are the lifetime high and low, and the next column is the contract month. The next three columns are the week's high, low, and closing prices, followed by

FIGURE 13.5

Foreign Currency Option Volume, 1982–1989

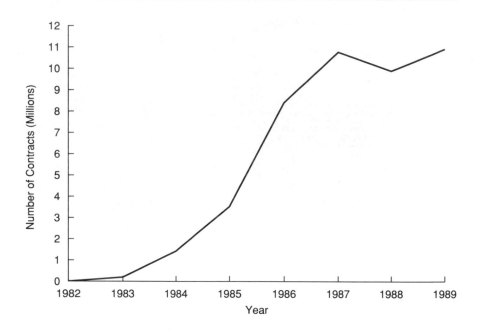

the net change in the closing price and the open interest. The remaining lines provide the spot price, sales (volume), and open interest statistics for all contracts.

Foreign Currency Options Markets

Foreign currency options were first introduced in 1982 at the Philadelphia Stock Exchange. Figure 13.5 illustrates the volume of foreign currency options over the first eight years of its existence. Although the volume is small relative to stock and index options and foreign currency futures, it has experienced rapid growth.

The Philadelphia Stock Exchange's options expire in the next two months and in March, June, September, and December. They trade from 7:00 p.m. to 2:30 p.m. the next day Eastern time; during daylight savings time they start at 6:00 p.m. The contract sizes are exactly one-half the sizes of the corresponding IMM futures contracts. The expiration date is the Saturday before the third Wednesday of the month. Each option has a European and an American contract. Appendix 13B gives the contract specifications.

Figure 13.6 illustrates *The Wall Street Journal*'s foreign currency options quotations.[1] As you can see, the system is similar to that used for ordinary stock options. It is important, however, to pay close attention to the contract size and the unit of quotation. For example, the British pound contract at the Philadelphia Stock Exchange is for 31,250 pounds and is quoted in cents per unit. Thus, the exercise price of 180 is $1.80 per pound and the price of the April 180 call is 1.50 cents per pound.

PRICING FOREIGN CURRENCY FUTURES AND OPTIONS

Foreign currency futures and options are priced according to the same arbitrage arguments we have used throughout this book. However, applying these arguments is less straightforward than it is for ordinary futures and options. In this section, we shall look at some basic principles of pricing foreign currency instruments.

Cross-Rate Relationships

One of the most elementary principles is the *cross-rate* relationship among foreign currencies. Let us consider three currencies: the U.S. dollar, the British pound, and the deutsche mark. We express the dollar/pound exchange rate as $/£, the mark/dollar exchange rate as DM/$, and the pound/mark exchange rate as £/DM. Notice what we get when we multiply these three rates:

$$\left(\frac{\$}{£}\right)\left(\frac{DM}{\$}\right)\left(\frac{£}{DM}\right) = 1.$$

If this relationship does not hold, an arbitrageur can make a riskless profit. For example, consider the spot rates for pounds and marks in terms of dollars on September 26 of a particular year. The rates are $1.437/£ and DM2.0465/$. These rates imply that the price of deutsche marks in pounds should be £.34/DM, since ($1.437)(2.0465)(.34) = 1. Now suppose the price of deutsche marks in pounds is £.36/DM. This means the deutsche mark is overvalued relative to the pound. An arbitrageur will want to convert marks to pounds. Here is how the transaction would be done.

Take 1 dollar and convert it to DM2.0465. Then arrange for a currency dealer to convert the 2.0465 marks to 2.0465(.36) = .7367 pounds. Then convert the .7367 pounds to .7367(1.4367) = 1.0585 dollars. This transaction is riskless and immediately earns a profit of 5.85 cents on a 1-dollar investment. The 5.85 percent return is the amount by which the mark is overvalued relative to the pound. In the

---

[1]*Barron's* foreign currency option quotes are not shown, because they are virtually identical to its stock and index option quotes, which have been covered in previous chapters.

FIGURE 13.6

Foreign Currency Option Quotations in *The Wall Street Journal*, Trading Day of March 22, 1991

Option & Underlying	Strike Price	Calls—Last Apr	May	Jun	Puts—Last Apr	May	Jun
50,000 Australian Dollars-cents per unit.							
ADollr	...71	r	r	r	r	r	0.09
77.34	...73	r	r	r	r	r	0.24
77.34	...76	1.32	r	r	r	0.52	r
77.34	...77	r	r	r	r	r	1.57
77.34	...78	r	0.46	r	r	r	r
31,250 British Pounds-cents per unit.							
BPound	170	r	r	r	r	r	1.95
179.01	.175	r	r	r	1.05	r	r
179.01	177½	r	r	4.86	r	r	4.67
179.01	.180	1.50	2.22	r	3.69	3.90	5.18
179.01	182½	1.05	r	r	r	r	r
179.01	.185	0.39	r	1.60	r	r	8.43
179.01	187½	0.20	r	r	r	r	r
50,000 Canadian Dollars-cents per unit.							
CDollr	...86	r	r	r	0.22	r	0.78
86.38	.86½	r	r	r	0.43	r	r
86.38	...87	r	r	r	r	r	1.49
62,500 German Marks-cents per unit.							
DMark	.. 58	r	r	r	r	0.24	0.60
60.86	...59	r	r	r	r	0.62	r
60.86	...60	r	1.46	r	0.58	0.92	1.28
60.86	...61	0.70	0.96	1.17	0.70	1.33	1.69
60.86	...62	0.40	0.58	0.84	1.57	r	2.23
60.86	.62½	0.28	0.48	s	r	1.89	s
60.86	...63	0.21	r	0.54	r	2.83	3.08
60.86	...64	0.11	0.20	0.40	2.83	3.65	3.92
60.86	.64½	0.06	r	s	r	r	s
60.86	...65	r	r	r	4.20	r	4.75
60.86	...66	r	r	r	r	r	5.52
60.86	...68	r	r	r	r	r	7.44
6,250,000 Japanese Yen-100ths of a cent per unit.							
JYen	... 68	r	r	r	0.04	r	r
72.82	...69	r	r	r	r	r	0.46
73.11	...70	r	r	r	0.18	r	r
72.82	...71	r	r	r	0.27	0.60	r
73.11	.71½	r	r	s	0.36	r	s
72.82	...72	r	r	1.94	0.52	r	1.40
72.82	.73½	r	1.01	s	r	r	s
72.82	...75	0.27	r	r	r	r	r
62,500 Swiss Francs-cents per unit.							
SFranc	..66	s	s	r	s	s	0.35
70.91	...68	s	s	r	s	s	0.78
70.91	...69	r	r	r	r	r	1.14
70.91	...70	r	r	r	r	1.11	1.71
71.32	...74	s	r	0.70	s	r	r
62,500 Swiss Francs-European Style.							
70.91	...69	r	r	r	r	r	1.12
70.91	...70	r	r	r	r	1.18	r
70.91	...71	r	r	r	r	r	2.08

Total call vol.   13,923   Call open int.   322,412
Total put vol.   14,386   Put open int.   264,719
r—Not traded.   s—No option offered.
Last is premium (purchase price).

Source: The Wall Street Journal, *March 25, 1991.*

real world, there would be a dealer bid-ask spread to cover and some modest transaction costs; however, we shall ignore these for this analysis.

The combined effects of numerous arbitrageurs would drive the exchange rate of marks for pounds down to £.34/DM. This is the cross-rate relationship among any three currencies. Any two rates imply the third rate. The transaction that upholds this relationship is sometimes called *triangular arbitrage*. These relationships will hold for spot, forward, and futures exchange rates.

Interest Rate Parity

Interest rate parity is an important fundamental relationship between the spot and forward exchange rates and the interest rates in two countries. It is the foreign currency market's version of the cost-of-carry forward and futures pricing model. Consider the following situation involving U.S. dollars and British pounds.

The spot exchange rate is S. This quote is in dollars per £. The British risk-free interest rate is ρ, and the holding period is T. You take $S(1+\rho)^{-T}$ dollars and buy $(1+\rho)^{-T}$ pounds. Simultaneously, you sell one forward contract expiring at time T. The forward exchange rate is F, which is also in dollars per pound. You take your $(1+\rho)^{-T}$ pounds and invest them in British T-bills that have a return of ρ.

When the forward contract expires, you will have 1 pound. This is because your $(1+\rho)^{-T}$ pounds will have grown by the factor $(1+\rho)^{T}$, so $(1+\rho)^{-T}(1+\rho)^{T}$ = 1. Your forward contract obligates you to deliver the pound, for which you receive F dollars. In effect, you have invested $S(1+\rho)^{-T}$ dollars and received F dollars. Since the transaction is riskless, your return should be the U.S. risk-free rate, r; that is,

$$S(1+\rho)^{-T}(1+r)^{T} = F.$$

This relationship is called *interest rate parity*. It is sometimes expressed as

$$\frac{F}{S} = (1+r)^{T}(1+\rho)^{-T}.$$

Consider the following example. On September 26 of a particular year, the spot rate for pounds was $1.437 and the 90-day forward rate was $1.421. The U.S. interest rate was 5.46 percent, while the British interest rate was 9.96 percent. The time to expiration was 90/365 = .2466. According to the formula,

$$\frac{F}{S} = \frac{\$1.421}{\$1.437} = .9889$$

and

$$(1+r)^{T}(1+\rho)^{-T} = (1.0546)^{.2466}(1.0996)^{-.2466} = .9897.$$

The difference is very small, as we would expect in an efficient market.

To illustrate an arbitrage transaction, assume the spot rate is correct but the forward rate is $1.43. An arbitrageur buys $(1.0996)^{-.2466} = .9769$ pounds for $1.437(.9769) = 1.4037 and sells one forward contract at a forward rate of $1.43. The .9769 pounds are invested at the British risk-free rate. When the contract expires, the arbitrageur will have 1 pound, which is delivered on the forward contract and for which $1.43 is received. Thus, the arbitrageur has invested $1.4037 and received $1.43 in 90 days. The annualized return is

$$\left(\frac{1.43}{1.4037}\right)^{1/.2466} - 1 = .0782,$$

which exceeds the domestic risk-free rate of 5.46 percent. The combined effects of numerous arbitrageurs would push the spot price up and/or the forward price down until the spot and forward prices were properly aligned with the relative interest rates in the two countries.[2] Of course, some transaction costs and the dealer bid-ask spread would prevent the relationship from holding precisely.

Interest rate parity is a powerful relationship and is used by all international currency traders. It is analogous to the cost of carry model for pricing other types of futures. The only difference is that the cost of carry in the two countries must be considered. For example, when funds are tied up in a foreign currency, the investor forgoes interest at the U.S. rate but earns interest at the foreign rate. The difference between the U.S. rate and the foreign rate is the cost of carry. The foreign interest rate thus is analogous to the dividend yield in the stock index futures pricing model.

As we saw in previous chapters, futures prices are not necessarily equal to forward prices. This depends on the stability of interest rates and the relationship among futures prices, forward prices, and interest rates. However, empirical tests by Cornell and Reinganum (1981) show that the differences observed in real data are extremely small. Thus, as we have done previously, we shall assume forward exchange rates and futures exchange rates are equivalent.

The Intrinsic Value of an American Foreign Currency Option

Most of the principles of option pricing we previously covered are equally applicable to foreign currency option pricing. Thus, we shall limit our discussion to the most important principles and those that differ slightly from ordinary options. We shall use the same notation as in the option chapters. C(S,T,E) and P(S,T,E) are the call and put prices, with subscripts a and e used when necessary to distinguish American from European options. S_T is the spot rate at expiration. The risk-free rates and time to expiration are r, ρ, and T, as in the preceding section.

---

[2] The arbitrage could also put pressure on interest rates in the two countries. The British rate would decrease, while the U.S. rate would increase.

The minimum value of an American foreign currency call is

$$C_a(S,T,E) \geq Max(0, S - E),$$

which is the same as for an equity call. The term $Max(0, S - E)$ is the intrinsic value. As an example, take the December 140 British pound call on September 26 of a particular year. The spot rate is 143.53 cents. Thus, the intrinsic value is $Max(0, 143.53 - 140) = 3.53$. The call price is 5.10 cents. The difference, $5.10 - 3.53 = 1.57$, is the time value.

The minimum value of an American foreign currency put is

$$P_a(S,T,E) \geq Max(0, E - S),$$

where $Max(0, E - S)$ is the intrinsic value. For example, on September 26, the December 145 British pound put has an intrinsic value of $Max(0, 145 - 143.53) = 1.47$. The put price is 4.90. The difference of $4.90 - 1.47 = 3.43$ is the time value.

As the options move closer to expiration, their time values erode, and at expiration the options are worth only their intrinsic values. These principles are exactly like those for their equity option counterparts. Now, however, we shall establish lower bounds for European options that differ somewhat from those we did for equity options.

The Lower Bound of European Foreign Currency Options

Consider two portfolios, A and B. Portfolio A consists of a foreign currency call priced at $C_e(S,T,E)$ and a risk-free bond with a face value of E and a present value of $E(1 + r)^{-T}$. Portfolio B is constructed by taking $S(1 + \rho)^{-T}$ dollars, converting it to the foreign currency, and investing it in a foreign pure discount bond with a face value equal to one unit of the foreign currency. The present value of that bond is $S(1 + \rho)^{-T}$ dollars. When the bond matures, it pays one unit of the foreign currency, which is converted back into S_T dollars.

Table 13.1 illustrates the payoffs from that portfolio. For portfolio A, if the spot rate at expiration does not exceed the exercise price, the call expires worthless but the bonds are worth E dollars. If the spot rate at expiration is greater than E, the call is worth $S_T - E$ and the bonds are worth E for a total of S_T. Thus, portfolio A is worth the greater of E and S_T. Portfolio B is worth S_T in either case. This is because the British bonds mature and are worth 1 pound in either case, and that pound is converted back into S_T dollars.

The outcome of portfolio A equals or exceeds that of portfolio B in both cases. Thus, portfolio A must sell for at least as much as portfolio B.[3] The current value

---

[3]Recall from Chapter 3 why this is true. If portfolio B sold for more than portfolio A, British investors would have an arbitrage opportunity. They could go short in portfolio B by selling their own currency. Then they would use the funds to construct portfolio A. This would enable them to earn a non-negative profit and have cash left over up front.

TABLE 13.1

The Lower Bound of a European Foreign Currency Call: Payoffs at Expiration of Portfolios A and B

Portfolio	Current Value	Payoffs from Portfolio Given Spot Rate at Expiration	
		$S_T \leq E$	$S_T > E$
A	$C_e(S,T,E) + E(1+r)^{-T}$	E	$(S_T - E) + E = S_T$
B	$S(1+\rho)^{-T}$	S_T	S_T

for portfolio B is $S(1+\rho)^{-T}$, while the current value for portfolio A is $C_e(S,T,E) + E(1+r)^{-T}$. We state this inequality as

$$C_e(S,T,E) + E(1+r)^{-T} \geq S(1+\rho)^{-T}.$$

This is frequently written as

$$C_e(S,T,E) \geq S(1+\rho)^{-T} - E(1+r)^{-T.}$$

Because an option cannot have a negative value, we can state this as

$$C_e(S,T,E) \geq \text{Max}[0, S(1+\rho)^{-T} - E(1+r)^{-T}].$$

The call price is greater than or equal to the spot rate discounted at the foreign interest rate minus the present value of the exercise price. This is similar to the lower bound of an equity call, which is the spot price minus the present value of the exercise price. In fact, if there were a dividend on the stock, these two boundaries would be equivalent. The dividend yield would replace the foreign risk-free interest rate.

Converting dollars into a foreign currency is similar to buying a stock with a known dividend. Suppose the dividend yield is equivalent to ρ. You buy the stock, hold it, and collect the dividend; then you sell the stock at S_T. In the case of a foreign currency, you buy the currency, hold it, and collect the interest; then you sell (convert) it.

Let us test the lower bound rule on a European option, the November 145 British pound European call on September 26. The spot rate was 143.53, the domestic interest rate was 5.46 percent, the British interest rate was 9.96 percent, and the option expired on November 14, 49 days later. Thus, $T = 49/365 = .1342$. The lower bound is

$$143.53(1.0996)^{-.1342} - 145(1.0546)^{-.1342} = -2.25.$$

Thus, the lower bound is zero. The actual price of the call is 1.80, so it does exceed the lower bound.

TABLE 13.2

The Lower Bound of a European Foreign Currency Put: Payoffs at Expiration of Portfolios A and B

Portfolio	Current Value	Payoffs from Portfolio Given Spot Rate at Expiration	
		$S_T \leq E$	$S_T > E$
A	$P_e(S,T,E) + S(1+\rho)^{-T}$	$(E - S_T) + S_T = E$	0
B	$E(1+r)^{-T}$	E	E

The lower bound for a European put is derived similarly. Portfolio A consists of a European put plus an investment of $S(1 + \rho)^{-T}$ dollars in a foreign pure discount bond worth one unit of the foreign currency at expiration. Portfolio B consists of a domestic pure discount bond worth E dollars at expiration. Table 13.2 illustrates the payoffs.

Portfolio A performs at least as well as portfolio B and therefore should be priced at least as high. We state this as

$$P_e(S,T,E) + S(1+\rho)^{-T} \geq E(1+r)^{-T}.$$

This is usually written as

$$P_e(S,T,E) \geq E(1+r)^{-T} - S(1+\rho)^{-T}.$$

Because an option cannot have a negative value,

$$P_e(S,T,E) \geq \text{Max}\,[0, E(1+r)^{-T} - S(1+\rho)^{-T}].$$

The put price must equal or exceed the present value of the exercise price minus the spot rate discounted at the foreign interest rate. This too is identical to the lower bound of a European put option on a dividend-paying stock when the dividend yield is equivalent to ρ.

As an example, consider the December 150 British pound European put on September 26 of a recent year. The lower bound is

$$150(1.0546)^{-.2192} - 143.53(1.0996)^{-.2192} = 7.69.$$

The actual put price is 8.50, so the put conforms to the boundary condition.

As was the case with equity options, these lower bounds establish the lowest possible price for European calls and puts. For American calls and puts, the lowest possible price is the intrinsic value.

TABLE 13.3
Put-Call Parity of Foreign Currency Options

		Payoffs from Portfolio Given Spot Rate at Expiration	
Payoff From	Current Value	$S_T < E$	$S_T \geq E$
Long foreign bonds	$S(1 + \rho)^{-T}$	S_T	S_T
Long put	$P_e(S,T,E)$	$E - S_T$	0
Short call	$-C_e(S,T,E)$	0	$-(S_T - E)$
Short domestic bonds	$-E(1 + r)^{-T}$	$-E$	$-E$
		0	0

Put-Call Parity

Suppose we construct the following portfolio. Take $S(1 + \rho)^{-T}$ dollars, convert it to the foreign currency, and buy a foreign pure discount bond worth one unit of the foreign currency at expiration. Also, buy one foreign currency European put, sell one European call, and sell short one domestic pure discount bond worth E dollars at expiration.[4] As Table 13.3 shows, this portfolio offers a zero cash flow at expiration regardless of the spot exchange rate.

Because the portfolio has a zero cash flow at expiration, it should have a current value of zero. This means that

$$S(1 + \rho)^{-T} + P_e(S,T,E) - C_e(S,T,E) - E(1 + r)^{-T} = 0.$$

Stated alternatively,

$$P_e(S,T,E) = C_e(S,T,E) - S(1 + \rho)^{-T} + E(1 + r)^{-T}$$

or

$$C_e(S,T,E) = P_e(S,T,E) + S(1 + \rho)^{-T} - E(1 + r)^{-T}.$$

This is put-call parity for foreign currency options. The only difference between it and put-call parity for stock options is the presence of the foreign discount factor times the spot rate. Once again, however, this is equivalent to a dividend on a stock. Put-call parity for dividend-paying stocks thus would be identical to the above statement if the dividend were paid at the rate ρ.

---

[4]Remember that this is equivalent to taking out a loan in which you receive the present value of E dollars today and pay back E dollars at maturity.

Consider the December 150 European put and call on September 26. The call price is $1. According to the formula, the put should be worth

$$1 - 143.53(1.0996)^{-.2192} + 150(1.0546)^{-.2192} = 8.69.$$

The actual put price is 8.50, so the put appears to be slightly underpriced. However, transaction costs could account for the difference.

Put-call parity gives the relationship between puts and calls denominated in one currency but exercisable into another. To fully understand foreign currency options, it is important to recognize another type of put-call parity: A call to buy currency A denominated in currency B with an exercise price of E is equivalent to a put to sell E units of currency B denominated in currency A with an exercise price of 1/E. For example, consider the December 140 British pound call. This is a call to buy 1 British pound at $1.40. It is equivalent to a put to sell 1.40 dollars at 1/1.40 = £.71. Let us see why this is so by considering the payoffs at expiration from these two options. If we buy the call to buy a British pound at $1.40, we shall receive the following payoffs:

$$S_T - \$1.40 \quad \text{if } S_T \geq \$1.40$$
$$0 \quad\quad\quad \text{if } S_T < \$1.40.$$

If we buy the put to sell 1.40 dollars at £.71, we shall receive the following payoffs:

$$0 \quad\quad\quad\quad\quad \text{if } 1/S_T \geq \pounds.71$$
$$(1.40)[\pounds.71 - (1/S_T)] \quad \text{if } 1/S_T < \pounds.71.$$

The expression $1/S_T$ is simply the £/$ exchange rate at expiration expressed in terms of pounds. The put pays off when $1/S_T < \pounds.71$. Recall that the exercise price of £.71 was simply the inverse of $1.40. Thus, the put pays off when $1/S_T < 1/\$1.40$, which is equivalent to $S_T > \$1.40$. The put payoff when this occurs is $1.40(\pounds.71 - 1/S_T) = \pounds1 - 1.40/S_T$. This amount is in pounds, so we convert it to dollars by multiplying by $\$S_T$, giving us $S_T - \$1.40$. Looking back at the call payoffs, we see that when the put pays off, the call pays off, and they both pay off the same amount in dollars. It follows that when the call is out-of-the-money, the put is also out-of-the-money, and neither pays off anything. Thus, the call and the put are equivalent.

Bodurtha and Courtadon (1986) examined the prices of currency options to determine if they conform to the lower bounds and put-call parity. Although there was a surprising number of violations, there were few that could be profitably exploited. Thus, foreign currency options, for all practical purposes, conform to these rules.

The Garman-Kohlhagen Foreign Currency Option Pricing Model

Garman and Kohlhagen (1983) derived an option pricing model for foreign currency options. Their model is a simple extension of the Black-Scholes model. The formula is

$$C = Se^{-\rho T}N(d_1) - Ee^{-rT}N(d_2),$$

where

$$d_1 = \frac{\ln\left(Se^{-\rho T}/E\right) + \left[r + \left(\sigma^2/2\right)\right]T}{\sigma\sqrt{T}}$$

$$d_2 = d_1 - \sigma\sqrt{T}.$$

Once again the foreign interest rate enters the problem like a dividend on a stock. In fact, this model is identical to the model for pricing stocks with a continuous dividend yield equal to ρ. Instead of using S, you substitute $Se^{-\rho T}$.

As an example, suppose we look at the British pound November 145 European call. The spot rate is 143.53, the exercise price is 145, the risk-free rate is $\ln(1.0546)$ = .0532, the British interest rate is $\ln(1.0996)$ = .0949, and the time to expiration is .1342.[5] The only other variable we need is the standard deviation. Recall from Chapter 4 that this would be the standard deviation of the logarithmic percentage change in the underlying variable—in this case, the spot exchange rate. There is no need to repeat our previous discussion about methods of estimating σ. Let us simply use a value for illustrative purposes. Here we shall use .15.

The values of d_1 and d_2 are

$$d_1 = \frac{\ln\left(143.53e^{(-.0949)(.1342)}/145\right) + \left[.0532 + (.15^2)/2\right](.1342)}{.15\sqrt{.1342}}$$

$$= -.26$$

$$d_2 = -.26 - .15\sqrt{.1342} = -.3149.$$

Now we look up the values in the normal probability table, Table 4.2 on page 122. We find that $N(-.26) = 1 - .6026 = .3974$ and $N(-.31) = 1 - .6217 = .3783$. Plugging everything back in gives

$$C = 143.53e^{(-.0949)(.1342)}(.3974) - 145e^{(-.0532)(.1342)}(.3783)$$

$$= 1.85.$$

---

[5]Recall that in the Black-Scholes formula, all interest rates must be expressed in continuously compounded form.

The actual price of the call is 1.80. Thus, the call is slightly underpriced.

Put options can also be priced by substituting the Garman-Kohlhagen formula for the call price in the put-call parity formula. Remember, of course, that the Garman-Kohlhagen model, like Black-Scholes, is a European option pricing model. The American options on the Philadelphia Stock Exchange would have higher prices and would tend to be underpriced by the model. Thus, to accurately price an American foreign currency option would require an American option pricing model. As we have noted previously, most of the American models are beyond the scope of this book; however, Appendix 4C presents the Barone-Adesi/ Whaley model, which gives an approximate American option price for a stock with a constant dividend yield. The BAW model can be used with American foreign currency calls by using the foreign interest rate as the dividend yield.

Tucker (1985) tested the Garman-Kohlhagen model in a manner similar to tests of the Black-Scholes model discussed in Chapter 4. A fairly large number of pricing errors were detected, but transaction costs prevented them from being fully exploited. Shastri and Tandon (1986a) compared results from tests of the Garman-Kohlhagen model with a more sophisticated American option pricing model. The results showed that the differences were small except when the foreign interest rate was high, which is exactly the condition that would trigger early exercise.

This concludes our discussion of pricing foreign currency futures and options. In the next section, we shall briefly overview several strategies using these instruments.

TRADING STRATEGIES IN FOREIGN CURRENCY FUTURES AND OPTIONS

In this section, we shall look at five applications of foreign currency instruments. The first two are long and short hedges using futures. The next two are simple speculative call and put strategies. The last is a foreign currency hedge using options.

A Long Hedge with Foreign Currency Futures

Recall that a long hedge with futures involves the purchase of a futures contract. In the case of foreign currencies, a long hedger is concerned that the value of the foreign currency will rise. Here is an example.

On July 1, an American automobile dealer enters into a contract to import 20 British luxury cars. Each car will cost £35,000. Payment will be made in British pounds on November 1. Over the next several months, the car dealer is exposed to the risk of an increase in the exchange rate for pounds.

For example, the spot rate for pounds currently is $1.3060. This means that the cars currently cost £35,000($1.3060) = $45,710 each. If the pound strengthens, the £35,000 will require more dollars, thus effectively raising the price of the

TABLE 13.4

A Long Hedge with Foreign Currency Futures

Scenario: On July 1, an American auto dealer enters into a contract to purchase 20 British sports cars with payment to be made in British pounds on November 1. Each car will cost 35,000 pounds. The dealer is concerned that the pound will strengthen over the next few months, causing the cars to cost more in dollars.

July 1

Spot market: Current exchange rate is $1.3060 per pound
   Cost of 20 cars: 20(35,000)($1.3060) = $914,200
Futures market: December pound contract is at $1.278
   Price per contract: 62,500($1.278) = $79,875
Buy 11 contracts

November 1

Spot market: Spot rate is $1.442
   Buy 700,000 pounds to purchase 20 cars
   Cost in dollars: 700,000($1.442) = $1,009,400
Futures market: December pound contract is at $1.4375
   Price per contract: 62,500($1.4375) = $89,843.75
Sell 11 contracts

Results

Profit on spot position: $914,200 − $1,009,400 = − $95,200
Profit on futures transaction: 11($89,843.75 − $79,875) = $109,656.25
Net profit: $109,656.25 − $95,200 = $14,456.25

cars. The actual car price in pounds is fixed at 35,000, but the price of pounds necessary for purchasing the car may fluctuate. Of course, the car dealer might get lucky and have the pound weaken, which will make the cars less expensive. The dealer does not want to take the chance, however, and decides to hedge in the foreign currency futures market.

Since the pounds will be paid in November, the dealer uses the December contract currently priced at $1.278. At 62,500 pounds each, the price of one contract is £62,500($1.278) = $79,875. The dealer is attempting to hedge pounds worth 20(35,000)($1.3060) = $914,200 with contracts priced at $79,875 each. Thus, the number of contracts is

$$\$914,200/\$79,875 = 11.4.$$

The dealer's concern is that the pound will rise. To profit if that occurs, the dealer must take a long position in pound futures. Thus, the dealer buys 11 contracts. The result of the hedge is shown in Table 13.4.

On November 1, the spot rate is at $1.442. This means that the dealer will have to pay £35,000($1.442) = $50,470 per car, or $1,009,400 overall, which is

$95,200 more. However, the pound futures price increased to $1.4375, or £62,500($1.4375) = $89,843.75 per contract. For 11 contracts, the profit is $109,656.25. The futures contract covered all of the cars' additional cost caused by the increase in the pound's value and left a profit of $14,456.25.

As long as the pound spot and futures rates move in the same direction, the hedge will be successful in reducing some of the loss in the spot market. Had the pound weakened, there would have been a loss in the futures market that would have offset some or all of the gain in the spot market.

A Short Hedge With Foreign Currency Futures

A short hedge involves a short position in futures and is designed to protect against a decrease in the foreign currency's value. Consider the following situation. On June 29, a multinational firm with a British subsidiary decides to transfer £10 million from an account at a London bank to an account at a New York bank. At a current spot rate of $1.357, the £10 million are now worth 10,000,000($1.357) = $13,570,000. However, the transfer cannot be made until September 28. During the next three months, the firm is exposed to the risk of the pound depreciating, which would result in fewer dollars upon conversion in September. The firm decides to protect its long position in pounds by selling a pound futures contract.

The nearest expiring contract after September 28 was the December contract.[6] The December contract is priced at $1.375. At 62,500 pounds, the contract price is £62,500($1.375) = $85,937.50. This hedge will require $13,570,000/$85,937.50 = 157.91, or 158 contracts. The outcome is shown in Table 13.5.

On September 28, the spot rate is $1.2375. This results in a conversion of the £10 million to $12,375,000, a loss of $1,195,000. However, the futures price was $1.238 and the futures profit was $1,352,875. The futures profit recovered all of the pounds' loss in value and left a profit of $157,875.

The hedging effectiveness of foreign currency futures has been verified in studies by Hill and Schneeweis (1982), Grammatikos and Saunders (1983), and Herbst, Kare, and Caples (1989). Chang and Shanker (1986) and Ahmadi, Sharp, and Walther (1986) compared the hedging effectiveness of currency futures and options. Though they claim futures may be better, there are nonetheless some advantages of using options. We now turn to some option strategies.

Buy a Foreign Currency Call

Following the notation used in Chapters 5 and 6, the profit from a single foreign currency call held to expiration is

$$\Pi = \text{Max}(0, S_T - E) - C.$$

---

[6]Since the time of this example, the IMM has added an October contract that could be used.

TABLE 13.5
A Short Hedge with Foreign Currency Futures

Scenario: On June 29, a multinational firm with a British subsidiary decides it will need to transfer 10 million pounds from an account in London to an account with a New York bank. The transfer will be made on September 28. The firm is concerned that over the next two months the pound will weaken.

June 29
Spot market: Current exchange rate is $1.357 per pound
   Amount in dollars: 10,000,000($1.357) = $13,570,000
Futures market: December pound contract is at $1.375
   Price per contract: 62,500($1.375) = $85,937.50
Sell 158 contracts

September 28
Spot market: Spot rate is $1.2375
   Convert 10 million pounds to dollars: 10,000,000($1.2375) = $12,375,000
Futures market: December pound contract is at $1.238
   Price per contract: 62,500($1.238) = $77,375
Buy 158 contracts

Results
Profit on spot position: $12,375,000 – $13,570,000 = – $1,195,000
Profit on futures transaction: –158($77,375 – $85,937.50) = $1,352,875
Net profit: $1,352,875 – $1,195,000 = $157,875

Just as we did in Chapter 5, we will look at the outcomes in both cases, $S_T \leq E$ and $S_T > E$, and the breakeven spot rates at expiration. However, the results are the same as they were for equity calls:

$$\Pi = -C \qquad \text{if } S_T \leq E$$
$$\Pi = S_T - E - C \qquad \text{if } S_T > E.$$

The breakeven spot rate at expiration is $E + C$.

Consider the December 140 British pound call on the Philadelphia Stock Exchange on September 26 of a particular year. One contract is for £31,250. The call costs 5.10 cents per pound. Figure 13.7 illustrates the profit graph.

Suppose that at expiration the exchange rate is $1.50. Then the pounds are worth £31,250($1.50 – $1.40) = $3,125. The profit is $3,125 less the cost of the option, £31,250($0.051) = $1,593.75, or = $1,531.25. If the spot rate ends up below $1.40, the call will expire worthless and the loss will be the option's cost, $1,593.75. To reach breakeven, the spot rate must be at least $1.40 + $.051 = $1.451.

When analyzing equity options, we looked at the factors affecting the choice of exercise price and the length of the holding period. We shall not discuss those

FIGURE 13.7
Buy Foreign Currency Call

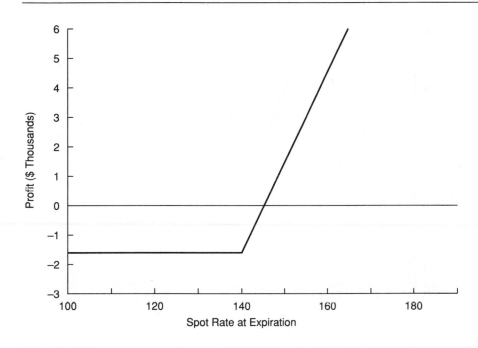

factors here; the same principles for equity options apply to foreign currency options. In addition, we shall omit a direct discussion of writing foreign currency options, as the principles are similar to those for writing equity options.

Buy a Foreign Currency Put

The profit from the purchase of a single foreign currency put held to expiration is

$$\Pi = \text{Max}(0, E - S_T) - P.$$

This is, of course, the same as the profit for an equity put. The outcomes for the two cases are

$$\Pi = -P \qquad \text{if } S_T \geq E$$
$$\Pi = E - S_T - P \quad \text{if } S_T < E.$$

The breakeven spot rate at expiration is $E - P$.

As an example, consider the December 145 British pound put on the Philadelphia Stock Exchange on September 26 of a particular year. The cost of the put is 2.5 cents. Figure 13.8 illustrates the performance of the strategy.

FIGURE 13.8

Buy Foreign Currency Put

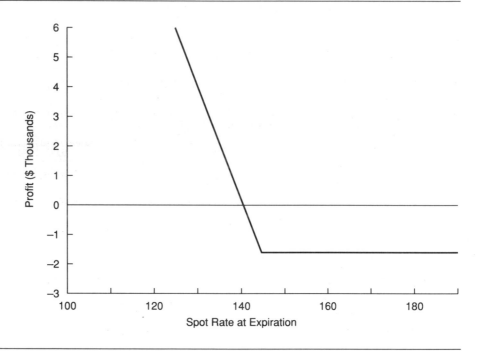

Suppose the spot rate at expiration is 138. Then the puts are worth 31,250($1.45 − $1.38) = $2,187.50. You paid 2.5 cents per put, or 31,250($.025) = $781.25. Thus, the net profit is $1,406.25. If the spot rate at expiration exceeds 145, the put will expire worthless and the strategy will lose the premium, $781.25. The breakeven spot rate is 145 − 2.5 = 142.5.

A Foreign Currency Option Hedge

Foreign currency futures clearly are a useful tool for managing exchange rate risk. Lest we leave the impression that foreign currency options are exclusively for speculation, we should look at an interesting hedging application using foreign currency options.

In some situations, one does not know for certain whether one will enter into a foreign currency transaction at a future date. For example, suppose an American firm is making a bid on a project. If it wins the bid, the foreign firm or government will pay the American firm in the foreign currency. A forward or futures contract will hedge the risk of a change in the exchange rate. Suppose, however, that the bid is awarded to another firm. This means the American firm will not receive the foreign currency. Had a forward or futures contract been used, the hedger either

TABLE 13.6

Comparison of a Foreign Currency Forward/Futures Hedge and an Option Hedge

Assumption: A firm is bidding on a construction project. If the bid is successful, payment will be made in a fixed number of British pounds. The table below indicates the outcome from the forward, futures, or option contract but does not consider the profit from the construction project itself.

Outcome of Bid	No Hedge	Short Forward or Futures Hedge	Option Hedge (Buy Put)
Successful:			
Pound increases	Gain on pound	Gain on pound reduced by hedge Small profit or loss	Put expires Premium lost
Pound decreases	Loss on pound	Loss on pound reduced by hedge Small profit or loss	Loss on pound reduced by exercise of put. Small profit or loss
Unsuccessful:			
Pound increases	No effect	Potentially large loss on pound	Put expires Premium lost
Pound decreases	No effect	Potentially large gain on pound	Potentially large gain on pound by exercise of put

would have a short position in the contract or, if it expired, would have to deliver the currency itself. This means the firm will be exposed to the risk of an increase in the exchange rate. An option can be used to avoid this problem.

For example, suppose an American firm is bidding for a contract to construct a large sports complex in London. The bid must be submitted in British pounds. The firm plans to make a bid of £25 million. At the current spot exchange rate of $1.437, the bid in dollars is £25,000,000($1.437) = $35,925,000. Once the bid is submitted, the firm must be prepared to accept £25 million if the bid is successful. Because it is an American firm, it will convert the pounds into dollars at whatever rate prevails on the date payment is made. If the pound weakens, the firm will effectively receive fewer dollars. To simplify the example somewhat, we shall assume the payment will be made as soon as the decision is made as to which firm is awarded the construction contract.

Table 13.6 summarizes the possible outcomes and compares the general results for a forward or futures hedge with those for an option hedge. The option would be a put, because the firm would need to protect itself against a decline in the pound's value.

If the bid is successful and the pound increases, the firm will receive the pounds, which now are valued at more dollars per pound. However, the forward or futures hedge will reduce this gain, because the hedge will be a short position. If the option is used, the put will expire worthless.

If the bid is successful and the pound decreases, the forward or futures hedge will reduce the loss caused by the decline in the pound's value. However, the option will also reduce the loss on the pound.

If the bid is unsuccessful and the pound increases, the forward or futures hedge will result in a potentially large speculative loss. This is because the firm will not receive the pounds if the bid fails but will have a short position in futures. If the option hedge is used, the put will expire worthless. The firm will have lost money—the premium on the put—but the amount lost will be less than it would have been with the futures hedge.

If the bid is unsuccessful and the pound decreases, the forward or futures hedge will become a speculative transaction. A potentially substantial profit will be earned, because the firm will be short futures and will not receive the pounds as a result of the failure to win the bid. If the option hedge is used, the put's exercise will result in a potentially large profit on the put.[7]

The option hedge is most beneficial when the bid is unsuccessful. Because the firm does not receive the pounds, the futures position generates a potentially large profit or loss. The option, however, can generate a large profit if the pound declines; if the pound rises, the loss will be limited to the premium. Of course, the option hedge requires payment of the option premium, while the futures hedge requires the initial margin deposit plus the margin calls from marking to market. Neither type of hedge dominates the other, but each has its merits.

Let us now look at some specific outcomes. The firm needs to hedge about $35 million of pounds. Each option contract is for £31,250, so let the firm use £25,000,000/£31,250 = 800 contracts. The premium for a put with an exercise price of 140 is 2.5 cents per pound. Thus, the price of a contract is £31,250($.025) = $781.25, and the total premium is $781.25(800) = $625,000. The current spot rate is $1.437, so the bid is effectively $35,925,000.

We shall look at four outcomes:

1. The bid is successful, and the pound increases to $1.48.
2. The bid is successful, and the pound decreases to $1.38.
3. The bid is unsuccessful, and the pound increases to $1.48.
4. The bid is unsuccessful, and the pound decreases to $1.38.

As a point of comparison, we shall also look at a futures hedge. Let the futures price be $1.424, meaning that one contract is priced at £62,500($1.424) = $89,000.

---

[7]Technically, we have not specified how low the pound goes, but we assume it is lower than the exercise price. There will be a profit only if the spot rate at expiration is less than the exercise price by the amount of the premium.

Since each contract is for £62,500, the firm will sell 400 contracts.[8] We assume the futures expires when the hedge is terminated.

In the first outcome, the firm wins the bid and receives £25 million, which is converted to £25,000,000($1.48) = $37,000,000. The puts expire out-of-the-money. Subtracting the cost of the puts of $625,000 leaves a net gain of $36,375,000. If the futures is used, the firm effectively sells the pounds for the futures price of $1.424, giving it $35,600,000.

In the second outcome, the firm wins the bid and exercises the puts, thus converting the currency at a rate of $1.40. Thus, it receives £25,000,000($1.40) = $35,000,000. Subtracting the cost of the puts leaves a net gain of $34,375,000. As in the first outcome, the futures hedge would have left the firm with $35,600,000.

In the third outcome, the firm loses the bid. At a spot rate of $1.48, the put expires worthless. The net effect is a loss of the put premium of $625,000. Had the futures hedge been used, the firm would have had to purchase £25 million pounds at $1.48 and deliver them for $1.424 per pound. This would have produced a loss of £25,000,000($1.48 − $1.424) = $1,400,000.

In the fourth case, the firm loses the bid and the put expires in-the-money. The firm exercises the put, purchasing £25 million at $1.38 for £25,000,000($1.38) = $34,500,000 and then selling the pounds at $1.40 for £25,000,000($1.40) = $35,000,000. Subtracting the cost of the insurance leaves a net loss of $125,000. Had the futures been used, the firm would have purchased the pounds for $1.38 and delivered them, receiving $1.424 for a gain of £25,000,000($1.424 − $1.38) = $1,100,000.

If futures were used and the firm loses the bid, the potential for a large loss or gain exists. Of course, the firm could choose not to bid, but this is unlikely because bidding on contracts is the nature of the construction business. The firm could choose not to hedge, but it could win the bid and lose dollars if the pound falls significantly. The option hedge provides an alternative that will be attractive to some firms, while the futures hedge will be better for others. The differences in their expectations and willingness to take exchange rate risk will determine whether they use options or futures.

Other Techniques for Managing Foreign Exchange Risk

As we saw in previous chapters, a variety of techniques can be used to manage risk. In this chapter, we have talked about currency forwards, futures, and options; however, there are a number of other, related ways to manage foreign exchange risk. We shall briefly look at a few here.

OTHER FOREIGN CURRENCY OPTIONS AND RELATED INSTRUMENTS In Chapter 12, we examined options on futures. There is also an active market for

---

[8]In both cases, we simply determined the number of contracts by dividing the contract size, in pounds, into the total number of pounds hedged. In practice, one might wish to obtain a more accurate hedge ratio, as was done in Chapters 4 and 10.

foreign currency options on futures at the Index and Option Market of the Chicago Mercantile Exchange. In fact, as we saw in Chapter 12, some of the foreign currency options on futures are the most active contracts. This is partially due to the fact that extremely active foreign currency futures markets operate side by side with the options.

There really is no need to spend time on the principles of pricing and examples of hedging. Most of these were well covered in Chapter 12 and require little, if any, adaptation to apply them to foreign currency options on futures. The Black model also can be used to price these instruments, recognizing, of course, that that model prices a European option. The Barone-Adesi/Whaley model, discussed in Appendix 4C for stocks and Appendix 12C for options on futures, can be used just as it is in Appendix 12C. We simply set the cost of carry to zero by letting the dividend (or foreign interest rate) be represented by the risk-free rate and insert the futures price in place of the stock price.

One increasingly popular instrument in foreign currency hedges is the over-the-counter option. We have briefly mentioned over-the-counter options, which preceded the days of the Chicago Board Options Exchange. These instruments have made a comeback, particularly in the foreign exchange arena. In fact, they have become the most popular type of hedging vehicle for corporations with foreign exchange risk.

An over-the-counter, or OTC, option is written by a bank or dealer firm and tailored to the specific needs of the hedger. For example, our firm that was bidding on a construction project in England might have chosen to obtain its put option from the OTC dealer market rather than from the Philadelphia Stock Exchange's listed options market. That way the hedge could be tailored with the exact exercise price and expiration date the firm needs. In addition, the listed options market for European options on foreign currencies is fairly thin. Thus, the firm might prefer to obtain a European option from a dealer, thus avoiding paying the premium for early exercise, which it would not use. Of course, OTC options, being tailored to buyers, have some disadvantages. They are more costly because they are specialized and the firms that write the options are then exposed themselves and must do some hedging. Moreover, the OTC options essentially have no liquidity, so the firms typically will be unable to offset their positions by selling the options back in the market.

In Chapter 14, we shall examine caps and floors. A *cap* establishes a maximum interest rate that a borrowing firm would pay, while a *floor* creates a minimum on the rate a lending firm would receive. In a similar manner, a firm could create caps and collars on foreign currencies. A firm that is short a foreign currency and thus would be harmed if the currency strengthened could buy a cap from a dealer firm. Likewise, a firm that is long a foreign currency and would be hurt if the currency weakened might buy a floor from a dealer firm. We shall learn more about these strategies in Chapter 14.

CURRENCY SWAPS   In Chapter 14, we shall cover interest rate swaps. Here we shall briefly examine a similar arrangement called a *currency swap*. In a currency swap, one firm borrows in one currency but needs to borrow in another. It goes to a swap dealer, which matches it with another firm holding the opposite position. The swap dealer arranges for the two firms to exchange cash flows. Of course, a particular firm's needs might not always be matched with another firm with exactly the opposite needs; in that case, the swap dealer will attempt to bring in other firms or, if necessary, take an exposed position itself. When it does that, however, it usually will attempt to hedge its own risk in another market.

Let us look at a currency swap example, Alpine Ski Equipment, henceforth called "Alpine," is a Swiss manufacturer of ski equipment. It is a well-known borrower in Switzerland and can easily issue bonds at a favorable interest rate and at low issue costs in Switzerland. It plans a bond issue of SF2.8 million at 7.5 percent interest but actually needs the equivalent amount in dollars, $2 million, for some purchases of American raw materials. Southern Technology, an American firm, specializes in computer circuitry and is a well-known borrower in U.S. bond markets. It plans to issue $2 million in bonds at 10 percent interest in the United States, but it needs SF2.8 million for some purchases of Swiss materials. Both firms go to a swap dealer.

The transaction is best understood by observing Figure 13.9. At the onset of the transaction, Alpine issues the bonds and receives SF2.8 million from the bondholders. It pays this to the swap dealer, which passes it on through to Southern. Southern, in turn, issues its bonds and receives $2 million from its bondholders, which it then sends to the swap dealer, which passes it through to Alpine. The net effect at the onset is that Alpine has received the $2 million it needs and Southern has received the SF2.8 million it requires.

Each year thereafter, interest payments are made. The swap dealer arranges for Alpine to pay interest on the $2 million at 9.75 percent and for Southern to pay interest on the SF2.8 million at 10 percent. Thus, Alpine pays the dealer (.0975)($2 million) = $0.195 million. The dealer, however, passes on $0.2 million to Southern, which then uses that money to pay the interest on its bonds. Southern, in turn, pays (.08)(SF2.8 million) = SF0.224 million to the dealer, which passes on SF0.21 million to Alpine, which uses it to make the interest payments to its bondholders. Note that the dealer nets an annual gain on the Swiss francs of .014 million, or SF39,200, and nets a loss on dollars of $0.005, or $10,000. Thus, the dealer, assuming it operates in dollars, takes a loss on the dollars and is exposed to the risk of fluctuations in the exchange rate at which it will convert the 39,200 in Swiss francs it receives. However, it can reduce and perhaps eliminate that risk with some hedging of its own.

Of course, the dealer might structure the interest payments so that it will face little or no exposure, but it must offer rates that will be attractive to the borrowing firms. In addition, the swap dealer is exposed to the credit risk that one of the firms will default.

At the maturity date, Alpine pays $2 million to the swap dealer, which passes on the $2 million to Southern, which uses it to pay off its American bonds. Southern pays SF2.8 million to the swap dealer, which passes it on to Alpine, which uses it to pay off its Swiss bonds.

The net effect is that Alpine converted its SF2.8 million bond issue at 7.5 percent interest to a $2 million bond issue at 9.75 percent interest. Southern

FIGURE 13.9

Example of a Currency Swap

Scenario: Alpine, a Swiss firm, issues SF2.8 million of bonds at 7.5 percent interest and needs $2 million. Southern, an American firm, issues $2 million of bonds at 10 percent interest and needs SF2.8 million. The firms arrange a currency swap through a swap dealer.

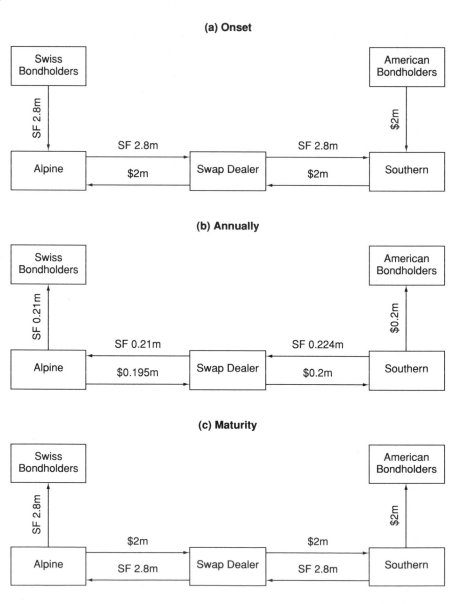

(a) Onset

(b) Annually

(c) Maturity

converted its $2 million bond issue at 10 percent interest to an SF2.8 million bond issue at 8 percent interest. The swap dealer profits off of the spread between interest payments received and interest payments made. It might also have incurred some hedging costs on its exposure to the Swiss francs.

It is helpful to recognize that the transaction is a series of forward contracts. For example, let us consider the final principal repayment. Alpine has promised to pay $2 million at maturity and will receive SF2.8 million. Thus, it has effectively taken out a long forward contract to buy SF2.8 million for $2 million, a forward price of $0.71/SF. Suppose the bonds have a ten-year maturity. Now, after four years, the price of a six-year forward contract to buy Swiss francs is, say, $0.60. The Swiss franc has weakened, so the long forward position should have lost value from its original value of zero.

Let the Swiss risk-free rate be 5 percent. Recall from Chapter 9 that the value of a forward contract during its life is

$$(F_t - F)(1 + r)^{-(T-t)}.$$

Here F is the forward price when the contract was established, $0.71, and F_t is the new forward price for contracts expiring at the same time as the original contract (or in six years). F_t thus is $0.60. Hence, the value of the forward contract is

$$(\$0.60 - \$0.71)(1.05)^{-6} = -\$0.082.$$

The weakening Swiss franc causes a loss on the implicit forward position established by Alpine. In other words, the new forward price of $0.60 implies that the $2 million Alpine must pay out at expiration would cost it (1/$0.60)$2 million = SF3.3 million if it went ahead and locked in that rate now. It is assured of receiving SF2.8 million at expiration. Of course, the actual exchange rate at maturity is uncertain, so the outcome could be even worse.

For Southern, the situation is just the opposite: It has gained from the weakening Swiss franc. In addition, the risk exposure we examined here was only for the final principal repayment. Each interest payment is a forward contract as well and exposes the firms to risk, which they might elect to hedge with other instruments covered in this chapter.

This concludes our discussion of foreign currency instruments. We gave them only a brief overview, but, as we noted, most of the principles of options and futures pricing already covered apply to foreign currency instruments and can easily be adapted to them. Some of the end-of-chapter problems ask you to do some of these applications.

Summary

This chapter examined foreign currency options and futures. We saw that understanding foreign currency options and futures requires an awareness of the special characteristics of foreign currency spot and forward markets. We observed how interest rate parity is the foreign currency futures counterpart of the cost of carry model. We examined several basic principles for pricing foreign currency options and found that they differ only slightly from those for equity options. In particular, we saw that the Garman-Kohlhagen foreign currency option pricing model is merely a minor modification of the Black-Scholes model.

We saw that foreign currency hedge and speculative strategies are straightforward extensions of previous principles. We also observed an example of the advantage of a foreign currency option hedge. The option can be an effective hedging device when it is uncertain whether the hedger will need to take a position in the currency at a future date. Other instruments we examined were forward contracts, over-the-counter options, and currency swaps.

In Chapter 14 we shall continue to look at some new and exotic instruments, some popular trading strategies, and some controversial issues that are associated with futures and options markets.

Questions and Problems

1. Explain the difference between the forward and futures markets for foreign currency.

2. Discuss the differences between the use of options and futures (or forward) contracts in hedging foreign exchange risk.

3. On December 10 of a particular year, the deutsche mark exchange rate was $.3937 while the Swiss franc exchange rate was $.4710. The exchange rate for Swiss francs in terms of deutsche marks is 1.21, that is, DM1.21/SF. Explain how an arbitrageur could make a risk-free profit.

4. Suppose you are an analyst with a firm that specializes in following foreign markets and making investment strategy recommendations based on its perception of changing conditions in other countries. You observed the growing Japanese trade surplus with the United States in the 1980s. You believe, however, that during the upcoming six months the trade surplus figures will narrow. Your opinion is contrary to that of most other firms. You would like to recommend a strategy that will be profitable if you are correct. Suggest one option and one futures strategy, and justify your recommendations. Then discuss the risks of your strategies and ways to manage the risks so that your clients will not be wiped out if you are not as prescient as you think.

5. On October 15 of a particular year, the following information was available:

   Spot rate for deutsche marks: $.3746
   December futures rate for deutsche marks: $.3775 (expires on December 16)
   U.S. risk-free rate: 7.57 percent (simple)
   German risk-free rate: 4.21 percent (simple)

   Determine whether interest rate parity holds.

6. On December 9 of a particular year, the Philadelphia Stock Exchange January Swiss franc call option with an exercise price of 46 had a price of 1.63. The

January 46 put was at 14. The spot rate was 47.28. (All prices are in cents per Swiss franc.) The option expired on January 13. The U.S. risk-free rate was 7.1 percent, while the Swiss risk-free rate was 3.6 percent. Answer the following:

a. Determine the intrinsic value of the call.

b. Determine the lower bound of the call.

c. Determine the time value of the call.

d. Determine the intrinsic value of the put.

e. Determine the lower bound of the put.

f. Determine the time value of the put.

g. Determine whether put-call parity holds.

7. Use the Garman-Kohlhagen model to determine whether the Swiss franc call in problem 6 is correctly priced. Use .145 as the standard deviation of the logarithmic percentage change in the spot Swiss franc.

8. Differences would be expected in American and European call prices for foreign currency options. How is the relative level of interest rates in the two countries involved likely to affect the spread between European and American call prices?

9. On June 17 of a particular year, an American watch dealer decided to import 100,000 Swiss watches. Each watch costs SF225. The dealer would like to hedge against a change in the dollar/Swiss franc exchange rate. The spot rate was $.3881, and the September futures price was $.3907. Determine the outcome from the hedge if it was closed on August 16, when the spot rate was $.4434 and the futures price was $.4436.

10. On January 2 of a particular year, an American firm decided to close out its account at a Canadian bank on February 28. The firm expected to have 5 million Canadian dollars in the account at the time of the withdrawal. It would convert the funds to U.S. dollars and transfer them to a New York bank. The current spot exchange rate was $.7564. The March Canadian dollar futures contract was priced at $.7541. Determine the outcome of the hedge if on February 28 the spot rate was $.7207 and the futures rate was $.7220. (All prices are in U.S. dollars per Canadian dollar.)

For problems 11, 12, and 13, determine the profit for each of the following spot rates at expiration: 32, 34, 36, 38, 40, and 42. Construct a profit graph. Find the breakeven spot rate at expiration.

11. On December 9 of a particular year, the deutsche mark January 38 call was priced at 1.57 (cents per deutsche mark). Construct a simple long position in the call.

12. On December 9 of a particular year, the March 40 put was priced at .72 (cents per deutsche mark). Construct a simple long position in the put.

13. Use the information in problem 11 to construct a covered call. Assume the spot rate at the onset is 39.

14. Suppose it is December 9 and an American firm is bidding on a contract to sell microcomputers to the German government. German officials have stipulated that the bid be made in deutsche marks and the firm receiving the bid be paid in deutsche marks. The decision will be made in January. The firm decides to use deutsche mark options to hedge its position. The current spot rate is $.3945. The firm will bid 11.5 million marks and use the January 39 contract. The call price is $.0079, and the put price is $.0025. Which option, call or put, should the firm use? Why? Assume the day German officials will make their decision is the same day payment will be made. Also on that day, the option expires. Determine the cash flow to the firm under each of the following possible outcomes.

   a.   The firm wins the bid, and the spot rate is 43.

   b.   The firm wins the bid, and the spot rate is 38.

   c.   The firm loses the bid, and the spot rate is 43.

   d.   The firm loses the bid, and the spot rate is 38.

15. Suppose you are a swap dealer. A French firm arranges to borrow FF10,000,000 from a French bank for 90 days at 12 percent interest. It will make three monthly payments of FF100,000 and then repay the principal with the last interest payment. It wishes to convert the loan to a dollar loan of $2 million (based on the prevailing exchange rate of FF5/$). You find an American firm with a $2 million, three-month loan at 9.5 percent that needs the money in French francs. You arrange a swap in which the French firm will pay 11 percent in dollars and the American firm will pay 8.75 percent in French francs.

   a.   Construct the payment schedule for all the payments involved in the swap.

   b.   Determine the swap dealer's exposure.

   c.   From the perspective of the American firm, evaluate the loan repayment as a forward contract. Assume a risk-free interest rate in the United States of 7 percent. Determine the value of the forward contract halfway through the loan if the franc weakens to FF5.2/$.

16. (Concept Problem) Using the information in problem 11, rework the problem under the assumption that the call expires on January 20 and is closed out on December 31. Use .22 as the volatility, .05 as the U.S. interest rate, and .04 as the German interest rate.

17. (Concept Probem) You plan to buy 1,000 shares of stock of Swissair. The current price is SF950. The current exchange rate is $0.7254/SF. You are interested in speculating on the stock but do not wish to assume any currency risk. You plan to hold the position for six months. The appropriate futures contract currently is trading at $0.7250. Construct a hedge and evaluate how your investment will do if in six months the stock is at SF926.50, the spot exchange rate is $0.7301, and the futures price is $0.7295. The Swiss franc futures contract size is SF125,000. Determine the overall profit from the

transaction. Then break down the profit into the amount earned solely from the performance of the stock, the loss or gain from the currency change while holding the stock, and the loss or gain on the futures transaction.

References

Ahmadi, Hamid Z., Peter A. Sharp, and Carl H. Walther. "The Effectiveness of Futures and Options in Hedging Currency Risk." *Advances in Futures and Options Research* 1, part B (1986): 171–191.

Biger, Nahum, and John Hull. "The Valuation of Currency Options." *Financial Management* 13 (Spring 1983): 24–28.

Bodurtha, James N., and Georges R. Courtadon. "Efficiency Tests of the Foreign Currency Options Market." *The Journal of Finance* 13 (March 1986): 151–162.

Chang, Jack S. K., and Latha Shanker. "Hedging Effectiveness of Options and Currency Futures." *The Journal of Futures Markets* 6 (Summer 1986): 289–305.

Chicago Board of Trade. *Commodity Trading Manual*, Chapter 17. Chicago: Board of Trade of the City of Chicago, 1989.

Chicago Mercantile Exchange. "Understanding Futures in Foreign Exchange." Chicago: Chicago Mercantile Exchange.

Cornell, Bradford, and Mark Reinganum. "Forward and Futures Prices: Evidence from the Foreign Exchange Market." *The Journal of Finance* 36 (December 1981): 1035–1045.

Duffie, Darrell. *Futures Markets*, Chapter 7. Englewood Cliffs, N.J.: Prentice-Hall, 1989.

Gadkari, Vilas. "Relative Pricing of Currency Options: A Tutorial." *Advances in Futures and Options Research* 1, part A (1986): 227–245.

Garman, Mark B., and Steven W. Kohlhagen. "Foreign Currency Option Values." *Journal of International Money and Finance* 2 (1983): 231–237.

Giddy, Ian H. "The Foreign Exchange Option as a Hedging Tool." *Midland Corporate Finance Journal* 1 (Fall 1983): 32–42.

Giddy, Ian H. "Foreign Exchange Options." *The Journal of Futures Markets* 2 (1983): 143–166.

Goodman, Laurie S., Susan Ross, and Frederick Schmidt. "Are Foreign Currency Options Overvalued? The Early Experience of the Philadelphia Stock Exchange." *The Journal of Futures Markets* 5 (1985): 349–359.

Grabbe, J. Orlin. "The Pricing of Call and Put Options on Foreign Exchange." *Journal of International Money and Finance* 2 (1983): 239–253.

Grammatikos, Theoharry, and Anthony Saunders. "Stability and the Hedging Performance of Foreign Currency Futures." *The Journal of Futures Markets* 3 (Fall 1983): 295–305.

Herbst, A. F., D. D. Kare, and S. C. Caples. "Hedging Effectiveness and Minimum Risk Hedge Ratios in the Presence of Autocorrelation: Foreign Currency Futures." *The Journal of Futures Markets* 3 (1989): 185–197.

Hill, Joanne, and Thomas Schneeweis. "The Hedging Effectiveness of Foreign Currency Futures." *The Journal of Financial Research* 5 (Spring 1982): 95–104.

Hull, John. *Options, Futures, and other Derivative Securities*, Chapters 2, 6, 11. Englewood Cliffs, N.J.: Prentice-Hall, 1989.

Kolb, Robert W., Gerald D. Gay, and James V. Jordan. "Managing Foreign Interest Rate Risk." *The Journal of Futures Markets* 2 (1982): 151–158.

Leuthold, Raymond M., Joan C. Junkus, and Jean E. Cordier. *The Theory and Practice of Futures Markets*, Chapter 12. Englewood Cliffs, N.J.: Prentice-Hall, 1989.

McMillan, Lawrence G. *Options as a Strategic Investment*, 2d ed., Chapter 34. New York: New York Institute of Finance, 1986.

Philadelphia Stock Exchange. "Foreign Currency Options." Philadelphia: Philadelphia Stock Exchange.

Philadelphia Stock Exchange. "Understanding Foreign Currency Options." Philadelphia: Philadelphia Stock Exchange.

Powers, Mark J. *Inside the Financial Futures Market*, 2d ed., Chapters 22, 23. New York: Wiley, 1984.

Ritchen, Peter. *Options: Theory, Strategy, and Applications*, Chapter 15. Glenview, Ill.: Scott, Foresman, 1987.

Rothstein, Nancy H. *The Handbook of Financial Futures*, Chapter 12. New York: McGraw-Hill, 1984.

Schwarz, Edward W., Joanne M. Hill, and Thomas Schneeweis. *Financial Futures: Fundamentals, Strategies, and Applications*, Chapter 13. Homewood: Ill.: Irwin, 1986.

Shastri, Kuldeep, and Kishore Tandon. "On the Use of European Models to Price American Options on Foreign Currency." *The Journal of Futures Markets* 6 (Spring 1986a): 93–108.

Shastri, Kuldeep, and Kishore Tandon. "Options on Futures Contracts: A Comparison of European and American Pricing Models." *The Journal of Futures Markets* 6 (Winter 1986b): 593–618.

Shastri, Kuldeep, and Kishore Tandon. "Arbitrage Tests of the Efficiency of the Foreign Currency Options Markets." *Journal of International Money and Finance* 4 (December 1985): 455–468.

Siegel, Daniel R., and Diane F. Siegel. *Futures Markets*, Chapter 7. Hinsdale, Ill.: Dryden Press, 1990.

Teweles, Richard J., and Frank J. Jones. *The Futures Game: Who Wins? Who Loses? Why?*, Chapter 21. New York: McGraw-Hill, 1987.

Tucker, Alan L. "Empirical Tests of the Efficiency of the Currency Option Market." *The Journal of Financial Research* 8 (Winter 1985): 275–285.

appendix 13A

Foreign Currency Futures Contract Specifications[1]

These contracts trade on the International Monetary Market. Smaller versions trade on the MidAmerica Commodity Exchange.

- Delivery months: January, March, April, June, July, September, October, December, and current month
- Daily price limit: None, except at opening
- Last trading day: Second business day before third Wednesday of month
- First delivery day: Third Wednesday of month
- Trading hours: 7:20 a.m. to 2:00 p.m. (local time)

[1]Source: *Consensus* (any issue). This material is believed to be current as of early January 1991. Contract specifications can change, especially margins and daily price limits. Investors should consult the exchanges for the latest information.

Contract	Contract Size	Minimum Price Change	Margin (Initial/ Maintenance)[a]
Deutsche mark	125,000DM	$0.0001/DM = $12.50	$2,025/$1,500
Canadian dollar	100,000CD	$0.0001/CD = $10	$810/$600
Swiss franc	125,000SF	$0.0001/SF = $12.50	$2,025/$1,500
British pound	62,500BP	$0.0002/BP = $12.50	$2,025/$1,500
Japanese yen	12,500,000JY	$0.000001/JY = $12.50	$2,025/$1,500
Australian dollar	100,000AD	$0.0001/AD = $10	$1,350/$1,000

[a]Check with the exchange for spread and hedge margins, which usually are much lower than the speculative margins shown here.

appendix 13B

Foreign Currency Options Contract Specifications[1]

These contracts trade on the Philadelphia Stock Exchange and are available as both American and European options. All contracts have expirations on the March cycle plus the two near-term months. The last trading day is the Friday preceding the third Wednesday of the month. The trading hours are 7:00 p.m. through 2:30 p.m. the next day, Sunday through Thursday, Eastern daylight time. During standard time, the session begins at 6:00 p.m. The French franc is also listed but trades very inactively.

Contract	Contract Size	Exercise Price Increments	Minimum Price Change
British pound	31,250BP	$0.0250	$0.0001 = $3.125
Canadian dollar	50,000CD	$0.050	$0.0001 = $5.00
Deutsche mark	62,500DM	$0.050	$0.0001 = $6.25
Japanese yen	6,250,000JY	$0.050	$0.000001 = $6.25
Swiss franc	62,500SF	$0.050	$0.0001 = $6.25
Australian dollar	50,000AD	$0.0100	$0.0001 = $5

[1]Source: *Futures* and *The Wall Street Journal*. This material is believed to be correct as of January 1991. Contract specifications can change. Investors should consult the exchange for the latest information.

ADVANCED STRATEGIES AND CONTEMPORARY ISSUES IN FUTURES AND OPTIONS MARKETS

> *If one advances confidently in the direction of his dreams,*
> *and endeavors to live the life which he has imagined, he will*
> *meet with a success unexpected in common hours.*
> HENRY DAVID THOREAU, Walden Pond, The Conclusion, 1854

In Chapters 2 through 6, we covered the fundamentals of option pricing and strategies; in Chapters 7 through 11, we examined the fundamentals of futures pricing and strategies; and in Chapters 12 and 13, we saw some different types of futures and options instruments. Now we are ready to conclude this book by exploring some advanced topics. We shall look at some of the newer and more exotic strategies and instruments that are similar to options and futures.

One consequence of an increasingly active market for these types of instruments is that many investors feel threatened by them. As a result, the problems and concerns that confront the market today often are blamed on options and futures. In the latter part of the chapter, we shall look at several of these issues and the role options and futures play in them.

ADVANCED STRATEGIES

In recent years, there has been an increased interest in the investment objective of market timing. *Market timing* involves forecasting the direction of the market rather than the expected performance of individual securities. Its current popularity should not be surprising. The Capital Asset Pricing Model, which we discussed in Chapter 8, says that all investors should hold the market portfolio and diversify away individual security risk. However, because successful market timing would be evidence against market efficiency, the CAPM and the Efficient Market Hypothesis do not recommend market timing. However, that is not our concern here; we shall assume there are market timers (you may be one yourself) who, if their forecasts are correct, could benefit from using futures and options.

A more general form of market timing has arisen in recent years. This is called *asset allocation*. In asset allocation, the investor recognizes the existence of several broad asset classes such as domestic stocks, bonds, real estate, precious metals, and foreign stocks. Of course, there are more classes, but for now we shall stick to these five groups. The asset allocator tries to predict which of these asset classes will do well and which will do poorly and then allocates his or her money across them. For example, an unweighted allocation would be one-fifth of the money in each class. If the asset allocator predicted that foreign stocks would do better and U.S. stocks worse, an allocation of, say, one-fourth of the money in foreign stocks and 15 percent in U.S. stocks plus 20 percent in each of the other groups might be chosen. Of course, such moves are predicated on a belief that one can successfully predict how the asset classes will perform in relation to one another. However, there are other asset allocation strategies that do not presume predictive ability and simply attempt to find the combination that will maximize an investor's utility.

Asset allocation and market timing decisions require occassional, if not frequent, trading. Futures and options can be used to offset some of the costs of these trades. In this context, we shall illustrate how one can use futures to adjust a bond's duration and use futures and options to adjust a stock portfolio's beta.

Market Timing in the Bond Market with Futures

In Chapter 10, we showed how hedge ratios can be constructed using futures. The procedure essentially combines futures so that the overall investment is insensitive to interest rate changes. In effect, this changes the duration to zero. Suppose a market timer believes that interest rates will move in one direction or the other but a duration of zero may not be appropriate. If interest rates are expected to fall, the timer may wish to increase the duration; if rates are expected to rise, the timer may wish to decrease the duration but not necessarily reduce it to zero.

Suppose a portfolio of bonds has a face value of S and a duration of DUR_S. The futures contract has a duration of DUR_f and a price of f. The timer wishes to change the duration to DUR_T, which we shall call the *target duration*. One way to do this is to put more money in high duration bonds and less money in low duration bonds. However, this would incur transaction costs on the purchase and sale of at least two bonds. Futures can be used to adjust the duration easily and at lower transaction costs.

The number of futures needed to change the duration to DUR_T is

$$N_f = -\left(\frac{DUR_s - DUR_T}{DUR_f}\right)\left(\frac{S}{f}\right)\left(\frac{1+y_f}{1+y_s}\right),$$

where y_f is the yield implied by the futures price and y_s is the yield on the spot portfolio. Appendix 14A presents the derivation of this formula.

Notice how similar this formula is to that in Chapter 10. That formula was

$$N_f = -\left(\frac{DUR_s}{DUR_f}\right)\left(\frac{S}{f}\right)\left(\frac{1+y_s}{1+y_f}\right),$$

which reduces the interest sensitivity and duration to zero.[1] If the target duration were zero in our new formula, we would obtain the old formula. Thus, the new formula is a much more general restatement of the optimal hedge ratio, because it permits the duration to be adjusted to any chosen value. If the investor expected falling interest rates and wished to increase the duration, DUR_T would be larger than DUR_S. Then N_f would be positive and futures would be bought. This makes sense because adding futures to a long spot position should increase the risk. If the trader were bearish and wished to reduce the duration, DUR_T would be less than DUR_S and N_f would be negative, meaning that futures would be sold. This is so because an opposite position in futures should be required to reduce the risk.

As an example, let us rework the T-bond hedging example that appeared in Table 10.5 in Chapter 10. In that problem, on February 25 the portfolio manager held $1 million face value of the 11 7/8s bond maturing in about 19 years. The bond price is 101, and the bond will be sold on March 28. In Chapter 10, we feared an increase in interest rates and lowered the duration to zero by selling 16 futures contracts. Suppose, however, that we wanted to lower the duration from its present level of 7.83 to 4. This would make the portfolio less sensitive to interest rates, but not completely unaffected by them. In that way, if the forecast proved incorrect, the positive duration would still leave room to profit.

The futures price was $70,500, the duration of the futures was 7.20, and the implied yield on the futures was 14.92 percent. Thus, the number of futures needed to change the duration to 4 would be

$$N_f = -\left(\frac{7.83-4}{7.20}\right)\left(\frac{\$1,010,000}{\$70,500}\right)\left(\frac{1.1492}{1.1174}\right) = -7.84.$$

By rounding off, the portfolio manager should sell eight contracts. Recall from Chapter 10 that the bonds fell in price to 95 22/32, resulting in a loss of $53,125.

[1] We should note that strictly speaking, both of these formulas apply only to extremely short holding periods. Any increment of time or change in yield will require recalculation of the number of futures contracts, so the number of contracts will need adjustment throughout the holding period.

The futures price fell to 66 23/32. The profit on the futures transaction would be

$$-8(\$66{,}718.75 - \$70{,}500) = \$30{,}250.$$

Hence, the net effect is a loss of $22,875, which is 2.26 percent of the value of the portfolio.

To determine how close the outcome was to the desired outcome, we need to know the change in the yield on the bonds. On February 25, the yield on the spot bond was 11.74 percent; on March 28, the yield that corresponded to a price of 95 22/32 was 12.50 percent. Recall from Chapter 8 that the following formula expresses the relationship between the change in the yield and the percentage change in the bond price:

$$\frac{\Delta B}{B} = -DUR\left(\frac{\Delta y}{1+y}\right),$$

where B represents the bond price. With a duration reset to 4, the formula predicts that for a yield change of .1250 − .1174 = .0076, the percentage price change would be

$$\frac{\Delta B}{B} = -4\left(\frac{.0076}{1.1174}\right) = -.0272,$$

or 2.72 percent. The actual change was 2.26 percent. Without the futures position, the duration still would have been 7.83. Plugging into the formula gives a predicted percentage change in the bond price of

$$\frac{\Delta B}{B} = -7.83\left(\frac{.0076}{1.1174}\right) = -.0533,$$

or a loss of 5.33 percent. The actual loss without the hedge would have been predicted to be − $53,125/$1,010,000 = −.0526, or 5.26 percent.

This example illustrates how market timing, specifically the timing of interest rate changes, might be done with bonds and futures. In the stock market, a timer would want to adjust the beta using stock index futures or options.

Market Timing in the Stock Market with Futures

In the case of bonds, a market timer would want to adjust the duration. If the portfolio consisted of stocks, the market timer would adjust the beta. Recall that in Chapter 10, we looked at an example in which a portfolio manager sold stock index futures to eliminate the systematic risk. At a later date, the futures contracts were repurchased and the portfolio was returned to its previous level of systematic risk. The number of futures contracts was given by the formula

$$N_f = -\beta(S/f).$$

In some cases, a portfolio manager may wish to change the systematic risk but not eliminate it altogether. For example, if a portfolio manager believes the market is highly volatile, the portfolio beta could be lowered but not reduced to zero. This would enable the portfolio to profit if the market did move upward but would produce a smaller loss if the market moved down. At more optimistic times, the portfolio beta could be increased. In the absence of stock index futures (or options), changing the portfolio beta would require costly transactions in the individual stocks.

Assume we have a portfolio containing stock valued at S and N_f futures contracts. The return on the portfolio is given as r_{sf}, where

$$r_{sf} = \frac{\Delta S + N_f \Delta f}{S}.$$

The first term in the numerator, ΔS, is the change in the price of the stock. The second term, $N_f \Delta f$, is the number of contracts times the change in the price of the futures contract. The denominator, S, is the amount of money invested in the stock. The expected return on the portfolio, $E(r_{sf})$, is

$$E(r_{sf}) = \frac{E(\Delta S)}{S} + N_f \frac{E(\Delta f)}{S} = E(r_s) + \frac{N_f}{S} E(\Delta f),$$

where $E(r_s)$ is the expected return on the stock defined as $E(\Delta S)/S$ and $E(\Delta f)$ is the expected change in the price of the futures contract.

Recall from Chapter 8 that the Capital Asset Pricing Model gives the expected return on a stock as $r + [E(r_M) - r]\beta$. If the market is efficient, the investor's required return will equal the expected return. If the CAPM holds for stocks, it should also hold for stock index futures; however, it would be written as

$$\frac{E(\Delta f)}{f} = [E(r_M) - r]\beta_f = E(r_M) - r,$$

where β_f is the beta of the futures contract, assumed to be 1. Although in reality β_f will not be precisely equal to 1, it is sufficiently close that we shall assume it to keep the model simple. Note that this CAPM equation seems to be missing the term r from the right-hand side. The risk-free rate reflects the opportunity cost of money invested in the asset. Because the futures contract requires no initial outlay, there is no opportunity cost; thus, the r term is omitted.

The objective is to adjust the portfolio beta, β_s, and expected return, $E(r_{sf})$, to a more preferred level. Since the CAPM holds for the portfolio, we can write the relationship between expected return and beta as

$$E(r_{sf}) = r + [E(r_M) - r]\beta_T,$$

where β_T is the *target beta*, the desired risk level. Now we substitute for $E(r_s)$ and $E(\Delta f)$ and get

$$E(r_{sf}) = r + [E(r_M) - r]\beta_s + N_f(f/S)[E(r_M) - r].$$

Setting this equal to $r + [E(r_M) - r]\beta_T$ and solving for N_f gives

$$N_f = (S/f)(\beta_T - \beta_s).$$

This formula differs only slightly from the previous formula for N_f. In fact, that formula is but a special case of this one. For example, if the target beta is zero, the above formula reduces to $- (S/f)\beta_s$, where the negative sign means that you would sell N_f futures. This is the same formula we previously used to eliminate systematic risk.

When the manager wants to increase the beta, β_T will be greater than β_s and N_f will be positive. In that case, the manager will buy futures contracts. That makes sense, since the risk will increase. When the beta needs to be reduced, β_T will be less than β_s, and the manager should sell futures to reduce the risk.

As an example, suppose that on August 29 of a particular year you are holding a portfolio of stocks worth $3,783,225. The portfolio beta is .95. You expect the market as a whole to be bullish over the next three months. You would like to increase the beta to 1.25. Rather than shift funds out of low-beta stocks and into high-beta stocks, you decide to use stock index futures. Table 14.1 shows the results.

The December S&P 500 futures contract is priced at 189.90. With a multiplier of $500, the contract price is actually $94,950. The target beta is 1.25. The number of contracts you should trade is

$$N_f = (\$3,783,225/\$94,950)(1.25 - .95) = 11.95.$$

So, you will buy 12 contracts.

The lower half of Table 14.1 presents the outcome. The market was indeed bullish, and the portfolio value on November 29 was $4,161,500. The futures price was 202.40 for a contract price of $101,200. The portfolio showed a profit of $378,275 and the 12 futures contracts produced a profit of $75,000, for a total profit of $453,275, not counting any dividends on the stocks. This was a return of about 12 percent compared to the 10 percent that would have been earned without the futures contract.

The futures contract succeeded in increasing the portfolio's systematic risk. As long as futures and spot prices move together, the strategy will work. However, there are no guarantees that the beta will increase to the exact level desired. In this example, the futures price increased by 6.6 percent while the portfolio itself increased by 10 percent. Thus, the portfolio beta without the futures was 10/6.6 = 1.51. With the futures, the portfolio return was 12 percent. Therefore, the

TABLE 14.1
Adjusting Beta with Stock Index Futures

Scenario: On August 29 of a particular year, you are holding a portfolio of stocks worth $3,783,225. The portfolio beta is .95. You expect the stock market as a whole to appreciate substantially over the next three months, and you want to increase the portfolio beta to 1.25. You could buy and sell shares in the securities, but this would incur high transaction costs and later the portfolio beta would need to be adjusted back to .95. You decide to buy stock index futures to temporarily increase the portfolio's systematic risk. The prices, number of shares, and betas are given below.

Stock	Price (8/29)	Number of Shares	Value	Weight	Beta
Beneficial Corp.	40.500	11,350	$459,675.00	.122	.95
Cummins Engine	64.500	10,950	706,275.00	.187	1.10
Gillette	62.000	12,400	768,800.00	.203	.85
K Mart	33.000	5,500	181,500.00	.048	1.15
Boeing	49.000	4,600	225,400.00	.059	1.15
W. R. Grace	42.625	6,750	287,718.75	.076	1.00
Eli Lilly	87.375	11,400	996,075.00	.263	.85
Parker Pen	20.625	7,650	157,781.25	.042	.75
Total value			$3,783,225.00		

Portfolio beta: .122(.95) + .187(1.10) + .203(.85) + .048(1.15) + .059(1.15) + .076(1.00) + .263(.85) + .042(.75) = .95
S&P 500 December futures price: 189.90
Price per contract: 189.90($500) = $94,950
$N_f = (\$3,783,225/\$94,950)(1.25 - .95) = 11.95$
Buy 12 contracts

Results

Stock	Price (11/29)	Value
Beneficial Corp.	45.125	$512,168.75
Cummins Engine	66.750	730,912.50
Gillette	69.875	866,450.00
K Mart	35.125	193,187.50
Boeing	49.125	225,975.00
W. R. Grace	40.750	275,062.50
Eli Lilly	103.750	1,182,750.00
Parker Pen	22.875	174,993.75
Total value		$4,161,500.00

S&P 500 December futures price: 202.40
Price per contract: 202.40($500) = $101,200
Profit on portfolio: $4,161,500 − $3,783,225 = $378,275
Profit on futures: 12($101,200 − $94,950) = $75,000
Net profit on transaction: $378,275 + $75,000 = $453,275

actual beta was $12/6.6 = 1.82.$[2] This confirms a point we made in Chapter 8: Betas are unstable.

Market Timing in the Stock Market with Options

Because stock index options also move with the market as a whole, it is possible to use them to adjust a portfolio's beta. Recall that the beta of a portfolio is the weighted average of the betas of its components. We want our portfolio beta to be the target beta, so let us specify that the target beta of a portfolio of stock and index options is as follows:

$$\beta_T = \beta_S w_S + \beta_C(1 - w_S).$$

Here w_S is the weight associated with the stock, which is the percentage of our wealth invested in the stock. Since the remaining wealth is invested in the call (or it could be a put), its weight is $1 - w_S$. The beta of the call is β_C. If V is the overall value of the portfolio, then $w_S = S/V$, where $V = S + N_C C$, N_C is the number of calls, and the weight of the calls, $1 - w_S$, is $N_C C/V$. If we substitute these values into the above equation and solve for N_C, we get

$$N_C = -\frac{V(\beta_T - \beta_S)}{C(\beta_S - \beta_C)}.$$

Without proving it, we shall use the fact that the formula for the beta of a call is

$$\beta_C = N(d_1)S/C.$$

Now let us rework the previous example in which we used stock index futures to change the portfolio beta. The following additional information is needed: The risk-free rate is .06, the dividend yield is .043, the call has an exercise price of 190 and an expiration in 93 days, the call price is 5.98, $N(d_1)$ is .5135, and the S&P 500 spot index is at 189.08. Thus, the beta of the call is

$$\beta_C = .5135(189.08/5.98) = 16.24.$$

Given that one call costs $598, the number of calls required is

$$N_C = -\frac{\$3,783,225(1.25 - .95)}{598(.95 - 16.24)} = 124.12.$$

The portfolio manager should buy 124 calls to increase the risk. The call expires on the date on which the portfolio will be liquidated. On that day, the S&P 500 was at 202.40; thus, the call will be worth 12.40 and the overall value of the calls

---

[2]These betas are not exactly the correct ones. A portion of the return would have reflected the risk-free rate. Nonetheless, the example illustrates the risk of beta instability.

will be $12.40(100)(124) = $153,760. Thus, the portfolio's overall value will be $378,275 + $153,760 = $532,035.

While the strategy worked quite well in this example, it should be noted that the call beta is never constant. Thus, while 124 calls is the correct number at the beginning of the trade, this number will change constantly throughout the holding period. The reason for adjusting the number of calls is the same reason we had to adjust the number of calls in the binomial model: The call's sensitivity to the stock price, here reflected in its beta, constantly changes, and thus the number of calls must change accordingly.[3]

Arbitraging Stock Index Futures with Stock Index Options

Recall from Chapter 3 that we examined put-call parity, the relationship between put and call prices and the price of the underlying stock, the exercise price, the risk-free rate, and the time to expiration. We derived the equation by constructing a risk-free portfolio. Now we shall examine parity with puts, calls, and futures contracts. To keep things as simple as possible, we shall assume the risk-free rate is constant. This allows us to ignore marking to market and treat futures contracts as forward contracts. We assume the options are European.

The first step in constructing a risk-free portfolio is to recognize that a combination of a long call and a short put is equivalent to a futures contract. In fact, a long-call/short-put combination is called a *synthetic futures contract*. A risk-free portfolio would consist of a long futures contract and a short synthetic futures contract. Selling the synthetic futures contract requires selling a call and buying a put. The payoff at expiration from this portfolio is shown in Table 14.2.

The payoff from the portfolio is $E - f$ regardless of the spot price at expiration. Thus, the portfolio is riskless. The current value of the portfolio therefore should equal the present value of $E - f$. The portfolio's current value is the price of the long put minus the price of the short call. Of course, the futures contract has a value of zero. Thus,

$$P_e(S,T,E) - C_e(S,T,E) = (E-f)(1+r)^{-T}$$

or

$$C_e(S,T,E) - P_e(S,T,E) = (f-E)(1+r)^{-T}.$$

Notice that whether the put price exceeds the call price depends on whether the exercise price exceeds the futures price. If this relationship is violated, it may be possible to earn an arbitrage profit.

A good instrument for examining put-call-futures parity is the S&P 500 index options and futures. The options are European and trade on the CBOE, while the

---

[3]This is the same point we made in footnote 1 with regard to futures, but it is even more critical when using options.

TABLE 14.2
Put-Call-Futures Parity

Payoff from	Current Value	Payoffs from Portfolio Given Stock Price at Expiration	
		$S_T < E$	$S_T \geq E$
Long futures	0	$S_T - f$	$S_T - f$
Short call	$-C_e(S,T,E)$	0	$-(S_T - E)$
Long put	$P_e(S,T,E)$	$E - S_T$	0
		$E - f$	$E - f$

futures trade on the Chicago Mercantile Exchange. On September 26 of a particular year, the S&P 500 index was 232.23 and the December futures was at 231.95. The December 225 call was at 12, and the put was at 5.5. The expiration date was December 19, and the risk-free rate was 5.46 percent.

Since there are 84 days between September 26 and December 19, the time to expiration is 84/365 = .2301. The left-hand side of the put-call-futures parity equation is

$$C_e(S,T,E) - P_e(S,T,E) = 12 - 5.5 = 6.5.$$

The right-hand side is

$$(f - E)(1 + r)^{-T} = (231.95 - 225)(1.0546)^{-.2301} = 6.87.$$

Thus, the synthetic futures contract (long call and short put) is underpriced. An arbitrageur could buy the call for 12, sell the put for 5.5, and sell a futures contract. The payoff at expiration would be f − E, or 231.95 − 225 = 6.95. The present value of 6.95 is 6.87.

While transaction costs might consume the difference, let us first assume that they do not and that this difference can be captured with an arbitrage trnasaction. Since we have shown that the call price minus the put price is too low, we should buy the call and sell the put. This will cost 6.5. Suppose we borrow 6.5 at the risk-free rate of 5.46 percent for 84 days. Then at expiration, we know that the payoff should be the futures price, 231.95, minus the exercise price, 225, or 6.95 minus the principal and interest in our loan of $6.5(1.0546)^{-.2301} = 6.42$. This leaves a difference of .53. It is likely that this difference would not be sufficient to cover transaction costs.

Hedged Dividend Capture Strategy

Options give corporate investors an opportunity to take advantage of special tax status they receive. Because dividends paid by a corporation are not tax deductible, they are effectively taxed twice: once at the corporate level and again when the shareholders receive them. If a corporation owns shares in another corporation, the dividends are effectively taxed three times. To help offset this inequity, the tax laws permit corporations that own other corporations to exclude 70 percent of dividends received from taxable income. This creates an incentive for corporations to try to capture as much dividend income as possible. Many corporations thus buy stock in other corporations around the dates of dividend payments. However, the tax laws require that the stock be held for at least 46 days. Thus, ownership of the shares puts the firm at risk. To offset some of this risk, firms could write calls on the stock. However, their ability to do this is limited. The tax laws specify that if the firm takes an opposite position to offset the risk, the dividend exclusion is lost.

Like many tax laws, there are loopholes. For a near perfect hedge, the call needs to be deep-in-the-money.[4] However, if it is too deep-in-the-money, the call will behave identically to the stock and the dividend exclusion could be forfeited. It has been determined that a qualifying call would probably need an exercise price of at least 80 percent of the stock price and be the call that is the least in-the-money. Also, the call should be as close as possible to expiration to maximize the probability of its being in-the-money at expiration. However, the law requires that the call have at least 30 days remaining. Despite this maze of restrictions, however, these requirements are not necessarily difficult to meet, as we shall show in the following example.

On August 24, a firm decides to try a hedged dividend capture with Eastman Kodak stock, which currently is selling for $38.875. The call that is the least in-the-money has an exercise price of 35 and is selling at 4. Note that the exercise price is more than 80 percent of the stock price. The call expires on October 19, 56 days later. Kodak is scheduled to pay a dividend of $0.89 on October 1. The risk-free rate of interest is 7.92 percent.

Suppose that at expiration the call is in-the-money, that is, the stock is selling for at least $35. It does not matter what price the stock is. Recall that at expiration, an in-the-money covered call will result in selling the stock at the exercise price to the holder of the call. Since we wrote the call for 4, the effective selling price of the stock is 35 + 4 = 39, giving us a profit of $39 – $38.875 = $0.125 on the stock. We received a dividend on October 1 of $0.89. Using 34 percent as the corporate tax rate, we shall owe $0.125(.34) = $0.0425 in taxes on the gain from the sale of the stock and .3($0.89)(.34) = $0.0907 in taxes on the dividend of $0.89 received.

---

[4]Recall that the delta of a deep-in-the-money call will be close to 1. Thus, one share of stock and one short call will be a near perfect hedge. As an alternative, the firm could buy $N(d_1)$ shares for each call written, as we illustrated in Chapter 4, and continuously adjust this ratio, but as a practical matter most firms simply hold one share per call.

Note that we pay taxes on only 30 percent of the dividend. Thus, the rate of return is[5]

$$\frac{0.125 + 0.89 - 0.0425 - 0.0907}{34.875} = .0253.$$

Note that the denominator is the amount we initially invested, 38.875, minus the premium on the call of 4. The annualized return is $(1.0253)^{365/56} - 1 = .1769$.

If the call ends up out-of-the-money at expiration, we will earn less. For example, let the stock end up at 32 at expiration. Then we have a profit of -2.875 on the stock and get a tax saving of $.34(\$2.875) = \$0.9775$, but we receive the dividend less the taxes paid on it. The return is

$$\frac{-2.875 + 0.9775 + 0.89 - 0.0907}{34.875} = -.0314,$$

which annualizes to $(1 - .0314)^{365/56} - 1 = -.1882$. Lower stock prices at expiration would produce lower returns.

One other possibility we must consider is that the call will be exercised shortly before the stock goes ex-dividend on September 4. If that happens, we will earn a profit on the stock of 0.125 less the taxes on it of 0.0425. Of course, we will not receive the dividend. Then the return will be

$$\frac{0.125 - 0.0425}{34.875} = .0024,$$

which annualizes to $(1.0024)^{365/11} - 1 = .0816$.

The returns shown here seem relatively high; however, this is due to the magnitude of the call premium. At the time of these prices, option premiums were high owing to unusual volatility in the market. This implies that the risk of such a position would be quite high. If stock prices fell substantially, the returns could be much lower. Thus, this strategy is in no way risk free and should not be undertaken without an appraisal of the attendant risks.

There have been empirical tests of the effectiveness of the hedged dividend capture strategy. Brown and Lummer (1986) achieved impressive returns in a test of writing calls on stocks owned. Zivney and Alderson (1986) also found excellent returns when the calls were written on index options. They claim that using index options produces better results because if the corporation holds a diversified portfolio of stocks, unsystematic risk is hedged while the index calls hedge the systematic risk.

---

[5]We are ignoring the slight effect of the interest earned on the reinvestment of the dividend for 18 days. Also, the taxes would not be due for awhile and thus would have a present value slightly lower than their full value.

Portfolio Insurance

The concept of insurance has been around for hundreds of years. Individuals and business firms routinely insure their lives and property against risk of loss. In recent years, more and more investors have been insuring their portfolios.

The idea of insuring a portfolio should not be new. In Chapter 5, we discussed how a put on a stock works like an insurance policy. The put establishes a minimum price at which the stock can be sold. If the market moves up, the put is not exercised, meaning that the insurance is not needed. In addition to puts, portfolios can be insured with calls, Treasury bills, and futures. Each type of portfolio insurance strategy establishes a minimum value for the portfolio.

The concept of portfolio insurance is more easily illustrated in the context of an option. However, option contracts that have the terms and conditions necessary for meeting the insured's needs are seldom available on organized exchanges. In many cases, however, futures contracts and Treasury bills can be used to accomplish the same effect. In this section, we shall illustrate the concept of portfolio insurance using stocks and puts and then calls and T-bills. Then we shall follow with illustrations of the more commonly employed portfolio insurance strategies, which use stocks and futures and then stocks and T-bills.

STOCK-PUT INSURANCE   Suppose we own a portfolio consisting of N_S shares of stock and N_P puts. The stock price is S, and the put price is P. The puts are European, and we assume no dividends on the stock. The value of the portfolio is

$$V = N_S S + N_P P.$$

Letting $N_S = N_P$ and calling this N, we have

$$N = \frac{V}{S + P}.$$

This tells us how many shares of stock and how many puts we can buy. At expiration the portfolio's value is

$$V_T = NS_T \qquad \qquad \text{if } S_T > E$$
$$V_T = NS_T + N(E - S_T) = NE \qquad \text{if } S_T \le E,$$

where S_T is the stock price when the put expires.

The worst possible outcome is that in which $S_T = 0$. Suppose we define V_{min} as the minimum value of V_T, which occurs when $S_T = 0$. Then $V_{min} = NE$ and, since N must also equal $V/(S + P)$,

$$V_{min} = \frac{EV}{S + P}.$$

This establishes the minimum insured value of the portfolio at expiration.

Let us illustrate how this works. Suppose that on September 26 the S&P 500 is at 232.23 and the December 265 S&P 500 put option is priced at $30.878. The option expires on December 19, which is 84 days away, so the time to expiration is 84/365 = .2301. The risk-free rate is 5.46 percent, stated as a simple annual rate or 5.32 percent continuously compounded. The standard deviation is .206.

Suppose we hold a diversified portfolio of stocks that replicates the S&P 500. The portfolio is worth $232,230, which is equivalent to 1,000 units of the index. Note that we cannot actually hold the index, but we hold a portfolio that is weighted exactly like it and is worth 1,000 times the index level.

The minimum insured level of the portfolio is

$$V_{min} = \frac{EV}{S+P}$$

$$= \frac{(265)(232,230)}{232.23 + 30.878}$$

$$= 233,900.$$

Thus, the minimum level at which we can insure the portfolio is $233,900. This means that if we own N shares and N puts, where

$$N = \frac{V}{S+P} = \frac{232,230}{232.23 + 30.88} = 882.64,$$

the minimum value of the portfolio on December 19 is $233,900. This is a guaranteed return of .0072 for 84 days, or

$$(1.0072)^{(365/84)} - 1 = .0317$$

per year. This figure must be below the risk-free rate or an arbitrage opportunity would be possible. After all, how could we guarantee a minimum return on a risky portfolio greater than the risk-free rate?

To keep the results as accurate as possible, assume we can buy fractional shares and puts. Thus, we buy 882.64 shares and 882.64 puts. Suppose that at expiration the S&P 500 index is at 275:

$$
\begin{aligned}
\text{Value of stock} &= 882.64(\$275) = \$242,726 \\
+\,\text{Value of puts} &= 882.64(\$0\,) \;\; = \underline{\hspace{1.5cm} 0} \\
\text{Total} & \qquad\qquad\quad = \$242,726.
\end{aligned}
$$

This exceeds the minimum value.

If at expiration the S&P 500 index is at 220,

$$\text{Value of stock} = 882.64(\$265) = \$233,900 \text{ (by exercising the puts).}$$

This is the minimum value derived earlier.

FIGURE 14.1
Insured Portfolio: Stock-Put

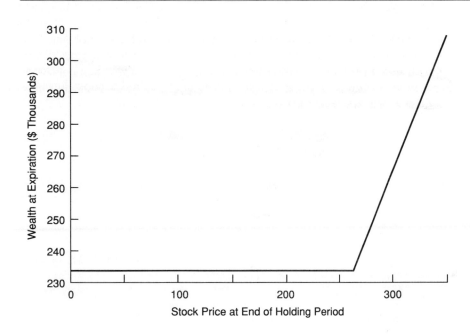

Figure 14.1 shows the value of the insured stock-put portfolio when the put expires. The exact minimum cannot be read from the graph but is mathematically equal to $233,900. The graph should look familiar. It is essentially the same as that of the protective put covered in Chapter 5. In this example, however, we are looking only at the value of the investor's position at expiration and not at the profit.

Like any form of insurance, portfolio insurance entails a cost. By *cost* we do not necessarily mean commissions, bid-ask spreads, and so on. These certainly are important, but the cost of portfolio insurance is the difference in the return of the insured portfolio and the return of the uninsured portfolio when the market goes up. In other words, it is the return that is given up in bull markets, in which the insurance was not needed. For example, when the S&P 500 ended up at 275, the insured portfolio was worth $242,726. Had the portfolio not been insured, it would have consisted of 1,000 shares valued at $275 each for a total value of $275,000. The cost thus is $32,274, or about 13.9 percent of the portfolio's original value. The difference between 100 percent and the cost of 13.9 percent, or 86.1 percent, is called the *upside capture*. It is the percentage of the uninsured return in a bull market that is earned by the insured portfolio. As Clark and Arnott (1987) point out, the loss in upside capture is a very important component of the cost of portfolio insurance. If the insurance is determined to be too costly, they show how the cost can be reduced by lowering the minimum value of the portfolio, insuring a smaller fraction of the assets, increasing the risk of the portfolio, or extending the holding period.

CALL–TREASURY BILL INSURANCE   An identical result can be obtained using calls and Treasury bills. This is sometimes referred to as a *fiduciary call*. Let us define B as the price of a Treasury bill and B_T as its face value when it matures. Suppose we own a portfolio of N_C calls priced at C and N_B Treasury bills. The portfolio's value when the call expires is

$$V_T = N_B B_T \qquad\qquad\qquad \text{if } S_T < E$$
$$V_T = N_C(S_T - E) + N_B B_T \quad \text{if } S_T \geq E.$$

The worst outcome occurs when $S_T = 0$; let us call that result V_{min}. Then

$$V_{min} = N_B B_T.$$

Thus,

$$N_B = \frac{V_{min}}{B_T}.$$

If we buy N_B Treasury bills, we can buy

$$N_C = \frac{V - N_B B}{C} \text{ calls.}$$

Without going through the algebraic details, it can be shown that N_C, the number of calls, will equal the number of shares of stock and puts from the previous example, in which we insured with stock and puts. Thus,

$$N_C = \frac{V}{S + P}.$$

In this example, the price of a European call with the assumed terms and conditions would be $1.33. We would need

$$N_B = \frac{\$233,900}{\$100} = 2,339 \text{ Treasury bills}$$

and 882.64 calls.

Suppose that at expiration the S&P 500 index is 275:

$$
\begin{array}{lll}
\text{Value of calls} & = 882.64(\$10) = \$ & 8,826 \\
\text{Value of T-bills} & = 2,339(\$100) = & 233,900 \\
\text{Total} & & = \$242,726
\end{array}
$$

This exceeds the minimum value.

If the S&P 500 is at 220,

$$
\begin{aligned}
\text{Value of calls} &= 882.64(\$0) &&= \$0 \\
\text{Value of T-bills} &= 2,339(\$100) &&= \underline{233,900} \\
\text{Total} & &&= \$233,900
\end{aligned}
$$

This equals the minimum value. Because these outcomes are the same as in the stock-put example, the cost of the insurance is also the same.

The value of this portfolio at expiration is shown in Figure 14.2. We see that the portfolio is insured at a minimum level of $233,900. In addition, the investor can profit if there is a strong bull market. This was also true of the stock-put portfolio. In fact, there is a correspondence between the call and T-bill portfolio and the stock-put portfolio. In Chapter 3, we learned that according to the put-call parity rule, a portfolio consisting of a call and a T-bill is equivalent to a stock and a put.

These examples illustrate how portfolios can be insured using options. Unfortunately, exchange-traded options seldom have the terms and conditions appropriate for meeting the insured's needs. For example, the options must be European and the expiration date must coincide with the investor's holding period. One alternative is for firms to write portfolio insurance that is tailored to the investor's situation. This is similar to what Lloyd's of London does in the area of property and casualty insurance. If someone has a specific need for coverage for which there is little demand, most insurance companies normally will not offer a policy to provide it. Lloyd's of London sometimes will write a policy designed specifically for the insured. For example, in 1980 NBC took out a policy with Lloyd's of London that protected it against a loss caused by a possible boycott or cancellation of the 1980 Summer Olympic games in Moscow. As it turned out, the United States did boycott the games and NBC collected on its policy.

Tailored portfolio insurance would work similarly except that a financial instititution would write the policy. The investment banking firm would offer European puts or calls that expire at the end of the investor's holding period and have the desired exercise prices. Because the terms are specialized, the insurance would be expensive. Many institutional investors with an ongoing need for such insurance have sought less expensive alternatives. One way to simulate portfolio insurance using stock index futures is dynamic hedging.

DYNAMIC HEDGING WITH STOCK INDEX FUTURES[*] A European put with the appropriate terms and conditions would be a means of insuring a portfolio. While such puts generally are not available, it is possible to replicate the behavior of the stock-put insured portfolio by continuously adjusting a portfolio of stocks and index futures. This technique usually is referred to as *dynamic hedging*. It involves selling a number of futures contracts such that the portfolio responds to

---

[*]This section requires the use of calculus.

FIGURE 14.2

Insured Portfolio: Call–T-Bill

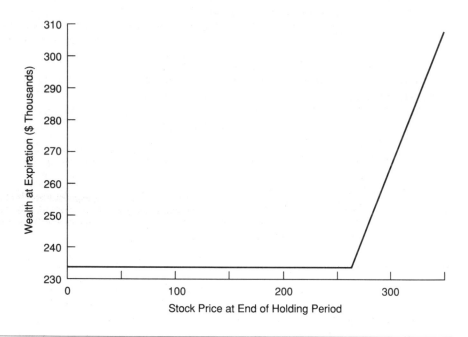

stock price movements the same way the stock-put insured portfolio would   respond.

The procedure for deriving the hedge ratio is presented in Appendix 14B. The solution is

$$N_f = \left[\left(\frac{V_{min}}{E} \right) \left(\frac{\partial C}{\partial S} \right) - \left(\frac{V}{S} \right) \right] e^{-rT}.$$

This gives the number of futures contracts. The hedger must also be sure to continuously adjust the number of futures contracts so that it always equals the value of N_f. As you can see, some of these variables will change as the stock price and time to expiration change.

Continuing with the same portfolio insurance example, we now need to know the value of $\partial C/\partial S$. From the Black-Scholes model of Chapter 4, $\partial C/\partial S = N(d_1)$. Here $N(d_1) = .122$. Plugging into the formula for N_f gives

$$N_f = \left[\left(\frac{233,900}{265} \right)(.122) - \left(\frac{232,230}{232.23} \right) \right] e^{-(.0532)(.2301)}$$

$$= -881.461.$$

We still need to make one adjustment. The actual futures price is 500 times the index, so we need only $-881.461/500 = -1.76$ contracts. We invest all of our money in stock by buying 1,000 shares at $232.23 each.

For illustrative purposes, assume the derivative accurately represents the change in the futures and put prices for a $1 change in the stock price. First, let us see how a stock-put portfolio, if we could construct one, would change for a $1 stock price decrease. The put delta is $.122 - 1 = -.878$.

From the previous example, we would own 882.64 shares of stock and the same number of puts. The outcome of the stock-put portfolio would be

---

Stock: 882.64 shares lose $1 each
   Profit $= -\$882.64$
Put: 882.64 puts increase by $0.878 each
   Profit $= 882.64(\$0.878) = 774.96$
Net profit: $-\$882.64 + \$774.96 = -\$107.68$

Now consider what the stock-futures portfolio would do. The futures price would decrease by $e^{(.0532)(.2301)} = 1.0123$. The outcome would be

---

Stock: 1,000 shares lose $1 each
   Profit: $= -\$1,000$
Futures: 1.76 futures contracts decrease by $1.0123 each
   Profit $= -1.76(500)(-\$1.0123) = \$890.82$
Net profit: $-\$1,000 + \$890.82 = -\$109.18$.

The difference between $107.68 and $109.18 is due to rounding. Thus, the stock-futures portfolio would react to stock price changes the same way the stock-put portfolio would.

Had the stock price gone up by $1, the insured portfolio would have produced a gain of about the same amount. The cost of the insurance is determined by noting that the uninsured portfolio would have increased by a value of $1,000. Thus, insuring the portfolio resulted in a cost of $1,000 - $109.18 = $890.82, or about .38 percent of its original value. Of course, this cost is incurred over a very brief time period.

The number of futures contracts changes with a change in any variable. For example, in this case we are trying to achieve a target portfolio value on December

19 of \$233,900. Suppose the stock price immediately increased. From the formula for V_{min},

$$V_{min} = \frac{EV}{S+P},$$

we can see that if S increases, P decreases by less than the change in S, and if V_{min} stays the same, we will need to increase E. Reworking the problem would reveal that we would need to sell fewer futures contracts. Had S immediately fallen, we would need to sell more futures contracts. Thus, when the stock price is higher, we need fewer futures contracts, which corresponds to less insurance. When the stock price is lower, we need more futures contracts for more insurance.

As we move closer to expiration, we shall also need to change the number of futures contracts. If the stock price is very high, achieving the target without futures is increasingly likely. Thus, we can reduce the number of futures contracts. However, if the stock price is low, we may need to sell more futures as we approach expiration. In the extreme case—if the portfolio value is well below the target—it may be nearly impossible to obtain a sufficient number of futures to insure the portfolio. However, if the hedge ratio has been frequently adjusted, the portfolio will be unlikely to fall too far off the track toward the target value.

One problem in dynamic hedging is that it requires continuously adjusting the hedge ratio. Continuous adjustment is, of course, not possible in practice, and it is not at all clear how frequently it should be done. Another, closely related problem is that the hedge ratio is but an approximation of the sensitivity of the put and futures to a stock price change. If there is a large stock price change, the approximation will not hold. Thus, in fast-moving markets, this simulated insurance strategy may not work.

It has been said that with portfolio insurance, you are buying futures when stock prices are high and selling them when stock prices are low. Thus, you tend to "buy high and sell low," which, of course, runs counter to the old investment adage "buy low and sell high." This point should not be of concern, however, since the objective is to provide protection. By its very definition, protection is a form of hedging, which means taking a position in the futures market opposite to that in the spot market.

Dynamic Hedging with Treasury Bills

An alternative to the use of futures contracts is the use of Treasury bills. It is possible to combine stock and Treasury bills so that the portfolio behaves like the protective put. The formula for the number of shares of stock is

$$N_s = \left(\frac{V_{min}}{E}\right)\left(\frac{\partial C}{\partial S}\right),$$

and the number of T-bills is

$$N_B = \frac{V - N_S S}{B}.$$

The derivation of the formula for N_S is also in Appendix 14B. As with the use of stock index futures, it is necessary to continuously adjust this hedge ratio. Continuing with the same example, the number of shares of stock will be

$$N_S = \left(\frac{233,900}{265}\right)(.122) = 107.68,$$

and the number of Treasury bills will be

$$N_B = \left(\frac{232,230 - 107.68(232.23)}{98.78}\right) = 2,097.$$

For a \$1 increase in the price of the stock, the outcome of the stock–T-bill portfolio will be as follows:

Stock: 107.68 shares lose \$1 each
  Profit $= -\$107.68$
T-bills: No change in value here because the stock price change does not cause the T-bill price to change
Net profit: $-\$107.68$.

This outcome is the same as that of the stock and put hedge and differs from the stock-futures hedge by a round-off error.

Thus, we see that portfolio insurance can be conducted either with European options expiring on the horizon date with the exact terms and conditions needed or by using a dynamic hedge with either stock and futures or stock and T-bills. Although portfolio insurance has been blamed for contributing to market volatility (a topic we shall explore in more detail later) and consequently has lost some of its appeal, it nonetheless remains a useful strategy for ensuring a minimum return.

NEW FUTURES AND OPTIONS PRODUCTS

In recent years, there has been an enormous increase in the number of new futures and options products offered by financial institutions. We already covered some of these, such as portfolio insurance, and briefly mentioned others. In this section, we shall take a more detailed look at some of the new and popular products that have characteristics of futures and options. Many of these instruments are called *hybrids*, because they have been developed by combining some of the more useful features of futures and options.

Swaps

In Chapter 13, we covered currency swaps. Similar in concept, an interest rate swap, or simply a *swap*, is an arrangement between two parties to exchange interest payments. Several types of interest rate swaps exist, but we shall cover only one here: the common and simple swap of fixed- for floating-rate payments, sometimes called a *generic* or *plain vanilla swap*.

Consider firm XYZ that is engaged in borrowing at a floating rate. Recall from Chapter 10 that we looked at a firm that was borrowing at a floating rate. It constructed a Eurodollar strip to hedge the uncertainty of the LIBOR rate over the life of its loan. Swaps provide an alternative way to hedge that risk. Suppose firm ABC is borrowing over the same period at a fixed rate. ABC would prefer to borrow at the floating rate, while XYZ would prefer to borrow at a fixed rate. Why would ABC want to borrow at the floating rate and thus incur more uncertainty? It is possible that ABC is simultaneously lending at a floating rate as well. If interest rates fall, it will earn less on its lending assets, so it would like to pay less on its liabilities.

There is a vast network of firms, called *swap dealers*, that arrange swaps. These dealers find firms that have offsetting needs and arrange the swap transactions for a fee. If there are no firms with such offsetting needs, swap dealers can combine swaps with several firms and even assume some of the risk themselves, hedging it in other markets. Let us assume that a swap dealer arranges the swap between ABC and XYZ.

Assume the principal involved in the loan is $50 million. This is referred to as the *notional principal*. The current date is December 15. ABC pays the LIBOR rate plus .5 percent on the 15th of March, June, September, and the following December. On December 15, one year from now, it pays the $50 million principal. XYZ is also borrowing $50 million and will pay a rate of 8 percent on the 15th of March, June, September, and December and will repay the $50 million on December 15, one year from now. The current LIBOR rate is 7.68 percent.

The terms of the swap call for XYZ to pay the fixed rate of 8 percent to ABC while ABC will pay the LIBOR rate plus .5 percent to XYZ. Depending on the course of interest rates over the next year, each payment date will involve one party paying more to the other. The usual arrangement is for the party that owes more to simply pay the difference to the party that owes less. Table 14.3 presents the schedule of payments.

On March 15, ABC will owe interest from December 15 to March 15, which is 90 days, at a rate of $7.68 + .5 = 8.18$ percent. Thus, ABC will owe

$$\$50,000,000[.0818(90/360)] = \$1,022,500.$$

TABLE 14.3

Schedule of Payments in Floating-Rate for Fixed-Rate Swap

Date	3-Month LIBOR Rate	Floating-Rate Paid	Days in Period	ABC Floating Payment	XYZ Fixed Payment	Net Cash Flow to Fixed
12/15	7.68	8.18	—	—	—	—
3/15	7.50	8.00	90	$1,022,500	$1,000,000	+$22,500
6/15	7.06	7.56	92	1,022,222	1,022,222	+0
9/15	6.06	6.56	92	966,000	1,022,222	−56,222
12/15	—	—	91	829,111	1,011,111	−182,000

XYZ will owe

$$\$50,000,000[.08(90/360)] = \$1,000,000.$$

The net payment will be $22,500 from ABC to XYZ. On that date, the new LIBOR rate is 7.50 percent. Thus, over the second quarter, ABC will pay interest at a rate of $7.50 + .5 = 8$ percent, which is the same rate XYZ pays.

As Table 14.3 shows, ABC pays XYZ the first payment and XYZ pays ABC the last two payments. The swap is for interest payments only, so neither party pays the other the notional principal. Both parties simply pay off their principals to their respective creditors.

There are a number of similarities between swaps and other types of financial transactions. For example, in Chapter 10 we illustrated the hedging of a floating rate LIBOR loan with a Eurodollar strip. Recall that a Eurodollar strip involves selling a series of Eurodollar futures contracts with different expirations. If interest rates rise, the higher interest paid on the spot loan is offset somewhat by profits from the short position in futures. This tends to lock in the Eurodollar rate implied by the term structure. In a swap transaction, the firm paying a floating rate and wanting to lock in a fixed rate is doing something very similar to a Eurodollar strip. The swap guarantees fixed payments, which should be made at approximately the rate implied by the term structure.

Since a Eurodollar strip is a series of futures contracts, it is not surprising that a swap is like a series of forward contracts. For example, when XYZ enters into the swap to receive the floating rate, it has entered into an agreement to receive

$$(\text{Notional principal})\left(\frac{\text{Days in period}}{360}\right)\left(\frac{\text{LIBOR} + .5 - 8}{100}\right)$$

or, effectively,

$$(\text{Notional principal})\left(\frac{\text{Days in period}}{360}\right)\left(\frac{\text{LIBOR} - 7.5}{100}\right).$$

Thus, XYZ has entered into n long forward contracts on the LIBOR rate at a price of 7.5. The number of contracts, n, is equal to (Notional principal)(Days in period/360)/100, which for the first period equals $50,000,000(90/360)/100 = 125,000. To see why this is indeed a forward contract, remember that a forward contract is an agreement in which a long and a short agree to exchange money for an asset at a price agreed upon today. In this case, ABC has agreed to pay XYZ the difference between the LIBOR rate and 7.5. If the difference is negative, XYZ pays ABC. This is exactly the payment schedule that would result if XYZ purchased 125,000 forward contracts on an asset called LIBOR with the forward price at 7.5.

This applies only to the first interest payment. Obviously there are forward contracts on each of the remaining interest payments. The number of contracts differs only according to the number of days between coupon payments. Thus, in total a swap is equal to a series of forward contracts. The fixed payer is holding the long forward position, and the floating payer is holding the short forward position.

There are many other types of swaps. For example, some borrowers have advantages in borrowing in short-term markets and others advantages in borrowing in long-term markets. A swap can be used to pass on those advantages to others while gaining the others' advantages. In most cases, however, swaps are designed to exploit differences in credit risk. Note that in the swap we just examined, there was no allowance for the possibility that one party will default. Like forward contracts, these transactions are not risk free. Thus, when borrowers with favorable borrowing rates enter into swaps, they may find themselves assuming the credit risk of borrowers with lower credit ratings. Although the swap market is enormous, there is some concern that these credit issues have not been fully appreciated and properly priced. This remains an issue of ongoing debate and research.

In addition to financial swaps, there are commodity swaps, which can involve the exchange of fixed payments covering a specified quantity of a commodity for floating payments as determined by the fluctuating market price of the commodity. There are also options to buy swaps. These instruments, sometimes called *swaptions*, are complex to evaluate, and we will not cover them in this book. Those interested in the swap market can refer to the excellent articles by Wall and Pringle (1989), Goodman (1990), and Smith (1989) listed in the references section.

Interest Rate Options

We already alluded to *interest rate options*. By these, we do not mean options on bonds or other interest-sensitive securities; rather, we mean options in which the payoff is based on an interest rate rather than on the price of a bond. Although there have been attempts to create a market for these products on an exchange, interest rate options have succeeded only in the over-the-counter market. In fact, they have been extremely successful and now are one of the primary vehicles used by corporate treasurers to hedge interest rate risk.

Interest rate options usually are written by large financial institutions, such as banks, and are tailored to the needs of a specific clientele. The options are European, meaning they can be exercised only at expiration. The expiration date is chosen by the buyer, and the exercise price usually is set at the current level of the spot interest rate. Thus, the options are written at-the-money. The options pay off on the basis of the difference between an interest rate, usually the LIBOR rate, and an interest rate designated as the exercise price, or strike. When exercised, the payment by the writer is made not at the expiration but at a future date that corresponds to the maturity of the underlying spot instrument.

For example, consider a call option written on the 90-day LIBOR rate at an exercise price of 10 percent, which is the current LIBOR rate, for a face amount of $20 million. This option expires in 30 days. At that time, the buyer determines whether to exercise the option, which depends on whether the 90-day LIBOR rate is above 10 percent. However, if the option is exercised, the payment from the writer to the buyer is made 90 days after the exercise, or 120 days from now.

Let us consider an example using this option. A firm decides that in 30 days it will borrow $20 million at the LIBOR rate plus 1 point. Fearing an increase in the LIBOR rate, it asks its bank to write it a call option on the LIBOR rate. The option will expire in 30 days and pay off 90 days thereafter. The bank charges a premium of $50,000.

In 30 days, if LIBOR exceeds 10 percent, the firm exercises the option. It pays off

$$\$20,000,000\left(\frac{90}{360}\right)\left(\frac{\text{Max}(0,\ \text{LIBOR} - \text{E})}{100}\right)$$

90 days after the expiration. If exercised, this amount helps reduce the increased cost of the loan. Table 14.4 illustrates how the option pays off.

The outcome is determined as follows. Suppose the LIBOR rate at expiration is 6 percent. Since the premium is paid today but the loan is taken out in 30 days, we must compound the premium forward for 30 days at today's spot rate plus the spread of 1 point. This gives us $50,000[1 + .11(30/360)] = $50,458. Thus, when we take out the loan, we shall effectively receive $20,000,000 − $50,458 = $19,949,542. The interest on the spot loan is based on the LIBOR rate of 6 percent plus 1 point, so it will be $20,000,000[.07(90/360)] = $350,000. The call is out-of-the-money, so the total amount paid is $350,000. As we have done previously, we should determine the annualized cost of the loan. We paid back $20,350,000 and received $19,949,542. The rate thus is ($20,350,000)($19,949,542)$^{(365/90)}$ − 1 = .0839.

If the LIBOR rate rises to 11 percent, the firm will exercise the option and receive $20,000,000(.11 − .10)(90/360) = $50,000 at the maturity of the loan. This reduces the amount paid from $600,000 in interest to $550,000. The annualized cost of the loan thus will be ($20,550,000)/($19,949,542)$^{(365/90)}$ − 1 = .1278. Therefore, the call caps the interest cost at 12.78 percent.

TABLE 14.4
Payoffs from Interest Rate Call

Scenario: A firm plans to borrow at the LIBOR rate plus a spread of 1 point. The loan will be for $20 million and will be taken out in 30 days. The loan matures 90 days after that and is paid back in one lump sum. The firm buys an interest rate call for $50,000 with a strike of 10 percent expiring in 30 days.

LIBOR Rate in 30 Days	Value of Call at Loan Maturity	Profit on Call at Loan Maturity	Interest on Loan at Loan Maturity	Total Paid	Annualized Cost of Loan
6.00%	0	−$50,458	$350,000	$350,000	8.39%
6.50	0	−50,458	375,000	375,000	8.94
7.00	0	−50,458	400,000	400,000	9.48
7.50	0	−50,458	425,000	425,000	10.02
8.00	0	−50,458	450,000	450,000	10.57
8.50	0	−50,458	475,000	475,000	11.12
9.00	0	−50,458	500,000	500,000	11.67
9.50	0	−50,458	525,000	525,000	12.22
10.00	0	−50,458	550,000	550,000	12.78
10.50	25,000	−25,458	575,000	550,000	12.78
11.00	50,000	−458	600,000	550,000	12.78
11.50	75,000	24,542	625,000	550,000	12.78
12.00	100,000	49,542	650,000	550,000	12.78
12.50	125,000	74,542	675,000	550,000	12.78
13.00	150,000	99,542	700,000	550,000	12.78
13.50	175,000	124,542	725,000	550,000	12.78
14.00	200,000	149,542	750,000	550,000	12.78

Figure 14.3 illustrates the total amount paid at the loan maturity as a function of the LIBOR rate at maturity. The three lines show the profit on the call, the interest paid on the spot loan, and the total amount paid. Up to the strike at 10 percent, the spot interest and total paid lines coincide. Notice how the profit line on the call looks like a traditional call profit curve. The only difference, however, is that the call pays off when interest rates are high. High interest rates are a bearish scenario; thus, this type of call is actually bearish in contrast to the calls we previously covered.

The line representing the spot interest reflects the results from an unhedged position. As you can see, the line continues down infinitely as interest rates become higher and higher. The interest rate call added to the spot loan allows the firm to lock in a maximum amount of interest it will pay and hence a maximum interest rate.

Table 14.5 illustrates an interest rate put. An interest rate put might be used by a firm, such as a bank, that lends at the LIBOR rate plus, say, a spread. It thus is

FIGURE 14.3
LIBOR Loan + Interest Rate Call

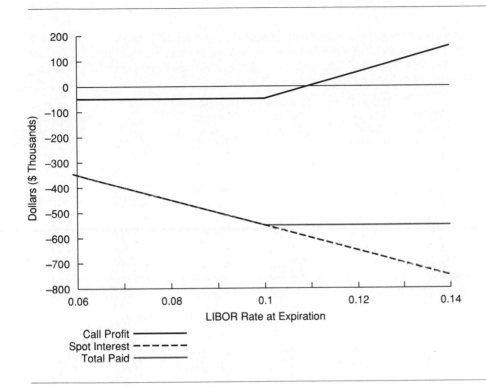

Call Profit ——————
Spot Interest – – – – – –
Total Paid ▬▬▬▬▬

vulnerable to a decline in interest rates. Although declining interest rates gener-ally are considered bullish, the firm nonetheless should buy a put on the LIBOR rate.

Here the bank plans to lend in 90 days at the LIBOR rate plus a spread of 1.5 points. The amount of the loan will be $10 million, and the loan will be for 180 days and be paid back in one lump sum. The bank finds a writer to sell it a put on the LIBOR with a strike of 9, the current LIBOR rate. The put premium will be $26,500.

Let us say that at expiration, the LIBOR rate is 7 percent. Then the put is worth $10,000,000(.09 − .07)(180/360) = $100,000. The put premium was paid today, so we must compound it at today's LIBOR rate plus the 1.5-point spread. This gives $26,500[1 + .105(90/360)] = $27,196. Thus, we effectively loaned $10,027,196. The interest we receive on the loan will be $10,000,000[.085(180/360)] = $425,000. The put payoff means that the total interest received is effec-tively $525,000. Thus, we paid out $10,027,196 and received $10,525,000. The annualized return is ($10,525,000/$10,027,196)$^{(365/180)}$ − 1 = .1032.

Figure 14.4 illustrates the payoffs from the put. The line indicating the put payoff has the traditional shape of a put; however, keep in mind that the horizontal

TABLE 14.5
Payoffs from Interest Rate Put

Scenario: A bank plans to lend at the LIBOR rate plus a spread of 1.5 points. The loan will be for $10 million and will be taken out in 90 days. The loan matures 180 days after that and is paid back in one lump sum. The bank buys an interest rate put for $26,500 with a strike of 9 percent expiring in 90 days.

LIBOR Rate in 90 Days	Value of Put at Loan Maturity	Profit on Put at Loan Maturity	Interest on Loan at Loan Maturity	Total Received	Annualized Return of Loan
5.00%	$200,000	$172,804	$325,000	$525,000	10.32%
5.50	175,000	147,804	350,000	525,000	10.32
6.00	150,000	122,804	375,000	525,000	10.32
6.50	125,000	97,804	400,000	525,000	10.32
7.00	100,000	72,804	425,000	525,000	10.32
7.50	75,000	47,804	450,000	525,000	10.32
8.00	50,000	22,804	475,000	525,000	10.32
8.50	25,000	−2,196	500,000	525,000	10.32
9.00	0	−27,196	525,000	525,000	10.32
9.50	0	−27,196	550,000	550,000	10.86
10.00	0	−27,196	575,000	575,000	11.39
10.50	0	−27,196	600,000	600,000	11.92
11.00	0	−27,196	625,000	625,000	12.46
11.50	0	−27,196	650,000	650,000	13.00
12.00	0	−27,196	675,000	675,000	13.54
12.50	0	−27,196	700,000	700,000	14.08
13.00	0	−27,196	725,000	725,000	14.62

axis is the interest rate and not the price of an asset. The upward-sloping line labeled as the "Spot Interest" is the payoff from an unhedged position. It increases if rates rise but decreases if rates fall. The total received line and the spot interest line coincide beyond the strike of 0.09. The interest rate put allows the firm to limit its minimum return to 10.32 percent. Again, remember that the put, while traditionally viewed as a bearish strategy, is used here to protect against falling interest rates, which normally is considered a bull market. This is because interest rate options, unlike most options, pay off according to interest rates and not bond prices.

Recall that we spent a great deal of time on how to value ordinary puts and calls on stock. We would like to be able to do the same with interest rate puts and calls. Unfortunately, the application of traditional methods, such as the Black-Scholes model, is not widely accepted for interest rates. There is considerable disagreement about the assumptions regarding the distribution of interest rates. The lognormal distribution, the assumption behind the Black-Scholes model, gen-

FIGURE 14.4
LIBOR Loan + Interest Rate Put

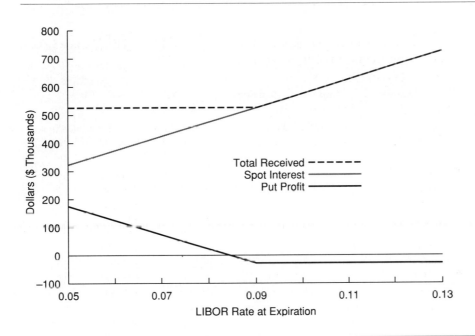

erally is not valid for interest rates. An examination of the literature on the pricing of interest rate options reveals that these instruments, like most new financial products, have generated considerable controversy, and the issues are too complex to cover here.

Interest Rate Caps

Another type of transaction that can be used to protect against rising interest rates is a cap. A *cap* is a series of European calls that mature at dates corresponding to interest payment dates on a loan. At each interest payment date, the holder of the cap decides whether to exercise the option based on whether the interest rate has risen above the exercise price, or strike. A price is paid up front for the cap. The price corresponds to the sum of the prices of the series of options that make up the cap. Each option is an interest rate call.

Let us look at an example. On January 2, a firm borrows $25 million over one year. It will make payments on April 2, July 2, October 2, and next January 2. On each date, starting with January 2, the LIBOR rate in effect on that day will be the interest rate paid over the next three months. The current LIBOR rate is 10 percent. The firm wishes to fix its rate at 10 percent, so it buys a cap for an up-

TABLE 14.6
Schedule of Payments for Interest Rate Cap

Scenario: On January 2, a firm takes out a one-year loan with interest paid quarterly at the LIBOR rate. The face value is $25 million. The firm buys an interest rate cap with a strike of 10 percent for a premium of $70,000.

Date	Days in Quarter	LIBOR Rate	Interest Due	Cap Payment	Principal Repayment	Net Cash Flow	Net Cash Flow without Cap
1/2	—	10.00%	—	-$70,000	$ 0	$24,930,000	$25,000,000
4/2	91	10.68	$631,944	0	0	-631,944	-631,944
7/2	91	12.31	674,917	42,972	0	-631,944	-674,917
10/2	92	11.56	786,472	147,583	0	-638,889	-786,472
1/2	92	8.75	738,556	99,667	25,000,000	25,638,889	-25,738,556

Effective annual rate
Without cap: 11.7%
With cap: 10.8%

front payment of $70,000. At each interest payment date, the cap will be worth

$$\$25,000,000\left(\frac{\text{Days in period}}{360}\right)\left(\frac{\text{Max}(0,\ \text{LIBOR}-10)}{100}\right).$$

The LIBOR rate is the rate that was in effect at the beginning of each quarter. Thus, as with an interest rate option, the decision to exercise is made at the beginning of the quarter but the payoff occurs at the end of the quarter. If the LIBOR rate is greater than 10 percent, the firm will exercise the option and receive a sum as given by this equation. This helps offset the higher interest rate on the loan. Table 14.6 shows the payments associated with this interest rate cap.

For the first quarter, the firm will pay the LIBOR rate of 10 percent in effect on January 2. Thus, on April 2 it will owe $25,000,000(.10)(91/360) = $631,944 based on 91 days from January 2 to April 2. Then, on April 2, the LIBOR rate is 10.68 percent. Because this is greater than 10 percent, the cap will pay off at the next interest payment date and the holder of the cap will receive a payment of

$$\$25,000,000\left(\frac{91}{360}\right)\left(\frac{10.68-10}{100}\right)=\$42,972.$$

This will help offset the interest of $674,917, based on a rate of 10.68 percent for 91 days from April 2 to July 2. The rate on July 2 is 12.31 percent, so the cap will pay off on October 2. The net effect of these cash flows is seen in column 7 of Table 14.6. On January 2, the firm received $25 million from the lender but paid out $70,000 for the cap for a net cash inflow of $24,930,000. It made periodic payments as shown and, on the next January 2, repaid the principal and made the final interest payment less the cap payoff. Note that because of the cap, the interest payments differ only because of the different number of days during each interest payment period and not because of the rate. The interest rate is capped at the LIBOR rate of 10 percent.

If we wish to know what annualized rate the firm actually paid, we essentially must solve for the internal rate of return. This was discussed in Chapter 8 and, as you may remember, requires a computer or financial calculator. We are solving for the cash flow that equates the present value of the four payouts to the initial receipt:

$$\$24,930,000 = \frac{\$631,944}{(1+y)^1} + \frac{\$631,944}{(1+y)^2} + \frac{\$638,889}{(1+y)^3} + \frac{\$25,638,889}{(1+y)^4}.$$

The solution is y = .026. Annualizing this gives a rate of $(1.026)^4 - 1 = .108$. The last column in Table 14.6 shows the cash flows if the cap had not been purchased. Solving for the internal rate of return using those numbers and annualizing the result gives a rate of .117. Thus, the cap saved the firm 90 basis points. This was because during the life of the loan, interest rates generally were higher than they were at the time the loan was initiated.

Interest Rate Floors

From the perspective of a borrower, an interest rate cap is a series of call options that protects the borrower if interest rates increase. From the viewpoint of a lender in a variable rate loan, rising interest rates help the lender but falling interest rates are harmful. Thus, the lender may want protection against falling rates. This type of protection can be purchased with an interest rate *floor*, which is a series of interest rate put options expiring at the interest payment dates.

At each interest rate payment date, the payoff of an interest rate floor tied to the LIBOR rate with an exercise price of, say, 8 percent and a principal amount of $15 million will be

$$\$15,000,000\left(\frac{\text{Days in period}}{360}\right)\left(\frac{\text{Max}(0, \ 8 - \text{LIBOR})}{100}\right).$$

As previously, the LIBOR rate is determined at the beginning of the interest payment period.

Suppose a bank makes a one-year, $15 million loan with payments made at the LIBOR rate on March 16, June 16, September 15, and next December 16. Currently, it is December 16, and the LIBOR rate is 7.93 percent. Thus, on March 16 the bank will receive $15,000,000[.0793(90/360)] = $297,375 in interest. The

TABLE 14.7

Schedule of Payments for Interest Rate Floor

Scenario: On December 16, a bank makes a one-year loan with interest paid quarterly at the LIBOR rate. The face value is $15 million. The firm buys an interest rate floor with a strike of 8 percent for a premium of $30,000.

Date	Days in Quarter	LIBOR Rate	Interest Received	Floor Payment	Principal Repayment	Net Cash Flow	Net Cash Flow without Floor
12/16	—	7.93%	—	−$30,000	$ 0	−$15,030,000	−$15,000,000
3/16	90	7.50	$297,375	0	0	297,375	297,375
6/16	92	7.06	287,500	19,167	0	306,667	287,500
9/15	91	6.06	267,692	35,642	0	303,333	267,692
12/16	92	6.25	232,300	74,367	15,000,000	15,306,667	15,232,300

Effective annual rate
  Without floor: 7.4%
  With floor: 8.1%

new rate on that day is 7.50 percent. Thus, the floor is in-the-money and will pay off

$$\$15,000,000\left(\frac{92}{360}\right)\left(\frac{8-7.5}{100}\right)=\$19,167$$

on the next interest payment day. This will add to the interest payment of $287,500, which is lower because of the fall in interest rates. The complete results for the one-year loan are shown in Table 14.7. The floor is in-the-money and thus is exercised on each of the last three interest payment dates. This is because in this example, the year was one of interest rates lower than 8 percent.

The lender paid out $15,000,000 up front to the borrower and another $30,000 for the floor. Column 7 in Table 14.7 indicates the periodic cash flows associated with the floored loan. Following the same procedure as in the cap, we can solve for the periodic rate that equates the present value of the inflows to the outflow. This rate turns out to be about 2.0 percent. Annualizing this gives a rate of 8.1 percent. The last column shows the cash flows if the floor had not been used. The annualized return associated with these cash flows is 7.4 percent. Thus, the floor boosted the bank's return by 70 basis points. Of course, in a period of rising rates, the bank will lose the opportunity to gain from the increase in interest rates.

Interest Rate Collars

Consider a firm planning to borrow money that decides to purchase an interest rate cap. In so doing, the firm is trying to place a ceiling on the rate it will pay on its loan. If rates fall, it can gain by paying lower rates. However, in some cases a

TABLE 14.8

Schedule of Payments for Interest Rate Collar

Scenario: On March 15, a firm borrows $50 million with interest paid quarterly at the LIBOR rate. The firm buys an interest rate cap with a strike of 10 percent for $250,000. To help offset the cost of the cap, the firm sells an interest rate floor with a strike of 8 percent for $175,000.

Date	Days in Quarter	LIBOR Rate	Interest Due	Cap Payment	Floor Payment	Principal Repayment	Net Cash Flow with Collar	Net Cash Flow with Cap only	Net Cash Flow without Cap or Floor
3/15		10.50%	$0	−$250,000	$175,000	$0	$49,925,000	$49,750,000	$50,000,000
6/15	92	11.56	1,341,667	0	0	0	−1,341,667	−1,341,667	−1,341,667
9/14	91	11.75	1,461,056	197,167	0	0	−1,263,889	−1,263,889	−1,461,056
12/14	91	9.06	1,485,069	222,181	0	0	−1,263,889	−1,263,889	−1,485,069
3/15	91	9.50	1,145,083	0	0	0	−1,145,083	−1,145,083	−1,145,083
6/14	91	7.62	1,200,694	0	0	0	−1,200,694	−1,200,694	−1,200,694
9/14	92	8.31	973,667	0	−48,556	0	−1,022,222	−973,667	−973,667
12/15	92	7.93	1,061,833	0	0	0	−1,061,833	−1,061,833	−1,061,833
3/14	89	7.50	980,236	0	−8,653	50,000,000	−50,988,889	−50,980,236	−50,980,236

Effective annual rate
   Without cap or floor: 10.08%
   With collar: 9.76%
   With cap: 9.91%

firm will find it more advantageous to give up the right to gain from falling rates in order to lower the cost of the cap. One way to do this is to sell a *collar*. The premium received from selling the collar helps offset the cost of the cap. If interest rates fall, the options that comprise the collar will be exercised. The net effect is that the strategy will establish both a floor and a ceiling on the interest cost. The existence of both limited gains and losses should remind you of a money spread with options.

Table 14.8 illustrates a collar in which a firm borrowing $50 million over two years buys a cap for $250,000 with an exercise price of 10 percent and sells a floor for $175,000 with an exercise price of 8 percent. The loan begins on March 15 and will require payments at approximately 91-day intervals at the LIBOR rate.

By now, you should be able to verify the numbers in the table. The interest paid on June 15 is based on the LIBOR rate on March 15 of 10.5 percent and 92 days during the period. The cap pays off on September 14 and December 14 because those are the ends of the periods in which the LIBOR rate at the beginning of the period turned out to be greater than 10 percent. The floor pays off on September 14 of the next year and on March 14 of the following year, the due date on the loan. Note that when the floor pays off, the firm makes, rather than receives, the payment.

Column 8 in Table 14.8 shows the cash flows associated with the collar. Following the procedure previously described to solve for the internal rate of return gives an annualized rate of 9.76 percent for the collar. Column 9 shows the cash flows had the firm done only the cap. The return associated with this strategy would have been 9.91 percent. The last column indicates the cash flows had the firm done neither the cap nor the floor. The rate associated with that strategy would have been 10.08 percent.

The cap by itself would have helped lower the firm's cost of borrowing. By selling the floor and thus creating a collar, the cost of the loan was lowered from 9.91 percent to 9.76 percent.

Primes and Scores

We now turn to several types of option-like products related to equities.

In the mid-1980s, a new type of financial instrument emerged on the American Stock Exchange. A firm called Americus Trust created new securities called *primes* and *scores*. These instruments represent claims on the components of the return from ordinary equity securities.

Recalling our previous notation for options, let S be the current stock price, E the exercise price of an option, C the call price, P the put price, and S_T the stock price at some future date. Investors buy shares in the trust, which is like a mutual fund. For each share bought, the trust in turn holds a share of a particular stock. Each unit of the trust can be subdivided into special units called primes and scores. The holder of a prime receives the dividends on the stock and any increase in the value of the stock up to a termination value, E. The increase is paid at the expiration date. Let us assume a dividend of D_t is paid and is received and reinvested at the risk-free rate, r, for the remaining period, T – t. Thus, the payoff from a prime is simply $Min(S_T, E) + D_t(1 + r)^{T-t}$.

The holder of a score receives the increase above the termination value, or simply $Max(0, S_T - E)$. We should recognize this as simply a European call.

Table 14.9 shows that the payoffs from the prime plus the score are equivalent to the payoffs from holding the stock. If we let PRIME be the value of the prime and SCORE be the value of the score, we can state that

$$PRIME + SCORE = S.$$

Thus, primes and scores break down a stock's return into two components. Some investors will prefer primes, and some will prefer scores. Primes and scores trade on the American Stock Exchange; thus, they can be easily bought and sold. In addition, units of the trust itself, which are equivalent to shares of the stock, also trade. If we designate their price as UNIT, we can say that

$$PRIME + SCORE = S = UNIT.$$

If this relationship does not hold, arbitrage can occur. In addition, investors holding units can redeem them for shares. However, there are some transaction costs that prevent these relationships from holding perfectly.

TABLE 14.9
Payoffs from Prime, Score, and Stock

Payoff From	Current Value	Payoffs from Portfolio Given Stock Price at Expiration	
		$S_T < E$	$S_T \geq E$
Prime	PRIME	$S_T + D_t(1+r)^{T-t}$	$E + D_t(1+r)^{T-t}$
Score	SCORE	0	$S_T - E$
		$S_T + D_t(1+r)^{T-t}$	$S_T + D_t(1+r)^{T-t}$
Stock	S	$S_T + D_t(1+r)^{T-t}$	$S_T + D_t(1+r)^{T-t}$

Each trust offered by Americus is on a different stock. There are about 25 stocks on which primes and scores trade. Their expirations tend to be somewhat long term, making the scores equivalent to long-term calls.

Let us look at an example. On August 24, 1990, there was an Americus trust for primes, scores, and units on AT&T. They mature on February 14, 1992. The termination value, or exercise price, was $30. AT&T was selling for 31 7/8, which was also the price of the Americus trust unit. The prime was selling for 25 3/8, and the score was selling for 7 1/8. Note that the sum of the prices of the prime and score was greater than the price of the unit. This is a common finding, as noted by Jarrow and O'Hara (1989), and most likely reflects costs that limit the ability to arbitrage away the difference.

Because the score is a European call, we should be able to use the Black-Scholes model to price it. Table 14.10 illustrates the procedure we should follow. First, we need an estimate of the volatility of AT&T stock. We obtain this by applying the Black-Scholes model to an October 30 call trading on the CBOE. This is a simple matter, and we need not be concerned with dividends because AT&T's dividend dates are February 1, May 1, August 1, and November 1. Thus, no dividends are expected before the call expires. The implied volatility obtained is .32.

Then we can price the score using the Black-Scholes model after taking out the present value of the dividends expected over the remaining life of the score. AT&T currently is paying $0.33 dividend. While this could change, we shall simply extrapolate forward. As Table 14.10 indicates, the present value of the dividends is 1.8618. Subtracting this from the price gives an adjusted price of 30.0132. Now we have the five inputs for the Black-Scholes model. The resulting call price is 6.1658. Our estimate of the prime price thus would be 31.875 − 6.1658 = 25.71.

TABLE 14.10
Valuation of AT&T Primes and Scores

Current date: August 24, 1990
Stock price: 31 7/8
Risk-free rate: .0763
Expiration: February 14, 1992 (539 days, T = 539/365 = 1.4767)

Estimation of volatility: An AT&T October 30 call (time to expiration = 56/365 = .1534) trades on the CBOE at 2.875. No dividends on AT&T are expected between August 24 and October 19. The Black-Scholes model can be used to obtain the implied volatility of σ = .32.

Pricing the score: The Black-Scholes model can be used to price the score as a European call with T = 1.4767, r = .0763, E = 30, σ = .32, and S = 31.875. However, there will be dividends on AT&T stock. Their present value must be subtracted from the stock price as follows.

AT&T has been paying a $0.33 dividend on February 1, May 1, August 1, and November 1. Assuming this pattern continues, we find the present value of these dividends.

Dividend Date	Dividend d_{t_i}	Days to Payment Date	Days/365 t_i	Present Value $d_{t_i}e^{-rt_i}$
11/1/90	$0.33	69	0.1890	0.3253
2/1/91	0.33	161	0.4411	0.3191
5/1/91	0.33	250	0.6849	0.3132
8/1/91	0.33	342	0.9370	0.3072
11/1/91	0.33	434	1.1890	0.3014
2/1/92	0.33	526	1.4411	0.2956
				1.8618

Adjusted stock price: 31.875 − 1.8618 = 30.0132

Plugging into the Black-Scholes model a with time to expiration of 1.4767 gives the price of the score as 6.1658.

Now our results can be summarized as follows:

Instrument	Market Price	Estimated Value
Prime	25.375	25.71
Score	7.125	6.1658
Unit	31.875	31.875

There are several cases of apparent mispricing. The prime appears to be slightly underpriced and the score slightly overpriced. In addition, the market price of the prime plus the score, $32.50, does not equal the market price of the unit. While in this case the unit does sell for the price of a share of stock, that will not always be the case. Again we caution that transaction costs may prevent these differences from being fully exploitable.

Breaking down a stock's return into component parts is not a new strategy. Mutual funds called *dual-purpose funds* do the same thing. In addition, there have been other instruments similar to the Americus Trust securities. We can expect to see more instruments of these types in the future as firms look for new and creative ways to repackage securities.

Market Indexed Securities

Banks have been no less innovative than corporations and mutual funds. In recent years they have found creative ways to offer deposits. One interesting type is the *market indexed security*. One of the first was a bank deposit introduced in 1987 by Chase Manhattan Bank. It pays a guaranteed minimum interest rate plus a portion of the change in a stock market index over the life of the security.

The analysis that follows is adapted from Chance and Broughton (1988). To understand a market indexed security, let us initially assume the investor deposits $1 in the bank. At that time, the stock is worth S_0. The deposit pays a percentage of the return on the S&P 500. Let us call this the *participation percentage* or γ, where γ could be .5, .75, and so on. The deposit guarantees a minimum return of i, which we shall assume is stated as a continuously compounded rate. Thus, $1 deposited for a period of T will be worth a minimum of e^{iT} at the end of the period. The return on the S&P over that period will be $(S_T/S_0) - 1$. The depositor will receive a return of $\gamma[(S_T/S_0) - 1]$ if this is more than the minimum return. Thus, at the maturity date, T, the value of the customer's account will be

$$e^{iT} \qquad\qquad \text{if } 1 + \gamma[(S_T/S_0) - 1] \le e^{iT}$$
$$1 + \gamma[(S_T/S_0) - 1] \quad \text{if } 1 + \gamma[(S_T/S_0) - 1] > e^{iT}$$

These expressions can be restated in a more workable form as

$$\lambda \qquad\qquad\qquad \text{if } S_T \le S_0\{[(\lambda - 1)/\gamma] + 1\}$$
$$1 + \gamma[(S_T/S_0) - 1] \quad \text{if } S_T > S_0\{[(\lambda - 1)/\gamma] + 1\}$$

where $\lambda = e^{iT}$, the minimum value of the account at T.

Now suppose we are at time t during the life of the deposit. We wish to find the value of the deposit. For an ordinary deposit this would be simple, as it would reflect the accumulated value of the interest in the account. For an indexed deposit, however, it must reflect the option-like component of the deposit. As we did in pricing options, let us appeal to an arbitrage approach.

The holder of an indexed deposit can turn the position into a risk-free portfolio by selling m call options on the market index, where $m = \gamma/S_t$ with S_t being the cur-

TABLE 14.11
Payoffs from Indexed Deposit and Short Call

Payoff From	Current Value	Payoffs from Portfolio Given Stock Price at Expiration	
		$S_T < E$	$S_T \geq E$
Indexed deposit	$I(\gamma, \lambda, T - t)$	λ	$1 + \gamma[(S_T/S_0) - 1]$
Short call	$-mC(S_t, T - t, E)$	0	$(\gamma/S_T)(S_T - E)$
		λ	λ

Note: $E = S_0\{[(\lambda - 1)/\gamma] + 1\}$, $m = \gamma/S_0$.

rent stock price. Each call should have an exercise price of E, where E is set at $S_0\{[(\lambda - 1)/\gamma] + 1\}$. Let $C(S_t, T - t, E)$ be the price of the call and $I(\gamma, \lambda, T - t)$ be the value of the indexed deposit, where γ is the participation percentage, λ is the minimum future value, and $T - t$ is the remaining maturity. We shall take r to be the risk-free rate and σ to be the volatility of the stock index. Table 14.11 shows the payoffs from this portfolio.

In both outcomes, the portfolio value at T will be λ. This is a known value at time t. Thus, the portfolio of the indexed deposit and the short call must currently be worth the present value of λ. Therefore,

$$I(\gamma, \lambda, T - t) - mC(S_t, T - t, E) = \lambda e^{-rT},$$

which means that the indexed deposit is worth

$$I(\gamma, \lambda, T - t) = mC(S_t, T - t, E) + \lambda e^{-rT}.$$

The indexed deposit thus is worth m calls and a risk-free bond with a face value of $\lambda = e^{iT}$. With this relatively simple formula, we can easily make some computations of its value.

Consider the following information about an indexed deposit issued on August 14 and maturing one year later. The risk-free rate is 5.49 percent, the volatility is .21, the dividend yield on the stock index is 2.3 percent, and the guaranteed return is 4 percent. At the time of the issue, the stock market index, the S&P 500, was at 333.99. The guaranteed future value of the deposit is $\lambda = e^{.04(1)} = 1.0408$. The deposit pays 30 percent of the return on the S&P 500. Thus, the exercise price is

$$E = 333.99\{[(1.0408 - 1)/.30] + 1\} = 379.41.$$

Plugging into the Black-Scholes model gives us the value of a call option with a stock price of 333.99, an exercise price of 379.41, and other values as given above as 15.1976. The value of a $1 deposit today is

$$I(.3, 1.04, 1) = (.3/333.99)(15.1976) + 1.0408e^{-.0549(1)} = 1.$$

This simply says that $1 deposited is worth $1 today. This is as it has to be. If the deposit were worth more than $1, the bank would be deluged with deposits and would have to lower the minimum rate or participation percentage. If the value of the deposit were less than $1, the bank would get no customers and would have to raise the minimum value or participation percentage. Thus, for a deposit of $1, the parameters in the market (the volatility and the risk-free rate) plus the time to maturity of the deposit determine the combination of minimum rate and participation percentage that the bank can offer. It can choose either the minimum rate or the participation percentage, but once one of these is chosen, the other is determined so as to force the deposit to be worth $1.

Later, however, during the life of the deposit, it can be worth more or less than $1. Let us say that three months later, the S&P 500 is at 344. We should expect this to make the deposit more valuable. Using a stock price of 344, an exercise price of 379.41, a time to maturity of .75, and the risk-free rate, volatility, and dividend yield as defined above gives the value of the call as 14.5185. Then the deposit is worth

$$I(.3, 1.04, .75) = (.3/333.99)(14.5185) + 1.0408e^{-.0549(.75)}$$
$$= 1.0118.$$

Thus, the deposit is worth 1.0118, or about 1.2 percent more. After three months, the depositor has earned an annualized rate of $(1.0118/1)^4 - 1 = .048$. This exceeds the guaranteed rate because of the increase in the S&P 500.

Indexed securities have appeared in several forms. Salomon Brothers has offered a product indexed to the stock market but in which the minimum return is tied not to a fixed-rate security but to a coupon bond. Chen and Sears (1990) analyzed the properties of this instrument. In addition, other types of financial transactions have indexed returns. In 1986, Standard Oil of Ohio issued bonds that paid interest on the basis of the excess of the price of oil over $25 a barrel. In 1987, Wells Fargo Bank issued a security that paid off on the basis of the change in the price of gold. In 1989, a ruling by the CFTC made it easier for firms to issue these hybrid securities. Thus, we can expect to see more and more of these types of securities in years to come.

ISSUES AND IMPLICATIONS OF INCREASED TRADING IN FUTURES AND OPTIONS

In this chapter, we have focused on some of the advanced strategies that employ futures and options and new instruments that have characteristics of futures and options. Hopefully you can appreciate the increasing popularity of futures and options and their related instruments. With the rapid growth of many of these

-the-counter instruments—whose volume is not publicly reported—it is becoming increasingly difficult to gauge the true magnitude of this market.

As any market grows and develops, it inevitably encounters problems. Unfortunately, futures and options have received much of the blame for these problems. Perhaps this is because any innovation that solves some problems may produce others. For example, the automobile certainly has brought considerable benefits to society, but it has also caused an increase in accidental deaths and injuries and a deterioration in the quality of the air. Computers have made us much more productive but have eliminated some of our privacy and a number of jobs.

As we noted earlier in this book, futures and options have always been somewhat controversial. Their image as speculative instruments has been a constant burden. Yet as we have seen, they offer many benefits if used properly. Moreover, speculation per se is not harmful—in fact, it is quite beneficial.

A number of issues related to futures and options have generated considerable controversy. Most continue to be debated today. Some, such as dual trading and program trading, we already have briefly discussed. In the remainder of this chapter, we shall take a more in-depth look at three critical issues involving futures and options: the triple witching hour, market crashes, and the implications of program trading and futures margins for volatility in the stock market.

The Triple Witching Hour

In Chapters 9 and 11, we discussed index arbitrage. Recall that this type of transaction occurs in the stock and futures markets when the futures and spot prices are not aligned by the cost of carry formula. If the futures price is too high, the arbitrage will require selling the futures and buying the stocks that make up the index. At expiration, the futures and spot prices automatically converge. As a result, the arbitrageur earns a risk-free profit in excess of the Treasury bill rate. If the futures price is too low, the arbitrage involves buying the futures and selling the stocks in the index. If the shares are not already owned, the sales of the shares must be short sales.

One key requirement for making the transaction work is the fact that the futures and spot prices converge at expiration. Because stock index futures contracts are settled in cash, the futures price at expiration is automatically set equal to the spot price. The arbitrageur who is holding stocks is required to sell the stocks at the expiration. For the transaction to work precisely as the model specifies, the stocks must be sold at their closing prices as the futures expires. For example, suppose the arbitrageur holds each stock in the S&P 500 index in the same proportions as in the actual index. The arbitrageur sells the stocks at the close of trading on the expiration day.[6] The actual closing value of the S&P index is determined by the final transaction price of each component stock. If the arbitrageur is successful in selling all the stocks at their closing prices, the overall portfolio

---

[6]These trades usually are done with *market on close orders*. This type of order instructs the broker to sell the shares at a price as close as possible to the closing price.

indeed will be liquidated at a value equivalent to the closing value of the S&P 500 index, which will be the closing price of the expiring futures. If, however, the stocks were simply sold near the close of the day or if other sales came in afterward and established a new closing price, the arbitrageur's portfolio would not close out at the actual closing S&P 500 index.

It should be clear by now that there is likely to be a mad rush to sell stocks at the close of trading on the expiration day. Of course, arbitrageurs who originally sold short stocks and bought the futures because the latter was underpriced sometime during its life would rush to buy stocks at expiration. It would be nice if this buying and selling pressure would offset, but it seldom does. There is frequently much more demand than supply, or vice versa. Consequently, prices can and often do move rapidly at expiration.

The index arbitrage just described is conducted with futures. Other arbitrageurs use index options and options on index futures. Index options expire each month, options on index futures expire every March, June, September, and December, and stock index futures also expire every March, June, September, and December. In each case, the expiration is the third Friday of the month. Thus, on the third Friday of March, June, September, and December, there are three different types of instruments.[7] The large price movements that occur on these days have led some to call the final 60 minutes of trading on those days the *triple witching hour*.

This colorful name has contributed to a media blitz in which these expiration day effects are blamed for unusually large price declines at the expiration. Because there usually is a lot of concern about rapid price decreases, the media typically report that the expiration of futures and options was the cause. When the price rises sharply at expiration, the press often reports simply that the price increase was illusory and of no economic significance as it was caused only by the expiration of futures and options. Naturally, there has been concern about the potentially harmful impact of these expiration day effects.

Stoll and Whaley have studied the triple witching hour at great length. In Stoll and Whaley (1987), they examined these effects over the 1982–1985 period. They found that over that period the number of arbitrage opportunities began to decline but arbitrage-related trading activity at expiration remained quite prevalent. They also found that the volume of trading around the expiration is substantially higher than that during otherwise normal trading periods. Yet they also observed that the magnitude of the price change was not all that large. They compared expiration day effects to those of a *block trade*, a transaction involving the purchase and sale of a block of 10,000 or more shares of stock. Block trades induce price movements comparable to those that occur at the triple witching hour. However, the timing of block trades is unpredictable. Stoll and Whaley argue that expiration day effects can at least be anticipated and investors can stay out of the market around the triple witching hour. They also found that the effect of the options

---

[7]There are actually four expiring instruments since each month, there are a group of expiring options on individual stocks. However, these are not believed to have much of an effect on the volatility of prices at the close.

expirations on these price movements was fairly minor; most of the volatility was a result of the futures expirations.

Although Stoll and Whaley saw no reason to make any changes to the system, the SEC recommended and the Chicago Mercantile Exchange and New York Stock Exchange adopted a new procedure for settling the expiration of their stock index futures contracts. The final day of trading would be the Thursday before the third Friday. Then the final settlement price of the expiring futures would be determined not on the basis of the Thursday closing prices of the S&P stocks but on the basis of the stocks' Friday opening prices. The idea behind this procedure is that the heavy trading at the close would shift to the opening, permitting more time to process orders and presumably leading to a greater balance of demand and supply. This might also give the volatility some opportunity to smooth out over the course of the day on Friday. Of course, the effect of this shift is partly psychological. When the media report on what the market did on a given day, they focus on the closing price of, say, the Dow Jones Industrial Average. By getting the volatility out of the close, even though it may be merely shifted to the opening, the public does not hear about it so easily.

In a follow-up study, Stoll and Whaley (1990) examined the effect of this new settlement procedure. They found that, as expected, volume has shifted away from the Thursday close to the Friday opening. Price effects have decreased slightly at the close but have shifted to the opening. Still, the opening price effects are not great in an absolute sense and amount to less than the bid-ask spread on an average stock. Stoll and Whaley concluded that the change in the closing settlement procedure has simply shifted the volatility and that the volatility is not that significant compared to other events known to induce volatility.

Thus, the triple witching hour probably is really no more than a colorful fairy tale. Yet it remains another obstacle that futures and options markets have had to respond to in their seemingly endless battle for recognition and survival.

Market Crashes

The great American bull market that began in the summer of 1982 came to a screeching halt on October 19, 1987, a day that has come to be known as Black Monday. It was the second Black Monday in stock market history. The first was Monday, October 28, 1929, on which the Dow Jones Industrial Average fell 38 points, a 13 percent decline, and was followed the next day by a 30-point drop, almost 12 percent of the average. Black Monday of 1987 saw the Dow Jones Industrial Average fall an unprecedented 508 points. The loss was over 22 percent of the previous day's average.

Options and futures markets are integrally linked to the stock market, and consequently they mirrored the behavior of the stock market. Some even say they played a damaging role in the events of that fateful day.

The stock market had risen sharply over the first nine months of 1987. The Dow Jones Industrial Average had reached a high of 2722.42 in August, up over 41 percent since the start of the year. Then things began to turn around. Amid

FIGURE 14.5
The Dow's Retreat

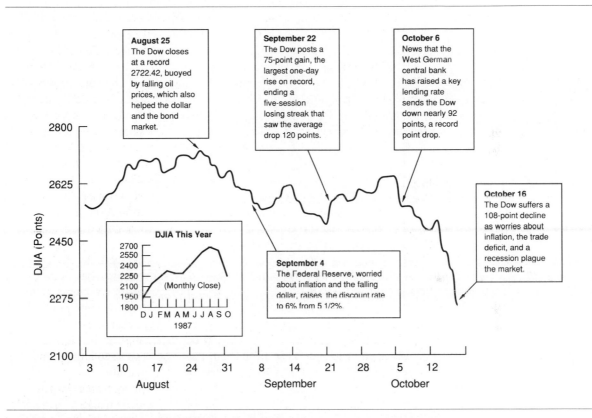

August 25
The Dow closes at a record 2722.42, buoyed by falling oil prices, which also helped the dollar and the bond market.

September 22
The Dow posts a 75-point gain, the largest one-day rise on record, ending a five-session losing streak that saw the average drop 120 points.

October 6
News that the West German central bank has raised a key lending rate sends the Dow down nearly 92 points, a record point drop.

October 16
The Dow suffers a 108-point decline as worries about inflation, the trade deficit, and a recession plague the market.

September 4
The Federal Reserve, worried about inflation and the falling dollar, raises the discount rate to 6% from 5 1/2%.

DJIA This Year

2700
2550
2400
2250
2100
1950
1800

(Monthly Close)

D J F M A M J J A S O
1987

DJIA (Points)

2800
2625
2450
2275
2100

3 10 17 24 31   8 14 21 28   5 12
August   September   October

Source: "Market at a Crossroads," The Wall Street Journal, *October 19, 1987.*

concern over growing budget and trade deficits, rising interest rates, fear of new legislation that could discourage takeover activity, and an increase in the prime and Federal Reserve discount rates, the market began to slow down. Yet somehow the bull market remained. The Dow reached a high of almost 2641 in early October, including a record 75-point gain on September 22. Over the next two weeks, sharp declines brought the average down significantly. The Dow fell 95 points on October 14, 57 points on October 15, and 108 points on Friday, October 16, closing at 2246.74.

Over the weekend, investors heard suggestions from Treasury Secretary Baker that the dollar might fall in international currency markets. It was also rumored that portfolio insurers would be selling heavily on Monday to adjust their hedge ratios to the proper levels. These circumstances raised concern over how the market would react on Monday.

On the morning of October 19, *The Wall Street Journal* presented the graph shown in Figure 14.5, an ominous recap of the Dow's recent decline. The events of that day are best described as earth shattering. Figure 14.6 indicates that with the

FIGURE 14.6

Dow Jones Industrial Average One-Minute Chart, Monday, October 19, 1987

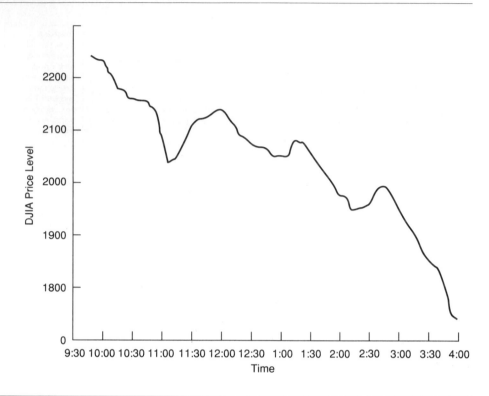

Source: Report of the Presidential Task Force on Market Mechanisms *(Washington, D.C.: U.S. Government Printing Office, January 1988).*

exception of a few brief rallies, the market fell for almost the entire day. At around 1:00 p.m., SEC chairman Ruder hinted that the exchanges might have to close, a message that may have fueled selling pressures. Computer systems that expedite and report trades were strained to capacity, and some became inoperative. Brokers were so deluged with phone calls that their customers were unable to get through to place their orders. Most important, the capital of specialists—those who buy and sell to the public and thus provide liquidity—was rapidly being depleted. When the day ended, volume stood at slightly over 600 million shares, almost double the record set just three days earlier.

The question on everyone's minds the following morning was whether the markets would continue to tumble or investors would see Monday's crash as an excellent opportunity to buy stocks at bargain prices. Foreign markets opened sharply lower. Before the U.S. markets opened, however, Federal Reserve chairman Greenspan issued a statement indicating the Fed's willingness to provide liquidity to banks that in turn would lend to specialists and others in need of credit. Many

FIGURE 14.7
MMI Spot and Futures, October 19, 1987

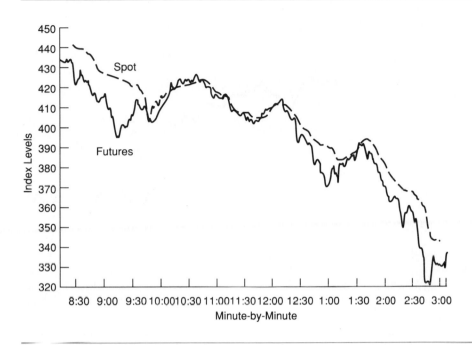

Source: Chicago Board of Trade, The Chicago Board of Trade's Response to the Presidential Task Force on Market Mechanisms, December 1987. Courtesy Chicago Board of Trade.

corporations announced programs for buying back their own stock. The New York Stock Exchange suspended the use of its DOT system, the automated procedure many program traders use to expedite transactions. The NYSE opened on time, but many stocks did not trade—surprisingly because of too many buyers and too few sellers. The stocks that did trade were up sharply.

The absence of stock trading presented special problems for options and futures markets. The American Stock Exchange, the Chicago Board Options Exchange, and the Chicago Mercantile Exchange halted trading in their index products. Although volume was light, the Chicago Board of Trade continued to trade its Major Market Index (MMI) futures, a contract designed to mirror the Dow Jones Industrial Average. Stock index futures contracts traded at well below the stock index level itself, an unheard-of experience and one ripe for arbitrage. However, arbitrage was impossible, because it would have required buying the underpriced futures and hedging the position by selling short the stocks in the index. Too few stocks were trading to do the arbitrage effectively. In addition, the unavailability of the DOT system prevented timely execution of arbitrage transactions.

Figure 14.7 presents the minute-by-minute Major Market Index spot and futures prices on October 19. Note the gap between the spot and futures for the first half of the day. As a point of comparison, Figures 14.8 and 14.9 present the

FIGURE 14.8

MMI Spot and Futures, October 16, 1987

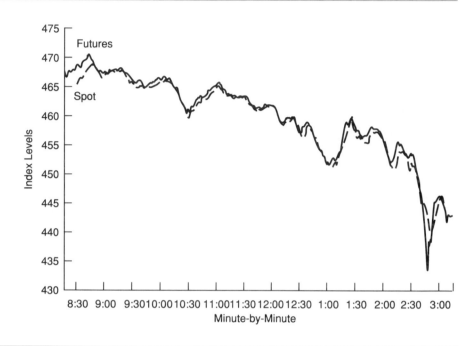

Source: Chicago Board of Trade, The Chicago Board of Trade's Response to the Presidential Task Force on Market Mechanisms, *December 1987. Courtesy Chicago Board of Trade.*

same items for the previous and following days, respectively. On Friday, October 16, the spot and futures moved in almost perfect tandem, with very little gap between them. On Black Monday, the spot price moved well ahead of the futures for about the first and last 90 minutes. During the middle of the day, however, the gap between the spot and futures prices was narrow, as it normally is.

At around 11:30 on October 20, the MMI contract staged a rally, with the futures price rising sharply on trades executed mostly by large institutions. Some have argued that the institutions may have colluded by initiating concerted purchase orders to inject a feeling of bullishness into the market, but later studies showed no such behavior. In any case, the market rallied. The futures rose sharply until it was well above the index level, investors began to buy stocks and sell the now expensive futures, and the arbitrage process was alive and well. The other options and futures products then began to trade. The market continued to rally and closed at 4 p.m., up over 102 points on a record-setting volume of 608 million shares. The next day, the market rose over 186 points.

In the aftermath of the crash investors, regulators, and legislators took a hard look at the markets' operations. The stock exchanges blamed the futures and options exchanges, the program traders, the portfolio insurers, and the CFTC. The futures and options exchanges blamed the stock exchanges and the SEC. The

FIGURE 14.9
MMI Spot and Futures, October 20, 1987

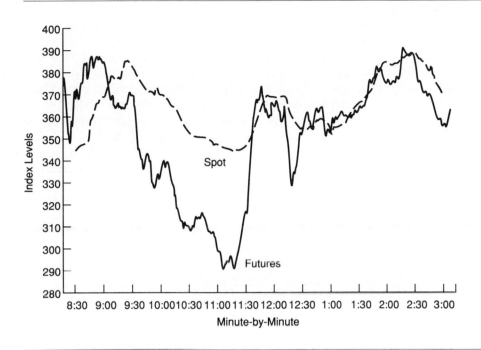

Source: Chicago Board of Trade, The Chicago Board of Trade's Response to the Presidential Task Force on Market Mechanisms, *December 1987. Courtesy Chicago Board of Trade.*

SEC, the CFTC, the New York Stock Exchange, the Chicago Board of Trade, and the Chicago Mercantile Exchange all conducted studies of the events surrounding the crash. President Reagan commissioned a task force headed by Nicholas Brady, chairman of Dillon, Read, a major Wall Street investment banking firm, and later treasury secretary in the Bush administration, to study the crash.

The Brady commission report, the most widely cited study of the crash, revealed a number of findings. It concluded that the crash was triggered by the erosion of market fundamentals, such as the aforementioned trade and budget deficits and rising interest rates. Surprisingly, however, only 3 percent of the total number of shares outstanding had changed hands. The commission also concluded that portfolio insurers had exacerbated the situation. For example, the wave of portfolio insurance selling was concentrated in only a few firms. The study reported that portfolio insurers sold about $4 billion of stock index futures on Black Monday, almost 70 percent of which came from three insurers. In addition, three portfolio insurers sold almost $2 billion in stocks, and index arbitrageurs sold about $1.7 billion in stocks. These figures were significant compared to those on otherwise normal trading days. However, other studies did not concur with these findings. For example, the CFTC's study found that portfolio insurers sold a much smaller percentage of the total number of futures contracts. Since portfolio insurance trading is not recorded as such, it is not surprising that there is disagreement over the amount of it that took place on Black Monday.

The Brady commission also outlined several proposals for changing the operations of securities, options, and futures markets. It argued that the current regulatory system, in which the stock and bond markets are regulated by the SEC and the futures markets by the CFTC, is inadequate for policing today's complex, highly integrated markets. It called for a type of super-regulator to oversee both agencies and suggested that the Federal Reserve perform this task. In light of the fact that most regulators seek to increase their powers, it was interesting that the Fed indicated it had no interest in assuming this responsibility.

The commission also recommended that the differential between margin requirements on stock and those on futures transactions be narrowed. Stock margins currently are 50 percent initial and 25 percent maintenance. Futures margins are about one-tenth of stock margins. The commission recommended not equalizing stock and futures margins but simply bringing them closer together. This particular recommendation was most distressing to the futures exchanges, which argued that futures margins really are not margins at all but performance guarantees and that any increases in margins on futures contracts would increase the cost of hedging. We shall look at this issue in more detail in the next section.

The Brady commission also asserted that the stock markets would benefit from the imposition of "circuit breakers," such as price limits or trading suspensions, that it believed would permit markets to "cool off" during times of panic. These suggestions were met with disdain by members of the Wall Street community, who see such devices as necessary only for futures markets.

Among the least controversial of the Brady commission proposals was its recommendation for a clearing system that includes both the stock and futures markets and its suggested improvements in the system of recording the identities of customers in trades executed by brokerage firms. Had the latter recommendation been in place, it probably would have made the commission's task much easier.

The entire story of what really happened on those two eventful days may never be completely known. Some people have described it—probably inaccurately—as a near financial meltdown, a system on the brink of total collapse. Others argue that it was simply the product of an overzealous investing public, benumbed to the continuing problems of the American economy. The market was simply adjusting itself to a more reasonable level. Index futures and options products may have sped up the revaluation of stocks sufficiently to occur in a matter of hours rather than months. Whatever the explanation, the crash ushered in an era of increasing stock price volatility.

Following the crash, some of the proposals of the Brady Committee were adopted. Circuit breakers, which halt trading when unusually large price movements have rapidly occurred, were instituted. However, an integrated clearing system, which might have reduced some of the panic selling to meet margin calls, is still not in place. In response to public pressures, many large institutions voluntarily stopped index arbitrage, and portfolio insurance was effectively dead. However, it is not clear that this was necessary. Roll (1988) found that of 23 countries studied, the U.S. market decline was the fifth smallest. A number of these countries' markets have extensive amounts of program trading. Roll found no relationship between the incidence of program trading and the size of the market's decline; in fact, countries with extensive program trading tended to have smaller declines. Roll concluded that the crash was truly worldwide in scope and was unrelated to futures and options activity.

Two years later, it was *déjà vu*. On Friday, October 13, 1989, the Dow fell 190.58 points, the second largest absolute decline and the twelfth largest percentage decline.[8] Volume was light early in the day, and it appeared the day might be uneventful. Almost all of the decline occurred in the last hour. The market break was primarily attributed to a takeover rumor in which UAL stockholders allegedly would be bought out by the firm's management. There was much speculative trading on this rumor, and at 2:43 p.m. the NYSE suspended trading in UAL. Ten minutes later, word arrived that UAL would be unable to obtain the necessary financing. Then the bottom fell out of the whole market. The circuit breakers took effect, closing the S&P futures market. This actually contributed to further confusion and an accumulation of unfilled orders in the futures markets. On the next trading day, Monday the 16th, the Dow fell 63 points in the first 40 minutes. However, it rebounded to close up 88 points.

Do index arbitrage trading and other forms of program trading produce this unusual volatility? Furbush (1989) found that index arbitrage trading indeed produces some price movements, as well it should, but the inability to do index arbitrage during the 1987 crash resulted in no relationship between volatility and the arbitrage. In other words, the market was quite volatile without index arbitrage. Harris, Sofianos, and Shapiro (1990) showed that program trading produces a modest increase in volatility.

Are we to conclude from this that volatility should be curtailed by restricting program trading? What is really happening is that futures prices are reacting more rapidly than spot prices to new information. This is as expected, because it is possible to trade in futures with less capital and the futures market is much more liquid. We should expect futures prices to move before spot prices. Futures are simply reacting quickly to the flow of new information. Although this may make the market more volatile, the lower volatility that previously characterized the market was but an illusion. When prices are more stable, it may well be that they simply have not reacted quickly enough. Futures trading enables prices to move more rapidly to their true values. Futures make the market more efficient. That this makes the market more volatile is merely a reflection of the fact that information is volatile and the market is now reacting more rapidly to the information.

A number of stock market participants have been hurt by the increased trading in futures and options. Brokers and institutions that specialize in stocks and do little, if any, futures and options trades have lost business as more trades have been diverted to the futures markets. Bad publicity and the tendency to look for a

---

[8] As you may have wondered, October has in fact been a particularly rough month for stocks. Of the 12 days in history with the largest declines in the market in both dollar and percentage terms, seven have been in October. The probability that this would occur by chance is less than .00002!

scapegoat have made many investors believe that these instruments are hurting them. Thus, the criticisms of futures are in many cases a result of individuals and institutions whose incomes have been damaged by lost business. Many firms and lawmakers have seized this issue as an opportunity to gain favor with the public. Thus, we should be aware that many criticisms often are self-serving.

Volatility and Margins

One recommendation of the Brady Commission was that margin requirements across stock and futures markets be made consistent. The commission did not define what *consistent* meant. However, it is clear from a reading of the report that the commission suggests raising futures margins, not necessarily to the level of stock margins but at least closer. Other critics of futures markets also have called for increases in futures margins. The primary means for accomplishing this would be to turn over the establishment of futures margins to a public regulator. Currently futures margins are set by the futures clearinghouses. By having a regulator such as the SEC, CFTC, or Federal Reserve set margins, it is likely that futures margins, like stock margins, would change infrequently and would be set considerably higher than they are now and higher than they would be on average if they were set by the futures clearinghouses.

The issue of whether margins can be used to control volatility is an old one. When the Federal Reserve was given margin setting authority over the stock market in 1934, it was stated that margin regulation was used to avoid the excess use of credit in the stock market, to protect investors from going too deeply into debt, and to control volatility. Over the years, the first two objectives are no longer considered of practical relevance. Yet there remains the belief that margins can be used to control volatility.

This issue has been studied extensively in both stock and futures markets. The monograph by Chance (1990) reviews the issues and evidence from about 70 documents on this subject. Here we shall take a brief look at this issue.

The general belief that margins can control volatility comes from the notion that margin trading is a cost of speculating. By making speculation more costly, there will be less of it and, if speculation causes volatility (an hypothesis that itself has not been proven), there will be lower volatility. The counterargument is that speculators provide valuable liquidity to the market. By making it more costly for them to trade, nonspeculators will have fewer investors to take the opposite side of the trade. This itself can increase volatility. Thus, by raising margin requirements it is actually possible to increase violatility.

The evidence on the effectiveness of margins in controlling volatility shows little support for their effectiveness. However, a series of papers by Hardouvelis (1988, 1990) claimed to have found support for the use of margins. Because these papers were done under the auspices of the Federal Reserve Bank of New York, they were highly publicized and opponents of futures and options markets seized the opportunity to use them as a basis for the argument for increasing futures margins.[9]

The methodology used in these papers has subsequently been attacked by Hsieh and Miller (1990) and several others. Correcting the Hardouvelis procedure, these authors show that there is no effect of margins on volatility. Extensive research by many other researchers on both futures and spot market prices shows no consistent impact of raising margins on volatility. In fact, in the futures markets, margins are raised in anticipation of increased volatility. Thus, higher margins do not cause volatility but are raised simply to better protect the markets from the effects of defaults when investors cannot meet margin calls. The futures markets have done an excellent job of responding to volatility by quickly raising margins. The alternative of having a government regulator set a margin would be far less efficient, because the government could not possibly react and change margins as quickly as the futures exchanges can.

As we briefly discussed earlier, it is important to recognize that futures margins actually are not margins at all. In the stock market, margin is an extension of credit. The investor puts down a fraction of the money and borrows the rest. In the futures market, the margin is simply a deposit that indicates that the futures trader is committed to the transaction. Unlike the margined stock transaction, the futures trader does not take title to an underlying asset. At the expiration of the transaction, the holder of the long position might take delivery and pay for it on margin, and at this point it would indeed be like a margin transaction in the spot market. However, this is not the proper comparison. Futures margins simply are not the same as stock margins.

The studies have revealed that futures margins are more than adequate to protect against defaults. If margins were increased, this excessive protection would be an economic waste. These funds could be used elsewhere. From the perspective of the hedger, margin represents the cost of insurance, and increased margins would make hedging more costly. Finally, arguments in favor of raising futures margins forget that highly liquid futures markets exist in other countries. If those countries do not raise margins on futures—and none have indicated a desire to do so—trades that formerly were done on U.S. exchanges will be done in other countries. The American futures industry, currently the world leader, could go the way of the automobile and steel industries.

This concludes our look at some of the critical issues that have dominated discussions of futures and options markets in recent years. It is obvious that the position taken here is one of strong support for futures and options markets. The more important conclusion is that you should carefully examine the evidence and not take a position based on emotion or popularity.

---

[9]As a matter of policy, the Federal Reserve banks, nearly all government agencies, and many corporations state that the views of their research economists represent independent thinking and are not necessarily the views of the institutition, agency, or firm.

SUMMARY

In this concluding chapter, we focused on three key points: understanding some advanced strategies that employ options and futures, learning about some new instruments that are similar to or contain imbedded options or futures, and addressing some controversial issues that have arisen as a result of the increased growth in the use of options, futures, and related instruments.

We saw how futures and options can be used to adjust the sensitivity of a portfolio to interest rate changes and stock market volatility. We examined how futures and options can be arbitraged with each other. We showed how options can be used to help capture dividends and earn certain tax breaks for corporations. We examined portfolio insurance, a now somewhat controversial practice that is designed to provide a minimum return on a portfolio.

We looked at interest rate options and a number of new, similar instruments, including caps, floors, collars, and swaps. We examined primes, scores, and market indexed securities, all of which have characteristics of equity, debt, and options.

Finally, we discussed the issues of the triple witching hour, the implications of market crashes, and the impact of margins on volatility.

This book has taken you on a journey into the world of options and futures. We have learned a lot since Chapter 1, but we have only begun to understand this fascinating and rapidly changing financial environment. You are encouraged to continue your study in this area by reading some of the advanced specialized books on these subjects. Many of the journal articles cited here provide important information about these markets. This book should be not an end but a beginning.

Questions and Problems

1. Studies have shown that the volatility of futures pricing during the triple witching hour is much greater when only futures expire than when only options expire. Why do you think this is the case?

2. Most of the portfolio insurance used in the real world is in the form of dynamically hedged portfolios of stock and futures or stock and T-bills. Opponents of portfolio insurance have argued that it can cause a falling market to fall more rapidly. Explain why this might be so. Then consider that portfolio insurance did not work as it should have during the market crash of 1987; that is, many so-called insured portfolios ended up falling below their targeted minimum values. Explain why you think this happened.

3. If futures margins, currently at 3 to 10 percent of the price of a contract, were raised to the level (or nearly the level) of stock margins, what would be the likely impact on the financial markets?

4. You are the manger of a bond portfolio of $10 million of face value of bonds worth $9,448,456. The portfolio has a yield of 12.25 percent and a duration of 8.33. You plan to liquidate the portfolio in six months and are concerned about an increase in interest rates that would produce a loss on the portfolio.

You would like to lower its duration to 5 years. A T-bond futures contract with the appropriate expiration is priced at ~~72 3/32~~ with a face value of $100,000, an implied yield of 12 percent, and a duration of 8.43 years.

a. Should you buy or sell futures? How many contracts should you use?

b. In six months, the portfolio has fallen in value to $8,952,597. The futures price is 68 16/32. Determine the profit from the transaction.

5. You are the manager of a stock portfolio worth $10,500,000. It has a beta of 1.15. During the next three months, you expect a correction in the market that will take the market down about 5 percent; thus, your portfolio is expected to fall about 5.75 percent (5 percent times a beta of 1.15). You wish to lower the beta to 1. An S&P 500 futures contract with the appropriate expiration is priced at 325.75 with a multiplier of $500.

a. Should you buy or sell futures? How many contracts should you use?

b. In three months, the portfolio has fallen in value to $9,870,000. The futures has fallen to 307.85. Determine the profit and portfolio return over the quarter. How close did you come to the desired result?

6. Determine the schedule of payments in a swap of floating- for fixed-rate interest payments. The notional principal is $20 million. The fixed-rate borrower pays the current LIBOR rate of 9 percent plus 2 points (i.e., 11 percent). The floating-rate borrower pays the LIBOR rate plus 1 point, with the rate determined on the first day of the interest period. Interest payments will be made in 90, 180, 270, and 360 days. The LIBOR rates that actually result are 10.5 (90 days from now), 10.2 (180 days from now), and 9.6 (270 days from now).

7. On September 12, the December S&P 500 futures was at 325.70. The December 320 call was at 18, and the put was at 14 5/8. The S&P 500 spot index was at 322.54. The futures and options expire on December 21. The discrete risk-free rate was 7.82 percent. Determine if the futures and options are priced correctly in relation to each other. If they are not, construct a risk-free portfolio and show how it will earn a rate better than the risk-free rate.

8. Evaluate the following hedged dividend capture strategy. On September 13, Coca-Cola stock was at 42 1/8. It was scheduled to pay a dividend of $0.20 on October 1. The November 40 call was selling at 3 1/4. The corporate tax rate is 34 percent, and the dividend exclusion is 70 percent. The call expires on November 16.

a. Determine the annualized return if the stock is at 35 when the call expires.

b. Determine the annualized return if the stock is at 46 when the call expires.

c. Identify the risk of this strategy.

9. On July 5, the S&P 500 index is at 192.54. You hold a portfolio that duplicates the S&P 500 and is worth 10,500 times the index. You wish to insure the portfolio over the period until September 20 at a minimum level slightly above its current value. You can buy T-bills maturing on September 20 with a face value of $100 for $98.78.

a. You plan to use S&P 500 puts, which are selling for $15.45 and have an exercise price of 208. Determine the appropriate number of puts and shares to hold.

b. Determine the value of the portfolio if the S&P 500 on September 20 is at 190.35.

c. Determine the value of the portfolio if the S&P 500 on September 20 is at 215. Compute the upside capture and the cost of the insurance.

10. On September 14, the S&P 500 index is a 318.65. You own a portfolio of shares that is equivalent to 150,000 shares of the S&P 500. You plan to sell the portfolio on December 20. You wish to insure the portfolio and plan to use S&P 500 calls with an exercise price of 325 and a price of $14.625 and T-bills worth $98.23 per $100 of face value. The corresponding puts are worth $18.25.

a. Determine the appropriate number of calls and T-bills.

b. Determine the portfolio rate of return on December 20 if the S&P 500 is at 332.5. Calculate the upside capture and the cost of the insurance.

c. Determine the portfolio rate of return on December 20 if the S&P 500 is at 305.45.

11. Use the information in problem 9 to set up a dynamic hedge using stock index futures. The continuously compounded risk-free rate is 6.83 percent, and the call delta is .27. Let the stock price increase by $1, and show that the change in the portfolio value is the same as it would have been had a put been used.

12. Use the information in problem 10 to set up a dynamic hedge using T-bills. The continuously compounded risk-free rate is 7.75 percent. The delta of the call is .53. Let the stock price decrease by $1 and show that the change in the portfolio value is the same as it would have been had calls and T-bills been used.

13. You are the treasurer of a firm that will need to borrow $10 million at the LIBOR rate plus 2.5 points in 45 days. The loan will have a maturity of 180 days, at which time all of the interest and principal will be repaid. The interest will be determined by the LIBOR rate on the day the loan is taken out. To hedge the uncertainty of this future rate, you purchase a call on the LIBOR rate with a strike of 9 percent for a premium of $32,000. Determine the amount you will pay back and the annualized cost of borrowing for LIBOR rates of 6 and 12 percent.

14. A large, multinational bank has committed to lend a firm $25 million in 30 days at the LIBOR rate plus 1 point. The loan will have a maturity of 90 days, at which time the principal and all interest will be repaid. The bank is concerned about falling interest rates and decides to buy a put on the LIBOR rate with a strike of 9.5 percent and a premium of $60,000. Determine the annualized cost of borrowing for LIBOR rates of 6.5 and 12.5 percent.

15. As the assistant treasurer of a large corporation, your job is to look for ways your company can lock in its cost of borrowing in the financial markets. The

date is June 28. Your firm is taking out a loan of $20 million, with interest to be paid on September 28, December 31, March 31, and June 29. You will pay the LIBOR rate in effect at the beginning of the interest payment period. The current LIBOR rate is 10 percent. You recommend that the firm buy an interest rate cap with a strike of 10 percent and a premium of $70,000. Determine the cash flows over the life of this loan if the LIBOR rates turn out to be 11 percent on September 28, 11.65 percent on December 31, and 12.04 percent on March 31. If you have a financial calculator or a spreadsheet with an IRR function, solve for the internal rate of return and annualize it to determine the effective cost of borrowing.

16. You are a funds manager for a large bank. On April 15, your bank lends a corporation $35 million, with interest payments to be made on July 16, October 15, January 16, and next April 16. The amount of interest will be determined by the LIBOR rate at the beginning of the interest payment period. Your forecast is for declining interest rates, so you anticipate lower loan interest revenues. You decide to buy an interest rate floor with a strike equal to the current LIBOR rate of 8 percent and a premium of $60,000. Determine the cash flows associated with the loan if the LIBOR rate turns out to be 7.9 percent on July 16, 7.7 percent on October 15, and 8.1 percent next January 16. If you have a financial calculator or spreadsheet with an IRR function, determine the internal rate of return and annualize it to determine your annualized return on the loan.

17. On January 15, a firm takes out a loan of $30 million, with interest payments to be made on April 16, July 15, October 14, and next July 15, when the principal will be repaid. Interest will be paid at the LIBOR rate based on the rate at the beginning of the interest payment period. The firm wants to buy a cap with a strike of 9 percent and a premium of $150,000. Its bank suggests that the firm sell a floor with a strike of 9 percent and a premium of $115,000. Answer the following questions.

    a. What is this transaction called? Why would the firm sell the floor in addition to buying the cap? What is the firm giving up if it adds the short floor to the long cap?

    b. If the LIBOR rates turn out to be 11.35 percent on April 16, 10.2 percent on July 15, and 8.86 percent on October 14, what are the firm's cash flows associated with the loan? If you have a financial calculator or spreadsheet, determine the internal rate of return and annualize it to determine your cost of borrowing.

18. Use the following information to estimate the price of an ARCO score. The current date is September 14, and ARCO stock is at 138 3/4. ARCO pays a dividend of $1.25 on the 15th of March, June, September, and December. ARCO scores pay gains based on whether the stock price rises above 116, and they expire on July 1, almost two years later. ARCO's volatility is .23, and the risk-free rate is 7.5 percent. Based upon the score price, how much should the prime be worth? (In counting days, ignore leap year.)

19. Consider the example of a market indexed security used in the chapter. Suppose that at the time the deposit was first offered, the bank wanted to pay 55 percent of the change in the S&P 500. Show that the guaranteed minimum rate would need to be zero.

20. (Concept Problem) In addition to market indexed securities that pay off in rising markets, there are market indexed securities that pay off in falling markets. These are called *put-style* or *bear market securities*. Using the procedure for deriving the call-style security, as presented in the chapter, develop a formula for a put-style security. Then use the data from the example in the chapter to determine the value of a put-style security on the day of initiation of its one-year life with a guaranteed rate of 4 percent and a participation percentage of 30 percent. What do you notice that is unusual about this result? (Note: The formula for the exercise price of the put-style security will differ from that of a call. It is $E = S_o / \{[(1 - \lambda)/\gamma] + 1\}$.

21. (Concept Problem) The formula we found for the minimum value of an insured portfolio of stock and puts is

$$V_{min} = \frac{EV}{S + P}.$$

In the problem used in the chapter, we established a minimum value of the portfolio of $233,900. Recall that $E = 265$, $V = \$232,230$, $S = 232.23$, and $P = \$30.878$. In that problem, we simply used the 265 put and derived the minimum value we could obtain with this put. However, a portfolio manager might want to choose the minimum value. This would require finding a put that would insure the portfolio at this minimum. Suppose that in this same example, the portfolio manager was willing to tolerate a 1 percent loss. Find the number of shares and puts that would be required. (Hint: The above equation for V_{min} must hold, but you must find a put with a different exercise price, which will result in a different put price, that will make the equation hold. You may wish to use a spreadsheet to do the repetitive calculations involved in the Black-Scholes model.)

References

Brown, Keith C., and Scott L. Lummer. "A Reexamination of the Covered Call Option Strategy for Corporate Cash Management." *Financial Management* 5 (Summer 1986): 13–17.

Chance, Don M. "The Effect of Margins on the Volatility of Stock and Derivative Markets: A Review of the Evidence." Monograph Series in Finance and Economics, Monograph 1990–2, New York University Salomon Center, 1990.

Chance, Don M., and John B. Broughton. "Market Index Depository Liabilities: Analysis, Interpretation and Performance." *Journal of Financial Services Research* 1 (1988): 335–352.

Chen, K. C., and R. Stephen Sears. "Pricing the SPIN." *Financial Management* 19 (Summer 1990): 36–47.

Clarke, Roger G., and Robert D. Arnott. "The Cost of Portfolio Insurance: Tradeoffs and Choices." *Financial Analysts Journal* 43 (November–December 1987): 35–47.

Duffie, Darrell. *Futures Markets*, Chapter 7. Englewood Cliffs, N.J.: Prentice-Hall, 1989.

Furbush, Dean. "Program Trading and Price Movements: Evidence from the October 1987 Market Crash." *Financial Management* 18 (Autumn 1989): 68–83.

Garcia, C. B., and F. J. Gould. "An Empirical Study of Portfolio Insurance." *Financial Analysts Journal* 43 (July–August 1987): 44–54.

Goodman, Laurie S. "The Use of Interest Rate Swaps in Managing Corporate Liabilities." *Journal of Applied Corporate Finance* 2 (1990): 35–47.

Hardouvelis, Gikas A. "Margin Requirements, Volatility and the Transitory Component of Stock Prices." *American Economic Review* 80 (September 1990): 736–762.

Hardouvelis, Gikas A. "Margin Requirements and Stock Market Volatility." *Federal Reserve Bank of New York Quarterly Review* 13 (Summer 1988): 80–89.

Harris, Lawrence, George Sofianos, and James E. Shapiro. "Program Trading and Intraday Volatility." Working paper no. 90–03, New York Stock Exchange, March 1990.

Hsieh, David A., and Merton H. Miller. "Margin Regulation and Stock Market Volatility." *The Journal of Finance* 45 (March 1990): 3–29.

Hull, John. *Options, Futures and Other Derivative Instruments*, Chapters 8, 10, 11. Englewood Cliffs, N.J.: Prentice-Hall, 1989.

Jarrow, Robert A., and Maureen O'Hara. "Primes and Scores: An Essay on Market Imperfections." *The Journal of Finance* 44 (December 1989): 1263–1287.

Marshall, John F., and Kenneth R. Kapner. *Understanding Swap Finance*. Cincinnati: South-Western Publishing Co., 1990.

Mid-America Institute for Public Policy Research. *Black Monday and the Future of Financial Markets*. Homewood, Ill.: Irwin, 1989.

O'Brien, Thomas J. "The Mechanics of Portfolio Insurance." *The Journal of Portfolio Management* 14 (Spring 1985): 40–47.

Rendleman, Richard J., Jr., and Richard W. McEnally. "Assessing the Cost of Portfolio Insurance." *Financial Analysts Journal* 43 (May–June 1987): 27–37.

Report of the Presidential Task Force on Market Mechanisms. Washington, D.C.: U.S. Government Printing Office, January 1988.

Ritchken, Peter. *Options: Theory, Strategy, and Applications*, Chapter 13. Glenview, Ill.: Scott, Foresman, 1987.

Roll, Richard. "The International Crash of October 1987." *Financial Analysts Journal* 44 (September–October, 1988): 19–35.

Rubinstein, Mark. "Portfolio Insurance and the Market Crash." *Financial Analysts Journal* 44 (January–February 1988): 38–47.

Rubinstein, Mark. "Alternative Paths to Portfolio Insurance." *Financial Analysts Journal* 41 (July–August 1985): 42–52.

Siegel, Daniel R., and Diane F. Siegel. *Futures Markets*, Chapters 4, 6, 10. Hinsdale, Ill.: Dryden Press, 1990.

Smith, Donald J. "The Arithmetic of Financial Engineering." *Journal of Applied Corporate Finance* 1 (1989): 49–58.

Stoll, Hans, and Robert E. Whaley. "Expiration Day Effects Revisited." Working paper, Futures and Options Research Center, Duke University, February 1990.

Stoll, Hans, and Robert E. Whaley. "Program Trading and Expiration Day Effects." *Financial Analysts Journal* 43 (July–August 1987): 44–54.

Tosini, Paula A. "Stock Index Futures and Stock Market Activity in October 1987." *Financial Analysts Journal* 44 (January–February 1988): 28–37.

Wall, Larry D., and John J. Pringle. "Alternative Explanations of Interest Rate Swaps." *Financial Management* 18 (Summer 1989): 59–73.

Yu, Zhu, and Robert C. Kavee. "Performance of Portfolio Insurance Strategies." *The Journal of Portfolio Management* 14 (1988): 48–54.

Zivney, Terry, and Michael J. Alderson. "Hedged Dividend Capture with Stock Index Options." *Financial Management* 15 (Summer 1986): 5–12.

appendix 14A

Derivation of the Hedge Ratio for Adjusting Duration with Treasury Bond Futures*

The value of the position can be specified as

$$V = S + V^f N_f,$$

where V^f is the value of the futures contract. Now we wish to find the effect of a change in r on V. Since $\partial V^f / \partial r = \partial f / \partial r$, we have

$$\frac{\partial V}{\partial r} = \left(\frac{\partial S}{\partial r}\right) + \left(\frac{\partial f}{\partial r}\right) N_f.$$

The overall portfolio of bonds and futures has a yield, y_v, and a target duration, DUR_T. We can use the chain rule to rewrite the above equation as

$$\frac{\partial V / \partial y_v}{\partial y_v / \partial r} = \left(\frac{\partial S / \partial y_s}{\partial y_s / \partial r}\right) + \left(\frac{\partial f / \partial y_f}{\partial y_f / \partial r}\right) N_f.$$

From the material on duration in Chapter 8, we know that by definition $\partial S / \partial y_s = -DUR_s S/(1 + y_s)$, $\partial f / \partial y_f = -DUR_f f/(1 + y_f)$, and $\partial V / \partial y_v = -DUR_v V/(1 + y_v)$. We make the assumption that the spot and futures yields change one for one with the yield on the overall portfolio. Thus, $\partial y_s / \partial y_v = 1$ and $\partial y_f / \partial y_v = 1$. Using this result, setting DUR_v to DUR_T the target duration, and making some algebraic rearrangements enables us to solve for the number of futures contracts:

$$N_f = -\left(\frac{DUR_s - DUR_T}{DUR_f}\right)\left(\frac{S}{f}\right)\left(\frac{1 + y_f}{1 + y_s}\right).$$

*This appendix requires the use of calculus.

appendix 14B

Derivation of the Dynamic Hedge Ratio for Portfolio Insurance[*]

STOCK-FUTURES DYNAMIC HEDGE

The stock-put portfolio of N shares and N puts initially is worth

$$V = N(S + P).$$

By this definition, N must equal $V/(S + P)$. The change in the portfolio's value for a small stock price change is given by the derivative of V with respect to S,

$$\frac{\partial V}{\partial S} = N\left(1 + \frac{\partial P}{\partial S}\right)$$

$$= \left(\frac{V}{S + P}\right)\left(1 + \frac{\partial P}{\partial S}\right).$$

We assume the put is not available, so we shall replicate the position with a portfolio of N_s shares of stock and N_f futures contracts. The value of the portfolio is

$$V = N_s S + N_f V^f,$$

where V^f is the value of the futures contract. Remember that the initial value of a futures contract is zero, so $V^f = 0$. The number of shares then will be $N_s = V/S$. The change in the portfolio's value for a small change in S is the derivative of V with respect to S,

$$\frac{\partial V}{\partial S} = N_s + N_f\left(\frac{\partial f}{\partial S}\right).$$

Note that we must include $N_f(df/dS)$ because $\partial V^f/\partial S = \partial f/\partial S$. Assuming no dividends, the futures price is

$$f = Se^{rT}.$$

[*]This appendix requires the use of calculus.

Thus,

$$\frac{\partial f}{\partial S} = e^{rT}.$$

We can substitute V/S for N_s and e^{rT} for $\partial f/\partial S$, giving

$$\frac{\partial V}{\partial S} = \left(\frac{V}{S}\right) + N_f e^{rT}.$$

The objective is to make the stock-futures portfolio respond to a stock price change in the same way a stock-put portfolio would. Thus, we should set these two derivatives equal to each other:

$$\left(\frac{V}{S+P}\right)\left(1 + \frac{\partial P}{\partial S}\right) = \left(\frac{V}{S}\right) + N_f e^{rT}.$$

Then we solve for N_f:

$$N_f = \left[\left(\frac{V}{S+P}\right)\left(1 + \frac{\partial P}{\partial S}\right) - \left(\frac{V}{S}\right)\right]e^{-rT}.$$

This formula might look somewhat simpler if we recognize that V/(S + P) is simply V_{min}/E and that $1 + \partial P/\partial S = \partial C/\partial S$. Thus,

$$N_f = \left[\left(\frac{V_{min}}{E}\right)\left(\frac{\partial C}{\partial S}\right) - \left(\frac{V}{S}\right)\right]e^{-rT}.$$

Of course, $\partial C/\partial S = N(d_1)$ from the Black-Scholes model.

STOCK–T-BILL DYNAMIC HEDGE

We just derived the sensitivity of a portfolio of N shares of stock and N puts. This value was shown to be

$$\frac{\partial V}{\partial S} = \left(\frac{V}{S+P}\right)\left(1 + \frac{\partial P}{\partial S}\right) = \frac{V_{min}}{E}\left(\frac{\partial C}{\partial S}\right).$$

A portfolio of stock and T-bills is worth

$$V = N_s S + N_B B.$$

Its sensitivity to a change in S is

$$\frac{\partial V}{\partial S} = N_s.$$

Note that the T-bill price does not change with a change in S. Setting this equal to the sensitivity of the stock-put portfolio and solving for N_s gives

$$N_s = \left(\frac{V_{min}}{E}\right)\left(\frac{\partial C}{\partial S}\right).$$

LIST OF SYMBOLS

A_2, A_1 = parameters in the Barone-Adesi/Whaley model

AI, AI_t, AI_T = accrued interest today, at time t, and at time T

b, b_t, b_T = basis today, at time t, and at expiration, T

B, B_T = price of bond or T-bill today, and at maturity, T

$\beta, \beta_S, \beta_f, \beta_p, \beta_c$ = beta, beta of spot asset, beta of futures, beta of portfolio, beta of call

β_T = target beta

C = (abbreviated) price of call

$C(S,T,E)$ = price of either European or American call on asset with price S, expiration T, and exercise price E

$C_e(S,T,E)$ = price of European call on asset with price S, expiration T, and exercise price E

$C_a(S,T,E)$ = price of American call on asset with price S, expiration T, and exercise price E

$C(f,T,E)$ = price of either European or American call on futures with price f, expiration T, and exercise price E

$C_e(f,T,E)$ = price of European call on futures with price f, expiration T, and exercise price E

$C_a(f,T,E)$ = price of American call on futures with price f, expiration T, and exercise price E

$C_u, C_d, C_{u^2}, C_{ud}, C_{d^2}$ = call price sequence in binomial model

χ = convenience yield

CI_t = coupon interest paid at time t

CP_t = cash payment (principal or interest) on bond at time t

CF = conversion factor on CBT T-bond contract

CF^t, CF^T = conversion factor on CBT T-bond contracts deliverable at times t and T

c = coupon rate

$\Delta S, \Delta f$ = change in spot price, change in futures price

δ = dividend yield

d = (without subscript) downward return on stock in binomial model

d_1, d_2 = variables in Black-Scholes model

D_t = dividend paid at time t

DUR, DUR_S, DUR_f = duration, duration of spot, duration of futures

E = exercise price

$E(x)$ = expected value of the argument x

e^* = measure of hedging effectiveness

f^*, f^{**} = critical stock prices for early exercise of call and put in the Barone-Adesi/Whaley option on futures pricing model

f, f_t, f_T = futures price or futures exchange rate today, at time t, and at expiration T

f^t, f^T = futures price today of contracts expiring at t and T

F, F_t, F_T = forward price or forward exchange rate today, at time t, and at expiration T

FV = face value of bond

γ = participation percentage in market indexed security

g = growth rate of stock

h, h_u, h_d = hedge ratios in binomial model

$I(\gamma, \lambda, T-t)$ = value of market indexed security

i = interest lost on storing a good; also guaranteed minimum interest rate on market indexed security

J = number of observations in sample

j = counter in summation procedure

K = number of stocks in portfolio; also a parameter in the Barone-Adesi/Whaley model

k = discount rate (required rate) on stock

λ = guaranteed minimum payoff from market indexed security m = number of implicit calls in market indexed security

M = value of market portfolio; also a parameter in the Barone-Adesi/Whaley model

MOS = number of months in computing CBT conversion factor

MOS* = number of months in computing CBT conversion factor rounded down to nearest quarter

μ_S = unsystematic return on stock

$N(d_1), N(d_2)$ = cumulative normal probabilities in Black-Scholes model

NPV = net present value of box spread

N_C, N_P, N_S, N_f, N_B = number of calls, puts, shares of stock, futures, and T-bills held in a position

N = parameter in the Barone-Adesi/Whaley model

n = number of time periods in n-period binomial model

Π = profit from strategy

P = (abbreviated) price of put

P(S,T,E) = price of either European or American put on asset with price S, expiration T, and exercise price E

P_e(S,T,E) = price of European put on asset with price S, expiration T, and exercise price E

P_a(S,T,E) = price of American put on asset with price S, expiration T, and exercise price E

P(f,T,E) = price of either European or American put on futures with price f, expiration T, and exercise price E

P_e(f,T,E) = price of European put on futures with price f, expiration T, and exercise price E

P_a(f,T,E) = price of American put on futures with price f, expiration T, and exercise price E

p = variable in binomial model

$PVBP_S, PVBP_f$ = present value of basis point change for spot, futures

PRIME = value of a prime

ϕ = risk premium

Q_1, Q_2 = quantity of good supplied at times 1 and 2

q_2, q_1 = parameters in the Barone-Adesi/Whaley option pricing model

r = risk-free rate

r(a,b) = interest rate over time interval (a,b)

R = implied repo rate

r_f = percentage change in futures price

r_S = return on stock or spot position

r_{St} = return on stock at time t

r_{Sf} = return on portfolio of stock and futures

r_M = return on market

r_{Mt} = return on market at time t

r^C = continuously compounded return

r_t^C = continuously compounded return at time t

$\bar{r}^C$ = mean continuously compounded return

ρ = foreign risk-free rate

s = storage costs

SCORE = value of a score

S^*, S^{**} = critical stock prices for early exercise of call and put in the Barone-Adesi/Whaley model

S, S_t, S_T = stock price (or spot price or spot exchange rate) today, at time t, and at time T

$S_u, S_{u^2}, S_{ud}, S_d, S_{d^2}$ = stock price sequence in binomial model

S_T^* = breakeven stock price at expiration

$S_T^\dagger$ = stock price at expiration at which straddle profit is equivalent to either strap or strip profit

S_D = stock price minus present value of dividends

S^* = ex-dividend stock price

$S_a^\ddagger$ = critical stock price for early exercise of put

$S_e^\ddagger$ = price at which European put price equals intrinsic value of American put

σ = standard deviation (σ^2 = variance)

σ_{xz} = covariance between x and z

σ_x^2 = variance of x

T = expiration or time to expiration from the current time

$T(1), T(2)$ = time points prior to expiration T

t = future point in time

τ = time value of option

θ = cost of carry

u = upward return on stock in binomial model

UNIT = value of a unit

V, V_t, V_T = value of a portfolio, asset, or contract today, at time t, and at time T

V_{min} = minimum or insured value of portfolio

V_u, V_d, V_{ud} = sequence of values of portfolio in binomial model

w_j = weight of asset j in portfolio

YRS = number of years in computation of CBT conversion factor

y, y_s, y_v = bond yield, yield on spot bond, yield on portfolio worth V

y_f = yield on deliverable bond implied by futures price

LIST OF FORMULAS

Intrinsic Value of American Call

$$C_a(S,T,E) \geq \text{Max}(0, S - E)$$

Maximum Spread of European Calls

$$(E_2 - E_1)(1 + r)^{-T} \geq C_e(S,T,E_1) - C_e(S,T,E_2)$$

Maximum Spread of American Calls

$$(E_2 - E_1) \geq C_a(S,T,E_1) - C_a(S,T,E_2)$$

Lower Bound of European Call

$$C_e(S,T,E) \geq \text{Max}[0, S - E(1 + r)^{-T}]$$

Intrinsic Value of American Put

$$P_a(S,T,E) \geq \text{Max}(0, E - S)$$

Maximum Spread of European Puts

$$(E_2 - E_1)(1 + r)^{-T} \geq P_e(S,T,E_2) - P_e(S,T,E_1)$$

Maximum Spread of American Puts

$$(E_2 - E_1) \geq P_a(S,T,E_2) - P_a(S,T,E_1)$$

Lower Bound of European Put

$$P_e(S,T,E) \geq Max[0, E(1+r)^{-T} - S]$$

Put-Call Parity

$$C_e(S,T,E) = P_e(S,T,E) + S - E(1+r)^{-T}$$

Stock Prices in Binomial Model

$$S_u = S(1+u)$$
$$S_d = S(1+d)$$
$$S_{u^2} = S(1+u)^2$$
$$S_{d^2} = S(1+d)^2$$
$$S_{ud} = S(1+u)(1+d)$$

Call Prices in One-Period Binomial Model

$$C_u = Max[0, S(1+u) - E]$$
$$C_d = Max[0, S(1+d) - E]$$
$$C = \frac{pC_u + (1-p)C_d}{1+r}$$

Call Prices in Two-Period Binomial Model

$$C_{u^2} = Max[0, S(1+u)^2 - E]$$
$$C_{d^2} = Max[0, S(1+d)^2 - E]$$
$$C_{ud} = Max[0, S(1+u)(1+d) - E]$$
$$C_u = \frac{pC_{u^2} + (1-p)C_{ud}}{1+r}$$
$$C_d = \frac{pC_{ud} + (1-p)C_{d^2}}{1+r}$$
$$C = \frac{pC_u + (1-p)C_d}{1+r}$$

Value of p in Binomial Model

$$p = \frac{r-d}{u-d}$$

Hedge Ratios in Binomial Model

$$h = \frac{C_u - C_d}{S_u - S_d}$$

$$h_u = \frac{C_{u2} - C_{ud}}{S_{u2} - S_{ud}}$$

$$h_d = \frac{C_{ud} - C_{d2}}{S_{ud} - S_{d2}}$$

Sequence of Hedge Portfolio Values in Binomial Model

$$V = hS - C$$
$$V_u = hS(1 + u) - C_u$$
$$V_d = hS(1 + d) - C_d$$

Black-Scholes Call Option Pricing Model

$$C = SN(d_1) - Ee^{-rT}N(d_2)$$

$$d_1 = \frac{\ln(S/E) + \left[r + \left(\sigma^2/2\right)\right]T}{\sigma\sqrt{T}}$$

$$d_2 = d_1 - \sigma\sqrt{T}$$

Black-Scholes Put Option Pricing Model

$$P = Ee^{-rT}[1 - N(d_2)] - S[1 - N(d_1)]$$

Stock Price Minus Present Value of Dividends

$$S_D = S - D_t e^{-rt} \text{ (one dividend)}$$
$$S_D = Se^{-\delta T} \text{ (continuous dividends)}$$

Sample Estimate of Mean of Continuously Compounded Return

$$r^c = \sum_{t=1}^{J} r_t^c / J$$

Sample Estimate of Variance of Continuously Compounded Return

$$\sigma^2 = \frac{\sum_{t=1}^{J}\left(r_t^c - \bar{r}^c\right)^2}{(J-1)} = \frac{\sum_{t=1}^{J}\left(r_t^c\right)^2 - \left(\sum_{t=1}^{J} r_t^c\right)^2 / J}{(J-1)}$$

Implied Volatility of At-the-Money Call

$$\sigma \cong C / (0.398)S\sqrt{T}$$

Profit from Call Transaction Held to Expiration

$$\Pi = N_c[\text{Max}(0, S_T - E) - C]$$

Profit from Call Transaction Terminated at T(1)

$$\Pi = N_c\left[C\left(S_{T(1)}, T - T(1), E\right) - C\right]$$

Profit from Put Transaction Held to Expiration

$$\Pi = N_p[\text{Max}(0, E - S_T) - P]$$

Profit from Put Transaction Terminated at T(1)

$$\Pi = N_P\left[P\left(S_{T(1)}, T - T(1), E\right) - P\right]$$

Profit from Stock Transaction

$$\Pi = N_s(S_T - S)$$

Ratio of Calls in Riskless Spread

$$\frac{N_1}{N_2} = -\frac{\partial C_2 / \partial S}{\partial C_1 / \partial S}$$

Bond Price Using Term Structure

$$B = \sum_{t=1}^{T} CI_t\left[1 + r(0, t)\right]^{-t} + FV\left[1 + r(0, T)\right]^{-T}$$

Bond Price Using Yield

$$B = \sum_{t=1}^{T} CP_t(1 + y)^{-t}$$

$$= CI\left[\frac{1 - (1 + y)^{-T}}{y}\right] + FV(1 + y)^{-T}$$

Duration

$$DUR = \frac{\sum_{t=1}^{T} tCP_t(1 + y)^{-t}}{B} = \frac{CI(1 + y)\left[(1 + y)^T - 1\right] + Ty(FVy - CI)}{CIy\left[(1 + y)^T - 1\right] + FVy^2}$$

Bond Price Percentage Change

$$\frac{\Delta B}{B} \cong -DUR\frac{\Delta y}{(1 + y)}$$

Constant Growth Stock Price

$$S = \frac{D_1}{k - g}$$

Capital Asset Pricing Model

$$E(r_S) = r + [E(r_M) - r]\beta$$

Beta

$$\beta = \frac{\sigma_{SM}}{\sigma_M^2}$$

Sample Estimate of Covariance between Returns on Stock and Market

$$\sigma_{SM} = \frac{\sum_{t=1}^{J} r_{St} r_{Mt} - \left(\sum_{t=1}^{J} r_{St} \sum_{t=1}^{J} r_{Mt}\right)/J}{J-1}$$

Sample Estimate of Variance of Return on Market

$$\sigma_{M}^{2} = \frac{\sum_{t=1}^{J} r_{Mt}^{2} - \left(\sum_{t=1}^{J} r_{Mt}\right)^{2}/J}{J-1}$$

Spot Price under Uncertainty and Risk Neutrality

$$S = E(S_{T}) - s - i$$

Spot Price under Uncertainty and Risk Aversion

$$S = E(S_{T}) - s - i - E(\phi)$$

Value of a Forward Contract at Time t Prior to Expiration

$$V_{t} = (F_{t} - F)(1 + r)^{-(T-t)}$$

Put-Call-Futures Parity

$$C_{e}(S,T,E) - P_{e}(S,T,E) = (f - E)(1 + r)^{-T}$$

Basis Today

$$b = S - f$$

Basis at Time t

$$b_{t} = S_{t} - f_{t}$$

Profit from a Short Hedge

$$\Pi = b_{t} - b$$

Cost of Carry Futures Pricing Model

$$f = S + \theta$$

Cost of Carry Futures Pricing Model with Convenience Yield

$$f = S + \theta + \chi$$

Stock Index Futures Pricing Model

$$f = Se^{(r-\delta)T}$$

Stock Index Futures Pricing Model with Discrete Dividends

$$f = S(1 + r)^{T} - \sum_{t=1}^{T} D_{t}(1 + r)^{T-t}$$

Futures Spread Pricing Model

$$f_{2} - f_{1} = \theta_{2} - \theta_{1}$$

Variance of Profit from Hedge

$$\sigma_\Pi^2 = \sigma_{\Delta S}^2 + \sigma_{\Delta f}^2 N_f^2 + 2\sigma_{\Delta S\Delta f}N_f$$

Duration of Futures

$$DUR_f \cong -\frac{(\Delta f/f)(1+y_f)}{\Delta y_f}$$

Minimum Variance Hedge Ratio

$$N_f = -\frac{\sigma_{\Delta S\Delta f}}{\sigma_{\Delta f}^2}$$

Price Sensitivity Hedge Ratio

$$N_f = -\frac{DUR_s S(1+y_f)}{DUR_f f(1+y_s)}$$

Stock Index Futures Hedge Ratio

$$N_f = -\beta_s\left(\frac{S}{f}\right)$$

Hedging Effectiveness

$$e* = \frac{\sigma_{\Delta S}^2 - \sigma_\Pi^2}{\sigma_{\Delta S}^2}$$

Number of Futures to Tail a Hedge

$$N = N_f(1+r)^{-(\text{days until expiration}-1)/365}$$

Beta of Portfolio

$$\beta_p = \sum_{j=1}^{K} w_j\beta_j$$

Conversion Factors for CBT T-Bond Contract

$$CF_0 = (c/2)\left(\frac{1-(1.04)^{-2*YRS}}{.04}\right) + (1.04)^{-2*YRS}$$

$$CF_3 = (CF_0 + c/2)(1.04)^{-.5} - c/4$$

$$CF_6 = (c/2)\left(\frac{1-(1.04)^{-(2*YRS+1)}}{.04}\right) + (1.04)^{-(2*YRS+1)}$$

$$CF_9 = (CF_6 + c/2)(1.04)^{-.5} - c/4$$

Conversion of IMM Index to Futures Price per $100

$$f = 100 - (100 - \text{IMM Index})(90/360)$$

Implied Repo on T-Bill or Eurodollar Cash and Carry

$$R = \left(\frac{f}{S}\right)^{(1/t)} - 1$$

Implied Repo on T-Bond or T-Note Cash and Carry

$$R = \left[\frac{f(CF) + AI_T}{S + AI}\right]^{(1/T)} - 1$$

Spot Price for Justifying Exercise of Wild Card Option

$$S_5 < f_3(CF)$$

Implied Repo Rate on T-Bond or T-Note Spread

$$R = \left[\frac{f^T(CF^T) + AI_T}{f^t(CF^t) + AI_t}\right]^{1/(T-t)} - 1$$

Intrinsic Value of American Call Option on Futures

$$C_a(f,T,E) \geq Max(0, f - E)$$

Intrinsic Value of American Put Option on Futures

$$P_a(f,T,E) \geq Max(0, E - f)$$

Lower Bound of European Call Option on Futures

$$C_e(f,T,E) \geq Max[0, (f - E)(1 + r)^{-T}]$$

Lower Bound of European Put Option on Futures

$$P_e(f,T,E) \geq Max[0, (E - f)(1 + r)^{-T}]$$

Put-Call Parity of Options on Futures

$$C_e(f,T,E) = P_e(f,T,E) + (f - E)(1 + r)^{-T}$$

Black Call Option on Futures Pricing Model

$$C = e^{-rT}\left[fN(d_1) - EN(d_2)\right]$$

$$d_1 = \frac{\ln(f/E) + (\sigma^2/2)T}{\sigma\sqrt{T}}$$

$$d_2 = d_1 - \sigma\sqrt{T}$$

Black Put Option on Futures Pricing Model

$$P = Ee^{-rT}\left[1 - N(d_2)\right] - fe^{-rT}\left[1 - N(d_1)\right]$$

Interest Rate Parity

$$\frac{F}{S} = (1 + r)^T(1 + \rho)^{-T}$$

Lower Bound of European Foreign Currency Call

$$C_e(S,T,E) \geq Max[0, S(1+\rho)^{-T} - E(1+r)^{-T}]$$

Lower Bound of European Foreign Currency Put

$$P_e(S,T,E) \geq Max[0, E(1+r)^{-T} - S(1+\rho)^{-T}]$$

Put-Call Parity of Foreign Currency Options

$$C_e(S,T,E) = P_e(S,T,E) + S(1+\rho)^{-T} - E(1+r)^{-T}$$

Garman-Kohlhagen Foreign Currency Call Option Pricing Model

$$C = Se^{-\rho T}N(d_1) - Ee^{-rT}N(d_2)$$

$$d_1 = \frac{\ln(Se^{-\rho T}/E) + [r + (\sigma^2/2)]T}{\sigma\sqrt{T}}$$

$$d_2 = d_1 - \sigma\sqrt{T}$$

Futures Contracts Required to Achieve Target Beta

$$N_f = (S/f)(\beta_T - \beta_S)$$

Calls Required to Achieve Target Beta

$$N_c = -\frac{V}{C}\left(\frac{\beta_T - \beta_S}{\beta_S - \beta_c}\right)$$

Futures Required to Achieve Target Duration

$$N_f = -\left(\frac{DUR_S - DUR_T}{DUR_f}\right)\left(\frac{S}{f}\right)\left(\frac{1+y_f}{1+y_s}\right)$$

Minimum Value of Insured Portfolio

$$V_{min} = \frac{EV}{S+P}$$

Number of Shares and Puts to Insure Portfolio

$$N = \frac{V}{S+P}$$

Number of Treasury Bills to Insure Portfolio with Calls and Treasury Bills

$$N_B = \frac{V_{min}}{B_T}$$

Number of Calls to Insure Portfolio with Calls and Treasury Bills

$$N_c = \frac{(V - N_B B)}{C} = \frac{V}{S+P}$$

Number of Shares of Stock in Dynamic Hedge with Treasury Bills

$$N_S = \left(\frac{V_{min}}{E}\right)\left(\frac{\partial C}{\partial S}\right)$$

Number of Treasury Bills in Dynamic Hedge

$$N_B = \frac{V - N_S S}{B}$$

Number of Futures in Dynamic Hedge with Stock Index Futures

$$N_f = \left[\left(\frac{V_{min}}{E}\right)\left(\frac{\partial C}{\partial S}\right) - \left(\frac{V}{S}\right)\right]e^{-rT}$$

Value of Market Indexed Security

$$I(\gamma, \lambda, T - t) = mC(S_t, T - t, E) + \lambda e^{-rT}$$

Exercise Price of Market Indexed Security

$$E = S_0\left\{\left[(\lambda - 1)\gamma\right] + 1\right\}$$

Payoff from Interest Rate Cap

$$(\text{Notional principal})\left(\frac{\text{Days in period}}{360}\right)\left(\frac{\text{Max}(0, \text{LIBOR} - E)}{100}\right)$$

Payoff from Interest Rate Floor

$$(\text{Notional principal})\left(\frac{\text{Days in period}}{360}\right)\left(\frac{\text{Max}(0, E - \text{LIBOR})}{100}\right)$$

GLOSSARY

Accrued interest The amount of interest accumulated on a bond since its last coupon payment date.

Against actuals *See* Exchange for physicals.

All or none order An order to purchase or sell a security or contract in which the broker is instructed to fill the entire order or not fill any of the order.

All or none, same price order An order to purchase or sell a security or contract in which the broker is instructed to fill the entire order at the same price or not fill any of the order.

American option An option that can be exercised on any day during its life.

Anticipatory hedge A futures transaction in which a hedger expects to make a transaction in the spot market at a future date and is attempting to protect against a change in the spot price.

Arbitrage A transaction based on the observation of the same asset selling at two different prices. The transaction involves buying the asset at the lower price and selling it at the higher price.

Arbitrage pricing theory A theory of asset pricing in which the expected return is a function of the asset's sensitivity to one or more underlying economic factors.

Arbitrageur An individual who engages in an arbitrage transaction.

Ask price The price at which a market maker offers to sell a security, option, or futures.

Asset allocation A type of general investment strategy in which funds are allocated across broad asset classes such as domestic stocks, foreign stocks, bonds, and real estate in an attempt to profit from those asset classes that are expected to provide the best performance.

Asset pricing theory The study of the economic processes through which prices and expected returns on securities are formulated.

Assignment The procedure in which the holder of a short position in an option is instructed to buy or sell the underlying asset or futures from or to the holder of the long position.

Associated person An individual affiliated with a firm engaged in any line of futures-related business but excluding individuals who execute trades, manage portfolios or pools, give advice, or perform clerical duties.

At-the-money An option in which the price of the underlying stock or futures equals the exercise price.

Backwardation A condition in financial markets in which the forward or futures price is less than the spot price.

Basis The difference between the spot price and the futures price or a nearby futures price and a deferred futures price.

Basis point A measure commonly applied to interest rates or yields equal to one 1/100 of 1 percent.

Bear market A market in which prices are falling.

Bear spread An option or futures spread designed to profit in a bear market. Also known as a *bearish spread.*

Best bond to deliver The bond that if delivered on the Chicago Board of Trade's Treasury bond or note contract provides the smallest difference between the invoice price and the cost of the bond.

Beta A measure of the responsiveness of a security or portfolio to the market as a whole.

Biased expectations A condition in which investors' expectations of a se-

curity price or return systematically differ from the subsequent long-run average price or return.

Bid price The price at which a market maker offers to buy a security, option, or futures.

Bid-ask spread The difference between the ask price and the bid price.

Binomial model An option pricing model based on the assumption that at any point in time the price of the underlying asset or futures can change to one of only two possible values.

Black model A pricing model for an option on a forward or futures contract.

Black-Scholes model A pricing model for an option on an asset.

Block trade The sale of at least 10,000 shares of stock normally conducted with considerable care so as to minimize the impact on the stock price.

Bond option An option to buy or sell a bond.

Boundary condition A statement specifying the maximum or minimum price or some other limitation on the price of an option.

Box spread A combination of a call money spread and a put money spread.

Breakeven stock price The stock price at which an option, futures, or stock strategy has a zero profit.

Broker A person who arranges a financial transaction by bringing a buyer and seller together and usually earns a commission.

Bull market A market in which prices are rising.

Bull spread An option or futures spread designed to profit in a bull market. Also known as a *bullish spread.*

Butterfly spread An option transaction consisting of one long call at a particular exercise price, another otherwise identical long call at a different exercise price, and two otherwise identical short calls at an exercise price between the other two.

Calendar spread   An option transaction consisting of the purchase of an option with a given expiration and the sale of an otherwise identical option with a different expiration.

Call   An option to buy an asset, currency, or futures. Also refers to the early retirement of a bond.

Call date   The earliest date at which a bond can be called.

Callability   A feature associated with many bonds in which the issuer is permitted to pay off the bond prior to its scheduled maturity date.

Callable bond   A bond that the issuer can retire the bond prior to its maturity date.

Cap   A transaction in which a party borrowing at a floating rate pays a fee to another party, which reimburses the borrower in the event that the borrower's interest costs exceed a certain level, thus making the effective interest paid on a floating rate loan have a cap or maximum amount.

Capital Asset Pricing Model   A model that gives the equilibrium expected return on an asset as a function of the risk-free rate, the expected return on the market, and the asset's beta or systematic risk.

Capital market   The financial market in which long-term securities such as stocks and long-term bonds are traded.

Carry   The difference between the cash received from holding an asset and the interest forgone or other costs associated with holding it.

Cash and carry   A theoretically riskless transaction consisting of a long position in the spot asset and a short position in the futures contract that is designed to be held until the futures expires.

Cash market   *See* Spot market.

Cash settlement   The feature of certain futures contracts or options that allows delivery or exercise to be conducted with an exchange of cash rather than the physical transfer of assets.

Cheapest to deliver   *See* Best bond to deliver.

Circuit breaker   *See* Trading halt.

Class   All of the options of a particular type (call or put) on a given stock, index, currency, or futures commodity.

Clearing firm   A company that is a member of a futures or options clearinghouse.

Clearinghouse   A corporation associated with an options or futures exchange that guarantees the performance of both parties to the contract, collects margins, and maintains records of the parties to all transactions.

Collar   A combination of a cap and a floor in which the purchaser of the cap also sells a floor or the purchaser of a floor also sells a cap. The sale of the cap or floor reduces the cost of the protection and forgoes gains if interest rates move in that party's favor.

Commercial paper   A short-term promissory note issued by a large, creditworthy corporation.

Commission   A fee paid by the parties in a transaction to a broker for arranging the transaction.

Commission broker   A trader on the floor of a futures exchange who executes transactions for off-the-floor customers.

Commodity   Any asset, but more frequently used to refer to an agricultural product or sometimes a metal or natural resource.

Commodity futures   Any futures contract, but primarily a futures on an agricultural product or sometimes a metal or natural resource.

Commodity Futures Trading Commission   The federal agency that regulates the futures markets.

Commodity option   An option on a commodity, but more often an option on a futures contract.

Commodity pool   An investment arrangement in which individuals combine their funds and the total amount of funds is used to trade futures contracts, with a large cash reserve set aside to meet margin calls. Essentially equivalent to a futures fund.

Commodity pool operator   The organizer or manager of a commodity pool.

Commodity trading advisor   An individual who specializes in offering advice regarding the trading of futures contracts.

Comparative statics   An examination of the effect on a model of the changes in the variables that influence the model.

Constant growth discounted cash flow model   A model that determines the price of a stock as the present value of a stream of dividends growing at a constant rate.

Contango   A condition in financial markets in which the forward or futures price is greater than the spot price.

Continuously compounded return   A rate of return in which the asset price grows continuously.

Convenience yield   A premium imbedded in the spot price that provides an extra return for those holding the commodity and is usually observed during shortages of the commodity.

Conversion   An arbitrage transaction consisting of the sale of a call and the purchase of a synthetic call.

Conversion factor   An adjustment factor applied to the settlement price of the Chicago Board of Trade's Treasury bond and note contracts that gives the holder of the short position a choice of several different bonds or notes to deliver.

Convertible bond   A bond in which the holder can convert into a specified number of shares of stock.

Convexity The mathematical relationship between the change in a bond price and the change in its yield that is not explained by its duration. Represents the change in the bond price for a given change in the yield. Knowledge and use of convexity is helpful in obtaining better hedge results.

Cost of carry The cost involved in holding or storing an asset that consists of storage costs and interest lost on funds tied up.

Coupon The interest paid on a bond.

Covariance A measure of the association between two random variables.

Covered call A combination of a long position in an asset, futures, or currency and a short position in a call on the same.

Cross-rate relationship The association among the exchange rates of three currencies.

Currency swap A transaction in which two parties each borrowing in a particular currency agree to swap interest payments, thus converting each party's loan in a given currency into a loan in another currency.

Daily price limits The maximum and minimum prices at which a futures contract can trade. These are established by the clearinghouse and are expressed in relation to the previous day's settlement price.

Daily settlement The process in a futures market in which the daily price changes are paid by the parties incurring losses to the parties making profits. Also known as marking to market.

Day order An order to purchase or sell a security, futures, or option that is cancelled if unfilled by the end of the day.

Day trader A futures or option trader who closes out all positions by the end of the trading session.

Dealer A person or firm who assists in a transaction by purchasing the security or contract from a seller and selling it to a buyer.

Deductible A concept in insurance representing the amount by which an insurance payoff is reduced as a result of the insured assuming some of the risk.

Deep in-the-money An option that is in-the-money by a significant, though unspecific, amount.

Deep out-of-the-money An option that is out-of-the-money by a significant, though unspecific, amount.

Delivery The process in which a futures contract can be terminated at expiration through the sale of the asset by the short to the long.

Delivery day The day on which an asset is delivered to terminate a futures contract.

Delta The ratio of the change in an option's price for a given change in the price of the underlying asset or futures.

Diagonal spread An option spread in which the options differ by both time to expiration and exercise price.

Diffs Futures contracts based on the difference between two prices, exchange rates, or interest rates.

Diversification An investment strategy in which funds are allocated across numerous different assets.

Dividend protection A feature associated with over-the-counter options in which the exercise price is reduced by the amount of any dividend paid on the underlying stock.

Dividend yield The ratio of the dividend to the stock price.

DOT An acronym for Designated Order Turnaround, the New York Stock Exchange's system for expediting stock transactions that is used frequently in program trading.

Dual trading The practice of a floor trader on a futures exchange trading for his or her own account as well as for a customer.

Duration A measure of the size and timing of a bond's cash flows. It also reflects the weighted average maturity of the bond and indicates the sensitivity of the bond's price to a change in its yield.

Dynamic hedge An investment strategy, often associated with portfolio insurance, in which a stock is hedged by selling futures or buying Treasury bills in such a manner that the position is adjusted frequently and simulates a protective put.

Early exercise Exercise of an American option before its expiration date.

Efficient market A market in which the price of an asset reflects its true economic value.

Empirical test A procedure in which data are subjected to various statistical measures to determine if a theory, model, or hypothesis is correct.

End-of-month option On the Chicago Board of Trade's Treasury Bond futures contract, the right to deliver any day during the last remaining business days of the month after the futures contract has ceased trading.

Equity option An option on a common stock.

Eurodollar A dollar deposited in a European bank or a European branch of an American bank.

European Currency Unit A composite measure of a U.S. dollar exchange rate based on a combination of European currencies.

European option An option that can be exercised only when it expires.

Exchange for physicals A method of delivery on a futures contract in which the long and short agree to delivery terms different from those specified in the futures contract.

Exchange rate The rate at which a given amount of one currency converts to another currency.

Ex-dividend date A day designated four business days prior to the holder-of-record date after which an investor purchasing a stock does not receive the upcoming dividend.

Exercise　The process by which a call option is used to purchase or a put option is used to sell the underlying security, futures, or currency or convert to their cash values.

Exercise limit　The maximum number of option contracts that any one investor can exercise over a specific time period.

Exercise price　The price at which an option permits its owner to buy or sell the underlying security, futures, or currency.

Exercise value　*See* Intrinsic value.

Expectations theory　An explanation for the shape of the term structure in which forward rates are considered to be the market's expectation of future spot rates.

Expiration　The date after which an option or futures contract no longer exists.

Extendible bond　A bond in which the holder can choose prior to maturity to extend the maturity date.

Face value　The principal amount borrowed on a loan.

Fiduciary call　A form of portfolio insurance in which funds are allocated to calls and Treasury bills such that the transaction is equivalent to a protective put.

Financial asset　An asset representing a claim of one party on another.

Financial futures　Futures on securities, sometimes including futures on foreign currencies.

Floating rate loan　A loan in which the interest payments are adjusted periodically to be consistent with current market interest rates.

Floor　A transaction in which a party lending at a floating rate pays a fee to another party, which reimburses the lender in the event that the lender's interest revenues are below a certain level, thus making the interest received on a floating rate loan have a floor or minimum value.

Floor broker　A trader on the floor of the options exchange who executes trades for others who are off the floor.

Foreign currency futures　A futures contract providing for the purchase of a foreign currency.

Foreign currency option　An option providing for the purchase or sale of a foreign currency.

Forward commitment　*See* forward contract.

Forward contract　An agreement between two parties, a buyer and a seller, to buy an asset or currency at a later date at a fixed price.

Forward discount　The relationship between the spot and forward exchange rates of a foreign currency in which the forward rate of a currency is less than the spot rate.

Forward market　A market in which forward contracts are constructed.

Forward premium　The relationship between the spot and forward exchange rates of a foreign currency in which the forward rate of a currency is greater than the spot rate.

Forward rate　The rate agreed upon in a forward contract for a loan or implied by the relationship between short- and long-term interest rates.

Free market　A market characterized by a high degree of efficiency and little or no regulatory influence.

Full carry　A condition associated with a futures contract in which the futures price exceeds the spot price by no less than the cost of carry.

Futures commission merchant　A firm in the business of executing futures transactions for the public.

Futures contract　An agreement between two parties, a buyer and a seller, to purchase an asset or currency at a later date at a fixed price and that trades on a futures exchange and is subject to a daily settlement procedure.

Futures fund　A mutual fund that specializes in trading futures contracts.

Futures option　An option on a futures contract.

Gamma　The rate of change of an option's delta with respect to a change in the price of the underlying asset or futures.

Garman-Kohlhagen model　A model for pricing European foreign currency options.

Generic swap　An interest rate swap involving the exchange of fixed interest payments for floating interest payments.

GLOBEX　A system of automated trading proposed by the Chicago Mercantile Exchange in which bids and offers are entered into a computer and executed electronically.

Good-till-cancelled order　An order that is in effect until cancelled and is used most often with stop orders and limit orders that may take some time to execute.

Grade　A measure of a commodity's relative quality.

Hedge　A transaction in which an investor seeks to protect a position or anticipated position in the spot market by using an opposite position in options or futures.

Hedge portfolio　A portfolio being hedged, often used in the context of a long stock–short call or long stock–long put in which the hedge ratio is continuously adjusted to produce a risk-free portfolio.

Hedge ratio　The ratio of options or futures to a spot position (or vice versa) that achieves an objective such as minimizing or eliminating risk.

Hedged dividend capture　A tax strategy in which a corporation attempts to earn dividend income by buying stock shortly before the stock's ex-dividend date and hedging the stock with short call options.

Hedger　An investor who executes a hedge transaction.

Historical volatility The standard deviation of a security, futures, or currency obtained by estimating it from historical data over a recent time period.

Holder-of-record date The day on which all current shareholders are entitled to receive the upcoming dividend.

Holding period The time period over which an investment is held.

Horizontal spread *See* Calendar spread.

Hybrid An instrument or contract that possesses some of the characteristics of an option, futures, or forward contract.

IMM Index The method of quoting the price of a Treasury bill or Eurodollar futures contract on the International Monetary Market in which the price is stated in terms of a discount from par of 100.

Immunization A bond portfolio strategy in which the return is protected against changes in interest rates and is obtained when the duration equals the holding period.

Implied repo rate The cost of financing a cash-and-carry transaction that is implied by the relationship between the spot and futures price.

Implied volatility The standard deviation obtained when the market price of an option equals the price given by a particular option pricing model.

Index arbitrage The purchase (sale) of a portfolio of stocks representing an index and the sale (purchase) of the corresponding futures contract. The trade is designed to profit from mispricing in the relationship between the spot and futures prices.

Index option An option on an index of securities.

Index participations Securities that pay off as if the holder had owned an index of securities. They represent a claim on the portfolio of securities that comprise an index.

Initial margin The minimum amount of money that must be in an investment account on the day of a transaction. On futures accounts, the initial margin must be met on any day in which the opening balance starts off below the maintenance margin requirement.

Institutional investor A term used to refer to a firm as an investor as opposed to an individual investor.

Interbank market An informal organization of banks that execute spot and forward transactions in foreign currency.

Intercommodity spread A futures transaction involving a long position in a futures on one commodity and a short position in a futures on another commodity.

Interest rate futures A futures contract on a fixed-income security.

Interest rate option An option on an interest rate rather than on a security, commodity, or futures price. Exercise is determined by whether the interest rate is above or below the strike.

Interest rate parity The relationship between the spot and forward exchange rates and the interest rates in two countries.

Interest rate swap A transaction between two parties who agree to swap interest payments on their respective loans.

Intermarket front running An illegal trading practice in which a party, aware of impending significant private information in the spot market, executes a trade in the futures or options market.

Internal rate of return The discount rate on an investment that equates the present value of the future cash flows with the price.

In-the-money A call (put) option in which the price of the asset or futures or the currency exchange rate exceeds (is less than) the exercise price.

Intracommodity spread A futures transaction consisting of a long position in a futures expiring in one month and a short position in an otherwise identical futures expiring in another month.

Intrinsic value For a call (put) option, the greater of zero or the difference between the stock (exercise) price and the exercise (stock) price. Also referred to as *parity value*.

Introducing broker A broker who arranges futures transactions for customers but contracts with another firm or individual for the execution of the trade.

Johnson-Shad Agreement The 1982 agreement between CFTC chairman Phillip McBryde Johnson and SEC chairman John Shad that established the lines of regulatory authority over options.

Kappa *See* Vega.

Lambda *See* Vega.

Law of One Price The principle that two identical assets cannot sell for different prices.

LEAPS Long-term Equity Anticipation Securities. Options on individual stocks with expirations of more than one year.

Leverage The use of debt to magnify investment returns.

Leverage contract A transaction in which the buyer deposits a small amount of money and agrees to purchase a commodity at a given price at a later date. The transaction occurs off of an exchange and is frequently used in metals trading.

Limit down An occurrence in which the futures price moves down to the lower daily price limit.

Limit move An occurrence in which a futures price hits the upper or lower daily price limit.

Limit order A request to purchase or sell a security, option, or futures that specifies the maximum price to pay or minimum price to accept.

Limit up An occurrence in which the futures price moves up to the upper daily price limit.

Liquidity A feature of a market in which transactions can be quickly executed with little impact on prices.

Liquidity preference theory An explanation for the shape of the term structure that assumes that long-term rates exceed short-term rates because of lenders' reluctance to make long-term loans.

Listing The offering of a security, option, or futures for public trading on an exchange.

Load fund A mutual fund in which the shareholders pay a portion of their money as a commission to the individual or firm selling the shares.

Local A trader on the floor of the futures exchange who executes trades for his or her personal account.

Lognormal A distribution of stock returns that is often used to develop option pricing models.

London Interbank Offer Rate (LIBOR) The interest rate on Eurodollar deposits.

Long A position involving the purchase of a security, option, or futures. It also refers to the person holding the long position.

Long hedge A hedge involving a short position in the spot market and a long position in the futures market.

Lower bound A value established as the lowest possible price of an option.

Macro hedging A strategy in which a firm hedges the combined exposure of all of its assets and liabilities.

Maintenance margin The minimum amount of money that must be kept in a margin account on any day other than the day of a transaction.

Margin Funds kept in a margin account for the purpose of covering losses.

Market efficiency A concept referring to a market in which prices reflect the true economic values of the underlying assets.

Market indexed security A security that promises a minimum return

plus a given percentage of any change in the market above a certain level.

Market maker A trader on an exchange who is responsible for buying and selling to the public.

Market-on-close order An order to purchase or sell securities, options, or futures that requests the broker to execute the transaction at a price as close as possible to the closing price.

Market order A request to purchase or sell a security, option, or futures in which the broker is instructed to execute the transaction at the current market price.

Market portfolio The portfolio consisting of all assets in the market.

Market segmentation theory An explanation of the shape of the term structure of interest rates in which long-term and short-term rates are determined by supply and demand in long-term and short-term markets.

Market timing An investment strategy in which the investor attempts to profit by predicting the direction of the market.

Mark-to-market *See* Daily settlement.

Micro hedging A strategy in which a firm hedges only specific transactions as opposed to hedging the entire firm.

Minimum variance hedge ratio The ratio of futures contracts for a given spot position that minimizes the variance of the profit from the hedge.

Money market The market for short-term securities.

Money spread An option transaction that involves a long position in one option and a short position in an otherwise identical option with a different exercise price.

Multiple listing The listing of identical options on more than one exchange.

Mutual fund A company whose shareholders' money is pooled and used to purchase securities.

Naked call *See* Uncovered call.

National Association of Securities Dealers An organization of firms that serve as market makers for certain stocks traded off of the exchanges.

National Futures Association An organization of firms engaged in the futures business that serves as the industry's self-regulatory body.

Net present value The present value of an investment's cash flows minus the initial cost of the investment.

No-load fund A mutual fund that does not charge its shareholders a load or sales commission.

Normal backwardation A condition in which the futures price is less than the expected future spot price at expiration.

Normal contango A condition in which the futures price is greater than the expected future spot price at expiration.

Normal probability The probability that a normally distributed random variable will be less than or equal to a given value.

Notice of intention day The second day in the three-day sequence leading to delivery in which the clearinghouse notifies the holder of the long position that delivery will be made the next business day.

Notional principal The principal amount or face value of a loan or bond. Often used to identify the size of an interest rate or currency swap.

Offsetting order A futures or option transaction that is the exact opposite of a previously established long or short position.

Open interest The number of futures or options contracts that have been established and not yet been offset or exercised.

Open outcry The process that occurs in a trading arena in which bids and offers are indicated by shouting.

Option A contract to buy or sell an asset, currency, or futures at a fixed price for a specific time period.

Option fund A mutual fund that uses options, often in the form of covered call strategies.

Option on futures An option to buy or sell a futures contract.

Options Clearing Corporation The firm that operates as a clearinghouse for the various exchanges that trade options on stocks and indices.

Order book official An employee of the Chicago Board Options Exchange who keeps public limit orders and attempts to fill them at the best available price.

Out-of-the-money A call (put) in which the price of the asset, currency, or futures is less (greater) than the exercise price.

Overnight repo A repurchase agreement with a maturity of one night. *See also* Term repo.

Overpriced A condition in which a security, option, or futures is valued at more than its worth.

Over-the-counter market A market for securities or options in which the transactions are conducted among dealers, brokers, and the public off of an organized exchange.

Over-the-counter option An option created in an over-the-counter market and in which there is no active secondary market.

Parity *See* Intrinsic value.

Participation percentage On a market-indexed security, the percentage of the market return that is earned by the holder of the security.

Payoff The amount of money received from a transaction at the end of the holding period.

Pit An octagonally or hexagonally shaped, multi-tiered area on the trading floor of a futures or options exchange within which a group of contracts trades.

Plain vanilla swap *See* Generic swap.

Portfolio insurance An investment strategy employing combinations of securities, options, or futures that is designed to provide a minimum or floor value of the portfolio at a future date.

Portfolio theory The study of the economic processes through which investors' portfolio decisions are made.

Position day The first day in the three-day sequence leading to delivery in which the holder of the short position notifies the clearinghouse of the intention to make delivery two business days later.

Position limit The maximum number of options or futures contracts that any one investor can hold.

Position trader A futures trader who normally holds open positions for a period longer than a day.

Preferred habitat theory *See* Market segmentation theory.

Price sensitivity hedge ratio The number of futures contracts used in a hedge that leaves the value of a portfolio unaffected by a change in an underlying variable, such as an interest rate.

Primary market The market for securities originally issued and not previously traded among the public.

Prime A security that pays off a value up to a maximum plus the dividends on a stock.

Program trading The trading of large blocks of stock as part of a program of index arbitrage or portfolio insurance.

Protective put An investment strategy involving the use of a long position in a put and a stock to provide a minimum selling price for the stock.

Pure discount bond A bond, such as a Treasury bill, that pays no coupon but sells for a discount from par value.

Put An option to sell an asset, currency, or futures.

Put-call-futures parity The relationship among the prices of puts, calls, and futures on a security, commodity, or currency.

Put-call parity The relationship between the prices of puts, calls, and the underlying security, commodity, or currency.

Quality option The right to deliver any one from a set of eligible bonds on the Chicago Board of Trade's Treasury Bond futures contract.

Quantity risk The risk involved in a hedge in which the hedger does not know how many units of the spot asset he or she will own or sell.

Ratio spread A spread transaction in which the number of contracts is weighted to produce a risk-free position.

Real asset A tangible asset such as real estate or equipment.

Registered option trader An options trader on the floor of the American Stock Exchange who trades options for his or her personal account.

Repo *See* Repurchase agreement.

Reportable position The number of contracts that if held by a futures trader must by law be reported to the regulatory authorities.

Repurchase agreement A securities transaction in which an investor sells a security and promises to repurchase it a specified number of days later at a higher price reflecting the prevailing interest rate.

Retail Automatic Execution System (RAES) A computerized system used by the Chicago Board Options Exchange to expedite the filling of public orders.

Retractable bond A bond in which the holder can choose to redeem prior to maturity.

Reversal *See* Reverse conversion.

Reverse conversion An arbitrage transaction consisting of the sale of a put and the purchase of a synthetic put.

Rho   The rate of change of an option's price with respect to the risk-free interest rate.

Risk aversion   The characteristic referring to an investor who dislikes risk and will not assume more risk without an additional return.

Risk neutrality   The characteristic referring to an investor who is indifferent toward risk.

Risk preferences   An investor's feelings toward risk.

Risk premium   The additional return risk-averse investors expect for assuming risk.

Risk-return trade-off   The concept in which additional risk must be accepted to increase the expected return.

Rolling strip hedge   A strip hedge with a relatively long hedge horizon in which the longer maturity futures are added as nearby futures expire.

Scalper   A trader on the floor of a futures exchange whose trading style involves short holding periods and small profits based on small price changes.

Score   A security that pays off at expiration any increase in the price of a stock above a given value. Equivalent to a call option.

Scratch trade   A trade primarily executed to adjust a dealer's inventory and in which no profit or loss is made.

Seat   A term used to refer to a membership on a futures, options, or stock exchange.

Secondary market   The market for assets that were issued previously and are now trading among investors.

Securities and Exchange Commission   The federal agency responsible for regulating the securities and options markets.

Securities Investor Protection Corporation   A federal agency that provides investors with insurance against failure of a brokerage firm.

Series   All of the options of a given class with the same exercise price and expiration.

Settlement price   The official price established by the clearinghouse at the end of each day for use in the daily settlement.

Short   A term used to refer to holding a short position or to the party holding the short position.

Short hedge   A hedge transaction involving a long position in the spot market and a short position in the futures market.

Short sale   An investment transaction in which securities are borrowed from a broker and sold to a buyer and, at a later time, repurchased and paid back to the broker.

Simple return   A rate of return that is not compounded.

Specialist   A trader on the floor of an exchange who is responsible for making a market in certain securities or options.

Speculation   Investments characterized by a high degree of risk and usually short holding periods.

Speculative value   *See* Time value.

Speculator   One who engages in speculative transactions.

Spot market   The market for assets that involves the immediate sale and delivery of the asset.

Spot price   The price of an asset on the spot market.

Spot rate   An interest rate on a loan or bond created in the spot market.

Spread   An option or futures transaction consisting of a long position in one contract and a short position in another, similar contract.

Spread delta   A measure of the sensitivity of a spread to a change in the price of the underlying asset, currency, or futures.

Spreader   A person or institution that engages in a spread transaction.

Stack hedge   A hedge in which the hedge horizon is longer than the expiration of the shortest-lived futures contract but due to lower liquidity of longer maturity futures, extra contracts of shorter maturity futures are used. Sometimes called a stack.

Standard deviation   A measure of the dispersion of a random variable around its mean, equal to the square root of the variance.

Stock index   A combination of stock prices designed to measure the performance of the stocks as a whole.

Stock index futures   A futures contract on an underlying stock index.

Stock option   *See* Equity option.

Stop order   An order to purchase or sell securities, options, or futures that is not executed until the price reaches a certain level.

Storage   The process in which an asset is held for a certain time period.

Storage cost   The cost of holding an asset, including the physical costs of storage and the interest lost on funds tied up.

Straddle   An option transaction that involves a long position in a put and a call with the same exercise price and expiration.

Strangle   A long put at one exercise price and long call at a higher exercise price.

Strap   An option transaction that involves a long position in two calls and one put, or two calls for every put, with the same exercise price and expiration.

Strike price   *See* Exercise price.

Strike spread   *See* Money spread.

Strip   An option transaction that involves a long position in two puts and one call, or two puts for every call, with the same exercise price and expiration. *See also* Strip hedge.

Strip hedge   A hedge in which a series of futures contracts of successively longer expirations are used to cover a hedge horizon longer than the expiration of the shortest-lived futures contract. Sometimes called a strip.

Stripped treasuries   Securities that represents claims on coupons and principal of Treasury bonds. The Treasury bond is purchased and stripped treasuries are sold against the coupons and principal on the Treasury bond.

Swap   *See* Interest rate swap or Currency swap.

Swap dealer   A firm that arranges an interest rate or currency swap between two other parties.

Switching option   *See* Quality option. Sometimes defined as the right to switch bonds in a cash and carry transaction using Treasury Bond futures although this right is a result of the quality option.

Synthetic call   A combination of a long put and long asset, futures, or currency that replicates the behavior of a call. It may sometimes include a short position in risk-free bonds.

Synthetic futures   A combination of a long call and a short put that replicates the behavior of a long futures contract. It may sometimes include a long or short position in risk-free bonds.

Synthetic put   A combination of a long call and short asset, currency, or futures that replicates the behavior of a put. It may sometimes include a long position in risk-free bonds.

Systematic risk   The risk associated with the market or economy as a whole.

Tail   The number of additional futures contracts purchased or sold to complete a wild card or quality option delivery.

Tailing the hedge   Adjusting the hedging ratio so that the effects of the interest earned or paid from the daily settlement are taken into account.

Target beta   The desired beta of a stock portfolio.

Target duration   The desired duration of a bond portfolio.

Term repo   A repurchase agreement with a maturity of more than one day. *See also* Overnight repo.

Term structure of interest rates   The relationship between interest rates and maturities of zero coupon bonds.

Theta   The rate of change of an option's price with respect to time.

Tick   The minimum permissable price fluctuation.

Time spread   *See* Calendar spread.

Time value   The difference between an option's price and its intrinsic value.

Time value decay   The erosion of an option's time value as expiration approaches.

Trading halt   A rule associated with futures or stock trading in which trading will temporarily cease if prices move by a specified amount during a specified period of time.

Treasury bill   A short-term pure-discount bond issued by the U.S. government with original maturities of 91, 182, and 365 days.

Treasury bond   A coupon-bearing bond issued by the U.S. government with an original maturity of at least 10 years.

Treasury note   A coupon-bearing bond issued by the U.S. government with an original maturity of one to ten years.

Triangular arbitrage   The foreign currency arbitrage transaction that forces the cross-rate relationship to hold.

Turtle trade   An arbitrage spread transaction in which a forward borrowing (or lending) rate is locked in on the Treasury bond or note futures market and a forward lending (or borrowing) rate is locked in on the Treasury bill futures market.

Two-state model   *See* Binomial model.

Unbiased   A characteristic of a forecast in which the prediction equals the actual outcome on average over a large number of predictions.

Unbiased expectations theory   *See* Expectations theory.

Uncovered call   An option strategy in which an investor writes a call on a stock not owned.

Underpriced   A condition in which a security, option, or futures is valued at less than its worth.

Unsystematic return   The portion of a security's return that is related to factors associated with the individual security and not to the market as a whole.

Unsystematic risk   The risk of a security related to factors specific to it and not to the market as a whole.

Upside capture   The percentage of the market value of an uninsured portfolio earned by an insured portfolio in a bull market.

Uptick   An increase in the price of a security or contract equal to one tick.

Utility   A measure of satisfaction usually obtained from money or wealth.

Value   A monetary measure of the worth of an investment or contract that reflects its contribution to the investor's wealth.

Variance   A measure of the dispersion of a random variable around its mean, equal to the square of the standard deviation.

Variation margin   Money added to or subtracted from a futures account that reflects profits or losses accruing from the daily settlement.

Vega   The rate of change of an option's price with respect to the volatility of the underlying asset or futures.

Vertical spread   *See* Money spread.

Volatility   The characteristic of fluctuations in price.

Warrant   An option issued by a corporation to buy or sell its stock. Usually has a life of several years when originally issued.

Wash sale   A transaction in which a stock is sold at a loss and an essentially identical stock, or a call option on the stock, is purchased within a 61-day period surrounding the sale. Tax laws prohibit deducting the loss on the sale.

Wild card option   The right to deliver on the Chicago Board of Trade's Treasury bond futures contract after the close of trading in the futures market.

Writer   A person or institution that sells an option.

Yield   The discount rate on a bond that equates the present value of the coupons and principal to the price.

Yield beta   The slope coefficient from a regression of the yield on a spot bond on the yield implied by the futures contract. Measures the relationship between spot and futures yields.

Yield curve   The relationship between yields on bonds and their maturity.

Yield to maturity   *See* Yield.

Zero coupon bond   *See* Pure discount bond.

Zero-plus tick   A situation in a financial market in which a trade takes place at the same price as the last trade but the last time a price changed, it increased.

INDEX